# Enemies on the Couch

# Enemies on the Couch

A PSYCHOPOLITICAL JOURNEY THROUGH WAR AND PEACE

VAMIK D. VOLKAN, M.D.

PITCHSTONE PUBLISHING
Durham, North Carolina

Pitchstone Publishing
Durham, NC 27705
www.pitchstonepublishing.com

Copyright © 2013 by Vamık D. Volkan

All rights reserved.
Originally published in hardcover by Pitchstone Publishing in 2013
First paperback edition by Pitchstone Publishing published in 2025
Printed in the United States of America

**Library of Congress Cataloging-in-Publication Data**

Volkan, Vamik D., 1932-
Enemies on the couch : a psychopolitical journey through war and peace / Vamik D. Volkan.
pages cm
Includes bibliographical references and index.
ISBN 978-0-9852815-5-7 (hardcover : alk. paper)
1. Political psychology. 2. Political science—Decision making. I. Title.
JA74.5.V65 2013
303.6'6019—dc23
2012051134

ISBN 978-1-939578-32-7 (pbk.)

*To Max, Liz, Thisbe, and Nehir*

# CONTENTS

# PREFACE

The aim of this book is to illustrate how psychological factors affect international relations and how an interdisciplinary facilitating team can use its knowledge about such factors to help establish peaceful coexistence among opposing large groups, whether ethnic, national, religious, or ideological. By revisiting case studies from multiple conflict zones spanning the last three decades, I invite readers to witness, through first-person accounts, facilitating processes in action as they deepen discussion between representatives from different countries and diverse cultures and create models to help societies after major trauma. This book explores how we conceptualize shared psychological journeys such as mourning after massive losses, and how we experience dangerous prejudices and transmit our sentiments about the Other to the generations after ours. It poses the question, "What is a large-group identity?" and ponders why people kill and maim in the name of shared tribal, ethnic, national, religious, or ideological sentiments.

In 1977, Egyptian president Anwar Sadat visited the Knesset and famously referred to a psychological "wall" between the Israelis and the Arabs—a wall, he stated, that accounted for 70 percent of the problems between them. Since that time, I have examined many such "walls" in international contexts, meeting world political leaders and framing my findings in theoretical terms and practical actions. This book summarizes these findings while guiding the reader to observe, across multiple cases, what is written on or embedded in such "walls." Even though incredible advances in technology and modern globalization have drastically changed how national, ethnic, religious, and ideological large groups relate to one another, the basic aspects of individual and large-group psychology remain the same. Therefore, findings in this book are applicable to present and future international conflicts and fundamentally relevant to all conflict resolution, conflict management, peacebuilding, and peacekeeping initiatives.

For scholars and practitioners, this book illustrates how facilitating teams can help opposing sides identify these "walls" and assist in separating reality from "psychic reality" in order to create a better atmosphere for more effective political negotiation. The studies and observations herein provide not only a new way of looking at recent historical events—from the former Soviet Union to the Middle East—but also offer a novel set of tools for dealing with major traumas and understanding and shaping the present and future.

For the general reader, the book's psychopolitical lens and my direct experiences provide a unique window onto watershed moments of the past three decades—such as the collapse of the Soviet Union, the fall of the Berlin Wall, the tragedy of September 11, 2001, and continued violence in the Middle East. Along the way the reader will meet ordinary citizens, refugees, victims of torture, scholars, diplomats, and political leaders, from Mikhail Gorbachev and Jimmy Carter to Yasser Arafat and Abdullah Gül, and learn, just as I have through the years, how different national, ethnic, religious, or ideological groups may perceive world affairs through their own unique histories and traditions. They do so, we will observe, using universal psychological mechanisms and processes.

I was trained to study human nature. Despite the fact that Sigmund Freud called my profession an "impossible" one, I have felt comfortable and confident as a psychoanalyst. When I found myself in situations where I needed to understand psychological processes shared by thousands or millions of persons, most of whom would never meet in their lifetimes, or to explore the role of political leaders, diplomats and ordinary persons in wars, war-like situations and terrorism, I often felt very humble and helpless. But through it all I continued to be actively curious about what has become known as "political psychology." And in this book I offer personal reasons for my stubborn optimism in such situations.

My method of telling about my involvement in political psychology has a model. In 2010 I published a book, *Psychoanalytic Technique Expanded: A Textbook on Psychoanalytic Treatment.* In it I attempted to put myself behind a metaphorical glass window and ask other clinicians to observe me while I treated patients or supervised the work of younger psychoanalysts in different countries. In this way, I hoped to provide a tool for those in this field to compare their own work with the way I have practiced psychoanalysis and to give them an opportunity to question and learn how psychoanalytic treatment is conducted at the present time. Psychoanalysis is facing a growth of pluralism, and we are witnessing many schools of psychoanalysis. Nevertheless, psychoanalysis had a "father," Sigmund Freud, and all psychoanalytic schools anchor their thinking, at least selectively or in modified ways, to the "father's" original ideas.

There are also many types of political psychology schools. Since political psychology does not have one recognized "father," its schools experience themselves as being even further apart than clinical psychoanalytic ones. In order to narrow down what I offer in this book, I must say that I am only referring to political psychology as conceptualized and practiced by psychoanalysts. Beginning with Sigmund Freud, psychoanalysts had for decades written about large groups, wars, and leaders, but there had been no application of psychoanalytic thinking to political and international issues in the field at the time this book's narrative begins. Many concepts that are introduced here were thus not available and were not—and still are not—included in the training of psychoanalysts and other mental health professionals.

In this book, once more I put myself behind the metaphorical glass window and ask the reader to observe my journey. I begin with stories of my first professional involvement with international conflict over three decades ago and gradually wind to my work in the present day.

And now the story of my journey begins.

—Vamık D. Volkan
Charlottesville, VA and Stockbridge, MA, USA,
and Ozanköy, North Cyprus, 2010–2012

# ACKNOWLEDGMENTS

I thank Gerard Fromm, Ph.D., Director of the Erik Erikson Institute of Training and Research of the Austen Riggs Center, Stockbridge, Massachusetts, as well as Edward Shapiro, M.D. and Donald Rosen, M.D., the former and present medical directors of the Austen Riggs Center, for giving me the opportunity to spend three months each year at this institute where time was provided for me to do most of my writing. I am grateful to Robert DiFazio, the Austen Riggs librarian, for his help in locating useful references. I also thank Dianna Downing, my long-time editor from Monterey, Massachusetts, for her help and valuable suggestions in preparing this book.

I am especially grateful to Joy Boissevain, who served as the Program Director of the Center for the Study of Mind and Human Interaction (CSMHI) at the University of Virginia School of Medicine and who passed away while I was writing this book. She helped to maintain many of the documents that I consulted while writing this book, most of which are now preserved at the Historical Collections and Services of Claude Moore Health Sciences Library at the University of Virginia. She is fondly remembered and greatly missed.

# PART I

# THE BIRTH OF POLITICAL PSYCHOLOGY

# 1

# SADAT AT THE KNESSET

## THE OTHER WALLS

In this fast-changing world, the career plans we made when young often look nothing like our professional lives as adults. For many of us, computers, new media, and other advanced technologies did not even exist when we entered the twentieth-century workforce. Social frameworks and political landscapes have shifted as well, many times in many places, as have our perspectives, from the personal to the global. We change with the times.

My career path is no exception. I have had three professions, all of them for decades. I spent a very long time preparing myself for my first profession—as a psychoanalyst—beginning in Turkey, where I attended the University of Ankara's Medical School, a natural choice since I was born on the Mediterranean island of Cyprus to Turkish parents. I came to the United States as a newly graduated physician in early 1957, interning at the Lutheran Deaconess Hospital in Chicago and receiving my psychiatric residency training at the Memorial Hospital of the University of North Carolina at Chapel Hill. Thereafter, I worked for two years at Cherry Hospital in Greensboro, North Carolina, then a state mental hospital that was only for black Americans, and Dorothea Dix Hospital in Raleigh, which was only for white Americans. Even in my medical school days I knew that I wanted to become a psychoanalyst, and my official psychoanalytic training took place at the Washington Psychoanalytic Institute, Washington, D.C.

By this time, 1964, I had moved to Charlottesville, Virginia, to join the faculty of the University of Virginia's psychiatric department. I remember years of traveling long hours between Charlottesville and Washington before the two lanes of old Highway 29 connecting these cities were turned into four, to receive my psychoanalytic education at the Institute and to lie down on my psychoanalyst's couch four times a week for my own training analysis. When I became an official member of the American Psychoanalytic Association in 1974, I felt well prepared for this profession and indeed was confident and comfortable practicing and teaching psychoanalysis.

As a psychiatric faculty member at the University of Virginia, I was given administrative responsibilities, such as directing the psychiatric in-patients services or functioning as the acting chairperson of the Department of Psychiatry. Eventually, I was appointed the medical director of the University's Blue Ridge Hospital, a 600-bed general hospital, and remained in this position for eighteen years while I continued to practice and teach psychoanalysis. Being a medical administrator was my second profession.

Unlike my years-long preparation to become a psychoanalyst and a medical administrator, I was completely unprepared for my third profession—as a "political psychologist." I did not give myself this title, but have accepted the fact that, for some decades now in many academic and political circles, I have become identified with this term.

My involvement in this third profession was accidental. Individuals who are planning a career in politics and international relations do not undertake psychiatric or psychoanalytic training, and psychiatric and psychoanalytic trainings do not include politics and international relations. Nevertheless, starting with Sigmund Freud, a number of psychoanalysts have shown interest in political leader-follower relationships, religion, and human behavior in large groups. In 1977 the American Psychiatric Association (APA) established the Committee on Psychiatry and Foreign Affairs, composed of psychiatrists who, for their own personal reasons, were involved or interested in American internal and external politics, but who did not have a special theory or methodology to study its psychological underpinnings.

In 1978 I was flattered when I was asked to join this committee. A few months later Demetrios Julius, a Greek-born American psychiatrist would become another new member.[1] During the late 1970s the Greek-Turkish relationship was tense, a product of a long, conflicted history. My ancestors, the Ottoman Turks, conquered Cyprus in 1570–1571 from the Venetian Empire. During the Venetian period the Greek Orthodox Church was suppressed on Cyprus and attempts were made to impose Roman Catholicism on the people there. The Ottomans restored the Greek Orthodox Church to its former status by recognizing it as the only official non-Muslim religious body on the island. The Ottoman administration lasted over three hundred years, until 1878 when Great Britain took Cyprus "in trust" by treaty with the Sultan. In turn, the British helped Ottomans protect themselves from the Russians. Although it remained nominally Ottoman territory during this period, Cyprus was finally annexed by the British in 1914 when World War I began. After the Ottoman Empire collapsed following the war, the new Turkey formally recognized British rule in Cyprus in 1923.

As this brief historical account indicates, when I was a child Cypriot Turks and Greeks had been living side by side for nearly four centuries under a strong centralized rule, either Ottoman or British. Throughout this time, Cypriot Turks and Cypriot Greeks living under a central authority had developed cultural and social customs in order to exist together.

In 1960 British rule had ended on the island and the Republic of Cyprus was founded with a controversial constitution that attempted to create political coexistence between Cypriot Greeks and Cypriot Turks. After three years, Cypriot Turks were forced by the Cypriot Greeks to live in enclaves within only 3 percent of the island in inhumane conditions for eleven years. A military force from Turkey came to Cyprus during the summer of 1974 and *de facto* divided the island into northern Turkish and southern Greek sections. At the time Demetrios and I were invited to join the committee, there was still no genuine peace between Cypriot Turks and Cypriot Greeks or Turks and Greeks in general.

I gradually began to sense that, although the senior members of the committee were most kind to the Greek-American and Turkish-American newcomers, both of us were chosen as "guinea pigs" to be observed by other members of the committee. Our inclusion was not, I humbly realized, due to our qualifications in the psychological realm of politics and international relations, but to our ethnic identifications. I felt that I was going to be observed as I interacted with my Greek-American colleague.

In truth, I welcomed the situation and felt actually driven to be a "guinea pig." I found myself wondering why I was excited about this new development in my professional life, a feeling that went beyond a superficial sense of being recognized by the APA and invited as a committee member. So I began a kind of self-analysis. When I was born in Cyprus in 1932 the island was a British colony, and in my preteen years my family lived in Nicosia, the capital city, in a rented house at a location where the Turkish section of the city joined the Greek section. Next to my family's house stood an identical house occupied by a Greek family. They had a daughter, Elena, who was probably a year younger than I. Our two families, living in identical houses next to one another, had no meaningful social contact in accord with the existing cultural tradition of those days in Cyprus. Although in mixed villages the two populations mingled, enough for the Cypriot Turkish villagers in those villages to speak Greek, in the cities, including Nicosia, the Turks and the Greeks remained mostly apart socially. Elsewhere Cypriot villages were exclusively Turkish or Greek.

During my latency years both Cypriot Turks and Cypriot Greeks were preoccupied with the impending danger coming from outside the boundaries of the island, dangers that as a child, my mind could not fully comprehend. After the Nazis' 1941 airborne invasion of another Mediterranean island, Crete, it was expected that they would next invade Cyprus. We dug a bomb shelter in our garden and took refuge there on many occasions, sometimes roused from our beds by sirens in the middle of rainy nights. Food was rationed and we were forced to eat dark, tasteless bread and taught how to wear gas masks. I began noticing Indian Sikh soldiers with turbans and long beards walking through the streets of my neighborhood. I witnessed a British Spitfire shooting down an Italian war plane just above my elementary schoolyard where I was playing with other kids. It can be said that during my childhood Cypriot Turks and Cypriot Greeks had a common "master" in the British and common external enemies in the Germans and the Italians.

The gardens of my house and Elena's were divided by a wall built of mud bricks, and as I grew taller, I could see Elena in her garden. I do not remember when she and I become acquainted, but we would often meet in the street in front of our houses. I would point at a car or bicycle that happened to be in the street and tell her their Turkish names. In turn she would point at things and try to teach me the Greek words for them. But soon she and I reached puberty and accepted cultural patterns that made us "taboo," as intermarrying between the two groups was considered to be as deeply forbidden as incest. Whatever I learned from Elena about real "Greekness" was thus denied more strongly. Without being aware of it during my childhood, I experienced concretely how large-group identities divide people.

There was one English school in Nicosia both teenage Cypriot Turks and Cypriot Greeks could attend, but most Turkish and most Greek youngsters went to schools in which the education was only in Turkish or Greek. I went to Turkish gymnasium and never learned to speak Greek, even though Greeks were everywhere on the island, and I would meet them almost every day without negative prejudice. We were different, but all of us were human. By the time Cypriot Turks and Cypriot Greeks became murderous enemies I had left that part of the world and was living first in Turkey as a medical student, and then in the United States as a physician.

After the island was actually divided into Turkish and Greek sections in 1974, my logic told me that the Cyprus of my childhood was lost forever. I believed that when I was asked to be a member of the APA committee, the idea of working with a Greek-American psychiatrist induced in me nostalgia for my lost childhood in Cyprus, a place where Turks and Greeks lived side by side without killing one another. Then I remembered an important event that I was told about throughout my childhood that provided a deeper meaning to my welcoming the role of "guinea pig."

One morning, at the age of two, I was kidnapped from the front of our house—a different one from the house next to Elena's—by a Greek woman. Ransom was not the motive. Apparently this troubled woman hoped to raise me as her own and intended me no harm. I was found in the late afternoon in Nicosia's electric factory, where she had hidden me away. I have no recollection of this incident, but I can recall my mother and grandmother's anxious expressions as they retold and relived the story. I was fascinated by it. Thus, this incident was mythologized in my mind. As a youngster, I had fears that I might be killed by electricity, but I was also curiously pleased that I, a Turkish child, had been a Greek person's object of desire. The APA committee's invitation had opened an emotional window for me to visit my childhood ambivalence and also my desire relating to Greeks. I realized I had never had a Greek friend in my adult life.

Soon, however, the committee's focus on having Demetrios and me as "guinea pigs" would be forgotten. The signing of the September 17, 1978 and March 26, 1979 Camp David Accords by Egyptian president Anwar Sadat and Israeli prime minister Menachem Begin in the presence of U.S. president Jimmy Carter changed the APA committee's focus. Sadat's famous November 19, 1977 visit to Jerusalem had played a significant role in starting the diplomatic dialogues at Camp David that resulted in these two agreements. On his visit to the Knesset, Sadat had referred to a psychological wall between Israelis and Arabs, which, he stated, was causing 70 percent of the problems in the Arab-Israeli conflict. Traditionally, approaches to peace in the Arab-Israeli conflict and all other international conflicts had been political and formally diplomatic. The psychological issue had remained largely dormant.

Sadat's speech in the Knesset had given an indirect challenge to the mental health professions as well as to politicians. Because of Sadat's stature in the United States, a great deal of attention was paid to his remarks there—so much so that the comment proved a boon to the development of political psychology.[2]

Since I was a new member of the APA committee, I do not know the full story of how the senior members found funds for the American Psychiatric Association's Committee on Psychiatry and Foreign Affairs to study the psychological wall President Sadat mentioned. Melvin Sabshin, who passed away recently and who was the medical director of the American Psychiatric Association when the committee was established, wrote in his book *Changing American Psychiatry: A Personal Perspective* that the American Psychiatric Association's project to study the psychological aspects of the Middle East process was funded by the U.S. Agency for International Development, the U.S. State Department, and the National Institute of Mental Health (NIMH).[3]

Senior members of the APA committee went to Israel and Egypt and, with the blessings of the American, Israeli and Egyptian governments, made arrangements to bring together influential Israelis and Egyptians for a series of meetings. An attempt would be made to define the psychological wall and try to remove it. Political psychology was a new approach to the Middle East conflict; there was no history to refer to, and no precedents by which to set hopes and expectations. Demetrios and I were not included in these preparations. I, for one, would have had nothing of value to offer at that time.

The first meeting of the Israeli-Egyptian unofficial dialogue under the sponsorship of the American Psychiatric Association's Committee on Psychiatry and Foreign Affairs took place at the Watergate Hotel in Washington, D.C., in January 1980. Two psychiatrists from Egypt and another two from Israel were among the selected participants. Also attending was a well-known Egyptian political figure, retired ambassador Tahseen Basheer, who had been an official spokesperson for the late Egyptian president Gamal Abdel Nasser and who was at that time an official spokesperson for Sadat. Other influential Egyptians and Israelis who did not have psychological training were also invited.

The Watergate Hotel meeting would be one of the first times Israelis and Egyptians met other than on a battlefield or perhaps around a diplomatic table since the 1967 War. The American Psychiatric Association's committee members were anxious since they had no experience and no methodology for bringing influential "enemies" together, for starting a series of dialogues, or for expecting something useful to emerge from such an effort. The first place the Egyptian and Israeli participants were to land in the United States was New York, and the American group had carefully orchestrated separate flights from there to Washington. We were afraid that if some kind of outburst of hostility between the groups occurred on the plane, our project would end before it began.

The two airplanes coming from New York would arrive at Dulles Airport at about the same time, and the American committee members were divided into two groups to meet them, each bearing a bouquet of flowers. One group went to one end of the airport to meet our Egyptian guests and one group went to the other end to meet the Israelis. At that time, without today's security procedures, people could easily meet disembarking passengers. Apparently, however, one of the planes designated to carry one group of our guests from New York to Washington had mechanical problems, and the airport officials in New York, without our knowledge, put all our guests onto the same plane. When the committee members realized this, we reorganized ourselves and all of us, with apprehension, waited at the same gate to meet both the Egyptian and Israeli participants. Since I had not gone to Israel and Egypt to select participants for the committee's project, I had no idea what the Egyptian and Israeli guests looked like. One of the first persons who came through the gate was a rather tall, thin man with a long beard who, wearing a cape around his shoulders, looked like an opera singer. Because of his manner of dress, I instantly decided that he was an Israeli. Soon I learned that he was Mohammed Shaalan, a charismatic Egyptian psychiatrist.

Looking back, I can say that this story of my very first experience as a member of a facilitating team with enemy representatives taught me two lessons: (1) it is necessary that a team that facilitates a dialogue between enemy representatives learns how to remain calm, and (2) it is a reality that enemies are often alike, at least in their physical appearance. I will describe later in this book other ways in which enemies, psychologically speaking, become alike, even while maintaining their obvious differences, whether in cultural expressions, religion, language, or methods of expressing aggression.

Senior members of the Committee on Psychiatry and Foreign Affairs had decided not to begin the dialogue between the enemy representatives right away. They preferred to initiate an intellectual exercise away from the Israeli-Arab conflict and engage our Egyptian and Israeli participants in a discussion that would not induce deep emotions. It was thought that this would help to calm the participants who would be seeing and talking to one another for the first time. The American group chose a mental defense mechanism known as "intellectualization" to deal with their own anxiety. "Intellectualization" refers to escaping an anxiety-provoking issue by being preoccupied with logical thinking. The Israelis and the Egyptians attended the APA committee meeting with the knowledge of their governments, but they did not wish to appear too eager to get together, most likely due to political pressure from their own countries. They demanded that they would only attend an international meeting where not only the Arab-Israeli issues would be discussed, but also other conflicts. This helped with the APA committee's plan. I would be a "victim" of this approach.

I was asked by the senior members of the facilitating team to be the first speaker after the welcoming remarks. In 1979 I had published a book, *Cyprus—War and Adaptation: A Psychoanalytic History of Two Ethnic Groups in Conflict,*[4] and I was to give a talk on the Cyprus problem, to tell the Cypriot Turks' and Cypriot Greeks' stories in order to keep the minds of the Israeli and Egyptian participants off of their own troubles. According to the senior members, this would allow a gradual opening for slowly approaching the Arab-Israeli conflict. A copy of my book had been sent to Nechama de Shalit Agmon, a child psychiatrist from Jerusalem, and she was asked to discuss my paper. She would be the second "victim" of the APA group's apprehension.

When I stood on the stage at the podium and spoke for forty-five minutes, not one Egyptian or Israeli cared about what I was saying and not one of them listened. I felt embarrassed and experienced a psychosomatic symptom, nausea. When Nechama discussed my paper, no one paid attention to her either. As soon as she finished her discussion, or even before she finished it, Egyptians and Israeli participants began focusing on their own conflict in emotional tones.

This event taught me another lesson: when people are chosen to represent their ethnic groups and come to a meeting where they meet representatives of their enemies, they are not interested in intellectualized exercises, especially when they include topics different from their own large-group issues. The facilitating group needs to learn about and be ready to deal with emotional issues right away.

At the Watergate Hotel meeting, the APA Committee on Psychiatry and Foreign Affairs arranged to begin a series of meetings with the Egyptian and Israeli participants who were present at this first gathering. In fact, we ended up meeting at least once per year over the next six years, each time for four days. New participants who had not attended the Watergate meeting were added to each group. Joseph ("Joe") Montville, a former diplomat who was familiar with the Middle East from his work with the U.S. Department of State, was present as a member of the APA committee team at the Watergate Hotel meeting. He would attend all but one of the APA committee–sponsored meetings. He and APA committee chairperson William ("Bill") Davidson would later name the APA group's activities "track-two diplomacy" and popularize this term.[5]

It was in April 1983 during the third year of this dialogue series that four Palestinians participated for the first time, at a place called the Mountain House in Caux, Switzerland. Two days before the meeting started the APA appointed me as the new chairperson of the committee and Demetrios Julius became the assistant chair. We remained in charge of the Arab-Israeli dialogues for the next three years. We also became good friends and later worked together in other conflict areas of the world. I suspect that a Turkish-American and a Greek-American working together at a time when tensions in the Turkish-Greek populations were active was a model to people from Israel and the Arab world, and later to members from other opposing large groups, that "enemies" can indeed cooperate.

On April 13, as the new leader of the APA committee, I walked into a large conference room at the Mountain House where other participants had already gathered. At that moment my career as a political psychologist began *in earnest*.

# 2

# MENTAL HEALTH PROFESSIONALS AT THE TABLE

## ETHICAL CHALLENGES

At the time the APA Committee on Psychiatry and Foreign Affairs was created, the psychiatric profession's public involvement in political and societal issues was discussed in the United States in relation to professional ethics. In 1964 *Fact* magazine conducted a mail survey about Senator Barry Goldwater's fitness to be the president of the United States. A questionnaire was sent to over 10,000 psychiatrists, with 2,417 responding. The majority of them described the senator using psychiatric terms such as narcissistic, paranoid, megalomaniac, or immature, and declared that Goldwater was not a suitable person to be in the Oval Office.[1] When the findings were published in the magazine's September/October 1964 issue, they created embarrassment and a major debate within psychiatric circles. The result was the APA Ethic Committee's so-called Goldwater Rule, which stated that it is unethical for a psychiatrist to express an opinion about an individual who has not been professionally examined. In many psychiatrists' minds, the "Goldwater Rule" encompassed all public political issues as off-limits. Therefore, the APA's decision to form the Committee on Psychiatry and Foreign Affairs was, in a sense, a courageous move.

The APA's initiative was also at odds with some firmly establish psychoanalytic traditions going back to well-known correspondence between Albert Einstein and Sigmund Freud. The year I was born, 1932, Einstein wrote to Freud, asking if the new science called psychoanalysis could offer insights that might deliver humankind from the menace of war. In his response to Einstein, Freud expressed little hope for an end to war and violence or for psychoanalysis to change human behavior beyond the individual level.[2]

In 2006, the year Austria served as head of the European Union, the country declared that year to be the Year of Mozart and the Year of Freud. I had the honor of being the Fulbright-Sigmund Freud Privatstiftung Visiting Scholar of Psychoanalysis in Vienna at this time, teaching political psychology at the University of Vienna for a semester, and having an office at 19 Berggasse, where Freud had lived and practiced. While working in Freud's house for four months organizing an international meeting between psychoanalysts and diplomats to celebrate Freud's 150th birthday, I pictured him at this same location in 1932 and wondered about his response to Einstein. Anti-Semitism surrounded Freud at that time, and a year later Adolf Hitler would become the dictator of Germany. Was Freud's response to Einstein an attempt to deny the impending danger to himself, his family, and his neighbors? I came to a conclusion that this might be true.

Even though some analysts have found indications of cautious optimism in some of Freud's writings,[3] his general pessimism about the role of psychoanalysis in international relations was mirrored by many of his followers. This, I think, created psychoanalytic traditions that limited for a long time—including when the APA Committee on Psychiatry and Foreign Affairs project first started—the contributions psychoanalysis could make to understanding the mental phenomena that exist within large groups and affect international relations, even though some analysts had tried to open doors to such investigations.[4]

In addition, Freud's large-group psychology reflected a theme that mainly focused on understanding the individual: the members of a group sublimate their aggression toward the leader and turn it into loyalty in a process that is similar to that of a son turning his negative feelings toward his oedipal father into identification with the father.[5] The members of a large group idealize the leader, identify with each other, and rally around the leader. Much later, others wrote about fantasies shared by members of a large group. They suggested that large groups represent idealized mothers who repair narcissistic injuries.[6] It is assumed that external processes that threaten the group members' image of an idealized mother can initiate political processes and influence international affairs. But, again, these theories primarily focused on individuals' perceptions, and they did not offer *specificity* concerning what exists within a large-group psychology itself and what might be useful in a diplomatic or political strategy to tame or prevent massive aggression.[7]

Freud was aware of widespread "war neurosis." However, beginning with Freud's own writings in 1917, only a relative emphasis was given to patients' experiences with war, war-like conditions, drastic political change, and reactivation of ancestors' historical events. Decades ago, as today, there were multiple psychoanalytic schools. All schools seemed to bypass, to a great extent, the influence of traumatizing external historical events. For example, the mother of so-called Kleinian psychoanalysis, Melanie Klein, paid no attention to the realities of World War II when she treated a ten-year-old boy named Richard in 1941.[8] During Richard's analysis, the terror of the Blitz under which Melanie Klein and Richard lived was not examined. We will never know for sure why she avoided the influence of the war while analyzing Richard.

There are other occasions when psychoanalysts' failure to pay attention to dangerous current or traumatic past events was clearly connected to their own resistance to recalling and/or reexperiencing troublesome affects and to their own resistance dovetailing with the resistance of their patients. Harold Blum's description of a patient who came to him for reanalysis illustrates the extent to which mutual resistances may prevail when both analyst and patient belong to the same large group that was massively traumatized by an external historical event. Blum failed to "hear" in the material of this patient, who like Blum was Jewish, their large group's shared trauma at the hands of the Nazis; as a consequence, mutually sanctioned silence and denial pervaded the entire analytic experience, leaving unanalyzed residues of the Holocaust in the patient's symptoms.[9]

We can wonder how many Jewish analysts after World War II were like Blum's patient's former analyst and how many of them, without being aware of it, influenced the application of psychoanalytic treatment in a way that tended to ignore Holocaust-related external reality. I suggest that some of them who were very influential in the field of psychoanalysis, both in the United States and elsewhere, exaggerated their bias in favor of a theoretical position called "classical analysis" that focused mainly on the analysand's internal wishes and fantasies and mental defenses against unacceptable ones. We now know that in post–World War II Germany as well, there was both German and German-Jewish analyst–supported (unconscious) resistance to exploring the intertwining of internal and external wars and the influence of Holocaust-related issues on analysands' psyches.[10] As time went on, however, psychoanalytic studies on Holocaust-related psychic processes, especially on transgenerational transmissions of trauma, were deepened.[11] But the argument for focusing on the patient's internal world, while not paying much attention to his or her large-group history or to transgenerational transmissions, continued.

The APA committee's initiation of a dialogue series between Egyptians and Israelis can be seen as a concrete event in changing ethical and traditional attitudes about mental health workers' involvement in external events in the public eye. Happenings during recent decades in the Middle East, Latin America, Africa, India, Turkey, the Soviet Union, Yugoslavia, Rwanda, and elsewhere and the appearance of international terrorism has motivated, perhaps forced, psychoanalysts to write about such things. Wars, war-like situations, terrorism, and international relations have increasingly begun to be addressed and examined through a psychoanalytic lens, with reference not only to traumatized individuals and individual psychology but also to shared social and political processes.[12]

After September 11, 2001, the International Psychoanalytic Association (IPA) formed the Terror and Terrorism Study Group. Norwegian analyst Sverre Varvin chaired this study group, which lasted for several years.[13] The IPA also established a committee on the United Nations. The theme of the 44th Annual Meeting of the IPA in Rio de Janeiro in the summer of 2005 was "trauma," including trauma due to historical events. In 2011, during her plenary lecture at the American Psychoanalytic Association's Winter Meeting in New York, outgoing president Prudence Gourguechon urged the members of the association to show their faces in areas already in the public eye. She stated that if psychoanalysts do not attempt to explain the causality of disturbing events and provide professional information about human behavior, statements by others with less knowledge on such matters will prevail.[14]

# 3

# MEETING THE ENEMY

## ACKNOWLEDGING ANXIETY

Our own conflicts, ambivalences, rage, helplessness, losses, feelings of revenge, guilt, hope, and other internal processes resulting from large-group conflicts—or simply due to some events in our personal environments—influence how we react to the idea of meeting those we consider to be our large-group's "enemies" and having dialogues with them. When we read descriptions of what *official* diplomats are doing, we seldom think about how these individuals' own psychological makeup and personal experiences at the time of negotiations might influence the process. For example, David Rothstein, a psychiatrist who served on the Warren Commission and the Eisenhower Commission, wondered about a meeting between Soviet premier Alexei Kosygin and U.S. president Lyndon Johnson that took place in New Jersey just after Kosygin's wife had died. Rothstein stated: "Could Premier Kosygin have no feelings or thoughts whatsoever about his wife's death while he was meeting with President Johnson, or could he have kept those feelings entirely isolated from his participation in the talks?"[1]

An example of how human emotions can play a significant diplomatic role comes from a moment in the Camp David meetings. Many books have been written about what happened there over thirteen days in September 1978 when official leaders of the United States, Egypt, and Israel met in a rather unofficial manner, days that included laughter, anger, and even tears. While most writers of these books focus on typical diplomatic processes, some describe, however briefly, a story which played a significant role and perhaps *the* role in turning the Camp David meetings from complete breakdown into success. President Jimmy Carter himself has written about this story, and years later, when I was a member of the Atlanta-based Carter Center's International Negotiation Network, I heard him refer to it directly.

During the last day of the conference Menachem Begin was adamant in his refusal to sign any accord. There was all-around frustration. Earlier, Begin had asked the three political leaders from the United States, Egypt, and Israel to sign photographs of the three of them together. He intended to give the photographs to his grandchildren. Anwar Sadat had already autographed the photographs, and Carter made his own inscriptions on them after obtaining the names of Begin's grandchildren. He took the photographs to Begin's cabin. When Begin saw his granddaughter's name on one of the photographs he started crying. He began telling Carter about his grandchildren and about the effects of war on young people. After this incident, Begin's mood changed dramatically. Carter spoke about "a love fest" between Begin and Sadat following this incident and the euphoric atmosphere that led to the signing of the Camp David Accords.[2]

Once at an unofficial meeting between "enemies," I noted one individual's personal distress during the sessions; sometimes he would suddenly perspire, and other times his face literally became purple. This person was a highly respected intellectual with important political contacts, and his influence in his society was palpable. This was why he had been selected as a representative of his own large group during the unofficial dialogues. When I, as the leader of the facilitating group, became keenly aware of his distress, I decided to speak with him privately. He informed me that his younger brother, whom he loved dearly, had been killed only a few years earlier during a bloody conflict with a neighboring large group with whom he was now engaged in discussion. Sitting in a room and talking to people who belonged to this, according to him, "murderous and barbarian" large group was overwhelming for him. He voluntarily decided to withdraw from participating in our meetings.

More than two years after the meeting at the Watergate Hotel, Nechama Agmon visited Charlottesville, and she and I had leisure time to talk. She told me the story of how she became involved in the APA committee's project. One evening a highly respected Israeli psychoanalyst, Rafael Moses, whom she knew professionally but not terribly well, called her, asking, "How would you like to go to Washington?" Apparently the senior members of the APA had first contacted Rafael and suggested that he call Nechama. Together they would choose people to represent Israel in the APA project. Her own life experiences and the very fact that she lived and worked in Israel made the proposed APA meeting a very exciting but bewildering idea.

As we will now observe Nechama's preparation for an unofficial dialogue process through her eyes, it is helpful to know her background. She was born in Atarot, a small village not far from Jerusalem, close to the Arab city of Ramallah. One meaning of Atarot is "crown," referring to the crown of hills that ridged the village. Her middle-class parents had both come to the area in 1929 from Russia attracted by the Zionist movement, and they were among the group of Israeli settlers known as pioneers, for building a new home for the Jewish people out of the desert.

Atarot was quite isolated from other Jewish areas, and there was a lot of interaction between the Jewish settlers and the Arab villagers. As a child Nechama played frequently with Arab children in the rocky hills surrounding the village. She informed me, however, that when she was two years old, the women and children in her settlement were evacuated because Arabs were attacking the village. Her earliest memory is of shouts and gunfire and then of being in a very big school in Jerusalem where she slept on the floor. Later they went to stay with one of her mother's friends. She did not recall exactly when they went back to Atarot. "When I was older I began to wonder how it was, that those who were your friends and neighbors could become your enemies in a day. That was how long it took—from one day to the next."

Arabs were friends and enemies. There were constant fears. She used to bicycle with her friends to Ramallah where the Arabs used to negotiate with the older children about buying a bride. They were probably joking, but she was terrified that she would be taken away and sold, like Joseph in the Bible. "When the water supply was down, we would go to buy water from a spring nearby," Nechama told me. "There was an old grandfatherly man that I liked very much who took care of the spring, and he was an Arab. So the Arabs could give us water, the essence of life, but they also could shoot us."

Life in Nechama's village was filled with ambivalence and flaring emotions now and then. At first sight it seemed a pastoral farming community, but lurking in the quiet fields were fears, aggression, and bloodshed. In addition to skirmishes with Jewish settlers and their Arab neighbors, peace was often interrupted by encounters with another world, the outside world. Near the village was a small airport that belonged to the British Army. Nechama recalled how as a girl she and her girlfriends found the British pilots handsome and dashing, smelling of tobacco and leather. To these young Jewish girls, the foreigners were exciting, adding an international flavor to life in the village and arousing in them a mysterious, eroticized longing for faraway places and tall rugged heroes. The outside world was Nechama's and her girlfriends' hope but also their disappointment. In the 1929 attack on the village, when all women and children were evacuated and the men protected the village with only a handful of rifles, the British force that was expected to reinforce them never arrived. Nechama and her friends, raised with this story, felt betrayed by another large group, which was supposed to be friendly and caring.

If third-party negotiators, such as those from the United States, do not study and learn the history and experiences of people in foreign lands, they may sometimes become easily frustrated when they note that delegates from such places have various prejudices. In the initial stages of a process, third-party facilitators' logical explanations will not easily influence or change the participants who have the prejudices.

Nechama told me that after she and Rafael Moses were asked to research English-speaking candidates for the APA project, rumor had it that the American delegation would be visiting Israel and would eventually choose the Israeli participants. This seemed a mixed message: you can make a list, but we will select from it—and we may not even select you. Even though trusting the friendly outsider was proving difficult, Nechama put aside her doubts and suspicions, and she and Rafael began to work on the list of names. They drew up a profile of what seemed to them the right kind of person. This person was intelligent, sensitive, and exposed to psychosocial, political, and historical issues through his or her profession—a writer, someone from the media or academia, or someone in a continuous dialogue with the public. They looked for people who were open to psychological thinking, familiar with its language, and capable of negotiating in a small-group situation.

One problem arose when they realized that all the names they had come up with were dovish, soft-liners. The list did not represent a realistic cross section of Israeli society. But whenever they thought of a name that represented the hawkish side, that personality in one way or another seemed to them psychologically unfit to participate in such a conference—some memory or event raised fears that the person was insensitive, abrasive, aggressive, or narrow-minded.

In retrospect Nechama admitted to me that this decision in itself showed a prevalent stereotype among liberal Israelis in the late 1970s, a stereotype of the Other. She added, "The 'others' can be the enemy—the Arabs—but they can also be our neighbors or allies, who look at events from a different perspective. This was a lesson we had to learn at the beginning—how difficult it was to give up stereotypes." Eventually they decided that their number-one priority was not to jeopardize the meeting, and they proceeded to put together the best group possible. This consisted of three psychiatrists and three nonpsychiatrists, as prescribed by the elites of the American Psychiatric Association and its Committee on Psychiatry and Foreign Affairs. The strict supervision of the Israelis' preparation by the American group apparently was worrisome for Nechama and Rafael. She said, "We felt that the Americans always wanted to have the last word on the composition of the group, and we saw this as a threat to our autonomy. This was not out in the open, but it was an undercurrent that was there all the time, from the very beginning."

While I know a great deal about how the Israeli delegates were chosen from having this conversation with Nechama, I know much less about how the APA helped the Egyptians to come up with their participants. Apparently the Egyptians were not given the option of choosing their own group. I was told that Rita Rogers, a senior member of the APA committee, had flown to Egypt and interviewed different Egyptians for the delegation one by one, all well-versed in the English language, rather than appointing a leader of the group.

"We have a phrase in Israel," said Nechama during our discussion in Charlottesville, "'the fog of the battle,' the mist that hovers over the battlefield and confuses the enemy." She added, "We didn't know if the Americans were trying to be mysterious, or if they were as confused as we were. We didn't know if this was going to be an academic endeavor, or if they were planning to use us as guinea pigs in some laboratory experiment." I had to laugh when I heard her referring to herself and other Israelis as "guinea pigs" since, as the reader knows, I had characterized myself and Demetrios as the same laboratory animals. She continued, "We didn't know if we were a part of some secret political agenda, or if they were naïve enough to think that we could go back and make a difference after this war was over."

As it turned out, the members of the Committee on Psychiatry and Foreign Affairs did not know any more than the Israelis. The fog came from neither side—it was generated by the heavy weather of the issues, of the whole situation. And though Israelis thought that their anxieties were theirs alone, they found out differently when they flew into Dulles Airport and met the American team.

# PART II

---

## THE ARAB-ISRAELI CONFLICT: PSYCHOLOGICAL FINDINGS FROM THE 1980–1985 DIALOGUES

# 4

# IS IT POSSIBLE FOR AN ISRAELI TO BE AFRAID?

## ON NOT HEARING THE OTHER

As soon as Nechama Agmon finished her discussion of my paper on Cyprus at the opening of the Watergate Hotel meeting, Israelis and Egyptians right away revealed stereotyped perceptions about their own group and the "enemy." There was a lot of hidden and sometimes open hostility and chaotic competition: Whose history is longer? Who has more grievances? There was even competition about which group wanted peace more than the other. For instance, an Egyptian would say something like, "We want to negotiate, because in our culture we negotiate every day!" revealing the Egyptians view of themselves as more open to communication and peacemaking than Israelis. Egyptians also seemed to be willing to write some things off to the will of Allah, at least on the surface. On the other hand, I sensed that Israelis presented their large group as an entity that demands intellectual mastery of each issue. The style of the Egyptians was different enough from that of the Israelis that misperceptions could not help but arise.

When we met in Charlottesville, Nechama told me that Israelis were also puzzled by the Americans. When people from different countries come together, even when they think they know about the Other's culture, misperceptions occur and induce uncomfortable feelings. I would never have guessed what had disturbed Nechama most about the Americans. Here is what she told me:

> There were things that I didn't understand, and the unfamiliar made me anxious. The Americans liked to meet for breakfast. I did not understand this tradition and found it very mysterious. In fact, the Americans turned out to be as mysterious to me as the Egyptians were, and this surprised me very much. When the Americans met for breakfast and I asked what they were doing, I was told they were having a *caucus*. I didn't understand what was meant by this word caucus. I kept mean-

> ing to ask someone about it, but I couldn't remember how to pronounce it. So, after awhile it symbolized for me the incomprehensible and inaccessible aspects of the meeting. It was like we were children, outside the closed bedroom door. The Americans were excluding us, talking about us.

Because Nechama told me this, later in my third career as a political psychologist I would meet with the members of my team when participants from other groups were not around, usually in the evenings after everyone else had gone to their rooms.

At the Watergate Hotel meeting the American group had no given issues or negotiation points to present to our guests. Our task at that time was to diagnose the nature of psychological obstacles keeping enemies apart. Such obstacles were present in the conference room right away: when enemy delegates are put in the same room for the first time, they dramatically become spokespersons for their own large groups, lose their individuality to a very great extent, bring stereotypes and prejudice, present "psychic realities" as if they are true, and do not hear each other.[1]

Imagine a very dark place with two (ethnic) sources appearing as search lights. Both sources are turning around and around beaming their lights quickly, all over the place in a chaotic fashion. Some search lights coming from opposite sources occasionally cross one another, but only for a few seconds. An observer watching this would become dizzy. I pictured the facilitating team's task as catching the moment the search lights touched one another and stopping the sources from continuing to move around at that moment. In this way, the area where beams of light cross would be the most illuminated space and catch everyone's attention.

The following story from the Watergate Hotel meeting relates an event that brought together and stabilized "search lights" from two ethnic sources. An Egyptian historian and journalist, Abdel Azim Ramadan, from the University of Monoufeia appeared to be extremely religious, but was also a Socialist and very anti-Zionist. From my perspective, he was doing everything in his power to stop any meaningful dialogue between Egyptians and Israelis. During the second day of the gathering, Ramadan was giving a "lecture" in favor of a Palestinian state. The usual response to this situation would be for an Israeli to start his or her own "lecture," usually in a more intellectual and academic fashion than an Egyptian would be inclined to present, and factually describe a rather stereotypical version of the Israeli position on the formation of a Palestine state. But this time Nechama responded to Ramadan as an *individual.* Nechama asked him how he could convince her not to be afraid of a Palestinian state. What guaranties could he give that would make her less afraid? Ramadan answered shortly, "I do not believe that you Israelis are afraid. Israelis are *never* afraid."

Nechama was appalled. "What? How can you say such a thing?" Ramadan continued to respond to Nechama as if she stood for all Israelis, "You, with a strong, long arm, you are never afraid."

Nechama: "How can you say so? What is happening here? Why don't you believe *me*? We are together for two days, we eat together, we talk together, and you should know better by now than to think I would lie to you."

After this bitter exchange, the encounter was over and participants went back to make competing statements about their large-groups' presumed political and cultural positions.

That evening Demetrios and I talked about the exchange between Ramadan and Nechama. On the surface, Ramadan was using his logic by saying that because of Israelis' success in military encounters, their military might, their planes and tanks, and their friendship with the United States, Israelis would not experience fear. However, the way he talked to Nechama and the way he used his body language suggested to us that his declaration—if you are an Israeli you will never experience fear—was in the service of degrading Israelis as a large group, even seeing them as nonhuman. Israelis would not have emotions, even negative ones. If there was going to be emotion, the Egyptians were going to have it. Ramadan wanted to have an ethnic or national "monopoly" on fear, on vulnerability.

The next morning when all of us got together Ramadan asked permission to speak. Apparently the emotional argument between him and Nechama had affected him greatly. He said that he had not slept the night before, thinking about what had happened. Apparently, there was no need for Demetrios or me to bring this topic back for discussion and "interpret" its hidden meaning of robbing the enemy of its human emotions. Ramadan, probably also sensing our amazement about his remarks the day before, said that his mind was busy wondering if he should trust Nechama or not. Are Israelis able to be afraid or not?

He had consulted the Koran that he brought with him to Washington. In it he found a passage that said three times that Moses was afraid. Ramadan read this passage to all present, in Arabic, and then in English. Then he said, "I never thought Moses was afraid. But now I know that if Moses was afraid, Nechama can be too. So after last night I believe *you*, Nechama."

For me, this was an important development. Ramadan was still under the influence of his religion and culture. He could accept whatever Nechama had to say only after he was able to integrate it into his own religion and culture. But he had made a step toward developing an empathic understanding of an Israeli and had spoken to her, not as a spokesperson of his large group, but on an individual level.

At this point the meeting changed. Suddenly there were individuals from Egypt and Israel in the room and not "puppets" mechanically programmed to sing their large-groups' songs. Demetrios later would write about the exchange between Ramadan and Nechama and the change in the room: "The forging of this personal and human link was the first step in the building of a trusting relationship between one Israeli and one Egyptian. What we saw, then, in the Washington Conference was the beginning of an understanding of the reality of *the other* as someone distinct from an internalized stereotype."[2]

I was learning another "technical" consideration for conducting dialogues between enemy groups. In such a project the facilitators would wish and expect the participants of opposing groups to remain as representatives of their large group, holding its sentiments, but these participants become more effective negotiators of their large-group conflicts when they held on to their individuality and began seeing those in the other group also as separate and distinct individuals—"yet in some ways like themselves, with similar feelings, aspirations, fears, and shortcomings."[3] The last two days of the Watergate meeting allowed a process of discovery in which Egyptians and Israelis revealed new things to each other. When the meeting came to an end, Nechama summarized it this way: "It was as if we learned things we had never known or imagined; it was like an inventor inventing a new machine."[4]

# 5

# A VISIT TO "MONT FREUD"

## THE ECHO AND ACCORDION PHENOMENA

I do not know the reasons why a year and half went by before the APA Committee on Psychiatry and Foreign Affairs called a second meeting with Egyptians and Israelis. Was this due to APA politics, American government sources not wishing to fund such a project, Israeli or Egyptian authorities' objections, or the disorganization of the committee itself? If APA elite communicated with the Israeli and Egyptian participants, I was not informed. Eventually I was invited to go to Mont Pelerin, a resort near Vevey overlooking Lake Geneva in Switzerland, for a second gathering of the Egyptians and Israeli delegates under the sponsorship of the APA Committee on Psychiatry and Foreign Affairs.

I noticed great tension at the beginning of the Mont Pelerin gathering. This meeting took place a few months after the June 7, 1981 Israeli bombing, using U.S.-made war planes, of a French-built nuclear plant near Baghdad, Iraq. The day of the strike BBC broadcasted the Israeli government's reasons for this surprise attack: "The atomic bombs which that reactor was capable of producing, whether from enriched uranium or from plutonium, would be of the Hiroshima size. Thus a mortal danger to the people of Israel progressively arose."

As I write this book long after the Israeli raid on the nuclear plant in Iraq, it is clear that the present-day Israeli popular view about Iranian nuclear activities still reflects this thirty-year-old statement. At the present time, distrust of Iranian president Mahmoud Ahmedinijad and other Iranian political figures is extreme in Israel. My personal belief is that Israel will not stop trying every way it can to hinder production of an Iranian bomb. Iranian security services announced that they succeeded in crushing a team of Mossad spies in Iran. According to this source, these spies were responsible for killing Iranian nuclear scientists, including physics professor Ali Mohammadi, who in January 2010 was a victim of a blast set off by remote control. On the other hand, Mohammadi had publicly supported Ahmedinijad's political opponent and perhaps because of this he might have been considered an "unwanted" person by some Iranian authorities. Obviously, we have no way of knowing the truth. The most recent assassination of an Iranian nuclear scientist, this time of Mostafa Ahmadi-Roshan, took place on February 9, 2012. U.S. secretary of state Hillary Clinton denied any United States involvement. I make this reference to present-day issues to illustrate that "never again" is very much kept alive in Israeli minds, and the reality of existing dangers and political circumstances in the Middle East do not create an atmosphere that tames this determination.

Let me return to the Israeli bombing of the Iraqi nuclear plant in 1981. This operation, which was known as "Operation Opera," killed ten Iraqi military men and one French civilian. As expected, it was controversial and had its critics everywhere, especially in the Muslim world. Later it was rebuked by the United Nations Security Council as well as by the United Nations General Assembly. It was also perceived by some as being related to internal political movement within Israel, since the attack took place three weeks before Knesset elections.

Because of Operation Opera, only three Egyptians showed up at Mont Pelerin in 1981; the others canceled their reservations at the last minute. The bombing had caused such great consternation among the participants that there were doubts about the continuation of the meetings. I noticed that the most obvious controversy was closer to home, so to speak. One of the delegates, Alouph Hareven from Van Leer Jerusalem Foundation, had apparently written a letter to some of the Americans and some of the Egyptians that seemed to be a kind of justification for the reactor bombing. It deeply disturbed the Egyptians. And, it confused others—Nechama, Demetrios, and me—because we had not received the letter, so initially we were baffled by the feeling of hostility that permeated the Mont Pelerin gathering.

Besides the bombing itself and Alouph's letter, there was another event that resulted in Egyptians feeling betrayed. Prime Minister Begin had met President Sadat three days before the bombing, and Begin did not warn Sadat about it. Egyptian participants stated that if Begin had told Sadat about the Israeli plans, their reaction to the bombing would not have induced such a feeling of betrayal.

Before I went to Mont Pelerin I had misgivings about the APA committee's plans for the second meeting with the Egyptians and the Israelis, which was to hold it as an academic forum. But I had no effective voice in changing minds. Participants were divided into three teams and were asked to prepare papers on three subjects: historical enmity, dehumanization, and victimization. Even though I came to the meeting to present a paper, high-level administrators, themselves psychiatrists from the American Psychiatric Association who were not members of the Psychiatry and Foreign Affairs Committee, were present too, and it was difficult to know who was in charge of the facilitating team.

This atmosphere was not conducive to this scholarly activity, and most of the discussion was not about the papers. It was about the absence of the Egyptians, about the letter, and about Egyptians feeling betrayed. Since the meeting was right after elections in Israel and there had been changes in the Likud Party, participants further escaped talking about emotions by analyzing the political changes in Israel and their effect upon the situation in Egypt. Following the idealization of the meeting at the Watergate Hotel, at Mont Pelerin the participants were testing reality and referring to real politics.

An important figure from Israel, Maj. Gen. (ret.) Shlomo Gazit, was present at Mont Pelerin, attending the APA Committee–sponsored meetings for the first time. He had become a hero during the Six-Day War in June 1967 and later served as the head of the Military Intelligence Directorate. At the time he joined us he was president of Ben Gurion University of the Negev in Beersheva. His presence was instrumental in turning the discussions away from the APA committee's aim and making it more like an official gathering. The meeting, I sensed, was difficult for Shlomo. He was trying to figure out how psychology could fit into what he had been doing for many years. He wanted to talk about politics and realities.

Participants as a whole remained tense and somewhat "paranoid." On two occasions, however, bonds were established and participants from different groups once again saw one another as individuals like themselves caught in a meeting that was frustrating for all. Ellen Mercer from the Washington office of the APA Medical Director was in charge of making arrangements for the Mont Pelerin meeting. She had arranged two excursions for the participants: to the Gruyère cheese factory and up to the nearby mountaintop in a cable car. These trips, especially going to the mountaintop, turned out to be "bonding excursions." All Egyptians and Israelis and most Americans had never traveled in a cable car before, which seemed to hang by a thread over an abyss of ice and snow. Jack Weinberg, a former president of APA, a fatherly and kind person who was not a member of the committee but who was present at the Mont Pelerin meeting, actually sat down on the floor of the cable car. The car shook and swayed; we joined Jack in fear, and then we all laughed about it together. As the cable car ascended, it gradually emerged from the clouds toward the top of the mountain. Someone said, "We'll come out of the clouds to find Sigmund Freud waiting on the mountaintop for us." Laughter and bonding grew.

I noted however that Israelis' and Egyptians' bonding would suddenly disappear, and once more they would maintain their distance. Sometimes closeness and feeling apart would appear dramatically within a very short time. For example, a period of closeness peaked when Egyptians and Israelis spoke of being "all brothers and sisters, descendants of a common grandfather, Abraham." Then suddenly an Israeli asked, "What is Egypt? Take away the Nile river and you have nothing!." This quickly alienated one group from the other. I noticed that after this event Egyptians and Israelis no longer were sitting near one another, but apart. I spoke about my observation and asked them to observe with me this nearly rhythmic alternation of togetherness and distancing. I suggested that what was happening between them was like the extension and contraction of an accordion. I suggested that we become curious about this phenomenon in order to have a dialogue without drastic mood changes.

At one time when the accordion was squeezed Nechama Agmon and Mohammed Shaalan became involved in a lively and somewhat humorous discussion about the meeting we were attending. They asked, "Is this a love affair, or a marriage, or a secret liaison with a concubine—are we going to have children? Will the Palestinians be our children? Should we bring them in or not?" Looking back, this was the first open discussion about having Palestinian delegates join us.

British psychoanalyst Wilfred Bion illustrated that when a small group cannot evolve as a *work group* and function in a corporative mature level, it functions according to three basic emotional assumptions: *dependency*, *fight-flight*, and *pairing*.[1] At Mont Pelerin we could not evolve and maintain ourselves as a work group. Dependency refers to the perception of the small-group leader as omnipotent and the membership incompetent. This assumption also could not be maintained at Mont Pelerin since there was confusion about leadership. Fight-flight small groups operate on a basis of suspicion. This clearly represented what happened to us at Mont Pelerin most of the time. In the third type of basic assumption, small groups focus on a couple rather than a leader. The couple need not be a man and woman. According to Bion the shared unconscious fantasy underlying this assumption is that a sexual union will reproduce the group and ensure its longevity and survival. The exchange between Nechama and Mohammed is a good example of Bion's pairing fantasies in the service of a shared wish for the survival of the APA group.

During unofficial diplomacy meetings, the facilitating team needs to pay attention to small-group dynamics such as the one described by Bion, without forgetting that such gatherings are not designed to treat individual delegates. The aim and the task is to help the participants from opposing large groups speak about the shared sentiments, thoughts, wishes, expectations, fears, and fantasies of their large groups while maintaining their individualities. Since participants in such small groups hold on to their opposing large-group identities, and since the aim is not to unify persons with opposing large-group identities for the benefit of only one large group, and since therapy for individuals is not an aim, enemy representatives in a conference room do not evolve as small therapy groups with which group therapists are familiar. But aspects of Bion's observations at times are present.

I learned a handful of things from the Mont Pelerin meeting that I would later incorporate into my technique for unofficial diplomatic dialogues aimed at creating an atmosphere for peaceful coexistence.

1. I appreciated not following an intellectual academic approach that includes paper presentations for a meeting among enemies if the aim is to have meaningful dialogue between them.
2. I observed the facilitating team's need to have a clear leader and clear task.
3. I noted how the shadow of an external event can fall over the meeting room and make a genuine dialogue impossible until this shadow moves away. I call this observation an "echo phenomenon." The facilitators should not minimize and deny it and force the delegates to follow the scheduled agenda. Shared feelings about the recent external event make delegates lose their individuality to an even greater extent than usual. Such feelings need to be vented before negotiation between enemies can begin.
4. I learned the usefulness of "bonding excursions," and I would include similar activities in my future work.
5. I observed and named an aspect of enemy representatives' behavior toward one another the "accordion phenomenon." As I stated earlier, the alternation of togetherness and separation, as it plays out during these meetings, reminded me of the extension and contraction of an accordion as it is played. Initial distancing between enemy representatives during a meeting is a defensive maneuver to keep the aggressive attitudes and feelings in check, because, were the opponents to come together, they might harm one another, at least in fantasy—or in turn become targets of retaliation. However, when representatives from opposing large groups are confined in a room, sharing a conscious effort for peace, at times they must deny their aggressive feelings and press together in a kind of illusory union. After a while this becomes oppressive; it becomes dangerous, as if large-group identities are fused and the luxury of projecting and externalizing bad thoughts, feelings, and images onto the Other is taken away. Then distancing occurs again. I thought that confidence-building and realistic dialogues would benefit from taming these fluctuations. Later in this book I will explain why agreements between enemies are most stable if they are made when the accordion is at neither extreme.

# 6

# PRESIDENT SADAT'S ASSASSINATION

## TO GRIEVE OR NOT TO GRIEVE?

Shortly after the Mont Pelerin meeting in the summer of 1981, Demetrios Julius and I found ourselves assigned to carry out the preparation for the third meeting with the help of Ellen Mercer. The meeting promised to be an unusual one as it would take place in Egypt. Demetrios and I were asked to go there and talk with Egyptians before definite plans were finalized. I believe the APA authorities were told by the Israeli, Egyptian, and American government authorities to "hide" the fact that only Egyptians and Israelis would be present at this next meeting. Thus, Demetrios was asked to visit the Republic of Cyprus and I was asked to visit Northern Cyprus on our way to Egypt to talk with the Cypriot Greek and Turkish authorities, respectively, as part of the pretense that our upcoming meeting was going to be a wider international gathering. We were supposed to explore Cypriot Greeks' and Cypriot Turks' interest in joining future unofficial diplomatic events. I was happy to have a trip to Northern Cyprus. I visited my family and had lunch with Cypriot Turkish leader Rauf Denktaş. I told him why I was in Northern Cyprus. Even then, I knew that I could not be on a facilitating team for any unofficial diplomatic effort dealing with the Cyprus issue. Would I put my mother or a close relative on my psychoanalytic couch? Of course not. Similarly, I knew that I could not be a facilitator or a neutral observer in any meeting where Cypriot Greek and Cypriot Turkish representatives were involved in negotiations, even unofficial ones.

I got together with Demetrios and Ellen in Cairo, my first visit there, and the first for Demetrios as well. We talked about Cyprus only very briefly, and then this topic was closed. Rita Rogers, who had been in Egypt before and who had played the key role in selecting the Egyptian representatives for the APA committee's project, joined us. A Romanian-born Jew, Rita was deported by the Nazis to a transport camp in Ukraine when she was a teenager. She survived and, after incredible difficulties, came to the United States. When she joined the APA committee, she was a child psychiatrist and a clinical professor of psychiatry at the University of California, Los Angeles. She also had devoted her life to international relationships and understanding human behavior in large groups.[1] She was in a sense our mentor in introducing us to some senior Egyptian political figures, including the foreign minister, who did not discuss the APA committee's project with us in detail except to offer his support. President Sadat was then still in power and huge pictures of him hung on the walls of offices and apartment buildings all over Cairo, constantly reminding everyone of his presence in the Egyptian capital city.

Demetrios and I wanted to observe the culture and the political atmosphere as much as we could. Obviously, in only one week we would see little and have only some surface impressions of life in Cairo. The difference between the inside of the fancy hotel where we stayed and the outside world was extreme; just one block from the hotel flies buzzed around meat hanging in open butcher shops. The fantastic Egyptian Museum stood for the glory of old Egypt, while the surrounding markets and neighborhoods at the time of our visit reflected the poverty in the city. Extreme traffic congestion and disorganization, with drivers not obeying simple traffic rules, further suggested a style of civic life far different from the Western standards to which we had become accustomed in the United States.

When we visited offices of important persons in an affluent section of Cairo, I witnessed how the intersection of religion and politics affected some well-known public figures. One important person we visited locked the door to his plush office, fetched a bottle of whisky that was hidden behind some books in his huge bookshelf, unlocked a desk drawer, took out glasses, and offered us drinks. When we finished drinking and talking, he again hid the whisky bottle, wiped out the glasses with his handkerchief, and placed them back in the desk drawer, locking it afterward. He did this as if it was a normal routine thing to do. As he unlocked his office door and we said goodbye. I realized that when in public he behaved as a good Muslim who would not touch alcohol, presenting an image acceptable to the Islamists.

Before going to Egypt, I read President Sadat's 1978 autobiography.[2] Since I am of Turkish origin, I was impressed that Sadat counted Kemal Atatürk, the founder of the Turkish Republic, as one of his inspirations. To me, Sadat was a charismatic leader, and my perception was that, like Atatürk, he would commit himself to being a reparative leader and do his best to modernize Egypt. His signing of the Camp David Accords, however, was perceived by many Islamists in Egypt and many Arabs in other countries as a betrayal. In fact, in 1979 the Arab League suspended Egypt's membership in the organization and moved its headquarters out of Egypt.[3]

While I knew some of these facts, I had no opportunity during my visit to examine and understand the mixed feelings Sadat created there. I observed that while some Israelis had already begun to go to Egypt as tourists, Egyptian tourists would not visit Israel; they were very cautious about appearing to be friendly with Israelis. While never saying "no" to our idea of having a meeting in their country, Egyptians with whom we discussed our APA project appeared cautious about our plans.

A month or so after I returned to the United States, we heard from the Egyptians that they preferred our meeting to take place in Alexandria instead of in Cairo, and it was clear to me that they considered Alexandria a more secure place to meet with the Israelis. Then we heard the news of President Sadat's assassination, and I watched its coverage on television. Sadat was "loved" by those Americans in my personal and professional environment who were interested in international relationships. Even after my visit to Egypt, when I sensed some tension and caution in Cairo about referring to internal political affairs, I did not think of Sadat as unpopular in his own country. His assassination was an unexpected horror for me. He had become president in 1970, but beginning in 1977, many Egyptians became increasingly upset with his economic strategies. Many rioted against the Egyptian governments' lifting price controls on items like bread in what become known as the "Bread Riots." There were mixed feelings about Sadat's regime in Egypt. His determination to keep peace with Israel was especially rejected by many segments of the society. During his last years in office there were also allegations of corruption in the Egyptian government.

After becoming the president of Egypt, he gradually allowed members of the Muslim Brotherhood who had been jailed before his presidency to be released.[4] But after signing the Camp David Accords, Islamists belonging to different organizations, including members of the Muslim Brotherhood, made their displeasure with Sadat known. In September 1981, Sadat permitted the roundup of about 1,500 Egyptians, including members of Egyptian Islamic Jihad, political activists, intellectuals, and even Orthodox Coptics. The roundup created anxiety in the society and was unpopular. Sadat's assassination took place a month after this roundup, on October 6, 1981. An Islamic group known as al-Gama'a al-Islamiyya apparently organized the assassination, which took place during a parade commemorating the 1973 Egyptian Third Army's surprise attack on Israel.

The assassination squad hid in one of the trucks in the parade, and as the truck passed the stand where the president and other dignitaries were located, the squad of assassins led by a lieutenant still in his twenties named Khalid Islambouli dismounted and murdered Sadat.[5] Within two minutes, twelve people, including Sadat, had been killed and twenty-eight were wounded, including Vice President Hosni Mubarak, who suffered a hand injury. A short-lived insurrection took place in Upper Egypt in conjunction with Sadat's murder, but Mubarak became the new president and government control over all of Egypt returned, with Mubarak reimposing the country's "emergency law," a kind of martial law that was enforced throughout his entire thirty-year presidency.

As I was writing this book, stunning developments in Tunisia, Egypt, Yemen, Bahrain, and Libya, and then horrible events in Syria, took place. After eighteen fascinating days of demonstrations at Tahrir Square in downtown Cairo, on February 11, 2011, Hosni Mubarak resigned from the presidency, left Cairo with his family, and moved to Sharm el-Sheikh. Many persons around the world have already commented on Mubarak's fall and the present events in the Arab world. In order to remain with this chapter's story of decades ago, I will only briefly refer to an editorial by Fouad Ajami, which appeared in the *New York Times* on February 26, 2011. While there were many reasons for these uprisings and revolutions, Ajami describes factors that have existed *within* the Arab world. His characterization that this "Arab Revolution of 2011 had a scent for the geography of grief and cruelty" is of interest to a psychoanalyst. He correctly states that to understand the present, we need to know the past. He adds: "The tumult in Arab politics began in the 1950s and the 1960s, when rulers rose and fell with regularity. . . . By the 1980s, give or take a few years, in Egypt, Syria, Iraq, Libya, Algeria and Yemen, a new political creature had taken hold: repressive 'national security states' with awesome means of control and terror." Ajami explains that the new leaders were pitiless and that they ordered killings. Thus cruelty settled upon the Arabs. The Arab population coped with this situation by going inward, and fear became the glue of politics. The rulers became 'country owners,' . . . devouring all that could be had by way of riches and vanity."

If Sadat had not been assassinated, would he have played a significant role in developing a very different Egypt than the one under Mubarak? Or would the roundup of people and increase in social anxiety have led to conditions described in Ajami's article? We can only guess. At the time of Sadat's assassination, however, he was seen as a key figure for lessening Israelis' anxiety and was appreciated by the West.

Despite the unfolding events in Egypt, the APA committee's third Egyptian-Israeli dialogue meeting took place in Alexandria soon after Sadat's assassination. The Americans and Israelis first flew to Cairo, and then in different cars we were taken to the Palestine Hotel in Alexandria. When I first heard the hotel's name I thought that the Egyptians deliberately wanted to remind the Israelis about another place important to them with the same name, and I wondered how the Israelis would feel about staying there. But when I arrived at the hotel, I realized that it was chosen for security. The Palestine Hotel, on the Mediterranean Sea, is within a walled 350-acre park a distance from the city. When the car taking me and others entered the gates, I was very impressed with the beautiful gardens. It did not take me long to realize that no guests other than the participants of the APA committee meeting were staying in the hotel. Of course there were hotel workers who served us, but I wonder if some of them, although dressed in civilian clothes, were assigned to protect us.

The meeting started with a late dinner. Egyptian and Israeli participants already knew one another and many of them sat side by side. There was plenty of good food served by polite waiters. Members of an Egyptian chamber orchestra played Western music at one end of the room. As I write this book thirty years later, I recall that one of the pieces they played was Mozart's "Eine kleine Nachtmusik," and listening to it in this big dining room, it felt like we were in Vienna! Conversation was social with no reference to Sadat's assassination. Just before 11:00 p.m., members of the chamber orchestra bowed, said goodbye to us, collected their instruments, and left. Soon a new group of musicians with *alaturca* musical instruments, accompanied by a belly dancer, appeared. I was not expecting this.

I wondered if, due to Egyptian cultural mores, our hosts were deliberately avoiding the mention of painful things such as Sadat's assassination in order to welcome us, show us Egyptian hospitality, and please us with Western music. Then it was their turn to show us something that belonged to their culture. When the belly dancer began performing, all Israelis one by one said "good night" and went to their hotel rooms. I do not think that any one of them deliberately wanted to reject something Egyptian—*alaturca* music and belly dancing—to humiliate their hosts. They seemed absolutely unaware that the Egyptians might be offended by their departure. With my Turkish background I am familiar with *alaturca* music and belly dancing. I got up from my chair and, walking around the huge dining room table, I whispered to the American facilitating team members not to leave the dining room and to accept gracefully the Egyptians treating us to something special from their culture. No American left the table. In fact most of us tried to dance with the belly dancer. The Egyptians appeared to appreciate our staying with them until after midnight.

The next day turned out to be a moving experience for many of us. Israelis wondered why Egyptians were not focusing on losing Sadat. The Israelis directed our attention to a complicated echo phenomenon which was present in the silence concerning the external events. Then they began to talk about these events, at first without showing emotion. The Egyptians explained to the foreigners how there was a severe ambivalence about Sadat's image in Egypt, and this was the reason they did not know how to feel. I thought that the Egyptians were still in shock. Meanwhile, Israelis were allowing their sorrow about losing Sadat to come out in an emotional way. This puzzled, and I sensed even angered, the Egyptians. Why were the Israelis feeling sad about a man who in fact was an Egyptian?

Things changed in the conference room when Israelis started to present Israel's role in inducing Islamic hatred toward Sadat and general ambivalence about him in the greater Egyptian society. At first they did this without being aware that they were experiencing empathy for the Egyptian participants' difficulty in experiencing grief and mourning. The Camp David Accords had not produced the hoped-for outcome, and this played a key role in changing Sadat's image from one of a courageous statesman who dealt with Israelis to that of an ineffective leader. Both of Sadat's images, however, existed side by side within the Egyptian society, and there remained societal ambivalence about him.

One of the Israeli representatives at the APA committee meetings was historian Shimon Shamir, who spoke fluent Arabic. Later, from 1988 to 1990, he would be the Israeli ambassador to Egypt and then the first Israeli ambassador to Jordan from 1995 to 1997. One of his interviews provides a good summary of what Israelis told the Egyptians during the second day of our stay in the Palestine Hotel:

> The Camp David Accord was signed without full agreement on both sides. Immediately after signing of the accord, the Begin government initiated the establishment of a wave of settlements in the West Bank, the expropriation of land, and an "iron fist" policy vis-à-vis the local populations. The expectations of the Egyptians were that in the wake of Camp David, there would be progress towards the realization of what was written in the agreement: a solution which would satisfy "the legitimate rights of the Palestinians."[6]

When Egyptians sensed Israelis' empathy, they began to express their grief. It was during the meeting in the Palestine Hotel that the Americans started small-group discussions, with one or two members of the American team facilitating. After separating into small groups and working in this way for long hours, we would all gather and share what had happened in each small group. It became clear that intense emotions were expressed, especially in one group against Israelis' treatment of Palestinians and their hurting Sadat's image in Egypt. Through the American facilitator's help, the Egyptian participants' intense emotions in this small group were successfully channeled to develop a more empathetic relationship between the "enemies" as individuals.

This led both parties to agree that there was a need to have Palestinian participation in the APA project. Demetrios would later write: "In Alexandria the members resolved to seek out Palestinian participation at the next meeting. It had taken two substantial meetings to lay the foundation of a secure atmosphere of trust so that so major a step in the process could be taken. And it was in Alexandria that the group began to recognize and to take greater initiative necessary to move on to larger emotional and political issues."[7]

After spending four days at the Palestine Hotel, different vehicles brought the American and Israeli participants to a hotel in Cairo. The next day we would leave Egypt. I arrived in Cairo late in the afternoon. There were not many senior APA people attending this meeting and Demetrios and I were filling the gap. I wanted to be sure that every Israeli and American returned to Cairo safely. I checked and learned that everyone was present except General Shlomo Gazit. No one knew what had happened to Shlomo. Where was he? The rest of us gathered in anxiety and waited. It was a great relief when he showed up. He told us that before returning to Cairo, he realized that he wanted to go to Mit Abu al-Kum, Sadat's home village in the Nile Delta. He had asked the driver to take him to Sadat's birthplace where he met one of Sadat's sisters and offered his condolences.

# 7

# THE MOUNTAIN HOUSE MEETING

## THE INEVITABILITY OF "MINICONFLICTS"

In Chapter 1 I mentioned how the chairmanship of the APA Committee on Psychiatry and Foreign Affairs was given to me two days before our meeting began on April 13, 1983, at the Mountain House in Caux, Switzerland. The Mountain House, built at the turn of the century in a location of great natural beauty overlooking Montreux and Lake Geneva, was and is now the World Center for Moral Re-Armament. A few months earlier the APA committee members had met with key representatives from Egypt and Israel at Arlie House, Warrenton, Virginia, and together we planned the upcoming Caux meeting—the first, we all agreed, that would include Palestinian delegates. We had by now learned the importance of proper preparation. The first day of the Caux meeting would have one morning and one afternoon plenary session, and during the rest of the meeting we would divide ourselves into three small groups for discussion. Participants from Egypt, Israel, and Palestine would have their own chosen leaders for the general meeting who would also conduct the three small groups. Rotating reporters were to be assigned to each small group. After small-group discussions, participants would gather in plenary meetings conducted by the leader of the American facilitating team.

Since Mountain House was the first such meeting that I conducted where enemy representatives met with a facilitating team, it has a special place in my memory. It was also a historical meeting, since I believe that it was the first meeting during those tense times in which Israelis and Palestinians interacted unofficially as individuals, openly expressed their own personal thoughts and feelings as well as their respective large group's sentiments, and were able to "hear" each other. In this book I have decided to give a more detailed description of what happened at the Mountain House than of other such APA Committee on Psychiatry and Foreign Affairs gatherings. The reader will notice that, even though there have been some major historical changes in the Israeli-Palestinian conflict over the last thirty years, certain sentiments and issues have remained the same. I will also illustrate how my psychoanalytic identity influenced me in conducting this type of gathering.

On the morning of April 13, 1983, a Wednesday, when I entered the conference room as the new chairperson of the committee, I found that Egyptians and Palestinian newcomers were somewhat loud and agitated. There were four Palestinians, two from the West Bank and two from Gaza. We had made sure that none of them were known members of the Palestinian Liberation Organization (PLO).[1] Elias Freij, an Orthodox Christian and at the time of the meeting the mayor of Bethlehem, was not a member of the PLO, but everyone on our committee suspected that, due to his position among Palestinians, he had access to the PLO authorities. I wondered if the presence of Palestinians had turned the Egyptians into instant protectors of "victimized Arabs" and that, without being aware of it, both Egyptians and Palestinians wanted to emphasize their presence in the room. By now I was very familiar with the echo phenomenon that occurs at the beginning of each gathering, and I knew that the shadow of the June–September 1982 Lebanon War would fall upon us at Caux. I was also aware that we were meeting during the first anniversary of the Israeli withdrawal from Yamit. According to the 1979 Egypt–Israel Peace Treaty, the Israelis had agreed to withdraw from the Sinai Peninsula. When the time came to leave the Yamit settlement, the settlers refused. On April 25, 1982, Israeli soldiers removed the Israeli settlers using brutal force and then destroyed the settlement. As a psychoanalyst I was cautious about inflaming feelings during "anniversary reactions." Soon, however, I realized that there was an acute and specific reason for the nervous excitement among the Arab participants, and it was connected with the Palestinian issue.

Three days earlier, on April 10, Issam Sartawi, a cardiologist who was known as an adviser and roving ambassador for Yasser Arafat, had been shot and killed in Portugal while attending the Congress of Socialist International. Arab participants at our meeting had learned of this tragedy just before they arrived in Switzerland. Sartawi had been meeting with Israelis and seeking an end to the Israeli-Palestinian conflict. Palestinian hard-liners did not like Sartawi's peace efforts. Sometime later, in fact, the Abu Nidal Organization, a ruthless militant Palestinian group, would take responsibility for having killed Sartawi.

When all of us settled in our comfortable chairs around long tables that formed a big quadrangle in the conference room, an Egyptian told me with a loud voice to ask everyone present to pay respects to the memory of Issam Sartawi by standing for a moment of silence. He also told me that if I refused to comply with his request he would go directly to the airport and fly back to Egypt. My first task as the brand new chairperson of the APA committee was to deal with this ultimatum. I knew that Israelis, even those who might have had a favorable view of Arafat's friend, would not stand up to honor the memory of a Palestinian. Then Alouph Hareven rose to describe how not long ago, on February 10 of that year, his friend, Israeli peace activist Emil Grunzweig, was also killed at a peace rally in Jerusalem, just twenty minutes after Alouph had met with him. Now, competing with the Egyptians, Alouph insisted that everyone in the conference room stand for a moment of silence to honor Grunzweig's memory. Soon a commotion ensued.

Through numerous experiences in my psychoanalytic office, I had learned that whenever an analysand had "emotional flooding" on my couch[2]—meaning peaked emotions would not allow the analysand to think logically—I should stay calm, maintain my curiosity, and respond without humiliating the analysand. And I would not hurry this, so that the analysand would have time to own his or her feelings and have freedom to express them. Therefore I stayed silent, while noises from many participants circled around the conference room for some time, and searched my mind for reasons for this emotional commotion that was started by an Egyptian participant. Two things came to me:

First, during the APA committee's last meeting in Alexandria, the Egyptian participants were experiencing shock and an inability to begin grieving President Sadat's assassination and changes in Egypt. At that time no Egyptian asked us to stand in silence to honor the memory of Sadat. Instead Israelis were the ones expressing open sorrow. By demanding that all of us in the conference room honor Sartawi's memory, the Egyptian participant (for himself and I believe for all Egyptians present) was reversing his former passivity, asserting himself and taking responsibility for his own sentiments concerning a loss. As I thought this, I also realized that the timing would not be right for bringing this realization to the participants' attention in the midst of the commotion. Furthermore, at this time the Egyptians might perceive as degrading any remarks about their difficulty in starting their grieving after Sadat's death. I said to myself: "Let them assert themselves."

Second, the Egyptian participant's demand initiated by a recent loss was not only related to issues from the previous APA meeting, but also to another recent and unexpected "loss" when the committee's previous chairperson, Bill Davidson, withdrew from the committee and decided not to come to Caux. Also, not long before, Jack Weinberg, a well-liked person and an APA representative to our project, had died unexpectedly. The Egyptians, joined by Israelis, were testing me as the new and unexpected chairperson.

I named this kind of an incident a "miniconflict."[3] Miniconflicts are apt to occur in a gathering of "enemy" representatives with a "neutral" facilitating team, usually at its start; this creates an atmosphere of crisis, giving the leader of the facilitating team a sense of urgency that the crisis must be resolved at once lest the meeting collapses. These conflicts may be connected with the event in an echo phenomenon. Or, a participant might use a personal issue to create a miniconflict: "My wife came here with me. I want you to accept her as a delegate of our group. I want her to join in our discussions. If you say 'no' I will leave this meeting!"

It should be recalled that the APA committee members at the first meeting of Israelis and Arabs at the Watergate Hotel had used "intellectualization" to hide their apprehension when they asked me to give the opening speech on Cyprus. Participants from opposing groups also may try to utilize intellectualization, but when they are flooded with emotions, intellectualization cannot be maintained. This is one reason for the miniconflict. Aside from the real and political aspects of a miniconflict, it provides a target whereon the participants from opposing large groups can displace the major large-group conflict with its personalized psychological implications and associated feelings. It provides an arena in which differing groups can posture, testing out one another before plunging into a discussion of major issues that will awaken more compelling emotions. Although the miniconflict is, in effect, a safety valve, it is connected with larger difficulties, and any leader of a facilitating team should heed it carefully, within the limits of reality and neutrality, and resolve it in a spirit of compromise in order to establish the tone of the dialogue.

In a setting such as the one that existed at Mountain House, there are many leaders, some of them in the conference room and some of them far away. Israeli participants looked to psychoanalyst Rafael Moses as their leader even before the Mountain House meeting. But, when things got tough and when there was an unconscious wish to strengthen narcissistic investment in Israeli identity, they would turn to General Gazit to lead and speak for them. Psychiatrist Mohammed Shaalan was the obvious leader of the Egyptian group, but diplomat Tahseen Basheer, who was not present at Caux, had overshadowed Mohammed on different occasions during the previous meetings because of his political standing. This was especially evident during diplomatic bargaining, even when it was done unofficially. Soon I would notice that Palestinians from Gaza did not necessarily see Mayor Freij from the West Bank as the Palestinian spokesperson. Furthermore, images of Anwar Sadat, Yasser Arafat, Menachem Begin, Hosni Mubarak, and other politicians both in the Arab world and Israel were looked up to by the participants.

In order to work together while holding on to different large-group identities and different leaders who are either at the conference or in faraway locations, the participants from opposing large groups need to accept the presence of a *special* leader above all other leaders during the gathering: the head of the facilitating team. Thus, miniconflicts may occur in the service of "creating" such a special leader. When there is doubt about his or her ability to function as the anchor of a ship in stormy weather, a commotion arises. If he or she can handle this conflict, the special leader is thereby "created."

Such a leader can maintain the facilitating role as long as he or she does not humiliate anyone in the room, while not shrinking from assertiveness. Looking back, I can say that I genuinely established myself as a psychoanalytic political psychologist when I found a solution to the miniconflict presented to me during the first minutes of the Mountain House meeting: I stood up, tapped the table in front of me gently to silence everyone and said, "Everyone will remain silent for a minute. But, everyone is free to think about whoever they wish to honor." Spontaneously all participants stayed silent for a minute. It was clear that through my behavior and words I had survived my initiation and established myself as the new and accepted chairperson of this gathering. The Mountain House Arab-Israeli dialogues could now begin.

Following my previous day's arrangements with the Egyptian, Israeli, and Palestinian representatives' leaders, I called upon selected persons from each group to speak. Since we had newcomers, we needed to orient them to our project, explain where we were, and help them to think about how they would fit in. Next it was the Palestinians' turn to present themselves. Iyad Al-Sarraj, a psychiatrist from Gaza, confessed that he had always hated Jews and Israelis until he encountered an Israeli soldier who asked him why he was so angry. He answered by saying that he was miserable because he dreaded what might happen to his family, whereupon the soldier confided that he did not really want to be a soldier, and was himself hoping for peace. This man-to-man exchange had transformed him. Aziz Shehadeh, a lawyer from Ramallah, not far from where Nechama had spent her childhood, spoke of having been dedicated to peace and active in the peace movement for decades, and of undergoing hardship because of his views.

During our afternoon plenary session the Arabs wanted to look at the "Reagan Plan." After the war in Lebanon and the expulsion of an estimated 15,000 PLO fighters from that country on September 1, 1982, President Ronald Reagan, citing the Camp David Accords, presented a plan for Israeli-Palestinian peace. Very briefly, this plan included full autonomy for the West Bank and Gaza Palestinians, a freeze of Israeli settlements, and negotiations on the final status of the West Bank, Gaza, and Jerusalem.

Mayor Freij began by saying that 1,300,000 Arabs had been governed by Israel on the West Bank and in Gaza for sixteen years. They lived under military occupation with all its frustrations and humiliations, and no Palestinian liked or accepted the occupation. He declared that Palestinians should challenge Israel for peace, and that Israelis and Palestinians should live as equals and neighbors within the boundaries of their own respective nations. Despite conferences held on the issue, nothing was changing, and there were no serious exchanges between the two peoples. Israel is here to stay, he said, but Palestinians should have their own home and govern themselves. He noted that the Israelis are continuing to colonize the

West Bank and Gaza in expectation of annexing them: "I have seen places where every town in the West Bank and Gaza, every Arab sector, will be turned into a ghetto surrounded by Israeli settlement."

I noted that he found the Reagan Plan a useful basis for negotiations, despite its official rejection by the Israelis. He said of the Committee of Psychiatry and Foreign Affairs that it had proved itself a success even before the conference opened, since it had succeeded in getting Palestinians and Israelis to meet. It became clear that as a newcomer he did not yet know what the content of such meetings was and he did not expect any significant achievement. However, his comment made me think that even if "the content" should prove useless, the possibility that the Palestinians and Israelis in the room might continue talking with one another after the meeting was enough to consider the gathering a success.

After Elias's remarks, other Palestinians focused on the situation in Gaza and on the West Bank and spontaneously brought up personal issues with few direct references to the Reagan Plan. Psychiatrist Iyad Al-Sarraj described the life of a Palestinian in Gaza in a way that everyone seemed to find moving, emphasizing the damage to one's sense of identity. "I am not allowed," he said, "to carry a passport to indicate my nationality. I must travel with a document in which my national identity is indicated as 'undetermined.'" Once, we were told, the Israelis changed the name of the Palestinian Medical Association to the Arab Medical Association. "Israelis do not regard us as equals, and harass us day and night. . . . Certain books are prohibited in Gaza, and our telephones are tapped." He had once been asked to give a lecture on the importance to children of identity, but had been forbidden to do so by Israeli authorities, as they considered it a breach of security. With rising emotion, Iyad went on to tell about a Palestinian working as a painter in a house occupied by an Israeli—but it was actually his own house! He told of an engineer who was working as a garbage collector, and of a psychiatric patient whose memory held nothing after the year 1948.

Other Palestinians also reported personal stories. Listening to personal stories helped the participants to maintain their individuality and be heard by Others more empathetically.

I asked Israelis to respond to Palestinians' statements. General Shlomo Gazit spoke first. "What the Palestinians have said is not subject to a practical solution," he stated, adding, "It could have been worse! What we have been told is almost unavoidable, a part of the cruel reality of using the military as an occupying force." Shlomo asked if we had thought about what would happen to the Palestinians under Soviet occupation. Certainly, they would not be permitted to attend a four-party conference and speak out. He wanted us to understand that the four Palestinians present, from Bethlehem, Ramallah, and Gaza, would return home and nothing would happen to them. "I was the coordinator of occupying forces," he continued. "During my day, no man was appointed to serve in the occupying administration without being grilled first to make sure that he was the right person to serve in Gaza or on the West Bank, but this is not the case today. We are told that the worst kind of military men are sent to serve in the occupied territories. Good, ambitious military people are interested in their careers, and a military career is generally not advanced by assignment to the occupied territories. This is the cruel reality. There's nothing we can do about it!" Addressing the Palestinians directly, Shlomo said that President Sadat had faced a great challenge when he went to Israel—the challenge of getting the Sinai back. He had not "fallen in love with Zionism." "Now," he went on, "there is a great challenge for the Palestinians. You have a potent card in your hands—the democracy of Israel. The present Israeli government is not going to change its policy. Change must come from the Palestinian leadership, especially the leadership outside the occupied territories. Time is running out. I know that in this room we can do little, but somebody has to start crying out."

Alouph Hareven then replied to the Palestinians, first recognizing their courage in coming to Switzerland. He suggested that the suppression of Palestinian identity by the Israelis had begun to distort the identity of the Israelis themselves. He theorized that the Holocaust had made the Israelis extremely vulnerable in respect to issues of security and intolerant of ambiguity, a state the Palestinians could not appreciate. This was a significant reference to the Holocaust, but Alouph did not stay with this topic.

During the Watergate meeting and the following APA committee–sponsored gatherings, any reference to the Holocaust possibly playing a psychological role in Israeli responses to the enemy was "taboo." If Arabs who were attending the APA committee meetings referred to it, they received an angry response from the Israeli participants and, I think, also from the Jewish-Americans present, and the subject was quickly closed. Israelis themselves would very seldom bring such a topic to the table, and if they did, it was brief and they changed the subject immediately thereafter. If the APA committee dialogue series took place today, I believe that there might be more flexibility to discuss the Holocaust and its continuing psychological effects on Israeli society and politics.

At the end of the first day I made two notes:

1. After sixteen years the Palestinians had internalized their sense of victimization and had become, in effect, "professional sufferers." When speaking of a devastating situation they exhibited a kind of anesthetized state that those witnessing it found most moving; it was, paradoxically, more effective in pleading their cause than emotionality could have been.

2. Sartawi's death just before the Mountain House meeting and the association between this murder and other loses also inhibited the expression of intense emotions after the miniconflict was resolved. No one exhibited anger openly. I thought there was an unconscious fear in the room that if aggression were expressed, the fate that befell Sartawi would fall upon us too.

I spoke to Demetrios Julius and Joe Montville about my second thought, and they agreed that they also felt that participants, including ourselves, were showing hesitation to express anger, and that there was anxiety about our well-being. With Ellen Mercer's help we got in touch with the Swiss authorities and asked them to provide security measures for all participants without being intrusive. All the doors of Mountain House were locked, and when we went out to dine in restaurants, security guards were assigned to us, especially to the Mayor of Bethlehem.

At dinner that first night, there were two psychiatrists, one psychologist, a lawyer, and an educator at our table. The subject of forensic psychiatry came up. We discussed how psychiatrists and lawyers were working on the concept of the insanity plea. This led to mention of John Hinkley, who had tried to assassinate President Ronald Reagan. I realized that our unconscious anxiety had found expression in our intellectual approach to Hinkley and "killers."

After eating, we circulated among the other tables, and I found myself next to the Mayor of Bethlehem. He was speaking in a humorous way of the security provided in a London hotel in which he had stayed. The hotel manager had denied his presence in the hotel to his wife when she returned there after an outing. When she demurred, "But I am his wife!" they continued to say, "There is no Mr. Freij registered."

This time I was sure of the participants' unconscious anxiety. All had been informed about the security measures with the hope they might calm the participants. I learned that after "formal" discussions end in conference rooms, thoughts and feelings about what had been discussed and felt linger and appear during social times, even though they may be expressed indirectly. The facilitating team must pay attention to these expressions in social settings too.

On April 14, Thursday, we looked further into the Reagan Plan and mutual and reciprocal recognition between Palestinians and Israelis. Here I will not dwell on what was said about the current events of the time or on the people who were involved in them. But I will say that we learned that communication between Israelis and Palestinians in Gaza and the West Bank was virtually nonexistent. Palestinians wanted to hear an offer from Israel, but the government of Israel at that time did not communicate with them at all. The Palestinians maintained that if they were given a "formula," they would talk with the Israelis, and the Israelis began to question their own perception that the "insider" Palestinians were totally "prisoners of the PLO." Only few known leaders in the occupied territories would talk directly to the Israelis. Mayor Freij had met with Begin only twice. He declared that no Arab mayor had ever refused to meet with Israeli authorities. Some Egyptians advocated for the idea of initiating a strong voice from inside the occupied territories and arranging get-togethers between "insider" Palestinians and Israelis. Also discussed was how each side was unable to see the other's problems and fears. Almost every Arab and Israeli agreed that extremism on either side supported the status quo.

Nobody had a problem with the issue of mutual recognition and, in fact, that concept was a problem chiefly of semantics. Nonetheless, one could sense the re-emergence of competition over who was to start the ball rolling. The Palestinians asked for a formula, while the Israelis were asking in their own way for stronger "insider" Palestinian leadership. When communication on these issues became difficult, the APA facilitating team brought the following observations to the Arabs' and Israelis' attention:

1. The models for peace envisioned by the two sides were conceptually different. Possibly, because of differences in cultural orientation and experience, the two sides were promoting different solutions while remaining emotionally and even cognitively unaware that their models were incongruent.
2. The Israelis seemed to be "process" oriented. As Shimon Shamir indicated, the State of Israel was the result of a process focused on gaining something and then seeking opportunities to gain more—and more. The Camp David Accords was consistent with this model in their view, which anticipated taking one step at a time.
3. The Palestinians wanted to have a concrete and final objective (or ultimate solution) without regard for process. The Reagan Plan seemed suitable to them.
4. The two sides were not hearing one another as long as they failed to realize the differences through which they were approaching the issue, and failed to acknowledge the emotional attachment each group felt for its own model.

Even at the Mountain House I was developing my technique to run such meetings. I was not there to give advice to the "enemy" participants. As a psychoanalyst I would offer empathetic explanations or interpretations to my patients about what lay behind their ambivalences and conflicts. I would not tell them what to do and how to manage their lives. While I was being trained to become a psychoanalyst, no one taught me how to manage other peoples' lives. Unlike psychotherapy as it is portrayed in many popular television shows, in real psychoanalysis the patient finds his or her own positive solutions.

We were taken for dinner that night to a small restaurant in the country where we had a room to ourselves. The security guards, to whose presence we were by now accustomed, also joined us. The curtains were drawn for greater safety, making the room dark and sensual. When a musician came in, Rafael pointed to his accordion and declared, "The accordion phenomenon!" He was referring to the analogy I had used at the Mont Pelerin meeting comparing the distancing and coming together of Egyptians and Israelis on that occasion with the push and pull of an accordion. He reminded people sitting in the dining room how I had stated that as the music goes on, the vacillation of distancing/coming together becomes more and more realistic.

The accordion player was an Armenian with an uncanny ability to respond to a diversity of ethnic interests. When he learned who we were he started playing Hebrew, Arabic, Turkish, Greek, and American songs. As he played, everyone danced. The Arabs found themselves dancing dances of Israeli origin, and vice versa. Our "celebration" became frenzied when Mohammed, after singing Arabic songs, invited us to join in singing the "Hymn of Joy" from Beethoven's 9th Symphony.

Among the personal contacts I made that night, one that stands out was my rapprochement with Hatem Abu Ghazaleh, a physician from Gaza. He told me about his and his family's previous contact with Turks, including stories about his elders' adventures with Turkish authorities during the centuries-long Turkish rule over what is known today as Palestine.[4] I sensed that he was disturbed by the present occupation of his land, and speaking of the occupation of the past gave him relief. We could laugh together, as a descendant of the occupier and a descendant of the occupied, at his humorous accounts of his family's dealing with the Turks, about which he expressed both anger and affection. As we rode back to Mountain House on the bus, Hatem sat behind Shlomo, and I sat across the aisle on his right. As we got up to disembark upon our arrival, I noticed that all rose at the same time. Spontaneously, and without thinking, I turned to Hatem, saying, "I allow you to go first. Let this Turk treat you nicely!" Overhearing my remark, Shlomo gestured for Hatem to move down the aisle ahead of him, saying, "I am the real Turk!" Then he confided that he had, in fact, been born in Istanbul. I think this event between the three of us gave symbolic reference to aspects of interaction between representatives of different ethnic groups: seeing myself as a representative of occupiers of the past with my gesture, I was acknowledging Hatem's hurt and trying to repair his pride. Shlomo then identified with me, acknowledging his being an occupier and announcing that he was "the real Turk." Moreover, he transformed himself into a reparative person by permitting Hatem to go first.

On April 15, Friday, we took a "bonding excursion." The next day, Saturday, the shadow of the 1982 Lebanon War fell on the meeting's discussion. During the war, a Lebanese Christian-Maronite Phalangist militia killed between 1,000 and

3,000 Palestinians, including children and other civilians in the Sabra and Shatila Palestinian refugee camps in Beirut. These camps were surrounded by Israeli forces when this tragedy occurred. The Maronites were responding to the assassination of Lebanist Phalangist leader Bachir Gemayel. Once more participants in our gathering made an association to an assassination, and its consequences would really touch a sore spot.

Shlomo, referring to the massacres at Sabra and Shatila, said, "We [Israelis] have no responsibility for the killings. Not one Israeli killed a Palestinian!" A Palestinian raised his voice in reply. "I can't believe what you are saying!" he exclaimed. "We know that the Phalangists were responsible for the killings at Sabra and Shatila. You [the Israelis] kept saying that Arabs were barbaric and that you were civilized. Then when you were around, killing occurred. The Israeli report on this incident [Kahan Report],[5] says that you are responsible, but it cannot say more than that. The report is partly political; it is emotionally motivated. You cannot wash your hands! You cannot say this was only a Phalangist business!" He then added, "I hope I am not offending anybody." Calm returned.

Copies of the Kahan Report that had been brought from Israel earlier were distributed to all participants. Referring to it, Alouph stated that one could see 3,000 years of Judaism in the study, with interpretation and reinterpretation of law dominating the society. With recent events in Lebanon, the issue of whether the law or the military controlled the country came into focus and led to the Kahan Report. He added, "I have deep doubts whether such an issue can be openly discussed in other countries." In response to this, Iyad spoke of how moved he had been at seeing the demonstrations in Israel in response to Sabra and Shatila; it had given him hope.

The rest of the discussion focused on observations that extreme religious fanaticism was increasing in the Arab world as well as in Israel. We also explored ideas of what could be done to strengthen the moderates in each national group. Earlier, after I consulted with the leaders of each group and other members of the facilitating team, it was decided that from that point on we would spend the last day of our meetings discussing what actions participants would try to take after the meeting was over.

On April 17, Sunday, we had a very early morning plenary session in which we considered actions such as reporting to appropriate people in governments concerning the ideas that had come to the surface in our meetings (Joe Montville would be the Americans' link to the U.S. Department of State); informing the American ambassadors in Jerusalem and Cairo about the meeting (with the Israelis and Palestinians going to see the U.S. ambassador to Israel together); visiting the West Bank and Gaza (by Israelis) to review the conditions there with the help of the Palestinian participants and to make recommendations for improvement and start joint projects on immigration, education, and press attitudes; conferring with each other by conference call after critical events; publishing a special issue of the *American Journal of Psychiatry* on the APA Committee on Psychiatry and Foreign Affairs–sponsored Arab-Israeli meetings; and considering inviting to regular meetings representatives of special professional groups, such as newspaper editors.

After the plenary session we took a train to Rochers-de-Naye, the snowy mountaintop above the Mountain House. It was a pleasant break of a few hours. That evening all of us got together again and everyone had a turn making farewell remarks. The Mountain House meeting came to a formal end. We had dinner at Château du Châtelard, where the Mayor of Montreux was our guest. We were welcomed to the château by some Swiss in native dress and the blowing of bugles. After the Israeli, Egyptian, and Palestinian participants left the next day, the Americans stayed in Switzerland to meet by themselves and to review the meeting.

On April 18, 1983, there was a suicide bombing attack on the U.S. embassy in Beirut that killed sixty people, mostly Americans working at the embassy, Marines, and sailors. We learned about this tragedy on April 19. Hezbollah, a Shi'ite Muslim militant group, took responsibility with the explanation that it wanted Americans out of Lebanon. With the knowledge of this new tragedy, and its associated death and destruction, the Americans flew back to their homes the next day.

# 8

# PALESTINIAN STONES

## THE SIGNIFICANCE OF LARGE-GROUP IDENTITY

In 1984, Kobenzl Hotel on the outskirts of Salzburg, Austria, was the location for the APA committee's next meeting with Israelis and Arabs. I felt confident and relaxed in my leadership role there. One reason for my confidence was my having been selected to be the fourth president of the International Society of Political Psychology (ISPP) in 1983 after the Mountain House gathering. With this, my career as a "political psychologist," in a sense, was crystallized and approved by many interested in this new field of inquiry. The founder of ISPP was Jeanne Knutson, a psychologist from the Department of Psychiatry and Biobehavioral Sciences, University of California, Los Angeles. Around the same time the American Psychiatric Association established its Committee on Psychiatry and Foreign Affairs, Jeanne became interested in the political belief systems of children and international terrorism and developed the right idea that to understand world affairs one needed input from different disciplines. She called some very well-known scholars from various fields of study—psychoanalysis, political science, theology, history, sociology, anthropology, diplomacy—shared her ideas with them, and asked if they would get together with her. I was one of the persons whom she called. With the little money that she was able to raise, we began to meet once or twice a year and sit around a table with Jeanne, increasingly infected by her enthusiasm. I realized that she was accomplishing something rather unusual: she brought together people who had firmly established themselves in their own professions and found ways for them to have dialogues, hear each other's terminology and concepts, and share ideas about politics and diplomacy. It was decided that this new society's presidency would rotate among persons from these various disciplines. This was how ISPP was born. I served from 1983 to 1984 as the first president with a medical background, and I take pride that ISPP's constitution was written during my presidency.

One significant development at the Kobenzl Hotel meeting was the addition of a new member to the APA committee's facilitating team, Harold ("Hal") Saunders. Hal was a well-known person in Washington, D.C., who had served on the U.S. National Security staff for twenty-five years beginning in 1961. He later served as deputy assistant secretary of state, as director of intelligence and research in the State Department, and lastly as assistant secretary of state for Near Eastern and South Asian Affairs. During the Nixon and Ford administrations, Secretary of State Henry Kissinger was involved in third-party mediations between Israel and Egypt, which became known as "shuttle diplomacy." Hal flew on Kissinger's shuttles. Ultimately, shuttle diplomacy ended in failure because the Israelis and Egyptians would not accept each other's goals. Hal was also present at the Camp David negotiations and participated in drafting the Camp David Accords.[1]

The interesting history of Kobenzl Hotel and its location goes back centuries. From the hotel a visitor can enjoy a panoramic view of Salzburg and its surroundings, including, on a distant mountaintop, Kehlsteinhaus, known to English-speaking people as Hitler's Eagle Nest. It was commissioned by Martin Bormann, who served as Hitler's private secretary, and was built in a little over thirteen months and presented as a gift to the Führer for his fiftieth birthday on April 20, 1939. To reach this building one has to take a fancy elevator straight up through the mountain. I was told that excavating the tunnel to build this elevator cost twelve lives. Even though we could not see Hitler's Eagle Nest clearly, its existence stimulated some of the Israeli participants during the first day of our meeting to refer to Hitler and the Holocaust, even though they knew that Hitler seldom visited the place. I believe that sharing their feelings and referring to some tragic stories gave them more freedom to discuss the existing conflict in the Middle East with the Egyptians and the Palestinians.

I will not give details of what the Israeli and Arab participants said during the duration of our meeting at Kobenzl Hotel, since this would be repeating many of their comments from the Mountain House meeting that I already reported in the last chapter. As Demetrios wrote, the Kobenzl Hotel meeting "was a more mature version" of the Mountain House gathering.[2] We paid more attention to disseminating our findings more widely, and the individuals with diplomatic background among us were mostly responsible for suggesting ways to reach important persons with political power in Cairo, Jerusalem, and Washington. Besides Hal's and Joe's presence, Ambassador Tahseen Basheer and a member of the Israeli embassy in Washington were with us in Salzburg. Shimon Shamir was already the head of the Israeli Academic Center in Cairo. The plan to open this center had come out of the APA project. Nechama would give a series of lectures on the children of Israel at the Israeli Academic Center in Cairo, exposing Egyptian intellectuals to some of the most poignant human issues involved in the conflict. Shlomo Gazit, then the president of Ben Gurion University, was responsible for planning academic collaboration between Egyptian scholars and members of his university. Alouph from the Van Leer Institute was encouraged and volunteered to be engaged in an examination of the way the image of the Arabs was being presented in Israeli schools. Because of the interest this awakened, a project for the rewriting of textbooks to eliminate distortions was later funded by the Israeli Ministry of Education. This project involved preparing new curricula and changing existing curricula throughout grades one through twelve, both in the Jewish and the Arab school systems in Israel. Alouph, who credited the APA conferences with nourishing his activities, already was bringing a number of Jewish and Arab teachers together for better mutual understanding. He spoke about a new project, in the planning stages that would examine what the occupation was doing to Israeli identity. We spoke about his searching for grants to realize his goal of producing a prime-time educational television series on Arab-Jewish relations. Already Israeli participants were meeting as a small group in their own country in the intervals between general meetings. They developed a network of personal contacts and talked about their APA experiences with many others, including some who exercised significant political power. They told us in Salzburg that they had begun contacting a number of Israelis who anticipated visiting Egypt, briefing them about the psychology of Egyptian people. Gabriel Cohen, from the Hebrew University and also a participant in our meetings, had joined Alouph, Rafael, and Shlomo in actively reflecting in print the APA meetings' influence.

Palestinians at Kobenzl Hotel shared with us that they had contacted Palestinian and Arab leaders outside the occupied territories and even some authorities of other nations and shared political perceptions gained at the Mountain House meeting. They told us that they would continue such activities. Meanwhile, Ramadan continued to write three pages of editorial comment in each issue of the influential periodical *October*, as well as writing regularly for the newspaper *Gumhuriyet*. We learned how he was disclosing attitudes clearly influenced by his experiences in the APA meetings. Psychiatrists Mohammed Shaalan and Adel Sadek also advocated in print many ideas formulated at our gatherings. We learned from Adel that he investigated the views of Egyptian medical students concerning Israelis, and initiated an examination of how people in one national group felt about those in another. This study was replicated by Shlomo at Ben Gurion University.

There was another event that took place at Kobenzl Hotel that taught me more about an abstract concept called large-group identity and its most significance role in international conflict, one that left a lasting impact on my mind. I learned that after the Mountain House meeting Israeli psychoanalyst Rafael Moses played a role in inviting the Palestinian psychiatrist Iyad Al-Sarraj to take part in some educational medical activities with Israelis. Iyad also participated in academic gatherings at Ben Gurion University. In Salzburg Iyad appeared to be more comfortable with the Israeli participants. During the first day of the Kobenzl Hotel meeting, in a small group, I was sitting to the left of Shlomo Gazit, with Iyad to the right of the general. While Iyad felt confident about talking to Shlomo openly and honestly about the conditions in Gaza, I sensed he was still nervous. At one point he turned to Shlomo, the first Israeli general assigned to manage the Gaza Strip, and said: "You were the first and the last Israeli general in charge of Gaza who was fair in dealing with the Arabs. I don't like living under Israeli occupation one bit. As a man, I respect you. After your tenure was over, however, none of the new military commanders assigned to Gaza have been fair to us as you were. Now, to be assigned as the Israeli military chief in Gaza is the end of a person's career. The Israelis send their unwanted military officers to us. These military officers know this, and they show their frustration by being unjust to us." As Iyad spoke, his emotions overtook him. He put his right hand into the right pocket of his trousers. I could see the frantic movements of his fingers under the cloth. Then, the Palestinian physician, almost screaming, declared: "As long as I have this, you can't take my Palestinian identity from me." While it was clear that he was speaking about an object in his pocket, I had no idea what "this" was.

Later, I learned the full story: "this" turned out to be a small piece of stone on which the Palestinian flag's colors were painted. Although Iyad never showed it to me directly, he described it and told me that most Palestinians in Gaza had a similar stone. It held great meaning to him, and he felt protective of it. Keeping his stone gave him an almost tangible sense of unity with other Palestinians. During a time of political turmoil and shared humiliation, these little painted stones had become the shared reservoirs in which Palestinians had, symbolically, placed externalized aspects of their ethnic identity. With these reservoirs tucked away securely and secretly in their pockets, away from the sight of Israelis, their sense of ethnic identity, or "we-ness," was placed in safekeeping.[3] Since my childhood I was exposed to various large-group identities: Turkish, Greek, British. But, it was the above interaction between Iyad and Shlomo that would genuinely turn my attention toward studying large-group identity from a psychological point of view and how this sense of identity becomes the central issue in conflicts among large groups.

I was very satisfied with the meeting at Kobenzl Hotel and looked forward to deepening the APA committee's unofficial role in the Middle East. I thought that we needed to have meetings without waiting too long, as we often waited many months or even a year. I hoped for the possibility of enlarging audience exposure to our findings. Soon I would be disappointed and frustrated. The APA committee would have only one more meeting with the Arabs and the Israelis, and then it would be dissolved.

The demise of the Middle East project was not due to pressure from Arabs or Israelis, but because of the internal affairs of the American Psychiatric Association. I never got involved in the APA's internal affairs, never ran for a position at the APA, and was never asked to take part in its administration, except for my leadership role in the APA's Arab-Israeli meetings. I understood that some psychiatrists in the APA who were moving up influentially in the organization felt that the membership of the Psychiatry and Foreign Affairs Committee needed to be changed. There were complaints that the committee's existing members had exceeded the accepted duration of their memberships according to the APA's constitution and that no exceptions should be made. Once at a professional meeting a psychiatrist told me, "You and your friends are traveling to marvelous places free. It is time that you stepped down and we have a chance to travel overseas." This person had no idea how hard we worked during each meeting, and it was clear that he thought that the APA was providing us with vacations.

The Committee on Psychiatry and Foreign Affairs' last meeting took place at the Aspen Institute in Wye, Maryland, in 1985. Originally it was planned that only the American, Egyptian, Israeli, and Palestinian participants who had gotten to know each other and who had gone through the discussion process would be present at Wye. But, at the last minute and without much consultation with me or Demetrios, APA expanded the plans, as Demetrious wrote, "precipitously."[4] The veterans of this project were mixed with "newcomers," some of whom, I was told, had been promised that they would take over running the dialogue series in the very near future. Later, Demetrios would write the following about the Wye conference: "It proved to be our most difficult conference to date. . . . [the participants] at this meeting might be described as having been, out of sync." The core veterans of the APA committee were told that, according to APA rules and regulations, this was the end of our membership on the committee and that new members would be in charge of the committee's activities. In fact, the new members never held even a single meeting with the Arabs and Israelis after the gathering at Wye. The committee was essentially "murdered."

Soon after the APA Committee on Psychiatry and Foreign Affairs ended, other former members of the committee and I learned that there had been a tragic and actual murder. On December 2, 1985, Aziz Shehadeh was knifed to death in the driveway of his home in East Jerusalem. It was said that his murder was politically motivated and that his murderer most likely was also a Palestinian. Aziz's efforts for finding peaceful ways of negotiating with Israelis apparently prompted this assassination. As far as I know, his murderer was never found, and I learned that Aziz's family and others complained about the inadequate investigation by the Israeli police. Learning of Aziz's demise shocked me and also induced some guilt in me. I wondered if his coming to the APA meetings played a role in his assassination. I realized that "political psychology" must consider the safety of its participants and be careful about real-world human cruelty.[5]

# PART III

---

# THE PSYCHOLOGY OF IDENTITY AND MOURNING

# 9

# THE DEVELOPMENT OF LARGE-GROUP IDENTITY

## THE PSYCHOLOGY OF "SYNTHETIC NATIONS"

In the previous chapter I told the story of Iyad Al-Sarraj's painted stone. Watching his interaction with General Shlomo Gazit at Kobenzl Hotel, I reacted like Isaac Newton in the popular myth when the apple supposedly fell on his head and led him to think about the Universal Law of Gravitation. Let us assume that before this event other apples had fallen on Newton's head or at least he had seen apples falling from trees. Only when the apple hit his head at this time was he ready for his insightful discovery. I had noticed since my childhood how people link their individual identities with their large-group identities. But it was Iyad's touching his little painted stone that led me to conclude that large-group identity, an *abstract* concept, is the main issue in international relations. Wars, war-like situations, terrorism, diplomatic efforts, and shared losses and gains associated with shared mourning or elation are all carried out in the name of large-group identity. This is true even though this psychological source is usually hidden behind rational real-world considerations—political, economic, legal, historical, moral, etc.

Sigmund Freud seldom referred to the term "identity." One well-known reference to identity is found in a speech Freud wrote for B'nai B'rith. In this text, Freud wondered why he was bound to Jewry since, as a nonbeliever, he had never been instilled with ethnonational pride or religious faith. Nevertheless, Freud noted a "safe privacy of a common mental construction," and a clear consciousness of his "inner identity" [as a Jew].[1] It is interesting that Freud's remarks linked his individual identity with his large-group identity. When World War I began he was even enthusiastic about his Austrian identity. In a letter to Karl Abraham written in July 1914, he stated, " For the first time in thirty years I feel myself to be an Austrian and feel like giving this not very hopeful Empire another chance."[2] But a few days later in another letter to Abraham, he was skeptical about getting involved in the shared excitement of Austrian nationalism. He wrote, "Can you perhaps tell me whether in a fortnight's time we shall be thinking half ashamedly of excitement of these days. . ."[3]

Some early psychoanalysts noticed the importance of large-group identity for individuals and large groups *without* using the term "identity" and without carrying out studies in diplomatic settings or in locations where enemies meet, whether peacefully or aggressively. For example, back in 1915, Ernest Jones, a close follower of Sigmund Freud, wrote, "Patriotism, or devotion, love and loyalty towards one country (or smaller unit), involves the willingness to fight for its interests, this taking the various forms of defending its material interests, avenging a slight on its honour, extending its prestige and importance, or resisting encroachments." He went on to state that love of one's country (or smaller units) is related to feelings about the self, the father, and the mother. The source concerning father is the least important of the three, "but is more prominent in some cases than others, leading then to patriarchal conceptions in which the head of state is felt to be the father, and the state itself the father's land."[4] Jones stated that the relation to the mother has more significance. He reminded us that a country, as a rule, is conceived of as being of feminine gender. He continued, "Most important of all is the source in self-love and self-interest, where the self becomes more or less identified with one's fellow-citizens and the state is a magnified self."[5]

It was Erik Erikson who made the concept of "identity" a psychoanalytic one. Referring to *individuals*, first he used the term "ego identity," and then dropped the word ego and used simply "identity." He described it as "a persistent sameness within oneself . . . [and] a persistent sharing of some kind of essential character with others."[6]

In psychoanalysis there is a consensus that an individual's "identity" refers to a subjective experience. It is differentiated from related concepts such as an individual's "character" and "personality," which are sometimes used interchangeably. The latter terms describe others' impressions of the individual's emotional expressions, modes of speech, typical actions, and habitual ways of thinking and behaving. If we observe someone to be habitually clean, orderly, or greedy, or if he uses excessive intellectualization and shows excessive ambivalence and controlled emotional expressions, we say that this person has an obsessional character. If we observe someone who is overtly suspicious and cautious, and whose physical demeanor suggests that she is constantly scanning the environment for possible danger, we say that this person has a paranoid personality. Unlike the terms "character" and "personality," "identity" refers to an individual's inner working model—he or she, not an outsider, senses and experiences it.

Salman Akhtar looked at individual identity from different angles. He stated that the sustained feeling of inner sameness is accompanied by a temporal continuity in the self-experience: the past, the present, and the future are integrated into a smooth continuum of remembered, felt, and expected existence for the individual. The individual identity is connected with a realistic body image and a sense of inner solidarity and is associated with the capacity for solitude and clarity of one's gender. Akhtar also connected individual identity with large-group identity, such as a national, ethnic, or religious identity.[7] Akhtar's last characteristic of individual identity refers to an oedipal link between one's personal identity and large-group identity.[8] He suggests that children's full assimilation of a large-group identity within themselves takes place when they are around four or five years old. At these ages children identify with their parents' prohibitions and ideals, and by extension, their large group's ideals and prohibitions. However, we know that the potential for a sense of "we-ness" in a human's mind exists very early in life.

Due to scientific observations of infants during the last few decades, we know that an infant's mind is more active than we thought it was when I began my psychoanalytic training. For example, Robert Emde's research on the evolution of an infant's mind suggests the existence of a psychobiological potential for "we-ness" and group-related behavior.[9] A recent interesting book by Paul Bloom, a professor of psychology at Yale, describes convincingly why we like what we like from early childhood on and how we are biased toward our own kind. He reminds us that a three-month-old baby is attracted to the face of a person from the same race and young children like to wear the same color or style shirt as adults in their group.[10]

Because the environment of an infant and small child is restricted to parents, siblings, relatives, and other caretakers, the extent of "we-ness" does not include a distinct dimension of large-group identity. An infant and a very small child is, to use Erik Erikson's term, a "generalist"[11] as far as tribal affiliation, nationality, ethnicity, religion, or political ideology are concerned; the subjective experience of belonging to a large group develops later.

Before I write about how children develop their individual identities, stop being generalists, and establish a firm sense of belonging to a large group, let me explore further what a large-group identity is. In psychoanalytic literature, the term "large group" sometimes refers to 30 to 150 members who meet in order to deal with a given issue. I have consistently used the term "large group" to refer to tens of thousands or millions of people who are linked by "a persistent sense of sameness" and who share subjective experiences—a *large-group identity*—whether it refers to a tribe, a clan, a class, an ethnicity, a race, a nationality, a religion, or a political ideology: "We are Apache," "We are FFVs (First Families of Virginia)," "We are Lithuanian Jews," "We are Kurds," "We are Polish," "We are white," "We are Muslims," "We are Communists," etc.

In such large groups, most of the individuals will never meet during their lifetimes. In fact, they will not even know of the existence of many others possessing the same large-group identity as their own. Yet, members of a large group share what John Mack called "cultural amplifiers,"[12] which are wide-ranging concrete or abstract identity markers such as physical body characteristics, language, nursery rhymes, food, dances, religious or other magical beliefs and myths, flags, and, most importantly—as I came to realize in international relations—images of realistic or mythologized figures or places and images of historical events and their consequences. These include the large group's difficulty or inability to mourn after massive losses stemming from such historical events.

A large group's "cultural amplifiers" are only associated with that particular large group; they are invested with shared narcissism (self-love) and usually accepted as "superior" and as a source of pride. If they relate to historical hurts, they are subjectively experienced as "bigger" than others' hurts. In 1982 when the APA committee meetings were still taking place, Rafael Moses wrote: "I was impressed with the predominance of narcissistic phenomena in the Arab-Israeli conflict. The exchange of narcissistic hurt and narcissistic counter-blow, the narcissistic rage engendered in the party which has been hurt and humiliated, are visible throughout the history of the Arab-Israeli conflict."[13]

The sharing of the large group's tribal, national, ethnic, religious, and other elements and the developing of ideas about large-group enemies as well as allies begin in childhood. This applies also to those whose family and community belong to a political ideological group, such as Communism for example. While growing up, they assimilate this ideology's specific identity markers and connected historical events as part of their large-group identity. To become a follower of a political ideology as an adult involves other psychological motivations.

First I will explore how an individual's identity develops and then how this person's large-group identity begins to be crystallized. The interplay between age-appropriate experiences and the maturation of the central nervous system in the development of what psychoanalysts call "ego functions" and the ability to form mental images of relationships with others ("object relations") have been scientifically studied, especially since the 1970s. One fact we learned is that no matter how much potential and ability an infant possesses, in infancy no one has a fully separate self; the infant's mind can be conceptualized as being in a creative state of confusion. A very small child's sense of genuine "I" evolves slowly.

One of the many tasks that infants need to accomplish is coming to see themselves as psychologically separate from their caretakers and clearly sensing the distinctions between others.[14] Another task is to learn that the mother (or other caretaker) who gratifies them and the mother who frustrates them is the same person and correspondingly, the loved and rejected infant is also a single individual. Infants need to accomplish the mending of opposites.[15] One of the pioneers of scientific observations of infants, Daniel Stern, reminds us that an infant is fed four to six times a day. Each feeding experience produces different degrees of pleasure. As the child grows up, in a sense, different experiences become categorized in the child's mind as "good" and "bad."[16] Loving and frustrating, as well as loved and frustrated, aspects of people connected with these experiences too are divided until the integrative function is effectively accomplished. The child's *subjective sense* of his or her integrated self is the child's personal identity. If the child cannot fully accomplish the integrative task, due to biological as well as environmental reasons, the individual's identity, even in adulthood, remains divided.

Once I had a young man as a patient—let us call him Saul—who divided his self-image into two parts. At times he thought of himself as a genius, and at other times he considered himself stupid. Being an average person would never cross his mind, since he never truly experienced being average. He also divided people around him into "good" and "bad" categories. During the third year of his analysis, he began coming to his sessions twenty-five minutes late. Without offering an excuse for this, or mentioning the subject at all, four times a week he would simply come to my office, lay on the couch with a smile on his face, and began talking. I sensed that this new pattern in his analysis reflected his developing an exaggerated transference—what psychoanalysts call "split transference"—toward me. He literally was dividing (splitting) his sessions/me into two parts in order to visit his childhood experiences fully and work on them.

To avoid interfering prematurely with this development, I waited for several weeks before I told Saul that he was losing half of his sessions each time he came to see me. I inquired if he was curious about this development, for I certainly was. My patient appeared very surprised—he seemed genuinely convinced that he was attending his full sessions. I stayed calm and continued to encourage him to be curious about our discrepancy regarding what time he arrived at my office. Slowly I came to understand what was occurring and learned that Saul was, in a way, telling the truth about coming to our sessions on time. He did in fact arrive at the scheduled time, but instead of entering my office, he would go into the bathroom next door where he spent twenty-five minutes holding an inner conversation with me during which he felt like an angry monster and likewise perceived me as a horrible person. He then would get off the toilet, come to my office, lay on my couch, and behave in an extremely friendly way and perceive me as friendly as well.[17] This patient much later went through a therapeutic process and mended his two sides, a process that in "normal" child development takes place before the child reaches the oedipal age.

I will reexamine what I describe above by referencing an important figure in psychoanalytic circles, Donald Winnicott. In 1963, Winnicott played with diagrams, using a circle to represent a person. He wrote, "Inside the circle is collected all the interplay of forces and objects that constitute the inner reality of the individual at this moment of time."[18] In 1969, Winnicott added that an individual who is mature enough to be represented as a circle is one who is capable of containing conflicts that arise from within and without, and that it is necessary to divide this circle by putting a line down its center, because "there must always be war or potential war along the line in the centre, on either side of the line there become organized groupings of benign and persecutory elements."[19] He continued by stating that only idealists "often speak as if there were such a thing as an individual with no line down the middle in the diagram of the person, where there is nothing but benign forces for use for good purposes."[20] According to Winnicott, "the individual" is a relatively modern concept. Until a few hundred years ago, he said, outside of a few exceptional "total individuals,"[21] everyone was unintegrated. When he wrote his papers on this topic he thought that even then, the world was mainly composed of individuals who could not achieve integration and be a total unit.

I believe that it would be less confusing to consider a circle with a line through its center as representing an individual who has achieved tolerance for ambivalence to one degree or another. Since opposite halves of the circle touch each other, metapsychologically speaking, such an individual has moved to a higher-level personality organization from the previous level—that of a personality organization—in that the person's opposite parts do not touch one another. I suggest that a diagram representing a truly unintegrated person would have not a line, but a definable gap between the two halves of the circle.[22] What Saul concretely exhibited was a representation of a truly unintegrated person; it also reflected a small child's "normal" internal world before the child was able to have an integrated self-representation.

Prior to an individual becoming a circle bisected by a line, one way of dealing with the tension created by having both unintegrated "good" and unintegrated "bad" elements is to repress one side of the unintegrated parts, meaning putting them away in the basement of the mind and locking the door. This would help the small child deal with the tension, at least temporarily. Another way is to put one side of these unintegrated parts into others or things, a process technically called "externalization." We see temporary externalizations every day when we watch children. A child who falls down and feels unhappy may say that he is not the one who fell down and that it is his toy bear that does not know how to run and falls down. Another child who observes the pleasure of someone eating an ice cream cone may declare that she is the ice cream eater herself. Usually what is externalized, "good" or "bad," does not stay out there, but comes back in. We call this process "internalization." Externalizations and internalizations follow one another.

We also see such externalizations and internalizations in adults who as children could not accomplish their internal mending. Here is another brief case-study to illustrate this.

Ricky was born with a deformity of his right arm and right fingers. This was unacceptable to his narcissistic mother who denied her son's deformity in peculiar ways, embarrassing and humiliating the growing child again and again. For example, she would give him rings on his birthdays, which in reality he could not wear on his deformed fingers. The mother's denial of his bodily reality combined with her other frustrating mothering functions played a role in Ricky's developing an unusual psychic organization. As a teenager he called his mother "Hitler," and himself "Goebbels," Hitler's "right-hand man," and read everything he could find on the Third Reich. Ricky's family was not Jewish, and his case illustrates what I wrote earlier: Nazi Germany and its leaders have become universal symbols for aggression and bad things in general.

Ricky came to see me for the first time when he was in his early twenties. When he sat in front of me in my office he began moving his mouth and making sucking sounds. Then he acted as if he was spitting something out. I learned that when he saw my name on my office door and heard my accent when I greeted him, he thought that I was German. He explained that the movements of his mouth and the sounds he made represented his drinking bad/Nazi German wine and then spitting it out. He had put Hitler's image into me and then was busy reinternalizing and then externalizing it through sucking and spitting. Since it is important to establish a "reality base" before beginning the treatment of patients like Ricky, I told him that I was not German, and that I had come from Turkey. Right away he asked me if Turks make wine. I replied, "Yes, both sweet and sour wines." I was giving him "permission" to take me in and put me out as both "good" and "bad" until we would begin building a therapeutic relationship.[23]

Earlier I developed a theory that children, as they grow up, especially at the peak of their putting their unmended sides together, are provided by adults in their environment what I called "shared targets" for their *permanent* externalizations. Such targets are mostly inanimate things supported and sponsored by adults. These permanent externalizations do not come back into the child. They initiate the beginnings of "we-ness" and the beginning of Others in a concrete way.[24] This preoedipal process later becomes combined with the oedipal child's more sophisticated understanding of concepts of clan, ethnicity, nationality, or other large-group labels.

To illustrate the application of my theory, let us consider Cyprus, where Greeks and Turks lived side by side for centuries until the island was *de facto* divided into two political entities in 1974. Greek farmers there often raise pigs. Turkish children, like Greek children, invariably are drawn to farm animals, but imagine a Turkish child wanting to touch and love a piglet. The mother or other important individuals in the Turkish child's environment would strongly discourage the child from playing with the piglet. For Muslim Turks, the pig is "dirty." For the Turkish child the pig is perceived as a cultural amplifier for the Greeks; it does not belong to the Turks' large group. Now the Turkish child has found a reservoir for externalizing permanently his or her unintegrated "bad" self- and object images. Since Muslim Turks do not eat pork, in a concrete sense what is externalized into the image of the pig will not be reinternalized.

When the child finds a suitable target for unintegrated "bad" self- and object images, the precursor of the Other becomes established in the child's mind at an experimental level. The Turkish child at this point does not fully understand what Greekness means. Sophisticated thoughts, perceptions and emotions, and images of history about the Other evolve much later without the individual's awareness that the first symbol of the enemy was in the service of helping him or her avoid feeling object relations tension. Since almost all Turkish children in Cyprus will use the same target, they will share the same precursor of the Other who may become the enemy if real world problems become complicated.

My coauthor of several books, Princeton historian Norman Itzkowitz, once told me how some children of Polish Jewish peasant origins living in America, far from the dangers of the old anti-Semitic world, were taught to spit three times when passing a Catholic church. This may be dismissed simply as superstition, but, according to Norman, it also partakes of the notion of the church as a suitable target of externalization. He added, "It is easier to give up 'bad' targets of externalization in an atmosphere of comparative safety, but memories of them linger on."[25] Nevertheless, with the exception of Native Americans and those who were brought as slaves, people from different countries with different religions and other belief systems came to the United States in order to be an American, the idealized image of the large-group identity for the citizens living in the United States. Because of this, the suitable target of externalization to which Norman referred might not be as stable as the suitable target of the Turkish child in Cyprus.

Unintegrated "good" self- and others' images too find suitable targets of permanent externalization which, as the child grows, represent "we-ness" and become significant cultural amplifiers for one's large group. Finnish children use the sauna for their "good" reservoir. Only when Finnish children grow up will they have sophisticated thoughts and feelings about Finishness.

In a more general way, certain cultural amplifiers, such as language, nursery rhymes, food, dances, religious symbols, or specific geographical locations, become "good" targets of permanent externalization. Certain historical events may increase a large group's investment in its own suitable target of externalization. In Scotland, Highland dress dates from the thirteenth century, but it was an event in the eighteenth century that transformed the tartan kilt into a shared "good" reservoir of Scottishness. When England defeated Bonnie Prince Charles at Culloden in 1746, the English banned the wearing of the kilt in Scotland under the Act of Proscription. The act was repealed thirty-six years later, and the kilt was adopted as Scottish military dress. When George IV made a state visit to Scotland in 1882, his visit strengthened Scottish investment in the kilt, which served to enhance Scottish "we-ness" in the face of a visit from the figurehead of powerful England. Many Scottish families even have their own tartan design, which they sometimes use in their personal clothing. Efforts to suppress the wearing of the kilt have been unsuccessful; the dress continues to serve as an ethnic reservoir signifying Scottishness.

Another psychoanalytic concept called "identification" is well-known for its role in how a child develops large-group identity. During repeated interactions with mother, father, siblings, grandparents, other family members, neighbors, teachers and important persons in their environment, children begin to "eat up" such experiences (internalization). Sometimes what is "eaten" is not externalized. When what is "eaten" is kept within the psyche of the child, we name this psychic event "identification." Recalling what I have said about the child's developing an integrative function, it is clear that very early identifications are split (or even fragmented). When the integrative function fully develops, a child will be able to put together his or her identifications.

Children identify with realistic, fantasized, wished-for, or scary aspects of important individuals in their environment and their psychological functions. Such individuals' mothering, fathering, sibling, and mentoring functions, psychological ways of handling problems, belief systems, investments in cultural amplifiers, large-group ceremonies, and related things are internalized and utilized to expand children's internal worlds in adaptive and sometime in maladaptive ways in relating to small as well as large groups. When a child stops being, in Erik Erikson's term, a "generalist,"[26] as far as tribal affiliation, nationality, ethnicity, religion, or political ideology are concerned, the subjective experience of belonging to a large group develops. A child growing up in a Catholic family, without even being aware of it, will slowly stop being a generalist and become a Catholic. If the child who grows up "eating" Catholic religion is molested by a Catholic priest, his investment in the religious large-group identity most likely will not be an integrated one, and one aspect of it will continue to "nauseate" him for the rest of his life.

At the foundation of who we would grow up to be, besides our biological and genetic potentials, lies our childhood experiences with suitable targets of permanent externalizations and identifications with important others and their functions. This depends on the degree of our ability to integrate our self-images. Existing conditions in the environment direct children to invest in this or that type of large-group belongingness. A child born in Hyderabad, India, for example, would focus on religio-cultural issues as she develops a large-group identity, since adults there define their dominant large-group identity according to religious affiliation, Muslim or Hindu.[27] A child born in Cyprus during the hot Cypriot Turk–Cypriot Greek conflict would absorb a dominant large-group identity defined by ethnonational sentiments, because what was critical in this part of the world at that time was whether one was Greek or Turkish, and less emphasis was placed on whether one was Greek Orthodox Christian or Sunni Muslim. Questions of investment in ethnicity versus religion, or nationality versus race, or one ideology versus another are not as essential to understanding large-group identity as are the psychodynamic processes of linking individual identity to large-group identity and how large groups use them in their interactions.

Some children have parents who belong to two different ethnic or religious groups. If an international conflict erupts between these two large groups, these youngsters may, even as adults, have severe psychological problems. For example, when I worked in South Ossetia years after my involvement with the APA committee's Arab-Israeli dialogue series, I noticed how wars between Georgians and South Ossetians especially confused and psychologically disturbed individuals with "mixed" lineage. The same was true in Transylvania for the children born of mixed Romanian and Hungarian marriages.

Identification and identity are related, but they are not interchangeable concepts. As Erik Erikson stated, identity starts when a process of identification ends.[28] A cohesive personal identity starts when identifications are assimilated within a self-representation that is clearly differentiated from other persons' mental doubles and that is integrated. During the adolescent passage there is a psychobiological review that is carried within oneself. Youngsters loosen their investments in the images of important others of their childhood, modifying, sometimes strengthening, and even disregarding their identifications with them. Furthermore, they add additional identifications, this time through their experiences with their peer group or far beyond their restricted family or neighborhood environment. Through these internal activities there is an overhauling of youngsters' persistent sense of inner sameness.[29] The formation of a solid identity finalizes during this period along with large-group identity and children's sense of how belonging to a specific large-group identity differentiates them from those with different large-group identities.

Belonging to a large group, after going through the adolescent passage, endures throughout a lifetime.[30] Sometimes an individual's belongingness can be a shadow identity, as we sometimes see in persons after voluntary or forced migrations or in individuals who become dissenters or in persons who, for ideological and politically influenced reasons, intellectually refuse to belong to any given large group and unconsciously or even consciously hide their original emotional investments.

One can find many phenomenologies in the literature of history, political science, sociology, anthropology, and philosophy that define tribal, ethnic, national, or political groups. Often, however, a description of a large group's title changes in scope and substance according to the discipline by which it is studied. For example, the word "nation" usually means a large group of persons with common territory, history, language, way of life, and economy. But another description of the word nation refers to a large group of persons living in a territory under the same government: a large group of persons having a state, living within a legal boundary. Others argue that the term "nation" should not be linked to the term "state." A simple definition of a large-group title is not sufficient to explain the power it has to influence political, economic, legal, and military initiatives and to induce seemingly irrational resistances to change.

Neither do surface descriptions explain how large-group identity raises substantial barriers to peaceful coexistence between former enemies. We should also keep in mind that tens of thousands or millions of individuals' shared investment in the existing identity markers change as time goes on due to historical events, revolutions, economic situations, occupations, migrations, the personality of political leaders, and other factors. For example, soon after the Turkish Republic was founded in 1923, the *fez*, a headgear for men, was no longer a cultural amplifier after the founders of modern Turkey became involved in modernization and Westernization of the new Republic. In today's Turkey, religious identity markers overshadow the nationalist ones; it was the other way around a few decades ago. I suggest those of us who have studied human psychology should pay more attention to the psychodynamic processes that take place within a large group and within its relationships with other groups, instead of being preoccupied with surface definitions of large-group identity terms.

I will use a psychological lens to examine one aspect of large-group identity within a legal boundary. Nation-states are born differently. Some are what historian and psychoanalyst Peter Loewenberg calls "synthetic nations," such as the United States and Israel, places where in broad terms people came from different places with different experiences to create a synthesis of disparate influences and to live together. They "invent" a nation. Loewenberg states that such nations need a mythic common past, usually glorious and sometimes persecuting, and develop self-worshipping in order to firm up the synthesis.[31]

The attempt to link people from different groups increases a need to externalize unwanted images and to project unwanted ideas and feelings that cannot be integrated within the developing synthetic large group onto Others. In the United States, a majority of white persons from different backgrounds aimed to create an idealized white-national large-group identity, an effort, psychologically speaking, that was supported by racism. I believe that in the United States Norman Itzkowitz's description of a Jewish-American child's using a Catholic church as a suitable target of externalization for the Other is much less powerful than another target of externalization in the United States: skin color. There is much work to be done around the subject of racism in the United States, even now after an African-American has been elected president.

I was a guest during the 52nd anniversary of the founding of the State of Israel at a ceremony at Mount Herzl on the west side of Jerusalem on May 10, 2000. The Speaker of the Knesset, Avraham Burg, gave a speech that day. I had met Burg at the Knesset just a few days earlier, when both of us participated in a meeting that dealt with the themes of cultural diversity and coexistence. At Mount Herzl he first mentioned that no other nation has managed to overcome circumstances like the Holocaust and the price Israel had to pay in each of its wars in building a country. But he was not satisfied. He referred to "a sour atmosphere in Israel" and added, "The scandals follow one another, the internal enmity, the sectarianism—we no longer follow the principle 'the Tribes of Israel together,' but rather 'Each man to thy tents, O Israel.'"

Burg's wish for an "integrated" Israel was clear, but he was aware that the implementation was difficult. He stated, "Israel will be a society of its beliefs and of its believers. It has one God and four religions: Jews and Christians, Muslims and Druze. The religious and the secular, Jews and Arabs, men and women, rich and poor, Westerners and Easterners, immigrants and those born in Israel." He was clearly aware of the identity problem in Israel. He urged, "From here on Mt. Herzl, we must bring the debate on identity into everyday life, into the classroom and into the workplace, into the Knesset and into the decision-making centres." After Burg's speech, representatives of twelve subgroups, such as European Israelis who had been most directly traumatized by the Holocaust, Israelis coming from Africa, and Israelis who immigrated from Russia, stood on the stage, symbolically unifying themselves through their speeches and behavior.

On the other hand, the Palestinian large-group identity evolved by linking ethnic Arabs living in specific territory who had undergone a series of massive traumas and major losses and had suffered from humiliation. The Palestinian identity developed as the number-one Arab large-group identity, as a flag for suffering. Utilization of a sense of suffering is often in the service of feeling morally superior, openly or in a hidden fashion, and represents the existence of "masochistic (victimized) large-group narcissism."[32] To complicate matters further, there was an unacknowledged competition about "victimization" between Palestinians and Israelis with the history of the Holocaust. In 2000 the Israelis were still trying to avoid "looking back" in regard to the Holocaust and its impact on Israel's politics. I am reminded of the Bible story in which God destroyed Sodom and Gomorrah and saved Lot and his wife, telling them that they were forbidden to look back toward the destroyed cities. Lot's wife looked back, and God turned her into a pillar of salt. "Looking back" thus can be painful to the point of numbness.

During a visit to Jerusalem in 2012, when I talked with influential Palestinians in the West Bank, I noticed that the investment in Palestinian identity—at least among the Palestinians from West Bank—is changing rapidly as the West Bank, financially speaking, is booming. Masochistic investment seemed to have disappeared. Furthermore, at the present time among some important Israeli politicians, acknowledgment of the impact of the Holocaust on politics seems to be verbalized more readily. There are still feelings of humiliation regarding the Holocaust past, and this avoidance might also be connected to those feelings.

Going back to my observations of 2000, it was reasonable to consider that developing a "synthetic" nation surrounded by enemies also psychologically needs to have enemies in order to externalize elements that cannot be synthesized, and a neighbor with masochistic large-group narcissism needs to collect sufferings to maintain this type of large-group identity, so we can imagine a major psychological reason why it was and still is so difficult to find a peaceful solution to the Israeli-Palestinian problems. This does not minimize real problems. Understanding a major underlying psychological factor does not erase real issues in an international conflict, but it does acknowledge obstacles to resolving such conflicts.

Let me return to Iyad's painted stone, where this chapter began. Members of a large group under the influence of an international conflict or a war-like situation regress. In such a circumstance, especially when they feel victimized and helpless, they may create adult versions of suitable targets of permanent externalization. In childhood, reservoirs are chosen because they have been culturally or religiously invested in by parents and other adults who direct the children to choose them. Adults who regress under a shared trauma, however, choose reservoirs that are related to their threatening environment. Iyad's story of Palestinians reaching into their pockets and touching colored stones is an example of this. Reaching into such targets for externalization and creating symbolic "we-ness" protects the shared large-group identity, especially when there is a danger from the Other.

In the next chapters I will examine the psychology of individual as well as large-group (shared) mourning. International relations and conflicts between large groups are always connected with individual and large-group mourning processes, because they always deal with some form of loss and gain, narcissistic blow, and narcissistic enhancement of large-group identity.

# 10

# INDIVIDUALS' RESPONSES TO LOSSES

## LINKING OBJECTS AND LINKING PHENOMENA

After the APA Committee on Psychiatry and Foreign Affairs' Arab-Israeli dialogue series ended in 1985, professional and personal relationships among its participants continued. I myself visited Israel yearly for some time, speaking at various professional gatherings where I began describing my psychopolitical observations by using psychoanalytic insights. I became more and more aware that knowledge about individual psychodynamics was not enough to adequately explain community affairs, especially large-group processes. There are echoes of individual psychology in large-group psychology shared by thousands or millions of persons, but large groups do not have one brain to think with or two eyes to cry. Thousands or millions in a large group share a psychological journey, such as going through a complicated mourning after major shared losses, or when they use the same psychological mechanism such as "externalization," making the Other a shared target. These journeys become social, cultural, political, or ideological processes that are *specific* for the large group under study. Considering large-group psychology in its own right means making formulations about a large groups' conscious and unconscious shared psychological experiences and motivations that initiate specific social, cultural, political, or ideological processes and that influence the large group's internal and external affairs. This is the same process psychoanalysts follow in their clinical practice when they make formulations about the internal worlds of their patients in order to summarize what their diagnoses and treatment will be.

There were constant direct or indirect references to personal and shared losses during the APA committee–sponsored Arab-Israeli meetings. In fact, Arab and Israeli participants, especially during the first years of the dialogue series, often competed by comparing their personal and shared losses. Listening to them, it was easy to recognize that international relations becomes contaminated by many painful losses, whether of individuals, land, or prestige, and a series of gains, such as the acquiring of power, influence, and new territory. Our observations of human behavior patterns, coupled with psychoanalytic theories that explain such patterns, inform us that after a significant loss a person is obliged to mourn. Complications in shared mourning constitute a key phenomenon in international affairs.

In this chapter I will describe clinical observations and theories of grief and mourning and illustrate them by telling the story of an individual loss—mine—and in the next chapter I will talk about a relatively small Israeli community's response to shared losses. Following this, I will describe a Palestinian community's response to its shared losses. Later in the book I will share my observations and theories about grief and mourning of large groups—including in the generations that follow the one that actually suffered the massive losses.

Let me begin by examining an adult individual's mourning process. Princeton University history professor Norman Itzkowitz wrote, "Although dictionaries give grieving and mourning as synonymous, for me they are not the same emotionally. To grieve and experience sorrow that accompanies it is a much more transitory matter than mourning. Mourning is a process, and you have to go through the entire process and emerge at the other end before you can let go of the deceased [or the lost thing]. As such, it takes time. Dictionaries neither grieve nor mourn, otherwise they would know the difference."[1]

I also refer to initial reactions to a loss as a "grief reaction." It includes a sense of shock if the person experiencing it was not prepared to lose a psychologically significant person or thing. The sense of shock alternates or is accompanied by some physical reactions, such as shortness of breath, tightness in the throat, a need to sigh, muscular limpness, and a loss of appetite. As shock and its physical symptoms abate, the grieving person shows signs of wishing to have the loss reversed. He or she may deny, at least for a while, that the loss actually took place. A more common phenomenon is the person's utilization of splitting.[2] This individual splits an ego function so that opposing perceptions and experiences can take place simultaneously. For example, a woman knows that her dead husband is lying in a coffin at a funeral home, but she "hears" her husband's car as it crunches the gravel in the driveway. Grief also includes the grieving person's bargaining with God, Fate, oneself, or others in order to reverse the death of someone or to undo the burning of a beloved house, as if such reversals were possible: "If I had not been stuck in traffic and had come home earlier, I would have prevented the accident that caused the death of my wife." The grieving person, in his or her mind, may become preoccupied with the idea of taking a different route when driving home that day and avoiding the heavy traffic, thereby reversing the tragedy.

In reality the lost person or thing never reappears and the grieving person feels guilty, to one degree or another, for not reversing the outcome of the tragedy and/or for continuing to live while someone else is gone or something is destroyed. This person's own guilt, however, is complicated, because—again to one degree or another—he or she is also angry that, by being lost, the person or thing has induced in the grieving person a narcissistic wound. Feelings of guilt and anger may be conscious, but most often they are repressed. We know these feelings exist if the grieving person seeks psychological treatment or is already undergoing treatment. The therapist then can "hear" a great deal about the grieving person's guilt and anger. Often the person displaces anger onto someone else or something else. He may feel anger toward a physician who had taken care of his now-deceased wife, for example, or she may become irritated with the manufacturer of the gas stove that ignited the fire that burned her house. Grieving persons may also turn their anger inward if they do not have a suitable target outside of themselves. The turning of anger toward oneself also becomes a maladaptive remedy for guilt feelings.

Most importantly and obviously, a person's grieving process is accompanied by pain, sorrow, and crying spells. Grieving people, in a sense, keep hitting their head against a wall, a wall that never opens up to allow the dead person or lost thing to come back. This itself induces hidden and sometimes open anger, but this type of anger is a healthy indication that the grieving person is beginning to accept the facts.

A typical grief reaction takes some months to disappear. In truth, there is no typical grief reaction, because the circumstances of a loss vary, and because each individual has his or her own degree of internal preparedness to face significant losses. The symptoms I described above may not even be visible if the person has been prepared for the loss, such as waiting for a long-bedridden grandmother to die. Grief reactions may reappear for a time at the anniversary of the event when the loss took place. A grief reaction itself can be complicated. There are adults who spontaneously cry and feel pain and anger whenever something in their environment reminds them of their original loss.

Mourning is a more silent and internal phenomenon. It begins when the individual still exhibits a grief reaction and, if everything progresses without complications, it typically continues for years before it is tamed and, for all practical purposes, ends. In fact, the mourning process as it will be described here, never really ends until the mourner dies. Sigmund Freud's 1917 paper "Mourning and Melancholia" contains a very good description of what a mourner goes through internally.[3] Let me try to restate what Freud said by using nontechnical terms and by modifying his theories using newer findings:

To understand what an adult person's mourning is, I will start with the description of a nontechnical term: "mental double." It stands for the technical terms "mental representation" or "object representation," a collection of images of another person or thing. We can understand what a mental double means if we close our eyes when alone, picture someone who is important to us—someone we love or hate—and allow ourselves to think of an event in which we had a memorable interaction with this person. Furthermore, if we allow ourselves to recall and sense our emotions associated with this event, we temporarily create a mental double of the person who is not in the room. We always have mental doubles of others and, if we have unfinished businesses with them, we may be preoccupied with inner relationships and even inner conversations with them.

Such mental doubles are based on the reality of our experiences, but also to one extent or another, on our modification of such realities according to our perceptions, wishes, expectations, and fears—in short, our fantasies. We also have mental doubles of things, such as our childhood environment, a special gift, or a professional position. The physical loss of a person or thing does not parallel the mental "burial" of the mental double of the lost person or thing. In fact, the physical loss, or even a threat of a physical loss, turns the adult mourner's attention to the mental double of the real or threatened loss. The sum of mental activities the mourner performs in reviewing and dealing with many images of the mental double of the lost person or thing constitutes an adult person's mourning process.

Very small children do not have a firmly established mental double of another person. As Edna Furman described long ago,[4] children cannot mourn as adults do. Children who slowly develop a lasting mental double of the Other, also slowly develop the concept of death. Even when they intellectually learn what death is on one level, belief in its reversibility remains, however hidden it may be. According to Martha Wolfenstein, the adolescent passage is the crucial process that separates one's ability or inability to genuinely mourn in an adult fashion.[5] This period includes youngsters' mostly unconscious examination of their internalized childhood attachments to and more developed relationships with mental doubles or special images of parents, siblings, and other important individuals in their rather limited psychic environments. During the adolescent passage, they loosen these attachments and internal relationships, modify them, replace them, or even give them up. This work allows them—now with the more established gender identity and personality formation of adolescence—to make new, or at least modified, kinds of investments in others, such as peer groups, movie stars, and musicians and their associated mental images or representations, and in issues of social, cultural ,and historical importance to them, thereby enlarging their psychic environments.[6] Wolfenstein argued that the "normal" adolescent passage provides a model for an adult type of mourning. In it, we learn how to modify or let go, to one extent or another, of mental doubles or specific images of others who were subjects of our attachments and of other types of intense relationships.

During the mourning process, the adult mourner identifies with some images of the mental double of the lost person and assumes functions associated with these images, and in doing so may enrich his or her psychic world. A year or so after his father's death, a wayward young man becomes a serious industrialist like his dead father used to be. A woman who depended on her husband to reinforce her sense of femininity may emerge from a "healthy" mourning feeling confident and more feminine. An immigrant who had lost his country may become an official or nonofficial representative of his lost country. Other mourners, instead of accomplishing enriching identifications, assimilate images that are invested heavily with both love and hate. The strong ambivalence that originally connected the mourner to the lost person or thing when they actually existed turns the mourner's internal world into a battleground, an internal fight between love and hate. In short, identifications with the lost person or thing and their functions can be "healthy" or "unhealthy."

Most images of the dead person or lost thing are not involved in identifications; they will remain unassimilated. A mourner is able to relate to unassimilated images of a dead person or lost thing as long as this mourner is alive and keeps his or her mental functioning. We can say that a mourning process is completed, for practical purposes, when the unassimilated images of the mental double of the lost person or thing become "futureless"[7]— that is, when the mental double or some of its specific images are no longer utilized to respond to the mourner's wishes or fears. A young man stops fantasizing that his wife who has been dead for some time will give him sexual pleasure, for example. Or, a woman stops wishing to boss her underlings at a job from which she was fired years before.

There are various reasons for the diverse outcomes of mourning processes. All of us experience "developmental" losses and gains during our childhood. A small child "loses" his mother's breast and "gains" the ability to psychologically and physically separate from his mother. If there are childhood traumas that interfere with the "developmental" loses and gains, an adult may not have enough "knowledge" about how to deal with significant losses in adulthood. Or, when the death of someone is connected with violence such as murder or suicide, the "normal" anger during the grief reaction, as well as the mourning process, unconsciously becomes connected with exaggerated violence and this creates complications.

Another major factor that complicates a mourning process comes from its contamination with reactions to a trauma. When a loss is associated with experiences of helplessness, passivity, shame, and humiliation, the mourning process is accompanied by other psychological tasks, such as turning helplessness and passivity into assertion and activity and reversing shame and humiliation. A loss itself may be traumatic in its own right, especially when it is sudden and unexpected, but above and beyond the loss itself, the combination of a loss with actual trauma complicates the mourning process in a serious way. Losses occurring during wars and war-like situations accompanied by humiliation, helplessness, terror, or terrorism would most likely complicate the mourning process.

Some images of the lost person or thing do not become futureless. If the mourner remains preoccupied with such images, we say that he or she is a "perennial mourner." The internal relationship with the unassimilated parts of a mental double is psychologically tiresome and bothersome, so the mourner puts the lost mental double "out there." A man came to see me in my clinical office complaining that his younger brother had been disturbing him daily and he did not know how to deal with the situation. He sought treatment in order to free himself from his brother's influence. He explained that while driving to work in his car his brother constantly talked with him, even when my patient wanted some time for himself or when he wanted to listen to the car radio. His brother gave him advice about everything. For example, he made suggestions as to how my patient should behave when meeting his boss or when talking to a particular secretary at work. My patient did not like his brother's advice. Sometimes he told his brother to shut up, but the younger man continued to talk and irritate him. I also learned that when both men were young my patient experienced considerable sibling rivalry.

I pictured my patient in his car with his brother sitting next to him. I even imagined that my patient and his brother lived together in the same house or at least nearby, which would explain their riding downtown together each workday. Therefore I was surprised when my patient, in his sixth therapeutic session, informed me that his younger brother had died six years before in an accident. The "brother" with whom he had conversations while driving to work was actually his brother's unassimilated mental double. Sometimes my patient sensed his brother's mental double as lodged in his chest. This sensation was very uncomfortable for him. He felt better when he experienced this mental double as a puppet-sized younger brother sitting on one of his shoulders and talking to him, literally a symbolized burden he carried on his shoulder. He did not experience any break with reality except when communicating with his brother's mental double located "out there."

Perennial mourners commonly create "linking objects" or "linking phenomena." These terms refer to inanimate and sometimes animate objects and things "out there" in which the unassimilated image of the mental double of the lost person meets the corresponding self-image of the mourner. For example, a son "chooses" a broken watch owned by his dead father and, psychologically speaking, makes it magical. In this case, the mental double of the dead father is externalized and meets the son's own mental representation "out there." The internal adult-type work on mourning that would make the images of the lost person or thing futureless is replaced by a continuous preoccupation and relationship with the broken watch.

The son thinks of fixing it, but never tries to do so. He feels a sense of relief in exerting control over the broken watch. He locks it in a drawer and thus distances himself from an internal struggle with the image of the dead. A realistic representation of the lost person, such as a photograph, can also function as a linking object. When perennial mourners "hide" a photograph that has become a linking object in a drawer, they also "hide" their complicated mourning process in the same drawer. Then there are linking objects I call "last-minute objects," something that was at hand when a mourner first learned of the death or saw the dead body. They relate to the last moment in which the deceased was regarded as a living person.

There are linking objects that connect a person with complicated mourning, not to a deceased person, but to a significant lost *thing*. Many years after the Arab-Israeli dialogues, I learned a most moving illustration of this. It was in 2006 when I was the Fulbright-Sigmund Freud Scholar of Psychoanalysis in Vienna, Austria, and I became close friends with the Austrian painter, visual artist, and architect Wolf Werdigier. Wolf's father was a Jew who had lost his wife and a son during the Holocaust. Later he married Wolf's German mother. Due to his background, Wolf has been very interested in human nature, large-group violence, psychoanalysis, and the Middle East conflict. During the 1990s as well as in the 2000s, he painted dozens of psychoanalytic concepts. One of his paintings is titled "Attachment to Ground." The painting shows the agonized face of a person, a Palestinian, whose body disappears in yellow sand. Old-fashioned keys protrude from the sand around the head of this individual. In reality the keys provide a linking object for many Palestinians. I learned from Wolf that when the Israelis bulldoze Palestinian houses, most of these Palestinians keep the keys to their front doors and become perennial mourners over losing their homes. They control the keys in order to "freeze" their mourning process; the hope that they might rebuild their homes and the expectation for revenge are locked within the keys. Later when I met some high-level Palestinian politicians in Europe, I noticed that the pins they were wearing on the lapels of their jackets showed a picture of a key. Right away I knew that, like the painted stones Iyad Al-Sarraj described, these pins had become shared linking objects, symbols of Palestinianess. A linking phenomenon refers to a song, a smell, a gesture, an action, or an affect that functions as a linking object. It was raining on the day a young woman attended her father's funeral. The song "Raindrops Keep Falling on My Head" came to her mind. Later, she utilized this song as a linking phenomenon whenever she needed to escape the internal pressure of her mourning process.[8]

Keepsakes cherished by a mourner should be considered a linking object. A typical keepsake does not function as a repository where a complicated mourning process is externalized. A typical keepsake provides continuity between the time before the loss and the time after the loss, or generational continuity if the lost person or item belonged to a previous generation. Persons without complicated mourning are capable of having keepsakes. On the other hand, perennial mourners with linking objects or linking phenomena are like people sitting on a fence. Unconsciously they feel that if they jump off one side of the fence the lost item will be recovered; if they jump off the other side they will accept the reality of the loss. They do not jump either way, but "freeze" their mourning process. Even in their dreams they see frozen, motionless items. Perennial mourning has various degrees of severity and some perennial mourners live miserable lives. Others express their unending mourning in more creative ways.

Starting in the early 1970s,[9] I studied perennial mourners in a hospital setting and thought of all of them as "pathological." Then one day years later I realized that I had been a perennial mourner myself. In the summer of 1956 I finished Ankara University's School of Medicine and six months later I came to America, where I remained. During the last two and a half years of my life in Ankara, first as a rather poor medical student and then as a newly graduated physician, I shared a small room in an apartment complex with another Cypriot Turk named Erol. He had come to Ankara, as had I, for his medical education and was two classes below me at the same medical school. He called me "*abi*" meaning 'big brother." Since I only had sisters and no brother, I considered him to be my brother. During the time we were roommates ethnic conflict began between the Cypriot Turks and Cypriot Greeks.

Three months after my arrival in the United States I received a letter from my father. In the envelope there was a newspaper article with Erol's picture describing how he had gone to Cyprus from Ankara to visit his ailing mother. While trying to purchase medicine for her at a pharmacy, he was shot seven times by Cypriot Greek terrorists. These people killed Erol, a bright young man with a promising future, in order to terrorize the ethnic group to which he belonged. After receiving the news of Erol's death, I felt numb. I did not cry. I was in Chicago in a foreign environment in which I was close to no one, so I did not share the news of Erol's murder with any other person. Even when I was undergoing my personal analysis some years later, I did not dwell on losing Erol. My "hidden" mourning process, I believe, largely remained just that—hidden.

As a young psychoanalyst I felt close to the late William Niederland and, in a sense, I thought of him as a mentor. At the time it never occurred to me that my seeking out Niederland, who had coined the term "survivor syndrome,"[10] as a mentor might have something to do with my own "survival guilt" over losing Erol. In 1979 I published a book called *Cyprus—War and Adaptation* in which I briefly described Erol's murder.[11] During the same year I began my involvement with the

APA committee's Arab-Israeli dialogue series and, as this text describes, a lifetime of similar involvement in other conflict areas. At the same time I was trying to understand the psychology of ethnic, national, religious, and ideological conflicts that are associated with massive losses. During these years I also visited Northern Cyprus on many occasions, but it never occurred to me to visit Erol's family or find his grave.

Thirty-some years after Erol's death I once more visited Northern Cyprus. One summer night some friends took me to a garden restaurant, and one of them who knew Erol's story pointed out a bearded man behind the bar and told me that this man was Erol's younger brother. I spontaneously got up from my chair, approached this man and said to him, "My name is Vamık. Does this name mean anything to you?" He began to cry and I found myself also crying out loud, right in the midst of people dining, with soothing classical music playing in the background. I had experienced an acute grief reaction, which was followed by the reactivation of my mourning process, which lasted many, many months. Upon reflection I realized that I had kept the newspaper clipping with Erol's picture, which my father had sent me, as a linking object. Erol's mental double now is futureless. But when I was keeping it "alive," I used what it represented for me psychologically as a motivational source for many of my professional activities.

My reaction to Erol's death included many elements that are discussed in Otto Kernberg's description of "normal" mourning after the death of a spouse.[12] As I had done previously,[13] Kernberg observed that even a normal mourning process is not time-limited. Erol's death obviously induced elements of survivor guilt in me. Furthermore, when we were sharing lodgings, there were times when I treated him as a younger brother and ordered him around, and now he was no longer available to forgive me. Losing him also initiated reparative efforts in me. I became fully aware of this after my mourning process was activated in the restaurant. I realized then that the main reason for my choosing to study the topic of mourning in individuals and societies was connected with my previously unconscious response to Erol's death.[14]

I was fascinated with my new understanding that my spending considerable time in conflict areas and refugee camps where victims constantly deal with losses—that will be described later in this book—was connected with my reparative efforts. I can say that I felt, using Kernberg's terms, a "moral obligation" or a "mandate" to work on behalf of Erol's wishes. In my mind his main wish was to remain alive and not to induce guilt in me. I wished that people under the influence of ethnic, national, religious, or ideological conflicts would not kill others belonging to opposing large groups. Instead, I wanted them to make peace. I realized that, besides my being an object of desire for a Cypriot Greek woman who kidnapped me when I was a small child and my nostalgia about my budding relationship with Elena that was stopped for cultural traditions, my response to Erol's death encouraged my membership in the APA committee and my stubborn continuation of work in international relations. I became fascinated with the realization that because of my perennial mourning I had also chosen a Greek-American psychiatrist, Demetrius Julius, as my primary coworker in our international efforts. I realized that for decades I had partnered with a Greek in another arena as well. I cochaired the American Psychoanalytic Association's so-called Sexual Deviations Study Group with the late Charles Socarides, another Greek-American, for ten years. I was not fixated on the past; I was able to find other "brothers," and some of them were even Greeks.

If we consider my "moral obligation" and "mandate" to work on reversing Erol's murder to be sublimated activities, it will be difficult to call my long mourning process pathological. I wish to believe that Erol would appreciate my efforts to find peaceful solutions to massive human aggression.

As time passed, my colleagues and I began noticing that many individuals who had become perennial mourners, but who were not patients in distress, created their own linking objects and phenomena in beautiful drawings, poetry, architecture, and music.[15] In some situations it was difficult to differentiate linking objects and phenomena from keepsakes that are helpful for keeping continuity with our past experiences, present lives, and future hopes and for supporting our personal and large-group identities.

While writing a book on the Holocaust,[16] Gabriele Ast and William Greer and I reviewed many studies on child survivors. While in Nazi camps, these children held on to material objects such as a dead mother's knit dress or a photo of a dead father in order to connect themselves to their parents and hold on to their generational continuity. As adults, those who were very young when in the camps could not recall any realistic aspects of their mothers and fathers, but all of them had formed fantasized mental doubles of these long-departed parents. Some of them used pets and even plants as "living linking objects"to "reincarnate" those who were the victims of the Nazis.[17] In one case, Judith Kestenberg tells of a woman who was attached to her cow and her plants, "with which she consciously conversed as if they were her parents."[18] Her living linking objects connected her, as a survivor, to images or mental representations of those who were lost during the Holocaust. I assume that this was crucial for this woman's own psychic survival.

I explored individuals' various reactions to losses in some detail deliberately. I think that a solid understanding about human reaction to loss is needed in the field of political psychology.

# 11

# THE ISRAELI WITHDRAWAL FROM OPHIRA

## A COMMUNITY'S MOURNING

The reader will recall that the Mountain House meeting had taken place during the first anniversary of the Israeli withdrawal from the Yamit settlement in the Sinai Peninsula. The Sinai was occupied by the Israelis in 1967, and after fifteen years they withdrew from it. During this occupation, starting in 1968, 7,000 Israelis were settled in fourteen locations in this peninsula of approximately 23,000-square miles that was home to native Bedouins. While Sinai was under Israeli occupation, Israel had become, in a sense, a "Greater Israel." All indications are that, in general, this withdrawal was perceived by the majority of Israelis as a great loss, a giving up of the idea of "Greater Israel." Popular remarks in Israel refer to this withdrawal as a most painful "sacrifice," involving the loss of realistic/fantasized riches such as the Alma oil field. The Sinai settlers felt that they had worked hard to build houses, plant trees, and open roads in the settlements and could not believe that such places would no longer belong to them. Ariel Sharon was the defense minister of Israel in 1982. A champion of building the Sinai settlements, he would now oversee the Israeli withdrawal from this peninsula. We can only imagine his ambivalence.

The evacuation of Yamit was a disaster. While some 2,500 Israelis who lived there left this settlement peacefully, others refused to do so. The disciples of Rabbi Meir Kahane in Yamit even declared that it would be better for them to commit suicide than to leave.[1] Some barricaded themselves on the rooftops. Israeli soldiers were raised by machine to the rooftops in order to deal with the resisters. The soldiers, men and women, sprayed those who refused to move with white foam, carried children and adults by force to buses, and, when the town was emptied, bulldozed the buildings. Yamit was erased from the face of earth. This event led to more emotional divisions in Israel between right-wingers and those with leftist leanings and induced bad feelings in Egypt.

We can describe the events at Yamit by simply making references only to historical and political facts. But large-group grief and mourning responses, a shared sense of facing a big loss, also need to be considered. People in Yamit, representing the sentiments in Israel, were like persons in acute grief reaction using splitting—knowing the reality of upcoming evacuation and at the same time denying it. The anger of narcissistic hurt, without a suitable outward target—there was no war with Egypt at that time—had turned inward. Anger at the Egyptians was expressed by razing Yamit from the face of the earth so that one group's loss would not be the other group's gain. I do not know any direct psychological examination of what happened during the evacuation.

A close look at the work of psychoanalyst Rafael Moses and his colleagues concerning another small community called Ophira, however, clearly illustrates the psychological contamination of the historical/political event of the Sinai withdrawal. While I describe the April 1982 forced evacuation of Ophira, I will make a few direct references to a report prepared by Rafael and his colleagues that Rafael gave me at the time.

Ophira was an Israeli settlement at the southern-most tip of the peninsula, today better known as Sharm el-Sheikh, the place Hosni Mubarak went after leaving the Egyptian presidency. This area is a few miles from the Straits of Tiran and controls access to what the Jordanians call Aqaba Gulf and what Israelis call Eilat Gulf. Sharm el-Sheikh is seabound on two sides, boasting coral reefs, exotic tropical fish, and even sharks. Ophira was very attractive to the settlers, and they began to move there in 1968, taking advantage of certain financial incentives offered by the government to inhabitants of all development towns. Mainly, however, they took delight in the environment. Israeli military instillations were placed in Ophira, and in 1976 an airfield was built, today known as Sharm el-Sheikh International Airport. On October 6, 1973, during the Yom Kippur War, an air battle took place over the settlement. Israelis shot down seven Egyptian war planes without suffering a single loss themselves. Thus, Ophira became a place of pride for the Israelis. By 1975 the population in Ophira peaked at 250 families or 1,000 people.

In 1982, four months before the settlers' withdrawal from Ophira, the settlement's Resident's Committee asked four Israeli mental health professionals to visit this little town and facilitate resolution of any problems concerning the upcoming forced evacuation that might arise. The four Israeli professionals were Rafael Moses and his wife Rena Moses-Hrushovski, also a psychoanalyst, and social workers Yona Rosenfeld and Reuven Beumel. They visited Ophira over a ten-week period, working in different combinations, six times in all. They interviewed forty families, reaching about 120 individuals (an average of three to a family) and specific classifications of people, such as policemen, unmarried men and women, teachers, seaside tourist workers, and two school classes. Each time they visited Ophira they also met with those who had invited them and sponsored their work.

The settlers, although a little suspicious at first, were ready to talk candidly about themselves and describe the pain they felt at giving up their creation, Ophira. Rafael and his coworkers initially learned that denial of the upcoming loss was quite common, and some people had made no plans about where they would go. "Many in Ophira simply refused to take the count-down of two months, a month-and-a-half, etc., into their consciousness, and put off their plans and their packing. When challenged they were likely to say, 'Well, who knows, maybe it will be changed, maybe we'll be allowed to stay here after all.'"

Fear manifested in many forms. Adults mostly talked about their children and the fate of their pets, denying their own fears. The local physician confirmed that many somatized their grief reactions with sighing, aches, pains, and sleep disturbances. During one interview, a man felt burning on his left cheek. He recalled that when he was an orphaned street beggar in Tunis as a child, a passerby once spat at him. The spittle that struck the cheek now burned with the unforgettable humiliation. Rafael and his colleagues also noticed that "persons in the unmarried group had grown together in the face of departure, in what seemed a reaction to the threat of separation-increased dependency." The initial bargaining with the Egyptians embittered the Ophirians, who resented the low prices offered for their property. They thought of pouring kerosene on their gardens so that the Egyptians would not enjoy their beautiful plants and flowers. One ten-year-old child wrote a curse on the Egyptians on a wall.

Facing significant loss or actually experiencing it reactivates the images of past significant losses with their associated affects. The reactivation of evictions and deportations of the past were very visible, especially among the Holocaust survivors in Ophira. One concentration camp survivor, describing how her husband turned pale when he took out the first screw to prepare a packing box, stated that "leaving is a kind of inner disintegration." One couple spoke of being regarded by Israelis in the north as avaricious; the wife recalled how Poles in Poland spoke of Jews with contempt as money grabbers. She thought it ironic that such an "anti-Semitic attitude" would be manifested by other Jews and Israelis toward those about to leave Sinai, where she had hoped for a different life and a different image, at least for her son. Now they would be despised again, and as a Polish Jew she would be again a member of a minority. Such tragic reemergence of the past was common. Rafael and his coworkers, by noticing how the Holocaust-related issues came to the surface and intertwined with the Sinai evacuation problem, were able to help the community to separate the images of past events from the images of the Ophira evacuation. This helped the community to deal more realistically with the issues they were facing at that time, without the burden of images from the past and the emotions connected with them.

About six weeks before the final evacuation, an advance group of forty Egyptians, led by a general, arrived. The representatives of Ophira at first preferred to destroy some of their equipment rather than hand it over for nothing. But an Israeli businessman, a pillar of the community, ended up inviting Egyptians to a sumptuous breakfast with Israeli delicacies delivered daily from hundreds of miles away. In the end, he was deeply touched when the leader of the visiting Egyptian group shyly told him how well he understood the intense pain and grief of having to leave and give up what had been home. The Israeli wept for the first time—a more direct expression of "normal" grief—in the arms of the Egyptian who shared his tears and his grief. Rafael and his coworkers reported: "We came to understand that leadership, as well as the populace, and the interactions between the two played an important role in the successful adaptation to evacuating Ophira. . . . It was very impressive to see how harmonious and good, and truly democratic the relationship between the leaders and the led was."

It was moving to see how Rafael and his colleagues exhibited modesty by not talking about their role in preventing a tragedy in Ophira. The reality of Ophira's being apolitical—unlike the situation in Yamit—obviously played a role in its peaceful evacuation. But I believe that we should also acknowledge that a successful utilization of political psychology took place in Ophira. The opening up of discussions and feelings concerning what would be lost, separating responses to an enormous historical loss from reactions to the problem at hand, and putting shared complicated grief and mourning processes into normal routes and thus dealing with a community's problem prevented potential tragedy.

I have no data on Egyptians who settled in Israeli homes in Ophira. I can, however, guess some of their reactions because of my previous work in Cyprus. After the Turkish Army came to Cyprus and the island was divided into northern Turkish and southern Greek sections in 1974, the Cypriot Turks escaping from the south were put in Cypriot Greek homes in villages vacated by the Greeks who had escaped to the south. During the first winter after these massive forced migrations took place, authorities in the north provided blankets for the new Turkish settlers. Soon unusual behavior could be witnessed in these former Cypriot Greek villages. The new Cypriot Turkish settlers began burning the blankets even though, logically speaking, they needed them to keep warm. An examination of these actions revealed that since the Cypriot Turks believed that the blankets were made from cloth left behind by the Cypriot Greeks, they unconsciously did not wish the symbolic images of their enemies to touch their bodies. This was their main psychological reason for burning the blankets, along with guilt feelings for living in the vacated houses of the enemy. At times of stress and major change in a society as a result of conflict with people who belong to another large-group identity, the members of this society do not want their large-group identity to “touch” the enemy’s large-group identity.[2]

In the next chapter I will describe the mourning process of a small Palestinian community.

# 12

# PALESTINIANS IN TUNISIA

## LIVING SYMBOLS

In the spring of 1990 I was encouraged by Israeli colleagues, with permission from the PLO, to observe Palestinian orphans in Tunis, Tunisia, at an orphanage named Beit Atfal al-Sumud (the House of Steadfast Children) and to then present my findings in Jerusalem at a conference on children of wars. Beit Atfal al-Sumud was first opened in Lebanon in 1976 to provide a place for orphaned Palestinian children from the destroyed Tel al-Za'atar district. Beit Atfal al-Sumud later had a branch in Tunis, located in the residential Alomran district. It had been a maternity hospital during the presidency of Habib Bourguiba, whose wife later gave it to the orphanage. After the 1982 war in Lebanon, another 1,300 Palestinian children needed looking after. Some were sent to Tunis. In the spring of 1990 Beit Atfal al-Sumud housed thirty-one boys and twenty-one girls, ranging from age seven to eighteen, who had lost one or both parents in the Middle East conflicts. Five had been rescued as infants from the massacres at Sabra and Shatila. Because the birth names of these five children were never known, each was given an individual first name and all were called by the surname "Arafat" after the chairman of the PLO. Some other children too were given the name Arafat because the identity of their fathers was not known. Chairman Yasser Arafat, we were told, would often spend time in the orphanage and would send the children presents.

My ten-day visit to Tunisia took place with my wife and two American colleagues of Palestinian background, a psychiatrist and a psychologist. After the war in Lebanon, the PLO moved its headquarters to Tunisia, so at the time of our visit Chairman Arafat, important individuals of the PLO administration, and many other Palestinians lived there. On October 1, 1985, the Israeli Air Force bombed PLO Headquarters in Tunis in an operation named Operation Wooden Leg. I have no idea why this peculiar name was used. This operation killed more than sixty individuals. As a group, the Palestinians in Tunis were in a state of perpetual alert and were afraid of unexpected secret attacks by Israeli commandos. Indeed, prior to our visit, one of Arafat's closest associates had been assassinated at his home during an Israeli raid.

Despite having been granted permission by the PLO to spend time with children at Beit Atfal al-Sumud, after arriving in Tunis we were made to wait for three days before being allowed to visit the orphanage, presumably for further background checks. First we were put in a run-down and rather frightening PLO hiding place at the outskirts of Tunis, and three days later we were transferred to a nice hotel in the center of the city. During our "waiting period," however, we were invited to and visited many Palestinian homes and the offices of high-ranking officials. The group's anxiety was palpable, and I had the impression that most of the Palestinians never had a good night's sleep. They would call or visit each other at all hours of the night just to check that nothing was amiss. After we moved to our hotel, they also began calling me and my wife in the middle of night, whispering on the telephone, "Are you alright?"

Chairman Arafat, I was told, would never stay long in one location, but would move around constantly for security reasons. The PLO used souped-up civilian cars that sped through the streets as if in perpetual motion. Pictures of PLO officials who had died during Operation Wooden Leg and other raids hung on the walls of PLO officials' hideouts, homes, oand offices. This was after the beginning of the First Intifada in 1987 in the Gaza Strip and West Bank, which was still unfolding. The waiting room of the official PLO Headquarters did not have chairs. I was told that to honor the suffering Palestinians in Palestine who were showing their courage by the Intifada, the PLO Headquarters in Tunis would have no luxury such as chairs in the waiting room. I remember getting tired from standing there for some time. However, at some PLO officials' homes, behind security lines and locked doors, there was abundant comfort and food.

All the Palestinians in Tunis with whom I met felt as if they had been forcibly exiled, and they yearned to return to a peaceful homeland. Even though the Tunisian government had given the PLO certain autonomy, these Palestinians considered themselves refugees of a sort. People cannot accept change without mourning what is lost from the past. Whether the loss is a homeland, as it is for immigrants or refugees, or a person or thing, the process of adapting to life after loss is necessary and sometimes complex. There are many variables involved in the immigrant or refugee experience. Newcomers differ with respect to their ages, psychological makeup, and the support system that is available to them. The circumstances surrounding individual or group movements from one location to another also affect their adaptation to a new place. Specifically, forced migration and the trauma associated with it cause complications that may not be present when relocation is voluntary. Nevertheless, at the foundation of the psychology of any kind of immigrant or refugee experience, we see aspects of grief, mourning, and difficulties in these processes.[1]

One morning we were received by Chairman Arafat. He was pleasant and in good spirits, exhibiting his leadership. I sensed that he wanted me to tell the Israelis that the PLO had not been involved in a recent sea raid on Israel and that the PLO was willing to talk with the Israelis. There was no official communication between the U.S. embassy in Tunis and the PLO officials. I joined Arafat and about twelve other individuals for lunch. They had a place for me at the long dining table just across from Arafat. Plenty of food had been placed in the middle of the table, and people were reaching forward, picking up of pieces of grilled chicken from a large platter. I made a "mistake" and tried to reach this plate with my left hand, which was contrary to the Palestinian cultural custom. Arafat stopped me and, picking up some chicken with his right hand, placed it on a fork, and fed me. This was one indication of how he identified strongly with their large-group identity. The PLO's Tunis period would last until 1991, and the Oslo Accords would take place in 1993.

During our "waiting period," I felt that the PLO officials were very interested in knowing what I would say about the Palestinian orphans at the conference in Jerusalem. I was directly and indirectly questioned to ensure that I would present my findings in a neutral way. I told them the truth, that I was an academician and that I would speak about my observations without getting involved in politics or taking sides. Finally the door of the orphanage was opened to us.

My first day at Beit Atfal al-Sumud revealed it as a house of hugs and kisses, as the children and youngsters were affectionate toward each other. Often they would get together and sing, and I learned that their songs described victimization. When dining with them in a big dining room, I observed that the atmosphere was lively but orderly. The orphans laughed and talked while eating, and their diet was very good. They had bananas, which were prized because they were not grown in Tunisia and because they had been sent to them by Yasser Arafat. They were proud to share their bananas with me. In the big yard surrounding the house they seemed especially engaged by soccer practice. My first day's impression of this lively environment persisted over subsequent visits.

My study involved observing all the orphans for a week, spending one afternoon only with the Sabra and Shatila kids, and conducting psychoanalytic interviews with fifteen other orphans who knew English or who talked with me with the help of an interpreter. Each interview lasted two to three hours and was designed to help acquaint me with the internal worlds of fifteen orphans: their fantasies, dreams, repeating dreams, affects, identity issues, and perceptions of external world events. Obviously, the success of each interview necessarily depended on the readiness of the orphan being interviewed to report introspectively and to put into words even those thoughts and feelings that seemed unacceptable. Psychological tests were given to each subject by one of the persons accompanying me from the Unites States, Nuha Abudabbeh, a psychologist of Palestinian birth who spoke Arabic. I also interviewed many caretakers and the director of this orphanage, who herself had been an orphan and who truly had dedicated herself to looking after the children.[2]

It soon became clear to me that each child or youngster at the orphanage lived in two worlds—the cheerful surface group life in which Beit Atfal al-Sumud provided abundant loving care, and a unique personal world that reflected the traumatic events to which they had been exposed, including losses of parents and siblings. Many of those whom I interviewed had crying spells after going to bed at night, and almost all of them had nightmares in which aggression usually was symbolized by Israeli soldiers. Most of them could differentiate fully between fantasy and reality. One eighteen-year-old girl was still bedwetting at least three nights a week, and one young man was afraid of tongue injury after learning that his older brother he had left behind was shot to death through his mouth.

When I first saw them, the five Sabra and Shatila children were playing together. They appeared as "normal" children do in play. I also observed that they would remain together as a "team," and if one of them was separated from the others, he or she would become agitated. On the fifth day of my visit to the orphanage, I attempted to speak with these children individually, with the aid of an interpreter. All of them then became "abnormal"—one hallucinated, and another one literally destroyed the interview room. As soon as they were placed together again as a "team" they appeared "normal" once more. I concluded that they must have difficulties in their sense of personal identity; on the other hand, they appeared "normal" when they were a team of "Arafats." This observation taught me a lot about replacing, to one extent or another, a person's individual identity with a "team" or large-group identity associated with ethnicity, nationality, religion, or ideology. Although the phenomenon was most pronounced in these five children, I easily noticed variations of it in the other orphans, as when the orphans called one another "brother" or "sister" even when they were biologically not related. Those who had linking objects, such as photographs connecting them with dead or disappeared parents, appeared more adjusted than those with no linking objects or no memory of their babyhood or childhood caretakers. Those with linking objects were preoccupied with these magical articles, which they protected as if their lives depended on them.

To focus on the role of linking objects and linking phenomena in the lives of these orphans, I will describe the case of one handsome seventeen-year-old whom I will call Farouk. When I met him he had lived in this orphanage for eleven years. He was the captain of the soccer team and knew perfect English. He told me that when he was five years old and living in southern Lebanon, his family tried to escape when the Israelis invaded his birthplace. They halted their flight to safety when Farouk's father wanted to go back and get something they had left behind in the house. An Israeli soldier captured his father and killed him. Hiding behind a boulder with an uncle, Farouk saw not only the death of his father, but the shooting of his mother, a sister, and a cousin. Farouk and his uncle were the only survivors, and later he was also separated from his uncle. He told me this story in a matter-of-fact way and informed me that he no longer remembered his parents' faces. He confessed that when alone he often wept. "I know it is a healthy thing to do," he said.

While he was talking, Farouk did something unusual. He kept rubbing his right shoe. When I became curious about what he was doing, he told me that once as a child, while watching his mother and grandmother cook sweets, he accidently stepped in a hot pan and burned his right foot. His father put ointment on the burn and tried to soothe his pain. This was Farouk's earliest memory. He still had a scar from this episode and, without my asking him to do so, he removed his right shoe and sock, showed me the scar and demonstrated his tender way of touching it. He confided that when he touched his scar, "I almost recall my parents from within, from inside of my body." He had recently received a scar on his left knee while playing soccer, but he said this was nothing; the old scar was everything.

Listening to him, I realized that his family identification was burned into him like an emblem. His scar stood for his lost parents and family, southern Lebanon, and as long as he could touch it, he was not, psychologically speaking, alone. His scar linked him to his past, now mostly fantasized images. Even if he wanted to stop the link to his traumatic past, he could not. Farouk himself was aware of this but had never spoken of it to others. However, I concluded that because he had this link to the mental doubles of his family, Farouk was one of the better-adjusted youngsters in the orphanage. He had an ability to sublimate. He liked soccer, at which the other orphans said he was a star, scoring more goals than anyone else, using his foot with the special scar, and perhaps discharging feelings of rage and revenge in this way. Even though he had not spoken openly to other orphans about what his scar on his right foot meant to him, everyone seemed to be aware of its specialness. When Farouk used his scarred foot to score goals, the little ones, including the Sabra and Shatila kids, would touch his right shoe and sometimes his scar and everyone's self-esteem would increase.

Farouk informed me that the Intifada awakened much emotion in him. "I have nobody left in Palestine," he said. "Watching Palestinian boys throwing stones at the Israelis on the television," he added, "I cannot just sit in front of the television. My body talks; I stand up and automatically move as if I am throwing stones." Then, sounding like a mature adult, Farouk said, "Life goes on. I may continue to cry from time to time, but I want to be an engineer." Most of the boys at Beit Atfal al-Sumud wanted to be pilots so they could bomb Israel. I was impressed with Farouk's having his own special vision for his future. The uncle who saved him when his parents were killed lived in Germany, and he hoped that this uncle would help him to attend college somewhere. Unfortunately, I have no follow-up information about what happened to Farouk.

One day when asked why I was not planning to interview Palestinian orphans older than age eighteen, I replied that the idea had not occurred to me, since from the outset the project had focused on younger children. I let my hosts know, however, that I would be willing to interview an adult candidate if one were interested. The next day at a luncheon with senior PLO officials I met a beautiful young woman in her twenties who asked to be interviewed. For four evenings she came to our hotel and we talked late into the night for a total of over sixteen hours. The young woman introduced herself to me in perfect English as the daughter of an airplane hijacker. When she was an oedipal child her father had hijacked a commercial airplane and forced it to land in Israel, demanding the release of certain Palestinians from Israeli jails. According to her account, her father was "tricked" by Israeli antiterrorist forces and shot to death during the hijacking episode.

Although anyone seriously interested can find out the true identity of this woman, and although I was given permission by her to use her name, I will refrain from doing so. Her story was a poignant one that revolved around being raised with a "hero ghost," the mental double of her father. Many of his friends who had high positions in the PLO treated her as a special being after the death of her father. She was idealized as a martyr's daughter and a symbol of Palestine. These influential men and women helped with her schooling; she gradually spent more and more time at PLO Headquarters and also worked as a secretary to Chairman Arafat. She was present at many official and social gatherings of PLO authorities and also accompanied them on various travels. When I attended the luncheon given by Chairman Arafat, for example, she functioned as a kind of silent hostess. My focus here is not to present her personal story per se, but rather to show how she played a significant psychological role for the PLO authorities and by extension for the Palestinians in Tunis.

Every Palestinian in Tunis knew who she was. This young woman was aware that she represented an idealized Palestine to which the exiled Palestinians wanted to return. When she came to her interviews with me, she wore a white dress. Despite her physical beauty and grace and despite being regularly pursued by men, she had remained "pure." She wanted me to know that she was still a virgin. I report this to emphasize that she physically stood for the concept "virgin white." Even though the Arab-Israeli conflict had been a bloody one and both sides had used violence, this young woman needed to remain like a flower in the battlefield. I learned that many men at PLO Headquarters found her very attractive, but she remained in a sense "unreachable," representing the Palestinians' longing for their own state, which at that time was also unreachable.

As our sixteen hours of interviews were coming to an end, I asked her why she had volunteered to come and tell her story late into the night, to reveal her personal wishes and fears, in short why she would open so completely to a stranger. She responded that while she was aware of her role as a "flag" for the Palestinian people in Tunisia, she also knew that she was made of flesh and blood, and had dreams of finding a mate, marrying, having sex, and being a regular person. The fact was that she wanted to be both an idealized symbol and a regular woman. She was aware that in order to be one type of person, she would have to give up the other. Having no solution for her internal struggle, she had developed a daydream in which she would lose both identities to escape the tension. She imagined being in an airplane with Chairman Arafat, her living hero/father figure. Their plane would explode in midair, killing both of them. Psychoanalysts may infer other meanings to her daydream, such as a wish for reunion with her dead pilot-father image, but here I simply want to remain with her inner struggle to be either a symbol or a regular woman. Her fantasy bothered her. She was well-read and knew something about psychoanalysis. Thus, when I, a psychoanalyst, appeared in Tunis, she wanted to share with me her internal dilemma, thinking that such sharing might help. Interestingly, she knew that I would not give her any advice.

To this day, I do not know if my empathic understanding of her internal struggle was helpful to her. I never met her again.[3] Of course, dramatic events relating to the PLO's political situation have taken place since then. Perhaps the return of Palestinians from Tunis to their ancestral land removed the external pressure on this young woman to serve as a nostalgic, physical representation of an idealized Palestine.

This young woman represented an external meeting ground between the "lost" but idealized Palestine and the reality that Palestinians living in Tunisia were exiles. She was a kind of "living linking object." As a mental double of their idealized state and what it meant to them, she helped the Palestinian community in Tunisia tolerate the emotions associated with being deprived of it. Historians who focus on the history of the PLO will probably never mention the role that this young lady played at PLO Headquarters in Tunis in the late 1980s and early 1990s.

Some analysts describe the mental representation of a state as a nurturing mother figure.[4] The PLO and Palestinians in Tunis had created a literal illustration of this concept. The young woman was both a nurturing figure as well as an unreachable virgin, which reflected the reality of their situation. She was a catalyst for their belief in a hopeful future, one that was defensively exaggerated and pure. I perceived that they used her image to give them strength to move on, to seek their statehood, and to hold on to their large-group identity.

# PART IV

## THE PSYCHOLOGY OF THE SOVIET COLLAPSE AND GERMAN REUNIFICATION

# 13

# UNDER THE SHADOW OF MONTICELLO

## FROM FIELDWORK TO THEORY

In 1914 the state of Virginia acquired a 142-acre site just east of Thomas Jefferson's Monticello and built a tuberculosis sanatorium there. Blue Ridge Sanatorium was opened in 1920 with a potential for housing 382 patients. As time passed, a half a dozen houses for the staff were also built on this site, including the Lyman Mansion as a home for nurses, a chapel, a dairy farm, and other buildings for outpatients and maintenance facilities. Since it was thought that sunshine and fresh air were necessary for individuals with tuberculosis, the hospital building itself was constructed to receive plenty of both. After 1962 no new patients were admitted, but the place remained as a tuberculosis sanatorium until it was turned over to the University of Virginia in 1978.

The university was planning to expand its existing hospital in Charlottesville and build a brand new medical center with the highest standards, but as this project would take many years to complete, an alternative location was needed to temporarily house some medical programs that did not require high technological support. The Blue Ridge Sanatorium was selected to house these medical programs and was renamed the Blue Ridge Hospital Division of the University of Virginia. It would be my professional home from 1978 until 1996 while I served as its medical director from its beginning until it began the closing process.[1] Its in-patient and out-patient programs and its various medical institutions slowly began relocating to the new medical center, and the place was completely shut down in 1998 and turned over to the University of Virginia Foundation. Since then, this site has not been used and the road entering the grounds has been chained off.

The Commonwealth of Virginia was expected to provide ten million dollars for the renovation of the Blue Ridge Hospital Division of the University of Virginia, but it only gave three million, and many buildings, including the Lyman Mansion, were never renovated. From the outside, the mansion looked beautiful, but inside it was collapsing. Nevertheless, the giant trees surrounding the hospital, the Lyman

Mansion, the chapel, and the many houses and other buildings gave this location a special aura of comfort. It appeared as if time slowed down at this place, separated as it was from the hustle and bustle of Charlottesville.

I selected a huge room with a balcony on the third floor of the hospital as my office. At one end of the room, in front of a bookshelf covering one wall, there was a big conference table around which twenty persons could sit. When I was at this end of the room I was a medical administrator. On the other end of this room, near the balcony overlooking a field with beautiful trees, I placed a couch for my psychoanalytic patients, a very comfortable chair behind it for me, and a desk. When I was at this end of the room I was a psychoanalyst. So I practiced my first two professions in this room.

Two years after I settled at Blue Ridge Hospital I became a member of the American Psychiatric Association's Committee on Psychiatry and Foreign Affairs. Before the committee ceased to exist, I found an empty house on the Blue Ridge Hospital grounds, and this house became the administrative home for my third profession, political psychology. We called this place the Division of Psychopolitical Studies. After the APA committee was gone, this place was restructured with the addition of a program director and an editor, and on October 20, 1988, it officially became known as the Center for the Study of Mind and Human Interaction (CSMHI). CSMHI moved to another, bigger house nearby with a basement that was turned into a conference room big enough for over fifty people a couple years later. When Blue Ridge Hospital was closed, CSMHI was relocated to a building next to the new University of Virginia Medical Center. As its founder, I would remain the director of CSMHI until my retirement in 2002.

CSMHI's connection to a medical school was justified because we considered it to be a place where we would try to expand the concept of preventive medicine to include an examination of societal responses to massive aggression due to wars or war-like situations and to develop methods to psychologically "vaccinate" large groups against violent acts. Under the umbrella of a medical school, CSMHI was the first of its kind. We planned to apply a growing theoretical and field-proven base of psychopolitical knowledge to issues such as ethnic tension, racism, large-group identity, terrorism, societal trauma, leader-follower relationships, and other aspects of national and international conflict. Because no single discipline can fully illuminate such deep-seated and complex issues, we decided that CSMHI's faculty and board would be interdisciplinary. They would include experts in psychoanalysis, psychiatry, psychology, diplomacy, political science, history, and environmental policy. Their combined perspectives and experience would provide in-depth analysis of political, historical, and social issues and the psychological processes that invariably exist beneath their surface.

I would not have been able to establish and maintain this interdisciplinary center without the support of two deans of the University of Virginia's School of Medicine, Norman Knorr and Robert ("Bob") Carey, along with William ("Bill") Massey of the Massey Foundation in Richmond, Virginia. Norman Knorr is a psychiatrist. Between 1977 and 1982 he and I were consultants to the United States Agency for International Development's Cyprus Mental Health Project for the design and construction of a 100-bed Community Mental Health Center in Nicosia, Northern Cyprus, and we had traveled together to my home country.[2] When Norman stepped down, the new dean, Bob Carey, from the Department of Internal Medicine, was as enthusiastic as his predecessor had been in supporting CSMHI. In fact, Bob would be the first chairperson of its advisory board and often traveled overseas with the CSMHI team while we carried out our projects. The foundation that Bill Massey headed was established by the Massey family in 1916 with profits from West Virginia coal mining. The family sold out its interest in the coal mines in 2000. The foundation's name was also associated with generous philanthropy, as it had given millions of dollars in grants to schools, colleges, institutions, and health-care organizations, the best known being Virginia Commonwealth University's Massey Cancer Center in Richmond. CSMHI received financial support to start its operation from the Massey Foundation and the foundation supported CSMHI throughout its existence.[3]

In creating this new center, I went back to my friends who had been involved in the American Psychiatric Association's Committee on Psychiatry and Foreign Affairs Arab-Israeli project and was delighted that some of them agreed to get together under the umbrella of CSMHI. Demetrios Julius and Joe Montville, who were already very involved with the Division of Psychopolitical Studies, joined me as faculty members of CSMHI. Since one lived in Richmond, Virginia, and the other in Washington, D.C., they could easily travel to Charlottesville for major faculty gatherings. Hal Saunders and Rita Rogers kindly accepted roles as CSMHI board members under the leadership of Dean Carey. Nechama Agmon became an international associate. As I recount stories of our activities in the chapters to follow, I will mention others who became very active at CSMHI as faculty, board members, or consultants.

When CSMHI was officially established, the University of Virginia and the Massey Foundation took care of our expenses. We did not have enough funds for major projects, and all faculty members, including me, were part time at CSMHI. I was still running the Blue Ridge Hospital as its medical director and still seeing psychoanalytic patients as a member of the Department of Psychiatry. We began publishing a quarterly journal titled *Mind and Human Interaction* in which we not only published papers by scholars from different disciplines writing about issues that would fit into our center's mission, but also provided a voice for younger professionals to support their enthusiasm and to help them find an audience for their ideas.[4]

Even before the Division of Psychopolitical Studies changed its name to the Center for the Study of Mind and Human Interaction, Demetrios, Joe, and I, with Hal's help, planned and later accomplished bringing together people, well-known at the time, in the field of political psychology for several days of dialogue in Charlottesville in April 1988. We learned from each other and realized that there is a great variety of focus under the general term "political psychology." Again, our guests and some of us were utilizing different names for similar activities, terms such as "track-two diplomacy," "cultural diplomacy," "supplemental diplomacy," "people-to-people diplomacy," "problem solving workshops," "interactive problem solving," and so on. Some of these approaches paid little attention to deep psychology.

Samuel Lewis, who was the U.S. ambassador to Israel from 1977 to 1985 and who at the time of the Charlottesville gathering was the president of the United States Institute of Peace (USIP), attended as an observer. I was very pleased with this, since the presence of Ambassador Lewis signified the importance of this meeting. USIP had been established in 1984 and would sponsor some future CSMHI activities. In 1991, Joe, Demetrios, and I published all participants' papers in two volumes as examples of different types of theories and applications of political psychology.[5] For a long time these two volumes would be sought after by the younger generation of political psychologists as a textbook-like resource.

Political psychologists who gathered in Charlottesville touched on topics ranging from the Holocaust to the murderous exploits of the Pol Pot regime in Cambodia, but mostly we talked about the Arab-Israeli conflict and the East-West relationship, especially the relationship between the Soviet Union and the United States. Because of my work with the APA committee's project, I was more familiar with Middle East issues than I was American-Soviet relations. In the middle of my involvement with the APA project, U.S. president Ronald Reagan had declared that the Soviet Union was an "evil empire." Addressing a religious group, in this case the National Association of Evangelicals in Orlando, Florida, on March 8, 1983, Reagan used a religious concept, "good" versus "evil," and urged the audience to be aware of "the temptation of pride, the temptation of blithely declaring yourselves above it all and label[ing] both sides equally at fault, to ignore the facts of history and the aggressive impulses of an evil empire, to simply call the arms race a giant misunderstanding and thereby remove yourself from the struggle between right and wrong and good and evil."[6]

Like most people around me in the United States, I also had a feeling that "we were good and Soviets were bad." We did not think much about actual ordinary people living in the Soviet Union—people who were from many different ethnic and religious groups—or that some of them were victimized and needed empathy and understanding. We treated the Soviet Union as if it were one "evil" unit, just as many tend to think about "Muslims" today.

My ease at joining the general U.S. perception of the Soviets was supported by my upbringing as a Turkish child. In Turkish history books that I read in school, there were no friendly references to Russians. The Russian Empire was a competitor of the Ottoman Empire. The main story that stands out in my mind—perhaps because it included reference to tricking someone with sex—is how Catherine the Great seduced an Ottoman grand vizier/commander in order to defeat his army. Of course, I never wondered if this story was true or false. In my young mind, Russians and Soviets were intertwined, and despite knowing intellectually many real truths about the Soviet Union, this "belief" remained in my mind as it did in the minds of many Americans in the 1980s. When Princeton historian Norman Itzkowitz and I started writing a psychobiography of Mustafa Kemal (Atatürk), the founder of modern Turkey, I learned about how many of the Soviets aided the Turks in their fight for independence. Later, however, Mustafa Kemal would speak openly and negatively about the Communist system.[7]

On February 24–25, 1956, Nikita Khrushchev, the first Secretary of the Communist Party of the Soviet Union, gave a special report to the 20th Congress of the Communist Party of the Soviet Union in a closed session and exposed crimes of the Stalin era. He opened his very long speech by referring to "the cult of the individual [Josef Stalin] and its harmful consequences." Khrushchev, as a leader of the Soviet Union, was trying to free the "spirit of Marxism-Leninism" by exorcising its evils. He said, "After Stalin's death the Central Committee of the party began to implement a policy of explaining concisely and consistently that it is impermissible and foreign to the spirit of Marxism-Leninism to elevate one person, to transform him into a superman possessing supernatural characteristics, akin to those of a god. Such a man supposedly knows everything, sees everything, thinks for everyone, can do anything, is infallible in his behavior. . . . Such a belief about a man, and specifically about Stalin was cultivated among us for many years." He added that the Soviet Union was now concerned "with how the cult of the person of Stalin has been gradually growing, the cult which became at a certain specific stage the source of a whole series of exceedingly serious and grave perversions of party principles, of party democracy, and revolutionary legality."

Khrushchev finished his talk with a promise to overcome the cult of the individual and to show the evidence of the great moral and political strength of the Communist Party.[8] It is clear that what was to be cleaned and saved was Communism, which in the West was still perceived as something very bad. It would take many years for a drastic internal transformation in the Soviet Union to take place and for Westerners, especially Americans, to slowly change their perceptions of the Soviets and the individuals living in the "Soviet Empire." The anxiety about the possibility of a nuclear war and its consequences evolving without our knowledge—as depicted in Stanley Kramer's 1959 movie, *On The Beach*, starring Gregory Peck, Ava Gardner, and Fred Astaire—had magnified the "badness" of the enemy. I remember the days of the 1962 Cuban Missile Crisis, worrying about my children's future in a nuclear world and wishing that Soviets never existed.

Mikhail Gorbachev was born in 1931 and was the General Secretary of the Communist Party of the Soviet Union from 1985 until the collapse of the Soviet Union in 1991. In late 2011, I was in St. Petersburg and Moscow and had a chance to speak with many young Russians. Obviously, I was not conducting a scientific survey, but my impression is that in today's Russia, specifically in these major cities, the majority of young Russians have a perception of Gorbachev as a "bad man" who ruined their "empire." In a group of young persons studying psychoanalysis in Russia, I heard remarks indicating that it was Gorbachev who had brought on disaster and humiliated the Russian people. I wondered if these young people knew that if the Communist system still existed, they might not be permitted to study psychoanalysis at all. For me, Gorbachev remains a man who dared to make a crucial change for millions of people in the belief that it would give them better lives.

President Reagan and General Secretary Gorbachev talked face to face for the first time in Geneva in 1985, followed by summit meetings in Reykjavik in 1986, Washington in 1987, and Moscow in 1988. On December 7, 1988, during Gorbachev's trip to New York to deliver his now well-known speech, he and Reagan met for the last time on Governor's Island in New York Harbor. This last summit between the two leaders symbolizes the end of the Cold War.[9] Here in the United States we like to credit Reagan for bringing the Cold War to an end, at least on paper. But I agree with those who thought that Gorbachev's determination played a bigger role.[10] Reagan was getting ready to transfer the presidency to George H. W. Bush, and president-elect Bush was present during the summit on Governor's Island. We now know that the incoming president and his key advisers did not trust Gorbachev as much as Reagan did and would not have the same chemistry relating to the Soviet leader as Reagan had developed. Strong public doubt about the Soviets prevailed in the United States, and the person on the street continued to perceive Soviet individuals as if they were a different species of human beings from Americans, as if the Soviets had horns on their heads. During my 2010 visit to St. Petersburg and Moscow, I saw many Soviet propaganda posters and cartoons for sale for the tourists. They showed Americans as less than human beings.

The Reagan-Gorbachev summit series, however, opened ways for unofficial citizen communication. My first attendance at a meeting with Soviet delegates took place in Chautauqua, New York, in June 1985. Joe Montville was also present. After checking into the hotel I went to the hospitality room for a drink. I was alone there when the door opened and four men came in speaking Russian. When I turned and looked at them, one of them smiled and said in English, "Do not worry. We do not eat people!"

There was a festive atmosphere at Chautauqua; Soviet and American musicians gave public concerts, and this created an atmosphere for friendly dialogues among the Soviet and American participants. Nothing was discussed in-depth, but both sides were able to "humanize" the other side. What moved me was my realization of a strong possibility that a complicated perennial mourning among the Soviet population existed. Two Soviet poets had come to Chautauqua: Yevgeny Yevtushenko and Andrei Voznesensky. My conversations with them were my first meaningful experiences with people from the Other's side of the world. As I got to know these poets, they took my breath away. Even though some of their poems dealt with fairly lighthearted themes, many were preoccupied with war and death.[11] For example, Yevtushenko's "Lament for a Brother" is about a goose grieving a brother goose that has been shot down, and he bemoans his own punishment for surviving, having been spared—this time. The poet is keenly aware that "survival guilt" complicates the process of mourning for lost victims or possessions.[12] Each poet functioned as a "mouthpiece," illustrating what existed within his large group.

During the Cold War, when Americans and Soviets were seeing each other through extremely prejudicial lenses, Americans seldom thought about the incredible Soviet military and civilian losses during World War II, estimated from 15 million to over 20 million people, and the suffering of the Soviet people at the time, and we rarely appreciated how such shared trauma affected their large-group psychology. Furthermore, exiles and other massive oppressions in the Stalin era added to this society's burden.

Listening to these two poets had a great impression on me. But I had no idea that one day I would work with Soviets intensively and, with my friends from CSMHI, indirectly play a role in opening a more direct and, psychologically speaking, more mature relationship between Americans and Soviets as the effects of the Cold War continued. This process began the same way I started my involvement in the APA Committee on Psychiatry and Foreign Affairs' Arab-Israeli project: I was at the right place at the right time.

After Gorbachev's *glasnost* and *perestroika*, the International Society of Political Psychology (ISPP) invited Soviet psychologists and other professionals dealing with peace issues to attend its annual meetings. For the first years after such invitations were sent out, no one from the Soviet Union showed up. Then, in the summer of 1987, the annual ISPP meeting was held in New Jersey. When I went to my hotel room, I found a handwritten note on a pink slip of paper waiting for me from the then president of ISPP. The note informed me that four Soviet delegates unexpectedly had arrived at the hotel as our guests. Since I was a former president of ISPP, the note continued, would I meet them and welcome them? I put my suitcase down and went directly to the hotel lobby, hoping to find some ISPP officials, get more information, and learn more about what I was supposed to do with the Soviet guests. But as soon as I arrived in the lobby I saw three men standing near the hotel entrance around a white-haired man who was shorter than the others, all smoking cigarettes and looking around. Intuitively I knew that they were the Soviets and that the white-haired man was their leader. Impulsively I approached them, introduced myself as a former president of ISPP, and welcomed them. One tall man turned to me and said in better English than mine, "Just a minute! First things first. Where can we get a couple of six-packs?" I was not expecting such a response, but I replied that there might be some grocery stores nearby. He motioned outside and the two of us quickly walked out to look for a place to buy beer.

My companion introduced himself as Stanislav Roschin, a psychologist at the USSR Institute of Psychology. I felt comfortable with him. Only much later would I learn more about Stanislav, such as that he had spent time in London as a KGB agent connected with the Soviet embassy. I would also later observe that he had a way with women, making them feel important and happy. If Stanislav wanted to impress a woman, he would hold one of her hands, rub it gently and seductively, look at the lines in her palm, and speak about her usually glorious destiny. He would become a fortuneteller in order to put a woman at ease. Later, I would joke with him about learning how to tell a woman's fortune while training to be a KGB agent. He apparently was also able to put me at ease during our half-hour walk, because it ended with my buying him two six-packs of beer.

As we walked through a parking lot near the hotel, I found myself telling Stanislav about the APA committee's work with Arabs and Israelis, how it ended, and how I was running a division of psychoanalytic studies that had an interdisciplinary approach to unofficial diplomacy. Just before coming to this meeting I had visited Norman Knorr's office. Without my asking, he had called someone in the medical school's business office and transferred $8,000 to the account of the Division of Psychopolitical Studies. I found myself asking Stanislav, "Can we get a group of Soviets and Americans together for a series of meetings so that we might find ways to understand one another? Then we can disperse this knowledge with the hope for better human relationships between Soviets and Americans." Then I added, "I have

$8,000 to start this. Perhaps we can find more funds." Stanislav responded, "Just a minute! First I want to tell this to Boris."

After we entered the hotel lobby, carrying two six-packs of beer, Stanislav approached the white-haired man and said something to him in Russian. I knew that he was passing along my offer to him. After listening to Stanislav, the white-haired man turned to me and said, "Just a minute!" Later I would wonder about hearing "Just a minute" so many times. I would conclude that in the Soviet system no one could easily make a decision, or more correctly, even think of making a decision, until the topic was sent to an official place where the decision would be reached collectively. In fact, I would learn that the USSR Institute of Psychology would be instructed by authorities to do "research" again and again to prove how a decision made collectively was better than a decision made by a single individual. The white-haired man was Boris Lomov, also a psychologist, assigned to the Soviet space program as the head psychologist. Some months later, after the Division of Psychopolitical Studies changed its name to the Center for the Study of Mind and Human Interaction, the Soviet Duma and CSMHI made an official contract, written in both Russian and English, allowing CSMHI and the USSR Institute of Psychology to start a dialogue series aiming to help the Soviet and the American people get to know one another better and to offer ideas to improve Soviet-American relationships.

Less than a month after CSMHI was founded, on November 15, 1988, the former Soviet nuclear physicist and dissident Andrei Sakharov was given the Albert Einstein Peace Prize in Washington, D.C. In the 1950s he had come out against nuclear proliferation, and in 1975, calling him the "spokesman for the conscience of mankind," the Nobel Peace Committee awarded Sakharov the Nobel Peace Prize. At that time, however, he was not allowed to go to Oslo to receive it in person. Now he was in Washington for the Albert Einstein Peace Prize. I was invited to this event, and after the ceremony Sakharov kindly spent some time with me. I told him about CSMHI, and its plans for opening an unofficial dialogue between the Americans and the Soviets to look into and work on psychological obstacles to a more peaceful coexistence. I noted that he, even as a physicist, was most interested in and appreciative of psychological issues. He said that psychopolitical activities would be crucial for improving the American-Soviet relationship. I was very happy to have the blessing of this great man for CSMHI's hoped-for projects.[13]

Exactly one year after the gathering of scholars and practitioners of "conflict resolution" in Charlottesville, in April 1989, thirteen people convened at CSMHI to exchange ideas about ways in which they could use their varied skills and experiences to work toward new methods of communication, primarily between the United States and the Soviet Union. The group came from a broad array of backgrounds and disciplines, including psychoanalysis, psychology, diplomacy, political science, and journalism, and included participants from the United States, Canada, and the Soviet Union. Boris Lomov and Stanislav Roschin had come from the Soviet Union. Earlier Stanislav had visited with us in Charlottesville as part of a planning process for the future work between the USSR Institute of Psychology and CSMHI. This was Boris's first visit.[14]

Boris and Stanislav left Charlottesville as my friends.[15] I learned a great deal about Boris's twin grandchildren. Much later Stanislav would confide in me that he lived with Vera Tulyakova, and because of this he was surrounded with many items from Turkey at home in his daily environment. Vera Tulyakova was the Russian wife of the famous Turkish poet Nâzım Hikmet, who had escaped to Russia in 1950, died there from a heart attack in 1963, and was buried in Novodevichy Cemetery in Moscow.

In May 1989 Alexander ("Sasha") Obolonsky visited CSMHI.[16] At that time Sasha was a senior research associate at the Institute of State and Law of the USSR Academy of Sciences. Trained as a lawyer and not as a psychologist, he would be the third important Soviet with whom we would continue to work.

In the next chapter, I will tell some stories of how we worked with the Soviets until Mikhail Gorbachev no longer ran the Soviet Union and until the Soviet Union, in fact, no longer existed. I will describe how, when we were in Moscow, Gorbachev's advisers became involved with us, and one time even took us to the Communist headquarters for a special meeting and asked our advice about what to do, not only with Americans, but also with their internal problems, such as the Baltic Republics' desire to have their independence. No one in the U.S. government asked me about our findings. Hal Saunders, Joe Montville, and Richard Arndt, who were involved in the CSMHI team's work with the Soviets, knew many politically influential persons in Washington and were free to talk with them. I never met President Reagan or President Bush or their advisers, although I would meet Mikhail Gorbachev in 1993.

The University of Virginia was planning to celebrate the 250th birthday of its founder, Thomas Jefferson, on April 13, 1993. Many months earlier the university president's office asked me if I could invite Gorbachev to take part in the celebrations. I got in touch with one of Gorbachev's former advisers, and the former leader of the Soviet Union accepted. In his speech Gorbachev spoke about how he was influenced by Thomas Jefferson's ideas. He said,

> Both Jefferson's time and our own are periods of profound and dramatic historical change. The changes, of course, are substantially different. Two and a half centuries ago humankind was entering the extremely promising era of industrial civilization. An era of machines which has benefited people a great deal, but has also brought about a multiplicity of problems, disasters, and tragedies. Today, human-

> kind is stepping toward a post-industrial civilization. No one can yet say what kind of civilization it will be. One thing, however, is clear: it must place humanity at its center. Without that we simply cannot survive.[17]

Gorbachev praised the man who had built and lived in Monticello under whose shadow our Center for the Study of Mind and Human Interaction was located.

# 14

# THE VIRGIN MARY AND JESUS RETURN TO MOSCOW

## THE PSYCHOLOGICAL EFFECTS OF TOTALITARIANISM

Members of the Center for the Study of Mind and Human Interaction (CSMHI) went to Moscow in April 1990 and stayed there for one week. There were seven of us, plus two spouses.[1] At the airport the customs officers checked our baggage thoroughly, and then we were met by some of our hosts and taken to one of the "Seven Sisters," a name given to seven skyscrapers that were built between1947 and 1956 in Moscow. The Moscovites call them *Stalinskie Vysotki* (Stalin's high-rises), after Josef Stalin's initiative to change the appearance of Moscow after World War II.[2] The high-rise where we stayed, Hotel Ukraina, like its sisters, exhibited a mixture of Gothic and Russian Baroque styles—not slim and trim, but heavy and strong. It opened in 1957 as the largest hotel in Europe and after subsequent renovation is today called the Radisson Royal Hotel. This new name illustrates the dramatic changes that have occurred during the last two decades in Moscow, and how symbols of globalization can be seen everywhere.

We arrived at Hotel Ukraina in mid-afternoon. In those days, each floor had a person sitting on a chair next to the elevator or in a nearby room watching who entered and exited the elevator. The guests would deposit their keys with this individual before leaving the floor and retrieve them from her or him upon returning. The woman on my floor would not even greet us, and her presence gave me an unpleasant feeling of being watched. In my mind she symbolized my old prejudiced thoughts about the Soviet system. Unfamiliar customs or sights, even when they also induce awe or envy, can result in negative prejudice.

Before our trip to Moscow we did our homework and familiarized ourselves with Soviet history and recent events in that part of the world. We studied *glasnost* (openness), *perestroika* (restructuring), *demokratizatsiya* (democratization), and *uskoreniye* (acceleration), all of which were initiated by Mikhail Gorbachev after he became the general secretary on March 11, 1985, to deal with the country's serious economic and political problems. While Gorbachev would work for a peaceful world, his new thinking—about streamlining and taming the Communist system so that it would survive, finding solutions for extremely difficult economic conditions, and dealing with increasing nationality issues—would not be successful in the long run.

At the time the CSMHI team arrived in Moscow, we had no idea that the Soviet Union would dissolve in December 1991; we still considered the Soviet Union with its nuclear missiles as the strongest opponent of the United States and the Western world, even though by then the Soviets were trying to present a friendly face. But their doing this was anxiety provoking for the Western world, as well as for the Soviets, since this attitude was new and unfamiliar. Before the trip I recalled what Alexander Obolonsky had told us when he visited CSMHI in May 1989:

> The Soviet Union is moving in two directions: one is toward the separation of power and checks and balances in government; at the same time it has a concentration of power in one charismatic leader.
>
> There are still many fears, of not knowing where lines will be drawn. Lithuanians, for example, are willing to go a certain distance, but they are unsure when the whip will fall. They are afraid of military extremism, of violence. . . . The boundaries of *glasnost* are constantly in motion, but they are not spontaneously generated. They come from the top.[3]

The fall of the Berlin Wall in November 1989 was an enormous historical event.[4] It represented a concrete change. Drastic changes had also occurred in Moscow during the four years before the wall fell and have occurred since then as well. Without a tangible symbol like the Berlin Wall in the Soviet Union, however, shifts in Moscow were not much in the public eye in the United States in those days. The American response to changes in the Soviet Union was slow. Most Americans, like me, had not seen what Moscow was like before the economic decline in the Soviet Union, so we could not imagine what was different in this city during the Gorbachev period. Furthermore, for the American man and woman on the street, the Cold War had built a resistance to accepting new, friendlier political movements in the Soviet Union. Now in Moscow I would observe things and events illustrating great changes in economics, politics, and shared psychology.

When we arrived at the hotel, I suggested that all of us meet that evening in the hotel dining room, which, at that time, was not a fancy place by any standards. The restaurant had a long menu, but soon it became clear that only very few items on it were available. I was not surprised. Before coming we were informed of the food shortages and poor conditions of Moscow's restaurants. After so many years I do not now remember who our informant was. We were also told about the existence of places where we could dine properly, but finding and gaining entrance to them would be a problem since their names and locations were not advertised and we would need local persons to take us there. We were advised to carry packages of cigarettes to bribe the "gatekeepers" of good restaurants so they would allow us in. If we found a good restaurant, we were told, its door would be closed. We were instructed to ring the bell and when a small window on the door or the door itself opened, we were to show a package of cigarettes to the doorman. If he took the package, he would let us in. I recall that our informant suggested that we carry Marlboros, as apparently they were the most sought-after brand. Indeed, we carried many packages of Marlboro cigarettes, and during this first trip to Moscow, we were able to bribe quite a few doormen to allow us some rather decent meals.

At the Hotel Ukraina restaurant when the bill came I thought that it was $420 and that they were taking advantage of us. I was mistaken. The bill turned out to be only $42 for meals, vanilla ice cream—despite the various types of ice cream on the menu, they only had vanilla—and vodka for nine individuals. During that evening not one of us would have dreamed that thirty years later as I write this book, Moscow would be known as one of the most expensive tourist cities on earth. To examine real historic changes in a community within a few decades, one has simply to compare Moscow of a little over two decades ago with Moscow today.

Before we began our meetings at the USSR Institute of Psychology, our Soviet hosts had arranged for a couple of young students to show us the city. Naturally, the Kremlin, Red Square, and museums were the places to see. But this is not a travelogue, so I will instead focus on my observations of a collapsing "empire," and peoples' reactions to it. When we visited GUM, the huge state department store on the eastern side of Red Square, the rows of drab stores told the story of the economic conditions of the Soviet Union. In a shoe store, for example, there were only about a dozen pairs of shoes for sale and the rest of the store was empty. People walked around without smiles. This situation presented a striking contrast to the many statues of persons with raised fists in locations all over Moscow, Communist symbols illustrating peoples' pride and the government's power.

The cover of the April 1990 issue of the Soviet political humor magazine *Krokodyl* (Crocodile) displayed a remarkable cartoon of a man wearing a low-brimmed hat and an overcoat with the collar turned up to hide his face as he wearily attempted to write "Long Live the Communist Party" on a wall in the middle of the night. Only a few years earlier when I was working on my book, *The Need to Have Enemies and Allies*,[5] I had perused some old copies of the same magazine; in those editions the pages were filled with cartoons portraying an aggressive American eagle devouring helpless populations.

On Moscow's Arbat Street, Soviet artists exhibited their paintings. Although most paintings depicted well-known landscapes and buildings, it was now common to see paintings for sale in which the artists had the freedom to express themselves about conditions in Moscow. One showed Gorbachev attempting to pull a broken-down Soviet ship to a safe shore. Another showed a toilet bowl as a boat, aimlessly drifting in the water with the Soviet flag as its sail. Exhibits depicting the Stalin era showed chained men and mountains of skulls under the shadow of the dictator. Where the dictator appeared, religious symbols appeared also—for example, a bleeding Jesus was nailed to a cross, presumably to counteract the evil. There were matryoshka dolls showing the likeness of Stalin on the biggest doll. You opened it up to see the next doll in the likeness of Adolf Hitler.

There were people on Arbat Street reading political poetry and orators giving political speeches to groups of listeners. It was like being in London's Hyde Park! Our taxi driver pointed out various KGB buildings as if they were historical relics. In the lobby of the Moscow Academical Theatre of Musicals on Pushkinskaya Street the portraits of Peter the Great, Ivan the Terrible, Nicholas II, and every other Russian czar were being shown on a large wall. The Soviets, as if they had suddenly discovered the freedom to review their czarist roots, stood in a group studiously examining the likenesses of their past leaders.

We were in Moscow on Easter Sunday, and the beautiful Orthodox churches and monasteries were filled with Soviets, old and young. There were two vans of police next to one crowded monastery, and that night on television I saw them helping the Easter crowd. For the second time in the Soviet Union, Easter ceremonies were being televised, for hours and hours. Cameras zoomed in on portraits of Jesus or the Virgin Mary, and then panned to the faces of awe-filled young girls in the crowd, bright-eyed and solemn. The grim-faced woman in my hotel who usually sat next to the elevator, watching who was coming and going, was absent from her seat the night before Easter. I noticed that she was in an empty room watching the ceremonies on television. Where was the godless Moscow we had all come to know? The guards, however, still watched over Vladimir Ilyich Lenin's tomb at the Kremlin, and busts and pictures of the leader remained in abundance throughout the city.

The Moscow conference took place at the Institute of Psychology of the USSR Academy of Sciences. The Soviet participants, besides coming from this institute, also came from the Center for Political Studies of the Institute of State and Law of the USSR Academy of Sciences, the Diplomatic Academy of the Soviet Foreign Ministry, the Association for International Dialogue, and the Central Committee of the Communist Party. Since we had participants from the Diplomatic Academy, the place where future Soviet diplomats were trained, one day the American participants were taken there. Along the walls of a long corridor leading to the director's office, glass cases displayed numerous pictures of Lenin, along with political declarations and documents exalting the Communist way of life. We were invited to listen to and interact with Soviet scholars who were speaking to future diplomats in a conference room. A translator, of course, was helping us. As we listened to the speakers, discrepancies became apparent. Some of them were holding on to Marxist and Leninist ideals perhaps, I thought, in order to assuage their fears about the rapid changes taking place in their world. Others were openly making anti-Communist statements while sitting under a picture of Lenin. Watching the latter speakers was like watching *The Man with Two Brains*, a popular 1983 comedy about brain transplant directed by Carl Reiner and starring Steve Martin and Kathleen Turner. Many other intellectuals whom I met in Moscow seemed to be gripped by this active paradox; some sidestepped it by going to the extreme right or left, while others were just bewildered by it.

One day Hal Saunders and I, accompanied by one of our hosts, Stanislav Roschin, appeared on the *Good Evening Moscow* program on Moscow Central Television. Having members of a visiting American team interested in the psychology of Soviet-American relations who were not official diplomats as guests on a popular Soviet talk show was something unusual for the people of Moscow—a symbolic illustration of people-to-people communication between Americans and Soviets. As far as I know, this was the first time something like this had happened. Before Hal and I went to the television studio, we got together with other members of the CSMHI team: Dean Robert Carey, Demetrios Julius, Richard Arndt, Norman Itzkowitz, and Molly Turner, the first program director of CSMHI. While we were discussing our upcoming appearance on *Good Evening Moscow*, Hal put his diplomatic hat on and warned us to be very careful talking publicly about American-Soviet relations. He suggested that instead of referring to United States-Soviet issues, he and I should talk about how we were involved in the unofficial Arab-Israeli dialogues and describe our observations of the Middle East conflict. We could talk about the importance of political psychology, but we should be tactful and not mention problems in the Soviet Republics of Armenia, Azerbaijan, Lithuania, or elsewhere.

Since February 1988 there had been armed conflict between Armenians and Azeris in the Nagorno-Karabakh region in southwest Azerbaijan.[6] The Reform Movement of Lithuania (Lietuvos persitvarkymo sąjūdis) began in 1988. In August 1989, Lithuanians, Latvians, and Estonians had held hands to form a human chain that stretched 600 kilometers from Tallinn, to Riga, to Vilnius. This brought worldwide attention to the three Baltic States and their wish to be independent from the Soviet Union. The month before the CSMHI members' arrival in Moscow, in March 1990, the Supreme Soviet accepted the reestablishment of Lithuanian independence. But within the month, the Soviet Union had demanded revocation of that independence. We together agreed not to speak on camera about the situation in the Caucasus region and the Baltic Republics.

When Hal and I were in front of the television cameras, I quickly became flooded with memories of the Watergate Hotel meeting where the senior APA committee members had asked me to talk about Cyprus during the first gathering of Egyptians and Israelis. At Watergate not one Arab or Israeli had paid attention to what I had said. As soon as *Good Evening Moscow* started, our Soviet television host made it clear that he had no interest in what Hal and I were trying to say about the Arab-Israeli conflict. He cut our remarks short. He wanted to know about Americans' views about the disorganization within the Soviet Union and ethnic and nationalist issues in Lithuania, Armenia, Azerbaijan, and other places in the USSR. For him, censorship was a thing of the past. He was excited about the changes and new freedom in the USSR and expected us to join him in openly discussing how people from the Soviet Union and the United States could begin communicating and getting to know one another. We relaxed and joined him. I suggested that drastic changes like those that were occurring in the Soviet Union should also be considered as losses of familiar and accustomed ways of life. I stated that human beings respond to losses by grieving and mourning and that a mourning process refers to reviewing what is lost and the expected replacements for those losses. Then I added that during the Moscow conference the CSMHI members would discuss with our Soviet friends ideas for finding ways to turn this acute large-group grief and mourning into a more organized process.

At the meeting at the USSR Institute of Psychology, Soviet scholars with different backgrounds gave papers and made intellectualized references to the "new way of thinking" and "mass consciousness," but also talked about their confusion about losing old ways and not yet knowing how to replace what was being lost. For example, Alexander Obolonsky described "compulsory collectivism" in the Soviet period and how this accustomed anti-individual social attitude now was one of the most serious obstacles for "restructuring." He listed Communist social issues such as "payless labor," which had blocked the positive transformation of a labor ethic.[7] Leonid Dobrokhotov from the Section of International Information of the Central Committee of the Communist Party stated that the economy was in very bad shape, but that they had ideas about solutions to these problems. He also wanted us to know that it was not only the Soviets who created vicious enemy images. We listened to such presentations respectfully. It was during informal discussions among the CSMHI members and the Soviet participants that emotionally tinged political concerns were verbalized more openly and all of us could put our heads together in order to understand them from realistic as well as from psychopolitical points of view. Large-group grief/mourning and large-group identity issues quickly appeared as the main characters on the stage. Deep concerns about what was going on in Lithuania, Azerbaijan, and Armenia surfaced.

After the December 7, 1988, earthquake in Armenia that killed tens of thousands of persons, humanitarian help was desperately needed. The Soviets even asked the United States for help for the first time since World War II. They also collected Azerbaijani blood for the Armenian victims, but were puzzled when Armenians preferred to die rather than accept their enemies' blood. When this topic came up at the Moscow meeting, we explained that an individual's personal identity is intertwined with his or her large-group identity and that during times of stress, contaminating one's blood with the enemy's blood is perceived as a psychological death of one's large-group identity. Armenians would prefer actual death over psychological death. Knowing this psychological finding might help governments to deal with problems such as the one the Armenians presented to the Soviet government.

Under the Soviet regime the ideological large-group identity, being Communist, was so idealized that the Soviets did not prohibit writing an individual's ethnic identity on "internal passports," which were used for travel and relocation within the Soviet Union—one person was an Armenian, another an Uzbek, still another an Estonian, and so on. In 1990 investment in ethnic identities at many locations in the Soviet Union was overshadowed by the holding on to ideological ones.

As a historian with psychoanalytic training, Norman Itzkowitz declared that human beings were entering into the ethnic phase of history. Also, he added, the question of religion had not been delved into deeply enough. He thought that America's basic distrust of the USSR stemmed from a view of it as a "godless country," and that America, generally speaking, was very conservative religiously. He stated that somehow Lithuanians were seen as holding on to their religion. We suspected that what the CSMHI members observed on that Easter Sunday in Moscow and the appearance of images of Jesus and the Virgin Mary on Moscow television screens for hours and hours would not be facts known by Americans in general.

At least in Moscow where we had direct observation, the economic and political changes were perceived by the public in the Soviet Union as losses, even though on a logical level many wanted certain changes to take place. Losses induced shared complicated grieving and mourning processes and this, in turn, reactivated images of losses from the past. It was clear to me that large-group mourning in Moscow piggybacked onto complicated mourning processes of the past. There seemed to be a feverish degree of emotional investment in "The Great Patriotic War," as Soviets referred to World War II. This was not at all surprising in light of the enormous and shattering losses suffered by the Soviet population during that war. But I also considered the possibility that feelings about losses during the Stalin era, about which our hosts could not talk openly, had been displaced onto feelings about the losses in World War II and condensed with them. There were also very good signs of opening up these wounds in a way that would be helpful to the society: monuments, books, and movies were being utilized for this purpose. In the Soviet Union no one could make a movie without first getting Soviet authorities' approval of its content.

Nikita Khrushchev's attempt to open up the wounds and losses of the Stalin era had failed. The Gorbachev administration was doing a better job, very slowly and sensitively. Monuments that linked people collectively with the shared meaning of their losses were being erected,[8] like the monument honoring Marshal Georgi Zhukov, a World War II hero denounced by Stalin. Anatoly Rybakov's *Children of Arbat* was one of several works dealing with the Stalin period.[9] My favorite turned out to be Tengiz Abuladze's 1984 film *Repentance*, which depicted a villain with characteristics that evoked memories of Stalin. The man dies, but his body is removed from the grave. They bury him again, but his body is removed again, and so on. The series of burials and "resurrections" that leads up to the final burial is a direct symbolic manifestation of the work of mourning that I described earlier in this book—the process of working through the loss until the reality of death is accepted and its meaning is assimilated.

Most likely it was Leonid Dobrokhotov who shared what happened at the Institute of Psychology with Gorbachev's advisers. I received a call at the hotel from the Communist Party of the Soviet Union headquarters inviting me to come to their building and meet with these advisers. I could bring a few of my CSMHI colleagues, but not all of them. I asked Hal, Demetrios, and Dean Carey to join me. Early the next morning we were ushered into a secure room at the Communist Party Headquarters and had a long conversation with Leonid and a group of advisers. I realized that Gorbachev and his advisers still believed in the superiority of the Communist large-group identity and that they were very surprised about how ethnic identity could be reactivated and threaten this ideological identity. We were told how Gorbachev had visited Lithuania recently, explained to the Lithuanians how he was democratizing the Communist system, and asked them for help in keeping the Soviet Union alive. Gorbachev was not received well in Lithuania, and this greatly disappointed and puzzled him. His advisers, referring to Gorbachev's reforms, kept repeating to us, "We are the good people; we are the good people." They continued, "Why can't the Lithuanians see this? Why can't they hear Gorbachev's words? Help us. Please help us!"

Gorbachev's advisers, I sensed, genuinely had no real idea about the psychological impact of ethnic identity. They were referring to political and economic issues and bypassing the power of shared emotions invested in ethnic symbols and images of history. They still wanted to utilize Communist ideals and symbols, now with more democratized modifications, to stop the unrest. They were very interested in the idea that Gorbachev should pay attention to emotions and try to speak with Lithuanians again, this time respecting the power of ethnic identity and being careful not to include statements that might be perceived as humiliating to ethnic groups. The advisers began to wonder about how to prepare new approaches. Gorbachev would not go to Lithuania again, but he could address the Lithuanians by radio and so on. I was surprised to hear that, for some technical reasons I did not understand—as I recall, some locations for transmitting verbal and visual messages were damaged—it would not be possible for Gorbachev to reach the Lithuanians very soon.

As members of CSMHI, we only presented our understanding of large-group behavior from academic and political psychology points of view during the gatherings at the Diplomatic Academy of the Soviet Foreign Ministry and Communist Party Headquarters. We sought no media attention, excepting the appearance on the *Good Evening Moscow* program. We published papers on this meeting only in *Mind and Human Interaction*, which at that time had a rather limited numbers of subscribers.[10] Once our "neutrality" was appreciated in Moscow, a door was opened to us to share our psychopolitical ideas with those inside Gorbachev's circle. Such a thing never occurred in Washington. The Soviets invited me back to Moscow, and this time I went there without any other member of CSMHI, just my wife, and spent days at the Diplomatic Academy lecturing on and discussing political psychology topics. I got to know Yuri Urbanovich from the Soviet Diplomatic Academy well during this visit. Yuri would join us as an International Fellow at CSMHI in Charlottesville in April 1992.

Exactly one year after the Moscow meeting, in April 1991, another major gathering of Soviets, CSMHI members, and other American guests, with the addition of scholars representing Lithuania and Estonia, took place in Charlottesville. On August 19–21, 1991, a coup d'état attempt occurred in the USSR, with a group of hard-liners wanting to take control of the Soviet Union from Gorbachev. It would be known as the "August Putsch." Three months after the putsch, I was rushed to Moscow as a guest of the Diplomatic Academy of the Soviet Foreign Ministry to meet representatives from the Sovereign States of the USSR. This, I think, was one of their last illusions to "save" the Soviet Union.

# 15

# THE END OF THE SOVIET UNION

## THE AGE OF ETHNICITY AND THE PSYCHOLOGY OF PURIFICATION

On August 19, 1991, one day before Gorbachev and a group of Soviet Republic leaders were due to sign a new liberalized union treaty, a coup was carried out under the leadership of eight individuals from the KGB, the Communist Party, and the military calling themselves the State Emergency Committee.[1] These hard-liners, some of whom had been Gorbachev's former allies, wanted to return to old party values and avert the new union treaty by removing Gorbachev, who was in Crimea at the time, from power. The Emergency Committee members announced that Gorbachev was ill and that he was no longer the president of the Soviet Union. Gorbachev was not allowed to return to Moscow. Meanwhile, Boris Yeltsin, who had been elected president of the Russian Soviet Federative Republic two months earlier, became the man of the hour, with the help of public demonstrations against the putsch, by successfully resisting the coup. He barricaded himself inside the Russian Parliament, called the persons who had planned the coup "traitors," and dared them to attack the building.

Three months later the Muscovites with whom I spoke could tell me where they were and what they were doing at the time news of the coup was broadcasted. Some were informed that Gorbachev had just been poisoned by Martians, an example of how crisis in a society initiates interest in the supernatural. Anatoly ("Tolja") Golubovsky had already been invited to join the Center for the Study of Mind and Human Interaction as an International Scholar for a year when he and his family, who were staying near Moscow at their country house, heard the first decree of the State Emergency Committee on the morning of August 19, 1991. They returned to Moscow right away, but on the way to their home just opposite the Kremlin walls in the center of Moscow, they were surprised not to see any troops or army personnel carriers. Soon, however, they heard the rumble of military vehicles moving under their windows. Tired and frightened, Tolja felt as if he were in a movie. The next day, despite an announced curfew, there were no military patrols in sight, and telephones and international communications continued to operate.

The situation was all the more bizarre because the plotters could have captured the Russian Parliament, detained Yeltsin, and celebrated victory at any moment during those first two days. It is hard to say why they did not, since, according to Tolja, the personal backgrounds, political orientations, and professional experiences of the men behind the coup testify to the fact that they would not have been averse to spilling blood. They seemed to have adopted the 1964 arrest of Nikita Khrushchev as their model. The plotters took steps that were in line with their own convictions, but they did not have, and could not have, any plan of action for the period after August 19. For them, the coup ended the moment Gorbachev was detained in Crimea. In fact, the plotters were betrayed by their own political views and by their thinking that the people would stay silent, listening and blindly obeying as they had done for more than seventy years. But the opposite occurred. Nearly two to three hundred thousand citizens gathered in the environs of the Russian Parliament, enough to minimize the escalation of the coup.[2]

Ill-prepared, the coup fell apart by August 21 and most of its leaders left Moscow, just as Gorbachev returned there, having been "saved" by Yeltsin. He might have been in shock, but in public Gorbachev tried to behave as if no dramatic events had taken place in the USSR and that the Soviet Union would continue to exist if he could purge the hard-liners from the Communist Party of the Soviet Union (CPSU). Yeltsin, however, had different ideas. Furthermore, starting the second day of the coup and continuing over the next two months, Ukraine, Belarus, Moldova, Georgia, Armenia, Azerbaijan, and the Baltic and Central Asian Republics would declare their intention to leave the Soviet Union. On August 24, after Yeltsin had ordered the CPSU to suspend its activities in all Russian territory, Gorbachev resigned as general secretary of the CPSU, but remained president of the Soviet Union. Meanwhile, the Russian flag was erected alongside the Soviet flag at the Kremlin. Against all odds, Gorbachev still hoped for a new union.

It was under these conditions that the Rector of the Diplomatic Academy of the Soviet Foreign Ministry, Oleg Peressypkin, the former Soviet ambassador to Libya and Yemen, informed me that, regardless of the regime in power, many factors—economic, legal, political, military, and ecological—would be contaminated with ethnicity and nationalism. He predicted that reaching an understanding of ethnic and nationalistic issues would be Moscow's most significant achievement. He and other Soviet diplomats made a plan to bring representatives from the different republics in the Soviet Union to the academy. I was asked to rush to Moscow and spend four days with these representatives to explore large-group psychology, leader-follower relationships, and peaceful ways of managing conflicts among neighbors. I sensed that my meeting with the representatives of the Soviet republics might also be in the service of Ambassador Peressypkin's and others' magical hope to keep the union alive, liberalized, and more democratic.

I asked myself, "Why me? I have no answers." Upon reflection, I think that during my previous interactions with Soviet colleagues I was able to maintain my psychoanalytic/academic identity. I did not communicate with them as someone who had answers to societal and political conflicts, but as someone who could listen to them while absorbing their anxiety and help them to separate their wishes and fears from realistic issues under discussion so they could deal with realities in a more comfortable way. Also, everyone knew that I, as well as other members of CSMHI, was not involved with the Soviets for any economic gain. I believe that they trusted me.

When my wife and I flew by Aeroflot from Washington and arrived in Moscow in the middle of the night three months after the coup, we were treated as if we were important dignitaries. Yuri Urbanovich met us at the airport accompanied by a younger man, Yalçın Nasırov, who was a postgraduate student at the Diplomatic Academy. Yalçın spoke to me in Turkish since he was from Azerbaijan. His wife's father, a prominent historian, was the permanent representative of Azerbaijan in Moscow. They took my wife and me to the huge building complex where the permanent representative of Azerbaijan had his home and offices. They told us that Moscow had changed a great deal during the last months and that it might not be safe for us to stay in a hotel. Yalçın excitedly told me that the Azerbaijanis would provide three bodyguards for us whenever we left the building without escorts from the Diplomatic Academy.

The next day when I paid a visit to the Diplomatic Academy, I was impressed with the changes in the long hallway in front of the rector's office. Previously this place had been filled with mementos of Lenin. Now these items were gone, along with the vice-rector who, a year and half earlier, had told me that only by drawing blood would the problem of the Baltic Republics be solved. Only one handmade rug depicting Lenin's likeness remained on one wall. Pictures of Gorbachev, Yeltsin, François Mitterrand, Margaret Thatcher, Bush, and even Dan Quayle were now displayed in the hallway. I was pleased to see a picture of a friend of mine, Princeton University political science professor Robert Tucker, who had written about changes in the Soviet Union.[3]

I was given a pass to make a special visit to Lenin's mausoleum. On my way there the next day, I was stopped by two women who presented me with Lenin pins and through my interpreter asked me to support efforts to keep Lenin's body at its present location. I had to remind myself that only the day before I had seen a broken statue of Lenin dumped in the yard of Tretjakovskaja Gallery, which was not too far from the Kremlin, alongside toppled statues of Stalin and Felix Dzerzhinsky, the founder of the KGB. I was witnessing confusion due to an atmosphere that was simultaneously honoring and dishonoring Lenin's memory.

Preoccupation with large-group identity was also visible in the streets. It would be at the borders of subgroups that the Soviet "Empire" would tear apart. As I walked with my three Azerbaijani bodyguards through a park, talking with them in Turkish, a group of Russian high school students shouted at us "Invasion! Invasion!" and made hostile gestures. It was clear that these students perceived Azerbaijanis as "foreigners," even though at that time 30,000 of them were living, to some degree, as "Soviets" in Moscow. One of the bodyguards shouted back, saying, "Thank you" (*spasibo*) in Russian. He accented the first syllable, *spa*, and this caused the Azerbaijanis to laugh among themselves. *Spa* is pronounced the same way as the Turkish word for donkey (*sıpa*). This was typical of the kinds of open and hidden expressions of prejudice that were prevalent in Moscow at that time.[4]

We also noticed lines of people everywhere. It made no difference whether they were trying to buy food or luxury items. On Tverskaja Street (this was the original name for Gorky Avenue; it was changed back just before the putsch) I saw a crowd gathered outside a large glass window to watch "rich" Muscovite women have their hair styled. A sign on the door stated that some hair treatments cost as much as 300 rubles, which was a one-month salary for an average highly educated person. A visible division between "rich" and "poor" had begun, even though at that time, due to the Communist ideology, an ambulance driver still earned more money than an emergency room physician. Overwhelming confusion was visible.

My hosts also arranged for my wife and me to visit the Yuri Gagarin Cosmonaut Training Center near Vladimir and Suzdal, just outside Moscow. We were met by a Soviet general whose name unfortunately I do not recall today. He did not look like the tough and mean Soviet military men depicted in many American movies during the Cold War, and he had brought his ten-year-old son to meet the Americans. The boy joined us as we were shown areas where sophisticated machines for training astronauts were kept. What made me sad was that hallways separating huge rooms with sophisticated machines, exercise rooms, and offices were being cleaned by ladies with brooms instead of vacuum cleaners, and that most of the walls of the surrounding hallways were falling apart. The contrast between pride and greatness and humility and poorness was striking.

The city of Vladimir and the town of Suzdal, sixteen miles from Vladimir, are historical places where one can see magnificent examples of very old Russian architecture. In these locations too the contrast between beauty and the beast tore me apart emotionally. For example, when we entered Vladimir through the Golden Gate, originally built in 1158–1164, expecting to see masterpieces such as the Assumption Cathedral and St. Demetrius Cathedral, we were met with dark yellow smoke billowing from the chimneys of several factories and hovering over the city. During the Communist regime, the Soviets had turned Vladimir into a center for the chemical and electrical industry. I wanted Stalin's ghost to appear in front of me so that I could shake him by the shoulders and shout, "How could you ruin such a beautiful place?" Probably he would have had me shot before I could touch him!

I still have very vivid memories of meeting with representatives of the Sovereign States as the Soviet "Empire" was collapsing. There were also representatives from the so-called autonomous regions. With Yuri Urbanovich as my interpreter, I met with them for four days from morning to evening. We took time for lunch and had coffee breaks, but instead of coffee I was usually given a shot of cognac. Looking back, it is almost as if my hosts and I, without being aware of it at that time, thought that one had to be under the influence of alcohol, at least a bit, to conduct and tolerate such a gathering. I had in mind the psychology of internalization. If people live under a centralized system through generations, especially a totalitarian one, and cannot escape its grasp, the system becomes internalized. Even those who are able to maintain their individuality more than others cannot escape internalizing the system to some extent. "Freedom" and "independence" in a political and legal sense do not mean that what is internalized can or should be changed overnight. I wanted to keep this in mind and not hurt anyone's feelings.

Michael Šebek, who now practices psychoanalysis in the Czech Republic, described the influence of the Communist regime on individuals and families in his country and its internalization soon after Communism's collapse. Later he would write about the psychopathology of everyday life in the posttotalitarian society. Šebek described internalization under the Communist system in the following way:

> While fascist totalitarian power emphasizes national justice, racial purity, and equality based on national identity, the communists emphasized international justice. With magical grandiosity and alchemic enthusiasm, the intellectual is transformed into an unqualified worker, the worker into a sophisticated man, the poor man into a rich one, and the rich man into a poor one.
>
> In the interests of this perverse justice, not even the biological differences between men and women are respected—women are allocated the same hard work as men, and this latently and unconsciously damages the family structure. Not only does it ignore the difference between men and women, but it also establishes an assumption about the right to make decisions concerning the lives of the children living in the state; education in the collective is elevated above the education in the family.[5]

Later Šebek used the term "totalitarian objects" in describing what people living under Communist regimes internalize and identify with from childhood on—to one degree or another, taking into account individual and family issues and belief systems.[6]

The gathering started as an intellectual exercise. The Soviets, from different republics and autonomous regions, wanted to hear exact definitions of concepts such as ethnicity. There were many other words that had meanings that needed to be changed intellectually and emotionally in the Soviet participants' minds. For example, "money" in the Soviet system was an item that could be exchanged only for a rather limited number of things, and recently it had begun to have a different meaning for them. Words such as "governments," "newspapers," and "political parties" too carried different meanings. In turn, the Soviet participants provided "scientific" statistics about ethnic groups in this or that location and talked about "borders" separating one large group from another and "histories" that were not taught under the Communist system and were different for each large group. I, as a foreigner, needed to develop empathy and the ability to understand their confusion. Those who harbored conscious or hidden desires to keep the Soviet Union alive in one form or another perceived the ethnonationalism of the people in the republics and in the autonomous regions as a threat. Those who saw the inevitability of republics going their separate ways were aware of the difficulties the independence movements would bring. No republic was made up of any "pure" ethnic group and no republic had enough latitude to go its own way completely. For example, one third of the inhabitants of Estonia were not Estonians; they were Russians or Others called "Russian speakers." If the union collapsed, facing a process that I had already named "purification"was a realistic expectation for certain locations of the USSR.[7]

Let me briefly explain what I mean by purification. Purification processes stand for large-group externalizations and projections. After a nation or large group emerges from crises such as war, the breakup of a political system, or drastic revolutionary change, a period of restabilization typically ensues. During this time of reassessment and redefinition, when a large group in a sense collectively asks, "Who are we now?" or "How do we define our large-group identity now?" attempts at purification often occur. Purification intensifies and modifies the group's identity by shedding its unwanted aspects and by solidifying its borders. It might drop certain words considered "foreign" from everyday use, as Greeks did following their independence from the Ottoman Empire, or the group might erase symbols of other cultures by, for example, destroying churches or mosques. These are instances of purification. Large-group purification activities involve a spectrum of practices, policies, and ideologies ranging from benign (purifying language) to malignant (ethnic cleansing). I mentioned above how the name "Gorky Avenue" was replaced with the original name for this street. We can certainly consider this a benign form of purification. When I was meeting with the representatives of the Sovereign States, the government in the Republic of Georgia was considering denying citizenship rights to people there who could not prove that their ancestors were Georgians who had lived in the territory before 1801. Dangerous purification possibilities were already looming on the horizon.

The conference room turned into a "laboratory," where the participants in a sense experimented on how various large groups would exist side by side if a new type of union were to be founded or if the Soviet Empire collapsed. The Russians, I sensed, were experiencing a heightened shared feeling of nationalism, but it was cloaked under the cover of the Russian Orthodox religion. Others, in a sense, were asking questions such as, "What is my history?" "How different am I from the Russians?" "How different am I from my neighbors?" "How can I maintain *my* group identity?" Then, the doubts and anxieties pertaining to the dramatic transformations that had taken place would surface with this final question, "What is my fate?"

Border issues were hot. It was known that some borders within the USSR were labeled as merely Stalin's, and even Khrushchev's, whims. Not long before this conference, one of Yeltsin's public relations officers had announced that if a republic left the union, its borders would become subject to new negotiations. Of course, the reactions of the republics, especially that of Ukraine, were very negative. When Moldavians spoke up and expressed their grievances against Moscow, Armenians and Azerbaijanis appeared to be listening, but without much emotional investment. But the Armenians listened very intensely to the Azerbaijanis' reports since Armenia and Azerbaijan shared a border and had different perceptions about its "correct" version.

The group of people I met with wanted to assess what characteristics of good leadership would be required for finding a balance between emotional and real social and political issues in order to moderate many potentially harmful processes. Could a leader in a "democratic" system summon whatever he or she required to balance such issues? If the participants at the meeting I was conducting were asked to be advisers to governments, how could they be good advisers? When intellectualization ended very early in this four-day meeting, the participants from different large groups became participant-observers in a highly dramatic period of their history. They experienced humanity, warts and all.

On the afternoon of the fourth day one Russian, Vlademir Pechkourov, chairman of the Oriental Languages Department at the Diplomatic Academy, raised his voice and addressed me. In heavily accented English, he said, "Professor Volkan, we learned a great deal and now we need to face our responsibilities because the cookie will crumble." There was nothing more to discuss.

A month later the cookie crumbled.[8]

# 16

# THE BERLIN WALL FALLS

## THE PSYCHOLOGY OF BORDERS, MODERN GLOBALIZATION, AND MINOR DIFFERENCES

As I worked with representative Israelis, Egyptians, and Palestinians and then with representatives of the Sovereign States and autonomous regions in the Soviet Union, I noticed they frequently referenced physical borders between large groups. This chapter examines the psychology of borders.

As my work with the Soviets was ending, I came to the conclusion that the *prototype* of large-group conflicts occurs in areas where two large groups are physical neighbors. Israelis and Palestinians, Armenians and Azerbaijanis, and Cypriot Turks and Cypriot Greeks are neighbors who often claim ownership of the same piece of land and are confused about the physical border separating them. When the Soviet Union collapsed, millions of Russians found themselves living in newly independent states. Over a million Arabs live in Israel and hundreds of Cypriot Turks and Greeks inhabit territory belonging to the Other. In the modern world, people with different large-group identities—from ethnic to racial to ideological—mingle everywhere. Another aspect of the modern world is that even if large groups are not neighbors geographically, all of them are linked, at least figuratively, by modern communication and transportation technologies as well as by economic, legal, and other commitments.[1] The modern phenomenon of globalization strives to make all large groups in the world neighbors. With the world shrinking in this way, is it possible to identify derivatives of behavior that are based upon the psychology of neighboring large groups in large groups that are not even close geographically?

In November 2006 at Cape Town University in South Africa I was honored to give the keynote speech for the celebration of Archbishop Desmond Tutu's seventy-fifth birthday and the tenth anniversary of the Truth and Reconciliation Commissions' work.[2] After this event my wife and I spent some time at Kruger Park, a preserve for wild animals and birds. People who visit this place remain in enclosed spaces to protect them from the wild animals. One day we took a four-hour jeep ride with a guide and driver to see the animals in their natural habitat. We were told that if we were lucky we would witness unusual animal activity. We were lucky on several occasions. I am not an expert on animal behavior, but what I will report here is what came to my mind while watching these animals.

During the ride I saw a kind of "oedipal story" performed by elephants. While we were being driven around, the air began to smell peculiar. The guide informed us that the smell was coming from a sexually aroused young male elephant; it was the smell of testosterone. This excited elephant had spotted an older male elephant with two female companions and two very young elephants. The sexually aroused male elephant rushed to this "family gathering" in a fury, causing the female elephants to take their "children" and slowly move away, while the two male elephants, the younger one and the older one, pulled up some trees with their trunks and started hitting each other. We watched them for some time in amazement. Then we were driven away before we could see the end of this fantastic battle. Other amazing sights at Kruger Park included rhinos pairing up, "dancing" around a pond and exhibiting a concrete example of "we-ness" when there was a thunderstorm that apparently frightened them. We saw a female lion whose cubs had been killed a few days earlier joining another female lion in tenderly taking care of this lion's newborns. We also saw a big wooden cross under a tree that marked the spot where a guide who had stepped out of his vehicle to urinate was eaten by a lion.

Sipping wine in an enclosed and secure place that evening, after witnessing these interesting sights and events, I decided to make a list of what I observed the animals doing at Kruger Park: searching for food, possessing a territory, having sex, making babies, protecting babies, losing a loved one, forming groups, males competing with other males in the same group, exhibiting aggression and submission, experiencing fear, developing species-oriented defenses, escaping from or fighting and killing the Other, and being preoccupied with individualized and group survival. The two elephants that were fighting belonged to the same species, but I was told that they would not kill one another. In the wild animal world at Kruger Park, the Others who are killed—like the unfortunate guide who stepped out from his jeep to urinate, or the many antelopes roaming in groups—in general belong to a different species than the killer does. I amused myself by thinking that no candidate in a psychoanalytic institute should be allowed to graduate without first visiting Kruger Park and observing wild animals illustrating elements that also underlie human nature. But, I also wondered why humans, in the name of large-group identity, do not hesitate to kill others, sometimes thousands or even millions of them, who belong to their own species.

I remembered Erik Erikson's idea that every human being is born a "generalist." He or she needs another person who provides mothering functions in order to survive, but later the child needs to psychologically separate from this needed "other" in order to individuate. To find objects for their sexual and aggressive desires and to develop more sophisticated minds, humans need even more Others, above and beyond mothers and their substitutes. Accordingly, the Other is both desirable and frightening. For their entire lives people continue to draw near, but also withdraw from, Others. They use Others when subjectively defining themselves, by focusing on the undesirable differences between themselves and the Others and to understand their own feelings of envy and jealousy by realizing unattainable but wished-for qualities that do not belong to them.

Through interaction in childhood with those to whom the child belongs and with those who their parents consider to be Others, and by finding suitable targets of externalization, the child no longer remains a generalist and becomes a member of a distinct large group. Earlier in this book I explained theories pertaining to how the human mind and the need to have enemies and allies evolve in childhood. I also mentioned that some research illustrates that an infant possesses some biological ability from birth on to sense "we-ness" and "otherness."

The concept of our needing enemies and allies receives further confirmation from another idea from Erik Erikson: his use of the term "pseudo species" in reference to the diversity of humankind. He stated that "man has evolved (by whatever kind of evolution and for whatever adaptive reasons) in pseudo species, i.e., tribes, clans, classes, etc., which behave as if they were separate species, created at the beginning of time by supernatural intent."[3] Erikson theorized that primitive humans sought a measure of protection for their unbearable nakedness by adopting the armor of the lower animals and wearing their skins, feathers, or claws. On the basis of these outer garments, each tribe, clan, or group developed a sense of shared identity, as well as a conviction that it alone harbored the *one* human identity. Based on Erikson's ideas, I thought that if large human groups felt that they belonged to different species, they would kill one another.

We can add another idea to Erikson's supposition, also speculative, that may further explain what happened during the course of human evolution. For centuries, neighboring tribes had only each other to interact with, due to their natural boundaries. Neighboring groups had to compete for territory, food, sex, and physical goods for their survival. Eventually, this primitive level of competition assumed more psychological implications. Physical essentials, besides retaining their status as genuine necessities, absorbed mental meanings as well, such as prestige, honor, power, envy, revenge, humiliation, submission, and loss, and evolved from being tokens of survival to becoming large-group symbols, cultural amplifiers, traditions, religions, and historical memories that embedded a large-group's self-esteem, narcissism, and identity.

Erikson's postulations are supported by references to the Other in many ancient documents and languages. Ancient Chinese regarded themselves as *people* and viewed the Other as *kuei* or "hunting spirits." The Apache Indians considered themselves to be *indeh*, the people, and all others as *indah*, the enemy.[4] The Mundurucu in the Brazilian rain forest divided their world into Mundurucu, who were people, and non-Mundurucu, who were *pariwat* (enemies), except for certain neighbors who they perceived as friendly.[5] Anthropologist Howard Stein stated that this type of pattern "cannot be literally generalized to all cultures, but it shows in the extreme a universal proclivity in feelings towards, perception of, and action taken against those who were not 'the people.'"[6] During the times about which written history is available, we constantly see interactions of Erikson's pseudo species and one group seeing the other as less than human. The Christian Europeans' treatment of Jews during the Middle Ages, the white Americans' treatment of black Americans in the United States, and the Nazis' treatment of Jews and Roma are examples of one large group dehumanizing another.

Late African-American psychiatrist Charles Pinderhughes also studied the universality of the shared Other. Although he recognized the validity of psychological and social causes, he theorized that the bedrock of the universal drive to dichotomize rested in biology and physiology. He referred to zoologist Konrad Lorenz's studies on animal bonding,[7] but he asserted that Lorenz only conceptualized bonding in affiliated terms. Pinderhughes focused on a broader level and also included aggressive behavior as a bonding phenomenon. He stated, "Differentiation, projection, repudiation, and aggression appear to be built on the bedrock of avoidance psychology."[8] Thus, Pinderhughes connected the need to have the Other with human biology and suggested that some degree of stereotyping is necessary for human adaptation. His ideas fit well with the psychoanalytic theory on the need to have enemies and allies that I wrote about earlier in this book and have explored elsewhere.[9] Studies in evolutionary psychology also refer to the creation of the Other and dehumanization as elements of human nature.[10]

There is also a need to put a "psychological border" between "us" and "them" due to our wish to keep what we externalized and projected onto the Other from returning to us. Even in the present world where persons from different large groups live in locations with mixed populations, most of the time the Other is still on the opposite side of some kind of physical border: a legal political border of a nation, a geographical border created by nature between tribes or ethnic groups, or a border created by force when an enemy surrounds another group. When there is no extensive conflict between neighbors, a physical border remains simply a physical border; when there is a conflict, the physical border assumes great psychological meaning as the border separating large-group identities.

My first return to Cyprus after spending eleven years in the United States was in 1968. From 1963 on, my family in Nicosia had lived surrounded by their enemies in a crowded enclave with no opportunity to leave their inhumane surroundings. They were "prisoners" on a small piece of land while they lived in their or their relatives' homes huddled together or sometimes even in man-made caves. After Turkey showed its military muscle against Cypriot Greeks with an air attack in 1968, the gates of the Turkish enclaves in Cyprus were opened to some extent. For the first time in five years my family left their Nicosia enclave and came to the Nicosia Airport on the Cypriot Greek side to meet my wife and me. At the airport they spoke to me in whispers, and in the car driving through Cypriot Greek territory they spoke so softly I could not hear them clearly. When we passed through the barricades separating the Cypriot Greek side from the Cypriot Turkish enclave, I was grief stricken when I saw the horrible physical conditions in the enclave. My voice was subdued, but my family members, now free to speak in a natural way, raised their voices. The barricades that surrounded their enclave had become the psychological border protecting their large-group identity.

I learned that within this border they had found a magical way to survive psychologically as a group by raising parakeets in cages. Parakeets are not native to Cyprus. Upon our arrival at my family's house where we would stay, my wife and I were immediately introduced to sixteen parakeets divided among three cages. I found it disconcerting to have my attention directed so insistently to the birds when I had been waiting for eleven years to see my family members and to meet those who had been born during my absence. But it was plain that my people thought it entirely natural that the birds had a higher priority. The parakeets were being raised as an extended family, as this type of family system had existed among the Cypriot Turks for centuries. The original pair of birds—the "mother and father"—were pointed out to me in one cage along with a "bride" who had been moved into her new "home." One enormously fertile but crippled hen was a special pet; her fecundity more than made up for her imperfections. The next day I became aware that the hobby of parakeet raising was not unique to my family's household, but was the hobby of all in the enclave. When I went to a small grocery store to buy a loaf of bread, I had to step over cages. When I investigated, I learned that there was no such shared hobby in Cypriot Greek–held areas; the hobby existed only in the 3 percent of the island where Cypriot Turks were forced to live in enclaves. Despite my sadness and sometimes unbearable guilt for being in the United States enjoying freedom while my family and my people went through, and were going through, such horrors, I was able to use my mind and figure out the psychological meaning of the shared bird hobby.

I had read a great deal about what had happened in the Nazi concentration camps and had worked with two patients intensively who were children of Holocaust survivors. One dissimilarity between the situation of the Jews in concentration camps and Cypriot Turks living as "prisoners" in enclaves surrounded by their enemies for years was immediately evident: the defensive-adaptive behavior of those awaiting certain death is not the same as that of persons who can still entertain the hope of survival or safety, no matter how long hope is deferred and how chronic the situation becomes. The Cypriot Turks kept alive the hope that their "mother," the Turks in Turkey, would come to their rescue. This in fact took place in 1974.

The birds in cages represented the externalized self-representations, mental doubles, of the Cypriot Turks. As long as the birds produced new birds, sang and survived, the Cypriot Turks could maintain hope for survival. They identified with the image of the rescuers and took care of the birds. As the physical borders became more permeable, the bird hobby disappeared. In 1974 the physical border between Cypriot Turks and Cypriot Greeks changed drastically as the island was divided into northern Cypriot Turkish and southern Cypriot Greek sections. Between 1963 and 1968, however, the cages protected the birds, and barricades evolved as psychological borders protecting the Cypriot Turks' psychological existence.[11] The present physical border in Cyprus remains controversial and in fact continues to function as an emotional border.

Here is a summary of my observations of another physical border between two antagonistic large groups and how it also became a psychological border: in 1986, when tensions between Israelis and Jordanians were high, as a guest of the Israelis, I visited the Allenby Bridge over the Jordan River that separates the two countries. A white line drawn in the middle of the bridge divided the two countries. At that time, as I recall, sixteen particular trucks were allowed to pass through the border. Trucks that went over the bridge looked like the factory had forgotten to finish them: doors and hoods were missing, and even the upholstery had been removed to allow no places to hide contraband items. In spite of this, Israeli customs officers would spend hours taking vehicles apart and putting them back together to assure that nothing was smuggled in from Jordan. At a "jewelry shop" located at the customs building, gold rings and bracelets of every Arab woman were evaluated as they came in and went out of Israel in order to ensure that these women left nothing valuable for their Arab relatives living in Israel. The idea was that if gold was left for Israeli Arabs, they might buy "dangerous" things to be used against Israeli Jews.

In another precaution, the Israelis routinely swept a dirt road that ran parallel to the border in order to detect the footprints of people trying to cross it. It should be noted that the border was amply supplied with sophisticated electronic surveillance devices; an Israeli officer informed me, perhaps jokingly, that through electronic surveillance the Israeli authorities could even know when an important person in Jordan went to the bathroom or when he visited a woman who was not his wife. Even if there was justification for the extra precaution, the idea of a psychological border was intertwined with the physical border at the Allenby Bridge, resulting in rituals that created a psychological gap between the two countries.

Borders between Cypriot Turks and Cypriot Greeks and between Israel and Jordan separate people belonging to different ethnic groups. Now I will tell the story of a border that separated people of the same blood but with different political ideologies. In Part III, I described how Donald Winnicott played with diagrams, using a circle to represent a person. His belief that most individuals are unintegrated led him to examine political divisions. He compared Berlin, which was still divided at that time, to his diagram of a circle with a line through its center that represents the unintegrated individual. He noted that some political divisions, such as the border between England and Wales, can be looked upon in terms of geography and mountains, but a man-made border like the Berlin Wall could never be associated with the word "beauty." However, he acknowledged *positive* aspects of the Berlin Wall; in the 1960s there would have been war without the wall. He argued that a dividing line between opposing forces, at its worst postpones conflict and at its best holds opposing forces away from each other for long periods of time. During this respite people may pursue the arts of peace, which speak to the temporary success of a dividing line between opposing forces, the lull between times when the wall has ceased to segregate good and bad.[12] When there is anxiety and regression within large groups in conflict, a simple physical border between them is not enough to protect the antagonists' identities. The physical border must evolve as a psychological border to defend against any possibility of interpenetration. During the Cold War, the Berlin Wall stood as the ultimate symbol of the physical as well as psychological border between the East and the West.

A few months after the reunification of Germany, I visited a friend who lived in a town on the west side of the former East German–West German border. He asked if I would like to see the former border and then drove us to a grassy area not far from Göttingen, a town that had been on the boundary between the two German states prior to 1990. My friend described how the trees had been cut down to help the border guards apprehend defectors. That day, of course, there were no soldiers, and the watchtowers were empty. I was, however, struck by the eerie silence of the place, and also by the fact that my friend was whispering. It was as though there was still danger in this former border region. We then drove across the old border and into former East Germany, something my friend had not done since before Germany's division. Even though they had been reunited, the physical disparities between the two former countries were immediately obvious: the eastern side's roads were poorly designed and maintained and even the shape of the power poles and street lights were different. It was indisputable that we were now in a different "country."

As we rode through the countryside, leaving heavy traffic behind, my friend took a deep breath and then asked me if I smelled something foul. I could not detect anything out of the ordinary, and told him so, but he did not accept my answer. He pointed to a car that was quite a distance in front of us and said, "You see that car? It's Communist-made. Those cars smell." I was certain he could not have realistically sensed anything emanating from the car because it was too far away. It seemed that since he "knew" Communist-made cars had an offensive odor, his senses played a trick on him. *Seeing* the car stimulated his *smelling* the car. As a psychoanalyst, I also came to another conclusion: my friend was externalizing, projecting, and displaying some unacceptable elements of his own onto East Germans. He was "clean"; East Germans "stunk." I did not verbalize my deduction but sensed that my friend, also a psychoanalyst, had come to a similar conclusion about his experience. He seemed embarrassed and quickly changed the topic of conversation. I realized that after the Berlin Wall was gone, former projections, externalizations, and displacements could boomerang!

Soon after the Berlin Wall was taken down, at a Center for the Study of Mind and Human Interaction meeting, we formed the following hypothesis: as a psychological border, the Berlin Wall, in the years when it was experienced as stable, allowed the societies with different political ideological large-group identities on either side to effectively externalize, project, and displace their shared unwanted self- or object images, thoughts, and affects onto the other side without feeling anxiety that these elements would be returned to them. Metaphorically speaking, the "smell" of the Communist-made car could never float over to West Germany. We also hypothesized that the initial elation we witnessed over the reunion of same-blooded people after forty years and over the loss of an "enemy," would be accompanied or followed by the more complicated psychological processes of facing the "boomerang" effect of externalizations, projections, and displacements. Individuals in both halves of the reunited country would struggle between wishing to hold on to and wishing to modify their existing large-group identity, and they would have to contend with mourning and adaptation. In short, we believed that if we studied people's internal experiences concerning the removal of a physical border between East and West Germany, we could understand the nature of a psychological border between two large-group identities. We could thus apply this knowledge not only to the case of Germany, but also to other large-group conflicts, recognizing that the psychodynamics of these relationships can be usefully compared even though the physical and historical realities would of course be very different.

We received funds to start working with Germans from both sides of the former border and to collect data about their shared, but mostly unconscious, perceptions of the border.[13] CSMHI's international member Gabriele Ast from Munich was involved in this project. Besides conducting interviews in German, she would help psychoanalysts from CSMHI interview other Germans in English. We planned to interview at least one hundred people. These interviews were envisioned as similar to psychoanalytic diagnostic interviews, with an emphasis on the individual's experience with the mental images of historical events, that is, how the images of such occurrences appeared in their free associations, fantasies, and dreams.

Note, for example, the dream of a twenty-five-year-old law student from former East Germany named Hans soon after German reunification. He had, in actuality, helped his parents build a house on a hill overlooking a lake. In his dream, however, a wealthy man builds a much larger house on the same hill. This man then tells Hans and his family to move out of their newly built home because it obstructs his view of the lake. As consolation, the wealthy man offers the second floor of his house to the family, and though Hans' parents quarrel with their "landlord," the rich man wins in the end. In the dream, the house explodes as soon as Hans and his family move in with the wealthy "landlord."

Hans' associations to this dream, apart from those relating to divisions within his childhood family, were to the German reunification. A former East German, Hans knew that the wealthy neighbor in the dream represented West Germany. His experiences with early emotional and physical divisions in his family (between his mother and father and between his mother and grandmother) were condensed in the country's division between East and West. While the luxury of the rich man's larger house was appealing to Hans, his old self (his family's house) in the German Democratic Republic was threatened and disappearing. He spoke of how he was paralyzed for half an hour and felt completely numb on the night of the official German reunification. He noted that "the danger was over" because he realized that the threat of a military confrontation was eliminated, "but he was overwhelmed by the anxiety that, with the two sides now united, the 'bad' representations symbolized by West Germany would destroy the 'good' representations symbolized by East Germany."[14]

Another interviewee was Martin, a physicist from West Germany who was thirty-three at the time of reunification. He was more direct than Hans—his fantasies associated with reunification caused a panic reaction. Martin's parents had divorced when he was a child, and his father had taken his siblings to another country. Martin did not have many realistic experiences with his father, but his mother told him that his father was "a monster, a brute." During his teenage years, Martin contemplated joining his father for a while, but he remained in West Germany with his mother, away from the "monster" father. His father's mental double was externalized onto East Germany and the Nazis. Martin had become consciously aware of the meaning of the Holocaust when he was a teenager. He believed that the GDR provided, in a disguised way, more derivatives of National Socialism than existed in West Germany. Thus, he could displace his negative feelings about West Germany onto the country across the border, and there they would be contained. Martin married a Turkish woman living in Germany—in his mind Turks in West Germany were the inheritors of the prejudices previously held against Jews. During the interview, it appeared that his marriage to a Turk helped bolster his wish to avoid becoming a Nazi, a symbolic representation of his "monster father," and helped convince him that he did not have untamed aggression.

It seemed that Martin utilized the division between East and West to keep the mental doubles of his parents separate from each other. Therefore, the German reunification implied the return of Nazism to his self-representation, in which his aggression had been denied; Martin's denial was no longer effective after the reunification. Martin then recalled how it was his mother, with whom he stayed after the departure of his father and siblings, who was openly prejudiced against Jews. During the interview, Martin reported, "The ideas written about Jews in *der Stürmer* [the Nazi propaganda magazine] are still in her mind [though she was a member of SPD, Social Democratic Party of Germany]."[15]

A West German woman, Sabine, in her late twenties at the time of reunification, also participated in our project. At the time, she was undergoing her personal analysis as part of her psychoanalytic training. The reunification pleased Sabine in some ways, but also instilled the fear that it would "recreate the murderer, the monster [Nazis, Hitler] that perpetuated so many horrors."[16] She, like Martin, had externalized, projected, and displaced her thoughts and feelings about the Nazis onto East Germans. Soon after the reunification, she had a dream in which people were standing in an open truck. "When I saw the truck I knew it was a picture from the Nazi era, of Jews being deported to Auschwitz. I felt very guilty for coming up with this picture."[17] Since her analyst was Jewish, she developed anxiety about reporting her dream to him. She and her analyst would speak of the Holocaust, but they could not fully explore this topic to analyze her fantasies and affects related to the Third Reich.

Our project was unfortunately truncated due to insufficient funds after Dr. Ast and I had conducted only twenty-one interviews. The interviews described above and the others, however, afforded us a glimpse into the way mental images of a historical event as significant as German reunification are accompanied by personal and large-group identity issues, emotions, and fantasies. Perhaps most conclusive was that some of these identity issues, emotions, and fantasies seem to be shared by many of the participants. We felt that these interviews supported our initial hypothesis that the forty-year-long separation between East and West Germany had created two different large-group identities and that the German reunification initially induced anxieties and other affects concerning personal and large-group identity issues in both East and West Germans.

Although this project could not be completed, our initial findings are supported by other researchers who have investigated the psychology of German reunification. Their studies also showed that certain images related to the Third Reich and the Holocaust (that individuals did not wish to own) and their associated affects and fantasies had been externalized, projected, and displaced from one side of the border to the other and that the reunification destabilized this situation. For example, in separate studies Dieter Ohlmeier, Irene Misselwitz, Hans-Joachim Maaz, and Adam Weisberger declared that the reunification of Germany was not only a major political change, but was also a major psychological event, prompting a new wave of renegotiations with the Nazi past.[18]

Among these renegotiations within German society was the "Nazi skinhead" movement, a maladaptive manifestation of shame and guilt derivations related to the mental representation of the Third Reich.[19] As Ohlmeier suggested, psychoanalytic considerations of the German reunification evoked questions of psychology for Germans, and the necessity of a psychohistorical reflection of the Germans since 1933. When Ohlmeier referred to "a psychology for Germans," he was considering large-group identity issues that became stirred up after the fall of the Berlin Wall, and that since then have been tackled by some in the German psychological community. For example, in July 1995, the Psychotherapeutic Study Group of Persons Affected by the Holocaust (Psychotherapeutischer Arbeitskreis für Betroffene des Holocaust, or PAKH) was founded by a group of ten people, mostly German and Jewish German psychoanalysts and psychotherapists, to initiate a dialogue to end the "silence" about the Holocaust in Germany and to start a "fresh" method for self-examination of the Nazi past and the "new" German identity. Since then PAKH has played a significant role in efforts to prevent the renewal of xenophobia and anti-Semitism in Germany. As the generation of persons with firsthand experience with the Holocaust has almost died out, PAKH is now making efforts to deal with the problems of those that follow them—already third or fourth generations—and to integrate them into its work.

Another aspect that became an important part of PAKH's work is dealing with the so-called Kriegskinder. These individuals were children during World War II and many of them were seriously traumatized. For a long time they were not able to talk about their experience because of the Holocaust atrocities. PAKH members are now able to moderate and facilitate, not only bringing back the memories, but also opening ways for comprehensive understanding within the whole political and ideological context. PAKH's visions for the future include preventive activities to discourage racist tendencies and prevent genocide anywhere. In 2007 PAKH's official name was changed to Study Group for Intergenerational Consequences of the Holocaust (Arbeitskreis für intergenerationelle Folgen des Holocaust).[20] Despite much work in Germany on the country's Nazi past, even ten years after the reunification, different cultural amplifiers could be seen among the two groups of Germans, previously East and West; even handshaking rituals were different.[21]

Since each side used the other for externalization, projection, and displacement purposes during the Cold War, when we met at CSMHI at the time of Germany's reunification, we expected that the push toward absorption would most likely create an urgency to pursue different containers to absorb these externalizations, projections, and displacements. Observations at that time strongly suggested that minority communities within the country began to serve as these "new" containers. Peter Suzuki collected data concerning the reactions of nonnative guest workers to German reunification that clearly indicated that these workers themselves sensed that they had become more suitable for externalization, projections, and displacements of "bad" elements. This was especially true in the former East Germany. Violence against foreign workers took place in all five states that comprise the former GDR. In 1991, Suzuki stated, "The situation in the East has become so grave that Amnesty International has recommended to Bonn to change its policy of automatically resettling in East Germany 20 percent of all refugees and asylum seekers entering Germany, a policy which took effect in December 1990."[22] Policymakers, with the help of psychologically informed consultants, need to recognize the strong likelihood that new reservoirs for "bad" images and thoughts will evolve after societal "absorptions" or "integrations," and they should develop strategies to prevent such processes from becoming malignant.

There are many terms such as absorption, integration, assimilation, unification, coexistence, federation, and conciliation that appear in scholarly literature or in diplomatic language that deal with both physical and psychological borders between neighboring large groups. There are also terms that refer to the "separation" of large groups into different political entities, as would occur with bloodshed after the collapse of the Soviet Union and later also after the end of the former Yugoslavia, and voluntarily and peacefully in the Czech and Slovak Republics. Descriptively speaking, "integration" refers to the efforts to bring together previously separated large groups within one legal boundary and to reunite them politically while each group maintains its own distinct large-group identity. If the integrated groups also combine their large-group identities, the situation can be described as "absorption." Since people living in East and West Germany were of the same blood, the expected result from the removal of the physical border between them was the evolution of "absorption" among the Germans.

When different large ethnic groups exist within one legal physical boundary, one or more of these groups usually are called "minorities." In some cases efforts are made to forcefully "absorb" the minorities; other times attempts are made to "integrate" them, and sometimes other ways, such as establishing "federations," are found for the groups to "coexist." After wars or war-like situations, neighbors from different countries also must learn how to "coexist" side by side peacefully. When there are large groups of the same blood but opposing political ideologies within a legal boundary, the situation is different; such a situation too may become malignant. Before proceeding further, however, I must say that, in practice, all these terms I have used here are perceived and utilized in different ways, peacefully or with force, in different places according to legal, diplomatic, political, cultural, and emotional considerations.

Besides their need to maintain a psychological border between them, two neighboring groups in conflict also become preoccupied with what I call a "principle of non-sameness."[23] One large group must not be the same as, or even closely similar to, a neighboring large group that is perceived as an enemy. Although antagonistic large groups usually have major differences in religion, language, and historical or mythological backgrounds, "minor differences" between antagonists can become major problems. When large groups regress, any signal of similarity is perceived, often unconsciously, as unacceptable; minor differences therefore become elevated to great importance to protect non-sameness, and this can lead to deadly consequences. Much earlier Sigmund Freud noted the narcissism of the small differences among small and large groups,[24] but did not study their deadly consequences in international relations.

The inhabitants of Andhra Pradesh in India often wear scarves around their necks, whereas members of the neighboring group, the Telanganas, do not. Between Croats and Serbs, dialect differences—such as the Croat *mlijeko* (milk) versus the Serb *mleko*—carry a heavy political-cultural load. Thomas Butler wrote about how in the former Yugoslavia differences in the pronunciation of certain words by Croats and Serbs increased in significance when antagonism between the two groups increased.[25] In times of stress and violent outbreaks, identifying minor differences may have deadly implications.

Cypriot Greek farmers and Cypriot Turkish farmers used to dress in black shirts and loose black trousers. The Greek would put a blue or black sash around his waist and the Turk would wear a red one. Under increased hostilities the difference in sash color became a matter of life or death.[26] Donald Horowitz reported that in 1958 Sinhalese mobs methodically victimized only men bearing earring holes in their ears and wearing shirts over their *vertis*. In the absence of differentiating skin color or other dissimilar characteristics, these features identified people as enemy Tamils.[27] When "minor differences" between antagonists become major problems that lead to deadly consequences, we recognize the existence of the maintenance of the non-sameness principle.

In the United States many are preoccupied with "illegal immigrants" and physical borders, especially the U.S.-Mexican border, and consider the Mexican or Latino as the Other. Policies and actions dealing with the Other who crosses or threatens to cross our borders are highly controversial.[28] I have not studied this, but I suspect that a closer look would suggest psychologically motivated issues are intertwined with legal and social ones. Border issues are everywhere.

During the last few decades, a modern form of "globalization" has become the buzzword in political and academic circles. The term represents an idea and attempt to promote prosperity and well-being for societies by standardizing economic, technological, ecological, and sociocultural elements and by bringing political democratic freedom to every part of the world. From a psychological point of view, this wished-for form of internationalism implies erasing "borders" and "otherness" and is, I believe, an impossible task. More locally, the establishment of the European Union may eventually create an emotional togetherness among its members, but this will take a long time.[29]

It is no wonder that alongside preoccupation with the modern version of globalization there is an "antiglobalization" movement that speaks out against what is perceived to be negative aspects of globalization.[30] The tragedy of September 11, 2001, and the Western world's response to it, especially that of the United States, the wars in Iraq and Afghanistan, and war-like conditions in Africa and elsewhere in my mind indicate that the idealized version of modern globalization is an illusion, at least at the present time. Today, in the twenty-first century, we are once more witnessing the amazing ability of the human mind to create incredible technological achievements, while the aggressive aspects of human nature and the killing of Others in the name of large-group identity remain the same. Thus, the best that technology creates is mostly in the service of "protecting" one large group by increasing its capability to destroy or often, in actuality, kill Others. Furthermore, globalization that includes prejudice, racism, and an indifference to large-group differences never brings about the well-being of the affected societies.[31] Despite all these realities, since World War II this modern version of globalization that mainly focuses on economic internationalism has been taking place. Lowering barriers to international trade under the auspices of the General Agreement on Tariff and Trade (GATT) and the establishment of the World Bank and the International Monetary Fund are making this possible.

Meanwhile, the Internet and related technological advances in communications, the incredible increase in international travel, and related activities have forced people around the world to become integrated socioculturally in ways that were not possible during earlier human history. These phenomena, in turn, have been modifying cultures. Younger generations especially, with their preoccupation with available communication technology, are carrying out shared tasks, most likely without being aware of what they are doing, to change the culture of older generations worldwide.[32] Thus, the advantages that modern globalization provide are accompanied by losses pertaining to traditional aspects of various cultures. Actual and threatened concrete or abstract loses initiate anxiety on individual and societal levels and make such individuals and societies face the task of mourning. Under situations where individuals and societies are not prepared for losses, their mourning processes become complicated, creating more anxiety and more individualized and societal adaptive and often maladaptive responses. In today's world there are some who also connect extremist Islamic terrorism with the negative aspects of modern globalization.[33]

In Part II, I described the accordion phenomenon during the series of dialogues between enemy representatives. The accordion phenomenon reflects border psychology. Those political psychologists working on reconciliation and coexistence issues between enemy groups in today's world are required to pay attention to the accordion phenomenon and the more general issue of border psychology, as I had to do when I was involved in the APA-sponsored dialogue series and when I was working with the Soviets. Practitioners of international "conflict resolution" may in fact do harm if they force the removal of identity differences between opposing large groups as swiftly as possible or focus on seeking "apologies" and encouraging "forgiveness" too hastily when dealing with coexistence. Forgiveness and apology can take place after shared feelings of remorse, guilt, revenge, helplessness, and depression that accompany a complicated shared mourning process are worked through and after such a process leads to acceptance of losses on both sides. The political psychologist's aim is not to remove the psychological borders, but only to narrow the psychological gap between enemy large-group identities and, during unofficial dialogues, to help opposing representatives hold on to their large-group identities so they can make more realistic agreements.

# 17

# MORE LESSONS ON LARGE-GROUP IDENTITY

## TRAUMA, LARGE-GROUP MOURNING, ENTITLEMENT IDEOLOGIES, AND TIME COLLAPSE

As the Soviet Union was coming to an end, the Russians I met with, besides discussing concerns about major political, economic, ethnic, and border issues, would often talk about the Great Patriotic War. This referred to the time between June 1941 when the Nazi invasion of the USSR began and May 1945 when the fall of Berlin took place, signaling the complete defeat of the Nazis. It is estimated that about 26 million Soviets lost their lives during the Great Patriotic War. In written history, no other country suffered such a gigantic loss during a war. The Russian participants also made references to Tatar-Mongol invasions that took place centuries ago.[1]

At the time of my meetings with them, the Russians in Moscow began exhibiting pictures of great czars at different locations throughout the city and also openly turned to their old traditional religious practices. The representatives of the Soviet republics often referred to their own specific historical events, heroes, or martyrs. For example, the shared feeling of hurt among Ukrainians that has lingered since 1654 when Russia was united with the Ukraine was reactivated.[2] Before leaving the account of my involvement with the Soviet Union behind, in this chapter I will explain why a large group, along with its preoccupation with contemporary societal issues related to identity, will also reactivate images of historical events—with associated heroes and martyrs—that are sometimes decades or even centuries old.

In the last chapter I explored how a physical border evolves as a psychological border that contains and protects a large-group identity. Through the years I worked with the Israelis, Egyptians, Palestinians, Russians and people from the other Soviet republics, and former East and West Germans, I also continued to observe what was going on in Cyprus and in Turkish-Greek relationships in general. And, as we will see below, I also tried to understand the horrors that were taking place in the former Yugoslavia. As I observed these scenarios, I shifted my study of large-group psychology from a focus on individuals' perceptions of the meaning of their large group, to the structure of large-group psychology in its own right.

I began to think of the classical Freudian theory of large groups by visualizing people arranged around a gigantic maypole,[3] which represents the group leader. Individuals in the large group dance around the pole/leader, identifying with each other and idealizing and supporting the leader. I have expanded this metaphor by imagining a canvas extending from the pole over tens of thousands or millions of people, forming a gigantic tent. In this revised metaphor, the people still surround the pole/leader and support it—especially when there is a conflict with those living under another tent—determined to keep it upright, but their underlying concern is to keep the canvas taut so it can form a protective overarching cover. The cloth of the canvas of this metaphorical tent represents large-group identity and its borders. I have come to the conclusion that essential large-group activities center around maintaining the integrity of the group's identity, but leader-follower interactions are just one element of this effort.

While individuals under this metaphorical gigantic tent wear their individualized garments (individual identities) and decorate them with symbols of subgroups to which they belong, social or political—families, neighborhoods, gangs, professions, political parties, and so on—in certain situations everyone under this tent also wears the canvas of the tent as his or her shared second garment. In peaceful times people turn their attention toward their individualized garments and their interactions with their families, relatives, clans, neighbors, schools, professional and social organizations, sports clubs, local and national political parties, and even social media networks. But when a large group is humiliated or threatened by Others who identify with another large group, the attacked population to a great extent abandons its routine preoccupations and becomes obsessed with repairing, protecting, and maintaining the canvas of the tent. The attackers who humiliate, maim, and kill in the name of their large-group identity and who live under their own metaphorical tent also wear the canvas of their tent as their shared second garment. Minority dissidents on both sides remain ineffective in the interaction between the enemy groups.

Tens of thousands or millions of individuals sharing a metaphorical garment is analogous to individuals who are not constantly aware of their breathing, but if they find themselves in a smoke-filled room or develop pneumonia, they notice every breath they take. Similarly, when a large group is under stress and the large-group identity is injured or threatened or when a large-group kills in the name of identity, the people who belong to such groups become keenly aware of their "we-ness" and quickly and definitively separate their large-group identity from the identity of the Other, the "enemy" large group. This is true of those who come to negotiation tables to face enemy representatives and even of ordinary people on the street.

Large-group psychology primarily deals with a shared need to repair, protect, and maintain the canvas of the tent. Thousands or millions of people, with or without being aware of it, assign themselves these tasks and respond to ethnic, religious, ideological, and international relations accordingly. If a foreign large group deliberately shames, humiliates, and destroys the lives of a number of individuals in, let us say, the northern part of a country, others belonging to the same large-group identity as the victims will also feel pain and rage no matter where they live. When al-Qaida attacked New York and Washington on September 11, 2001, Americans living in Louisiana or California felt as if they were attacked too. Large-group identity connects people under the metaphorical gigantic tent in emotional ways wherever they live. Influences and consequences of traumas that are caused by Others belonging to another large-group identity do not remain regional.

Once I was told by a colleague that the "split" in Israel just before and during the Second Lebanon War from July 12 to August 14, 2006, when the north suffered while the rest of the country seemed to continue its daily routine in an environment in which the stock markets were doing fine, contradicted the idea that pain and rage are shared by all who belong to the same large-group identity. This "split" in Israel was possible because, underneath it all, Israelis everywhere shared *chronic* threats to their large-group identity and because the war itself took place on Lebanese soil.

We can visualize different colorful designs that are stitched on the canvas of each large group's metaphorical tent. Such designs on a canvas belong and are meaningful only to the tens of thousands or millions of people living under it. In Part III I referred to shared identifications, suitable targets of externalization, and cultural amplifiers. They represent such specific designs. There are other types of designs.[4] In this chapter my focus is on the type of design that represents specific realistic or mythologized past historical events and the heroes and martyrs associated with them. Such historical events can be categorized as glorified or traumatic; usually they are both. For example, the Great Patriotic War was glorified, illustrating the heroism and determination of the Soviet people, but it was also unbelievably traumatic.

In 1991 I described the terms "chosen glory" and "chosen trauma" for the first time.[5] Writing about these concepts, Bruce Edwards stated,

> Although a large group's unique identity is based upon a vast and sometimes vague array of elements, critical and specific elements of it manifest through explicit utilization, sustained recollection, and generational transmission of shared glories

> and traumas in its history. But it is not necessary for the historical or popular accounts of these past events to be accurate, consistent, logical, or indisputable. What is important for the group is that the mental doubles of these traumas and glories are shared by all members of the group and thereby help to define their collective identity, promote a persistent sense of "we-ness," and support the group in times of collective stress.[6]

Chosen glories are shared mental images of pride and pleasure evoking past events and heroes that are recollected ritualistically. Past victories in battle and great accomplishments of a political or religious nature frequently appear as chosen glories. For example, large groups celebrate their independence days. Some chosen glories and heroic persons attached to them are often heavily mythologized over time. The late psychoanalyst Robert Furman wrote that much of what most Americans believe to be historical facts of the first years of Pilgrim life in North America, including the celebration of Thanksgiving, are myths and romantic fantasies. Thanksgiving thus represents a type of chosen glory that idealizes the "birth" of the American nation.[7] Sometimes traumatic events in due time are celebrated as chosen glories. Reverend Ben Campbell noted that Americans typically portray Jamestown and the early history of Virginia in an idyllic way that is in sharp contrast to the harsh reality of the period. Because English colonists ultimately overcame adversity in Virginia, and the territory became a successful colony and later a state that produced so many notable figures in American history, the traumatic nature of seventeenth-century Virginia has been replaced by mythologized chosen glories that have displaced the reality of the horrifying conditions of starvation, warfare, slavery, abuse, and pervasive violation of what we today call human rights.[8]

Chosen glories are passed on to succeeding generations in parent/teacher-child interactions and through participation in ritualistic ceremonies. They link children of a large group with each other and with their large group, and the children experience increased self-esteem by being associated with such glories. It is not difficult to understand why parents and other important adults pass the mental doubles of chosen glories to their children; this is a pleasurable activity. In stressful situations political leaders reactivate the mental doubles of chosen glories and heroes associated with them to bolster the shared identity of their followers. During the first Gulf War Saddam Hussein made many references to Sultan Saladin's victories over the Crusaders, even though Saladin was not an Arab, but a Kurd.

A chosen trauma is the shared mental double of an event in a large group's history in which the group suffered catastrophic loss, humiliation, and helplessness at the hands of its enemies. While chosen glories increase collective self-esteem, they do not burden the next generation(s) with complicated shared psychological tasks as chosen traumas do. Below I will explain such tasks and illustrate why chosen traumas, in supporting large-group identity and its cohesiveness, are more complex than chosen glories and why chosen traumas are much stronger large-group identity markers than chosen glories.

Massive traumas are of various types. Some are from natural causes, such as tropical storms, floods, volcanic eruptions, forest fires, or earthquakes. As I was writing this book a tsunami hit Japan and also caused a nuclear disaster, creating a massive trauma for the Japanese and serious concerns for people in other countries. Germany, for example, decided to close its nuclear plants. Some societal traumas are accidental man-made disasters, like the 1986 Chernobyl accident that spewed tons of radioactive dust into the atmosphere. Sometimes, the death of a person who functioned as a shared "transference figure" (a symbol that mostly unconsciously stands for a parent figure and/or represents the large group's identity) for many members of the large group provokes traumatic societal responses—as did the assassinations of John F. Kennedy and Martin Luther King, Jr. in the United States,[9] Yitzhak Rabin in Israel,[10] Prime Minister Olof Palme in Sweden, the National Democratic Party leader Giorgi Chanturia in the Republic of Georgia, former prime minister Rafik Hariri in Lebanon and the deaths of the American astronauts, especially teacher Christa McAuliffe, in the 1986 space shuttle *Challenger* explosion.[11] Other massive traumas are due to the deliberate actions of an enemy group, as in ethnic, national, religious, and political ideological conflicts. Such catastrophes themselves range from chronic mistreatment or oppression of a group by Others within one national boundary, to terrorist attacks, wars, and even genocide, and from the traumatized group actively fighting its powerful enemy in desperation, to the traumatized group being rendered completely passive and helpless.

When nature shows its fury and people suffer, those affected tend ultimately to accept the event as fate or as the will of God.[12] Following man-made accidental disasters, survivors blame a small number of individuals or governmental organizations for their carelessness. When a leader is killed (not by Others but by an individual belonging to the same large-group as did the leader) the rage is against that killer and, if one exists, against the political organization to which the killer belongs. However, when a trauma results from oppression, war, or other ethnic, national, religious, or political conflict, especially when the victimized large group is rendered passive and helpless, there is an identifiable enemy large group that has *deliberately* inflicted pain, humiliation, environmental restriction, destruction, and death on its victims. Such collective trauma takes place because the affected large group and the perpetrators belong to different large groups and the killing and the destruction is in the name of large-group identity. Only this kind of trauma may evolve as a chosen trauma.[13] A large group does not "choose" to be victimized by another large group and to subsequently lose self-esteem, but it does "choose" to psychologize and dwell on a past traumatic event and make it a major design to be stitched on the canvas of a large-group tent.

After a massive trauma at the hands of the Other, members of a society (and also "perpetrators") will face difficult tasks taming and rendering harmless the following psychological features:

- Sense of victimization and exposure to dehumanization;
- Sense of open pain and open, although often hidden, shame and humiliation due to helplessness[14] (or [hidden] shame for hurting others);
- Sense of guilt for surviving while others perished;[15]
- Difficulty being assertive without facing humiliation (or [hidden] shame for hurting others);[16]
- Increase in externalizations and projections and thus exaggeration of "bad" prejudice;
- Increase in narcissistic investment in large-group identity;
- Envy toward the victimizer and (defensive) identification with the oppressor (or [hidden] guilt for being the oppressor and [hidden] fear of losing power);[17]
- Difficulty, or often inability, to mourn losses.[18]

When such shared psychological experiences continue and the members of a large group cannot find adaptive solutions for them, they become involved in the next shared experience:

- Shared transgenerational transmission of psychological tasks to deal with the influence of the trauma.[19]

Let us first look briefly at how transgenerational transmission occurs between an adult and a developing child and second how collective transgenerational transmission takes place: there is fluidity between a child's "psychic borders" and those of the mother and other caretakers, and the child-mother/caretaker experiences generally function as a kind of "incubator" for the child's developing mind. Besides growth-initiating elements, however, the caretaker from the older generation can also transmit undesirable psychological elements to the child. One of the best-known examples of a relatively simple negative form of transgenerational transmission comes from Anna Freud and Dorothy Burlingham's observations of women and children during the Nazi attacks on London. Freud and Burlingham noted that small children under three did not become anxious during the bombings unless their mothers were afraid.[20] The fluidity mentioned above also may occur among adults under certain conditions of regression, such as during and after massive catastrophes at the hand of others. There are many forms of transgenerational transmission. Besides anxiety, depression, elation, worries, and fantasies, there are various psychological tasks that an adult may assign to a child.

An adult may "deposit" his or her own injured self-images within the child along with images of others who were involved in the traumatic event—even sometime the image of the perpetrator—and then give psychological tasks to these transferred images that aim to ease the pain and terror of the original trauma or control the outcome of the trauma. Depositing is closely related to "identification" in childhood, but it is in some ways significantly different from identification. In identification, the child is the primary active partner in taking in and assimilating an adult's images and owning this person's ego and superego functions. In depositing, the adult person more actively pushes his or her specific images into the developing self-representation of the child. In other words, the adult person uses the child (mostly unconsciously) as a permanent reservoir for certain self- and other images belonging to that adult. The experiences that created these mental images in the adult are not accessible to the child; yet, those mental images are pushed into the child, without the experiential/contextual framework that created them. Memories belonging to one person cannot be transmitted to another person, but an adult can deposit his or her traumatized self- and other images into a child's self-representation and assign tasks to such internal images.[21]

To illustrate this, let me refer to the well-known phenomenon of the "replacement child":[22] A child dies; soon after, the mother becomes pregnant again, and the second child lives. The mother "deposits" her image of the dead child—including her affective relationship with the dead child—into the developing identity of her second child. The second child now has the task of keeping this "deposited" identity within him- or herself. There are different ways for the child to respond to this task: the child may adapt to being a replacement child by successfully "absorbing" what has been deposited. Alternately, the child may develop a "double identity," experiencing what clinicians call a "borderline personality organization." Or, the second child may be doomed to living up to the idealized image of the dead sibling within, becoming obsessively driven to excel. Similarly, adults who are acutely traumatized may deposit their traumatized self-images into the developing identities of their children. A Holocaust survivor who appears well adjusted may be able to behave "normally" because he has deposited aspects of his traumatized self-images into his children's developing selves and has given the children "tasks" to deal with these images. His children, then, are the ones now responding to the horror of the Holocaust, "freeing" the older victim from his burden. As with replacement children, such children's own responses to being carriers of injured parental self-images vary because of each child's individual psychological makeup that is independent of the deposited images.[23]

Depositing in the large-group psychology, however, refers to a process shared by thousands or millions that starts in childhood and becomes like "psychological DNA," creating a sense of belonging. After experiencing a collective catastrophe inflicted by an enemy group, affected individuals are left with self-images similarly (though not identically) traumatized by the shared event. Tens of thousands or millions of individuals deposit such images into their children and give them tasks such as "Regain my self-esteem for me," "Put my mourning process on the right track," or "Be assertive and take revenge." It is this transgenerational conveyance of long-term "tasks" that perpetuate the cycle of societal trauma. Though each child in the second generation has his or her own individualized personality, all share similar links to the trauma's mental double and similar unconscious tasks for coping with that representation. If the next generation cannot effectively fulfill their shared tasks—and this is usually the case—they will pass these tasks on to the third generation, and so on. Such conditions create a powerful unseen network among thousands or millions of people.

Depending on external conditions, shared tasks may change from generation to generation. For example, in one generation the shared task is to grieve the ancestors' loss and to feel their victimization. In the following generation, the shared task may be to express a sense of revenge for that loss and victimization. But whatever its expression in a given generation, keeping alive the mental double of the ancestors' trauma remains the core task. Similar processes also may appear in the descendants of victimizers. Among the descendants of perpetrators there is more preoccupation with consequences of shared feelings of guilt than preoccupation with the shared feeling of humiliation. Both groups share a severe difficulty or inability to mourn.

All images and tasks that are passed from generation to generation contain references to the same historical event and heroes and martyrs associated with this event. As decades pass, the event's mental double continues to link all the individuals in the large group. For the new generations, the meaning of the above tasks go through what psychoanalysts call "change of function";[24] now the mental double of the event emerges as a most significant large-group identity marker and becomes a chosen trauma.

Not all past massive tragedies at the hands of others evolve as chosen traumas. Mythologizing victimized heroes and telling moving stories associated with a collective trauma popularized in songs and poetry, and political leaders of later times creating a preoccupation with a past trauma and related events, all play a role in turning a historic event into a chosen trauma. Sometimes a combination of events sets the stage for the future evolution of a chosen trauma. On April 10, 2010, Polish president Lech Kaczyński, his wife Maria Kaczyńska, and many of Poland's highest military and civilian leaders were killed in an airplane crash while approaching Smolensk Air Base in Russia. They were on their way to commemorate the Katyn Forest massacre of Polish nationals by the Soviets that had occurred in April–May 1940. The massacre was carried out by the Soviet secret service with the knowledge and approval of Josef Stalin and the Soviet Politburo. About 22,000 Poles, including military and police officers, intellectuals, business people, and priests were murdered. It was not until 1990 that Mikhail Gorbachev acknowledged that the Soviet secret service had executed the Poles and confirmed two other burial sites similar to the site at Katyn.

A Polish citizen who responded to questions by Kamil Dabrowa on TOK FM Radio regarding the plane crash stated, "Our Polish collective awareness tries to find in this tragedy something phenomenal, of historic, religious importance." He warned that such "irresponsible, emotional reactions" are from those "who should watch the words they say because such words enter collective awareness and live there very long and then bear fruits totally unintended." The plane crash, I believe, will provide the extra element that will turn the Katyn massacre into a chosen trauma.

There are firmly established chosen traumas: Russians recall the "memory" of the Tatar-Mongol invasions in the thirteen and fourteen centuries; Greeks link themselves when they share the "memory" of the fall of Constantinople (Istanbul) to the Turks in 1453; Czechs commemorate the 1620 Battle of Bila Hora, which led to their subjugation under the Hapsburg Empire for nearly 300 years; Scots keep alive the story of the Battle of Culloden of 1746 and the failure of Bonnie Prince Charlie to restore a Stuart to the British throne; the Dakota people of the United States recall the anniversary of their decimation at Wounded Knee in 1890; and Crimean Tatars define themselves by their collective suffering during their deportation from Crimea in 1944. Israelis and Jews around the globe, including those not personally affected by the Holocaust, all define their large-group identity by direct or indirect references to it, but the Holocaust is still too "hot" to be considered a truly established chosen trauma as described above. However, it has become a large-group marker. Orthodox Jews still refer to the 586 BC destruction of the Jewish Temple in Jerusalem by Nebuchadnezzar II of Babylonia as the chosen trauma of the Jews. Some chosen traumas are difficult to detect because they are not simply connected to one well-recognized historical event. For example, the Estonians' chosen trauma seems unrelated to one specific event, but to the fact that they lived under constant dominance (Swedes, Germans, Russians) for thousands of years.

Certain religious events are also utilized as chosen glories or traumas or a mixture of them. One might say that the crucifixion of Jesus Christ could be considered a very special and very major chosen trauma for Christians. For Shi'ites, the

Battle of Karbala that took place in 680 (year 61 of the Islamic calendar) has the most significant place in Shi'ites' religious large-group identity. It was during this battle that Husain, a son of the fourth Caliph Ali ibn Abi Talip and grandson of the Prophet Muhammad, together with his family and followers, were deprived of water and killed upon the desert plain by soldiers of Yezid, the claimant of the caliphate. Shi'ites believe that after the death of Muhammad in 632, religious leadership of the Islamic faith belonged to Ali ibn Abi Talip, Husain's father. Ali was passed over, however, and when he was finally proclaimed caliph, his rule was opposed by Mu'awiyah ibn Sufyan. Ali was succeeded by his son Hasan, who Shi'ites believe was poisoned at the behest of Mu'awiyah, who then became caliph. Husain reportedly refused to pledge his allegiance to him, and was attempting to lead his family to safety when he was attacked by Mu'awiyah's son Yezid in Karbala. As a chosen trauma, Shi'ites relive this historical atrocity on the anniversary of the Karbala Battle. Those Westerners who are interested in present-day Iran's internal and external affairs need to study the psychological influence this Shi'ite chosen trauma has on the Iranian large group's social, cultural, and political processes.

When he was an International Fellow at CSMHI in 1998, Turkish psychiatrist Mehmet Âkif Ersoy applied the concept of chosen trauma in his analysis of the Alevi population in Turkey. People of Alevi faith, a sect of Islam in Turkey, are followers of the fourth Caliph Ali, but they differentiate themselves from Shi'ites. Contemporary Alevis of Turkey embody a mixture of cultural norms from pre-Islamic Turkish religions, Shamanism, Zoroastrianism, Christianity, and Paganism.[25] Alevis in Anatolia have encountered, on and off, discrimination by the Sunni majority since early Ottoman times. One of their heroes, Pir Sultan Abdal, was a famous folk poet and religious leader who lived in the sixteenth century and was executed by the Sunni-dominated Ottoman government. This event evolved as a chosen trauma for Alevis in Turkey, and they have kept the mental double of Pir Sultan Abdal "alive." Interestingly, the Alevis in Turkey also borrowed the "memory" of Karbala, a chosen trauma of Shi'ites, as a chosen trauma. Ersoy wrote, "I suppose that the traumatic events that the Alevis of Anatolia experienced, as well as their historical proximity to Shi'ites, have played an essential role in the acceptance and adoption of Shi'ite cultural norms such as Karbala, and its incorporation as an Alevi chosen trauma."[26]

Affective aspects of some chosen traumas may remain dormant, and some chosen traumas may only be recalled during anniversaries. However, those that become connected with what I term "entitlement ideologies" are prone to reactivation by emotions, and play a significant role in large-group social, political, and military affairs. Entitlement ideologies refer to a shared sense of entitlement to recover what was lost in reality and fantasy during the collective trauma that evolved as a chosen trauma and during other related shared traumas. Or they refer to the mythologized birth of a large group, a process that later generations idealize. They deny difficulties and losses that had occurred during it, and imagine their large group as if it is composed of persons belonging to a superior species. Holding on to an entitlement ideology primarily reflects a complication in large-group mourning, an attempt both to deny losses as well as a wish to recover them, a narcissistic reorganization accompanied by "bad' prejudice for the other.

Each large group's entitlement ideology is specific. Some entitlement ideologies are known by specific names in the literature. What Italians call "irredentism" (related to Italia Irredenta), what Greeks call "Megali Idea" (Great Idea), what Turks call "Pan-Turanism" (bringing all the Turkic people together from Anatolia to Central Asia), what Serbs call "Christoslavism," and what extreme religious Islamists of today call "the return of an Islamic Empire" are examples of entitlement ideologies. Nancy Hollander describes how the American entitlement ideology, usually called "American exceptionalism," was inflamed after September 11, 2001.[27] Such ideologies may last for centuries and may disappear and reappear when historical circumstances change and chosen traumas are activated. They contaminate diplomatic negotiations. They may result in changing the world map in peaceful or, unfortunately too often, dreadful ways.

I have studied in-depth two chosen traumas and their related entitlement ideologies and reported on them in detail elsewhere. Therefore, in this chapter I will describe both of them very briefly. The first one is the Greek's chosen trauma of losing Constantinople (Istanbul) in 1453, an event that ended the Byzantine Empire and is linked to the Greek entitlement ideology. I carried out this study with my friend, historian Norman Itzkowitz.[28] Here I will let Kyriacos Markides, a Cypriot-born Greek sociologist, describe his own large-group's preoccupations and their role in the "Cyprus problem" that I referenced in earlier chapters. Markides refers to Greeks' Great Idea as

> a dream shared by Greeks that someday the Byzantine Empire would be restored and all the Greek lands would once again be united in Greater Greece. . . . The "Great Idea" found expression in . . . parts of the Greek world, such as Crete and the Ionian Islands. One could argue that the "Great Idea" had an internal logic, pressing for realization in every part of the Greek world which continued to be under foreign rule. Because the Greeks of Cyprus had considered themselves historically and culturally to be Greek, the "Great Idea" has had an intense appeal. Thus, when the church fathers called on the Cypriots to fight for union with Greece, it did not require much effort to heat up emotions. . . . Enosis did not originate in the church but in the minds of intellectuals in their attempt to revive Greek-Byzantine civilization.[29] However, being the most central and powerful of institutions, the church contributed immensely to its development. The church embraced the movement and for all practical purposes became its guiding nucleus.[30]

Markides' description of "Megali Idea" is brief, but thorough. Note that when he referred to "Cypriots" who were called upon by the church fathers to fight for union with Greece, he meant only Cypriot Greeks. Cypriot Turks had their own ideas. After Greece joined the European Union, I came to the conclusion that the influence of Megali Idea on Greeks' political movements has decreased. But, even today it is obvious to me that keeping Megali Idea alive, especially in the Greek Church, is one of the big obstacles to finding a "solution" to the "Cyprus problem."

The other chosen trauma that I studied in-depth is the Serbian chosen trauma, the shared mental double of the Battle of Kosovo in 1389, along with the entitlement ideology Christoslavism to which it is linked.[31] I believe that this is critical to understanding the contributions of large-group psychology in the tragedies in Bosnia in 1992 and in Kosovo in 1999. Despite the fact that in 1389 the leaders of both sides—Ottoman Sultan Murad I and Serbian Prince Lazar—were both killed during the Battle of Kosovo, and despite the fact that Serbia remained autonomous for over seventy years after the battle, the shared mental double evolved as the major Serbian chosen trauma, marking the end of a glorious period of Serbian power and the beginning of the Serbs' subjugation by the Ottoman Empire. In certain periods, Prince Lazar's image was used to cement a shared sense of victimization and martyrdom under Muslim rule; during others, his image became a symbol of the Serbs' desire to reverse the humiliation of the loss by reconquering Kosovo. As decades passed, Prince Lazar became associated with Jesus Christ, and in fact icons showing Lazar's representation decorated many Serbian churches throughout the six centuries following the battle. Even during the Communist period, when the government discouraged hero worship, Serbs were able to drink (introject) a popular red wine called "Prince Lazar." Even after Kosovo Province was taken back from the Ottoman Turks in the late nineteenth century, Lazar's "ghost" was still not put to rest.

After the collapse of Communism, mental doubles of Lazar and the Battle of Kosovo were resurrected by Slobodan Milošević, along with some members of the Serbian church and some members of the Serbian academic community. As the six-hundredth anniversary of the Battle of Kosovo approached in 1989, with the permission and encouragement of Milošević, Lazar's 600-year-old remains, which had been kept north of Belgrade, were placed in a coffin and taken, over the course of the year, to almost every Serb village and town, where they were received by huge crowds of mourners dressed in black. Again and again during this long journey, Lazar's remains were symbolically buried and reincarnated, until they were buried for good at the original battleground in Kosovo on June 28, 1989. The Serbian people began feeling, without being intellectually aware of it, that the defeat at the Battle of Kosovo had occurred only recently, a development made possible by the fact that the chosen trauma had been kept effectively alive for centuries.

On June 28, 1989, the six-hundredth anniversary of the Battle of Kosovo, a helicopter brought Serbian president Slobodan Milošević to the burial ground, where a huge monument made of red stone symbolizing blood had been built. In the mythology, Prince Lazar had chosen the Kingdom of Heaven over the Kingdom of Earth. By design, Milošević descended from a helicopter, representing Prince Lazar/ Jesus Christ coming to earth to find a new kingdom, a Greater Serbia. Propaganda prepared an atmosphere that allowed the inflammation of the Serbian entitlement ideology, Christoslavism, which gave permission to create a Greater Serbia. Atrocities would eventually be committed against Bosnian and Kosovar Muslims, whom modern Serbs came to perceive as extensions of the Ottoman enemy of distant history. Thus, the Serbian large-group identity was reinforced and reinvigorated by the lasting emotional power of this ancient event—at terrible cost to non-Serbs.

Reactivation of a large group's chosen trauma and an entitlement ideology linked to it lead to "time collapse." Feelings, thoughts, wishes, and fears stimulated by the shared reactivation of the chosen trauma and the entitlement ideology collapsed into perceptions and affects about a current international conflict and magnified dangers. Milošević and his associates were able to create this time collapse that led to genocidal acts in Europe at the end of the twentieth century.

Reactivated chosen trauma and entitlement ideology strengthen the people's sense of belonging to the same group, their shared large-group identity. Their reactivation may become a crucial resistance to finding a peaceful solution to the group's problems involving its current enemies. Even though a chosen trauma refers to ancestors' victimhood, the current group does not wish to give up its investment in it. To do so would mean giving up a significant aspect of the shared large-group identity, so the large group resists making peace with its contemporary enemy.

Imagine that a serial killer such as Jack the Ripper or Ted Bundy is murdering his victims by strangling them with a red scarf. Also imagine that this serial killer is caught, tried, and put away. What happens to his murder weapon, the red scarf? It stays in a dusty box in the basement of a court or police building as evidence used during the trial. In short, in the future no one else will use this scarf as a tool for murdering people. Let us go back to Milošević. He died on March 11, 2006, while on trial because the United Nations considered him responsible for mass murder, among other things. His "red scarf" was a chosen trauma and an entitlement ideology. Since his "red scarf" belonged to a large group and not to one lone individual, is it possible to use it again in the future? Milošević was not the first person to inflame the mental doubles of the Battle of Kosovo and Prince Lazar. For example, on June 28, 1914, during an anniversary of the Battle of Kosovo, a Serb named Gavrilo Princip assassinated Archduke Francis Ferdinand of Austria-Hungary (Austria-Hungary had replaced the Ottoman Empire as the "oppressor" of the Serbs) and his pregnant wife in Sarajevo, thereby beginning World War I. I think that the question I asked above is a legitimate one.

The political and legal systems have no effective methods to deal with a "tool" that can be used for massive destruction when it belongs to a large group rather than to just the man or woman who makes use of it. It can be better understood by the application of psychological insights that illuminate large-group processes in their own right than by logical *realpolitik* conceptualizations. I suggest that those who are interested in psychoanalytic political psychology are best equipped to do so if they are willing to venture beyond their offices, conduct field work, and collaborate with scholars and practitioners from other disciplines in an effort to understand collective human issues. As a psychoanalyst starts analyzing a new individual, making a "formulation" (an assessment) about the internal world of the person lying on the couch is necessary for good analysis because it gives the psychoanalyst direction about what he or she will be treating. Similarly, making a formulation about what exists in the psychology of a large group can give us directions to help those dealing with that large group to develop helpful strategies. The following is a schema that can provide guidelines for a formulation if the political psychologist notices inflammation of a chosen trauma and/or entitlement ideology in a society under study.

Massive Trauma at the Hands of Others

↓

Depositing and Transgenerational Transmission

↓

Change of Function

↓

Chosen Trauma: Large-Group Identity Marker
(a *psychological gene* of the large group)

↓

Reactivation of Chosen Trauma and Entitlement Ideology

↓

Enhancement of Leader-Follower Interaction

↓

Time Collapse

↓

Entitlement for Revenge or Revictimization

↓

Increased Prejudice and Magnification of Current Large-Group Conflict

↓

"Irrational" Decision Making

↓

Tendency for Purification and Mobilization of Destructive Large-Group Activities

I will expand this schema when I examine the psychology of political leaders and their relationships with their followers later in this book. In the next chapter, I will return to stories of my work in international relations. After the collapse of the Soviet Union, my friends from CSMHI and I started to help the Baltic Republics, especially Estonia, work toward a peaceful "divorce" from the former Soviet Union and develop "new" large-group identities. The first gathering for our new project took place in April 1992 in Kaunas, Lithuania. The reader will note from this and the previous chapters that by the time members of CSMHI arrived in Kaunas, we had greatly expanded our understanding of psychoanalytic political psychology and its application.

# PART V

## THE PSYCHOLOGY OF "DIVORCE" IN THE BALTIC REPUBLICS

# 18

# THE KAUNUS MEETING

## THE NEED FOR THE OFFICIAL IN UNOFFICIAL

After a brief period of national independence was brought to an end by alternating invasions by Soviet and German forces in the early 1940s, Lithuania, Latvia, and Estonia were incorporated into the Stalinist Soviet Union in 1944. This forced occupation was followed by mass deportations and collectivizations. By the time of Stalin's death, national life in these republics was, at least in public, "effectively numbed," but "Baltic nationalism remained a strongly entrenched force which the regime was unable to eliminate or fully co-opt."[1] After the collapse of the Soviet Union, members of the Center for the Study of Mind and Human Interaction met in Kaunas, Lithuania, April 27–30, 1992, with interdisciplinary colleagues from Russia, Lithuania, Latvia, Estonia, and Byelorussia.[2] The meeting was conducted in English. When we planned the Kaunas meeting, our aim was to focus on the relationship between Russia and the Baltic Republics, especially Lithuania. We knew that this relationship could not be separated from each republic's internal ethnic issues, for in each case Russians constituted (and still constitute today) the largest ethnic minority and found themselves in extremely volatile situations. When we met in Kaunas, the Russians living in the Baltic Republics, together with a lesser number of non-Russians who came from different parts of the former Soviet Union during Soviet times, were widely regarded as "immigrants."

Although only 9 percent of the population in Lithuania was Russian, the percentage was much higher in Latvia and Estonia. While Lithuania remained overwhelmingly agricultural during the Soviet period, thanks to a successful "nativization" of the Communist Party in Lithuania and the consequent comparative protection of the country's natural resources, large numbers of Russians had been sent to work in the new industrial complexes erected in Estonia and Latvia. In Estonia, therefore, 30 percent of the population was Russian, as opposed to less than

9 percent before World War II. In Latvia, the figures were even higher: only 52 percent of the population was ethnic Latvian, while 34 percent was Russian. In 1935, 75.5 percent of the population in Latvia had been ethnic Latvians.

The situation in each Baltic republic was further complicated by the fact that there were several subgroups of Russians, distinguished by their length of residency and the conditions of their "immigration." The above figures, moreover, did not include Russian members of the Soviet Army still stationed in the Baltic Republics when CSMHI went to Kaunas. In Lithuania, the Ignalina Nuclear Power Plant was operated almost entirely by "immigrants." Lithuanians would tell us at the Kaunas meeting that Snieckus, the city where this plant was located, was a "secret city," as apparently the indigenous population did not even know of its existence until after independence. When CSMHI later went to Estonia, we found a similar situation in that country: another nuclear power plant and another "secret city" called Paldiski.

The significant Russian presence necessarily complicated relationships between Russia and her Baltic neighbors. When two other colleagues from CSMHI and I were taken to the Communist Party headquarters in Moscow for consultations, I sensed that Mikhail Gorbachev's advisers perceived the native populations in the Baltic States as "ungrateful." Addressing the people in the Baltic Republics, they seemed to be openly asking: "Look, why would you want to separate from us after all the good things Communism and the Russians have done for you?" In Kaunas we would become keenly aware that these "ungrateful " people had from the beginning perceived the Soviet authorities as "colonialists" and Russians living in the Baltic Republics as "immigrants" who were the principal threat (real in Estonia and Latvia, potential in Lithuania) to their national existence.[3] After the collapse of the Soviet Union, "ungrateful" people in the Baltic Republics were in charge in their own countries, and overnight the Russians living in these places became helpless, full of profound confusion and ineffective rage.

Before we went to Kaunas, the adoption of a law on citizenship in Estonia and preliminary parliamentary approval of a bill on citizenship in Latvia had given rise to fears that both countries would deny civil rights to or impose stringent residency qualifications upon hundreds of thousands of nonindigenous "immigrants." Fear that there would be protective intervention by Russia was in the air. Just before CSMHI went to Lithuania, Andronik Migranyan, who was close to the government in Moscow, wrote: "It remains to be hoped that the instinct of self-preservation will prevail and prompt the authorities in both Russia and the Baltics to address citizenship and other ethnic issues in a democratic fashion. Otherwise there is a danger that the decision will be taken out of their hands, and together with it will go the democratic gains of recent months."[4]

In the Baltic Republics the added presence of smaller minorities made for an intricate ethnic mix. In Latvia, for example, the 14 percent of the population that was neither Latvian nor Russian was, in decreasing numerical order, Byelorussian, Ukrainian, Polish, Lithuanian, Jewish, Estonian, German, Roma, Tatar, and "other."[5] Under the influence of what Norman Itzkowitz called "the age of ethnicity," each ethnic group in these countries was openly trying to express its desire for official recognition of its separate identity. One participant at the Kaunas meeting from Lithuania, Halina Kobeckaite, who then was the director of the Lithuanian government's Department of Nationalities, reported to us that there were 109 officially recognized ethnic minorities in her country, of which only 36 had more than one hundred members.

While brand new governments of the three republics seemed to respond democratically to ethnic issues, potential problems were surfacing. For example, in September 1991, considerable tensions had arisen over the Lithuanian authorities' decision to dissolve councils in the predominantly Polish districts of eastern Lithuania on the grounds that the Polish party Apparatchiki, which dominated them, had supported the August 1991 putsch. Furthermore, the Jewish community in Lithuania was voicing its grievances and its perception that Lithuanians had minimized their participation in the Holocaust.[6]

The Baltic Republics were the first in the former Soviet Union to conduct democratic elections and to declare independence. Failure of democracy in the Baltic Republics would have a profound impact on the prospects for democracy elsewhere in the former USSR. We went to Kaunas to help the Baltic Republics have a peaceful "divorce" from the Russians, evolve their democracies, and deal with complicated problems of "the age of ethnicity."

We wanted to do this silently and slowly, without getting involved with the media, and by holding fast to a most significant technical psychoanalytic principle: the facilitating team—members of CSMHI—had no formulas for solving the Baltic Republics' problems; each country would find its own solutions. We would only try to be helpful by removing psychological obstacles standing in the way of their utilizing peaceful "real world" solutions. Even though CSMHI's faculty was multidisciplinary, by now all of us were working as a team by following this principle of refraining from devising plans to resolve others' problems, and by helping them to find their own solutions. Hal Saunders referred to this attitude as creating "ideas in the air."[7] We were also well aware of former Israeli minister of foreign affairs Abba Eban's warning: "There is little to be gained from unofficial contacts that are totally alienated from the official communications system."[8] Whenever possible we would share our findings with the officials in the Baltic Republics and see if they could use some of these "ideas in the air."

Before I describe what happened during the Kaunas meeting, it is important to provide a summary of historical and cultural differences in the Baltic Republics. If there was a tendency among outsiders to view these three republics as the "same" under the umbrella of the Soviet system, when we met in Kaunas we became keenly aware that Lithuania, Latvia, and Estonia each had its own large-group identity. Here are some distinctions among the Baltic Republics: both Lithuanians and Latvians speak an Indo-European language. They differ, however, in matters of traditional religion. While the majority of Latvians are Lutheran, their Lithuanian neighbors are overwhelmingly Roman Catholic. The majority of Estonians, like the majority of Latvians, are Lutheran, but they speak a Finno-Ugric tongue and are related to the Finns. Even during the Soviet period, Estonians had access to the Finnish media, especially television, and thus were exposed to Western sources of information not available to other Soviet nationalities.[9]

The Baltic Republics had different historical experiences and also shared a certain historical fate. Lithuania emerged during the Middle Ages as a powerful state in its own right, whose borders extended to the Black Sea and included Byelorussia, most of Ukraine, and parts of Russia. In the late fourteenth century, Lithuania accepted Western Christianity when its Great Prince married the heir to the Polish crown and united the two realms in what became known later as the Polish-Lithuanian Commonwealth. Although the bulk of Lithuania came under Russian imperial rule in the eighteenth century, parts of the country reverted to Polish control between 1918 and 1939; as one example, we saw the evidence of strong Polish cultural influence in monuments and plaques around the capital city Vilnius when we went to Lithuania. In 1918 Lithuania was reestablished and it remained independent until the beginning of World War I, when it was occupied by the Soviet Union. During World War II Nazi Germany briefly took over Lithuania before the country once more was absorbed into the Soviet Union.

Unlike Lithuania's great past, Latvia and Estonia were conquered by crusading Teutonic knights in the Middle Ages and subsequently dominated by a local German elite, whoever their ultimate political rulers may have been: Danish, Swedish, and, beginning in the eighteenth century, Imperial Russian. Like Lithuania, both Latvia and Estonia won sovereign independence soon after World War I ended, some twenty years before the beginning of World War II, but their independence came to an end when they were occupied, illegally according to the West, under the auspices of the Molotov-Ribbentrop Pact by the Soviet Union in June 1940. From 1941 to 1944 they were incorporated into Nazi Germany until its surrender, and then the Stalinist Soviet Union occupied Latvia and Estonia once more, just as it occupied Lithuania.

By design, before arriving in Kaunas, CSMHI members and our American guests who were ethnically connected with Lithuania spent two days together in the capital city Vilnius. We wanted to reconstitute ourselves as a team and to be introduced to some realities of the host country. We were impressed by the cleanliness of Vilnius (and later Kaunas). We were told that keeping the country clean had been, for Lithuanians under the Soviet rule, a mode of discreet resistance to the Soviet system. But food in most restaurants, as we found in Moscow before the collapse of the Soviet Union, was not appetizing. If you ordered a chicken dish you would get a bird which had only a thin piece of meat between its bones and skin.

Believing in Eban's advice mentioned to keep officials informed, we met with representatives of the Lithuanian government and told them who we were. We also met with some members of the Jewish community in their new center and museum, and heard them speak hesitantly but passionately—beneath the fading outline of a now-removed plaque of Lenin—of resentment over what they perceived as the too hasty rehabilitation of Lithuanian "war criminals" of the Nazi occupation. Part of one afternoon was spent with the small Karaim community in Trakai. Previously I did not have any information about this community but, as I will describe later, I would soon learn a great deal about it. Finally, some of the CSMHI members attended Mass in a crowded Roman Catholic cathedral. At Vilnius University, the oldest in Central Europe, we saw murals painted in 1985 that depicted scenes from Lithuanian mythology. Stained glass windows in the same room contained miniature inscriptions that spoke of "the importance of preserving our heritage" and of the preservation of the national language as the most important means to that end.

Most moving to us was a visit to the city's TV tower where thirteen Lithuanians had been killed by Soviet tanks on Bloody Sunday, January 13, 1991. The site had quickly become a kind of national shrine, with folk carvings, ornamental crosses, and photographs of the dead. My visit to this shrine would lead me to come up with a concept that I call "hot places."[10]

While undergoing psychoanalysis, an analysand reports certain dreams that reveal in-depth unexpressed feelings and thoughts and the reasons for them. Although a large group does not share one brain and does not dream, I noted that when people who belong to the victimized large group, together with those who were perpetrators, visit a place that has become a symbol of shared trauma at the hands of Others—a hot place—they are stimulated to express their most intense feelings and talk about shared large-group issues that might not surface in meeting rooms. Listening to people who become spokespersons for their large groups at a hot place is like listening to a patient on the couch free associating intensively about a dream. Later in my psychopolitical work in various parts of the world, I would visit hot places with victims' representatives or with representatives of perpetrators, and this would help me to make a better assessment of the situation I was preparing to work on.

Before going to Kaunas we also studied a survey conducted in all the Baltic Republics a month before our arrival in Lithuania.[11] The survey showed that many were "depressed" by their economic prospects, worried by the rise in reported crime, and fearful of unemployment and ethnic conflict. Residents of Latvia and Estonia, it was clear, had a bleaker view of ethnic relationships than their counterparts in Lithuania. I mention these studies to emphasize the facilitating team's preparation in conducting a meeting where many ethnic and religious perceptions, wishes, and fears would be expressed and attempts for peaceful solutions would be considered. I had come a long way since my initial participation in the American Psychiatric Association's Egyptian-Israeli dialogues. Now my team members and I were doing serious homework before we brought together representatives of opposing large groups for dialogues.

The Baltic Republics' independence would not be instantaneous like the severing of an umbilical cord. It would be protracted. The republics were still dealing with complex issues, such as establishing their own currencies. When the Kaunas conference began on Monday April 27, I, as leader of CSMHI, suggested that the "separation" between Russia and the Baltic Republics would give rise to human emotions that might become entangled with "real world" political concerns. I spoke briefly of the individual psychology of separation, change, and loss, referring by way of illustration to the psychology of death and divorce. I predicted out loud that during the meeting certain emotionally charged questions would arise: "Who are we without the other group?" "What will be our new identity?" "What will we do about old hurts, humiliation, helplessness, and loss?" "Can we keep something from the old 'togetherness'?" "What should we discard?" "How will we relate to our old oppressors?" "How do we establish and observe our new boundaries?" I invited representatives of large groups to speak of this process of separation during the first days of the meeting, and stated that the CSMHI team's aim was to be a catalyst for analysis and for discovery of ways to make the process a peaceful one. I was like a clinician at a patient's first session explaining how we would work together. I asked Norman Itzkowitz to briefly compare the demise of the Ottoman, British, and Soviet Empires. We were careful not to turn the meeting into an intellectual exercise, but we chose to do this comparison in order to send the participants an implicit message: "You are not alone in experiencing complications during a time of drastic historical change."

Drawing on our previous experiences in bringing "enemies" together, we knew that despite our attempt to set up the topics and the mood of the meeting, initially participants would compete with their expressions of historical grievances and one group would externalize its unwelcome attitudes onto an opposing group as a means of delaying or preventing the development of empathy. Sometimes there would be a flight into "intellectualization." In fact, Halina Kobeckaite's report to the group on the history of ethnic relationships in twentieth-century Lithuania, in which she referenced how many ethnic groups in Lithuania had more or fewer than one hundred members, became a prime example of "boring" intellectualization. Only some days later would I learn how lovely and vibrant a person Halina was. But when the meeting started she apparently felt, as an official person from the Lithuanian government, that she had no choice but to read from a prepared paper filled with statistics and to try to illustrate how politically correct Lithuania was.

It was when Triin Vihalemm from the Sociology Department of Tartu University in Estonia spoke that emotions were ignited. After referring to the past "Soviet colonization policy," she told us how new professional requirements would be imposed in Estonia. For example, we learned that non-Estonian physicians working in Estonia were now required to speak a minimum of 1,500 Estonian words. During the Soviet period, Estonians had learned Russian. Now Russians in Estonia were required to understand and speak Estonian. While Triin told us how she herself had observed feelings of helplessness and defensiveness in many Russians, I thought without telling anyone that she was describing a process of purification and identification with the oppressor in Estonia. A Russian charged that requiring 1,500 Estonian words of non-Estonians was the beginning of dehumanization. "The subjects were no longer physicians, but 'things.'" A Lithuanian countered with a description of the linguistic hardship suffered by his people and the shameful distinction between *de facto* and *de jure* regulations under the Soviet regime.

Despite occasional encouragement from the CSMHI members to personalize the narratives of hurts and grievances, speakers were reluctant to venture further on the first day into areas of emotional risk. It was during the next day's gathering that Danute Bieliauskas, one of CSMHI's American guests of Lithuanian origin, brought a personal narrative to our attention. She spoke of arriving in Kaunas as a premed student in 1939. She recalled the sudden Russian occupation in 1941, when Russian planes flew overhead and Russian tanks rolled up Freedom Avenue.[12] Russian people, Russian songs, Russian language followed. In those days, Danute said, no one spoke of Soviets; the enemy was Russian. There were killings, deportations, and overnight disappearances. She remembered her best friend's family being herded into cattle trucks for deportation to Siberia. "We had to march to the Red Flag if we wanted to stay at the university. We had to listen to long speeches extolling the virtues of Communism. There were spies in the classrooms. Later I learned that my best friend, with whom I lived, had been signed up by the KGB. She had been threatened with the death of her whole family if she didn't cooperate." Even though Danute eventually left Kaunas, finished her studies in Vienna, and settled in the United States, she still had nightmares.

Lithuanian participants felt encouraged by Danute's story and began to tell their own stories, describing how none of them spoke to their children of the horrible things they had witnessed. Once more I was noticing that transgenerational transmissions do not occur simply from hearing previous generation's oral accounts of traumatic memories. An unusual event occurred and interested me as a psychoanalyst. One Lithuanian, speaking in English, was reporting his bad feelings about the intruders, the Russians, and could not find the English word for a Lithuanian one. Then he turned to other Lithuanian-speakers and asked for the English translation of this specific word. An extraordinary number of English synonyms were suggested before "hostility" was chosen. I thought that the Lithuanian who started this discussion, on the surface, was exhibiting his fear of directly expressing his hostility against the Russians. On the other hand this experience gave way to finding many words to express the oppressed persons' bad feelings. In the end, the "taboo" against speaking publicly about personal "hostility" was broken.

The response of the Russian participants to these Lithuanian testimonies was two-fold. First, the Russians wanted the Lithuanians to acknowledge that crimes against the Lithuanian people had been committed not only by Russians but also by their fellow Lithuanians. The villains, in other words, were not "Russians" but "Soviets." Second, the Russians wanted to insist that they, too, had experienced horrors at the hands of the Soviet regime. They believed that they shared "a common fate" with Lithuanians. Then we noticed an "accordion phenomenon" in the room. Empathy for the Other alternated with hostility toward the same. CSMHI allowed the "accordion" to continue to play for some time until extreme squeezing and extreme opening actions disappeared.

We turned our attention to a real world issue when we heard a Russian helicopter flying over the conference room: the continued presence of the Russian/Soviet military in the independent Baltic Republics. Representatives from the Baltic Republics declared that the presence of the Russian/Soviet military in the three republics made any serious, peaceful negotiations between them and Russia impossible. How could they be relaxed and not afraid when their former "partner" was living in their place while carrying a big stick? What kind of "divorce" was this? We learned that the presence of the Russian/Soviet military occasionally allowed the Russian minority to sustain the illusion that it was still in charge and made the Lithuanian, Latvian, and Estonian people fear that the military would be used to "solve" ethnic problems. "It would be useless," one Lithuanian said, "to attempt any serious discussion before the army's withdrawal." The absence of Russian ambassadors to the Baltic Republics and its inducing anxiety, fear, and confusion were absolutely clear.

Our Russian veterans of psychopolitical gatherings, Stanislav Roschin and Alexander Obolonsky, remarked that, despite the "real world" problems involved in

Soviet/Russian demobilization, the Russians should acknowledge the Baltic Republics' fears. Stanislav raised his hand and exclaimed: "I know the solution. Let the Russian army stationed here on the Lithuanian soil surrender to Lithuania!" Everybody laughed and tensions dissipated until we heard another Russian/Soviet helicopter flying low overhead.

On the third day we divided ourselves into three small groups with the expectation that this would allow participants from different locations to get to know one another better and interact in order to come up with "ideas in the air." Indeed, such ideas came up concerning the continuing presence of the Russian/Soviet military, national minorities, conflicting claims of ethnic allegiance and state citizenship, the influence of residual anger and resentment, and restoring trust.

That day the CSMHI team and other participants also visited with the representatives of the ethnic Russian community in Kaunas. These representatives and other Russians present spoke of their economic fears, their hesitation to speak Russian in public, and their wish to organize themselves culturally. Halina assured them that the Lithuanian government guaranteed their right to organize themselves culturally.[13]

During the last day of the meeting we discussed various action possibilities. Prominent among them were ideas dealing with the existence of the Soviet/Russian military in the Baltic Republics. We learned that a plebiscite was scheduled in Lithuania for June 14: voters were to be asked whether the Lithuanian government should demand the unconditional withdrawal of the former Soviet Army in 1992 along with suitable compensation for damages. It was clear that the vast majority would say "yes." We assumed that the Russians, for their own internal reasons, would not be able to comply at once with the expressed wishes of the Lithuanian people. But if the Russians were simply to ignore the referendum, this might induce strong feelings of helplessness in Lithuania.[14]

Accordingly, we discussed at great length the urgent need to appoint Russian ambassadors to the Baltic Republics. This action would verify the republics' independence and bear great symbolic weight. We even discussed the kind of personality that would be best suited for such appointments. While ambassadors should, of course, represent the interests of their own government, it would in this instance be particularly important that they be men and women capable of empathic understanding of the Baltic Republics' anxieties, especially in regard to the Russian/Soviet military still present there. The withdrawal of the military should be carried out according to the existing realities. For example, the security concerns about the nuclear plants in the three countries, their closure, and the opening of the "secret cities" to the native Baltic people should be done carefully. In addition, the ambassadors should do their best to ease the Lithuanians', Latvians', and Estonians' fears about Russian interference with the Baltic Republics' fair and democratic ways of handling issues related to their ethnic minorities. The Russian delegates then even proposed specific names to put forward for appointment as ambassadors to one or another of the Baltic Republics and promised to discuss this issue seriously with the Soviet authorities when they returned to Moscow. Later we would learn that indeed a report of the Kaunas meeting was presented to the Russian Ministry of Foreign Affairs and to the Russian State Committee on Ethnic Policy.

Within a matter of months of the Kaunas meeting, the first Russian ambassadors to the newly independent Baltic Republics presented their credentials. In July 1992, Alexander Rannikh was appointed ambassador to Latvia; in August 1992 Nikolai Obertyshev was appointed ambassador to Lithuania; in September 1992 Alexandre Trofimov, the ambassador of the Russian Federation to Estonia, presented his credentials in Tallinn. One of the ideas in the air had been taken seriously and been acted upon. One year after the Kaunas meeting, April 5–8, 1993, when CSMHI once more brought representatives of the Baltic Republics and Russia together, this time in Riga, Latvia, two of the ambassadors, Ambassador Rannikh and Ambassador Trofimov, joined us, along with other politically influential representatives from each country. I would develop a good personal working alliance with Trofimov when CSMHI eventually began working in Estonia.

Indeed, before leaving my recollections of Kaunas behind, I would like to point out that personal relationships are often important for such processes—and that the process we undertook taught and encouraged individuals in positions of authority to listen to and for psychologically informed material at other points in their careers, so they might do a better job of finding humane solutions to difficult domestic and international challenges. A brief illustration of this comes from Halina Kobeckaite. Just before we left Kaunas, she invited the CSMHI members and other meeting participants for a social reception at the small Karaim religious community's worship place, a *kenesa*, in Vilnius.

Karaims are descendants of Crimean guards brought to Lithuania in the tenth century. The community has preserved its own language and its own religion (a syncretic mix of Judaism, Islam, Christianity, and totemism) for almost a millennium. But, because the Soviet regime suppressed the Karaim culture, there were at the time of our visit to Lithuania only about a hundred Karaim speakers left, and they were trying to revive the language in the younger generation. Halina and her husband were important members of the Karaim community.

At the reception, Norman Itzkowitz and I, while speaking to one another, overheard a private conversation between Halina and her husband in Karaim. Surprisingly, I and Norman, who knows Turkish, could understand that Halina and her husband were discussing preparations for the dinner they would have after the reception. They were speaking in a form of Turkish peculiar to us. I approached Halina and told her how surprised I was that I could understand Karaim. She and her husband were also surprised that I understood their language—Turkic with Hebrew influence. Until then I was just an American to Halina; now she learned that I was a Turkish-American. Her husband disappeared briefly and came back with books written in the Karaim language and presented them to me.

From this moment on Halina and her husband and I were good friends. I kept in contact with Halina after we left Lithuania and a year later, when I saw her at the CSMHI meeting in Riga, she was still in charge of minority issues in Lithuania, where she played a most significant and humane role in preventing serious ethnic minority problems. Later, after CSMHI started to work in Estonia, Halina was appointed the Lithuanian ambassador there. The CSMHI team happened to be in Tallinn when Halina arrived as the new ambassador. One of my most delightful memories of my long work in international relations is visiting her one evening, with other members of CSMHI, at the newly opened Lithuanian embassy building in Tallinn. It did not have any furniture yet, so all of us sat on the floor, drank wine, and celebrated with great pleasure Halina's becoming an ambassador. Later, she became the Lithuanian ambassador to Turkey, and after that, the ambassador to Finland. I followed her career from a distance. She would often appear at meetings in different countries and lecture on ethnic identity. She would argue for a notion of "circles of personal identity." Last time I saw Her Excellency Dr. Halina Kobeckaite was when she was ambassador to Turkey. She, some of her family members, my wife, and I had a private dinner in Istanbul and talked fondly about our past work in the Baltic Republics after the collapse of the Soviet Union.

# 19

# THE RIGA MEETING

## THE ROLE OF PURIFICATION RITUALS

The Center for Study of Mind and Human Interaction's second meeting in the Baltic Republics took place at the Latvian Academy of Sciences' Science House in Lielupe on the Baltic Sea a few miles outside Riga, April 5–8, 1993. This was a much larger meeting that the one we had in Kaunas the year before.[1] It was designed to include, in an unofficial capacity, more high-level policymakers (ambassadors, government officials, and members of important parliamentary commissions), and thereby strengthen CSMHI's efforts to pass along important psychopolitical findings to official decision-making bodies.[2]

We prepared ourselves for the Riga meeting by conferring with the East European Studies Department at the University of Virginia. We wanted to know the real-world issues that had developed in these countries since our Kaunas meeting. The reader once more is reminded that today's incredible electronic communication systems were not available at that time. We regularly read issues of the English-language *American Baltic News* and the *Baltic Observer.* From these sources we learned of Latvia's introduction of a new currency (the *lat*), of heated debates over citizenship laws in Latvia and Estonia, of new visa requirements, and that the Russian troop withdrawal from Lithuania was proceeding on schedule but withdrawals from Latvia and Estonia were delayed because of fears of "human rights abuses" against ethnic Russians in those countries. We learned of Russian violations of Estonian air space, the Lithuanian battle to take control of the former Soviet military airport in Zuokaniai, and also of the controversy over Latvian plans to remove the graves of Soviet Army officers and officials during the restoration of the Cemetery of the Brethren in Riga.

Members of the CSMHI faculty were received in Washington, DC, by Ambassadors Vlademir Lukin of the Russian Federation and Ojārs Kalniņš of Latvia, and both expressed their strong support for our project. When I was lecturing at the Diplomatic Academy of the Soviet Union in 1991, Vera Gracheva from Latvia had been an active participant. Before CSMHI went to Latvia, Vera was the counselor to the Latvian ambassador in Washington, and she worked on humanitarian cooperation and human rights. She was highly sympathetic to CSMHI's work. She would join us in Riga.

We arrived there a few days before the meeting started and spent a day "sightseeing." In those days the only splash of color in the city came from two huge Pepsi Cola and Philips advertisements, symbolic perhaps of yet another "invasion," this time by the forces of the free market. Right away we could observe typical and not so dangerous examples of repeated "purification." For example, one of the main thoroughfares—unattractive compared to the cobbled streets and baroque buildings of old Riga that, however, were in darkness and rather empty during our visit—had been called Alexander III Avenue when Latvia was under the Russian Empire. Between 1918 and 1940, during Latvia's first period of independence, it was renamed *Brivibas Iela* (Freedom Avenue). After the Nazi occupation, it became *Hitler Straße*, and after the Soviet "liberation," its name was changed to Lenin Avenue. When we passed through, it had once more become known as *Brivibas Iela.* We also visited the Cemetery of the Brethren. This place had become a "hot place" just before our arrival in Riga, and we knew that a purification attempt at this location could have serious and dangerous consequences.[3]

The Cemetery of the Brethren is a Latvian military cemetery. At its heart is a thirty-foot limestone statue of Mother Latvia weeping over some 2,000 of her sons. Built between 1924 and 1936 at the site of mass burials of Latvian riflemen killed in the battles of 1915, it contains the remains of soldiers who perished in World War I and II, as well as fighters for independence. What I found most striking and psychologically powerful was the fact that this cemetery clearly and concretely symbolized the fragmentation of the Latvian population and its alliances. Walking through the rows of soldiers' gravestones, I was most surprised to see some marked with Nazi Swastikas directly next to others marked with the star of the Soviet Red Army and still others marked simply by a cross or a Star of David—all Latvian.

Earlier I wrote about how Israel is a synthetic country with a need to bring Jewish people from different backgrounds together in order to have a cohesive Israeli nation and how there is indeed a Ministry of Immigrant Absorption in Israel. At this Latvian military cemetery, I sensed in a similar but not identical way that, following Latvia's independence from Soviet domination, it would be necessary to bring different Latvian fragments together in order to establish an integrated Latvian nation. In this process each section of the Latvian community, with past investment in Nazism, Communism, nationalism, and even Judaism, would need to find a new target upon which to project and externalize its unwanted aspects. I realized that Latvians had found a reservoir in the approximately 200 "undesirable" corpses of Soviet Army officers and officials that had been buried in a section near the cemetery's entrance, segregated from the Latvian corpses.

Two months before we came to Latvia, a dispatch in the *New York Times* reported that the Latvian Parliament had voted on February 2 "to remove the remains of Soviet Army soldiers" from the Cemetery of the Brethren. Yanis Freimanis, a Latvian lawmaker, was quoted as saying, "Soldiers who served in the Red Army under Stalin's command were deliberately buried there to defile the cemetery."[4] Reading the article, I sensed the possibility of a kind of "ethnic corpse cleansing." When the CSMHI team visited Vladimir Lukin, the Russian ambassador to the United States, this issue came up. We were told that reports of the Latvian vote had alarmed the Yeltsin government and the Russians in general. Later we were informed that communication between the two governments had clarified the matter, and that there would be nothing done to humiliate the Russians.

Shortly before the CSMHI team left for Latvia, we read in the *American Baltic News* that the original vote in the Latvian Parliament had been misinterpreted in Russia and had infuriated ethnic Russians living in Latvia who were dependent on the Russian media for their news. It was now claimed that this distorted version had been repeated in the Western press. The truth, this article asserted, related to an effort to restore the cemetery to its original design: "In the process, the bodies of about 200 Communist leaders and Soviet army officers will need to be relocated to other sites." The idea of "removing" the Soviet corpses was downgraded to "relocating" them. A delegation of Russian "peace marchers composed of war veterans had traveled to Latvia to protest the decision, but had left reassured that nothing 'objectionable' would take place."[5] Whatever the truth, and whatever the real aesthetic or moral justification for restoring the cemetery by disinterring Soviet officials and army officers, it was clear that there were understandably strong feelings about the previous "Sovietization" of the Latvian national cemetery and the corresponding wish to purify it. I think that there were attempts at corpse purification and that attempts were stopped when the Latvians realized Russia's strong reaction. While the CSMHI team had no direct involvement in these developments, other than through the discussion it had with Ambassador Lukin at the Russian embassy, this story informed our meeting in Riga, as I will describe later in this chapter.

Once in Riga, we had four days to meet. We asked the participants from the Baltic Republics and Russia to answer the following questions on the first day: "Who were you before the fragmentation of the Soviet empire?" "Who are you now?" "What are your historical glories and traumas?" On the second day, the questions shifted the focus to the Other: "Who are they?" "How has the fragmentation of the Soviet Union affected them?" "Who were they before?" "Who are they now?" "What kind of neighbors are they?"

The reader can guess that completion of grievances and appearances of the accordion phenomenon dominated the first two days' often heated discussions. I will not repeat them here. During the third day, CSMHI wanted to identify psychological barriers and examine them with the other participants so that they could come up with ideas for becoming better neighbors. In order to stimulate this investigation, CSMHI brought the story of the Cemetery of the Brethren to everyone's attention. Emotions flared. CSMHI members' function was to "absorb" these emotions so that talks would go on until opposing sides could listen to one another with empathic ears. A Russian said to the representatives of the Baltic Republics: "I saved you." The singular pronoun "I" rather than "we" was spoken from his metaphorical ethnic tent, where a people lives as a single unit. "You" referred not so much to the Baltic Republics as to Western civilization as a whole. He told of the Russian chosen trauma/chosen glory, of which the CSMHI members were already familiar: the Russians had in the thirteenth century stood alone between the Mongols/Tatars and the West. The Lithuanians, he added, were then the enemies of Russia and had tried to come to the aid of the Mongols. Fortunately, the Lithuanians arrived one day too late. Had they successfully joined forces with the Mongol horde, the history of Russia and Western Europe, he suggested, would have been very different. In this mental double of the past, present stereotypes were reversed: the Lithuanians were the villains and the Russians the saviors of Western civilization.

Once more the reader will notice how chosen traumas and glories appear associated with feelings when representatives of opposing large groups come together to discuss their relationships, leading a "time collapse" to occur. The psychologically informed and trained facilitating team "allows" this to happen, since taming emotions about chosen traumas and glories can only be possible after they appear in the open. The facilitating team then helps the representatives of the opposing large groups create a "time expansion," to separate the mental double of a chosen trauma/glory and feelings linked to it from current issues and feelings attached to them. This leads to a more realistic discussion of the issues at hand and a better chance of finding solutions for them.

After "time expansion" was established during the third day of the Riga meeting, participants from the Baltic Republics could hear the Russians' concerns about the appearance of radical nationalism in the Baltic Republics. A Russian introduced a monument into the discussion. General Chernyakhovsky had been commander-in-chief of the Soviet force that liberated Lithuania from the Nazis. After his death at the German front in 1944, a monument honoring him was placed in the center of Vilnius. After independence, however, Chernyakhovsky's statue was removed to his hometown in Ukraine. When the Russian spoke of how upsetting this had been for him and the Russian people, a Lithuanian reminded him that Chernyakhovsky's family had requested this action. But for the Russian this "fact" made no difference. When a Lithuanian admitted that he felt uncomfortable sending Chernyakhovsky back, the participants as a whole agreed that Baltic-Russian relationships would have been improved had Chernyakhovsky stayed in Vilnius and had the graves of the Soviet military officers and Soviet officials in Riga been treated with more care. After an Estonian described how his son had once prepared a blue dye in order to make an Estonian flag, which was prohibited under the Soviet regime, a Russian replied, "I no longer object to you having an Estonian flag." Suddenly, everyone in the room seemed to have a measure of their self-esteem repaired.

A Lithuanian compared the Baltic Republics to three small boats tied to a larger boat. The cord that bound them should be severed, he said, but it should be done thoughtfully and carefully lest the small boats sink. At this point I felt that the participants were ready to accept that the complexities of the relationship between the Baltic Republics and Russia were a shared problem. Having expressed their emotions and developed empathic ties, the participants were at last ready, on the fourth day of our Riga gathering, to consider suggestions and actions for the external political world that might defuse tensions between their respective countries.

Such suggestions and action possibilities included introducing findings from the Kaunas and Riga meetings for facilitating adaptive discussions regarding citizenship laws between the Baltic Republics and the Office of the Secretary-General of the United Nations. The language tests required for citizenship should be standardized, rendering them as far as possible resistant to arbitrary and (worse) xenophobic influences. The idea arose to find ways to increase fluency and literacy among Russians in the Baltic Republics in the national language of the country in which now they lived. People from the Baltic Republics felt that such educational programs would be costly. CSMHI members also heard that there might be strong resistance from the Russians living in the Baltic Republics because they would perceive such programs as humiliating.

The participants would encourage the Baltic governments to actively help in the formation of political organizations to represent Russian-speaking noncitizens in dialogues with government officials. A message for President Yeltsin's press secretary would be prepared. It would include suggestions to remove from official statements language that the people of the Baltic Republics perceived as humiliating. For example, the Yeltsin government should give up "the language of totalitarianism" and should not refer to Lithuanians, Latvians, and Estonians simply as "ethnic groups." Also, the Yeltsin government should speak of people sent to other parts of the former Soviet Union from the Baltic region not as "exiles," but as "deportees." The participants of the Riga meeting would send messages to their own authorities asking that a moratorium be imposed on all unilateral changes in cemeteries, memorials, and monuments. Such changes should be made only after consultation with all the parties whose heroes or other dead are involved.

After the Riga meeting Halina Kobeckaite wrote to me stating that the Riga meeting was a "great success" and remarking that "this conference proved the fact that very often people outside governmental institutions might be more effective [than those within the government] in assisting official bodies . . . to deal with issues directly associated with human conflicts." After the Riga meeting I heard from Ambassador Trofimov, who also called the Riga meeting a success, because it responded to "the vital need for promoting sincere and candid dialogue between ethnic communities in [the] Baltic states." He added, "I am looking forward to the next meeting in Tallinn." We also received a letter from Ambassador Lukin informing us of his appreciation for our "noble mission."

After the Riga meeting CSMHI was accepted as an interdisciplinary organization able to play an important role in the "separation" between Russia and the Baltic Republics. CSMHI referred to what we were doing in the Baltic Republics as a "vaccination" against possible malignant political infections. After this meeting, CSMHI was ready to move on to the next step in its "vaccination" process.

# 20

# THE CARTER CENTER

## THE LIMITATIONS OF LOGIC

After the meeting in Riga, the CSMHI team planned to have a smaller meeting in April 1994 in Tallinn, the capital city of Estonia, where we would meet leaders of its ethnic communities together with high-level officials and scholars from both Estonia and Russia. Two participant observers from Lithuania and two from Latvia would also be invited. Besides the citizenship issue, the question of language examinations,[1] and the "Soviet" military presence,[2] Estonia was facing a "border adjustment issue" and intense frustration with this process. The Russian Federation had for some time maintained a belief that a strip of land along the border, which Estonians believed belonged to them, was Russian territory. All the inhabitants there were Russian.[3] Although the Helsinki Declaration prohibits a realignment of borders between nation-states, during our Riga meeting we saw some indications that in this instance it might be a realistic solution to this complex problem. During our Tallinn meeting we planned to look into all these matters and come up with some possibilities for action.

Hal Saunders' and my involvement with the Carter Center in Atlanta some years earlier, however, led to a drastic change in our plans. The Carter Center would collaborate with CSMHI as we applied a highly improved "vaccination"—in this case, of the societal/political situation in Estonia—that we had been fine-tuning over many years.[4] Thus, starting in April 1994, CSMHI's and the Carter Center's Conflict Resolution Program's (CRP) Baltic Project would involve *only* Estonians, Russians (and Russian-speakers) who had continued to stay in Estonia as citizens or noncitizens, and Russians from the Russian Federation. We would, however, welcome participant observers from the other two Baltic Republics. We had two meetings in 1994, seven meetings in 1995, and another two meetings in 1996. All of them took place in Estonia, except for one in 1995 for which we went back to Riga and two meetings in Charlottesville in 1995 and 1996.[5] After these dialogue series and this collaboration with the Carter Center ended, CSMHI was involved in projects for the next three years that took place in three locations in Estonia, applying what we learned during these CSMHI/CRP series to problems at the citizen level and evolving concrete models for peaceful coexistence between ethnic Estonians, Russians, and Russian-speakers living in Estonia. These projects continued until April 1999.

In the next chapter I will begin to illustrate this highly improved version of "vaccination," which we named the "Tree Model," that was applied to the Estonian situation for finding peaceful solutions for complicated large-group processes. In this chapter I will describe my involvement in the Carter Center and meeting people associated with it.

The Atlanta-based Carter Center was founded in 1982 by former U.S. president Jimmy Carter and former first lady Rosalynn Carter. In partnership with Emory University, the Carter Center was and still is committed to advancing human rights and alleviating unnecessary human suffering, with major programs that work toward waging peace, fighting diseases, and building hope. In 1987 it established the International Negotiation Network (INN) under the umbrella of the Carter Center's Conflict Resolution Program (CRP).[6] INN would be a flexible, informal network of eminent people. Through INN, CRP would coordinate third-party assistance, expert analysis and advice, workshops, media attention, and other means to facilitate constructive prevention or resolution of international conflicts. In the year INN was established, there were 111 armed conflicts in the world, and only 10 percent of them could be addressed by international agencies. The rest of these conflicts were domestic struggles such as civil wars that did not fall within the jurisdiction of organizations like the United Nations. The purpose of INN was to fill the "mediation gap."

Dayle Powell (later Dayle Spencer) had been a trial lawyer for ten years before she became in 1985 a fellow and then the director of the Carter Center's Conflict Resolution Program (CRP). I do not remember the exact date, but it was in the very late 1980s when I first met Dayle at a meeting in Washington, DC, a meeting that, I believe, was organized by the United States Institute of Peace. She asked me to be a consultant to INN's executive council members. At that time INN's executive council members included, besides President Carter, about a dozen well-known persons, including former president of Costa Rica and Nobel Peace Prize Laureate (1987) Oscar Arias Sánchez; former president of Nigeria General Olusegun Obasanjo; the widow of the assassinated (in 1986) Swedish prime minister Olof Palme and member of the Swedish Committee for UNICEF (later chairperson of UNICEF), Lisbet Palme; Archbishop Desmond Tutu from South Africa, also a Nobel Peace Prize winner (1984); and Elie Wiesel, still another Nobel Peace Prize winner (1987) . Jimmy Carter would also receive the Nobel Peace Prize in 2002.

I accepted Dayle's invitation and began visiting Atlanta and meeting other INN consultants, who were all new to me, with the exception of Hal. I was the only psychoanalyst who was process oriented, meaning that for me, finding solutions to large-group problems would involve individuals, small groups, and large groups going through psychological journeys. Most of the other consultants' orientation, I felt, was to utilize logical thinking in order to get to "yes" as soon as possible, solutions that I believed would not take into consideration strong psychological obstacles. Dayle and her husband, William Spencer, did their best to help the consultants get to know one another. I was willing to learn more about how official and nonpsychoanalytically oriented unofficial diplomacy was generally practiced. These methods used "psychology" to enable one party to obtain the upper hand in dealing with the opposing party, or, when a facilitating team was involved, to enable the team leaders to manipulate the parties involved.

Often we had lunch with Jimmy and Rosalynn Carter. My initial impression of the 39th President of the United States was that he was a very intelligent person with high idealistic expectations for the world's well-being. I sensed that he and Rosalynn were in a kind of "twinning": they seemed to be a very close, almost inseparable couple, doing most of their thinking and activities together. I sensed that Jimmy Carter had deep religious beliefs and had heard he was a devout Christian in media reports. (Later, after President Carter presented me with signed copies of his books, my reading of them confirmed this impression.) But not even once during our "formal" or social meetings did he refer to his or anyone else's religion. His spiritual convictions most likely played a role in his personal thinking, activities, and motivation to become a leader, but unlike other leaders I would meet much later in other countries, especially in the Middle East, Jimmy Carter, in his conversations with INN members or diplomatic guests, never used religion to justify his political thinking. I also never heard him refer to his loss of a second term as president, although Rosalynn Carter now and then would make direct or indirect references to it. I thought that the 1980 election represented a great personal loss for both of them, but I was impressed by how they used his postpresidency to turn this loss into a personal investment in improving human affairs. I liked them both.

In January 1992 President Carter asked me to give a paper that approached ethnic conflicts from a psychological point of view at a conference titled "Resolving Intra-National Conflicts: A Strengthened Role for Non-Governmental Actors" and to conduct two workshops. This conference brought together over two hundred invited guests from forty countries and more than 150 international organizations and governments. Among the participants were influential persons from eight selected conflict areas: Afghanistan, Angola, Burma/Myanmar, Cambodia, Cyprus, the Korean Peninsula, Liberia, and Sudan.

Different INN members conducted workshops on these eight regions. One of the workshops that President Carter wanted me to lead was on the Cyprus problem. High-level participants had come from both the Greek and Turkish sides of the island, from Turkey, and elsewhere. I was reluctant to try this since I was concerned I would not be able to maintain my neutrality. But I sensed Carter's genuine interest in observing a meeting directed by a psychoanalytically informed person instead of watching another meeting where the facilitator would help the opposing parties to bargain. He was an engineer and I was a psychoanalyst. Could we learn useful ways of thinking and conducting dialogues between "enemies" from one another? I ended up conducting the Cyprus workshop. Afterward, President Carter offered to go to the island and help both sides of the conflict negotiate a peaceful solution. No invitation came from either side. There was no process at the Carter Center conference that could help to prepare opposing parties for next steps.[7]

I would get to know President Carter even more closely when the INN held a regional meeting of NGOs in Dakar, Senegal, in September 1992. By then the former consultants to the executive council of the INN, myself included, had become full members; there would be no more consultants.[8] About a dozen of us joined President Carter and Rosalynn Carter in a Dakar hotel, which had been built (or paid for) a year earlier by King Fahd of Saudi Arabia for the meeting of the Organization of the Islamic Conference.[9] I suspect that for security reasons there were no guests besides the Carter Center people and the security staff in the entire hotel for the duration of our gathering. The meeting itself was not useful for me. I wanted to learn as much as possible about certain large-group problems in Africa. Those who presented papers, however, focused on statistics, charts, and logical mechanical ways for ending conflicts. I concluded that questions such as "who are we now?" and border issues could not be handled as easily as the statistics, charts, and mechanical measures suggested.

Landing Savané, the husband of INN member and former director of the United Nation's Africa Division Marie-Angélique, was running for president of Senegal as a member of the opposition. One day President Carter and those of us who had accompanied him to Dakar unofficially became involved in Savané's campaign during a visit to his house, when we were greeted by a huge crowd dressed in wonderful, colorful dress, chanting and dancing. In the evenings we would gather around the hotel's big swimming pool, which was filled with hundreds and hundreds of frogs. In this setting Jimmy Carter and the rest of us were able to relax, tell jokes, drink beer, and take a break from the seriousness of Africa's deadly large-group issues. One evening Jimmy Carter and Rosalynn left our gathering by the frog-filled swimming pool early. We learned the next day that they and Dayle had flown to Liberia in a small plane, landed near a place where a deadly struggle was taking place, and tried to talk people from opposing parties into stopping the bloodshed. I do not know many details of this mission, but I do recall our worry for their safety until we heard from them; I think it was two days later.

In Senegal with us was Dr. Joyce Neu, the assistant director of the Carter Center's Conflict Resolution Program. A linguist and former Peace Corps volunteer in Senegal from 1972 to 1974, she had tried unsuccessfully to start an academic exchange program between her then university, Pennsylvania State University, and the University of Dakar in 1987. I had met Joyce before this trip, but had never had the opportunity to work with her. Since she had friends in Senegal, I was able to visit some private homes with her in Dakar and to learn, with her help, something about Senegalese culture. To further do so, she, Lisbet Palme, and I spent two days driving around the country.

Norman Itzkowitz and I joined Joyce Neu in 1998 to carry out another project for the Carter Center's Conflict Resolution Program (CRP), when the three of us went twice to Albania to investigate the legacy of Enver Hoxha's totalitarian rule. We studied the societal split between those who were associated with the torturers and those who were related to the torture victims.[10] I saw Joyce again in 2001 when there was a dedicatory conference for the Joan B. Kroc Institute for Peace & Justice, which was founded at the University of San Diego in 2000. Joyce came from the Carter Center to the Kroc Institute as its founding director.[11] Jimmy Carter attended this meeting, and it was the last time I saw him. Earlier, Dayle and Mark had moved to Hawaii, and the Carter Center's Conflict Resolution program, as I had experienced it for about ten years, came to an end when Joyce moved to San Diego.

Joyce Neu was also involved in the CSMHI/CRP Estonia project, joining the CSMHI facilitating team in April 1994 as a representive of the Carter Center, while Hal Saunders and I represented both CSMHI and the Carter Center.[12] When we landed at the Tallinn Airport for the first time, the airport facilities were dysfunctional, and the immigration and customs officers had set up two long tables in front of the terminal building's door that faced the runways. This was our first indication that this was indeed a traumatized country. Before coming to Estonia, we were aware that in 1992, Max van der Stoel, the Conference on Security and Cooperation in Europe (CSCE) High Commissioner on Minorities, had identified Estonia as a country with the potential for violent conflict. Both Estonian and Russian authorities were aware of this prospect as well, and because of CSMHI's previous work in Russia and the Baltic Republics, both countries welcomed us and willingly became involved with the CSMHI/CRP project.

Former Chairman of the Presidium of the Supreme Soviet of the Estonian SSR, Arnold Rüütel, who negotiated with Michael Gorbachev for the restoration of Estonian independence, joined our CSMHI/CRP work. He later became the second president of Estonia after it regained its independence in 1991. For our dialogue series Rüütel was accompanied by parliamentarians (both Estonian and Russians living in Estonia), the presidents of Tartu University and LEX University, leaders from the Russian-speaking community, and other well-known figures in Estonia. Similarly, Russia would send influential persons to our dialogues, including Yuri Voyevoda, vice-president of the State Duma Committee on International Affairs. I kept the Russian ambassador to Estonia, Alexandre Trofimov, informed of our work throughout the project. Sometimes he, his family, and I would have dinner at the ambassador's home in Tallinn. Since we had funding for several years of the vaccination process, in addition to conducting dialogues among participants representing Estonia, Russia, and Russian-speakers in Estonia and Russia, we initiated other activities designed both to help us assess and reassess the situation in Estonia before and during the dialogue series, and to enhance the influence of the societal/political vaccination process in general.

Elsewhere, I have described the Tree Model in detail and told the stories of its application in Estonia.[13] In the next two chapters I will keep repetitions to a minimum and share other recollections of our work in Estonia.

# 21

# THE "TREE MODEL" IN ESTONIA

## PSYCHOPOLITICAL ASSESSMENT AND DIALOGUE

Some time ago when I was asked to describe the Tree Model at a professional gathering, I recalled CSMHI's Ambassador-in-Residence Nathaniel Howell's description of official diplomacy and I modified it to define the Tree Model. A tall man who played basketball in his youth, Nat compares good official diplomatic negotiation to playing basketball: opposing teams rush from one side of the court to the other using rules and regulations trying to score points. In the end, one team wins, but the other team also scores points and some measure of self-esteem for being a good competitor. According to Nat, involvement in a well-managed and fair official diplomatic activity is as pleasurable as watching a well-played basketball game. Expanding Ambassador Howell's metaphor, let us imagine that someone spills a huge barrel of olive oil onto the basketball court. Now the game becomes chaotic. The first thing required is to wipe off the oil spill and clean the floor. In an international relationship, the oil spill that makes a routine play impossible primarily relates to large-group identity and its protection and maintenance. When large-group identity issues become inflamed and problematic, conducting international relations only through "typical" official diplomatic efforts becomes slippery—very difficult and sometimes impossible. The application of the Tree Model, with necessary modifications for the specific conflict at hand, can be compared to cleaning up olive oil on a basketball court.

The Tree Model describes a *process* that grows over time and branches out like a tree. It is rooted in the facilitating team's initial careful assessment (and repeated assessments) of the situation at hand, and continues through a series of psychopolitical dialogues between influential members of the opposing groups (the trunk). The aim of psychopolitical dialogues is to reduce poisonous emotions and resistances to change (both conscious and, more importantly, unconscious), and thus allow more realistic discussions and strategy planning to take place by a limited, but influential, number of members of the opposing groups. The third part of this process entails implementing practical projects and building institutions (branches of the tree) while the facilitating team is still present, which will be left behind when the facilitators depart, so the insights and new attitudes gained from the dialogues will continue to grow and develop by the people who were involved in the conflict. Tree branches go upward, reaching the authorities, and also downward, reaching the community.

One of the unique aspects of the Tree Model is that it is carried out by an interdisciplinary facilitating team that includes not only psychoanalysts and psychiatrists, but also former diplomats, historians, other social and behavioral scientists, and even environmentalists. With such a diverse team, the complexities of real-world political, economic, legal, and military issues and environmental problems are examined in their own context, and also through *a psychoanalytic lens*. Therefore, starting with the first part, the initial assessment phase, attention is paid to unconscious (as well as conscious) psychological factors that most likely will blur realistic considerations, create resistances to change, and impede progress toward adaptive negotiations during the second part of the model.

Before and during the Estonian dialogue series, the facilitating team visited many towns and villages and met with local officials, business people, teachers, students, young persons, older individuals, men, women, ethnic Estonians, ethnic Russians, and Russian-speakers. Psychoanalytically informed clinicians among us spent hours talking with them, listening to their life experiences, perceptions of world events, and fantasies about their own and the Other. We even listened to recounting of dreams, helping us recognize the intertwining of external events with internal ones. Members of the facilitating team then met among themselves and tried to find shared themes that related to large-group conflicts in Estonia.

The facilitating team's visits to national cemeteries, memorials, monuments, museums, an abandoned former Soviet air base, dangerous nuclear waste sites, and other "hot" locations—sometimes only accompanied by an "official" guide and other times accompanied by other dialogue series participants—proved very useful in diagnosing the mental images of recent and more distant events. At such locations, listening to Estonians' and Russians' remarks helped the CSMHI/CRP team to better comprehend what the sites represented and the psychological impediments that likely would emerge during opposing group interactions. The visits also revealed what otherwise might have remained unexpressed during dialogues.

The major Estonian "hot spot" was the former Soviet nuclear submarine base in Paldiski on the Gulf of Finland, west of Tallinn. In spring 1994, the project's American team and its Russian and Estonian participants took a tour of Paldiski.

At the time, the heavily fortified base had been mostly shut down, and it looked like a huge garbage dump. The guide, a local history teacher fluent in English, referred angrily to Paldiski as "the carcass the Russians left" and repeated several times, "The devil himself sat here." Seeing Estonian and Russian participants' reactions to this place as well as hearing the guide's interpretation of its role in Estonian history provided the facilitators with a "shortcut" to understanding general emotions associated with the Soviet occupation of Estonia.

After reindependence, the Estonians had assigned an ethnic Estonian mayor to Paldiski, but the population in this nuclear base and town was still entirely Russian. Before our visit, the Russian Embassy had asked a Russian person who lived in Paldiski to be our guide. A personal verbal fight took place between the Estonian guide who had come to Paldiski by bus with the program participants from Tallinn and the Russian guide who was waiting for the bus's arrival. The facilitating team did not interfere. In the end, the Estonian authority in Paldiski allowed only the Estonian guide to accompany us. It was under this circumstance that the Estonian guide felt free to express his rage openly against the Soviets/Russians. This was unusual because, unlike the guide, ethnic Estonian participants did not themselves express negative feelings during our initial visits to various locations or in the dialogue. Instead, they remained silent. At times the faces of two of them in particular would literally change color, but they never verbally expressed rage or other negative feelings. Russians, meanwhile, freely expressed any kind of emotion.

It took me some time to understand this. The Estonians, having lived since the early Middle Ages—except for twenty years or so—under the authority of people who belonged to another large-group identity, were very careful about provoking unwanted responses from the Russians. During our initial assessment of the situation there, we realized that Estonians shared a mostly unconscious fantasy that Russians in Estonia represented a dragon's egg. If they were not careful, the dragon's egg would hatch and a new dragon would swallow them. The Estonian race would disappear! Thus, their rage was expressed only indirectly and most of the time they were not even aware of their feelings. Among other circumstances, this behavior would show itself in the behavior of many Estonian language examiners. Russians who were subjected to such examinations would sense the hidden rage. Since the language examination for citizenship for the Russian-speaker was a political issue, poisoning this process might have dangerous consequences.

People like me whose ancestors had empires, kingdoms, or strong and long-lasting states, including Russians, had trouble easily understanding the reasons for Estonians' inability to verbally express anger or other negative feelings toward their victimizers, the "enemy," in front of them. For example, Jaan Kaplinski had written poems about hurts and humiliation as well as the dignity of his people, but during the dialogue series, he was a very gentle person in front of the Russians. Estonians' shared fantasy of "disappearing" as an ethnic group and their expressing their rage in indirect ways were key obstacles to negotiating with the Russians. Even during the initial assessment part of our project, it became clear to me that the facilitating team would need to find the right time to empathically explain to both Estonians and Russians this psychological obstacle blocking direct communication between them.

On September 28, 1994, the cruise ferry *MS Estonia* sank in the Baltic Sea, killing at least 852 passengers. It was believed that the bow door of the ship opened or was never properly closed by the crew.[1] When we were in Parnu, Estonia, in October 1994 for another meeting, we heard of a belief among Estonians that the experienced Russian-speaking crew on the ship had been fired (by Estonians) and replaced by an inexperienced Estonian crew just before the tragedy took place. The idea behind this belief—true or false—indicated that Estonia (ship or country) needed Others to be in charge of important and crucial matters. If Estonians took over such activities they would sink and disappear.

In October 1994 clinicians among us clearly noticed how the sinking of the *Estonia* had become a concrete symbol for the dreaded fantasy that the Estonian race would disappear following reindependence. Again, logically speaking, the Estonians happily and joyously embraced freedom, but psychologically speaking, they had become more and more anxious. This increased the psychological resistance against direct and realistic negotiations between participants from the opposing groups. At the next two dialogue meetings following the one in Parnu—in January in Charlottesville and in Estonia—I joined Maurice Apprey in giving explanations on disappearance fantasies to all participants.[2] It was not until the second year of the dialogue series that Estonian participants began to feel free to express their negative emotions.

Our typical dialogues took four consecutive days. Most of our meetings took place as small groups of ten to twelve members, followed by plenary sessions with several hours allotted for eating meals and attending social events together. The facilitating team observed, explained, and helped the participants to work through echo and accordion phenomena, miniconflicts, competition of grievances, preoccupations with minor differences, reactivations of chosen traumas and glories (Estonians did not focus on a single chosen trauma; living under Others for centuries was their mental double for a chosen trauma), time collapse, magical thinking, various projections and externalizations, identifications with the opposite group, and so on.[3]

During the meetings the facilitating team always tried to speak "from the side of the ego," and not "from the sides of the id or the superego." Let me explain: if I tell a patient on my couch, "You are full of rage," I speak from the side of the id; if I tell him "Don't be so angry," I speak from the side of the superego. But, if I explain in an empathic fashion why the patient is angry and what the conscious and unconscious reasons are for her anger, then I speak from the side of the ego. In plain English, the facilitating team members tried to make sure that they did not humiliate any participants from the opposing groups or order them around. The idea was to allow them to develop their own autonomy and to find their own realistic solutions by "playing" seriously.

One day in the second year of the dialogue series, Arnold Rüütel turned to the leading Russian delegate Yuri Voyevoda and said: "You Russians are an elephant. You have a huge federation. We Estonians are a rabbit. We have a small country. If a rabbit becomes friendly with an elephant, it will not be careful around the elephant. It will face more danger because the elephant, even though it may not be aggressive, may step on it." Then another Estonian noted that Russians living in Estonia were like elephant eggs in the rabbit's nest—at any moment they might hatch and squash the rabbit and its home. Referring to the Russians' perception that they had done much good for Estonia when Estonia was a part of the Soviet Empire, Voyevoda replied: "All along I used to think that Estonians were ungrateful people. Now I understand that is not the case. You are telling me that Estonians are careful, not ungrateful. I can easily accept this. Let's see how an elephant and a rabbit can remain side by side without either of them getting hurt or humiliated."

Symbolic effigies of large-group identities were created. In a playful fashion, negotiators played elephant and rabbit games for days, and the facilitating team did not interfere. During this time while I was observing the negotiators I felt that I was watching children at play. Anxiety gave way to freer expressions of negative feelings. Estonians were angry since the elephant in the past had stepped on the rabbit. Now, should the elephant take care and watch out for the rabbit as it takes steps? Or, should the rabbit keep the necessary distance from the elephant in order to protect itself and also take responsibility for a peaceful coexistence?

While playing elephant and rabbit games, Estonians and Russians experienced another accordion phenomenon, and then the "border" between them was stabilized in a friendly way. As the play with effigies between Estonians and Russians continued, laughter replaced anxious and angry feelings, and both parties understood that a rabbit does not need to love an elephant and be too close to it, and that they can be friendly with a necessary distance between them. Russians "rehumanized" Estonians as careful people rather than people seeking ways to humiliate their former rulers, and Estonians appreciated that people with past and present empires are simply proud and sensitive about being powerful and they do not need to use their power to smash others.

Rüütel told us a personal story: once when he was the head political figure in Estonia, he was in Moscow to discuss Estonian reindependence with Mikhail Gorbachev. He had to wait in a waiting room for hours before Gorbachev asked him to come in. This humiliated and angered Rüütel. After playing elephant and rabbit games and after openly discussing the incident in Moscow, I felt that Rüütel no longer felt humiliated and angry at Russians.

Four months later, when the participants came together for another four-day dialogue, they continued, on and off, to play elephant-rabbit games. This development represented a turning-point in the dialogue series.[4] The participants were now more willing than ever to join in and help the facilitating team to develop and institutionalize projects to firm up peaceful coexistence between Estonians and Russians and Russian-speakers in Estonia.

The branches of the "tree" began to appear even while the CSMHI/CRP-sponsored dialogues were taking place. After the dialogue series was completed, three big additional branches began developing. In the next chapter I will describe these branches and tell stories of wonderful persons who took genuine responsibilities to see that the branches would grow strong and beautiful.

# 22

# EXTENDING THE TREE BRANCHES IN ESTONIA

## THE NEED FOR A VACCINATION PROCESS

Those working in the psychopolitical realm know that it sometimes involves accepting and tolerating, with good humor, unusual situations that arise and that nurturing unusual personal relationships are important. I begin with the story of an event that took place in a sauna.

Russian participants in our psychopolitical dialogue series were suspicious of our intentions. One evening three Russians asked me to join them in a sauna. I took Yuri Urbanovich with me since these Russians did not speak English and I needed an interpreter. Occasionally I like to sip good bourbon. After all, I have lived in Virginia for a long time and Virginians and Kentuckians are neighbors, but I am not fond of drinking a lot of alcohol. In the sauna the Russians insisted that I drink one small glass of vodka after another, and soon I noticed that one of them, Yuri Voyevoda, was interrogating me to find out if I worked for the American government and asking about the U.S. government's intentions concerning the future of the Russian Federation. I did not let on that I was aware of his reasons for inviting me to this sauna party and why he was so generous in encouraging me to get drunk. I told him that I was not an agent of any government, and I also gave him a brief history of how CSMHI began. He continued to interrogate me off and on for the next two hours while all of us sat in the sauna drinking vodka. Then Voyevoda spoke loud and clear: "Confucius says: 'The color of a cat is not important. What is important is whether the cat can catch mice!'" Pointing his finger at my chest in a friendly way he added: "You can catch mice!" The interrogation ended and was never repeated. The Russians in the sauna, now all under the influence of alcohol, began telling jokes. Yuri Urbanovich had no need to interpret them. I, also under the influence of alcohol, "understood" every joke in Russian and joined in the laughter!

Estonians never questioned the CSMHI members' intentions. In the spring of 1995 in Tallinn some of us visited the Estonian Foreign Ministry. Paul Lettens, who was then a councilor to the Estonian prime minister and was connected with the Foreign Affairs Department, and who also a participant of our dialogue series, had initiated this visit for us to explain our project to some officials. We were received very well, except by one Estonian-American lady who then held a position in the Estonian Foreign Ministry. After the Baltic Republics separated from the Soviet Union, some people originally from the Baltic Republics and/or their offspring, as one may expect, had returned to offer their services. Some with diplomatic experience were assigned to positions in the realm of foreign affairs. The Estonian-American lady was rather nasty, and I thought that perhaps she perceived the CSMHI/CRP team as other Americans competing with her. She started by saying that there was no role for psychologists in Estonian affairs. Because of this lady's attitude, someone on our team—I do not recall now who—came up with the idea that we should also visit the Estonian president's office and inform the president's advisers as to why we were in Estonia. In reality, there was no such need since the former "president" of Estonia (former Chairman of the Presidium of the Supreme Soviet of the Estonian SSR), Arnold Rüütel, Paul Lettens, Estonian parliamentarians, and other influential persons were already our partners in the psychopolitical dialogue series. They certainly had talked to higher authorities about what we were doing in their country. But, again with Yuri Urbanovich, I ended up going to President Lennart Meri's office to meet one of his very close advisers, Ants Paju.

When we entered Paju's office, I saw a big man, younger than I, holding a wooden stick like a huge baseball bat, giving me the fanciful impression that I was meeting a cartoon character from the Stone Age. He did not shake our hands, but kept staring into my eyes sternly for several minutes. All of us remained silent. After that Ants Paju asked Yuri to inform me that since I did not blink when he was staring at me while holding a big stick, he could trust me. In situations like this I gratefully reactivate my psychoanalyst identity. In my clinical practice I had seen many weird behavior patterns and had become accustomed to automatically remaining curious instead of defensively reacting to them. After this initial unusual welcome, I was able to tell Ants about our CSMHI activities and cooperation with the Carter Center in Estonia. From that time on, whenever I was in Estonia, Ants would come to see me. If I were away from Tallinn he would drive hours in order to spend some time with me. In fact, he took English lessons so we could communicate directly. He referred to me as his "teacher."

I learned that some of his family members had been exiled to Siberia during the Soviet regime and that he had grown up deeply disliking the Soviets. What really hurt and humiliated Ants the most was that when he became an Olympic-level discus thrower, the Soviet authorities did not choose him to participate in the Olympic Games. Like Arnold Rüütel, he was a "nationalist" and wanted to do his best for Estonia. Ants knew that he would be more helpful to his own large group if he gave up hating Soviets/Russians and learned to work with them. I think that his awareness of this is why I became what psychoanalysts call a "positive transference figure" for him: he perceived me as someone with whom he could identify so he could discard his hateful feelings, sublimate his aggression, and work for peace. Whenever he met me he would give me a hug so hard that my bones hurt. He was a big man. I never complained, never abused my role as his "teacher," never gave him advice about what to do, and respected his struggle to change. As he wrote to me in a March 1995 letter, "People change." He was an excellent example of this fact.

Before I met Ants for the first time in January 1993, Estonian president Lennart Meri had established the Estonian Round Table, a government-sanctioned multiethnic body to serve as a forum for discussion of interethnic issues and as an advisory body for the Estonian Parliament. Members of the Round Table came from different groups in Estonia, including Russian-speaking communities, other smaller ethnic groups, and the Parliament itself. Business, educational, and cultural interests were represented as well. Ants Paju was the head of the Round Table as the representative of the Estonian president. He never participated in our psychopolitical dialogue series, but he accepted four members from the series (Estonians, including Jaan Kaplinski who by then also was very close to me,[1] and Russians living in Estonia) to join his Round Table discussions and activities. Thus, we were able to grow a branch of our tree that would go upward reaching Estonian authorities. This "branch" allowed us to transfer what was learned and experienced in our dialogue series to the highest levels of decision making in Estonia's government. When Ants was elected to be a member of the Estonian Parliament he was replaced as the head of the Round Table by one member of our dialogue group.[2] As a member of the Parliament, Ants visited many towns and villages with Russian and Estonian populations on the Estonian-Russian border, helping mayors and other community leaders achieve peaceful coexistence between Estonians and Russians. History books most likely will not report this. But, I have the privilege of knowing about it.

In 1995 the president of Estonia met with Yuri Voyevoda and another Russian parliamentarian from the dialogue group, told them how much he appreciated our work in Estonia, and promised to look into concerns about the language examination requirement for citizenship. Another time, the Russian State Duma representatives from our dialogue group were invited to the Estonian Parliament to meet with their counterparts. Among other things, they discussed in productive ways Russia's reactions to Estonia's desire to join NATO. Eventually the border disputes between Estonia and Russia were resolved. The Estonians in the dialogue group even experienced grief and mourning in "letting go" of approximately twenty miles of territory east of Narva to the Russians. But, if this territory—where all the inhabitants were Russians—had been returned to Estonia, it would have increased the number of "dragon hatchlings" and frightened the Estonians. It was better to lose this land and mourn than to increase shared anxiety.

I hope that the reader now has a clear idea of how we tried to link our unofficial work with official considerations dealing with the minority issues in Estonia and with the Estonian-Russian relationship in general. There were other efforts, such as consultations with the Organization for Economic Co-operation and Development (OECD) mission in Estonia and with people from the European Union in order to share information and obtain different perspectives. Ambassadors to Estonia from the United States, Russia, Sweden, and Norway would come to some of the facilitating team's and participants' social gatherings and learn about our activities in such settings. The Finns, we knew, were most helpful to the Estonians, but for some reason, the Finnish ambassador never attended any of our social gatherings. When we went to Estonia, there were not many NGOs working there, but we contacted all the Estonian and Russian NGOs we could find.

One major tree branch we helped to grow dealt with changing the negative emotional nature of the language examinations and preventing possible dangerous consequences of its use. Facilitating team discussions concluded that if some of us were permitted to sit in while Estonian examiners tested Russians or Russian-speakers, we might prevent humiliating situations for the non-Estonians. We had no way of knowing if the Estonian examiners were actually rather sadistic, but non-Estonians' perceptions had to be taken seriously and something needed to be done as soon as possible.

The Estonian government gave its permission for CSMHI/CRP team involvement in the language examinations and Joyce Neu took on the leadership of this project. Several times she actually sat in the room when language examinations were taking place so no examiner could behave in a sadistic manner; the bad "reputation" (symbolic or realistic) of the examinations could no longer be maintained.[3] Joyce worked very closely with the Estonian authorities, bringing examples from different parts of the world to illustrate how to standardize the language examination and how to administer it in dignified ways. The Estonian authorities, with the help of the parliamentarians in our dialogue group and Ants Paju, accepted CSMHI/CRP recommendations and made them official.

The charismatic Vladimir Homyakov, a medical doctor from the Narva City Council, was the one who had always found a way to complain loudly about the language examination. I fully realized how humiliating it would be for him to be forced to learn over one thousand Estonian words in order to keep his medical license. After Joyce Neu was successful in the process of standardizing the examinations, I recall how he came to one meeting in Tallinn and right away, with a big smile on his face, told all of us how his daughter had just passed her language examination. It was at this moment that I realized how we had played a role in allowing himself to be a proud father and how our "vaccination" had taken away the poison of this citizenship requirement.

There was, however, one vaccination process that was not successful. After hearing Vladimir's daughter's story, a person in the dialogue group—I do not recall who—said: "We should bring some young persons, both Estonians and Russians living in Estonia here and listen to them." Most participants agreed with him. The general perception was that the younger persons, both Estonians and Russians, were not like their parents or grandparents and that they already had found ways to coexist peacefully. Four Estonian and four Russian university students living in Estonia were selected. One day we asked all the regular participants of the project to make a big circle. Eight students sat in the middle of this circle and Maurice Apprey and I, after asking the older people to stay silent and not to interfere, conducted a dialogue among the students. At first these young people declared that they were indeed different from their parents and grandparents. After all, the world was changing fast and they were willing to be citizens of this new world. It took perhaps twenty or thirty minutes before these eight very nice students clearly began repeating what the older participants had gone through: completion of grievances, increased narcissistic investment in their own large-group identities, reactivation of historical images, creation of a psychological border between them and the Other, preoccupations with minor differences, and so on.

The Carter Center offered to sponsor a visit by these eight young persons to the United States. The eight students came to America for a couple of weeks with the idea that this would cement their developing bonds. They first visited Charlottesville and then went to the Carter Center in Atlanta. On the morning of their return flight to Estonia, two of the Russian students announced their decisions to remain in the United States, where each knew someone with whom they thought they could stay. Instead of attending a planned farewell brunch, the students went to the Carter Center to have a discussion with Joyce Neu. Even two Estonian students shed tears over the two Russians' "defections" and their lack of understanding of how difficult life in Estonia could be for a noncitizen. Joyce called me and we—she in the room and I on the phone—spent hours with the students. Joyce and I explained to the two Russian students that by not returning they were violating the trust of the entire student group and the sponsoring organization. The two students in the end agreed to go home as planned. Once more I learned the lesson of not initiating a joint program for individuals from opposing groups in "hot" conflict without serious preparation, even when the program seems wonderful. The two Russian students did not maintain their involvement with our subsequent meetings in Estonia, but we were able to keep some contact with the others. Even though our wish to learn from the young people did not go so well, it did not harm CSMHI/CRP's continuing activities and did not negatively affect the adults' continuing dialogues.

Another branch that we tried to develop in Estonia dealt with environmental and related health issues. The northeastern section of Estonia was often called the most polluted area on the European Continent. I will very briefly refer to three of the environmental issues Estonia faced after it regained its independence, to illustrate how overwhelming these problems were:

- By Estonian estimates, there were more than 500 military bases in Estonia that had been previously occupied by the Soviet Union. The Estonians used the term "military pollution" synonymously with military bases, because of existing high levels of surface, water, and air contamination within and near these bases. Furthermore, because the Soviets removed all protective equipment, including wire boundary fences, many of these former bases were accessible to the public and to neighborhood children whose play could expose them to highly contaminated soil.
- Narva, a city of about 80,000 (the third largest in Estonia), is situated forty kilometers east of Sillamäe and across the Narva River from Russia. The main serious sources of pollution in Narva were two of Estonia's largest power plants that were then situated within five kilometers of the city proper. Baltic Thermal Power Plant, the largest of the two, consumed annually more than 10 million tons of shale from deposits in Estonia that yielded 4.5 million tons (almost 50 percent) of residual waste ash and slag that had been stored in the open and had formed heaps as high as 30–40 meters near the city. Additionally, 1.5 million cubic meters of waste water containing numerous chemicals were discharged annually and stored in a large man-made pond (earthen with no lining) near the plant with an elevation above the city.
- In Sillamäe (population 20,000) there was a metallurgy plant that, until the Estonian reindependence, was managed by the USSR Ministry of Medium-Scale Engineering and produced enriched uranium for military and civil use. It resulted in Sillamäe's most serious environmental public health problem at the time of Estonia's reindependence: a large radioactive dump located near the town's center and on the shores of the Gulf of Finland.

Obviously, the new Estonian government inherited these huge environmental public health problems from the Soviet Union and was well aware of them, as were the United Nations and the European authorities. For example, we knew that the Swedish Radiation Protection Institute of Stockholm had made sound and objective recommendations concerning the environmental problems in Sillamäe. Certainly remediation would require vast sums of money and decades of work. Why did our facilitating team decide to investigate them?

Many Estonians were moving into vacated former military bases to find free or cheap housing and they and those Russians and Russian-speakers who remained in these areas (mostly women and children since men often moved elsewhere to find jobs) needed to know more about the environmental dangers and health hazards they faced there. Such a "learning" process would increase cooperation, prevention of tragic health consequences, and a sense of peaceful coexistence. The populations of Narva and Sillamäe were entirely Russians or Russian-speakers, and rightly or wrongly, they thought that Estonians would not rush to make towns where they lived cleaner and safer. Open and clear interest in Narva's and Sillamäe's tragic environmental challenges by Estonian government officials would go a long way toward creating an atmosphere for a peaceful future for all Estonia's residents. If some members of our facilitating team visited these polluted and dangerous areas and talked with local officials and people living there, we thought we might initiate activities that encouraged Estonians of authority to also visit these sites and increase positive interethnic communications. Then the Russians and the Russian-speakers living there would not feel so much like rejected and forgotten children.

George Moein was the director of Earth 2020–Center for Environmental and Hazardous Materials Management Institute at the University of Virginia. We briefed him about CSMHI's work. In February and April of 1995 he joined many of us from the CSMHI facilitating team as we visited Narva and Sillamäe with the knowledge of the Estonian authorities. I still remember the horrible sight of a man-made pond containing waste material near the Baltic Thermal Power Plant and storage tanks for liquid nuclear waste in Sillamäe. George advised us about what to touch and what not to touch, and we only drank bottled water. Still, when we get together and recall these trips, my friends and I laugh nervously when we visualize how we used to take showers using bottled carbonated water instead of the available local water. Over four days we met and had long discussions with more than two dozen people in Sillamäe and Narva, including the mayors of these two places, a Narva City Council member, the director and technical director of the Baltic Power Plant, and dialogue series participant Vladimir Homyakov. After this exhausting trip, George Moein, representing CSMHI, attended the Ecological Security of the Baltic States, Nordic Countries and North-West Estonia, International Conference in Lohusalu, Estonia, and reported what we had seen at Sillamäe and Narva to representatives from different countries. These included the Estonian minister of environment; the head of department, Russian Institute of Scientific and Technical Information; two parliamentarians from Sweden; the director of the Olof Palme International Center in Sweden; the director of the Tampere Peace Institute, Finland; and the executive director of the Belona Foundation, Norway. Our Narva and Sillamäe visits played a big role in increasing the dialogue between group participants and capturing government authorities' attention to all our activities in Estonia. George Moein's report on how to investigate pollution-related problems and find technical assistance was most welcomed.

As our psychopolitical dialogue series began, we helped to establish an Estonian Contact Center. Endel Talvik, then a young psychotherapist and the president of the very small Estonian Psychoanalytically Oriented Society and a participant in our psychopolitical dialogue series was appointed to be the leader of the Contact Center. He maintained frequent communication with CSMHI when the facilitating team was not in Estonia. Soon he would undergo his personal psychoanalysis in Finland by traveling to Helsinki from Tallinn to lie on his psychoanalyst's couch and then start his psychoanalytic training. Today Endel is a member of the International Psychoanalytic Association.

After CSMHI/CRP joint venture in conducting the dialogue series ended, CSMHI alone initiated three multiyear community projects in a suburb of Tallinn called Mustamäe and in the Estonian towns Mustvee and Klooga. These projects represented new and major branches of the Tree Model. Endel Talvik was the key person in Estonia to assist us in these community projects.[4] Another person from our dialogue series who was also helpful was Peeter Vares, then the deputy director of the Institute for International and Social Studies in Tallinn.

Since I already described elsewhere details of the fascinating and moving stories of our involvement in Mustamäe, Mustvee, and Klooga,[5] here I will only briefly refer to our work in these places. These three sites were chosen because approximately 50 percent of their populations were indigenous Estonian-speakers and fifty percent were indigenous Russian-speakers. In these locations we provided $50,000 to a civic organization composed of equal membership from each group to develop and operate a project together. At that time in Estonia this was a large amount of money.[6] The formation of these civic organizations and the implementation of the three projects became models for peaceful coexistence in Estonia. Every third person—the Other— in Estonia had no place to go. Since they had to remain in Estonia, the necessity of peaceful coexistence then and in the future had to be accepted.

Mustamäe is a crowded suburb of Tallinn. The population is highly educated and cosmopolitan, and people there live a real "city life." Mustamäe at that time was fairly divided—50 percent Russian and 50 percent Estonian. They shared the same location, but there was very little social contact between the groups. We learned that in this suburb, throughout the fifty years of Soviet occupation, anti-Russian sentiments among Estonians remained high. Also, because of the growing presence of the Russian mafia, Estonians perceived many Russian or Russian-speakers as criminals. Fears and stereotypes of the Other prevailed at our first psychopolitical dialogue, and as the series progressed and participants felt safer, more perceptions of the Other were brought out. For example, we learned how some Estonians were even concerned about how Estonians and Russians typically arrange themselves on the beach. Estonians allow twenty to thirty meters distance between parties, reflecting a high value on privacy. Russians sat only two to three meters away from other parties, making Estonians feel their space was invaded. Even the Russians' fondness for a certain shade of blue was distasteful to Estonians.[7] Most Estonians were in favor of segregating Estonian and Russian children, because, in their minds, children from the two large groups had different "biological and psychological" makeups. Even the most "liberal" Estonians in our dialogue series "believed" that if four or five Russian children were put together with fifteen or twenty Estonian children in a kindergarten class, within a few months all the Estonian children would learn how to speak Russian and none of the Russian children would learn how to speak Estonian, because Russian children would be aggressive. This was an example of "magical thinking."

In Mustamäe, Russian and Estonian schools were segregated, and while many Russians in Mustamäe were Estonian citizens, there was a real problem with few Russian children learning the Estonian language, since education of each ethnic group was totally separate. There were thousands of children in Mustamäe, and the focus of any inquiry into interethnic relations centered especially on them.

Mustamäe was "a two tiered project: the first part involved teaching the Estonian language to 240 Russian children in nine Russian kindergartens; the second part provided opportunities for interaction where the Russian children communicated in Estonian to Estonian children. They played together, sang together, and undertook beneficial projects."[8] A model for teaching the Estonian language to young Russians was created. Two editions of a textbook (previously nonexistent) were written by Moscow-trained Estonian teacher and administrator Ly Krikk who, in addition to Endel Talvik, was a key person for us in Mustamäe. This project was successful. Once the Russian children had sufficient knowledge of the Estonian language, they were able to assist their parents, who spoke no Estonian or very little Estonian, in shops and other public places. Gradually, word about this program spread through the community, and the schools offering it were favored over others. Estonians found money to continue this program after CSMHI left Estonia.[9]

The Mustvee project involved a traditional eastern border town of approximately 4,000 that lies along the coast of Lake Peipsi, which divides Estonia from

Russia. When we first went to Mustvee, the border was still disputed by the two countries. The demographic makeup of the region is approximately 50 percent Russians and 50 percent Estonians. A special religious life exists in Mustvee, primarily consisting of a historic Russian sect called the "Old Believers" that left the official Russian Orthodox Church after 1666. In the late-seventeenth century and eighteenth century a large number of them settled in the Mustvee area and lived rather peacefully with Estonians for centuries. Old Believers operate four different churches in town. When the Soviet Union was in existence, Mustvee exported agricultural goods and fish, but after Estonian reindependence the economic structure collapsed, increasing difficulties between the two ethnic groups.

When we first went to Mustvee for an assessment of the community situation there, we noted that both Russians and Estonians in this town had one thing in common: for the most part, the community still thought in the "Soviet way"—i.e., its members suppressed their feelings about many things and they looked elsewhere for leaders to take charge of the future of their community. As a result, Mustvee's residents had never developed the skills necessary for participating in collaborative ventures. The Estonian government had not taken up that role—in fact, many political leaders had never even visited Mustvee.

We selected ten Russians and ten Estonians and began to bring them together. We told them that if they came up with a community project, we would give them $50,000 to develop it. These twenty individuals started to meet regularly with Endel Talvik, and when I was in Mustvee, I conducted the dialogues between them. When Estonians spoke during community group meetings, the Russians ignored them and talked among themselves. Conversely, the Estonians behaved the same way when the Russians spoke. Such reactions suggested keeping up or returning to old ways—surely someone in a position of power would tell them what to do, so why bother listening? We noticed the same behavior in Mustamäe, but it stemmed from an entirely different perspective when dialogues between Russian and Estonian teachers started. There, when a member of one group spoke, he or she was intentionally ignored by members of the opposition in order to show deliberate disrespect for the other group.

Our dialogue series in Mustvee slowly "taught" the Estonian and Russian participants to gain autonomy and learn to bargain realistically about issues among themselves and to agree on projects that would benefit the whole community. In 1997, the then mayor of Charlottesville, Elizabeth Waters, an experienced consultant in group consensus building and effective problem solving in community issues, accompanied the CSMHI team to Mustvee. We also worked closely with Gulnara Ishkuzina-Roll, who lived about forty-five minutes away in Tartu and was director of the Peipsi Lake Project. This NGO was active in the Mustvee community and had designed programs for environmental cooperation in the region. Eventually, with increased guidance, democratic leadership began to develop in the Mustvee group and the members were able to make decisions on possible projects.

Their focus was on programs to develop ecotourism in their part of Estonia as a way to improve their economy. The reader who is interested in how the CSMHI group became the first "tourists" to give the Mustvee population an experience in ecotourism can read my humorous accounts of this venture in my book, *Killing in the Name of Identity.*[10] Ants Paju visited Mustvee, and some Estonian parliamentarians and other dignitaries and scholars accepted CSMHI's invitation to come to a social event in the town. We also took a few important Mustvee persons to meetings in Tallinn. The aim was to "verify" the community building of the Mustvee community group and to give them greater connection to other parts of Estonia. When CSMHI's involvement came to an end, the group evolved as an NGO (Mustvee Ecotourism), an entity that would play a significant role in improving social, political, and economic conditions in Mustvee.

The Klooga project took shape in a small town located approximately twenty-five miles west of Tallinn. Before the dissolution of the Soviet Union, Klooga was a major Soviet military center. Newcomers, Estonians, shared the town with former "occupiers" when our project started, and virtually no relationship existed between them. It was a town without industry, and the only businesses were a small grocery store and a coffee shop. As an expression of their rage, looting by Estonians had left the place looking like a huge garbage dump in which people lived. Psychologically, Klooga represents a dark past, as it had been the site of a Nazi concentration camp. After their reindependence, Estonians would not make reference to the Nazi times but associated Klooga as a "Russian place," even though many Estonians had come to live there looking for free lodgings.

Only six people came to the first meeting held in Klooga, and they were so depressed they focused only on whether they would have heat for the winter and if they could provide the basic necessities for their children. Under the Soviet system, the Russian community had been taken care of by the army, but after Estonian reindependence, no new power or leadership had taken responsibility for this mixed community's well-being. The concept of community, in fact, was entirely missing. The roads were full of potholes, the seventy-five-year-old sewage system was in disrepair, the crime rate was high, and there was rampant unemployment. Most Russian men had escaped elsewhere, leaving their wives and children behind in this miserable place.

The first order of business was to begin the process of forming an NGO. We selected ten Estonians and ten Russians and Russian-speakers to the executive board, and they selected a Russian woman, Olga Kamyshan, as their leader. Endel

Talvik and other CSMHI members, including me, became involved in the arduous, bureaucratic process of the Klooga group becoming an NGO by opening a bank account and so on. The closest two constabularies were located ten miles away in Paldiski. Most problematic for the CSMHI team was the fact that, unlike Mustamäe and especially Mustvee, the Estonians and Russians in Klooga had no history of coexistence. Endel's house was between Tallinn and Klooga and he made regular weekly visits and held psychopolitical discussions (as he had learned from us) with the Klooga group. For some time he would feel depressed after each meeting and, as he told me later, needed a stiff drink when he returned home or to his job.

The Klooga group's top priority turned out to be the safety of children, who had become used to playing in and around the abandoned but still dangerous military base. Therefore, as a project, the Klooga group chose to create a community center. After incredible difficulties, and using the money we provided to them, they acquired the deed to a building that had once been a Soviet library. Renovations began in earnest. In fact, many Estonian and Russian residents would go to this building, clean it, repair fallen plaster, the leaky roof, and broken windows, and get to know the Other. Fights between residents, and crime in general, decreased. In the end, a comfortable multiroomed, multipurpose community center with an office and auditorium was completed.

During Christmastime in the first year of the project, the community group hesitated to decorate a public Christmas tree because they were sure that the ornaments and lights would be stolen and the tree vandalized. But Klooga's first community Christmas tree went untouched through the Christmas season and became a symbol for the success of our Tree Model.

In July 1997, CSMHI organized a July 4th celebration in Klooga, which was attended by officials from the U.S. Embassy and the Estonian Parliament and leaders of Russians and Russian-speakers in Tallinn. The gathering highlighted and validated Klooga as a functional community.

Due to the circumstances in Klooga, CSMHI expected less progress there than in the other two locations. In the end we found that we were wrong, and we were successful in Klooga beyond our imagination, especially due to Endel's and Olga's unending patience and commitment. Another positive and influential factor in Klooga's successful establishment of an integrated community was the making of a documentary film on the community project. Allan King, a Canadian filmmaker with numerous awards to his credit, had become interested in CSMHI's work in the Baltic Republics and had attended one of the psychopolitical dialogues in 1994. In the summer of 1997, after several years of research, development, and fundraising for the film (which cost approximately $500,000), the filmmaker traveled to Estonia and spent seven weeks filming in Klooga. King's presence had a significant impact on the Klooga community. The unique experience of being closely observed for nearly two months let the community know that they were important and that what they were attempting to do created a model worthy of following elsewhere. Allan King's film, *The Dragon's Egg: Making Peace on the Wreckage of the Twentieth Century*, carried a constructive message about the community-building process in Klooga as a big branch of the Tree Model. I recommend that those who are involved in psychopolitical work and especially in community-building and coexistence projects view this film.[11]

During our entire work in Estonia from 1994 to 1999, we avoided media attention. This was primarily because of my psychoanalytic identity and the confidentiality that went with it. In a sense, we kept our work in Estonia private. It was important not to contaminate it with public fantasies, sensationalism, and other interferences. I think that if we were to try the project today, due to the availability of an incredible electronic communication frenzy (a new civilization), we might not be able to protect the privacy of our work in Estonia.

In April 1999 Endel Talvik, Paul Lettens, Peeter Vares, Ly Krikk, and a Russian faction parliamentarian in Estonia and one of our psychopolitical dialogues members, Sergei Ivanov, came to Charlottesville. We had a public meeting and together we summarized our work in Estonia. Then, formally, the CSMHI work in Estonia came to an end.

I learned from Endel that people from Loksa, a shipbuilding town during Soviet times, which the year before had the dubious distinction of being named "the Most Unhappy Town in Estonia," and others from Narva-Jöesuu, approximately fifteen kilometers from Narva, had been in touch with him and wanted us to start community projects in their locations. On May 1, 1999, I wrote to Melissa Wells, the U.S. ambassador in Tallinn about this and asked if there might be some funds to establish projects in Loksa and Narva-Jöesuu. No funds could be found.

I did not go back to Estonia until 2003 to take part in a gathering in Haapsalu of the Han Groen-Prakken Psychoanalytic Institute for Eastern Europe. Endel Talvik was there too. Our psychopolitical dialogues participant Arnold Rüütel at that time was the President of Estonia. Before leaving I spent a day in Tallinn, then already a beautifully renovated city. Recalling my 2003 stay there, I later wrote how I amused myself remembering how many Estonian friends used to tell the CSMHI team that they would put our statues in the old city of Tallinn because of how much we had invested in their country. I added:

> There I was, some years later, walking alone in the old city of Tallinn. . . . suddenly, my psychoanalytic identity took over. I sensed that I was experiencing a feeling that used to come over me at the end of my analysands' analyses. . . . Through various unconscious identifications with me, [my former analysands] would carry me

> within themselves for the rest of their lives without being aware of doing so. They would not be in physical contact with me any longer or even call me, as should be the case. This realization made me feel good. Somehow, I thought, I existed somewhere in this beautiful country just as I exist in my former analysands, and somehow Estonia would exist in me for the rest of my life.[12]

I went back to Tallinn in the winter of 2011, again to attend a meeting of the Han Groen-Prakken Psychoanalytic Institute for Eastern Europe. Endel, now a fully trained psychoanalyst and a member of the International Psychoanalytic Association, was at the airport waiting for me. Now he had a white beard, as do I. Time passes. Since he was one of the organizers of the Institute's meeting, even though we met every day for about a week, we were not able to have long private conversations. It was freezing outside and I decided not to leave the small hotel, which was also the meeting location just at the outskirts of Tallinn, to look for some of my old friends, so I asked Endel if he could get in touch with them. He was able to reach Paul Lettens. One night Paul, who had become an important figure in the Estonian Foreign Ministry and an ambassador, stopped by the hotel on his way home after returning from a foreign trip. We sat in the dark basement drinking beer. We ended up talking about his son who would attend a university next year. Maybe he would go to Cambridge or Oxford in England, and so on. Old preoccupations in Estonia I knew were absent. Perhaps my narcissism led me to ask for verification for CSMHI's and my long years in his country. Referring to the old days, I wondered if what we had done in Estonia was useful. He looked at me as if I was asking a stupid question. He briefly answered me: "Of course!"

# PART VI

## THE PSYCHOLOGY OF TRAUMA, DICTATORS, THE DISPLACED, AND THE DISPOSSESSED

# 23

# TORTURERS AND THE TORTURED IN ROMANIA AND ALBANIA

## SOCIETAL SPLITS

In this section of the book I will relate my observations on the *immediate* effects of massive traumas related to large-group identity and how they initiate changes in societies during the years and initial decades following the traumas. I will also illustrate signs of disorganization in, as well as progression toward, the well-being of large groups.

Societal disorganization can be seen as parallel to individual regression and it is acceptable in my view to use the term "large-group regression" interchangeably with "large-group disorganization." This issue needs some explanation. Individuals are capable of individuating adaptively and moving up to levels where they utilize more sophisticated psychological capabilities that keep their less-sophisticated ones in the shadows and harmless. In individual regression we say that a "normal" person, due to an external trauma or an internal one such as an anxiety-creating nightmare, psychologically goes back and utilizes more "primitive" mental mechanisms like projection, introjection, fragmentation, splitting, disassociation, and denial to deal with the external world.

On the other hand, large groups, especially while dealing with large-group identity issues, even in "normal" times extensively utilize primitive mechanisms and are always ready to hold on to prejudicial conceptions about other large groups and "swallow" propaganda about their own superiority. In other words, when a large group "goes back," its regression starts from an already regressed position. Politics and diplomacy are in the service of stabilizing "normal" large-group regression. For this reason, I am searching for a better word to describe societal regression. I will use "societal disorganization" and "societal regression" interchangeably, although perhaps we should use Earl Hopper's term "societal incohesion."[1] More important than finding the proper term, however, is understanding the concept of societal disorganization itself.

I will start by recalling my observations on societal traumas that occurred internally within the *same* national large group and inflamed the question, "Who are we now?" as severe societal split or fragmentation occurred in the affected society.

Before our work in the Baltic Republics began and after curtailing our visits to Estonia, CSMHI members were involved in other psychopolitical programs in other parts of the world.[2] I observed societal processes after two dictators, Nicolae Ceauşescu and Enver Hoxha, were gone from Romania and from Albania, respectively. I accompanied Joe Montville in 1993 and 1994 to Romania and joined Joyce Neu and Norman Itzkowitz in Albania in 1998. In these two countries terror had come from above, from the leadership. People belonging to the same large-group identity were divided into "oppressors/torturers" and "oppressed/tortured."

I described what I saw in Romania in my book *Bloodlines: From Ethnic Pride to Ethnic Terrorism* and what I observed in Albania in *Blind Trust: Large Groups and Their Leaders in Times of Crisis and Terror*.[3] Here, rather than give detailed histories of Romania and Albania or repeat my recollections of individuals who told me their stories,[4] I will report on what happened in these countries under their respective dictators and soon after these dictators were gone. Examining these societies gives us glimpses of some current events in the news as I write this book, such as events in Tunisia, Egypt, and Libya after oppressive leaders were toppled and in Syria where a "dictator" is still in power.

Ceauşescu was a proverbial dreaded father figure. He ruled Communist Romania with an iron hand from 1965 until a quick bloody revolution ousted his government in December 1989. His titles included: Head of State, Chief of the Communist Party, Commander in Chief of the Army, Chairman of the Economic Council, and the architect of a "new" Romania. In the 1980s he announced a plan to raze eight thousand of Romania's thirteen thousand rural communities in order to build a better Romania. He clearly targeted the Hungarian settlements in Romania in order to get rid of this particular population. He became paranoid as he got older, hiring tasters to make sure his food was not poisoned. Even the children who were selected to present flowers to him on public occasions were first sent to hospitals to be certified free of infection before they were permitted to proffer their cheeks for his kiss.[5] During the revolution Ceauşescu and his wife, Elena, were captured, and after a very brief "trial" were executed by firing squad on Christmas Day 1989. Following this, Romania started to experiment with democracy. My observations of Romania took place four and five years after the killing of the dictator and his wife.

From 1944 until his death in 1985, Enver Hoxha ruled Albania. He had been one of the country's partisan leaders who liberated Albania from Axis hands only to deliver it to what became a complete Stalinist-type dictatorship, despite a short flirtation with the Chinese Communists from the late 1960s to the late 1970s. Albania became preoccupied with physical borders and evolved into a society isolated from the rest of the world and, as time went on, became increasingly "paranoid."

Enver Hoxha had transformed Albania from a semifeudal remnant of the Ottoman Empire—it remained under Ottoman rule from the fifteenth century until 1912—into an industrialized economy. But improvement in economy does not always make for the well-being of a society, just as being a millionaire does not guarantee the physical and mental health of an individual. In truth, Enver Hoxha's society was a "sick" society.

Albanians were a relatively homogenous ethnic large group in spite of religious divisions and two major subgroups: the Gegs and the Tosks. But during Enver Hoxha's long reign, societal "basic trust" disappeared. The term "basic trust," first described by Erik Erikson,[6] is a concept that describes how children learn to feel comfortable putting their own safety in a caretaker's hands; by developing basic trust, children discover, in turn, how to trust themselves. If a child cannot trust his mother and father, then he will have difficulty trusting himself. In a healthy society, adults also depend on trusting themselves and others to remain functioning citizens. Albania became divided into those who were followers of the leader and those who had a "black spot" on their family. If someone was perceived to be against Enver Hoxha and his brand of communism, even if they had merely complained about not finding freshly baked bread in the bakery or were caught playing backgammon, which was considered an Ottoman pastime, this person could risk acquiring a "black spot" of ostracism, and even face prison, torture, or even death.

There appeared a rigorous division of loyalty and disloyalty and goodness and badness. People who were considered "bad" by the regime would often endure torture or exile to certain areas of the country. A person could try to remain "good," but a relative who became "bad" could ruin the entire family. For example, young people who had someone in their family with a black spot would be unable to obtain a university education. Divorce was a frequent method used to purge a family of its black mark, which led to a society rife with broken homes. Even if families did not have a black mark against them, they tried to avoid allowing their children to marry into families that did have black marks.

Due to many historical, political, and cultural circumstances and external interferences, each large group that lives under an oppressive regime for decades reacts differently when that regime disappears. I went to Albania for the first time thirteen years after the dictator's death, and my observations there and in Romania suggest that there are also similar psychological reactions to getting rid of a dictator. People, especially the previously oppressed ones, appear jubilant and group cohesion evolves among them. Yet, seemingly illogical reactions—such as sharing unconscious guilt for removing or killing a long-time transference figure—a "bad/strong/dreaded" father figure—may also appear, something not usually mentioned by popular media.

In Romania when I met and interviewed many former dissenters, most of whom were persecuted or tortured—their finger nails were removed or they were subjected to waterboarding—I was unexpectedly struck by their depressive mood. My logical mind told me that they should be happy, but they were not. Some of them behaved like robots. I could understand their emotional reaction to the disappearance of Ceauşescu only by assuming that they felt guilty for wishing the dictator's death or, psychologically speaking, for "killing" the dictator. Some of their statements supported my assumption. Shooting Ceauşescu and his wife on the sacred day of Jesus Christ's birth also created psychological problems and led to Romanians' unconscious fantasies that the dictator had been "reincarnated."[7]

In Albania, Enver Hoxha was buried at a special location after his death from natural causes. A big statue was erected on his tomb. When Albanian "democracy" evolved and communism was left behind, the body of Enver Hoxha was taken to a regular cemetery at the outskirts of the capital city Tirana where there were hundreds and hundreds of graves. Enver Hoxha's new grave was given a simple ordinary tombstone like the others around it. However, when I visited this cemetery in 1998, I could identify Enver Hoxha's grave from a distance, because only on his grave was there a huge pile of flowers, many of them plastic so they would last. It was clear that thirteen years after the death of such a horrible dictator, many Albanians still related to his mental image and wanted to honor him or, better, "obey" him, since it is difficult for many individuals to give up behavior patterns they have been accustomed to for decades. In 2000 I went back to Albania, this time alone as a temporary consultant to the World Health Organization, but I have not been to Albania since then and I do not know if the pile of flowers still exists on the dictators' grave. I doubt that this is the case anymore since almost three decades have past since the dictator's death and during this period people who had lived under his regime have become exposed to images of new leaders, repressing the internal relationship to the mental double of Enver Hodxa. I cannot think of any drastic event in Albania during the last years that would reactivate the dictator's image within the society.

In oppressive regimes people "obey" the leader and those who function as the leader's extensions in order to feel secure and avoid punishment by the authorities for disobeying the regime's "rules," often developing behavior patterns that are initiated by fear. In Albania, for example, parents would not say a word against the dictator or his regime in front of their small children. They knew that Enver Hoxha's secret agents visited schools regularly and questioned the children about their parents. If these agents heard that a parent had complained about Enver Hoxha or his regime in the privacy of his or her home, the adult most likely would be punished severely by torture or exile to a remote area. The children, of course, would sense their parents' anxieties and worries. Without being aware of it, for decades—since most oppressive leaders remain in power for decades—people internalize what Michael Šebek called "totalitarian objects,"[8] or what we can call "oppressive objects," and blindly follow their leader by giving up many aspects of their individuality.[9] When at last a revolution takes place, adjustment to a "democratic environment" will usually be complicated. This is not only due to new external realities such as competition for power by those who want to be the new leader, splits among followers of candidates for new leadership, or economic difficulties and interferences from other countries, but also to unconscious struggles with internalized "totalitarian/oppressive objects."

My observations in Romania and Albania support the idea that sometimes after a revolution the people will wish to return to the historical/religious customs of a time just prior to the oppressive regime or even further back. This may create problems between the younger generation and those who would be the new political leaders in that country. In order to remove the effects of oppression by moving up to a societal level—such as a true democratic and secular level—with which they are not familiar, people find it easier to recreate customs of their elders or ancestors. They also may have a tendency to externalize "totalitarian objects" on an "enemy" outside of their legal borders and continue to struggle with this enemy, especially if the new leadership manipulates them to do so.

After a revolution topples an oppressive regime, the personality of a new political leader will play a crucial role in maintaining stable relationships both with those who are in the leader's immediate entourage and with the much larger group of people who comprise his or her followers. The leader-follower relationship is a two-way street: it is influenced and determined by the leader's personality and from the followers' shared conscious and unconscious wishes and needs. If the new leader is "reparative" and "transformative" the large group may modify its large-group identity in a way that increases its shared self-esteem. [10]

Reparative leaders have an increased narcissistic investment in their own selves, are very intelligent, feel entitled to be "number one," and are comfortable in this role. It is important for them to be loved and admired by their followers. If they devote their lives to improving mental and physical conditions of their followers in order to be admired and loved by people on a "higher" level of human existence without choosing a large group or a subgroup to devalue or destroy, they are truly reparative. I believe that my description of a reparative leader finds an echo in political science professor James MacGregor Burns' idea of a "transforming" leader. Burns identified two types of leaders: "transactional" and "transforming."[11] The transactional leader depends on—and in fact thrives upon—bargaining, manipulating, accommodating, and compromising within a given system. He or she acts according to political polls and national "climate" and follows existing societal sentiments, becoming a spokesperson for them. On the other hand, a transforming leader "responds to fundamental human needs and wants, hopes and expectations" and may "transcend and even seek to reconstruct the political system, rather than simply operating within it."[12]

In a stable democracy that is not experiencing economic, military, and political stress, the personality of a transactional leader typically is not of critical importance, and even a transforming leader will not cause fundamental changes in society or initiate drastically different policies. The formal and informal systems of "checks and balances" in a well-functioning democracy prevent a leader's habitual ways of behaving and feeling from exerting undue influence over government and the governed. Even when many followers are excited about a transforming leader's personality, behavior, and agenda, and identify with them, changes that may result typically are not drastic. Or, when they do take place, the population in a sense shares the responsibility, making them happen. People do not think about a leader's personality organization alone as causing major changes.

However, under certain circumstances, such as after a revolution or ousting of a dictator or after establishing a large group's independence, the personality of a political leader can clearly influence outcomes or policies, and at times even be a major factor in creating new and drastic societal and political processes. If adjustment to a drastic change in a country and modification of the large-group identity take a long time, some reparative leaders too may stay in power for decades, but unlike tyrants they do not create destructive processes.

If the new leader's manipulations of the society are "bad," two types of splitting will develop. First, a splitting between "us" and "them" (an enemy outside postrevolution society) may become pronounced and the Other may become a target for further dehumanization. Second, after the initial rallying around the "new" leader following a massive trauma, a severe split (or fragmentation) may occur within the society itself, such as between tribal or ideological subgroups—if the new leader cannot induce and maintain the shared feeling of "basic trust"within the large group.[13] The shared "basic trust" will be lost, especially when the new leader cannot differentiate between where real danger ends and where the fantasized dangers begin. Without this differentiation the large group cannot maintain hope and cannot tame shared aggression.

In the next chapter, I will turn again to Albania. Referring to certain events in that country, I will illustrate how the lingering influence of a deep split within the same large group interfered with attempts to improve the societal well-being there thirteen years after an oppressive regime had disappeared.

# 24

# LOOSE SCREWS THAT HINDER SOCIETAL WELL-BEING

## THE RETURN OF HISTORICAL MEMORY

It is difficult to assess and measure the health of a society, since its well-being involves a very long list of external factors, some of them closely intertwined with shared psychological motivations that caused societal disturbances in the first place. Some of these factors may include bad economics, unfair trade, mismanagement of human rights, criminal activities, increased abuse of women and children, absence of humane approaches for taking care of mentally disturbed or physically disabled individuals, lack of education, destructive religious or political ideologies, natural calamities, endemic diseases, pollution, man-made accidental disasters, assassinations of political leaders, dictatorships, the collapse of political or ideological "empires," terrorism, wars, and war-like conditions.

Another reason it is difficult to define and assess the well-being of a society is that very often no single professional discipline can fully understand and evaluate factors that cause unhealthy social circumstances. An interdisciplinary approach is then required to investigate the causes of problems and subsequent remedies that enable social progress. Building interdisciplinary teams takes time and often cannot be achieved, mainly because of competition between disciplines. Accordingly, and more often than we would like, understanding key aspects of what causes disturbances, and achieving progress informed by this understanding, remain illusive.

It is generally thought that global transformations take place within three major dimensions: economic, political, and social. Such transformations not only affect the adult populations but also children and youth, the future generations.[1] When there are crises in these transformations, we usually look to a number of "hard" macrolevel factors to explain the causes of social problems. For example, in an economic crisis what comes to mind first are visible factors such as austere budget cuts, high interest rates, and strict monetarist policies.

In the book *Poverty and Psychology*, Stuart Carr, Tod Sloan, and their colleagues remind us that there are "softer" microlevel processes hidden behind the "harder" macrolevel considerations, including psychological ones.[2] They state that soft microlevel factors have been increasingly recognized by economists since the days of Scottish social philosopher and economist Adam Smith (1723–1790). They focus on the importance of communicating human perceptions and motivations, both within and between community and organizational groups affected by economic crises. Such communications will improve efforts to combat downward spirals into poverty. Despite the optimism implied in this book, too often macrolevel factors of a society's problems overshadow the microlevel factors, and the latter are overlooked. This happens despite the reality that sometimes microlevel factors must be taken into consideration if there is to be a reversal of conditions within the society. By analogy, this is like a big machine that requires tiny screws to be in their proper places for it to function well, or even to function at all.

Albania in the 1990s provides a good example of this concept. A few years after Enver Hoxha's death, communist rule in Eastern Europe collapsed and the effects of this were felt deeply there. With the collapse of the state, the banking system—what little of it there was—collapsed too and was replaced by private banking that developed into pyramid schemes. Albania's first free elections since the 1920s took place in 1989, and by 1996 a large number of Albanians thought that they were rolling in new wealth. During that year 85,000 Mercedes cars were registered in Albania. But this wealth was imaginary, balanced upon pyramid schemes that grew into murky empires.

Pyramid schemes are not an Albanian invention. In England there was the famous South Sea Bubble of the first quarter of the eighteenth century, and in the United States we still call them Ponzi schemes after Charles Carlo Ponzi, an Italian immigrant who arrived in the United States penniless in 1903. In 1919 and 1920 he defrauded untold numbers of people of millions of dollars by means of a scheme based on postal reply coupons. Ponzi died in 1949.

The Albanian pyramid scheme arose in the absence of any real banking system once the country emerged from Enver Hoxha's isolationism, and money poured in from overseas Albanians wanting to help relatives back home. Those who received this money had little or no investment opportunities and few safe places to put their money. Starting around 1994 and culminating at its disastrous height in mid-1997, there were around twenty pyramid schemes in operation. They offered enormous rates of interest on deposits, starting at first at about 4 percent a month for each three-month period. But then, when competition increased as the real pyramid schemes entered the picture in 1996, interest rates ran as high as 49 percent a month. Some of those banks maintained they were investing in companies and real estate abroad, but that was largely fraudulent. Paying Peter from funds invested that day by Paul was bound to collapse, a process that started late in 1996. By mid-1997 as the schemes collapsed, investors began to find themselves defrauded of their lifesavings. The city of Vlore in southern Albania was the center of ensuing street demonstrations that escalated into armed conflict as armories and police stations were plundered for their weapons. Unofficially, some two thousand people were said to have been killed.

Some tranquility was restored with the assistance of international peacekeeping forces, and many Albanians illegally entered Italy and Greece. The tumbling down of the pyramid schemes swallowed an estimated $1.2 billion in savings. A good deal of this money found its way into the pockets of politicians and into the political system to fund the many elections that were held during the time of the schemes and their demise. This amount was about half of Albania's gross domestic product. The economic disaster touched "everything from Liberian shipping companies and German salami plants, to New York bank accounts."[3]

Auditors from PricewaterhouseCoopers and Deloitte & Touche from the United States, as well as other experts in economics from the World Bank, Italy, Greece, and Turkey, arrived in Albania to scrutinize "hard" macrolevel factors in an effort to unravel the pyramid finances. Their success was very limited. It was said that some powerful and influential Albanians, who were themselves connected with the missing money, stonewalled and interfered with the investigation. The failure of the pyramid system ushered in new social disorganization.

In the second half of 1997, alongside the international auditors and experts in economics, and even before some of them entered the scene, the Carter Center, at the initiation of former President Jimmy Carter, wanted to help the social disorganization in Albania, mainly through a political/social approach to correct macrolevel economic factors. It proposed to assist Albania in the development of a National Development Strategy (NDS) through a broad "participation" process. The Carter Center was following the World Bank's definition of the term "participation": "Participation is a process through which stakeholders influence and share control over development initiatives and the decisions and resources which affect them."[4] The World Bank was outlining methods for stakeholders' consultation and various outreach techniques to garner public input. A few years earlier, the Carter Center's National Development Strategy in Guyana had been a success story. Thus, it expected similar success in Albania when a former diplomat, Tom Forbord, who had worked on the Guyana project, went to Albania as the Carter Center's representative.

Armed with well-prepared plans, Forbord identified influential Albanians, chose participants for meetings to design economic strategies, and, once these strategies developed, obtained feedback from the Albanian government and opposition to help revise and improve the plans. But Forbord, who rented a house in Tirana and stayed in Albania many months, immediately noticed that something was seriously wrong. Even with the prestige of a former U.S. president behind him and access to the Albanian government and opposition officials at the highest levels, it was difficult for the diplomat to gather a group of influential Albanians willing to participate in serious discussions on the economy or future prospects regarding the country's social disorganization.

This led, in February 1998, to another collaboration between CSMHI and the Carter Center. Joyce Neu, then the assistant director of the Carter Center's Conflict Resolution Program, Norman Itzkowitz, one of the leading authorities on Ottoman history, and I from the CSMHI (I was also at the times a member of the Carter Center's International Negotiation Center) arrived in Tirana to see what had gone wrong.[5] We learned that the enduring psychological effect of societal trauma on the Albanian society, which happened under Enver Hoxha's regime, was a major factor in the Albanians' difficulty in utilizing the Carter Center's attempt to develop a strategy for economic recovery and Albania's well-being. The so-called "soft" psychological issues were like little screws that needed to be inserted in their proper places before the big Albanian machine worked. Our findings were primarily based on many psychoanalytically informed interviews we conducted with Albanians from different backgrounds.

When "democracy" came to Albania, the psychological effects of the decades-long societal split did not disappear. If a mother had a son in high school, she might wonder if the headmaster was the son of a person who had tortured her father. "Basic trust," which had fled the country under Enver Hoxha, had not returned to Albania. We noted in 1998 that it was extremely difficult to get twenty to thirty people there to sit down to discuss the future without splits such as torturers and tortured or despoilers and despoiled manifesting themselves. We concluded that this was the obstacle Tom Forbord had faced in his efforts to be helpful in Albania. The Carter Center's generously funded logical and intellectual approaches to consider a program for economic recovery could not be initiated without first recognizing and doing something about the "soft" psychological factors infecting the society.

The severe societal split between "good" and "bad" families was also reflected in severe splits in other large-group processes. For example, the Albanian main opposition party and the ruling party were so far apart that the opposition's elected members would not even attend the regular meetings of the Albanian Parliament. This alone was a factor in the country's inability to formulate a program for economic recovery.

In 1998 there were other manifestations of societal disorganization within Albania since the death of its paranoid dictator that were influencing the splitting in that country. Albania had become Europe's only avowedly atheistic nation in 1967 with the forced closing of the vast majority of its mosques and churches. In 1998 Albania's population was about three and a half million. The distribution of Albania's population by religion set the Muslims at 70 percent, the Greek Orthodox at 20 percent, and the Catholics at 10 percent, but during a massive trauma the Albanian people could not openly utilize religion for a hopeful future.

While I was working in the Soviet Union I noticed that as the Communist system was dying the peoples' rush to religion was palpable. After atheistic and paranoid Enver Hoxha was gone, Albanians returned to religion as well, but they also increased efforts to find other "magical" solutions to their problems, and we can surmise that the evolution of the pyramid schemes was part of this impulse. For Albanian society, putting together a religious structure after emerging from atheism proved to be a rather tall order for the religious groups. Even though, on the surface, there were no observable conflicts among Muslims, Orthodox Christians, and Catholics, we sensed that the increased competition among them also worked against Tom Forbord's attempt to bring twenty to thirty Albanian economic experts together.

In 1998 it was difficult to find an Albanian imam, an Albanian Orthodox bishop, or an Albanian Catholic bishop. For the Orthodox, they did not even know to whom they belonged as a group. After much research they determined that they fell under the jurisdiction of the Patriarchate of Constantinople (Istanbul), and the Patriarch sent them a Greek bishop, which did not please them very much. The Catholics were assigned the priest who had headed the large Albanian Catholic Church near Haverstraw, New York, off Route 287, a man of enormous fundraising ability.

Norman and I arranged to meet with each of the three religious leaders who were housed in the capital Tirana. We met first with the imam, then the Greek Orthodox stand-in since the bishop was out of town—the stand-in turned out to be an American from California—and finally the transplant from Haverstraw. The imam had his office in one of the few old remaining Ottoman buildings in Tirana, the first two floors of which were being used as a medical clinic. The Greek bishop was housed in a beautifully rehabilitated structure, and the Catholic bishop met us in his brand new residence-office building just off the main street of downtown Tirana. We asked each of these gentlemen what they and their staff would do in Albania. We received about the same answer from each of the three: we will go back to "*our* villages" and rehabilitate our mosque or church, our school, and construct an infirmary.

The return to historical memory was encapsulated in the concept of "our villages" uttered by the three religious dignitaries. "Our village" is a reference to the Ottoman Empire's institution of the *millet* system in which large-group identity was based on religious affiliation. The Jews of the empire were in the Jewish *millet*, the Greek Orthodox in the Rum *millet*, while the Muslims were the *ummah*, the people of Muhammad. Essentially, in Albania in Ottoman times—that is from the early fifteenth century to 1912—villages were predominantly composed of people of one religion, while the Jews were largely urban people centered in such Ottoman places as Istanbul, Salonika, and Izmir. In post–Enver Hoxha Albania, religious identity as it had been in Ottoman times was again in the forefront of social structure. Once more, I witnessed that societal disorganization, which can be seen as parallel to a condition in an individual called regression, elicits historical "memory."

In regressed Albania, it was not surprising that one of the institutions that Enver Hoxha seriously tried to suppress—the blood feud that existed during Ottoman times—surfaced again. This was also partly due to the demand for revenge for those killed during the fighting related to the collapse of the pyramid schemes. It was almost impossible to assess how much of it was related to this or to land issues engendered by collectivization under communism or to the military actions in neighboring Kosovo, where many Albanians live, that was taking place at the time of our visit.

We were lucky to find an Albanian organization, a kind of "think tank," that was cochaired by two intellectuals; one came from a family who had been loyal to Enver Hoxha and the other came from a family with a "black spot." Both of them were aware of the severe psychological division in their country, and they had formed their organization to study and do something about it. We began making plans to bring a group of influential Albanians, especially those knowledgeable in economics, to this "think tank" and *first* help them remove the effects of the social splitting and develop "basic trust." Then we would support them in their efforts to make an economic recovery plan for Albania. We also met with the then leader of the opposition, Sali Berisha, a cardiologist who was a former president of Albania (1992–1997). As I write this chapter, Berisha has been the prime minister of Albania since 2005. Interestingly, when we met him in 1998, we found him receptive to our ideas; he himself was aware that the severe social division that psychologically remained from the days of Enver Hoxha was paralyzing Albania. In fact, after Berisha and his people talked with us, he ordered his party deputies to resume attending Parliament. However, this was short-lived.

We were not able to implement our plans to start a psychologically informed economic recovery process in Albania due to events that took place in the former Yugoslavia. Ethnic Albanians in Kosovo began to suffer Serbian attacks; the NATO bombing of Serbia followed. In the summer of 1999, some 450,000 Kosovar Albanians sought shelter in Albania. When these refugees flooded Albania's disused factories, sports stadium, and city parks, it looked like the chaos would reach its peak. This tragedy, however, in a peculiar and unexpected way, had a significant impact on both the economy and the psychology of Albania.

When I revisited Albania by myself at the end of 2000 as a temporary consultant for the World Health Organization, I learned that taking in the refugees during the upheaval in Kosovo had improved the economy (officially by 8 percent), as various officials from foreign countries, journalists, and others poured in from abroad, stimulating the Albanian private and governmental security industries. Interestingly, I observed that having an external enemy in the Serbs began to heal splits within Albania and appeared to remove the malignant large-group psychology that interfered with work on macrolevel social, economic, and political issues. As noted, I have not visited Albania since 2000 and thus I cannot offer any observation about its present "societal health."[6]

There are many causes for a society's entry into paralyzing chaos or well-being. Some of these causes are visible, while others require psychological assessments in order to be noticeable and definable. In Albania a tyrannical man and his extensions inflicted trauma on another group of people of their own kind. Elsewhere, man-made shared societal traumas that affect large-group identity issues occur due to other causes. In the next chapter I will share my observations of a country, Kuwait, after it became free following occupation by another country.

# 25

# THE INVASION OF KUWAIT

## TRAUMA AND CULTURAL CUSTOMS

Kuwait is an oil rich country smaller than the state of New Jersey that borders the Persian Gulf between Iraq and Saudi Arabia. It has a population of about three million, 80 percent of whom live in Kuwait City. Kuwait is a society of immigrants. In the eighteenth century three families in search of a better life migrated to this location from the north central Arabian Peninsula. Over the centuries these first "Kuwaitis" were joined by other immigrants of both Arab and Persian origin; together they created the Kuwaiti "ethnic" identity. Many others subsequently came to Kuwait to work and settled there, but were considered non-Kuwaitis. In order to be eligible for Kuwaiti citizenship one has to be able to trace his or her ancestry in Kuwait back to the eighteenth century and the original Kuwaiti immigrants. There are about one million such Kuwaiti citizens—many fewer, in fact, than non-Kuwaiti persons in their own country. The non-Kuwaitis are divided into two categories: those with residency permits and those who are called *Bedoons*, stateless individuals without residency permits.

Kuwait's government is a parliamentary constitutional monarchy. Since 1759, the Kuwaitis have been ruled by the Sabahs, one of the three founding families. Starting in 1899, when Ottoman influence in the region disappeared, the British "protected" the Kuwaitis, running their foreign relations and national defense. In 1961, Kuwait gained independence from Great Britain, and in 1963 Iraq officially recognized Kuwait as an independent nation. Before the discovery of oil, the Kuwaitis lived, socially, economically, and politically, by their wits. After oil exportation began in 1946, the wealth it brought benefited not only the Sabah family, but also Kuwaiti citizens in general. During the Iran-Iraq War (September 1980–August 1988), Kuwaitis supported Iraq and many developed very positive feelings toward Saddam Hussein, then the Iraqi leader. Because of this, Kuwaiti oil tankers came under frequent attack by Iranian forces. After July 1987, therefore, U.S. Navy warships began escorting Kuwaiti tankers in the Persian Gulf. During the Iran-Iraq War, the United States also supported Saddam Hussein because it was believed that he could protect the eastern flank of the Arab world from Iran's Ayatollah Khomeini and his type of Muslim fundamentalism and anti-Western attitudes. Some Muslim fundamentalists, however, considered Saddam Hussein a Marxist who impiously attacked the Islamic Ayatollah. But slowly Saddam Hussein's image changed, even for many fundamentalists. For many Arabs, including Kuwaitis, Saddam Hussein was a role model.

The night of August 1, 1990, the people in Kuwait went to sleep feeling secure. The next morning they awoke surprised and terrified to discover that more than 100,000 well-armed Iraqi troops, backed by 700 tanks, had invaded Kuwait. On August 2 Iraqi jets dropped bombs on Kuwait City and Iraqi Special Forces landed at the Kuwaiti Defense Ministry. The news media reported that on this day at least 200 people were killed. On August 28 Iraq annexed Kuwait as its 19th province.

Kuwait's Amir, Al-Ahmad Al-Jaber Al-Sabah, and other Kuwaiti leaders managed to escape to Saudi Arabia as the Iraqi invasion started, establishing a government in exile. The rest is history. Saddam Hussein declared that he would turn Kuwait into a "graveyard" if other nations interfered. But there was international condemnation of this invasion and annexation. In the United States, on our television screens, we watched the verbal confrontations between President George H. W. Bush and Saddam Hussein intensify. The United Nations authorized a coalition force of thirty-four nations led by the United States to liberate Kuwait, and this led to "Operation Desert Storm" (the First Gulf War). We witnessed the amazing technology of modern war machines and saw emotionless and sterilized versions of death and destruction that resembled a video game more than the brutal combat that we associate with earlier wars. For the second time in history, Baghdad was destroyed (it was first destroyed in 1258 by the Mongols).

During the occupation, shops, museums, hospitals, the zoo, and some private homes were looted in Kuwait City. Beaches were lined with trenches, mines, and other obstacles designed to prevent invasion from the U.S.-led coalition forces. And, in their withdrawal from Kuwait, the Iraqis set Kuwait's oil fields ablaze, causing an inferno that left skies choked with smoke and soot. The highway leading from Kuwait City to Basra in southern Iraq, with its graveyard of smashed and abandoned military vehicles, would be renamed "Death Highway." After seven months of brutal occupation by Iraqi forces, in late February 1991, the liberation of Kuwait was complete within forty-two days, and by mid-March the Amir had returned. It is estimated that during the occupation 300,000 Kuwaitis had fled the country and 1,000 civilians had been killed.[1]

When the invasion came, thousands of foreign nationals, including the U.S.

ambassador, W. Nathaniel Howell, were trapped in Kuwait City. His wife Margie was the head nurse of the psychiatric in-patient units at the University of Virginia Hospital when I was the medical chief of these units in the late 1960s through the 1970s. About a week before the invasion, Margie had left Kuwait and returned to Charlottesville expecting her husband to join her soon. For seven months Margie was very concerned about her husband and the other Americans at the embassy. After Nat returned to the United States, we were honored to have him as CSMHI's Ambassador-in-Residence. We would benefit from his extensive knowledge in diplomatic affairs, and Margie Howell would become a new, and dedicated, CSMHI Advisory Board member.

In 1993 and 1994, as Ambassador-in-Residence at CSMHI, Nat Howell would be in charge of our Kuwait project after we received an invitation from the Social Development Office of the Amiri Diwan (State of Kuwait) to identify harmful sociopsychological effects of the Iraqi invasion. Noting that it would be impossible for Kuwaitis to resume their precrisis identity as if nothing had happened, the Amir established the Social Development Office to help traumatized individuals, not only to meet their needs but also to promote societal well-being. In 1993 Nat Howell wrote: "Iraq's attack, and its subsequent defiance of the will of the international community, inflicted upon Kuwait a serious trauma. The tragic suffering of both those who endured the occupation and those who were displaced from their homes; the sense of betrayal, loss and victimization felt by the entire society; and the feelings of vulnerability, rage and grief: all have become part of the collective psyche. The issue and challenge is not whether this residue exists, but how Kuwait deals with and works through this trauma."[2] He added that an attempt to help Kuwait was of particular importance to him because of the unique opportunity he had while ambassador there to make many good friends among the Kuwaiti people and gain appreciation of the society and its historic experience. Other principle figures in this project were CSMHI board member Margie Howell, and faculty members Andy Thomson and Gregory Saathoff.[3] Greg, like Andy, is a psychiatrist. At the present time Greg heads the Critical Incident Analysis Group at the University of Virginia. During two field trips to Kuwait in December 1993 and January 1994, Andy and Greg interviewed more than 150 Kuwaiti adults and children individually and carried out other tasks such as observing children in schools and listening to participants in *diwaniyas*, traditional gatherings of adult males. Our aim was to find shared themes in order to develop ideas about lingering societal responses to the invasion and subsequent liberation.

The *diwaniya* serves as both an important societal institution and a gathering place for social activities. Thirty to sixty men from the same neighborhood and their guests meet on selected evenings at halls or huge rooms connected to the home of a special person who is the host. They usually wear ankle-length robes with long sleeves called *dishdasha* and closefitting skullcaps called *gahfiah* and sit on soft low benches along the walls drinking coffee, eating snacks, smoking, and talking for hours, usually about the events that influence their district and country. "Socially, the *diwaniya* has performed, and continues to perform, an essential integrative function, encouraging an exchange of views, providing for forging consensus, and underpinning Kuwait's attachment to parliamentary practice."[4] This is a tradition from the Bedouin times when gatherings would take place in huge tents. The *diwaniya* was historically a male institution. Today a few parallel institutions for women exist.[5]

In the fall of 1993, before Andy and Greg's work in Kuwait, I accompanied Nat and Margie Howell for a week-long visit there. We flew Kuwaiti Airlines first-class as guests of the Kuwaiti government and were welcomed officially when we arrived in Kuwait. I could easily sense that Nat was perceived by our hosts as a special person, a hero, not only because he was the former U.S. ambassador to their country, but also because he had remained at the U.S. embassy during the Iraqi invasion, loved Kuwait, and was committed to do his best for that country. From my hotel window I could see the embassy where Nat had stayed when it was surrounded by Iraqi soldiers. I knew that while he and other Americans were stranded at the embassy, uncertainty about the duration of their plight dictated austerity. For example, they would not flush the toilets each time they used them in order to conserve water. I imagined an Iraqi soldier sitting in the room where I was staying, holding a gun while watching the embassy below. But now from this height the embassy looked like a peaceful place. When we went out and drove through the city, with its modern buildings and infrastructure, I could see little evidence of war damage. I saw only two houses that bore the marks of warfare—visible bullets holes, burnt windows, cracked walls. Within three years after the invasion the city had been quickly repaired, because, I thought, Kuwaitis had money to do so.

My first impression was that there might be denial of the trauma of invasion there. Quickly cleaning and repairing Kuwait City provided support for "forgetting" horrors that had occurred. Then I noticed the loss of some old trees that had lined both sides of several major streets in Kuwait City. Some may have been destroyed by fire, but most likely they died from neglect during the occupation. Kuwait, after all, is built on a desert. The dead trees had been replaced by new trees much smaller than the original ones planted years ago. Thus, there was a break in uniformity. The "flow" of trees was broken. This stuck in my mind as a symbol of trauma on many levels. In a psychological sense, I was reminded of an individual whose normal life is broken or ruptured by a trauma that is difficult to bridge. Now, I sensed that there would be a disjuncture in Kuwait's collective sense of self.

When, as part of an investigative model that Andy and Greg would follow, I interviewed some Kuwaiti citizens—from children, to government officials, to storeowners in the marketplace—and visited homes of Nat's and Margie's friends, I realized that the effects of the societal trauma was fully present in the citizens' minds. With Nat and Margie, I observed locations where "unofficial monuments" like disabled Iraqi tanks were displayed along the main road leading to Iraq. I also accompanied Nat when we observed Kuwaiti males interact in three *diwaniyas*. Although, unlike Nat, I do not know Arabic, in these three *diwaniyas* there were many Kuwaitis who had attended universities in England and the United States and who spoke perfect English. With their help I had no difficulty learning about customs in such gatherings and what was taking place in discussions.[6]

I was very impressed by the *diwaniyas* I attended. In my mind I compared them to group therapy sessions. Obviously *diwaniyas* are not designed to treat people; but certainly participants of *diwaniyas* were sharing ideas and emotions, looking for solutions for shared problems, making compromises, and forging consensus. I thought that *diwaniyas* would be, psychologically speaking, extremely useful for Kuwaitis' adjustment to postinvasion life. I came to a conclusion that they already had a custom for going over psychological wounds, sharing and comparing them, and thus opening up the societal mourning process. I was also present later, in 1994, when representatives of the Social Development Office of the Amiri Diwan visited CSMHI in Charlottesville to learn about our findings and discuss ideas to improve postinvasion Kuwaiti society's well-being.

Although my focus is on societal reactions to a massive trauma that became closely linked with large-group identity issues, I want to tell a couple of personal stories in some detail that reflect the horrors of war. These stories are not samples of data collected by psychoanalytically informed in-depth interviews such as those we conducted in other countries for assessing shared societal processes. In Kuwait, at the time the interviews were conducted, citizens' descriptions of trauma and crises would overwhelm them. Hearing such stories was necessary in order to imagine and formulate shared responses to this crisis. Such stories show how some Iraqis behaved inhumanely under the influence of their large-group psychology.

Sometimes people who would not hurt anyone in their routine lives become capable of torturing others whom they consider, or imagine, are "dangerous" when they wear the canvas of their large-group tent as if it were their main garment. This may be further manipulated by leaderships' propaganda and open or suggested permission to act in inhumane ways. Make no mistake: some Iraqis under Saddam Hussein's regime behaved in inhumane ways, but members of any ethnic, national, religious, or ideological group—even in well-functioning democratic countries—have done or are capable of doing similar things under the influence of shared psychology that provides them with a feeling, an illusion, that torturing people from the "enemy" large group protects their own large-group identity.[7] I am not, however, equating the degree of horrible acts carried out by tyrannical regimes and leadership with open or secret "permissions" from the authorities of truly democratic countries to torture only a selected few. Democratic countries question such policies and demand legal actions to address them.

Gregory Saathoff learned the story of a Kuwaiti man whom he called "M"[8] who was a torture survivor. I choose to report his story here since, according to Greg, he had become a *living statue*. I used the term "living statue" for the first time in reference to a Turkish Cypriot man whose wife, three sons (the youngest ten-years-old), seventy-two-year-old father-in-law, fifty-five-year-old mother-in-law, and twenty-two-year-old sister-in-law were killed by Cypriot Greeks, as were many other Cypriot Turks from the village of Maratha. He was away at the time and thus his life was saved. The Turks managed to remove eighty-eight bodies from mass graves before they had decomposed. Someone took a picture of this man as he watched the exhumation, and when the picture was published he became a living statue for the Cypriot Turks. I still vividly recall my interview with him. "My last glimpse of this man came as he rode away from me on his bicycle. He left me feeling that I must offer him an apology for what had been meted out to him by the human race to which I belong. But I felt that he was beyond hearing any apology; he was already a national monument rather than a man."[9]

M was picked up by the Iraqis at his home in Kuwait. Apparently some of his friends in the resistance had been captured earlier. M believed that one of them gave his name to the Iraqis while being tortured. M supported the resistance emotionally but had not taken any action against invading Iraqis. He was taken to Baghdad by some Iraqi officers and put into a holding cell at a Baghdad prison. Apparently when he was captured the Iraqis searched M's house very carefully and had much information about him. When they began his interrogation, he was surprised at how much they knew about him. For example, the Iraqis knew that M had visited Baghdad twice in 1981, visits he had in reality enjoyed. The interrogators also knew a great deal about his family.

M described three different rooms in the Bagdad prison where he was taken: the yellow room, the red room, and the black room. He stated:

> In the weeks to come, I was to learn the terrible secrets of these places. In the yellow room, there is light from a small yellow lamp, which gives the room a yellow glow. This is the best room to be in, although it is very bad. I would be taken there for periods of questioning, and then they would tell me personal things about myself, asking me questions about my family and friends. After they would stop questioning me, they would take me back to the holding cell, and tell me that they

> would come back the next day, but sometimes they would wait three, maybe four days, I could not tell.
>
> In the holding cell, there was no way to tell night from day. The time went forever. There was only the smallest hole in the top of the ceiling, and from there I could see the sky when the hole was not covered. It was covered most of the time, so I was usually in the dark. For questioning, they would pull me out of the room in a way that caused the greatest pain. I was physically tortured in terrible ways, and they would call me filthy names.[10]

Finally M would not give his interrogators any more information about his friends. He told the torturers that if they wanted to kill him, they should go ahead. Thereupon, a new type of torture began. They told M that they had brought his wife and children to the same Baghdad prison. After staying in the holding cell without any light for quite a period, M heard the voices of his wife and children in the next room and he was told that if he did not talk they would be harmed.

M continued:

> I now know that they were using video-taped family films stolen from my home during the occupation. It made me very upset, and I began to cry, thinking that my family would be harmed. I did hear voices and screams of women from another room. I said, "Give me a blank piece of paper and I will sign it. On the paper, you can write whatever you want." They said: "We will write that you have asked us to kill you for your crimes." I didn't care, and signed the paper.[11]

M also described experiencing hunger in the holding cell following the above events. In his mind he recalled eating lunch with his sister once when he was a very young boy when a cat was begging for food and mewing. He could not get this memory out of his head. He began hallucinating and was sure that his mother and grandmother were in the prison with him eating their meals comfortably without noticing him. He identified with the hungry cat from his childhood and found himself calling out loud "meow, meow. . . meow, meow"; then more loudly, "meow, meow . . . meow!!" Only after he made these sounds did he realize with a start that these women were only a vision in his head. "I knew then how sick I had become, not knowing the difference between reality and fantasy, more like an animal than a man."[12]

Much later M was brought to the red room. Here is his description of the red room and his experience in it:

> In this red room, there was a hook on the ceiling running over a moving belt. As the belts of the machinery hummed, the hook lifted me up slowly off my feet from the floor to the ceiling, like a take-off, above an area which looked like a small

> swimming pool. I thought, "Oh well, so what? They will pick me up and drop me into water. That is not so bad!" Over the pool, the hook was stopped suddenly. I looked down into a quiet pool.
>
> The Iraqi officer said, "In this pool we have acid. Now, for the last time, tell us about your friends, or we will drop you in the pool!" I looked down into the pool, and said nothing. I waited on the ceiling, with my hands bound, prepared for death. He did not drop me into the pool, but reversed the machinery, which landed me back on the floor. I was dragged back to the dark holding cell. I knew that the last room for me was the black room. . . . this is the room for torture, death, and no return. I knew this and was prepared to die.[13]

M was saved because the central prison building was hit by an Allied missile. M heard and felt a thunderous blast, a most terrible boom. It was followed by shouting and screaming of Iraqi soldiers. Prisoners were herded into a central area. M noticed how shaken the Iraqis were. The prisoners were allowed to go back to Kuwait in buses, and once home, M remained as if frozen, a living repository of Kuwaitis' collective trauma.

Greg Saathoff also spoke with H, a twenty-two-year-old, on four different occasions. Here is part of H's story:[14]

> Since you asked me my name, I will tell you that my family came from Saudi, but was not in the first group to settle in Kuwait, then called the Arab Peninsula. They came in the second caravan, I think. . . . Although I am Sunni, I do not have feelings against the Shii or any particular group. . . . I think in Kuwait, we have a tradition of more tolerance.
>
> I understand that you want to hear my story, but I will tell you that it is unremarkable. . . . You see, I was in Egypt at the time of the occupation. . . . I was in a hotel and noted a Reuters headline going across the screen. It said that Iraq had crossed the border. I minimized this. . . . I went to sleep, and was awakened by a friend, who called and said that the Iraqis were in Kuwait City. I couldn't believe it, and thought he was joking. . . . I rushed to the lobby without even washing my face, and found that women were crying as it was being shown on TV. But what really hit me was when I saw that the hotel would not take Kuwaiti currency. They said: "We are sorry, but there is no more Kuwait." My credit card was not acceptable either.

H managed to go to Saudi Arabia to his uncle's house, which is apparently very near the Kuwait border. His parents also escaped to Saudi Arabia and then to Switzerland, but money was tight. Once when the weather was cold H went to a store to look for a coat. A Palestinian happened to be at the same store. When the Palestinian noticed that H did not have enough money to pay for the coat, he said, "He (H) is a Kuwaiti, but he cannot afford to buy a coat since he has no country. See, he is nothing without his money." Apparently this Palestinian was envious of rich Kuwaitis. H recalled burning with anger despite the cold weather after hearing the Palestinian's comments. He felt that he had to do something for his country. He left his family in Switzerland, returned to Saudi Arabia, and made a decision to join the United States military. He sent a short message to his family telling them about his decision. He knew that his mother would be very worried and cry. H ended up at Fort Dix in New Jersey for basic training. He felt that he was doing what he had to do as a man, for his country.

H was among the first twenty-five Kuwaitis who returned to Kuwait to take part in its liberation. He was relieved to find his family home still standing, his and his father's school certificates still hanging on the walls. But, he learned that one of his classmates who worked for the resistance had been shot by the Iraqis while his family members were forced to watch. Another friend was tortured. As he spoke to Greg, H began crying and told how some young Kuwaiti men were forced at gunpoint to have sex with their sisters while Iraqis watched. H continued:

> I have another story for you. . . . On February 26, with the liberation, we were told that a Kuwaiti woman had been taken into the zoo grounds by the Iraqis. There were so many stories in the chaos, it was hard to know. But we kept hearing this story again and again. After four days we went to the zoo. What I saw, I will never forget: A naked woman *was* there in a cage. I cannot describe her body, she was so bruised, but she was still alive.
>
> In the cage she acted like an animal, moving around madly on her hands and feet. I tried to calm her, saying, "Look, we are free now, we have come to help you." I laid down my rifle to show her I meant no harm, but she became more agitated. She could not be calm, and acted angrier, upset and like an animal. I talked to my captain and we agreed that we could not let her out of the cage since she was not in her right mind. We decided to wait with her until the proper people arrived to take her to a psychiatric hospital. Remembering these events still disturbs me terribly. I cannot get them out of my mind.

Every Kuwaiti Andy, Greg, and I interviewed exhibited, to one degree or another, some combined manifestations of post-traumatic states, which constitute serious and lasting changes in arousal, thinking, emotion, and memory. They result in chronic anxiety, psychosomatic symptoms, sleep disturbances, nightmares, flashbacks, explosive outbursts, low frustration tolerance, dissociation, depersonalization, changes in self-perception and in the perception of the perpetrators, and loss of basic trust that modifies relationships with others.[15] CSMHI did not have as long a time in Kuwait as we had in Estonia for assessing large-group and psychopolitical processes. To notice every societal and cultural aspect of the postinvasion period would be impossible and would require hundreds of additional interviews and other observations. We did, however, clearly observe three kinds of splits in postwar Kuwait society.

The first split might be more accurately called a fragmentation. As I stated earlier, Kuwait's beginnings go back to the early eighteenth century when the Al-Sabah family and two other Arab families moved there from surrounding areas. Slowly others—Arabs and Persians—joined them and Kuwait's society and large-group identity was born, an amalgamation of diverse immigrants. The first split (or better, fragmentation) the CSMHI members observed in Kuwait in 1993 and 1994 was not related to place of origin or who was Sunni or Shi'ite or who had relatives in Saudi Arabia or Iraq or Iran. The fragmentation within the society was due to who did what during the invasion. The causes for the situation in Kuwait were very different from those that resulted in the societal split in Albania that I described in the previous chapter.

Some Kuwaitis actively resisted the invasion, some were involved in the liberation process, some escaped to other countries, some collaborated with Iraqis, some were tortured by the Iraqis. H, like many others we interviewed, was aware of this fragmentation. While talking with Greg, he said: "Some Kuwaitis have disappointed us. . . . Many did nothing. They stayed in their homes and watched television, much as a coward might do. Others waited in other countries. It is a cause of increasing tension here. Do you know that I was accused of joining the U.S. Army just so I would be among the first to return to Kuwait? Can you believe that someone would say such a thing after they had done nothing?" Many others we interviewed had noticed an increase in physical fights among men and verbal fights among women.

The second split, we noted, was directly related to reports of incidents when Iraqi soldiers raped women and forced young male Kuwaitis to have sex with their sisters. I cannot tell how widespread this was in reality. Sexual abuse of Kuwaiti women by Iraqis had an enormously negative impact on Muslim Kuwait. The story of the raped and tortured woman in a cage in the zoo became the shared symbol of what had happened to Kuwaiti women during the invasion. The people would not talk about this event openly. I first heard about it very indirectly, in a joke. After a societal trauma, traumatized people tell jokes connected with the trauma. On the surface this sounds like an unreasonable thing to do. A closer look, however, illustrates that by telling jokes people share a tool that celebrates staying alive; they reverse their affect and laugh instead of cry, but at the same time discharge emotions. If the trauma does not break the society's backbone, jokes are usually connected with the society's own lost things and individuals. This way, surviving citizens link themselves to images of lost objects; telling jokes, in a peculiar way, becomes part of the grieving and mourning process. Here are two examples:

On September 19, 1985, a magnitude 8.1 earthquake struck Mexico City. It was followed by strong aftershocks. This natural disaster killed at least 100,000 people. Ten days after this tragedy I went to Mexico City. My host, an intelligent lady and mother of four children, met me at the airport. During the long drive to the city she asked, "What is the similarity between a doughnut and Mexico City?" She was telling me a joke. The answer was: "The middle of both is missing." I knew then that Mexico's backbone was not broken after this earthquake and, by telling a joke and laughing, this nice lady was remembering her and her country's huge loss.

In another example, after the January 28, 1986, space shuttle *Challenger* disaster in the United States, there was a shared trauma. The main reason for this was the death of teacher, Christa McAuliffe from Concord, New Hampshire, along with the other six crew members. In classrooms all over the United States televisions had been tuned in to the event so school children could witness and celebrate a teacher going into space. Instead, they witnessed a terrible tragedy and, starting with children, the whole country was traumatized. Soon tasteless jokes were heard countrywide. One described how the shampoo, Heads and Shoulders, could be found on Miami Beach, symbolically referring to body parts of dead crew members. Even though this joke was horrible, psychologically speaking it was part of the shared grieving and mourning processes.

When a country is invaded by Others, its backbone is broken. Under such a condition jokes do not appear right after the trauma. When the danger seems to be over, one hears them, but they are different: they do not refer to their large groups' lost objects and they are not helpful for grieving and mourning. Under such situations, the reference is to the enemy's image, which is belittled and rendered stupid. Thus, the main psychological aim of these jokes refers to a shared wish to make the enemy less dangerous. This is because a shared fear that the enemy will cause more losses still exits. Many who were interviewed in Kuwait three years after the liberation still expressed anxiety that Saddam's forces would return. They thought or dreamt about it. One popular joke was about Iraqi soldiers who thought that when you knocked on certain walls in Kuwait City money would pour out. It referred to Iraqi soldiers' unfamiliarity with automated teller machines (ATMs). It implied that Iraqis were not as rich or sophisticated as Kuwaitis.

The shared joke that would bring the most anxious laughter had to do with the Kuwait City zoo. In the jokes, "stupid" Iraqis do not know the difference between animals, especially which ones are eatable and which are not. They open the cages at the zoo and eat uneatable animals. When I first heard this joke I did not yet know the story of how the Iraqi soldiers put a Kuwaiti woman in a cage. When I learned the story I came to the conclusion that this woman's horrible fate and the Iraqis' inability to differentiate between a human being and an animal stimulated the content of this joke. Shame and anxiety about what had happened in the zoo was covered up by the storyline of the joke, reversing horror and making it laughter.

I do not know what happened to the woman who was taken to a psychiatric hospital. My hunch is that this incident has been repressed in today's Kuwait because it was so humiliating. In 1993 and 1994, however, our interviews revealed that the idea of a Kuwaiti woman being abused sexually in such an unimaginable way combined with many other stories about raped women, including teenagers, creating a shared "psychic reality," a concept that I described earlier in this book. In this psychic "truth," Kuwaiti women, especially from the younger generation, were *unconsciously* tainted. This unconscious "reality" was generalized and settled in the minds of Muslim Kuwaiti males. Many young Kuwaiti men spoke openly about postponing their marriages. I believe that this was due to the unconscious "psychic reality" that every young woman in Kuwait might no longer be a virgin. Young Muslim Kuwaiti males would not consider marrying a young woman who was tainted. H told Greg that he was serious about a young woman for six months and thinking about marriage. Marrying at his age was a culturally accepted and expected event. But H was hesitating.[16] There was a clear split between young men and women.

Some women who were interviewed spoke about women being afraid of men and avoiding them. They seemed to indicate two kinds of reactions. Some wanted more freedom to assert themselves as independent women and complained that "religious zealots" were taking over. One said: "Now everything is forbidden. In ten years we will be all covered in black: we will go backward." Others consider giving in and become more religious.

Besides the fragmentation among people according to what they did during the invasion, and the split between young men and women due to the spread of a "psychic reality," there was a third unwelcomed split, this time between fathers and their children, especially their male children.

In 1993 and 1994 CSMHI members found that many Kuwaiti children were identifying with Saddam Hussein.[17] For example, at an elementary school play that staged the Iraqi invasion, the children vociferously applauded the youngster who played the role of Saddam. As expected, the children were also involved in "war games." While playing them, the children repeated in play what had once been a dangerous reality in order to master the harsh experience.[18] In these war games, too, children were identifying with Saddam.

One Kuwaiti woman had a boy soon after the invasion and the family named him George Bush. This family was not the only family to do so. A few years after the liberation, as we understood it, most of these families ended up changing their childrens' names, since George Bush was not an Arabic/Muslim name. The family I mention here also gave their son an Arabic name, but they kept "Bush" as a nickname. When Gregory Saathoff interviewed three-year-old Bush's mother, she described how all her children (the others older than Bush) were obsessed with a particular video game depicting war and violence. She said:

> Anyway, whenever they play, they all want to be Saddam, and fight over who gets to be Saddam. Even little Bush wants to be Saddam. Sometimes, if Saddam loses, I tell him now aren't you happy that you aren't Saddam? Bush won! He will then acknowledge that it is OK to be Bush. But still, they *all* really want to be Saddam. You know, I was so concerned about all of this, and I *hid* the Sega game! But they looked all over and actually found it. So now, they still play it all the time.[19]

Before the invasion of Kuwait, there seemed to be many Kuwaitis who admired Saddam Hussein as an Arab leader, and then they felt he *betrayed* them. Adults' preinvasion feelings about Saddam alone do not explain their children's stubborn attempts to identity with Saddam. After the invasion, Kuwait was bombarded with Saddam's images on billboards and on television. This too does not fully explain the children's holding on to the Iraqi leader's image.

"Identification with the aggressor" is a psychoanalytic term for a period during which a child identifies him- or herself with the parent of the same sex with whom the child has been involved in a competition for the affection of the parent of the opposite sex.[20] In childhood, this process results in emotional growth. For example, through identification with the father, whom he perceives as an "aggressor," a little boy makes a kind of entrance into manhood himself. In other situations, however, like those of many Kuwaiti elementary school children, identification with the aggressor—in this case Saddam Hussein—can obviously create problems.

During the invasion and occupation, many Kuwaiti fathers were humiliated in front of their children by Iraqi soldiers, who sometimes spat on them, beat them, or otherwise rendered them helpless before their children's eyes. In cases where their humiliation and torture had occurred away from their children's view, fathers often wanted to hide what had happened to them. Without necessarily being aware of it, fathers began to distance themselves from certain crucial emotional interactions with their children, especially their sons, in order to hide or deny their sense of shame.

Most children and adolescents (who themselves were afraid and regressed and in search of a strong father figure), however, "knew" or sensed what happened to their fathers, whether they had personally witnessed these events or not. Thus, children and youngsters who were regressed due to the turmoil around them turned to Saddam's image as a figure for identification—so they would not sense their predicament of being forced to have "distant fathers" who would not protect them and respond to their psychological needs. Furthermore, identification with Saddam would protect them from experiencing fear.

Identification with the aggressor, with Saddam, was also connected with another issue: many school buildings in Kuwait City were used as torture chambers during the Iraqi occupation. Adults did not speak to children about what had happened in the schools during the invasion, but the children knew; and, when they returned to their renovated schools, that "secret" quite naturally caused them psychological problems and fear.[21]

The reiteration of the "distant father" scenario in Kuwaiti families, I believe, also set in motion gang formations among teenagers. To some degree "gang formation" is normal in adolescent development as youngsters loosen their internal ties to the images of the important persons of their childhood and expand their social lives through investment in members of their peer group and new "objects."[22] When many parents are affected by a catastrophe inflicted by Others, the adolescent gangs that form after the acute phase of the shared trauma tend to be more pathological. In Kuwait, the new gangs were heavily involved in car theft, a new social process involving emergence of crime that essentially had not existed in preinvasion Kuwait.

The CSMHI's team members' first concern was to asses the fragmentation within the society and the splits mentioned above and do whatever was possible to begin to heal them. As Nat Howell stated, "Persons suffering the stress of trauma desperately seek strong leadership to guide them in difficult times. They need to believe not only that the leaders understand and care that they are suffering but also that their feelings are not unique. Most, perhaps all, of their countrymen and women are also experiencing painful and disruptive aftershocks. They need to realize that their feelings are normal human reactions and not evidence of personal weakness. For the individual, as for society, it is important to develop a coherent narrative to replace isolated, disturbing images, nightmares, and flashbacks of terror and helplessness."[23]

Because Kuwait is a relatively small society and because they have *diwaniyas*, we felt that opening dialogues among "fragmented" parts of the society and sharing experiences and mending fragmentations would be possible, while also discussing other splits and helping fathers to work on their "distancing" themselves from their children. We heard that the Amir visited many homes with his official entourage, hugged people, and all cried. He was also asserting his traditional leadership. One visible example that evidenced the Amir's caring leadership was his establishment of the Social Development Office. Ambassador and Mrs. Howell's visit to Kuwait, to the *diwaniyas*, and the CSMHI members' presence at the *diwaniyas* were attempts to openly support the aims and efforts of the Social Development Office. Andy's and Greg's presence at the *diwaniya* demonstrated that participants in most *diwaniyas* seemed eager to look at themselves and their postliberation psychology. For example, at a *diwaniya* called "Wichita State," where members were mostly middle-class males, a Kuwaiti man said, "Instead of building the country, we ought to be building the postinvasion Kuwaiti personality." Andy and Greg witnessed an intense discussion about how hot-tempered men had become in Kuwait and their difficulty controlling themselves. A Kuwaiti judge at this meeting connected the increase in impulsive actions, traffic violations, and traffic causalities with the societal trauma and started a dialogue for solutions. Andy and Greg also heard at various *diwaniyas* how anger was also beginning to be expressed against the United States—the United States had played the most significant role in the liberation of Kuwait, but could not, we felt, tame the psychological effects of the shared trauma. Thus, there was ambivalence toward the United States.

When I was in Kuwait I walked through an old marketplace in Kuwait City with Nat and Margie. When Nat bought a gold piece to give as a present to a friend in the United States, the storeowner would not accept Nat's payment. He said that it would be a shameful act for him to accept money from Ambassador Howell, a friend of Kuwait, who had stayed in the county throughout the invasion and suffered. I noticed how, at that time, Nat was a symbolic transference figure for many Kuwaitis, as well as an integrating force. His and CSMHI members' visits to various *diwaniyas*, we hoped, would be—and as later we noticed were—important in opening or maintaining dialogues for Kuwaitis sharing their stories and feelings about the societal trauma. By interviewing many persons whom they met at various *diwaniyas*, Andy and Greg brought direct attention to psychosocial issues and to the *diwaniya* as being a proper place to focus on them. We considered such actions as part of keeping the process of societal mourning open.

The CSMHI members' travel expenses were paid by the Social Development Office of the Amiri Diwan. After our visits came to an end, under Ambassador Howell's leadership, we shared our findings in tactful ways with the members of the Social Development Office. For example, we did not go into detail about what we heard about rapes, since culturally this would be a very humiliating topic. Andy and Greg described the well-known effects of trauma on individuals, and we urged Kuwaitis to educate mental health professionals in the area of dealing with posttraumatic states. We emphasized the need to open the shared mourning process and spoke of how *diwaniyas* could play a role in this and in mending splits. We discussed with the Kuwaiti government the idea of creating specific means of commemorating those who lost their lives during the invasion, occupation, and liberation of Kuwait—ceremonies of remembrance, memorials. Nat told them to collect stories and reminiscences from a broad spectrum of Kuwaiti people and publish them in Arabic and English. He explained to them that such a major collection of personal accounts would provide an authoritative and cathartic record of the society's experience. We especially suggested finding programs to help youngsters speak about their feelings concerning the invasion that would help prevent them from becoming carriers of the shared trauma with its psychological implications. We stated that CSMHI would provide models based on our work with schools in Estonia. We also told the Kuwaitis that their society was recreating itself after the shared trauma and that this would take time. We listened to their political and educational strategy proposals, mostly referring to networking, that dealt with our findings.[24]

My CSMHI friends and I sensed that the Kuwaiti authorities wished to take care of their own problems, without any further involvement from outsiders. Soon after the liberation there was a great deal of discussion in the American and Western press about postwar liberalization and further democratization in Kuwait. But, CSMHI members, after having been involved in very intense work during their visits to Kuwait, and with the help of Nat and Margie, could understand the role of traditions in this country and the political savvy of the Sabahs. The leadership in Kuwait had been exposed to close scrutiny and potential criticism in a way not previously experienced. The governing family's intention to reassert its authority was firm. This psychologically would be helpful in easing the fragmentation among the Kuwaiti citizenry. I also sensed that Kuwaitis would try to go back to their religious customs to mend fences among themselves. This meant that outsiders like us, Americans, would not have a practical role in how they dealt with our findings.

The Kuwait government did not invite us back for a follow-up. I wondered how the children who identified with Saddam Hussein would handle these identifications as adults. I hoped that in time, due to new external and internal circumstances, the identifications would be discarded, or at least strongly repressed.[25] One follow-up opportunity occurred in 1997 when CSMHI members had a chance to hold round-table discussions with a dozen young Kuwaiti diplomats who were being trained at the University of Virginia. From this, I formed the impression that, above and beyond the intellectual knowledge of what had happened in Kuwait, the Kuwaitis in general were continuing to deny their helplessness during the invasion and occupation and the need to mourn. Traditional religion was utilized to calm internal storms: God had allowed the Kuwaitis to suffer in order to have stronger "togetherness."

In November 2011, while attending a meeting in Byblos, Lebanon, I interviewed two important and knowledgeable Arab scholars—one who had been living in Kuwait for some years and one who had lived there previously—to learn about societal concerns in that country two decades after the liberation. The Kuwaiti society remains rich financially, but it is not a settled society, since preoccupation with

Others remains a continuing problem. After Kuwait was liberated, an estimated 400,000 Palestinian Arabs, noncitizens, were expelled from Kuwait for supporting Saddam Hussein. (It is estimated that only one-fourth actually collaborated with the Iraqis.) One can imagine, and could expect, that this is an example of "purification" when, following liberation and an attempt to mend societal fragmentation, Kuwaitis asked: "Who are we now?" Another reference to purification can be made in relation to Kuwait's treatment of Bedoons, about 300,000 of them, most originally Syrian and Palestinian Arabs. A Human Rights Watch report of August 1995 states: "After decades of treating Bedoons as citizens and repeatedly promising to confer formal citizenship on them, the Kuwaiti government reversed its practice and declared them illegal residents of the only country they have ever known. Although the policy was adopted before the Iraqi invasion, it has intensified since the Kuwaiti government was restored to power following the victory of the Desert Storm military campaign. Kuwaiti authorities have justified their policy on the theory that Bedoons are illegal aliens and therefore are not entitled to live in Kuwait or enjoy the basic rights to which citizens and lawful residents are entitled."

Kuwaitis believed that, correctly or in fantasy, Bedoons destroyed any legal paper they might own when liberation came, with the idea that they would fool the Kuwaiti authorities by declaring that their papers were lost during the invasion and that they were in fact Kuwaiti nationals. In today's Kuwait concerns about Bedoons' human rights, living conditions, and legal status continue. People who are residents of Kuwait but who possess residency cards are also divided into categories. Some of them are "golden" foreigners, some are "platinum," and still others, such as those who had come from Pakistan, Sri Lanka, and Philippines are "lower" kinds of residency card holders.

As mentioned, when CSMHI was in Kuwait we predicted that investment in religion would increase in that country as there would be psychological attempts to find traditional ways to deal with trauma. There is strong evidence that using religion in a way to dominate what goes on in the society has happened in Kuwait. Most likely there are reasons other than the consequences of societal trauma for increased use of religion and increased power of religious "authorities" in Kuwait. Activities of al-Qaida, the image of September 11, 2001, the Western world's response to terrorism, division between the Muslim and Christian/Western worlds, and associated large-group identity issues have certainly strengthened a turn toward religion in the Arab world, including Kuwait.

I learned from interviews I conducted in Lebanon that not long ago young men and women students at the American University of Kuwait, a private university, ended up dancing together. A Salafi, a follower of the Islamic "Salafiyyah" movement, in order to protect a puritanical and fundamentalist tradition, took pictures of the dancing youngsters. This caused an uproar in Kuwait. Since then, freshmen and sophomore classes are segregated at the American University of Kuwait. Junior classes are not segregated, but boys sit on the left side and girls on the right side in classrooms. The university library's upper level, where most books are located, is only for young men. The segregation of Kuwait State University is much more stringent. In spite of all these things, at the present time there are four women in the Parliament. There seems to be "confusion" about the role of women. The divorce rate in Kuwait was high before the invasion. Now it is higher. According to statistics published in 2011 by the Kuwait Ministry of Justice, divorce lawsuits filed in Kuwait far outnumber other legal cases. In 2010 Kuwait's courts handled 27,500 divorces. The ministry's report also showed that the 2010 caseload indicated a 10 percent increase from the previous year in the number of all lawsuits filed in Kuwait's courts.

The real world issues also dovetail with the psychological ones in creating anxiety in present-day Kuwait, fear of Iran being the most significant. About 25 percent of Kuwaitis are Shi'ites, mostly of Iranian origin. Kuwait is playing a balancing act between its interest and the United State's interest in the region, with accompanying mixed feelings.

In May and early June 2011 Ambassador and Margie Howell spent a week in Kuwait. They felt emotional when they learned that the old U.S. embassy, where they had lived, had been completely torn down and bulldozed. There were significant physical changes in the city, including lots of tall skyscrapers with unusual architecture and new shopping complexes. Nat and Margie were in Kuwait to take part in a cultural event that is a symbol of Kuwaiti large-group identity and pride. Before the invasion Nat and Margie had discussions with Sheikha Hussah, the sister of the present Amir and the daughter of an earlier one, about preserving old buildings important in Kuwait's history. During the invasion the Iraqis had ruined the Kuwaiti Museum. Now it was recreated by Sheikha Hussah and her husband in the restored American Hospital where, a hundred years ago, American missionaries introduced modern medical care and education. Ambassador Howell gave the first lecture in this restored building.

After Kuwait I would be involved with two more postwar locations: the Republic of Georgia and Croatia.

# 26

# THE GEORGIAN–SOUTH OSSETIAN CONFLICT

## HELPING THE HELPERS

In this chapter I will relate some of my memories of the Republic of Georgia with an emphasis on Georgia's conflict with South Ossetia and describe what I call an "experiential teaching and training" program for local professionals to improve their dealing with traumatized individuals and societies.

The Center of Mind and Human Interaction's involvement in the Soviet Union and the Baltic Republics apparently was noticed by other newly independent republics. In June 1991 we had an unexpected visit from Giorgi Khoshtaria, then the foreign minister of the Republic of Georgia, asking us to come to his country and help with the ethnic conflicts they were facing. Soon we would receive formal invitations from two more governments, Moldova and Azerbaijan, to explore ethnicity and political change in their newly independent countries.[1] Although local costs would be covered by the governments involved, CSMHI needed grants to cover travel and administrative expenses. We had no funds to quickly take action after each invitation. Those who invited us were not familiar with grant applications, yearly grant cycles, and all the other things that a center like CSMHI had to deal with to raise money.

I knew that Jimmy Carter had a special relationship with Eduard Shevardnadze. Shevardnadze was the Soviet minister of foreign affairs between 1988 and 1990 and close to Mikhail Gorbachev. He was also a Georgian and, in fact, he had been the head of Georgia from 1972 to 1985 as the First Secretary of the Georgian Communist Party. Carter was from the U.S. state of Georgia and Shevardnadze was from the country called Georgia. When Giorgi Khoshtaria asked for CSMHI's help in June 1991, Shevardnadze did not have authority in Georgia. At that time the Georgian president was Zviad Gamsakhurdia, the first to be democratically elected. But I thought that CSMHI could, once more, collaborate with the Carter Center if we started a project in the Republic of Georgia. However, the emotional reason for my turning CSMHI's attention to Georgia had a great deal to do with my personal relationship with Yuri Urbanovich, CSMHI's international fellow, whose help in our work in Estonia was crucial. Yuri's mother was Armenian and his father Lithuanian, but he was born in Georgia. At the time of Giorgi Khoshtaria's asking us to help his country, Yuri's mother and other relatives were living in Tbilisi, the capital of the Republic of Georgia. Yuri could speak both Russian and Georgian and, if CSMHI worked in Georgia, once more his help to us would be crucial.

The Republic of Georgia, with a population of 5.3 million, had seceded from the Soviet Union on March 9, 1990, but was facing big problems. Two semiautonomous regions (autonomous oblasts) of the former Georgian Soviet Socialist Republic, Abkhazia and South Ossetia, demanded fuller recognition. Zviad Gamsakhurdia's fervent nationalism—he would declare such statements as "Georgia is only for Georgians"—did not help, and we feared bloodshed in this part of the world soon.

South Ossetian nationalists declared their independence from Georgia in September 1990 and refused to participate in the first free national election—the same election that made Gamsakhurdia the first Georgian president after the collapse of the Soviet Union. In January 1991 the Georgian National Guard entered Tskhinvali, the capital of South Ossetia, starting the Georgian–South Ossetian War. It ended in 1992, exactly one year after Giorgi Khoshtaria's visit to CSMHI. South Ossetia was left with the option of negotiating an arrangement with the Georgians. Tensions remained high as South Ossetians continued to entertain a wish for union with North Ossetia in the Russian Federation. About 100,000 South Ossetians residing in various parts of Georgia fled, mainly to North Ossetia. About 40,000 Georgians who lived in South Ossetia were driven from their homes and became internally displaced persons (IDPs) in Georgia.

Another war, this time between Georgia and Abkhazia, would take place during 1992 and 1993. It caused a huge exodus to Georgia of Georgians (300,000) who had lived in Abkhazia for generations. While there was no more fighting with South Ossetia, Georgians would face repeated skirmishes with the Abkhazians afterward. (There was a bloody flare-up in 2008 between Georgian forces and South Ossetians, Abkhazians, and the Russian military after Georgians' attack on South Ossetia.) Large-group identity issues would be repeatedly and greatly inflamed in this part of the world.

To top it all, there would be a civil war furthering confusion about the question "Who am I now?" among Georgians themselves who, in fact, are composed of about a dozen centuries-old "tribes." A coup d'état occurred on December 21, 1991, against Gamsakhurdia. In 1993 he and his followers would be involved in an unsuccessful uprising in order to regain power. But, under still debated circumstances, Gamsakhurdia died while, in a sense, he was still formally president. Eduard Shevardnadze became president of Georgia in 1995.[2]

Throughout this period, CSMHI maintained contact with Tedo Japaridze, who had accompanied Khoshtaria to Charlottesville in 1991. Khoshtaria would be known as the first intellectual in Gamsakhurdia's circle who would oppose him. Japaridze became the Georgian ambassador to Washington. Our contacts with him intensified and Ambassador Japaridze visited Charlottesville three times. I kept the Carter Center informed of our communication with Japaridze, and the Center helped us to start the CSMHI project in Georgia.

The preliminary assessment of the situation in that part of the world was carried out by Joyce Neu of the Carter Center and Yuri Urbanovich from CSMHI.[3] In the fall of 1995, the Carter Center sponsored a meeting in Charlottesville and we brought twelve representatives of U.S. NGOs to learn what was being done unofficially to help the ethnic conflicts in that part of the world and to deal with tens of thousands of traumatized individuals. At the time all U.S. NGO work involved projects dealing with the situation in Georgia or on Georgia-Abkhazia problems. CSMHI decided not to duplicate such projects and chose to focus on the Georgia–South Ossetia conflict.

Georgians are proud that they can trace their history back to times before Christ. They still use their own alphabet and speak about being among the first large groups to become Christians. South Ossetia, a landlocked territory, is an approximately 3,900 kilometers-square mountainous area with a population of about 70,000 persons, and is separated from North Ossetia, which is part of the Russian Federation. Ossetians who became Christian during the early Middle Ages are descendants of Alans, nomadic people during the first century after Christ who spoke an Eastern Persian language.

My wish was to carry out a multiyear project based on the Tree Model. In order to start a project based on this model, there is a need to find water (money) so that the tree can grow. However, those U.S. foundations that provided grants for international work, at that time, were not interested in providing funds for such a project. They were willing, however, to give CSMHI money to carry out programs—usually each running for a year or two—that would deal with traumatized individuals and train Georgian and South Ossetian caretakers to deal with them. We assumed that mental health professionals themselves were traumatized in this part of the world and that by understanding better the trauma within themselves, they would be better able to mitigate it in others.

CSMHI planned to teach by performing what we named "experiential teaching and training." This method was meant to go above and beyond simply lecturing Georgian and South Ossetian caretakers about how to recognize the symptoms of trauma among refugees and others and giving them some general technical suggestions. Our plan was to join local helpers in their existing and/or future work with the victims of trauma, both adults and children. Together we would observe the ongoing work, supervise its process, deal with issues such as guilt, shame, and mourning, and try to significantly improve what such local helpers could do for their own societies. Through working with children we aimed to illustrate why the next generation could potentially be "infected" and how this might be prevented.

CSMHI also maintained the hope that while helping the helpers we would find ways to apply knowledge of the Tree Model experiences to psychopolitical difficulties between Georgians and South Ossetians. We thought that once we were in that part of the world, besides conducting dialogues between mental-health workers from opposing large groups, we would also reach out to political authorities both in Georgia and South Ossetia.[4] At that time, as far as we knew, there was no formal and effective political communications between these two opposing groups. A border was established between Georgia and South Ossetia that Georgia did not recognize as legal.

During his second fact-finding tour to Georgia, Yuri Urbanovich linked CSMHI with a Georgian NGO called the Foundation for the Development of Human Resources (FDHR) in Tbilisi,[5] headed by a charismatic psychology professor, Nodar Sharjveladze.[6] FDHR had received a substantial grant from the Norwegian Refugee Council (NRC) with instructions to promote meaningful communication between Georgian and South Ossetian experts to deal with traumatized individuals, especially children. Accordingly, FDHR initiated contact with counterpart caretakers in South Ossetia. In 1996 they organized a week-long youth camp at Kobuleti near the city Batumi for sixteen Georgian and South Ossetian children accompanied by counselors from both groups.

In 1998, FDHR began a program to be conducted jointly with South Ossetian counterparts at the Youth Palace of Child Creativity in the capital city of South Ossetia, Tskhinvali.[7] The name of this children's center comes from the Soviet times when children would gather there for creative activities. The Youth Palace was headed by Venera Basishvili, a woman in her sixties with three university degrees. We learned that Venera knew that after the war many traumatized South Ossetian children needed psychological help. Having been the teacher of many of the current parents in town, Venera represented authority and benevolence and was successful in attracting students to programs at the Youth Palace. When FDHR began collaborating with the Youth Palace, sixty (and later ninety) South Ossetian children between the ages of nine and fifteen began attending meetings with their teachers/counselors aimed at dealing with the effects of trauma on these children. None of the South Ossetian adults working at the Youth Palace or, as a matter of fact, throughout South Ossetia, had training in providing psychological help to children. Every month or so Georgian members of FDHR, who had much better psychological training for work with children than their South Ossetian counterparts, went to the Youth Palace and also met with the traumatized South Ossetian children and their caretakers.[8]

The United States had an embassy in Tbilisi, but no presence in South Ossetia. The United Nations High Commissioner for Refugees (UNHCR) had few representatives in South Ossetia, but focused more on physical restoration and repatriating persons displaced by the Georgian–South Ossetian conflict. The Youth Palace project was the only activity to address psychological problems after war. On the surface it sounded like a noble movement. But no one, including people from the Norwegian Refugee Council who supported this project, seemed to consider that the helpers themselves most likely had been traumatized and that when helpers from "enemy" large groups come together they might bring psychological obstacles against collaboration with the Other.

I went to Georgia, sometimes three times a year, from May 1998 until March 2002, usually staying in the region eight days each time. Yuri accompanied me almost every time. Andy Thomson and Greg Saathoff, who had done most of the work in Kuwait, and a few CSMHI guest experts joined me on some of the trips. During my first trip CSMHI formalized its partnership with FDHR and accepted the mission to apply its "experiential teaching and training" to both South Ossetian and Georgian helpers in the Youth Palace project. We also agreed to help the FDHR members in their work with Georgian IDPs in Tbilisi and other parts of Georgia.

In May 1998, CSMHI's assessment of the situation both in Georgia and South Ossetia included in-depth interviews with psychologists, historians, teachers, government officials, university professors, students, writers, NGO representatives, and IDPs and observation of people at devastated locations.

Tbilisi is a beautiful city. But when I first went there many of its areas depressed me. Its infrastructure for the most part was not functioning. When I visited the main building of the University of Tbilisi, dirty water from broken sewer lines covered the first floor. I had to walk through it in order to reach a stairway that would take me to the upper floors. The electricity was frequently off. During evenings I would not see one single neon light illuminating a store or advertising a product. I recall that the first big neon light to appear in Tbilisi was a huge Pepsi-Cola sign, signaling the appearance of Western influence in that city. During my first two years in Tbilisi crime was not yet high. During my later visits, my Georgian friends accompanied me and other members of CSMHI whenever we went out in the evenings as kidnappings were possible. On several occasions the police stopped our cars and if we did not bribe them they would harass us. The most depressing sight in the city was a former sixteen-story luxury hotel, Hotel Iveria, where thousands of internally displaced Georgians were living, their clothing and bed linen hanging from the building's windows to dry. "Refugee, Go Home" was written on walls throughout the city, illustrating a societal split.

Tbilisi was like heaven compared to Tskhinvali, the capital of South Ossetia, three hours by car from Tbilisi. Yuri, Andy and I, despite warnings from the U.S. embassy in Tbilisi, visited the South Ossetian capital for the first time in May 1998. We were accompanied by Nodar Sharjveladze, Amiran Dolidze, and Jana Javakhishvili from FDHR. The effects of the fighting and siege were evident everywhere. Buildings were dilapidated and riddled with bullet holes; roads were filled with potholes. Unlike the renovations I had observed in Kuwait City, none had taken place in Tskhinvali. Some parts of the first floor of the Youth Palace of Children's Creativity were like the University of Georgia's first floor, but much worse, filled with floating human excrement. This two-story building with its broken windows could not have been more incongruous with the word "palace."

Considering the economic problems the people in Tbilisi, including the FDHR members, were facing when CSMHI went to Georgia, we decided not to stay in a luxury hotel or even an expensive-looking hotel during our visits. In fact, at that time there was only one luxury hotel in Tbilisi. Most of its guests, we were told, were Americans assigned to Georgia to carry out some type of U.S. government work or American business. For security reasons they would seldom leave the hotel and get to know Georgians. We did not wish to create a psychological barrier between us and our new Georgian friends. During our visits a professor living on the eighth floor of the building where Nodar and his family lived moved himself and his family to a relatives' home for eight days in order to rent the family apartment to us. On many occasions, for serious meetings, members of FDHR and CSMHI gathered in Nodar's apartment, which was on the first floor. But we also ate, drank, and sang songs as most Georgians love to do—in a most pleasant and friendly way—with someone playing guitar or Nodar's wife's piano.

When Yuri and I returned to Georgia and South Ossetia for a second visit in late October 1998, CSMHI's "experiential teaching and training" of nine Georgian FRHR members and six South Ossetian participants in the Tskhinvali Youth Palace project began earnestly since we already had sufficient information about their large-group processes. CSMHI's program included my conducting, often accompanied by Andy and/or Greg, separate and sometimes joint psychodynamically oriented group meetings with the Georgian and South Ossetian participants. These were aimed at helping them to verbalize feelings and thoughts that could not be verbalized earlier and to understand how their own trauma might interfere with their work with others. Many Georgian and South Ossetian participants spoke

English, to one degree or another. Yuri, as if my twin, was my interpreter. We observed the caretakers' work with children at the Youth Palace and, following each activity, we brought together South Ossetian and Georgian participants to examine the details of the caretakers' performance and children's expressions in order to improve our approaches to the children's problems. Whenever it was possible we accompanied the FDHR members when they worked with Georgian IDPs or supervised their work after ethnic skirmishes at locations near Abkhazia, where the CSMHI members did not travel.

We worked with these Georgians and South Ossetians for four years. Opening and sustaining dialogues between those from two opposing large groups dealing with the effects of shared trauma is itself a psychopolitical activity, a kind of "folk diplomacy." But CSMHI went one step further. While working with the FDHR members and South Ossetians from the Youth Palace, CSMHI developed connections with many who were involved in internal and international politics and societal improvements.[9]

In order to illustrate what I mean by "experiential teaching and training," I will briefly describe my activities—accompanied by Yuri—during the October–November 1998 visit to Georgia and South Ossetia.

On October 31, I conducted the first small-group meeting with the FDHR members in Tbilisi, with no South Ossetians present. I will not write about the technical issues of conducting psychodynamically informed small-group sessions aimed at helping participants look at themselves in relation to a joint task they are performing. If colleagues working in international conflict areas realize that local helpers are traumatized and need help for themselves prior to becoming effective helpers for others, and if they wish to become involved in "experiential teaching and training" as CSMHI performed it in Georgia and South Ossetia, they should consider including a psychoanalytically oriented member in their facilitating team. Here I will focus on what these small-group sessions during this visit revealed. I think that this information itself is useful for all NGOs that work with traumatized local helpers.

During the first small-group session with the FDHR members—each such session would last three hours with short breaks—Nodar Sharjveladze, the leader of the small group, dominated the discussion by revisiting the meeting in Kobuleti two years earlier, in 1996. I heard many details about how Georgian and South Ossetian youngsters drove to this gathering place in the same bus, how they competed, what they wore, what they sang, and related events. I kept wondering why Nodar "went back," but did not question him, since asking such a question would usually lead to intellectualization. It was clear to me that talking about Kobuleti was a psychological defense for Nodar as well as the other Georgians: instead of staying with the task at hand and feeling emotions about the present situation, they were "regressed" to 1996. Slowly another deeper meaning for their preoccupation with the Kobuleti meeting surfaced.

Georgian and South Ossetian youngsters who met in Kobuleti for a "peaceful interaction"—as suggested by the Norwegian Refugee Council without first taking into consideration that these kids needed a great deal of preparation before meeting with youngsters from the opposite large group—were highly traumatized. For example, the father of one of the Georgian boys had been taken hostage when the boy was seven years old. Afterwards, the boy would sit by a window every day waiting for his father's return. Nodar was aware of this child's and others' psychological situations.

According to Nodar and other Georgians who were at Kobuleti, the leader of the South Ossetian group, a man named Phillips who was the deputy director of the Tskhinvali Youth Palace, constantly presented himself as a South Ossetian "nationalist" who did not wish to collaborate with Georgians. Phillips made the Georgian caretakers very angry, and one day Nodar expressed his rage openly and prohibited Phillips from attending an event. After the Kobuleti meeting Phillips remained as a key contact person in South Ossetia for the Georgians and continued to irritate Nodar and other Georgians. In 1998 the Georgians learned that Phillips had died in a motorcycle accident.

Listening to them, I slowly became aware that after Phillips' unexpected death, FDHR members, following Nodar, began to share a "psychic reality" that Nodar's anger and wish that Phillips disappear from his life had "killed" Phillips.[10] The image of Phillips represented "bad" South Ossetians for the Georgians. They used this "psychic reality" unconsciously to support their denial of aggressive thoughts and feelings every time they worked with South Ossetians in order to remain "civilized persons." This itself would disturb their effectiveness as long as it remained a "secret" from them. This "psychic reality"—they were unconsciously enemy-killers—also helped them, without their being aware of it, to tame their open fear of alienation when many of their compatriots perceived them as traitors and enemy-lovers.

During the first group dialogue with the FDHR members, I made the following remarks in order to bring to their consciousness previously unspeakable thoughts and feeling. I want to remind the reader that what they will read below is a summary of my statements, and that I did not deliver them as if I were giving a lecture.

> I do not know your individual motivations for becoming members of FDHR and doing a noble job, but it is clear that you want to establish a peaceful working relationship with South Ossetians. Nevertheless, you are accused of doing a job that is contrary to the sentiments of many individuals in your own ethnic group and

> sometimes you feel like traitors. The sense of ambivalence you feel about South Ossetians and about your own work with them is to be expected, even normal.
>
> It appears that you have unconsciously linked Philips' death with your aggression toward him—and this induced guilt feelings in you. We can let Nodar (and other Georgians who went to Kobuleti and got to know Phillips) continue to have the illusion of power so that he can kill people by being angry at them, or we can remind him that wishing an irritating individual to disappear does not kill people.

The small group responded to this explanation of their guilt feeling with a long nervous laughter, indicating that they had heard me clearly. I continued:

> You are discharging your troublesome feelings with laughter. Becoming more aware of the complexity and range of the emotions can reassure you and make you better equipped to carry on with your tasks. The facilitators from South Ossetia with whom you work, I imagine, have the same emotions and struggles. Recognizing your internal obstacles toward working with the "enemy" may lead to more and more genuine and effective approaches to your work.

On November 1 I conducted another three-hour small-group meeting. I noted that the previous day's experience initiated further curiosity in the FDHR members about examining themselves. I would hear about their on-and-off experiences of helplessness and depression, then their struggle to deny such feelings and hide them from other helpers. Canadian psychoanalyst Sheldon Heath in 1991 wrote a book complete with case reports to illustrate how, while treating depressed patients, a psychoanalyst or therapist is vulnerable to depression.[11] The analyst or therapist at times absorbs and experiences the patient's depressive affect for various psychological reasons, including for developing empathy and better understanding the patient. Other times patients "transfer" their "bad" feelings to the analyst in order to protect themselves from remaining in uncomfortable moods. During this group session the FRHR members "chose" to report one tragic event after another until we all understood what they were trying to verbalize openly and why they were prone to experience depressive affects. Below are two examples of stories I heard.

The father of a five-year-old IDP child died at Tbilisis Zgva (Tbilisi Sea), a former resort outside Tbilisi, which at that time housed 3,000 IDPs who had fled Abkhazia. One FDHR member doing work with kindergarten children at Tbilisi Sea heard about the child's father's death. She decided to go to the wake and pay her respects. When she arrived, she found the child crying. But what shocked her, and what has remained in her mind vividly ever since, is the fact that the dead man's shoes had holes in them. The IDP family did not have enough money to provide the dead man with appropriate shoes. Whenever the image of the dead man with torn shoes comes to her mind she is filled with depressive feelings.

An old couple living as IDPs in Kutaisi in western Georgia lost two sons during the initial phase of the Georgian-Abkhazian conflicts. The couple was taking care of their five grandchildren, ranging from four to twelve years of age. Pictures of their dead sons adorned the walls of the place where they lived. When one FDHR member visited the old couple he learned that the old woman had hidden in the basement in Abkhazia for a year before escaping, because she wanted to find where her sons were buried. One of her dead sons was a poet and his daughter recited one of her father's poems for the visiting FDHR member. But the family seemed at peace; they did not express any hostility toward the enemy. The old woman's name was Jajuna, which means "joyful." The FDHR member thought about how ironic it was that despite the severe blow dealt her by the conflict, she still maintained her joyfulness. As for himself, the FDHR member felt despair.

The FDHR group members gradually began to realize something that they had not previously been truly aware of—they were periodically the carriers, at least temporary, of the feelings of helplessness and depression of the people with whom they were working. They now knew that when this phenomenon was not recognized, it could lead to struggles within the group since unconsciously each one of them tried to hide his or her helplessness and depressive episodes from the others. No one wanted to appear as an ineffective helper. This was causing unnecessary frictions among them.

On November 3 Yuri, Nodar, Jana, Amiran, and I and also Nino Makhashvili, a child psychiatrist and member of FDHR, went back to Tskhinvali. In the morning I conducted a small-group meeting with the South Ossetian teachers and psychologists at the Youth Palace. I noted a disparity between Georgian and South Ossetian team members. While the Georgians from FDHR, with one exception, had not experienced the war directly, South Ossetians had been in Tskhinvali and had lived through bloody fighting and shelling. I asked the South Ossetians how this difference in the experiences of the trauma might affect their interactions as they got to know the Georgian team members better. This led one South Ossetian to comment that, although the South Ossetian caretakers had their government's blessing to collaborate with FDHR, many of their neighbors and friends in Tskhinvali were against the project. However, parents knew that their children had nightmares and they needed help. Ninety percent of the young participants of the Youth Palace project who were brought from the countryside to a location in Tskhinvali had lost one or both of their parents. As long as the parents and caretakers of those children understood that this collaboration with the Georgians of FDHR was in the service of helping their children, it appeared that the project would survive.

The South Ossetian culture of being good hosts, I sensed, played a role in the South Ossetians' politeness and kindness toward me. Once they began describing their and their neighbors' experiences, however, their pain was palpable. I noted that there had been many mixed marriages in Tskhinvali. Two members of South Ossetian helpers themselves were from mixed marriages. Their leader, Venera, then a widow, was a Georgian who had married a South Ossetian. She was revered by professionals working under her at Youth Palace and as far as I understood, by many South Ossetian government officials who had been her students. I sensed that before the war there was no malignant racism between South Ossetians and Georgians. When the war broke out many cousins fought one another, and after the war they had a difficult time restoring their relationships. Many family ties were broken. Many Georgians, former neighbors, or relatives had moved away. The South Ossetian helpers themselves, unlike their Georgian counterparts, were still in shock. I decided to go easy and not to stir up emotions by examining their hesitations, their concerns, and their own obstacles against being helpful to the children.

I was involved in a most unusual project—the Youth Palace project—that was not designed by me or by members of CSMHI. In typical cases, a foreign trauma expert helps local caretakers when their work with traumatized individuals is with their own large group, as would be the case when the Georgians worked with Georgian IDPs. At the Youth Palace helpers from one "enemy" large group were getting together with the helpers from the other "enemy" large group on behalf of the children of only one large group.

Twenty-five South Ossetian children, from age nine to age twelve, were gathered in a room, sitting on low wooden benches in three concentric circles. Jana and Nino sat in the outer circle; they would be the instructors of this two-hour session with South Ossetian children. Everyone would speak in Russian. Other South Ossetian caretakers, Nodar, Amiran, Yuri, and I sat on one side of the room on higher benches ready to observe what would happen. Nino threw a soft ball about the size of a tennis ball toward the group of children. Whoever caught the ball was to introduce him- or herself and name something he or she liked. Then this child would throw the ball to another who would do the same. The children spoke about liking soccer, music, wrestling, folk dancing, and so on. After everyone had a chance to speak, the instructors introduced a new twist to the game. After catching the ball, each child was to name one "rule" of social behavior in the group. Children identified rules such as smiling in friendship, accepting others' appearance, listening more and speaking less, and being polite. The interactions became more interesting when the children were asked to make up a story as a group and then to draw pictures. Through these activities, the instructors were creating a canvas onto which the children could externalize and project aspects of their internal world. Once out in the open, such externalizations and projections could be discussed.

Of course, if the instructors were ready emotionally and willing to conduct such discussions in an appropriate therapeutic manner, that would be helpful for the children.

The story the children created and drew involved someone sailing in a boat to an island where he searches for food. At one point, a stick figure on the island appeared on one drawing. The figure shouted, “Help! Help!” I noted that the instructors did not notice or did not want to notice why the stick figure was asking for help. South Ossetia does not border any sea. Most drawings showed sea water. One meaning of this might refer to the traumatized children’s wish to move away from their traumatizing environment. But this theme was not examined. It was as if water was present everywhere in the room. Another thought came to my mind: the fact that the children were being forced to walk through dirty water on the first floor of the building in order to come to this meeting room might be linked to their preoccupation with water. Instead of “swimming” in water with human excrement, they were wishing to swim in clean and blue waters. From my clinical experience with traumatized children I also knew their preoccupation with water in their dreams often is connected with their symptom of bedwetting.

When the session with the children ended I had another small-group session with the helpers, this time South Ossetians and Georgians together. The instructors admitted that they were afraid of touching upon painful topics, such as when the stick figure shouted, “Help! Help!” One South Ossetian told us, “It is too much for the teachers to talk about hurtful things, so we do not let the children talk about them either.” I suggested that the helpers consider that by references to water the children might be trying to send adults another message. I told them about the link between water dreams and bedwetting among traumatized children. My remarks surprised Venera. She was the only one who knew that most children whom we had just met were suffering from bedwetting. Their parents had confided this information to Venera and had also told her that most children were dreaming about water. The parents did not wish other caretakers to know this, because talking about their children’s bedwetting would be humiliating.

Quickly Venera perceived me as someone who was a *real* authority in understanding traumatized children, since I was able to discover the children’s and her “secret.” Her relationship with me drastically changed, as did the mood in the room. No longer were South Ossetian helpers hiding behind niceties and politeness. Confirmation of the children’s bedwetting opened discussion of how to address this symptom without humiliating them. While no immediate solution was found, identifying it as a concern initiated a more genuine collaborative discussion among the South Ossetians and Georgians. Now and then I would notice the appearance of the accordion phenomenon. We left Tskhinvali late and returned to Tbilisi.

On November 4 I directed my last small-group meeting, this time again only with Georgians from FDHR, including four who had been to Tskhinvali the day before. Jana told a story about the trip that revealed more clearly how anxiety over meeting "enemies" can create symptoms. During the social hour after the joint session, she was sitting around a table when a rather tall man entered the room. Her immediate reaction was fear that the newcomer was a South Ossetian who had come to take her hostage. She recounted: "I thought I had never seen him before and did not know who he was. Then someone asked him to sit down with us, and I realized that he was the driver of the car I had ridden in from Tbilisi."

During the session with children Amiran had left the room to smoke a cigarette. He now explained that his main reason for leaving the room was not his addiction to tobacco. Through the window he had seen some men hanging around one of the cars in which the Georgian group, Yuri, and I had travelled to Tskhinvali. He knew that the men had noticed its Georgian license plate, and he had left the room to make sure they did not damage or tamper with the car. Nino and Amiran's stories also reflect the reality of danger in "enemy" territory, but they also illustrate anxiety that often appears when enemies get together.

This summary of my observations from October 31 to November 4, 1998, is one illustration of what I mean by "experiential teaching and training." I was aware that these sessions with FDHR and Youth Palace members would not be enough to "complete" our experiential teaching and training. I would continue to have many more similar sessions with them during my subsequent visits. In 1999, with the permission of South Ossetian authorities, the South Ossetian team began for the first time to come to Tbilisi for joint sessions. This was a success story, since even business dealings between Georgians and South Ossetians were legally forbidden in that period. Our joint sessions were followed by social events during which we would eat together and sing and dance, and participants got to know each other very well. I recall that some of our sessions would last for seven hours—one even lasted twelve hours. Andy Thomson, Greg Saathoff, and I gave talks and seminars on large-group psychology for FDHR members, as well as for larger audiences at the University of Tbilisi.

FDHR group members truly became very skilled and confident helpers for traumatized individuals, and accrued vast knowledge of how shared trauma not only disturbs individuals but also influences societal processes. I also learned a great deal from them. It took South Ossetian helpers longer to demonstrate more confidence in their ability as helpers and to be more and more appreciated by the South Ossetian authorities. It helped that the uncle of one of the South Ossetians was the South Ossetian president. In 2000, I sensed that they were crystallizing their large-group identity as members of a "breakaway state"—a state that was determined not to be a part of Georgia again—and leaving behind the large-group identity they had when the Soviet Union existed and when there were many intermarriages between Georgians and South Ossetians. At some meetings they would freely express their anger against Georgians instead of always trying to be polite. But at the same time, for the sake of the children and the psychological welfare of their society, they participated in "realistic" collaboration with the FDHR Georgians, whom they trusted.

In late summer 1999 and winter 2000, violent events in nearby Chechnya caused many Chechens to flee, and thousands of them came to Georgia. Ultimately four thousand Chechen refugees would seek safety in Georgia and thousands more in other countries such as Turkey, Azerbaijan, and Iraq.[12] Chechen refugees' physical needs became a focus for the funders in the United States and raising money for our Georgian–South Ossetian project became impossible. CSMHI was able to receive a new generous grant from the International Research & Exchanges Board (IREX) to study gender issues and family violence in the Black and Caspian Sea region, with participants from Georgia, South Ossetia, Armenia, Abkhazia, and Turkey.[13] While carrying out the "IREX Black and Caspian Sea Collaborative Research Program," we were able to bring six FDHR members together with the South Ossetian participants, along with participants from Armenia, Abkhazia, and Turkey. For the IREX project, we had meetings in Tbilisi, Istanbul, and Izmir. Thus, we continued to maintain the collaboration between Georgian and South Ossetian counterparts through 2001 and 2002.[14] During this time FDHR also became involved in crisis intervention at Chechen refugee camps in Georgia.

During the IREX research program, CSMHI did not go to South Ossetia, where catastrophic economic depression and infrastructure collapse was accompanied by an epidemic of child prostitution, drug abuse, and criminality. We learned that the gender balance of the workforce had changed drastically in South Ossetia since the war, because many men left South Ossetia to find jobs elsewhere, usually in parts of the Russian Federation. Women had to work outside the home to make money to feed their children and themselves, such as by opening market stands. But, according to tradition, a woman who worked with the public was considered a "loose" woman. When husbands came back, some of them physically abused their wives.

In a society under stress, sometimes old traditions appear in new forms. Large groups turn to their traditions to strengthen the identity of the large group, but in a regressed state, the traditions may become exaggerated or linked with aggression that, turned inward, goes haywire. The ritual of a young man "kidnapping" a young girl—with the knowledge of the families—and then marrying her was part of traditional South Ossetian culture. After the brutal war and ensuing economic and political turmoil, this tradition of "kidnapping" reappeared in a more sinister fashion in the late 1990s and early 2000s. These "kidnappings" became more haphazard and were carried out with aggression; and they often did not end in marriage. Because of the societal dysfunction and the area's economic collapse, many girls turned to prostitution. This in turn set in motion a new cultural phenomenon: men began marrying younger and younger women. In a culture where the virginity of brides was important, the notion was that the younger the bride, the more likely she was to still be a virgin.

As prostitution and crime became generalized in Tskhinvali, younger and younger girls were involved in it. I was told that sexual favors would cost only a dollar. Young girls and younger males increasingly included criminality in their daily activities. Research carried out by Madina Gazzaeva and her associates in Tskhinvali showed that none of the ninety youngsters at the Youth Palace were involved in prostitution or crime. While I cannot say how scientifically accurate this finding was. Even if it might be flawed, it illustrates how the Youth Palace program was important and successful, and how it enhanced the participating children's self-esteem.[15]

In this chapter I focused on experiential teaching and training and our role in opening and maintaining communications between Georgians and South Ossetians. I wish to tell the reader that one third of my book, *Killing in the Name of Identity*, is devoted to other findings from my work in Georgia and South Ossetia.[16]

# 27

# POLITICAL PROPAGANDA AND MALIGNANT PURIFICATION

A simple definition of political propaganda, in its widest sense, would encompass any communication and manipulation from a source of political authority that is directed to its followers and its opposition at home and/or abroad, as well as to those who might be described as "neutrals" or "bystanders." Its aim is to further the propagandist's wishes and ideas. Political propaganda exists in all politically organized open or closed societies. In the United States we are always exposed to both Republicans' and Democrats' propaganda machinery. Due to the present incredible communication technology, winning elections and running a government in democratic states have also become intertwined with propaganda machines and raising huge funds to support them. Men and women in democratic countries must struggle more and more to maintain their individuality and integrity while separating "bad" from "good" propaganda, and their discernment concerning ideas and information dished out by propaganda machines.

Since propaganda and manipulation exit in every politically organized society, one can argue that differences between the type of propaganda utilized by the leader and his/her associates in one large group and that of another large group will be only a matter of degree. However, such a comparison is not always fair and becomes problematic when societal crises, ideology, type of government, existing laws, economic conditions, and political and military aims are taken into consideration. Furthermore, the psychology of the leaders and leader-follower relationships in different large groups, especially when a large group is in crisis, makes this comparison difficult.

The historical precursors to political propaganda may be the tribal battle sounds of earlier times "meant to encourage one's own group, frighten the foe, and impress those who did not participate in fight."[1] The ancient war cry, called *alala*, accompanied by nonverbal symbols such as banners and uniforms, is said to have been a significant factor for the Greeks and for their enemies. The ancient Roman armies used shouts and accompanying trumpet blasts, called *clamor*, and later adapted the Teutonic battle cry, *barditus*: "Tacitus describes it as an explosion of raucous sounds, made more prolonged and more resounding by pressing the shield against the mouth."[2] Beginning as a murmur, it would steadily increase into a roar, rousing the soldiers to intense excitement.

As human history proceeded, other means of influencing feelings and behavior and generating support for political and military decisions and actions in times of conflict superseded the battle sounds, and the use of such methods in peacetime as well as in war became more common. The appearance of propaganda in its broadest sense became more closely connected with religious issues. The battle cry of the Ottoman Empire was simply their God's name, as if their battles were sanctioned by God and as if any Ottoman soldier killed in battle would be taken care of by Him; Ottoman Janissaries (elite Ottoman troops) shouted "Allah! Allah!" as their colorful marching band, the *Mehter*, provided energizing background music. About fifteen years ago I was attending an international meeting in Istanbul with hundreds of participants from different countries, including those in the Balkans. One evening, the Turkish hosts gave a big dinner party in the gardens of the Turkish Military Museum. Everyone was having a very good time. Then the Turks entertained the guests by having a group of men dressed in Janissary uniforms play *Mehte*r music. When they appeared with their drums and horns and began calling their God's name, "Allah! Allah!" some people from the Balkans who were with me literally had anxiety attacks and left the party. The religious battle cry of the past and the music that accompanied it was still frightening to the descendants of a "victimized" large group centuries later.

Christians too used religion as a tool for propaganda and for protecting religious investment. Garth Jowett and Victoria O'Donnell describe how the concept of "propagating" (propaganda comes from the Latin "to propagate") ideas lost its neutrality: in 1622, *Sacra Congregatio de Propaganda Fide* (the "Sacred Congregation for Propagating the Faith" of the Roman Catholic Church) was established by the Vatican. The term "propaganda" thus became pejorative in Protestant Western Europe because it was associated with the project of spreading Catholicism in the New World at the expense of and in opposition to the "reformed" faiths.[3]

Historian Bernard Lewis explained at a meeting that I attended that political propaganda in its modern sense did not begin until after the French Revolution (1789–1799). Before then, there was essentially no meaningful contact between the rulers and the ordinary people. Those in power had no need to communicate with or manipulate the public; they simply ruled.[4]

Franz Anton Mesmer, a Viennese physician, appeared on the European scene at the beginning of the nineteenth century with his new "science" called hypnotism, which fascinated nobles, scientists, and the public. Although in the end he was declared a charlatan by a commission of the French Academy of Sciences,[5] the influence of hypnotism in shaping the psychological considerations of societal events continued. In 1895 Gustave Le Bon, a French social psychologist who was born two decades after Mesmer's death, published *The Crowd: A Study of Popular Mind* and, perhaps without being fully aware of it, he echoed the dynamics of hypnotism.[6] Le Bon held that an individual in a group loses much of his or her distinctiveness and acts in accordance with the group's consensual urges. The effects are readily apparent. When we observe any group, even a purely functional one such as a marching band, we see a unified body behaving according to a common goal, wish, or need—individuality displaced by common identity. Individuals' achievements or acquisitions become notable only relative to their success or failure in furthering or hindering the group's functioning. Without carefully differentiating small groups, in which participants see and get to know one another, from large groups, Le Bon noted that crowds crave illusions. The leader can supply such illusions, using them to manipulate and control the crowd. In other words, the leader can act as a kind of hypnotist.

Anyone who studies psychoanalysis is aware of how Sigmund Freud's psychoanalytic ideas about large groups were influenced by Le Bon's study of the crowd.[7] However, Le Bon's influence on the development of modern malignant propaganda is not common knowledge among psychoanalysts. After visiting India he developed an idea that the white race might be in danger, and in his 1910 book *La Psychologie Politigue, et la Défense Sociale*, he created a kind of blueprint for fascism.[8] I will return to Le Bon's influence on malignant political propaganda.

Harrold Lasswell, a pioneer in the study of psychosocial warfare, suggested that the "discovery of propaganda by both the man in the street and the man in the study" took place during World War I (1914–1918).[9] When the war began there was no public outcry about oppressed large groups, and no interest in secret diplomacies; the war was fought by soldiers with little knowledge of why they were fighting. Movies such as the 1981 Australian film *Gallipoli*, directed by Peter Weir and starring Mel Gibson, depict soldiers in World War I shooting and killing the enemy without hatred or even contempt. But as the war dragged on and began to affect peoples' lives more intimately, there appeared a dual need to stimulate the soldiers' will to fight and to explain the need for privation to the public at home. In order to justify the cost of operations it became necessary to inflate the fruits of victory with vague but lofty-sounding notions such as "self-determination" and "the war to end all wars."[10] Thus, Lasswell argued, propaganda was "discovered" and was more startling, he said, to the man in the street than to the man in the study. "The layman had previously lived in a world where there was no common name for deliberate forming of attitudes by the manipulation of words (and word substitutes)."[11]

In World War I, besides printed material, telegrams and the wireless were routinely available to influence the masses. Though motion pictures were still a relatively new technology in the second decade of the twentieth century, their use for propaganda purposes nevertheless began during this war as well. Germany came late to deploying movies as a means of propaganda; German propaganda was ineffectual during World War I. During World War II, however, an elaborately developed German film propaganda machine reached its apotheosis in the well-known works of Leni Riefenstahl and others.

Adolf Hitler devoted two chapters in *Mein Kampf* to the proper design and execution of political propaganda. It should be aimed "only to a limited degree at the so-called intellect. . . . The art of propaganda lies in understanding the emotional ideas of great masses and finding through a psychologically correct form, the way to attention and hence to the heart of the broad masses."[12] Hitler found an especially talented confederate in Joseph Goebbels who was ultimately responsible for creating Hitler's image and many of his signature gestures.

Psychoanalyst Ernst Kris reminded us about Le Bon's influence on fascism and Nazi propaganda. When Benito Mussolini came to power in Italy he professed that he was influenced by Le Bon's ideas. In turn, Le Bon, then almost ninety years old, became an admirer of the "new order" in Italy. Kris wrote: "The student of history of ideas will note in Le Bon the parallel with Nietzsche and reaction to Marx, but he will also be able to quote chapter and verse in order to prove how closely statement by Le Bon reappears in the concepts of propaganda developed by Hitler and Goebbels."[13] In Le Bon's scheme the function of political propaganda is clear: the leader as an orator/hypnotist drives the crowd into submission and promotes its regression.

After the political and economic humiliation experienced by the German people, Nazi propaganda created a shared psychic reality in which the "Aryan" identity of the German people was built up, while millions of Jews, Roma, and others were dehumanized and killed. The main characteristic of the Nazi propaganda was to build up the Fuhrer's and the Nazi authorities' omnipotence and provide satisfaction for the Germans in their belief that they were followers of a mighty leader who would lift up their self-esteem and make them special super beings. Elsewhere, I studied the psychology of Nazi propaganda, which included disturbances in the family system, such as severing children and youth from their natural object of love and attachment and then filling this vacuum with collective grandiosity and National Socialist "morality." I also examined how the propaganda engineered by Joseph Goebbels tried to ensure that Nazi publicity typically presented Hitler as a good man who was personally ignorant of any violent atrocities. Nevertheless, there were times when the satisfaction Hitler derived from his "aggressive triumphs" was publicly apparent.[14] Genocide occurred in order to prevent the contamination of super beings by those whom the Nazi propaganda rendered subhuman, like dangerous germs. Personal and shared historical and economic hurts and humiliations within German society could then be effectively denied. The Nazi propaganda used political ideology instead of religion as a tool. But this requires a closer look. Since Hitler was presented as if he were a God, we really cannot clearly differentiate ideological and religious tools for political propaganda in the case of the Nazis.

Contrary to the Nazis' propaganda, the Allies' propaganda during World War II allowed criticism, even while it stressed the gallantry of military forces and distracted attention from defeat. After World War II, international law tried to specify legal exceptions to freedom of speech. Hate speech that incites racism was banned, for example. The United States did not join the other countries in accepting the international law concerning hate speech, since it interferes with the First Amendment of the U.S. Constitution. In the United States hate speech is unregulated unless it is proven that it leads to clear and present danger. On the other hand, in Germany even hate speech that harms human dignity can be prosecuted. In Israel some laws go back to the Ottoman period and colonial times and the definition of incitement is connected with rebellious acts; this creates certain legal confusion. In short, propaganda and freedom of speech issues, even in democratic societies, often cause heated legal debates.

Throughout the world we can always find societies subjected, to one degree or another, to what might be considered a "malignant" type of propaganda—"brainwashing" or "thought reform" coming from above—for example, as existed during the growth of Chinese Communism between 1921 and 1948. The experiential world in this case was divided into "good"/pure and "bad"/impure categories, just as observed in the internal worlds of patients who have "borderline personality organization." What is pathological for the individual was the prescription for reform in Communist China.[15]

Iran's Ayatollah Khomeini depended on long-distance telephone calls and tape recorders to spread his religious fundamentalist revolution. ABC's *Nightline* reported in December 1991 the first recorded use of the fax machine for propaganda purposes in Riyadh. Notices describing how to prepare for a chemical warfare assault, presumably sent by Saddam Hussein's propagandists, came through thousands of Saudi Arabian fax machines. Poland's Lech Walesa once commented that the underground Solidarity movement could not have succeeded without video technology.

Now the internet is available for making propaganda and it can be said that even space technology is utilized to influence the masses. Some sources who were close to Ronald Reagan tell the story of when the president had a dream in which he wore a helmet. The next day, focusing on this dream, he slowly evolved the idea of creating a "helmet" for the United States to protect it from Soviet missiles. Thus Ronald Reagan's Strategic Defense Initiative (SDI) (commonly called "Star Wars") was initiated. It is also rumored that U.S. scientists went along with Reagan's "dream" in order to acquire funds to evolve space technology, which as we know, did happen. SDI as a notion was also used as U.S. propaganda. The evermore rapid proliferation of communication technologies during the last several decades and the use of the Internet have predictably diversified the means and methods of political manipulation and influence. Now, in our daily lives we are constantly exposed to political propaganda. And, also now, we are wondering what will happen to state ideologically tinted propaganda in North Korea since the death of Kim Jong-il in December 2011 and religiously tinted propaganda in Iran and other places in the so-called Muslim World.

When a large group wonders, "Who are we now?" the personality of the political leader or the new leader after a revolution becomes an important factor in the scenario, one that has considerable influence on societal and political processes. The leader may tame or inflame other large-group sentiments; he or she may lead the large group toward peaceful coexistence with Others, or fuel a war-like atmosphere, even playing an actual role in starting a war. Leaders can be reparative or destructive.[16] A reparative leader tries to increase the followers' narcissistic investment in large-group identity without malignantly devaluating or hurting Others, whether they are within the same legal boundary of the large-group to which the leader belongs or outside of this boundary. A destructive leader aims to enhance and/or modify the large group's identity by destroying, one way or another, an opposing and/or devalued group as an action of purification.

A destructive leader's and his or her associates' political propaganda that creates an atmosphere for malignant purification usually follows these steps:

- Enhancing a shared sense of victimization or unfair situation within the large group following an attack by an enemy or another disaster, such as an economic one, or even in situations without any visible victimization or unfair condition;
- Reactivating a chosen trauma or a past shared trauma;
- Creating a time collapse that mixes up the image of a past enemy with the present devalued group;
- Devaluing the opposing group and dehumanizing it;

- Presenting the large-group leadership as an omnipotent "savior";
- Elevating large-group identity to be more important than individual identity, such as through interference with home life and the family system, education in schools, and other means;
- Increasing a sense of "we-ness" (large-group narcissism) that is contaminated with an entitlement ideology usually linked with the reactivated chosen trauma;
- Expressing preoccupation with the large group's psychological borders through an obsession with physical borders;
- Turning an entitlement ideology into revengeful actions and malignant purifications and thus allowing mass murders to be committed.

Psychoanalysts have not written much about political propaganda.[17] An exception, as referenced above, was Ernst Kris. Kris also described people whom he named "opinion leaders," or "wicked agitators."[18] Also helpful in spreading political propaganda are "opinion leaders"—the doctor, the vicar, the teacher, the barber, the union organizer both inside and outside the framework of a political group or institution, and the "wicked agitator"—the person who polarizes his or her negative and positive attitudes and projects them toward specific targets while striving for applause. When Kris expressed his opinion about political propaganda decades ago, he could not have imagined today's communication technology and streamlined dissemination of information.

In the next chapter I will discuss the malignant political propaganda spread by Serbian leader Slobodan Milošević and his associates after the collapse of the former Yugoslavia and describe my observations of its tragic consequences in Croatia.

# 28

# SERBIA AND THE BALKANS

## REACTIVATION OF A CHOSEN TRAUMA

In June 1998, one month after I went to the Republic of Georgia for the first time, I also made my first visit to independent Croatia. I had been to the area once before in 1974 when Croatia was part of Yugoslavia. My family and I had bought a car in Munich and had driven along the Adriatic coast of Yugoslavia from Rijeka to south of Dubrovnik before turning east, making our way through Bulgaria to Istanbul. This trip through Yugoslavia and Bulgaria gave me a first glimpse of a Communist country.

My 1998 visit to Croatia was due to an invitation from Professor Eduard Klain from the University of Zagreb Medical School. Eduard had studied psychoanalysis,[1] and was leading and supervising efforts dealing with war trauma following the breakup of the former Yugoslavia. This breakup began in the summer of 1991 with the secession of Slovenia from the Yugoslav Federation. Eduard Klain invited me to come to Croatia after learning about CSMHI's work in Estonia and reading my papers on ethnic conflicts.

Before I received Eduard's invitation, I had examined how then Serbian leader Slobodan Milošević and the circle of academicians and religious persons around him had reactivated the six-century-old Serbian chosen trauma—the mental image of the Battle of Kosovo that took place on June 28, 1389—and its association with the Serbian entitlement ideology known as Christoslavism.[2] This reactivation and Milošević and his associates' wish to create a "Greater Serbia" had played a significant role in the Croatian "independence war" that started in 1991 and ended in 1995 and the Bosnian war that started in 1992 and also ended in 1995.

After becoming independent from Byzantium in the twelfth century, the kingdom of Serbia thrived for almost two hundred years under the leadership of the Nemanjić Dynasty, reaching its climax under Emperor Stefan Duśan. By the end of his twenty-four-year reign, Serbia encompassed territory from the Croatian border in the north to the Aegean Sea in the south, from the Adriatic Sea in the west to Constantinople (Istanbul) in the east. Duśan died in 1355 and the Nemanjić Dynasty came to an end a short time thereafter. In 1371, Serbian feudal lords elected Lazar Hrebeljanović as leader of Serbia, though he assumed the title of prince or duke rather than king or emperor.

The decline of Serbia that followed is primarily attributed to the expansion of the Ottoman Empire into Serbian territory, culminating in the Battle of Kosovo at the Kosovo Polje (the Field of the Blackbirds). There is no eyewitness account of the Battle of Kosovo, and, in fact, Serbian, Turkish, and Italian sources give us around twenty-five versions of what happened during this event.[3] We know that the Ottoman Turkish Sultan, Murad I, was fatally wounded by a Serbian assassin during or after the battle.[4] We also know that before he died, the wounded sultan, or his son Bayezid, ordered the execution of Prince Lazar, who had been captured during the battle. Chroniclers have disagreed, however, on some of the battle's other outcomes. With heavy losses on both sides, and the death of both leaders, many consider the immediate result of the battle to be indecisive. Ottoman forces apparently returned to Adrianople (Edirne) after Kosovo, and Lazar was succeeded by his son, Stefan Lazarević, who reportedly became an ally of Murad's successor, Sultan Bayezid. The new Turkish sultan also married Lazar's youngest daughter, Olivera, in 1389. Sending Olivera to the sultan's harem might have been humiliating for the Serbs, but the Serbs and the Turks, in a sense, "made love" instead of war.

Seventy years after the Battle of Kosovo, the Ottoman Turks gained substantial control over Serbia. Despite a gap of seven decades between the Battle of Kosovo and the total occupation of Serbia by the Turks, a belief gradually developed that equated the two events. One reason is that the Serbs removed Lazar's remains from Kosovo and, after a long trip north, they buried them at a location north of Belgrade. This event was accompanied by mythologized tales, folk songs, and epic poems. The Battle of Kosovo slowly evolved into a chosen trauma for the Serbian people. It became a societal "sacred grief,"[5] and the shared mental image of the battle was transmitted from generation to generation through a strong oral and religious tradition. What is important in this case, as in others, is the impact of the chosen trauma on a large group's identity.

As the chosen trauma evolved, several historical factors were repressed, including the disunity of the Balkan Slavs and even of Lazar's own family, Lazar's apparent ineffectiveness as a leader, and the continued existence of Serbia for many decades after the battle. The image of Prince Lazar initially had to be absolved for sealing the fate of Serbia. According to legend, Saint Ilya, in the shape of a gray falcon, appeared before Lazar on the eve of the battle with a message from the Virgin Mary. Lazar was given two choices: (1) if he wished, he could win the battle and find a kingdom on earth, or (2) he could lose the battle, die a martyr's death, and find a kingdom in heaven.[6] The legend says that Lazar "chose" a Christ-like sacrifice. Through the proliferation of this legend, the Serbs collectively tried to deny shame and humiliation, but also experienced an ongoing inability to mourn as a large group. They held on to the "martyrdom" of the legend and the image of Lazar as a kind of crucified Jesus Christ.

The sense of martyrdom fit well with their pre-Ottoman perception of themselves. Even during the Nemanjić period, the Serbs thought that they had sacrificed themselves for other Christians in Europe, as they had served as a "buffer" against the advancing Muslim Turks. The Serbs, belonging to the Eastern Orthodox Church, received no appreciation from their Roman Catholic neighbors in Europe for their "sacrifice." After Serbia was occupied by the Ottomans, this reality supported and increased their sense of victimization. The Church and folk singers, *guslars*, effectively kept the chosen trauma in the public's awareness. June 28, the day of the Battle of Kosovo, was commemorated as St. Vitus Day and through the centuries became the subject of other legends that strengthened the victimized large-group identity.

Without dwelling on the details of Serbian history, let us come to the nineteenth century, when the decline of the Ottoman Empire coincided with the awakening of nationalism in Europe. In Serbian minds Lazar's image was transformed from a saint and martyr into an avenger. But still there would be no shared Serbian identity outside the context of the symbol of Kosovo, whether it induced a shared sense of victimization or shared sense of revenge. Mothers began to greet their children as the "avengers of Kosovo"—the direct and indirect message was to reverse not only shame and humiliation, but also the large group's image of unending large-group mourning and helplessness. In 1878, after much political scheming and many wars, the Serbs (as well as the Montenegrins) were declared independent from the Ottoman Empire by the Treaty of Berlin. The treaty, however, placed them under the control of Austria-Hungary, which in turn tried to suppress Serbia's Kosovo spirit. Serbia soon found itself in the Balkan Wars of 1912–1913, but was finally able to "liberate" Kosovo after more than five hundred years.

Less than two years after Kosovo's liberation, on St. Vitus Day of 1914, a Bosnian Serb named Gavrilo Princip assassinated Archduke Francis Ferdinand and his pregnant wife in Sarajevo, thereby initiating World War I. What is known about Princip is that as a teenager he was filled, as were most other Serbian youngsters, with the transformed images of Lazar and his son-in-law Miloš, who supposedly had fatally wounded Murad I, as avengers. Although Serbia was now "free," the Austro-Hungarian Empire exerted significant influence over much of the region after the Ottomans. It appeared that in Princip's mind, the old and new "oppressors" were condensed, and the desire for revenge was transferred to the Austro-Hungarian heir apparent.

After World War I, the attempt to bring all the South Slavs into one kingdom slowly succeeded and the kingdom of the Serbs, Croats, and Slovenes was founded, later to be known as Yugoslavia, which means "land of the Southern Slavs"—distinguishing them from northern Slavs such as Poles, Slovakians, and Romanians. Yugoslavia was formed of five "lands": Serbia, Montenegro, Slovenia, Croatia, and Bosnia-Herzegovina (or simply Bosnia). Many Bosnians had become Muslims under the Ottoman rule, and the term "Bosniaks" stands for Bosnians who are Muslims and who are the majority in Bosnia. As one might expect, the kingdom was fragmented by frequent quarrels. In 1941 Yugoslavia surrendered to the Nazis, and while what happened in the Nazi period is another story that tells much about the present-day Serbian-Croat-Muslim enmities, I will not dwell on it here.

In 1945 Yugoslavia was reorganized as a Communist state with Marshall Josip Broz Tito as its head. The new Yugoslavia included the original five "lands," now called republics, plus Macedonia. Kosovo and Vojvodina, in southern and northern Serbia, respectively, remained "autonomous" republics. Under the Communist regime in Yugoslavia, Serbs, Croats, Muslims, Slovenes, Montenegrins, and others lived together in relative peace, although this was not the case at all times. For example, in the late 1960s and early 1970s Croat nationalists demanded the formation of an independent Croatia. To combat such problems, the Communists had been attempting to create a "Yugoslav man" similar to the Soviet ideal of a "Soviet man," in which all peoples were considered equal and connected through the higher objectives of Communist ideology. For a Serb, turning into a Communist "Yugoslav man" meant that he (or she) would no longer possess the most important Serbian large-group identity marker, the image of the Battle of Kosovo and the image of Prince Lazar who symbolized the events of this battle. Thus, Lazar's representation was officially degraded as a "symbol of reactionary nationalism."[7] In spite of this, the Serbs continued to drink red wine named after Lazar; symbolically speaking they continued to take in his image. During the Communist regime in Bosnia-Herzegovina, more than one-fourth of all marriages were mixed and less than three percent of all Muslims attended prayers in a mosque. But we now know that each group in Yugoslavia strongly held on to its own identity rather than become a single "Yugoslavian" people.

After Mikhail Gorbachev's introduction of *glasnost* and *perestroika* in 1987, the Socialist Republic of Yugoslavia began to show cracks: each group began to ask "Who are we now?" and "How are we different from others?" Then the breakup of Yugoslavia occurred with most deadly and dreadful consequences, in which political propaganda associated with the deliberate reactivation of the Serbian chosen trauma played a key role.[8] Slobodan Milošević's and his associates' reactivation of the Serbian chosen trauma primarily was accomplished when Prince Lazar's remains—whatever was left after six hundred years—were placed in a coffin and taken on tour to Serbian villages and towns where they were received by huge crowds of "mourners" dressed in black. A new monument was built at the Field of Blackbirds. After a year-long tour Lazar returned from "exile" and was placed in this monument, which has a sign that reads "1389–1989," symbolizing time collapse. On June 28, 1989, the 600th anniversary of the Battle of Kosovo, Milošević arrived at this location by helicopter, like the reincarnated Lazar/Christ returning to earth from heaven, now entitled to build his "kingdom" on earth.

The Serbian propaganda machinery was well organized. It was also a malignant form of propaganda that led to ethnic and cultural cleansing, a malignant purification. Malignant purification is different from some politicians' efforts to support their or their followers' wish to get rid of illegal immigrants or guest workers in a stable, democratic country. Even though such efforts may lead to human tragedies such as forced physical separation of some family members, they are carried out under a legal system and do not include murder. On the other hand, during malignant ethnic and cultural cleansing, many persons become murderers and destroyers of physical environments.

Serbian malignant propaganda focused on writing by the Bosnian Muslim leader Alija Izetbegović that envisioned a huge Muslim empire extending into Europe. Serbian propagandists modified and exaggerated Izetbegović's statements, sounding the alarm that Islamic fundamentalists would establish an Islamic enterprise in Bosnia and raise a generation of Janissaries in the territories. In order to do so, they warned, a fourfold crime would be committed against the Serbian woman: "to remove her from her family, to impregnate her by undesirable seeds, to make her bear a stranger and then to take even him away from her."[9]

This propaganda, with deliberate modification, aimed to reactivate the "memory" of the old Ottoman *devşirme* system in which Christian orthodox youth, such as Serbian youngsters, were collected under very strict rules as an extraordinary tax levied by the sultan, taken away from their families, converted to Islam, and educated to serve the sultan. One of the greatest grand viziers of the Ottoman Empire, Sokollu (Sokolovich) Mehmet Pasha was one of them, originally a Serb who was raised in the *devşirme* system. Most youngsters, however, would be enrolled in the ranks of the empire's feared Janissary infantry force or as the sultan's household bodyguards. This system started with the reign of Murad I in 1359 and was abandoned in 1826. More than 170 years after its abandonment, Serbian propaganda, based on pure fantasy, stated the return of Ottoman power. It created not only a sense of victimization and a time collapse but also a fusion between Ottomans of previous centuries and Bosniaks of the 1990s.

As time passed, new Serbian propaganda replaced the old campaign and it proclaimed that a child born to a non-Serbian woman raped by a Serb would be a Serb and would not carry any vestige of the non-Serbian mother's large-group identity.[10] The other side of the coin was now shown to the Serbian public: when Serbian boys were conscripted under the Ottoman *devşirme* system and transformed into Muslim Ottomans, their original large-group identity, their "psychological genes" from their parents, were rendered irrelevant. Now Serbs were trying to disregard the "genes" of non-Serbian women, by using these women as vessels to produce more "Serbs" to fight against Muslims (and Croats) and create a "Greater Serbia."

Bosniaks suffered horribly at the hands of the Serbs. Even though rapes occur during any war, raping Bosnian Muslim women was a deliberate attempt supported by Serbian propaganda to create more "Serbs" for the psychic reality of Greater Serbia. It is estimated that between 20,000 and 50,000 Bosniak women were raped during the Bosnian war. Meanwhile, Bosniak men were killed in part because, to the Serbs, they represented Muslim Ottoman Turks. Bosniaks were subjected to genocide in Srebrenica in July 1995.

Croatians' biggest tragedy occurred much earlier during the eighty-seven-day siege of Vukovar by the Serbian-dominated Yugoslav army between August and November 1991. Vukovar is in the Eastern Slovenia region of Croatia near the Croatia-Serbia border. Before the siege it was a modestly prosperous town with Baroque architecture. It was totally destroyed as Serbs took control of it on November 18, 1991. Hundreds of Croatian soldiers and civilians were massacred and it was ethnically cleansed of Croats—around 31,000 Croats from Vukovar and surrounding areas were forced to become refugees in Croatia. A cease-fire took place a few weeks after the Serbs took over the destroyed Vukovar. Prior to events there, the Croatians had attempted to get rid of Serbs living in Croatia, leading to casualties. But, as expected, the story of Vukovar induced deep emotions within Croatians.

Eduard Klain invited me in December 1997, first to come to Zagreb and participate in the 18th Danube Symposium of Psychiatry at the beginning of June 1998 and then to go to Dubrovnik to attend the School of Traumatology meeting. He wrote to remind me that the United Nations mandate in Eastern Slavonia, where Vukovar is located, would come to an end in the near future and that intensive interethnic tensions were expected between Serbs and Croats. He continued:

> Strained relations are already observed in other regions of Croatia where the Serbs who ran away after the military action of the Croatian army are coming back. As you probably know, these regions were occupied by the Serbs during the war. Nowadays, especially in Eastern Slavonia, but in the other regions of Croatia also,

> Croats and Serbs are to live together, as well as Hungarians and other nationalities in Slavonia. In my opinion, building the interethnic reliance is very important, but very hard to realize, due to severe traumas experienced by both sides. The Government essentially doesn't want reconciliation. Unfortunately, the Government wants the national state with as few Serbs as possible coming back to Croatia. It is important that you know that, because of my following request, I have read once again your report about the workshops in Tallinn, as well as in Kaunas. . . . I personally, along with many intellectuals with advanced views in Croatia, would like the reconciliation process to begin, and your model to be implemented.

Eduard continued to explain to me that he had been in touch with the Soros Foundation (Open Society) and that he hoped to receive support to start a reconciliation process.[11] I was asked to give three lectures on large-group rituals, transgenerational transmissions, and the Tree Model to participants of the Danube Symposium of Psychiatry. But, as a more important contribution, I was asked to direct one afternoon dialogue between Croatian, Serbian, and Bosnian psychiatrists who would attend this meeting. After Zagreb I would go with Eduard to Dubrovnik and take part in the School of Traumatology activities. In Dubrovnik too I would give lectures and conduct dialogues between Croatian, Serbian, and Bosnian psychiatrists, this time including psychologists from the same countries.

In Zagreb seventeen chairs were placed in a circle in a meeting room surrounded thirty or so chairs forming an outer circle. Eduard and I sat on chairs in the inner circle with five psychiatrists, two women and three men, from Serbia and one woman psychiatrist from Bosnia. Croatian psychiatrists sat on the remaining chairs in the inner circle. Colleagues who had come to observe this dialogue exercise took their places in the outer circle. What happened in this initial dialogue in Zagreb between psychiatrists from opposing large groups, as the reader can expect, was similar to dialogues I had conducted among members of opposing large groups elsewhere. The participants exhibited investment in large-group narcissism, accordion phenomena, and competitions of grievances, for example. Because of this I will not tell their stories, except one most moving story from a young Croatian psychiatrist.

The young psychiatrist was very proud to have been assigned by the Croatian Ministry of Health to work in Vukovar. He was the first Croatian mental health professional to go to this city after it was destroyed and worked at the Vukovar Hospital. He thought it his national duty to play a role in changing the emotional atmosphere of the city so that former Croatian residents would want to return. As Eduard had written to me, the UN mandate over this region would end soon and the town would be reintegrated into Croatia. Before going to Vukovar, the young man was told that 30,000 Serbs were still "occupying" the city and that only three Croatian refugees had returnedthere.[12] His ethnic sentiments were highly enhanced. When he arrived in Vukovar, he was met in the hospital by colleagues who were of Serbian origin. The Serbian psychiatrists wanted to be friendly with the newcomer and, in addressing him, used his first name. But soon, working daily with Serbian colleagues who spoke to him as if nothing had happened infuriated him.

The young man knew that after taking over the city, Serbs had brought many Croatian patients and staff members from the hospital and other Croatians from Vukovar to a place called Ovčara, which is five kilometers from the city and which had been turned into a prison camp. Many were killed there. The Croatian doctor became convinced that one of the Serbs at Vukovar Hospital had been involved in making an "extermination" list of Croatian patients and their Croatian caretakers for the Serbs. He felt like a traitor working with this Serb. When at the meeting he told the participants his story, he felt paralyzed. I felt for him and tried to help him as much as I could.

There was only one Bosnian at the Zagreb meeting. Nine Bosniaks, both men and women from Sarejevo, were present in Dubrovnik. People in many areas of Croatia and Serbia were not traumatized directly during the war. For example, the war was concentrated in a quarter of Croatian territory. Almost all Bosniaks, on the other hand, were directly affected. When I conducted dialogues among Croat, Serb, and Bosniak mental health workers, the nine Bosniaks stayed rather silent. I thought that their silence was mainly due to their shared feeling that no one would understand what they had gone through. But in their traumatized state and regression, they felt closely related to me when they learned that my ethnic origin is Turkish. The Serbian propaganda had enhanced the Serbs' idea that Bosniaks and Turks were the same. In fact, while killing Bosniak men, for example, in Srebrenica, the Serbs would call them "Turks." In turn, these nine Bosniaks now perceived me as their extensions. In the evenings they gathered around me without the other participants and told me horrifying personal stories and even presented their own symptoms.

A Bosniak woman, a psychiatrist, had to pass through streets amid gunfire to reach a hospital. A young man she knew well before the war was wounded by the Serbs and taken to this hospital. Here, the psychiatrist witnessed the amputation of one of the young man's legs. After this event, she developed a symptom of periodically checking to see if her legs were attached to her body. She would wake up in terror in the middle of the night to check whether her legs were still there. I helped her to understand that her symptoms were caused by her identification with the young man whose leg amputation she had witnessed. She had not previously been conscious of this connection and expressed great relief at this "discovery." I think their sharing their stories was helpful for the Bosniaks. They later sent faxes to me at CSMHI asking me to come to Sarajevo. Sadly, I could not find ways to start a program in Sarejevo and was unable to find opportunities to spend more time with them.

Unlike my frequent visits to the Republic of Georgia, my visits to Croatia took place once a year or once every other year. On one occasion we saw NATO planes fly over Dubrovnik and then heard them bombing Serbian areas. The School of Traumatology continued to have international summer gatherings in Dubrovnik until 2009, under the directorship of Eduard Klain and after his retirement under the directorship of Rudolf Gregurek. Serbs and Bosnians would also attend these meetings. Every time I joined them I gave lectures and conducted dialogues.

My role in helping the helpers was much less in this part of the world than it had been in the Republic of Georgia and South Ossetia. While I could not develop frequent contacts with the Bosniaks when I was away from this part of the world, I was able to keep meaningful contact with a group of Croat psychiatrists and one Serbian psychiatrist. I also met some of them at other international meetings.[13] Boris Drozdek, who had become the medical director at Psychotrauma Centrum Zuid in the Netherlands and was originally from Croatia, became a key figure at the Dubrovnik meetings and one of the important figures in Europe to deal with trauma, torture, and refugee issues.[14]

In Georgia I spent considerable time at Tbilisi Sea getting to know an internally displaced family and, through my work with them, I was able to be helpful to other IDPs too.[15] In Croatia I visited, only once, a group of Croatian refugees from Vukovar who were living in an apartment complex in Zagreb. Through my lectures, however, Croatian colleagues became aware of how, by looking for and finding refugees' linking objects, they could find a way to help them with complicated mourning. There were others in Croatia who had lost relatives during the war and who were also experiencing complicated mourning. The Office for the Detained and Missing Persons of the Republic of Croatia stated in March 2001 that there were 3,052 persons who had disappeared during the 1991–1995 war in Croatia and that only 1,529 bodies had been exhumed from 126 graves. They still did not know what had happened to the other 1,523 missing persons. One can easily understand how under such conditions there would be thousands and thousands of individuals who were mourning a loved one in a psychologically complicated manner.

Ivan Urlić, the head of the Department of Psychiatry, Split University School of Medicine, with Slavica Jurčević from the same institution, carried out a study examining linking objects of twenty-six mothers of disappeared Croatian soldiers. They found that all had linking objects and also described one kind of linking object that I had not mentioned in my writings on this topic. They called this type of linking object the "memorial shrine." They found this in eight homes, reflective of the Croatian religious culture and tradition: "A photograph of the missing person or person whose remains were identified long after he had gone missing occupied a central place at the shrine, and was surrounded by other symbols of the Catholic iconography (Virgin Mary, Crucifix), flower, and candle. The memorial shrine to the beloved son who disappeared was always located in the room where the family spent most of their time and/or where guests were received (living room or kitchen)."[16] Jurčević and Urlić stated that the "memorial shrine" bore a character of an altar and represented an expression of patriotism and sacrifice for the Homeland. They not only linked the mourner with the lost one, but also ascribed saint-like dimensions to the disappeared.

My most recent trip to Dubrovnik was in 2009. Near the main gate where one enters this historical and beautiful old city and within the old city itself, billboards were erected with maps of the area. Dozens and dozens of black spots on the maps illustrated locations that had been targets of the Serbian shelling. Thousands of tourists walking around were paying no attention to these billboards, but I knew that each black spot also represented a scar in a Croat's heart.

# 29

# THE IMMIGRANT EXPERIENCE, INTEGRATION, AND RACISM

There is a major issue that often accompanies societal disorganization, especially when it is associated with conflicts with the Other, within or outside of the legal boundaries in which a large group lives: many persons are forced to leave their familiar surroundings and become internally displaced persons or refugees as happened in the former Yugoslavia and in the Republic of Georgia. Also, modern globalization, which has lowered barriers to international trade, especially since World War II, has resulted not only in substantially increased travel but also greatly increased dislocation. "Globalization is likely to be one of the dominant forces in the psychological development of the people of the 21st century."[1] The task of learning to live together peacefully falls on both the newcomer and the host. This task also stimulates societies' preoccupations with large-group identity issues and initiates new social/political movements. As population profiles change worldwide, sometimes societies appreciate the beauty of ethnic, racial, or religious diversity, but sometimes xenophobic reactions and racism show their ugly faces.

The issue of illegal immigration, and even legal immigration, is a hot political issue. Questions associated with the influx of immigrants comprise a vast topic, and its comprehensive study requires input from different disciplines. Here I will examine only the psychology of voluntary and forced immigrants and also try to point out some political ramifications of worldwide massive dislocations.

My visits to Georgia and Croatia, combined with what I observed in North Cyprus much earlier, taught me a great deal about the psychology of internally displaced persons and refugees. This led me to compare the internal worlds of involuntary and voluntary immigrants.[2] I was a voluntary immigrant myself when I came to the United States, and I worked with others who were involuntary immigrants, some intensively such as IDPs at Tbilisi Sea, and some briefly such as those in Zagreb. The internal worlds of voluntary immigrants are vastly different from those of IDPs, refugees, and asylum seekers. Nevertheless, there are also common elements that underlie the psychology of both the voluntary immigrant and the traumatized forced immigrant, since moving from the home place to an unfamiliar location involves loss of people, familiar surroundings, language, music, dances, food, and smells. In addition, all such dislocation involves the need to mourn these losses and to struggle with both external and internal adjustment, especially the need to learn a new language.

In cases of "voluntary" immigration, dislocated persons' integration into a new country is—if the individual's psychological makeup does not present complications— smoother than the adaptation of another dislocated person who is "forced" to migrate. However, there is also difficulty in differentiating what is truly "voluntary"' and what is truly "involuntary" when moving to and settling into an unfamiliar place. I came to the United States voluntarily to expand my medical training with the idea that I would return to Cyprus when I finished my studies. But events in my life "voluntarily" led me to become a U.S. citizen. Intimate narratives in the book *Immigrant Experiences: Personal Narratives and Psychological Analysis*, edited by Paul Elovitz and Charlotte Kahn, describe various authors' voluntary immigrant experiences. Some of them "volunteered" to come to America in order to escape disturbing family conditions, and others could not wait to find freedom in America to escape devastating historical or political situations.[3] It is clear that individuals make the decision to settle in a new location for various reasons.

At the beginning there is, to one degree or another, "culture shock" for all dislocated individuals: the voluntary immigrant activates a fantasy that the past contained "good" images of self, others, and things. When the reality of dislocation sets in, such images are felt to be missing. The immigrant then experiences a sense of discontinuity.[4] At the present time, generally speaking, due to increased communication technology and modern globalization, "culture shock" has lost its impact for many. But it still exists. If the newcomer can mourn his or her losses while keeping the memory of the "good" lost persons and things, "culture shock" disappears.

In many cases of "forced" immigration, the dislocated person will have difficulty mourning, and the "culture shock" will linger, manifesting in different ways. For example, the immigrant might remain in deep yearning for "good" things left behind and show no eagerness to find pleasurable things in the new location. Furthermore, in cases in which people have escaped severe persecution or genocide, some of these newcomers have difficulty even developing a fantasy or nostalgia about "good" objects of the past due to an unconscious fear that if one imagines good things they will also be destroyed. This can leave the person in a horrible psychological state in which he or she will have no continuity with the old familiar objects and no true links to new objects in the new location.

I want to remind the reader that not all people who escaped the Holocaust or other terrible genocidal situations suffer from these conditions. Multiple psychological mechanisms can help keep resilience active. The legal ability to visit the country of origin and the degree of acceptance found at the new location help the dislocated person adjust to new surroundings. Still, adaptation is always slow, especially if there is a need to learn the nuances of a new language.

Salman Akhtar suggests that immigration initiates a "third individuation."[5] The first individuation occurs in childhood when children slowly go through psychological developmental steps and find their individuality.[6] The second individuation takes place during the adolescence passage when youngsters review, mostly unconsciously, the images of important people and things from their childhood. They continue to keep some, modify others, while adding new images from their expanded world and thus change their own internal worlds and identities.[7] The third individuation of the immigrant allows this person to experience biculturalism, resulting in a sense of belonging to neither the one left behind nor the one he or she has now entered, while neither excludes the other.[8] In fact, he or she will belong, as Demetrios Julius stated, "totally to both." Referring to his own experiences, Demetrios explained how he slowly came to appreciate the importance of intrapsychic cultural complementarity. As he reached an acceptance of the vast cultural differences between the two countries (Greece and the United States), he said he "began to accept certain psychological paradoxes and feel myself truly bicultural."[9] My own experiences are *almost* identical to Demetrios'. Nevertheless, he has no accent when he speaks English and I do. Also, after living in the United States for so long, now I have an accent when I speak Turkish. This sometimes creates uncomfortable situations in which I am treated as an Other. On many occasions during recent years, while shopping or ordering meals at a restaurant in Turkey, a shopkeeper or waiter will ask me, "Where did you study Turkish? How did you learn to speak it so well?" I always answer, "I had no choice. My mother taught me how to speak Turkish."

If children settle into a new country prior to their second individuation without external complications, their adjustment to and assimilation of the new culture will be, in general, easier. They will learn how to speak the new language without accent. However, adult immigrants with or without being aware of it, pass to their children aspects of traditions and history that had supposedly been left behind. As Ernst Kris stated long ago, "Under the disguise of full compliance with the new environment, cultural heritages of the past, though attenuated by time and intermarriage, live on among men."[10]

In 1993 we held a conference at CSMHI in Charlottesville on the topic of immigrants and refugees. One of the participants was Howard Stein, an anthropologist of East European Jewish ancestry who was born in the United States. Among his important works was his study of the Slovak- and Rusyn-American experience in the Steel Valley of western Pennsylvania. For this study he visited many Slovak and Rusyn homes. One day he realized that all interviews were taking place in kitchens and occasionally an adjacent dining room. He felt uneasy because in the culture in which he was raised visitors were made comfortable in the living room or family room. Then he learned that in the patriarchal Slavic world, in the second- or third-generation of the Slovak- and Rusyn-American houses, the kitchen was the authentic visiting room in the home, a place where family and friends could relax, eat, and drink for hours. Traditions had been passed from generation to generation. Only priests, politicians, dignitaries, and other official guests were brought into the formal "living room."

Howard's research also illustrated that both in Eastern Europe and the United States, despised and envied out-groups helped define Slovak and Rusyn boundaries. He wrote:

> To a degree, the role of Jews and Gypsies as outcast in eastern Europe was transferred to Blacks in the United States. Blacks became the new outgroup to embody the 'bad' counter-image to Slovaks and Rusyns, whose positive self-image was that of industriousness, thrift, generosity, familiality, non-violence, and sexual probity. At the same time, immigrant Slovaks and Rusyns were themselves stigmatized by more mainstream Americans who were anxious about their own social standing as real Americans. They lumped Slovaks, Rusyns, Maygars, Croats, Serbs, Slovenians, Macedonians, and others into a single degrading image, that of "Hunkies," whom they characterized as stupid, fat, brutal, drunk, and only suitable for hard labor.[11]

Elsewhere in America, in big cities, we can observe similar findings: an ethnic or racial group that lives in the same neighborhood holds on to its traditions and other psychological elements as it separates itself from another ethnic and racial group that lives in the adjacent neighborhood.

Forced immigration includes the impact of an *actual* trauma associated with fear for one's life, survival guilt, humiliation, helplessness, and sometimes torture, which is then piggybacked onto the trauma of losses caused by a dislocation. It becomes very difficult and often impossible for IDPs, refugees, and those who are exiled to go through the work of mourning in adaptive ways. These individuals need to deal with the effects of the actual trauma before they can become like ordinary, "normal" immigrants and begin to genuinely do the work of mourning. External factors before dislocation and after arriving at a new location that become intertwined with internal psychological conditions will be crucial in determining the degree of resilience and whether a forced immigrant will ever one day be able to feel like an ordinary immigrant.

Immigrants use linking objects like perennial mourners do. Their investment in such objects is withdrawn slowly as their adjustment to the new environment takes place and they feel comfortable with their biculturalism. Two or three years after I came to the United States and after I knew that the United States would be my new country, I collected pictures from my parents, sisters, other relatives, and friends and my own pictures from my days in Cyprus and made a photo album. On the cover of this album I wrote: "My life before I came to America." At the time I had no idea why I had made such an album. After I became a psychoanalyst I realized that this album was my linking object. I still keep it somewhere, but it has lost its original emotional power. I wrote earlier about how I kept the newspaper clipping that announced the murder of Erol, my roommate from my medical school days in Ankara. This newspaper clipping is also a linking object. Both the album and the newspaper clipping are personal items; they belong only to me and they have emotional meaning only for me.

Now I will begin to focus on large-group psychology. When a historical situation occurs and thousands of people volunteer or are forced to leave their familiar place and settle in a new location, they in a sense become a subgroup. They create a shared linking object or phenomenon. The family I worked with for years at Tbilisi Sea had its own linking object. It was a living one, a dog that was given a very special place in their crowded and poor hotel apartment where they were forced to live. When this family escaped from Abkhazia under horrible conditions, they had to leave their dog behind. I was told that the new dog at Tbilisi Sea looked like and was named after the dog that had been left behind. The dog at Tbilisi Sea connected this family with the lost past familiar place, but also illustrated that what was left behind (the first dog representing all the losses) could be reborn in a new location.

In this family's apartment there was a yellow telephone, the *only* telephone for the three thousand IDPs at Tbilisi Sea. This was a time when none of these dislocated persons possessed a mobile phone, so the yellow telephone emerged as a shared linking object for all of them, linking them to news from their lost locations as well as their new surroundings.[12] Similarly, I think that we can consider that family and friends gathering in the kitchens of the Slovak- and Rusyn-Americans in Steel Valley in western Pennsylvania served as the shared linking phenomenon for these people.

Refugees and IDPs living together at a new location create societal and political problems, of course, to one degree or another. When the city Tbilisi was filled with IDPs who were housed in special places, "Refugee, Go Home" signs were posted on many walls in Tbilisi. A split was observable in the city. Some of the IDPs were heroes and others were beloved teachers, respected writers, well-known sportspersons, and regular men, women, and children. Many local people who belonged to the same ethnic group, however, developed a psychic reality that the IDPs were dangerous persons or persons who would ruin the economy in Tbilisi. In time, this problem worked itself out without causing a major disaster.

A large group can also become refugees *without* leaving the physical location they live in. This occurs when the enemy ruins the physical environment, restricts activities, and kills relatives and friends. Then without actually going somewhere else, the large group loses familial places, people, and customs. As discussed in chapter 10, recall the phenomenon of Palestinians keeping the keys of their bulldozed houses. Such keys began to symbolize the reality of the loss and the hope of recovering the loss. As time passed, the symbol of a key became a shared linking object and also the symbol of Palestinian identity, and Palestinian politicians began coming to international meetings with a picture of a key pinned to their coat lapels.

As the twenty-first century approached, some felt that Europe was on the verge of an unprecedented era of social, economic, and political cooperation. It was, after all, almost fifty years since international war had ravaged the continent. Moreover, the Iron Curtain had melted, and the former client states of the Soviet Union were eager to join a united Europe. However, as old enmities between nation-states faded and borders became more porous, there were signs that all was not well in Europe. In Eastern Europe, many fragments of the old Soviet Empire and its sphere of influence disintegrated further into ethnic violence and even genocidal warfare. Furthermore, there was evidence of resurgent racism and xenophobia in Western Europe.[13] These phenomena were primarily due to the creation of new ethnic minorities, dislocated persons, and asylum-seekers who had come to Europe from many parts of the world legally and illegally. In Western Europe these minorities faced discrimination in employment and housing, abusive identity checks, threatening phone calls, attacks by Ku Klux Klan–style gangs, bombings, beatings, murders, and desecration of graves. The police reported seven thousand racist incidents in 1989 in London alone.

What was happening in Europe was called "neoracism." Variations in skin color, hair texture, facial features, and general physique have for centuries been thought to be manifestations of distinct human "races." Making such distinctions took on the character of racism when they were assumed to reflect diverse stages of human development and when rights and privileges were granted to the members of one group, while such rights and privileges were withheld from members of another. Racist theory was inadvertently given pseudo-scientific credence in the middle of the nineteenth century by the publication of Charles Darwin's *On the Origin of Species*.[14] From the data assembled by Darwin supporting the theory of biological evolution, various theories of social relations were extrapolated and came to be known collectively as "Social Darwinism." Arguments against the protection of the unfortunate, for example, were made on the grounds that it would hinder natural selection and survival of the fittest. The "natural superiority" of the white race was claimed to be the result of the "objective" process of biological evolution. Racist views were expounded as if they were scientific facts.

There is no need in this book to go into detail about the long history of this kind of racism in the United States. After I arrived in the United States and after I finished my internship in Chicago, Illinois, and psychiatric residency training in Chapel Hill, North Carolina, I worked for about two years at Cherry Hospital in Goldsboro, North Carolina. At that time, Cherry Hospital was a segregated place that only admitted African-American patients. It was just under fifty years before an African-American, Barack Obama, would become the president of the United States. My work at Cherry Hospital allowed me to observe racism at close range.[15]

Neoracism evolved as a new term that was used for the situation in Western Europe in the 1990s. It included hatred toward perceived cultural, and not just genetically determined, characteristics. This invited confusion between the concepts of race and ethnicity and between racism and ethnic hatred.

In the 1950s and 1960s, West Germany signed agreements with Greece, Turkey, Morocco, Portugal, Tunisia, and Yugoslavia to recruit workers for West Germany's industrial sector. Those foreigners who came to Germany for work would become known as "*Gastarbeiter*" (guest workers). By 1973 there were more than one million guest workers in Germany. Foreigners also began working in other Western European countries, brought their families to join them, and had children. Today, for example, it is estimated that more than four million Turks and German citizens with part or full Turkish ancestry live in Germany alone. It is clear that this situation is reflected in German and Turkish internal politics, as well as in German-Turkish relations. Neoracist video games, bearing titles such as *Concentration Camp Manager*, *Total Auschwitz*, and *Turk Village* were distributed in Austria, Germany and Sweden. These games, portraying Turks as "dangerous non-Aryans," had commentaries like "Play in Treblinka" and "Clean society of all parasites."[16]

In the 1990s, like people from other countries living in Germany and other Western European countries, the Turks were targets of neoracism. In 1993 Gündüz Aktan, then the Turkish permanent representative to the United Nations in Geneva, approached me and CSMHI and offered to sponsor us to form a CSMHI committee to study the psychology of Western European neoracism. He felt that it was important to have a report on the psychology of racism while the United Nations was intensively dealing with its political, societal, and legal aspects. I formed a CSMHI committee from its members and invited guests. Some members were from foreign countries or had close relationships with foreign countries, such as Turkey, Germany, Russia, and Ghana.[17] The committee met regularly over many months. We studied European Parliament and UN reports, newspaper accounts of many neoracist events, theoretical and especially psychoanalytical papers about how bad prejudice and racism evolve in individuals, the psychology of perpetrators and victims, and psychological mechanisms that trigger violence. Our report was presented to the Office of the Turkish Permanent Representative to the United Nations in Geneva and was distributed to officials dealing with the problem of neoracism in Western Europe. I cannot say what type of role CSMHI's report played in the official handing of this serious issue, but I know that Ambassador Aktan insisted on spreading psychological knowledge that the inevitability of prejudice does not mean submission to its malignant forms.

The CSMHI committee's work was one of the reasons we welcomed the study of societal issues in the Blackwell District of Richmond, Virginia. The inhabitants, all African-Americans, know this district as "Southside, Richmond." Crime and drug trafficking were present there and the Massey Foundation, also located in Richmond and a donor to CSMHI from its beginning, wanted us to get to know the Blackwell community and its religious leaders, teachers, and Richmond city authorities. They wanted us to consult with them in their efforts to make Blackwell a better place for its inhabitants and especially to prevent its young people from turning to drug use and criminality. CSMHI faculty member Maurice Apprey led this project,[18] and I accompanied him to Blackwell and Richmond city offices on several occasions.

During the time this district was known as "Southside, Richmond" to its inhabitants, there were still local jobs available. Residents would wake up in the morning to the smell of tobacco in the air, and the smell of tobacco told them to go to work, mostly at tobacco factories. Then a catastrophic change took place: a new highway system was built around the city, shifting the sewer lines. Now, instead of smelling tobacco and knowing it was time to go to work nearby, they smelled feces and knew it was time to figure out how to get to work in another part of town where their jobs had been relocated. This was easier said than done, as we learned one day when we examined the city bus lines on a map. We discovered that an "invisible border" had been erected around Blackwell, making it difficult to get in and out of this district. We took the map to the Richmond city officials who seemed surprised to see how Blackwell had become isolated. They were cooperative and serious in working with us to find a solution for how to integrate Blackwell's fractured community into the general city. As one tool for "treatment" for the youngsters' isolation and for turning them toward more adaptive occupations, CSMHI used project funds to buy a very nice bus for the Blackwell school system. With this bus, the teachers could break through the invisible wall and take children to places like the Richmond Museum or sporting events.

The Blackwell situation reminded me of another time I observed an "invisible wall." It was when I visited Skopje, the capital and largest city of the Republic of Macedonia, which had an invisible wall surrounding a district where Roma people lived, creating an "invisible enclave." I suspected that besides building a new highway system, a lingering investment in racism had played a role in isolating Blackwell, especially its young students, from the rest of the city.

# 30

# RETURNING TO THE MOUNTAIN HOUSE

## AN EXPANDING FIELD

From 1980 to the early 2000s our quarterly journal, *Mind and Human Interaction,* gave voice to psychoanalysts and scholars from different disciplines and countries who were writing about various forms of social traumas, losses, terrorism, identity issues, and related political changes around the globe. At CSMHI, meanwhile, through academic meetings, such as the November 1990 dialogue between well-known U.S. journalists and CSMHI members on the reasons for war, I continued to learn how people from other disciplines and countries were viewing large-group processes. Later CSMHI members, together with interdisciplinary and multicultural experts, studied the psychology of refugees, prejudice, racism, religious cults and fundamentalism, and terrorism, as well as movies and other forms of art that expressed these political/societal issues. Important scholars and authorities from different countries continued to visit CSMHI.

I was giving lectures at many universities in different countries during that time. Many students began writing to me for my opinion about their psychopolitical theses. At the same time many people working in traumatized locations of the world were also writing me, sharing their observations and asking questions about psychological resistances to carrying out peaceful solutions. I received an invitation to address an international audience of over five hundred people, including government ministers and ambassadors, at the United Nations in New York on April 23, 1999, during the Eighth International Conference on Health and Environment: Global Partners for Global Solutions.[1] This was one indication that interest in CSMHI's and my observations was spreading. During my talk at the United Nations, by giving examples from my observations in Croatia and Georgia, I referred to many psychopolitical concepts that have been described in this book. By then concepts such as large-group narcissism, chosen trauma, chosen glory, entitlement ideology, transgenerational transmissions, minor differences, accordion phenomenon, large-group mourning, linking objects, and purification had begun to appear in psychopolitical writings. Interestingly, psychoanalysts' interest in psychoanalytically informed psychopolitical findings developed very slowly. In 2005 psychoanalyst Howard Levine published a long summary of my findings on large-group dynamics in the *Journal of the American Psychoanalytic Association*.[2] Later, another psychoanalyst, Salman Akhtar, included my psychopolitical terms in his excellent *Comprehensive Dictionary of Psychoanalysis*,[3] and I gave keynote speeches during American and British psychoanalytical association meetings on what psychoanalysis can offer to politics. I also addressed the German Psychoanalytic Association and various other psychoanalytic organizations in many countries on the same topic.

As the millennium was coming to an end, CSMHI was approached by two Greek-Americans, Dr. Demetris Keridis, executive director of the Kokkalis Program on Southeastern and East-Central Europe at Harvard University's Kennedy School of Government and Dr. Elizabeth Prodromou, who at that time was at Princeton University. They were ready to raise funds to open a dialogue between politically influential Greeks and Turks. The two Greek-Americans asked CSMHI if we could join them and assist in removing resistances so that the Greek and the Turkish participants could engage in more realistic discussions about contentious issues, develop realistic strategies or suggestions for their respective authorities, and thus help to improve the relationship between the two countries. In January 1996, Turkey and Greece had come close to starting a war over two rocks in the Aegean Sea three miles from the Turkish coastline named Imia by the Greeks and Kardak by the Turks. These unpopulated islets occupy no more than ten acres. The "border psychology" between the Turks and the Greeks had become inflamed.[4] Another major contentious issue they wished to address was the Cyprus problem.

CSMHI accepted this invitation. However, because of the possibility that I might not remain "neutral," I refused to conduct psychopolitical dialogues between the representatives from Turkey and Greece. After some hesitation, a solution was found: first we would meet with the all-Turkish team and the all-Greek team separately at CSMHI and prepare them for the dialogue series. When joint meetings started later, Joseph Montville, who was a CSMHI member but who had also become the director of the Preventive Diplomacy Program, Center for the Strategic and International Studies (CSIS), in Washington, DC, would conduct the dialogues. Elizabeth Prodromou, who had become the executive director, Cambridge Foundation for Peace, Cambridge, Massachusetts, would assist Joe. Demetrios Julius, Norman Itzkowitz, Joy Boissevain, and I from CSMHI would join Joe and Elizabeth in forming the facilitating team during the joint meetings. Demetrios, as a Greek-American, would be the liaison between the Greek team and the facilitating team and I, as a Turkish-American, would be the liaison between the Turkish team and the facilitating team.

In April 1999 the all-Turkish team, including one Cypriot Turk, came to Charlottesville.[5] I led a CSMHI group, including Norman Itzkowitz, Andy Thomson, and Joy Boissevain, in welcoming them and conducting a three-day preparatory meeting for future dialogues between Turks and Greeks. The first day was spent on defining modern Turkish identity.

As American historian Justin McCarthy described in detail, between the Greek War of Independence (1821–1832) and the Turkish War of Independence (1919–1922), five and a half million Muslim Ottomans died due to conflict and five million became refugees. The Muslim communities in an area as large as all of Western Europe was diminished or destroyed.[6] The Turkish War of Independence followed World War I, during which the demise of the Ottoman Empire was sealed. Turks were proud to have survived partial occupation by some European forces during World War I. In the end their empire was gone, but they regained a sense of security as they established a new nation and found in Mustafa Kemal Atatürk a charismatic reparative leader.

Atatürk's focus in the new Turkish Republic, a land of recent refugee in-migration and massive mortality, was on a new secular concept of Turkishness for all citizens, whether they were ethnic Turks, Kurds, or Circassians or from Macedonia, Bulgaria, Cyprus, or elsewhere. Because of this chain of events, Turks could not properly mourn the loss of the Ottoman Empire. The consensus was that Atatürk's reforms after the birth of the Turkish Republic in 1923 had resulted in Turks retaining only selected aspects of their Ottoman past in their conscious collective memory.[7] They were holding on to what they considered "good" parts of their Ottoman history and denying the existence of the "bad." The full process of mourning would include a more complete recollection and working through the whole range of issues from Ottoman history. The Turkish participants complained that Christian suffering between 1821 and 1922 was kept alive in the Western world, while Christians would not even talk about the European Ottoman Muslim communities' tragedies, the largest loss of life and emigration since the Thirty Years' War.[8] Furthermore, participants referenced the terrorist activities of the Kurdistan Workers' Party (PKK) in Turkey, which I will describe in part VIII of this book.

The meeting participants reviewed Turkey's relationships with each of its neighbors as they existed in 1999. While the border between Turks and Iranians had remained unchanged for 350 years, the Turkish-Greek border had been in question either directly or indirectly (as on Cyprus) since the 1830s. Turks saw the Hellenistic ideas that dominated Greek policy as seeking to gather under one umbrella all the lands Greeks consider Hellenic (an entitlement ideology called "Megali Idea"). The Turkish team perceived the Greeks as being in constant struggle with the contradiction between this psychological border (that included lands outside the current territory of Greece) and their existing political borders. They described the asymmetry between the two countries as physical, military, demographic, and especially psychological. They saw managing this asymmetry as one of the greatest challenges to the bilateral relationship.

Four months after the all-Turkish team came to Charlottesville, on August 17, 1999, a massive earthquake hit a wide area of western Turkey, killing more than 20,000 persons. I was vacationing in North Cyprus at the time, and a few days after the earthquake I went to Istanbul and tried to be helpful to a small number of mental health workers who were already in the earthquake area or planning to go there. Here my focus is on how this natural disaster played a role in taming high Turkish-Greek tensions in the years following the Imia/Kardak rocks incident. When the then Turkish minister of health made a remark stating that injured Turks would not need Greek or Armenian blood, I was reminded of the Armenians' refusal to accept Azeri blood after the Armenian earthquake of 1988.

The Turkish minister became a target for rage on the part of many Turkish citizens and the Turkish media. Many Turkish intellectuals wanted the minister to resign. After a Greek team arrived to the earthquake zone to help, one Turkish newspaper thanked Greeks in Greek and described the heroic efforts of a female Greek firefighter. The picture of this woman firefighter and other members of the Greek team who had come to Turkey to help began to appear in many newspapers, making her and her coworkers known throughout the country. The sting poisoning the Turkish-Greek relationship was removed. Cafes, bars, and restaurants in Istanbul began playing Greek music to attract customers, and you could see Greek flags in many places. Nostalgia for the old "togetherness" of Turks and Greeks in Istanbul developed.

In January 2000 CSMHI hosted an all-Greek team, which included one Greek Cypriot.[9] Demetrios Julius was in charge of the preparatory meeting with the Greek guests. I was not present at the gathering, but I knew that they would examine modern Greek identity and historical events influencing this identity.

The first joint meeting took place at the Mountain House in Caux, Switzerland, in October 2000. Since I did not conduct the dialogues at Caux, I will not go into detail. Briefly, the participants from the opposing large groups showed themselves able and willing to engage fully with each other and to struggle with issues central to the Turkish-Greek relationship, including the Cyprus question, the Aegean Sea dispute, national identity, the collective memory of historical losses, and the future security and aspirations of each country. Many of the participants had attended other gatherings on Greek-Turkish affairs, and they acknowledged that this meeting was different, that it went beyond the intellectual debate that often characterizes such meetings.[10]

The second joint meeting took place in Istanbul in 2001 and the third and last one occurred in Thessalonica, Greece, in 2002. By the time we met in Thessalonica, I noticed something: while participants as representatives of Turkey and Greece held onto their governments' "official" positions and sometimes were involved in heated and seemingly intractable disagreement, as individuals they had become real friends. I had not seen this degree of friendship among opposing group representatives when Israelis and Arabs, or Russians and Estonians, or Croats and Serbs met. I wondered if my friendship with Demetrios was a role model for this, but most likely the groups' long history of togetherness, in spite of big differences in religion, who dominated who, and bloody wars, led Turks and Greeks to enjoy sharing culturally close things such as food and music. I noted when we met in Thessalonica that the Greek and Turkish participants seemed bored spending time discussing political matters. They behaved as if they wanted to leave such "nonsense" to official government authorities. At that time the FIFA World Cup was taking place and the Turkish national soccer team was doing well. On June 29, 2002, the last day of the meeting in Thessalonica, the Greek hosts took all the participants to an auditorium and all of us, instead of having a dialogue, watched Turkey play South Korea in Daegu Stadium in South Korea. There was much cheering by Turks and Greeks, and both watched Turkey beat South Korea 3-2 for third place. I sensed the dialogue series would not be repeated, and I was right.

October 2000 was the first time that I had returned to the Mountain House at Caux, Switzerland, since April 1983, when I was elected chairperson of the American Psychiatric Association's Committee on Psychiatry and Foreign Affairs and where I conducted a psychopolitical dialogue between Israelis, Egyptians, and Palestinians. Coming to Caux was an emotional event for me. This time, however, I was not the one conducting a dialogue between representatives of opposing large groups. At that time I was already thinking of a promise I had made to myself: I would retire from my medical school position when I reached the age of seventy. I had begun thinking about placing the running of CSMHI in new hands. But, on September 11, 2001, dramatic and horrible events would focus my immediate attention toward terrorism and its connection to fundamentalist religion.

# PART VII

## THE PSYCHOLOGY OF TERRORISM AND RELIGION

# 31

# KILLING IN THE NAME OF IDENTITY

## THE PSYCHOLOGY OF TERRORISTS

Since I began working in the international arena in 1979, global terrorism has become more and more of a serious problem worldwide. A survey of nearly two hundred terrorist acts carried out between July 1968 and November 1981 revealed that the vast majority were directed against carefully selected military, political, or foreign business targets.[1] There were exceptions. For example, the Irish Republican Army (IRA) bombers sometimes targeted civilian areas, and "skyjackers" took hostage whoever happened to be on their targeted airplane. However, especially in the latter case, Israeli or American passengers were often singled out for mistreatment. Contrary to popular perception, during this time period, a surprisingly small number of terrorist attacks involved random killings of unimplicated targets. By the late 1980s the number of international terrorist attacks had increased. In 1989 there were 533 incidents. But in 1990 the number of incidents dropped to around 450, of which bombings represented 63 percent of all international terrorist attacks, and the United States remained by far the most popular target of international terrorists that year. Most of the anti-U.S. attacks occurred in Latin America. During this period the United States listed Cuba, Iran, Iraq, Libya, North Korea, and Syria as state supporters of terrorists.[2]

UN Resolution 40/61, adopted by the UN General Assembly on December 9, 1985, encouraged the study of underlying causes of terrorism.[3] Today, general use of the term terrorism implies acts of violence "from below," intended to disrupt, topple, or express rage against a political order. In history, however, judging from the sheer number of its victims, terror "from above" far exceeds any other form of terrorism. In the twentieth century, for example, one thinks of the Holocaust, Josef Stalin's reign of terror, and the Pol Pot regime in Kampuchea. Terrorism from above—which included such methods as targeting, arresting, kidnapping, and executing innocent citizens or creating "death squads" to silence the opposition—was not included in Resolution 40/61's condemnation of mass and flagrant violations. This resolution restricted the word "terrorism" to violence coming from below.

Many studies focused on social, economic, and political conditions to explain what prompts certain individuals to take human lives, sometimes including their own, in attempts to effect radical change. Investigators easily recognized that there was no one type of terrorist personality. Furthermore, it was not easy to separate terrorism from below from other forms of violence that closely resemble it. For example, some authors distinguished assassins from terrorists, while others described the attacks on Anwar Sadat, Aldo Moro, and Indira Gandhi and assassinations of judges by the Colombian drug cartel as terrorist operations.[4] The acts of a "madman" who arbitrarily opens fire on a group of schoolchildren or the eruption of mob violence (even if it is politically motivated) may well induce a widespread public sense of vulnerability, but these events are not considered acts of terrorism. A satisfactory definition of terrorism was as notably elusive then as it is today.

In 1993 CSMHI was again approached by Ambassador Gündüz Aktan, the Turkish permanent representative to the United Nations in Geneva. We were asked to examine those less visible but no less potent causes of terrorism through a psychological lens. Therefore, when CSMHI established a committee that year to study neoracism in Europe, we also established another committee on the psychodynamics of ethnic and sectarian terrorism.[5] In the interest of consistency, we followed the United Nations' lead and confined our use of the term "terrorism" to the practice of violence by subordinate groups lacking political power. By the time we formed our committee, ethnicity had replaced political ideology as a driving force of terrorism. This was after colonial powers had left Africa and the Cold War had ended—an "age of ethnicity," as Norman Itzkowitz suggested, in which ethnic separatism occasioned considerable ambivalence among world leaders, even when unaccompanied by violence.

In my birthplace terrorism was carried out in the name of ethnicity, but it was also related to religious differences since Greek Cypriots are Christians and the Turkish Cypriots are Muslims. Sectarian aspects of violence were more visible in, for example, Northern Ireland, Lebanon, and Pakistan. In South America in the 1980s and early 1990s the primary targets of terrorists, along with guerrillas and narcotic traffickers, were domestic—government and law enforcement officials, opinion makers, and politicians. But, roughly two-thirds of all anti-U.S. attacks were taking place in Latin America by terrorists under the influence of shared identity colored by leftist ideology. In short, terrorism from below was connected with large-group identity issues.

Woodrow Wilson's well-publicized principle of a people's right to self-determination was still widely recognized as a significant political principle when the

CSMHI committee to study terrorism began its work. Resolution 40/61 reaffirmed "the inalienable right to self-determination and independence of all peoples under colonial and racist regimes and other forms of alien domination" and it upheld "the legitimacy" of "national liberation movements" in their struggle for independence. But the sheer number of peoples and groups who claimed or would claim such a right rendered the practical application of this principle extremely problematic. In 1993, there were fewer than two hundred nation-states seated in the United Nations. Twenty new countries, however, had emerged during the two years before the CSMHI Committee on Ethnic Terrorism was formed, constituting a 10 percent increase in membership. "If we allow each minority to have its own nation state," then UN secretary-general Boutros Boutros-Ghali remarked, "we will finish by having 500 members."[6]

Applying the principle of self-determination across the board would be to invite international chaos. And even if such a move were feasible, the existing nation-states would be unlikely to permit their own radical dismemberment, and the United Nations would also be against it.[7] Furthermore, populations were rarely cleanly divided and some ethnic minority groups did not aspire for independence. Under such confusing situations and confusing UN declarations, violence was appearing in many parts of the world that was directed against civilian targets and others not actively engaged in warfare, carried out by members of clandestine groups with political motives and the intention of inducing shock and fear.

The CSMHI committee members observed that in many places terrorists tended to ground their sense of legitimacy in a portrayal of the dominant large group as an occupying army and its civilians as colonizers, and to see acts of violence against this "foreign" people as legally sanctioned acts of war. A large group's own sense of being an afflicted people produces what psychoanalyst John Mack has called an "egoism of victimization," in which continued hostility against the Other is fueled by a "narcissistic focusing of empathy upon one's own people" and a "consequent inability to identify with the suffering of the other group." This "egoism of victimization," Mack observed, "removes one of the central emotional deterrents to the waging of war."[8] We concluded that it is equally effective in dismantling emotional barriers to terrorism. Indeed, even among those not actively involved in terrorism, there was generally a degree of overt or covert sympathy for the terrorists from their own large group and correspondingly little sympathy for their victims.

Despite this inherent tendency to sympathize with acts of violence directed against the "enemy," members of a large group sometimes found themselves targeted by their own terrorists in acts of "random" violence. So strong was the terrorists' perceived need to silence opposition and establish an unassailable "authority" within their own large group, that a campaign of internally directed terror could be considered essential to an effective campaign of terror against the Other, usually a dominant large group. Fear was generated both to crush internal opposition and to disrupt the enemy.

Our committee focused on answering a puzzling question from a psychological point of view. As others had already observed,[9] we noted that terrorism rarely furthered the terrorists' proclaimed ends. When they were rarely successful, no one called them terrorists, and they were better known as "freedom fighters." In general, we noted the terrorists would derail possibilities for peaceful solutions. For example, on a number of occasions in Northern Ireland horrendous terrorist acts managed to spoil a peaceful movement just when its success appeared to be in sight. Similarly, Hezbollah often derailed the Arab-Israeli peace talks. We asked what unspoken goals might drive their actions. To answer this question we focused on the concept of large-group identity, chosen traumas, chosen glories, and related concepts that have already been described at length in this book.

Terrorist groups develop their own special subgroup identity tent. As terrorist activities continue, even former bystanders who belong to the same large group as the terrorists are drawn toward concentrating under the terrorist tent's canvas. Making peace would mean losing the terrorist subgroup's identity. The shared need to protect this identity, knowingly or unknowingly supported emotionally by a huge number of others who do not actually murder people, leads terrorists to derail peace processes with the enemy. The deep psychological aim is to protect the terrorists' subgroup's identity, which in turn raises the self-esteem of the members of the large group to which they all belong. As more people gather under the tent, more people with different personality organizations become involved in violent acts in the service of the protection and maintenance of the terrorists' tent.

Real world and psychological issues become intertwined, for the more stress a subgroup or large group experiences, the more it wants to retain, at all costs, its own identity. The fear of large- or subgroup identity loss, of the tent collapsing or being torn to shreds, is a fear of psychological death. It occasions such anxiety that physical death may be preferred. As the terrorist group's shared externalizations, projections, and displacements of unwanted parts multiply, the preservation of the terrorists' subgroup tent, which plays a key role in separating the large-group identity with which it is linked from the large-group identity of the Other, becomes of paramount importance; to be the same as the Other is to risk the return of outward mechanisms. The terrorist subgroup, especially its members but often many members of the large group to which all belong, experiences a shared inclination to "kill" the targets of its outward mechanisms, because externalizations, projections, and displacements that are destroyed along with the enemy can no longer "boomerang."

We sensed that in such an atmosphere, terrorism gains wide support, since a terrorist group that lacks conventional political/military power and effective representation may find terrorism a way of discharging ethnic or sectarian stress. This may then be met with detention, torture, arbitrary executions, and even state-supported "counterterrorism." These, in turn, are taken as justification for further terrorism from below. Even if the state respects international standards of human rights and freedoms and uses only proportional force in its response to terrorist acts, terrorism may continue to increase, because repressive violence, no matter how "legitimate," breeds further terrorist violence.

As we developed psychological theories about ethnic and sectarian terrorism in general, it was proper to ask why some individuals—and not others whose investment in large-group identity may be just as intense—actually become terrorists. The answer, we believed, lies in ways in which personal history and individual psychology become intertwined with large-group processes. Despite what popular media sometimes leads us to believe, terrorists are not "crazy." "The last thing an effective terrorist group wants or needs is an unstable, unreliable operative."[10] Psychiatrist Jerrold Post cited a number of studies, including his own, which concluded that "the psychology of terrorists does not reveal major psychopathology."[11] Nevertheless, we noted that certain patterns do emerge from studying individual terrorist psychology: we see a link between a personal trauma or a trauma suffered by relatives or friends, and the internal preparedness to become an actual terrorist.

One member of the CSMHI Committee on Ethnic Terrorism, Katherine Kennedy, who was studying cross-cultural communications and conflict resolution and who had founded an organization called Natural Bridges, interviewed twenty-three state-labeled or self-proclaimed terrorists in Northern Ireland. Her experiences and the contents of her interviews helped us understand the idea of a connection between suffering from a humiliating trauma and preparedness for becoming a terrorist. We also received information about Northern Ireland from Joseph Montville, who was the only member of CSMHI who had done some work in Northern Ireland, although not under the sponsorship of CSMHI. While Joe was not a member of the Committee, he was generous in sharing his insights with me. They also supported our formulation about this common factor among terrorists. But when we prepared our report we wanted to remain tentative about such psychological patterns, since we did not have the access to the terrorist's mind that is available to a psychoanalyst or psychotherapist working with an individual in intensive treatment.

Kennedy's twenty-three subjects had experienced personal traumas in their formative years. One, for example, had an alcoholic father who physically abused him as a child. Most were also victims of sectarian violence. One person, before becoming a terrorist, was sexually harassed when stopped at a checkpoint at age nineteen; later he was so badly beaten in jail that his mother failed to recognize him. We considered the idea that a humiliating personal trauma initiated from personal surroundings and a trauma at the hand of the enemy come together in a future terrorist's mind. Montville reminded us that each of the original IRA hunger strikers of 1981 had what may have been a "conversion experience." These ranged from being stopped and badly beaten at a checkpoint operated by a unit of the Local Ulster Defense Regiment at age seventeen (Francis Hughes) to being shot in the foot by a member of the British Army at the age of twelve (Patsy O'Hara).[12] Such violations of individual boundaries induce a narcissistic hurt and profound loss of the sense of personal safety.

The merging of personal and ethnic or sectarian wounds sometimes even explained the selection of "random" terrorist targets. Kennedy reported, for example, an interview with a terrorist whose organization had assigned him to kill a policeman, though which policeman was left to his discretion. The man told Kennedy that he had chosen his victim because he "didn't like the policeman's smile." We surmised that the terrorist externalized an unwanted image from his own personal history onto the policeman before he killed the man.

Suffering from trauma at home and/or at the hand of the enemy does not produce one single psychopathology or personality type. Most individuals with similar traumas would not kill other persons. It appeared to us that existing terrorist cells created a place for future terrorists in which a psychological tool, what I call collecting of "aggressive triumphs," could be found to "repair" an injured self-esteem. Cell leaders or those who plan rather than carry out acts of terrorism, we found, were often older than those who actually were involved in murdering people. These leaders and the cell itself provided almost a parental atmosphere and therefore a sense of strong belonging for the future terrorist. The sense of belonging seemed to be wanted and perhaps needed for the future terrorist's maintenance of continuous good self-esteem. We examined a study by Robert Clark on the social backgrounds of members of the Basque separatist group Euskadi Ta Askatasuna (ETA) and found it to be instructive in this respect.[13] Clark provided us with forty-eight fairly detailed personal case histories and 447 other cases with lesser information about personal backgrounds. He found a much higher percentage (more than 40 percent) of ETA members were of mixed Basque-Spanish parentage than was true of the Basque population as a whole (no more than 8 percent). Since in the Basque region of Spain those of mixed Basque-Spanish parentage are generally reviled as half-breeds, Clark surmised that those "outcasts" who joined ETA were trying to demonstrate that they truly "belonged" to their chosen ethnic group.

If the need to belong is such an important motive for the terrorist, then the survival of his or her terrorist group will also be of central psychological importance.

This brings me back to the puzzling question that I referred to earlier: why do terrorist groups often protect themselves against success? Jerrold Post stated that, "For any group or organization, the highest priority is survival. This is especially true for the terrorist group. To succeed in achieving its espoused cause would threaten the goal of survival."[14] If the terrorist group is dissolved, its members will lose their target that supplies answers for their needed sense of belonging.

We also wondered about common psychological mechanisms in people who plan or who execute killings in the name of large-group identity. When not thinking about death and destruction, how do such killers and would-be murders act during their daily lives? While being preoccupied with terrorism, a person may even be compassionate and sensitive in his or her family relationships. Kennedy recounted an interview with a leader of the Ulster Defense Association, who played lovingly with his infant son while boasting of having ordered a bombing two weeks earlier in which a mother and two children were killed. The day after the interview, while warming up his car to drive his son to daycare, he was killed by a car bomb triggered by the ignition switch. On another occasion, a representative of the IRA interviewed by Kennedy in unheated offices in the middle of winter interrupted his description of personal involvement in terrorist activities to find a coat to protect the interviewer from the cold. Planners and executors of terrorism do not have a so-called "multiple personality" organization. Instead they utilize various psychological mechanisms that enable them to behave as if they have two parts.

These psychological mechanisms, related to one another and sometimes confused with each other, are known by different names: *splitting of the self representation*, which means relating to one's own self and others by alternately exhibiting severe opposing attitudes such as love and hate; *splitting ego functions*, which means that while knowing what is real one also experiences another imagined perception as real; *dissociation*, which means having an altered state of consciousness (usually short-lived) with the help of amnesia; *disavowal*, which means maintaining two contradictory attitudes while sensorium and perception remain clear but while the meaning of one experience is rejected; and *doubling*, which "means a complete reorganization of the self in which the old values, ideals, and ambitions are completely replaced by new ones."[15]

The frightening observation we made was that in time the actions of a terrorist cell lead to the contamination of the "healthy" segments of the larger group. By shaking the large-group identity tent, the cell stimulates broad anxiety about ethnic and/or sectarian identity, and many who have no personal traumatic stories or personal identity diffusion gravitate toward the terrorist group as a potential "cure" for ethnic wounds and for finding "glory" as a protector of the tent.[16]

Even before September 11, 2011, I studied terrorism further, this time including a much closer look at how the colors and designs of religion become deep stains on the large-group identity tent. I had an opportunity in early 1996 to study the siege of the Branch Davidians' ranch at Mount Carmel near Waco, Texas, a siege that began on February 28, 1993, and lasted for fifty days. This gave me an opportunity to see a religious cult's involvement in violence and how it also induced a violent response from the Federal Bureau of Investigation (FBI). There were forty-two men, forty-six women, and forty-three children of various ethnic backgrounds living at Mount Carmel just prior to the beginning of the siege, first by the U.S. Bureau of Alcohol, Tobacco and Firearms (ATF) and then by the FBI. The Davidians had initially become involved in an illegal gun trade to support themselves, but by 1991 or 1992 they had come to believe that Armageddon could begin at Waco (rather than Israel), and that keeping weapons on their compound was therefore a necessity. When the FBI siege was over, the Davidians camp at Waco was destroyed by fire and seventy-six Davidians, including their religious cult leader David Koresh and more than twenty children, were dead.

My study of the life of David Koresh and the Waco incident would prepare me to look at how religion can contaminate violence. In the next chapter, I will tell the story of my involvement in the Waco tragedy two years after it was over and then examine terrorism in the name of religion.

# 32

# TERROR AT WACO

## THE PSYCHOLOGY OF CULTS

One day in late 1995 while at work at Blue Ridge Hospital, I answered a telephone call. A man, without introducing himself, informed me that he was calling from the FBI and that the FBI was forming a commission to investigate the Waco, Texas, incident. This commission would be charged with examining how behavioral sciences' insights might be useful in enhancing the agency's ability to respond to future such crises. I was also informed that Attorney General Janet Reno was insisting on the formation of this commission. In my own mind I surmised that after the horrifying tragedy at Waco, the FBI wanted to look into its agents' behavior, and this especially involved a communication gap between the agency's tactical commanders and its behavioral scientists during the siege of Mount Carmel.[1] The "voice" told me that the FBI wanted me to chair this commission. Automatically I asked, "Why me?" There was a brief silence and then the "voice" said: "We know all about you."

After I accepted this invitation, another special agent, this one giving his name, spoke with me. The FBI wasted no time, and by mid-January 1996 the Select Advisory Commission to the FBI's Critical Incident Response Group (CIRG) commenced its first meeting at the FBI Academy at Quantico, Virginia. I drove to the academy and, after registering at the front desk, I was escorted to my room where I would stay for a couple of evenings. This place was like a hotel, but the rooms did not have keys. I thought that this was because no one would dare disturb or rob a guest in the FBI building! Walking through the grounds, the FBI trainees greeted me, always calling me, "sir."

The next day serious work began. I already knew two members of the commission. Gregory Saathoff, whose involvement in CSMHI's work in the Republic of Georgia, South Ossetia, and Kuwait has been mentioned earlier in this book, was one of them. Due to our mutual interest in psychobiography, I also knew Elizabeth Wirth Marvick. I had read one of her fine books, *Louis XIII: Making of a*

*King.*[2] The other members of the commission, whom I would meet for the first time at Quantico, were Michael Barkun, professor of political science at the Maxwell School of Citizenship and Public Affairs, Syracuse University; Joseph Krofcheck, a psychiatrist from Fairfax, Virginia, specializing in security issues; Stephen Sampson, director of psychology at Georgia Regional Hospital, Georgia State University in Atlanta; Allen Sapp, professor of criminal justice, Central Missouri State University in Warrensburg; and Robert Washington, professor of sociology from Bryn Mawr College in Bryn Mawr, Pennsylvania. After the commission's work was over, besides continuing to work with Greg at CSMHI, I also kept professional contact with Michael Barkun, who specializes in political extremism in the United States and the relationship between religion and violence.[3]

The incident at Waco involved fundamentalist believers. Even though, in general, we have a tendency to consider "fundamentalism" and "fundamentalist" as pejorative words, there are fundamentalist groups within practically every faith tradition. They hold on to specific doctrines of faith and often are preoccupied with protecting their groups and beliefs from interference from outsiders. The term "fundamentalism" as it relates to religious self-definition was coined in the late 1920s in the United States. In California two Union Oil tycoons, Lyman and Milton Stewart, financed the publication of a series of pamphlets called *The Fundamentals*, which enumerated five points essential for Christian orthodoxy: biblical inerrancy, the virgin birth, Christ's atonement and resurrection, the authenticity of miracles, and dispensationalism. At that time Christian "fundamentalists" were simply defenders of these five doctrines.[4]

There was a reason for the appearance of religious fundamentalism in America during the late 1920s: the United States was going through a drastic change as economic power was shifting from rural environments to urban ones. Furthermore, a large number of immigrants caused ethnic shifts in many locations throughout the country. As I indicated earlier, major changes in societal structure and large-group disorganization usher in magical thinking, and I believe that strict religious beliefs stand for shared magical thinking. Even though the term "fundamentalism" was popularized in the 1920s, I do not mean to suggest that people in the United States (or anywhere else in the world) did not turn to increased religiosity and/or specific doctrine during earlier times. Human history is full of exaggerated religious movements, both nonviolent and violent.

Here is an example of one person killing under the influence of his religious/ideological beliefs: just about two years before the FBI Commission was established, on February 24, 1994, Benjamin Goldstein, a physician who was then known as Baruch Goldstein, showered bullets on Palestinians worshipping in Ibrahimi Mosque (Mosque of Abraham) in Hebron, killing twenty-nine and injuring hundreds. The crowd subdued him with a fire extinguisher and then beat him to death. Baruch Goldstein was a follower of Rabbi Meir Kahane, who had evolved a religious, ideological, and political movement known as Kahanism. Kahanism focused on adopting *Halakha* (Jewish law) in public life in Israel, limiting Israeli citizenship to Jews only, forcibly expelling all Arab Muslims from Israeli-controlled lands, and annexing the biblical land of Israel. Kahane openly supported the use of terror against Arabs. He was assassinated in New York on November 5, 1990, by el Sayyid Nosair, an Egyptian Muslim, who obviously also killed in the name of religion.[5]

It is not, of course, only those who belong to Judaism or Islam who kill in the name of religion. For example, people of the Indian Subcontinent who are sometimes known for their peaceful nature exemplified in the great persona of Mahatma Gandhi are also known for the vicious religious atrocities that have occurred between Sikhs, Hindus, and Muslims. In fact, a close look illustrates striking similarities between Islamic extremists and Sikh youth who prepare for a holy war and their own "martyrdom."

At the time the FBI Commission members gathered at Quantico, an extreme version of religious fundamentalism was defined "in terms of its disciplined opposition to non-believers and 'lukewarm' believers alike."[6] As the millennium approached, according to Michael Barkun, 25–35 percent of the population in the United States was fundamentalist Christian and about 20 percent of this group (that is 5–6 percent of the total U.S. population) was extreme fundamentalist. These were people such as the millennialists who were convinced that Jesus Christ would return to earth, establish a kingdom, and rule from Jerusalem for one thousand years.[7]

While religious fundamentalism increased in the United States and the world after September 11, 2001, in the United States and Europe, the term "fundamentalist" practically disappeared from public speeches when used in reference to Christianity. Instead, Christians with exaggerated preoccupation with religion and some of its "fundamentals" would be referred to as "conservatives" or "extreme conservatives." The term "fundamentalist" or "extreme fundamentalist," for all practical purposes, was only attached to Muslims and was linked with danger.

Our FBI hosts showed us many areas of the academy and also gave us information about its behavioral science section. Perusing the library in this section I was surprised to note how many psychoanalytic concepts were being taught at the FBI academy. For example, the concept "repetition compulsion," a tendency to repeat painful experiences, was clearly used, even though in a modified way, in searching for a criminal with repeating behavioral patterns or a serial killer who continues to leave similar signs at crime scenes.[8]

During the first gathering the FBI showed us many films of Waco and provided information about the life of David Koresh (born Vernon Wayne Howell in

1959), the dead leader of the Branch Davidians. I also studied David Koresh from other data I could find about him,[9] and learned how the Branch Davidian group at Mount Carmel represented an especially fundamentalist strain of one tradition in American Christian millennialism. The Davidians believed that prophesies and statements of the King James Version of the Bible could be deciphered to interpret present events and to predict the end-time. For them, this specific version of the Bible was the true word of God, and other translations were filled with falsehood. This special, literalist devotion to a particular text was one of the elements that most clearly marked Davidians as a fundamentalist group.[10]

I was correct in my first assumptions about why the FBI had established this commission. We were asked what direction the FBI should take in the area of behavioral science and what to do to increase communications between the FBI's behavior scientists and those present at crisis zones making tactical decisions. What type of training would provide senior-level FBI managers with the ability to avert internal breakdowns? How could the FBI field personnel diffuse pressure from FBI headquarters? What would be the most creative way to apply behavioral sciences to a protracted crisis such as Waco? How can the FBI be more proactive? In what particular area, if any, does the FBI need to improve data collection? How can the FBI evaluate and streamline its relationships with other federal agencies? What should the FBI know about international terrorism? Our most senior FBI host made it clear that in all these considerations, legal limits should be taken into account. Throughout our stay, we heard statements attesting to the fact that the FBI's most important task is saving lives. We were given the impression that we should come up with ideas to "humanize" FBI operations in a way that would not interfere with its main task of criminal investigation.

The commission existed for a little over five weeks. We met at Quantico once more and also communicated among ourselves and our FBI hosts when we were not together. There was no time to examine the many questions that arose. We were therefore left to ponder two questions: how can an outside group have an impact on "FBI culture," seen as "inbred" by the attorney general? And, in practical terms, what do the behavioral sciences have to offer toward this end?

In February 1996 I signed the final commission report and it was presented to the FBI. Briefly, our report focused on opening a dialogue between the "FBI culture" and other paramilitary professionals and scholars in the "outside world," especially when managing problematic organizations such as religious cults involved in violence or breaking the law. The commission's report suggested the creation of two positions: that of "resource analyst" and that of "futurist." The resource analyst should have a current or recent academic career and would serve as a bridge between academic scholars/experts and the FBI's Crises Management Unit. There was a problem in considering this position. The FBI already had a Rolodex full of behavioral science experts available for "practical and user-friendly" advice. We did not wish the resource analyst to become another person hired to help reorganize the Rolodex. We described how he or she would be a special person who would open a dialogue between "FBI culture" and "outside culture," be able to effect change, and not get lost in the FBI's hierarchy.

The futurist should have significant academic status and experience. The role of the futurist would be to "scan the horizon," always with care and always without breaking laws, and to assist in developing an early-warning methodology on the domestic and international fronts. He or she would be linked to the FBI's Investigative Support Unit. Our report gave suggestions as to how to avoid the possibility that the futurist might be too easily co-opted within the FBI culture. On the other hand, ideas were expressed about how to avoid the futurist giving a false sense of security. We also dealt with the possibility that the futurist's activities might seem irrelevant to peers or supervisors who might stress short-term law-enforcement issues rather than the long-term approach necessitated by the position.

Both figures would retain their academic or organizational positions and would work with the FBI on a part-time basis. The FBI established these two positions. Both were filled by members of the commission: Gregory Saathoff became the resource analyst and Allen Sapp became the futurist. I had no further connection with the FBI. My aim in telling about my chairing the FBI Commission is to indicate how these five weeks of work—hearing FBI agents' own stories about Waco and researching the Branch Davidians—taught me a great deal about violent religious cults and the psychology of their leaders and followers. I hoped that this knowledge would help me to enrich my understanding of the psychology of terrorist leaders and terrorists who plan or execute murder in the name of their god.

Before proceeding further I must state that not every fundamentalist religious group is violent or destructive. For example, when I was working in Estonia, I got to know the peaceful Old Believers community and their leader in the Lake Peipsi area very well.[11] From the seventeenth century their ancestors faced violence and destruction. Therefore, I suggest that we need to be careful and not use terms such as "fundamentalist" or "cult" or "temple" or "*tarikat*" (an Islamic order or sect) loosely and only as they reflect aggression. We also need to be aware that religious movements do not always create "cults," "temples," or "*tarikat*s." When we use such terms, therefore, we always need to describe specific issues attached to them. For example, Branch Davidians at Mount Carmel were insular, a "restricted" fundamentalist religious group. The followers of Osama bin Laden were not "restricted" to one location and had a very different organization, reminding us of the organization of a huge international commercial business.

Most leaders of restricted fundamentalist communities who support and plan violence seem to share certain psychological characteristics: during their developmental years, they did not receive adequate parenting and are left with deep confusion, anger, and feelings of being rejected, and as a result they respond to such an environment with an unconscious search for an omnipotent parent, a god. Again, psychologically speaking, they cannot "kill" a god; this protects them from feeling guilty for their "murderous" rage. Also, they submit to a god, become an extension of him or her, and then feed their own narcissism. They search for life circumstances that will allow them to actualize this internal phenomenon. By creating a "cult," having adoring and submissive followers, they unconsciously establish a "family" that they (also unconsciously) hope will be different than their original family, since it will be run by a person who is an extension of a god. However, the aggression that accompanied their childhood frustrations remains and then turns toward the Other who is perceived as a threat to the new "family." Accordingly, both exaggerated narcissism and paranoia coexist. Sometimes "repetition compulsion" takes over as the leader "mistreats" followers as his own parents mistreated him. Then the leader turns the aggression to the newly created "family" itself, and members of the cult may commit mass suicide.[12]

Followers of violent fundamentalist restricted religious leaders appear to have a psychology similar to that of followers who are under the influence of or who obey planners of ethnic or sectarian terrorism, as I described in the previous chapter. Joseph Salande and David Perkins studied cult members with relatively healthy personalities and noted that these individuals "begin the cult experience with relatively good ego strength, which is methodically chipped away through experiences that lead to ego-weakening, and thus the activation of primate defensive operations, which in turn further exacerbates this ego-weakening process."[13]

There are countless examples of *restricted* extreme religious movements, cults, or *tarikat*s, such as David Koresh's Branch Davidians at Waco, Jim Jones' Temple in Jonestown, Shoko Asahara's Japanese Aum Shinrikyo, Joseph DiMambro's Order of the Solar Temple, Gush Emunim in Israel, and, even, in their initial stages, Hamas in Lebanon and Mullah Omar's Taliban in Afghanistan.[14]

I came up with a list of common characteristics of these restricted extreme and violent fundamentalist religious organizations, and even peaceful ones such as the Old Believers community in the Lake Peipsi region of Estonia. I believe that this list provides a necessary platform on which we can stand and take a closer look at more generalized or globalized violent fundamentalist religious movements like al-Qaida.

Restricted religious communities demonstrate these common characteristics:

- *A divine text.* As mentioned earlier, *The Fundamentals*, published in the 1920s, included five specific areas illustrating one group's specific religious self-definition. Likewise, each restricted extreme religious fundamentalist movement has its own "divine text," whether it is written on paper or passed along orally. For example, the text may be a specific version of the Bible, or an interpretation of certain verses of the Koran. The "divine text" is irrefutable, nonnegotiable. For example, for Gush Emunim in Israel, giving up areas that were included in the "Land of Israel" violates God's command and for the members of this organization such a belief is nonnegotiable.
- *An absolute leader who is the interpreter of the divine text.* The leader of a restricted fundamentalist religious movement is the sole interpreter of the group's divine text. No other interpretations are acceptable. The leader usually is a man. Only rarely is the leader a woman, such as "Prophet" Lois Roden, who led the Branch Davidians at Waco before David Koresh.[15] Sometimes a leader who does not possess enough charisma may choose a "front man." For example, Joseph DiMambro built his own temple preparing for the return of Jesus Christ in solar glory. But a physician, Luc Jouret, became the leader of the Order of the Solar Temple, with DiMambro pulling the strings backstage.
- *Total loyalty.* Membership in an extreme restricted religious community, cult, or *tarikat* provides a sense of belonging for its followers. Total loyalty to the leader and to the divine text "removes" anxiety they might have due to intrapsychic and interpersonal conflicts. In a well-run extreme religious organization, all the believers' actions and thoughts are highly organized and institutionalized. Most groups create tangible incentives and economic dependence to ensure that members never leave the group. Once an individual is involved in the network of an extreme restricted fundamentalist religious group, it becomes difficult for that person to quit the membership. The putative divine rule infiltrates members' everyday existence and intimate personal relationships, fundamentally changing them.
- *Members feel omnipotent, yet victimized.* Restricted extreme fundamentalist religious groups are pessimistic movements.[16] Pessimism exists because the members perceive their specific religious "fundamentals" to be continually under attack by nonbelievers or even lukewarm believers, Darwinists, scientists, and even rival religious fundamentalist groups that cite other texts as truly divine. Paradoxically, because they believe that their text is the true divine guide and their leader is the only true spiritual leader, a sense of omnipotence exists among the members of such groups. The contamination of a shared sense of pessimism with a shared sense of omnipotence creates a special condition that

allows extreme masochism or sadism to become tolerable, especially under the guidance of the leader.

- *Extreme sadistic and/or masochistic acts.* When a restricted extreme religious fundamentalist group perceives a threat to the divine authority of the leader and to the survival of the group and its identity, the protection of the group and its identity become its primary preoccupations. Since the members' pessimism is contaminated with omnipotence, the group feels entitled to destroy Others who are seen as threatening to the group identity's survival. Sometimes, with paranoia, they preemptively attack to remove the opposition and possible threat. For example, in 1980 in Kano, Nigeria, sect leader Alhaji Mohammadu (Maitatsine) Marva, who had proclaimed a new era of antimaterialist reformed Islam, led his followers to the central mosque in Kano where "nonbelievers" or "lukewarm believers" of his ideas were gathered. This event led to the killing of an estimated eight thousand people. However, a group can also express its omnipotence through a grand masochistic gesture such as massive suicide. Those who kill themselves believe that through death they will merge with the divine leader and/or god, the omnipotent object, and thus crystallize their omnipotence and continue their existence in heaven. Annie Moore, a twenty-four-year-old nurse who belonged to Jim Jones' People's Temple and who was the last to die in the mass suicide in Jonestown, provided an illustration of an escape from pessimism in her suicide note that says, "We died because you would not let us live in peace."[17] Extreme sadistic and masochistic acts reflect psychological purification in the service of maintaining the group's identity.
- *Alteration of the shared "morality".* What we observe in an extremely violent restricted religious fundamentalist group is the existence of an altered shared "morality," now colored by specific religious doctrines and beliefs that create permission for killing Others, as well as suicide. Codes of conduct change, for example, allowing the acceptability of the leader to have sex with children and teenagers. For example, David Koresh was "married" to teenage girls, even as young as twelve and fourteen.
- *Creation of borders.* Even during "safe times" when there is no imminent threat to the group's security, a restricted extreme religious fundamentalist organization builds physical borders such as walls or barricades. But more importantly, they also build psychological borders around themselves, such as wearing a specific color or style of dress that separates them from others. In Israel, men in the Haredi community seclude themselves in Yeshivot, institutions in which they study the Holy Scriptures without maintaining contact with general culture and knowledge. In today's Turkey we witness various religious fundamen-

talist movements that demand women wear scarves. But each group's scarf is different or worn in a different style. Thus, the group's scarf is like a uniform that defines a border between the group and Others.

- *Changing of family, gender, and sexual norms within the "borders"*. As the leader of an extreme and restricted religious fundamentalist movement becomes more divine and omnipotent, he or she may become "the father," "the mother," and "the lover" to all the followers. Routine family systems become disturbed and child-rearing practices drastically change. So-called family values are replaced by the leader's interpretation of the "divine text." The perception of women is usually reduced to their giving sex (pleasure) and food (milk) to the leader or other men belonging to the same group. Sometimes the leader in a restricted extreme religious fundamentalist organization "owns" all the women and children and even men in the group. This development in the community most likely reflects the leaders' unconscious wish to "change" their early troubled childhood by creating a new "family" with themselves as the new and wished-for parent. When this does not work out, however, the fate of the new family follows the fate of the leader's original family—it becomes dysfunctional. David Koresh "owned" all the women among his followers and had sex with underage girls. Men at Koresh's compound at Waco were to be celibate. "Pastor Jim Jones claimed that he was the only person who knew how to love, and frequently had the women and men he had had sexual relations with stand up and testify to what an excellent lover he was."[18] The leader's having sex with underage girls or boys is a kind of symbolic, but pathological, act to revise the leader's original internalized "bad" mother-child relationship. These acts, however, are usually explained by "magical" religious beliefs. For example, David Koresh (who was born out of wedlock when his mother was a young girl and who, until age five, believed that his mother was his aunt) was convinced he could not be Jesus Christ since Jesus did not have children. Accordingly, he modeled himself after a messiah referred to in Psalm 45, "Who married virgins and whose children ruled the earth."
- *Inducing negative feelings among outsiders.* Because a restricted extreme fundamentalist religious group feels special, divine, secretive, magical, omnipotent, masochistic, or sadistic, and because they erect borders around themselves, they induce negative feelings in people who live outside their borders. Outsiders perceive such groups as a threat to their own religious or other belief systems. If a restricted extreme religious cult or organization develops a reputation as a group that degrades women, abuses children, and ruins the traditional family system that is accepted by the surrounding society at large, the bystanders' negative feelings increase. During my work with the FBI Commission, I

noted that Branch Davidians in the Mount Carmel compound had induced negative feelings in the FBI agents at the location. I suspected that this was one of the (unconscious) motivations for responding in a deadly fashion against Branch Davidians and burning their compound. I also believe that the aggressive negative feelings held by the authorities against David Koresh and his Branch Davidians during the "siege" at Waco unintentionally fed the Branch Davidians' millennial expectations of a catastrophe and increased their daring and resistance to the FBI.

An extreme fundamentalist religious movement starts to become generalized when the majority of "bystanders" within the large group, instead of having and maintaining negative feelings about the movement, begin to support it directly or indirectly. An interesting example of this generalization was observed during the spread of the Taliban in Afghanistan in 1994. The Taliban, whose name means "religious students," originally recruited mostly from among young Pashtuns, Afghanistan's largest ethnic group. The group first came to notice in late 1994 when it was hired to drive local bandit groups away from a thirty-truck convoy that was trying to open a trade route between Pakistan and Central Asia. The Taliban leader, Mullah Omar, was then in his mid-thirties. As they refused to deal with warlords and fought local police forces as well as roving bandits, the Taliban applied an exaggerated interpretation of Islamic law to combat the corruption and chaos that plagued post-Soviet Afghanistan.

Kabul, the capital of Afghanistan, was still under President Burhanuddin Rabbani's control, however, and the Taliban were divided as to their next course of action. At this critical time, in one key act, Omar sealed his divine leadership: after climbing onto the roof of a mosque in the middle of Kandahar, he publicly displayed and put on the cloak of the Prophet Muhammad, which had been kept for over 250 years in a marble vault in Kandahar's Shrine of the Cloak of the Prophet Muhammad.[19] Donning the cloak publicly was certainly a gamble since the act could easily have been seen as blasphemous. However, by successfully fusing his image with the image of the Prophet in the minds of his followers and bystanders, Omar blurred the reality that he and the Prophet lived centuries apart. He was able to use the cloak to solidify both his image as the commander of the faithful and the shared political-religious identity of his followers. This act went a long way toward generalizing the Taliban movement, or at least toward crystallizing the movement's previous attempts to become generalized.

Taliban began to "purify" the society of elements they perceived as unwanted and to create a new large-group identity and culture. It was only a few months after Omar merged his image with the image of the Prophet that the Taliban captured

Kabul, began to enforce their oppressive laws within the Afghan population, and allowed Osama bin Laden and his well-funded al-Qaida organization to thrive in Afghanistan. The Taliban eventually grew from that original core group of about one hundred into a cohort of tens of thousands of men from at least forty-three countries. It is beyond the scope of this book to summarize the United States' and its allies' involvement with the Taliban and al-Qaida, except to point out that today the United States and its allies are still fighting them both.

In one of my previous books, I wrote a psychobiographical portrait of Osama bin Laden in an attempt to understand his personal psychology.[20] Even though it would be impossible to know his internal world in detail from a distance, information that was available to me about his life illustrates that he shared typical characteristics of extreme fundamentalist religious leaders described above. I also wrote about how some key events in his personal life directed him to devote himself to what became al-Qaida (The Base): the base of globalized militant terrorism fed by fundamentalist religious ideas.

On the surface, the characteristics of al-Qaida appeared very different than those of restricted extreme religious groups. Before its backbone was broken after a decade of "war" against it, especially after the murder of Osama bin Laden on May 2, 2011, in Pakistan, it resembled a giant global corporation with secret funds, high communication technology, and representatives in various countries. Al-Qaida seemed to strive to become a world power itself under the sponsorship of a god by using any means, from engaging in effective political and religious propaganda, to making financial deals while performing horrendous acts of violence. The characteristics that we can see more clearly in restricted extreme fundamentalist religious movements, however, were and still are present within this globalized example of this type of movement.

A "divine" ideology is present and its "interpreters" exist—primarily Osama bin Laden before he was killed. The al-Qaida leadership complained about the Western world's merciless commercial, technical, cultural, and religious organizations that have infiltrated the Islamic world and humiliated Muslims, especially starting in the nineteenth century and continuing through the present time by modern "globalization." Osama bin Laden had declared the United States, and the West in general, the enemy and "received permission" from Koranic passages (such as Surah 8, verse 17) to strike at the "enemy." Followers obediently followed the leader(s) and the ideology. They felt victimized but omnipotent, and experienced an altered "morality." They built "borders" around themselves in order to hide and maintain their large-group identity. It took many years to find out where Osama bin Laden was hiding. The "divine" ideology replaced some family values and many old peaceful traditional and religious beliefs, including beliefs about suicide and homicide. This radical Islam induced extreme negative feelings in "outsiders" in faraway locations, but many people in the locations where radical Islam is present, although not terrorists themselves, expressed direct or hidden sentiments supporting the movement.

In the next chapter I will examine aspects of history that created an atmosphere for the globalization of this particular type of fundamentalist religious Islamic terrorism.

# 33

# "MUSLIM RAGE"

## ANOTHER LOOK AT TERRORISM AND SUICIDE BOMBERS

---

In the lead-up to September 11, 2001, Islamic religious fundamentalism and even its extreme forms had for many years found emotional support among various large groups, especially in the Arab world. I noticed this particularly when I was involved in the Kuwait project. What historian Bernard Lewis called "Muslim rage,"[1] and what Ambassador Nathaniel Howell referred to as the "nostalgia movement,"[2] supported the globalization of Islamic religious fundamentalism. Back in 1990 Lewis noted: "Islamic fundamentalism has given an aim and a form to the otherwise aimless and formless resentment and anger of the Muslim masses at the forces that have devalued their traditional values and loyalties and, in the final analysis, robbed them of their beliefs, their aspirations, their dignity, and to an increasing extent even their livelihood."[3]

What are the causes of this "Muslim rage" or "nostalgia" for past chosen glories? As I attempt to answer this question, I would like to remind the reader that I am not a historian and my remarks will be very brief and many important historical events will by necessity be left out. My intention is to describe this history in a way that might be useful to understanding how these factors played a role in Osama bin Laden's unconscious search for a father figure (a caliph) to start a new "family." In addition, this discussion should not create a false impression that every person of the Muslim faith was or is involved in this "rage." I am simply referring to large-group processes that influence political and societal direction.

Less than a century after the death of the Prophet Muhammad, Muslim armies had established a huge Arab-dominated Islamic empire, stretching from India to Spain, in which Islamic culture blossomed. But the unity of Islam was actually broken up very early after the death of the Prophet Muhammad, and there were bitter divisions and regional power struggles almost from the beginning. The most important division occurred after the fourth Arab caliph, Ali, a cousin and son-in-law of Prophet Muhammad, was killed. A group of Muslims known as Shi'ites (from the Arabic *Shiat Ali*, the party of Ali) rejected the legitimacy of the first three caliphs in the line of Muhammad. Shi'ites considered Ali to be the first imam and the rightful successor to Muhammad. They accepted Muhammad as the Prophet and the Koran as divine revelation, but proposed their own interpretation of Koranic law.

The present world's Muslim population is estimated to be 1.6 billion. Today Sunni Islam is the largest branch of Islam, followed by the Shi'ite branch. There are other much smaller "schools." Shi'ites make up some 10 to 15 percent of the world's Muslim population. The majority of Muslims in Iran and Iraq are Shi'ite. Shi'ite territories in Iran and Iraq together possess the world's largest petroleum sources.

During the reign of Ottoman Sultan Selim I (1512–1520), the Turks took over Syria and Egypt, and in 1517 the Arab Sunni caliphates came to an end. The Ottoman sultan assumed the title and "inherited the role of the defender of the holiest places in Islam, the cities of Mecca and Medina, which were the cradle of Islam."[4] Islam was clearly one of the dominant elements of Ottoman identity, as the Ottomans took many lands in Europe and Arab lands in the Middle East, even though they allowed the conquered people to keep their religions. Arabs, who were the first Muslims and who now lived under the Ottoman Empire, had to submit to Islamic newcomers.

After the seventeenth century the relationship between Europe and the Ottoman Empire slowly began to change in favor of the European powers. The dominant relationship between the Christians and Islamists until the nineteenth century, when the Ottoman Empire clearly began to decline, was between Europe and the Ottoman Empire.[5] Ottoman identity was not connected with an ideology that called for bringing all Muslims under one political umbrella. There were no Western or Islamic historians articulating such a possibility until the nineteenth century,[6] when two developments defined the Western world's perception of the Ottoman Empire and, by extension, of Islam. The first was Europe's preoccupation with "pan" movements, such as Pan-Germanism and Pan-Slavism, movements that reflected a striving to create massive entities under the umbrella of Germanic or Slavic ethnicities. The European elite also quickly imagined "Pan-Islamism" originating in Ottoman lands. They were seeing the East through the lens of the West. The second development was the European powers' interest in the Ottoman lands, as the Ottoman Empire was perceived as the "Sick Man of Europe." These developments and other associated events, the study of which is beyond the scope of this book, magnified the idea of an Islamic power, even though the Ottoman Empire was just as powerless in the nineteenth century after the "pan" movements as it had been before. Nevertheless, the European powers thought that it would be a good move to make the "sick man" completely helpless so that the danger of a "Pan-Islamic" movement could be contained or removed.

Meanwhile, while competing among themselves, European powers colonized many Muslim communities outside Ottoman territory, especially in India and North Africa, and expanded their domination of the Middle East. Islam started to become "the banner of cultural authenticity and communal identity under which the elite could mobilize the masses against the 'colonial power.'"[7] Since the literacy rate was low, new Islamic images filtered in "by several indigenous institutions: the *caliphate*, the *tarikat*, the *madrassas* [Islamic educational schools], and the mosque."[8] Similar processes continued in the twentieth century as these institutions also promoted nationalism, such as Turkish, Persian, Arabic, and Bosnian nationalism, supported by Islamic symbols.

Before the First World War (1914–1918) started, Germans bought a number of Ottoman newspapers and sent representatives throughout the Ottoman lands. Their propaganda began influencing the Ottoman elite and the public in general, including the idea that England and France were leading an anti-Islamic movement, while Germany was supporting an Islamic movement. The propaganda reached an absurd level when it was rumored that Kaiser Wilhelm had converted to Islam and gone to Mecca for a pilgrimage. Germany utilized a strategy to destabilize regions where British and French influence was dominant. The Ottoman elite, by and large, identified with this German propaganda,[9] and the Ottoman Empire entered World War I on the side of Germany. The British continued to busy themselves developing a negative image of Islamist Ottomans. Propaganda spread fear among the British public about a possible united Islamic world under the Ottoman sultan/caliph ("a Pan-Islamic Movement") that would destroy the British Empire with the help of Germany. Using this feared and imagined movement to divide and conquer, the British government put out the suggestion that it would prefer to support a "caliph" of Arab origin, such as someone from among the rulers of Mecca.[10]

The Ottoman sultan's double role as religious leader (caliph) and political defender of the Islamic world lasted until the end of the Ottoman Empire and until the establishment of the secular Turkish Republic, which rose from the ashes of the Ottoman Empire in 1923 under the leadership of Mustafa Kemal (Atatürk). When modern Turkey was born and the caliphate—in a sense Sunni Islam's "papacy"—was abolished, the centuries-long established leadership of Islam disappeared overnight. With the Ottoman Empire, the former defender of Islam, in a state of collapse and Turks busy with the establishment of a new large-group identity and with their so-called "Westernization" struggles,[11] the Arabs and many other Muslims remained helplessly open to more and more influence and manipulation by Western powers. Even before the caliphate was abolished, as mentioned, the British continued to raise and dash hopes for establishing a caliphate outside of the Ottoman territory. They also deliberately created divisions among Indian and Arab Muslims by saying they would support the establishment of the caliphate in either India or in one of the Arab countries.

Elie Kedourie analyzed the British government's disastrous handling of the Middle East after the collapse of the Ottoman Empire and its humiliation of the Arabs and other Muslims.[12] According to Kedourie, the widely used ten volumes known popularly as the Chatham House (the Royal Institute of International Affairs) version of history, written or edited by British historian Arnold J. Toynbee, who died in 1975 at the age of eighty-five, and his followers,[13] was untrustworthy and humiliating to the Arabs. To some extent, Western scholars follow Toynbee's footsteps even today.

It is difficult to pinpoint one definitive and symbolic beginning that marks the attempt in *recent* decades to reverse this humiliation and rejuvenate the chosen glories of Islam. There were, however, multiple events that can be considered starting points. One of them was the establishment of *Dar al Tabligh al-Islami* (The Institute for the Propagation of Islam) in Iran, not an Arab country.[14] This institute played a role in nurturing an atmosphere in Iran for Ayatollah Khomeini's leadership, which embraced an apocalyptic, millennialist vision for a "perfect" theocracy.[15] But the prestige of the Iranian Shi'ite revolution among other Muslims (especially among Sunnis) declined in the late 1980s, and Iran ceased being a model for Islamic radicals of all kinds, a result of economic mismanagement, widespread torture, executions, human rights violations, and the war between Iran and Iraq. Later and continuing until today, the president of Iran, Mahmoud Ahmedinijad, has been trying to revive Iran's reputation and fundamentalist ideology through his determination to develop nuclear power, which, as it is perceived in the West and by the Israelis, also includes developing nuclear weapons. This, of course, has at the present time and will have in the near future major international consequences. Ahmedinijad's Holocaust denial exhibits a magical and illusionary thinking pattern that inflamed and still inflames fear in the international arena, especially in Israel. Response to the Iranians' continued work on developing nuclear bombs—work believed to be real despite Iranian denials—could create a new human tragedy of historic proportions if an Israeli attack on Iran becomes a reality.

As extreme Islamic fundamentalism evolved as an ideology that focused on the Western world as enemy, sought out a grandiose and millennialist savior, and wished to return to a realistic and imagined glorified past, Osama bin Laden's appeal found fertile ground. Nat Howell wrote: "The elements which distinguish bin Laden's al-Qaeda . . . is not the appeal to the alienated and anxious elements among Arabs and Muslims, but the grandiosity of his world vision, the use of modern technology to extend his reach and explore the vulnerabilities of contemporary societies, and the absence of spatial or humanitarian limits to his target-list."[16]

In my past writing on Osama bin Laden, I tried to illustrate how his troubled childhood and his personal internal revengeful psychological motivations were reflected in his actions in the external world. Prophet Muhammad was an orphan who later evolved as a spiritual leader and then took up a sword to protect Islam. bin Laden himself was in essence an "orphan," as his biological mother, originally from Syria, was "exiled" from his father's harem when he was one year old, leaving him in the care of his "stepmothers" who called him *Iban al Abeda* (son of the slave). This was certainly a factor in why he developed a revengeful character.[17] He frantically searched for a father figure, psychologically speaking, to pull him out from an environment of "bad" mother figures in order to reach up in his developmental ladder. All indications are that his father, with fifty-four children, did not have much time for him. Osama's father died in a plane crash when Osama was ten years old, and his older brother Salem, who could have been a father or big brother figure for Osama, was also killed in an air tragedy, this time a helicopter accident.

Peter Olsson, a psychoanalyst and a friend of CSMHI, wrote a psychobiography of Osama bin Laden and arrived at the same conclusions.[18] Peter's work included the examination of a long poem coauthored by Osama bin Laden. Peter noted that eighteen of the forty-two verses of this poem were written by Osama. His verses mention father, son, brother, child, or family and only one line mentions mother. When mentioning father, Osama asks, "Father, where is the way out?"[19] After reminding his readers that certain types of poetry provide access to the unconscious levels of a poet's psyche, Peter Olsson wrote: "Osama seems to have both found and become his own lost father, brother, mother, and family in the far-off terror training camps of Afghanistan. Osama's painful losses and unconscious disappointment in his parents led to a fixation in the form of his search for his grandiose omnipotent father/himself."[20]

I must add here that if Osama bin Laden did not have an estimated 80 million dollars inherited after his father died he might have remained harmless. Financial resources made it possible for him to effectively use propaganda and manipulation along with supplies of weapons and technical support. Like the orphan Muhammad who later became a warrior, the "orphan" Osama wanted to become a warrior. Therefore, when the opportunity arose, Osama bin Laden presented himself as a supreme leader who knew what to do for Islam and what Islam permits its followers to do, including suicide bombings.[21]

The appearance of suicide bombers for religious purposes (and for ethnic, nationalistic, or seemingly nonreligious ideological reasons) is nothing new. We can go back to a biblical story: "And Samson said, 'Let me die with the Philistines!' And he bowed himself with all his might; and the house fell upon the lords, and upon all the people that were therein. So the dead which he slew at his death were more than they which he slew in his life" (Judges 16:30). From Samson's suicidal destruction of the Philistine temple onward, there are numerous examples of this kind of deadly action in the history of humankind. Today suicide bombings have become directly associated with Islamic terrorism.

Before September 11, 2001, we had basic information about how Palestinian suicide bombers were trained.[22] Most of these suicide bombers were chosen as teenagers, "educated," and then sent off to perform their duty in their late teens or early to mid-twenties. Briefly, the technique for creating suicide bombers in the Middle East typically included two basic elements: (1) finding people whose personal identities were already disturbed due to humiliation of themselves or their families and who were seeking a second identity to stabilize their internal worlds; and (2) forcing the large-group identity, in this case religious, into the cracks of the recruits' damaged or subjugated individual identities. Once people were "educated" for suicide attacks, the ordinary "rules and regulations" of individual psychology no longer applied to their patterns of thought and action. Killing one's self (one's personal identity) and others (enemies) did not matter; what mattered was what the act of terrorism brought to the large group.

In clinical practice we sometimes see a similar phenomenon in isolated individual cases: a youngster who cannot maintain a cohesive sense of personal identity may become psychotic as an adult and have religious delusions, such as believing he or she is the reincarnation of an old religious leader or a defender of his or her religion. In such cases, persons replace their damaged personal identities with an identity that is "made up" and obviously *false* to outsiders. But suicide bombers, those who had to be trained, were not psychotic. In their cases, the created identity fitted well with external expectations and was *approved* by the trainees and many bystanders in their own society. The psychological priority was the repair and/or enhancement of the large-group identity (through a sadistic and masochistic act), which actually enhanced the suicide bomber's modified personal identity as the carrier, the agent, of the group's identity.

Osama bin Laden tried to provide leadership for the idealized future image of an Islamic world contaminated with a divine omnipotence. But this image was under attack in fantasy and in reality. Therefore, more "normal" Muslims were attracted to al-Qaida, not only psychologically but also bodily (destroying physically others' and one's own body) to protect the idealized/divine large-group image. No longer was it necessary to find youngsters who had actually been humiliated and to train them for months until they "graduated" as suicide bombers. Indeed, the events of September 11 caused the press to begin reporting about the existence of a new breed of extreme Islamic fundamentalist suicide terrorists. These terrorists were not "directly" humiliated Palestinians; they were mostly from Egypt and Saudi Arabia. These reports also said that the "profiles" of those in this new group of terrorists did not fit those of the standard suicide bomber. They were generally older, educated, and came from wealthy families, while the standard Palestinian suicide attacker had been a young malcontent who usually came from a traumatized family with a history of losses. In many ways, the hijackers of September 11 (such as Mohamed Atta) did appear to belong to a new breed. However, the mechanisms for creating terrorists and Islamic fundamentalist suicide bombers that I have explained apply to this new group of terrorists as well.

# 34

# GROUND ZERO

## HOW I BECAME A "MUSLIM"

There are events in people's lives which can be likened to a "period" after the last sentence of a chapter in a long book. After such an event a new chapter, good or bad, opens in life. The moment a young person realizes that he or she is in love, or the moment a mother witnesses the unexpected death of her small child, are such times. Sometimes such unforgettable occurrences are shared by tens of thousands or millions of persons. Images of the landing of Apollo 11 on the moon on July 20, 1969, and astronaut Neil Armstrong's words as he stepped onto the surface of the moon on July 21, 1969—"That's one small step for [a] man, one giant leap for mankind"—are still vividly in my mind as they are to millions around the globe. These moments may be tragic ones, as when John F. Kennedy was assassinated on November 22, 1963, a day marked by nearly everyone who was old enough to understand what was happening. The horror of September 11, 2001, its drama, and its symbolic meaning—the strongest country on earth was no longer a safe place—also temporarily stopped time for most Americans and others worldwide.

On that September day my wife and I were in our North Cyprus home as our vacation was drawing to an end. She was watching news on an English television channel, when she saw footage of an airplane "accidentally" hitting one of the Twin Towers in New York City. She called me to join her and we ended up observing in horror the events that unfolded. Our first concern was for our children and their families in the United States. We were able to reach them by phone, but even after hearing that they were safe, we remained in a most uneasy mental state, riveted to the television as if waiting for some signal to end our horror.

Personally, I first became familiar with tragedies caused by terrorism long before September 11, 2001, when my friend Erol was killed by Cypriot Greek terrorists in 1957. And, for years I had followed the tragic and deadly events caused by the PKK in Turkey and the Turkish government's military response to it. When I went to psychiatric conferences or visited medical centers in Turkey, I met people traumatized by terrorism or heard detailed reports on other individuals suffering from the same kinds of violent circumstances. The number of people killed in the United States on September 11, 2001, was small in comparison to an estimated 40,000 killed due to terrorism-related events in Turkey. Yet, the pictures of the collapsing Twin Towers, smoke coming from the Pentagon, people in shock, relatives searching for missing family members, the heroism of the firefighters—in short the human drama and symbolism of September 11 on the television screen and my wife's and my personal fears for the safety of family members—all stunned me.

The very next day we received a telephone call from the Center for Psychoanalytic Research and Training at Columbia University, New York. I was very surprised that they had found my North Cyprus number and were able to reach me. I was asked to come to New York as soon as possible to meet with the members of Columbia's psychoanalytic center, speak to them about the psychology of terrorism, and assist them in their effort to help the people of New York.

I spoke on the one-month anniversary of September 11 at Smith College in Massachusetts, and exactly two months after the terrorists attacked the Twin Towers I was in New York City at Columbia University to address hundreds of psychoanalysts and other concerned people. As I entered the auditorium I met a senior respected psychoanalyst whom I knew. While I was greeting him I noted that his eyes were darting all over the place as if he were trying to spot terrorists in the auditorium. This filled me with sadness as I walked to the podium.

I had prepared a three-part talk answering three questions: What is a traumatized society? What is religious fundamentalism? What is extreme Islamic fundamentalism? As I looked at the audience before me, I clearly realized that I was *not* present in this well-known auditorium for an intellectual exchange. This gathering, without being designed so on a conscious level, aimed to be a "therapeutic" one for the very large audience and for me. I spontaneously started my talk in the following way:

> While on the train to New York, I recalled occasions when I gave advice to outside speakers who were on their way to traumatized societies and I reminded them that in a traumatized society everybody is traumatized, including the caregivers. On my way to New York I decided not simply to give an academic lecture here, exactly two months after the terrorist attack on your city; instead I wanted to reach out to your hearts. I will end up describing certain things intellectually, but please help me by staying connected to your hearts.

I do not recall exactly how long I stayed behind the podium after my speech was over, but I know it was several hours. The auditorium turned into a place to discharge emotions and also to find strength to deal with trauma. It was also a most unusual, moving, and therapeutic experience for me. When the meeting ended and someone handed me a generous check for giving the talk, I spontaneously felt angry. How dare someone try to pay me for an event that had raised my self-esteem and contributed—as small a contribution as it was—to dealing with the trauma in New York! Without showing my anger, I simply asked that the check be forwarded to the firefighters.

That evening while going to my hotel I noticed an airplane flying above. I stood in the street and watched it until it flew away, as if making sure that it was not another plane hijacked by terrorists. I was identifying with my senior colleague whose eyes were scanning the auditorium for danger. Early the next morning I returned to Charlottesville. I would visit Ground Zero at a later time.

As I stated earlier, I had promised myself that I would retire when I turned seventy years old. In 2001 we were already busy thinking about the future of the Center for the Study of Mind and Human Interaction and were looking for someone to replace me as the director, since assistant director Andy Thomson had made it clear that for personal reasons he would not be able to assume the full-time job of running CSMHI. Two months or so after my heart-warming experience in New York, and while I was preoccupied with the future of CSMHI, in a hallway at the University of Virginia's main hospital I noted a close friend of CSMHI, a physician, walking fast as if she were late for something. I asked her where she was going. She informed me that she was rushing to a meeting with some U.S. military generals who had come to Charlottesville to meet with University of Virginia experts, mostly from CSMHI, to learn about the psychology of terrorism. No one at CSMHI had told me about this meeting, even though I was still the head of the center. When I expressed my dismay, she spontaneously answered, "You were not invited because you are a Muslim!"

That is how I became a "Muslim"—the Other, the "enemy," and the "unwanted one"—in my own university, in my own center, in a place I considered "home." I thought of a man named Frank Roque in Phoenix who, on September 15, 2001, under the influence of the September 11 tragedy, embarked on a shooting rampage in which he murdered a Sikh (whom he mistook for a Muslim Arab) and attacked an Afghan family and a Lebanese store clerk. When the words of this friend of CSMHI hit me, I thought, "Thank God they are not real bullets."

I was being exposed to a relatively small illustration of an inevitable large-group's regression after a massive trauma: within hours of the attack on the World Trade Center and the Pentagon, U.S. citizens rallied dramatically around their president. The slogan "United We Stand" and flags flying everywhere reflected loss of individuality and a rally around the leader. The American chosen trauma, Pearl

Harbor, was reactivated. Preoccupation with border psychology was initiated. Acts of "purification" took place and my becoming a "Muslim" was an expression of it. In certain circles, especially among radical Christian fundamentalists, we saw magical thinking that read the tragedies as divine punishment for "sinful acts" of homosexuals, feminists, or civil libertarians in the United States. The country's leadership increased its reliance on an "us-and-them" attitude. A severe division occurred between "Americans" and "terrorists," but also between Americans and anyone who might be easily (though often unjustly) associated with "terrorists." This itself magnified the danger, erased large-group "basic trust," and lead to fantasized and exaggerated "belief" in what had popularly become known as a clash of religions and civilizations.

At this point I must add that an understanding of large-group processes following a massive trauma does not eliminate the specter of additional terrorist attacks. Nor does it remove the need for realistic attempts to provide security. The main aim of terrorism is to kill innocent people and induce fear in the society as a whole. It is a crime against humanity, regardless of the reasons behind it. Attempting to understand some of these reasons does not change this fact. What I want to illustrate here is that, psychologically speaking, the United States began dividing the world into "good" and "bad," as the enemy had done and continued to do, instead of emphasizing the complexity of international process. President George W. Bush's reference to the "war on terror" as a "crusade" and his advocacy of prayer as a "shield of protection against the evil" in a sense brought religion into the political realm.[1] When the physician told me that I was an "unwanted one" in a University of Virginia Hospital hallway, she had essentially wrapped my identity into a religious cloth.

I did not like being wrapped in a religious cloth, since this image does not fit into my subjective feelings about myself. The Ottoman Empire had collapsed some years before I was born, and the young Turkish generation on Cyprus, especially the educated, had become close followers of the founder and first president of the Turkish Republic, Mustafa Kemal (Atatürk), his revolution, and his "Westernization" policies in Turkey. Looking back, I appreciate how strongly my parents and other Turkish Cypriots of their generation, both educated and uneducated, identified with the new "Turkishness" to balance their feelings of being like orphans living outside of mainland Turkey, which they referred to as *Ana Vatan* ("Mother Country"). They became, I believe, more Westernized than the Turks in Turkey and more dedicated followers of Atatürk's revolution. Among other things, this meant that women abandoned their Islamic head covers and became true believers in secularism.

As I was growing up, my family followed certain religious customs, such as circumcision. We also celebrated religious holidays, and I remember receiving money from relatives and enjoying nice cookies. Although no one "fed' me religion, I of course identified with my community's many Islamic cultural customs. I had religious education only during one year of secondary school, when once a week we had an hour-long class with a religious teacher. He tried to teach us to recite prayers in Arabic, which we did not understand. I remember the kids giggling throughout his class. I learned to recite one prayer, which I no longer remember, and I have never been to a mosque to pray in my life. Instead, as part of our "Westernization," my two sisters and I took violin lessons starting in our early teens from an Armenian music teacher and learned to play Western classical music.

Every Turkish friend I played with in my neighborhood and in my schools during my childhood and teen years were like me in their lack of investment in religion. It simply did not have a prominent role in our lives. When I went to Turkey for my medical school training, there, too, religion found no place in my daily life. I never observed any of my medical student friends preoccupied with religion and, unlike the situation in today's Turkey, there was no pressure on me or my friends to become religious.

Only a week or so after I arrived in the United States as a newly graduated physician in 1957, a young woman came to see me at the Lutheran Deaconess Hospital in Chicago, where I had just started my medical internship. She told me she had learned that I was a newcomer to the United States, and she wanted to be my friend. She invited me to go out with her. I was delighted about this unexpected visit and invitation. The next weekend the young woman appeared at the hospital and told me that she would drive me in her car to her place. I was surprised, as I did not know this American "custom" of a young woman taking a young male stranger to her place. I had various fantasies, but none of them included religion. It was only when we arrived at our destination that I realized she was a nun who lived in a convent and that her reason for being nice to me was in the service of trying to convert me to Christianity. She presented me with a Bible written in Turkish!

I never read the Bible she gave me. I never read the Bible or Koran until the 1990s, when I studied sections of these books as part of my study of religious violence and terrorism. Looking back, I feel rather good, even lucky, that I did not invest energy in religious matters and become preoccupied with their rituals. This does not mean that I do not enjoy and appreciate beautiful music, paintings, and architecture that celebrate or recall religious stories. I also do not detect any bad prejudice in myself against people who have religious beliefs and who keep such beliefs to themselves. In my daily life I simply respect people's personal belief systems. I also know that to be a good person one does not need to be religious.

My becoming a "Muslim" and being rejected was short-lived. Over the next two years or so—even after my retirement in 2002—I was invited to six major meetings on terrorism (only one of which took place in Charlottesville). They involved interdisciplinary investigation of the threat against the United States and included officials from the Central Intelligence Agency, the Federal Bureau of Investigation, other governmental security organizations, and the military, along with academicians and experts on terrorism. I was happy and honored to be asked to join such groups on these occasions.

My general impression from these meetings was that there was an appreciation of both the rage that was present in the United States after the 9/11 terrorist attacks (and in other countries where cities were attacked, including Madrid, Casablanca, Istanbul, Mombasa, Taba, and London) and the attendant wish for revenge that arose from the attacks. There was also a focus on efforts to protect against future disasters and tragedies. But instead of discussing and examining the causes of globalized terrorism, especially terrorism against the United States, and trying to develop effective strategies for dealing with it, the participants turned their attention to "quick solutions." There was a tendency to invest a great deal of time focusing on tactics—such as sharing stories of how terrorists could be "tricked" and caught. I was most impressed by some high-level CIA participants who had sophisticated knowledge of world affairs and wanted to learn the topic under discussion in-depth. Sometimes at these meetings there were people who were experts in the field of "popular propaganda," and they directed us to come up with words or phrases for the president and other government officials to use when talking about Muslim terrorists that would not be offensive to the Muslim population at large.

At these meetings I suggested that when "God versus the Devil" thinking begins to dominate enemy relationships, it means that a severe regression exists in international relationships. In such a situation, the large-group psychology and the leaders' individual psychologies begin to severely and sometimes illogically contaminate political, legal, economic, military, and other real-world issues. I wanted us to be humble about coming up with very quick new strategies for bringing the world into more peaceful and saner times. Obviously, if someone who planned to kill us was discovered, our first priority would be to capture him and make him harmless. I suggested however that examining the psychosocial foundation on which the planning and execution of terrorism was built should also be one of our main tasks. I used the metaphor of a ladder that extends up to terrorism and stated that one key place to study is the ground on which the ladder stands.[2]

When I was invited to attend still another such meeting, this time I was asked to fulfill a requirement: I should allow the U.S. government—I presume the FBI or CIA—to conduct a security check on me. I surmised that the unidentified FBI agent's remark, "We know all about you!" when I was asked to chair the FBI Commission on Waco was no longer enough. I thought about this condition. I had nothing to hide and wished to be helpful as much as I could. However, I felt that if I began going to such meetings under the conditions required by government officials, I would lose my identity as an academician and a freethinker. I was writing books and papers and frequently giving lectures on my psychopolitical findings. Anyone could learn from me. I decided not to accept the offer and remained a "free" individual. I attended no more meetings.

Years later, however, during the fall of 2010, I received an invitation from the Interagency Strategic Communication Network to address U.S. government communications professionals from the Department of State, the Department of Defense, the intelligence community, and the Broadcasting Board of Governors. They wanted me to describe my concepts of "chosen traumas," "chosen glories," and associated myths. The chairperson of this group who invited me added that it would serve them well to become much more aware of the group's existence and power. I accepted this invitation right away and spoke to this group. I have no information as to whether or not I was helpful. There was no follow-up.

In a paper written in 2001 on the regression in the United States following September 11, I expressed the hope that this regression would be an "average expectable" one after such a horrendous tragedy and that diminishing civil liberties, hurting the American way of life, and evoking "god" and "devil" in politics would not linger too long.[3] Over a decade has passed since the horrors of that day. Often a decade is not long enough to calm shared large-group processes that are initiated after a massive trauma. Today, with the added anxiety of economic problems and unemployment—related, among other things, to the so-called war on terror—the focus on "good" and "evil" remains a factor within U.S. external and internal politics. Continuing terrorism and the fight against it maintain the strong connection between religion and politics and other large-group societal issues worldwide. In the next chapter I will summarize what psychoanalysis tells us about religion and try to come up with a theoretical formulation that explains religion's connection with violence.

# 35

# ON FAITH

## THE PSYCHOLOGY OF RELIGION

There are millions and millions of individuals in every region of the world who have their own brand of religious belief that propels them to do good. Reportedly Archbishop Desmond Tutu once said: "Religion is like a knife. If you use it to slice bread, it is good. If you use it to slice off someone's hand, it is bad."[1] When studying international relations, we have no choice but to examine "bad" things done in the name of religion, since they are implicated throughout international relations and politics. Nonetheless, even though humiliating, maiming, or killing the Other is carried out in the name of gods, it is difficult to explore and write about the negative uses of religion; it is as if this makes one "antireligious." Fear of this label may turn people away from joining in the *needed* investigation of how people use religion to sanction cutting off hands—and most often heads—a reality throughout human history. This chapter offers a summary of what my first profession, psychoanalysis, taught me about this topic.

According to Sigmund Freud, any individual's religious commitment is an expression of unresolved psychological issues from childhood. The terrifying impressions of helplessness in childhood arouse the need for protection, which can be provided through the love of a father. The duration of one's sense of helplessness—overt or covert—throughout life, Freud concluded, makes it necessary to seek an omnipotent father, an image of God, to assuage the feeling of vulnerability. Thus, religion is related to shared illusion.[2] In 1901, he famously rewrote the well-known text of Genesis, "God created man in His own image," as "Man created God in his."[3] After noticing a close similarity between obsessive acts and religious practices, he viewed obsessional neurosis as a distorted private religion, and religion as a kind of universal obsessional neurosis.

For a very long time after Freud, few psychoanalysts dealt with the topic of religion or seriously questioned Freud's assumptions in any depth. I imagine in those days psychoanalysts were hesitant to disagree with the "psychoanalytic god." And if they agreed with him, I suspect it was difficult for them to risk raising eyebrows by voicing their opinions in scientific journals or in public. As expected, an "animosity" between religion and psychoanalysis also evolved, and psychoanalysts in general ignored the topic. It was the work of British pediatrician and psychoanalyst Donald W. Winnicott in 1953 on "transitional objects" and "transitional phenomena" that momentously enlarged psychoanalytic theory on the foundation of religious beliefs and feelings and in a sense took it from being considered "pathological" to being associated with a "normal" development of early childhood.[4] Winnicott understood the existence of transitional objects and phenomena to be universal.

The transitional object is a thing like the blanket of the well-known cartoon character Linus. During the early part of the first year of life, each infant or toddler chooses an item—a transitional object—from whatever is available on the basis of texture, odor, and mobility. Sometimes even an infant's own hair can become a transitional object. Usually, the child chooses a soft thing such as a teddy bear, which is, psychologically speaking, under the child's absolute control. A transitional phenomenon is an inanimate thing, like a nursery rhyme, that functions as a transitional object.

During the first years of a child's life, the transitional object or phenomenon becomes the first item that clearly represents "not-me" in his or her mind. Though this first "not-me" image corresponds to a thing that actually exists in the world, the transitional object is *not* entirely "not-me," because it is also a substitute for the child's mother (or mothering person), whom the child's mind, psychologically speaking, does not yet fully understand as a separate individual in her own right and whom the toddler perceives to be under his or her absolute control. This is why playing with a teddy bear or repeating a specific melody can soothe the child and, conversely, why on certain occasions the child can discharge aggression against the toy (or make the soothing melody sound ugly) without fearing that it will retaliate when the child again treats it as a soothing object. The transitional object or phenomenon, like the actual mother, responds to the child's need to be comforted and does not abandon the child when the child rejects it—it stays around. If you take the blanket that is used as a transitional object and replace it with another, the child will not respond to the second blanket as an object of attachment. A blanket, more a transitional object than the actual mother, is under the control of the toddler, who firmly clings to it and rubs it, for example, in order to go to sleep. In my clinical practice, I met mothers who were jealous of their infants' transitional objects.

Through hundreds and hundreds of repeated interactions with the teddy bear or the melody, the child begins to get to know the surrounding world. The teddy bear or the melody is not part of the child, so it signifies the reality "out there" beyond the child's internal world—the "not-me" that the child slowly discovers, "creates," and needs. What is "created" at first does not respond to reality as perceived by an adult through logical thinking. The child's "reality," while playing with a transitional object or phenomenon, is a combination of reality and illusion. The infant's experience, Winnicott observed, throughout his or her life, "is retained in the intense experiencing that belongs to the arts and to religion and to imaginative living, and to creative scientific work."[5] Long before Winnicott's description of transitional objects and transitional phenomena, Freud, in a letter to Swiss psychiatrist Ludwig Binswanger, described himself as dwelling in a basement while distinguished aristocratic guests such as art and religion visit an upper floor. Freud added, "If I had another working life ahead of me, I should undertake to find a place in my low hamlet for these aristocrats."[6] It can be said that Winnicott brought these distinguished guests to Freud's basement.

In the 1960s important figures in classical psychoanalysis began questioning some of Freud's assumptions, including his thoughts on religion. For example, Robert Waelder concluded that Freud's ideas "may well be correct for the father religions, the latecomers in religious history, but [they] do not offer a complete elucidation of this psychogenesis."[7] In 1978 another well-known psychoanalyst, Hans Leowald, admitted that "under the weight of [Freud's] authority religion in psychoanalysis has been largely considered a sign of man's mental immaturity," an illusion "to be given up as we are able to overcome our childish needs for all-powerful parents."[8] Leowald associated religion with the primary process, better known in lay terminology as illogical thinking. But he also stated that the secondary process—logical thinking in lay terminology—is nourished by the former. Leowald helped to open a way for psychoanalysts to discuss the topic of religion, question Freud's assumptions, and add their own views.

William W. Meissner was a Jesuit priest (Society of Jesus) as well as a psychoanalyst and member of the American Psychoanalytic Association. Also beginning in the 1960s, Meissner wrote a series of papers and books examining the relationship between psychoanalysis and religion.[9] He eventually returned to Winnicott's concepts, concluding: "If beliefs and belief systems facilitate psychic growth and contribute to the maintenance of psychic health and mature responsible living, they are not pathological—any more than the illusory play in the transitional space between mother and child is pathological. Or for that matter, any more than Freud's own cultural creation—psychoanalysis."[10]

Meissner also concluded that individuals, in general, would have a hard time maintaining a commitment to something as abstract as a religious belief without concrete symbols. He stated: "Communion itself, the act of consuming the sacred host, is a form of concrete symbolic action."[11] He reminded his readers that just as a transitional object can degenerate into a (pathological) fetish, "transitional religious experience can be distorted into less authentic, relatively fetishistic directions that tend to contaminate and distort the more profoundly meaningful aspects of the religious experience."[12]

Meissner, however, went no further in examining the relationship between religion and violence. His work was in the service of making peace between religion and psychoanalysis, and such attempts still continue.[13] In psychoanalytic writings on religion, especially before September 11, 2001, besides having little or no detailed interest in Islam, there was little emphasis on the relationship between religion and destructive acts.[14]

When I began to study terrorism in the name of religion, I attempted to come up with a theoretical formulation that explains religious fundamentalism using Winnicott's ideas as a starting point.[15] Elaborations on transitional objects and transitional phenomena by psychoanalysts, such as Phyllis Greenacre,[16] Arnold Modell,[17] and myself,[18] have allowed us to see more clearly the progressive, healing, and creative aspects of religious beliefs and feelings, as well as their regressive, destructive, and restrictive aspects. In order to illustrate additional considerations concerning the progressive and regressive functions of transitional objects and phenomena, one can visualize an imaginary lantern with one transparent side and one opaque side located between infants or toddlers and their actual environment.

When toddlers feel comfortable, fed, rested, and loved, they turn the transparent side toward the real things that surround them. By illuminating these things, they begin slowly, psychologically speaking, to perceive them as entities separate from themselves. We now know that an infant's mind is more active than we once believed; yet, the infant or toddler still needs exercises in which illusion and reality is mixed before the child develops better perceptions and ideas about the real world. When infants or toddlers feel uncomfortable, hungry, or sleepy, they turn the opaque side of the lantern toward the frustrating outside world. This "wipes out" the surrounding real things. Most mothers have observed that when their toddlers are falling asleep, they hold on to their blankets as if their whole world consists of child and blanket; at such times, the transitional object serves as a mother-substitute that cuddles and "protects" the children from the rest of the real world beyond. When the lantern is thus turned opaque-side out, we imagine that their minds experience a sense of cosmic omnipotence.

In "normal" development, toddlers play with their "lanterns" hundreds and hundreds of times, getting to know reality in one direction and succumbing back to lonely, omnipotent/narcissistic existence in the other direction. Eventually their minds begin to hold on to unchangeable external realities, such as having a mother psychologically separate from them who is sometimes gratifying and at other times frustrating. I am not discarding the infant's inborn psychological ability to differentiate between certain items, even colors. Here, I am referring to a more general, developmental differentiation. During such repeated "play" toddlers' minds learn both to separate and to fuse illusion and reality, omnipotence and restricted ability, suspension of disbelief and the impact of the real world. By using blankets, teddy bears, or other transitional objects or transitional phenomena, children are involved in a watershed concept.

If a child's development is normal, he or she eventually develops an acceptance of the "not-me" world, even the indifference of the universe, and adjusts to logical thinking and gives up the childhood use of a transitional object or phenomenon. However, the "function" of the transitional object or phenomenon remains part of our psychic life and reveals itself during what I call "moments of rest" from adult-type mental activities that include a necessity for logical thinking. During "moments of rest" there is no need to differentiate between what is real and what is illusion, a time when logical thinking need not be maintained. Indulging in intense love or hate or what is known as spirituality are examples of such moments.

When I first visited Jerusalem in the 1980s, a friend of mine, Avner Falk, took me to the old city. Instead of walking in the streets, he guided me to walk from one rooftop to another, looking down upon the old historic city from above. That experience caused one of my most memorable "moments of rest." The feeling was indescribable. With logical thinking I can only define my illogical experience as allowing centuries of human history into my body and soul and knowing what it is to be a human being. In these moments, our relation to the function of the transitional object or phenomenon and how we play with it echoes throughout a lifetime.

The need or duration of "moments of rest" varies from individual to individual and from group to group. During these moments a Christian might know that it is biologically impossible for a woman to have a baby without the sperm of a man but also believe in the virgin birth. Rationally, people might know that no one really sees angels, but they may behave as if angels exist. Some people declare that they do not require religious "moments of rest," but perhaps they refer to-the same function by different names. For example, they may "play" the game of linking magical and real in astrology, or paint abstract paintings that represent a mixture of illusion and reality.

The biggest and most organized and socially sanctioned "propaganda" for a better way of life comes from religious organizations to which parents, teachers, and neighbors belong. Children, who are, as Erik Erikson would say, "generalists,"[19] not only identify with their parents' religious beliefs but, as they grow up, also often continue to be exposed to religious "propaganda." Religion, a mixture of illusion and reality, becomes crystallized in peoples' minds as "psychic reality." It provides "moments of rest" regularly and becomes intertwined with large-group identity—or a subgroup identity—often mixed with a sense of nationalism or ethnicity. It functions in a way similar to how a very special chosen glory or chosen trauma functions. The "normal" range of religious beliefs and religious involvements, like the "normal" range of psychological health, is usually socially determined.

I consider religious beliefs and feelings to derive from *normal developmental processes* in early childhood and from the times when we require a "moment of rest" in adulthood. An investment in religion is not *only* due to mental conflicts of childhood associated with feelings of helplessness and the corresponding desire for an omnipotent father, as Freud thought. Nevertheless, the image of God incorporates many different sources as the child grows, and is modified according to an individual's own psychology, sociocultural experiences, education, and the degree religious items are used as symbols or "protosymbols."[20] Unlike a symbol, in the individual's mind a protosymbol stands not for another item, but *as* the other item. A painting of Jesus Christ in a church can be perceived as a symbol or protosymbol in individuals' minds; in the latter case individuals feel the presence of Jesus Christ in front of them.

As individuals go through the life cycle, they may use religion to gratify or to defend against various needs, wishes, and internal tensions and conflicts. For some people, Freud's original description of the emotional link between God and a father-image does indeed hold true. But, for each individual, the image of God represents a source of various combinations of maternal or paternal love, fear of punishment, hatred, omnipotence, and so on—including, very significantly, the sense of "belonging" to family, clan, and large group.

Returning to the lantern metaphor, theoretically speaking, we can say that the extreme religious fundamentalist is preoccupied with keeping the opaque side of the lantern turned against the real world. Unlike infants who can probably block out the external world more thoroughly when they grasp their transitional objects (for example, before going to sleep), adult extreme fundamentalists remain aware of a real environment that they perceive as threatening. Therefore, such an adult's "moment of rest" is *not* a restful one. An excessive preoccupation with religion—as a transitional phenomenon—that tries to block the external world is accompanied by complicating factors, such as feeling omnipotent and helpless, submitting to or fusing with divinity, searching for total perfection yet fearing failure, needing a nurturing mother but not really obtaining one, and reaching to an omnipotent father but ending up being his absolute "slave."

Persons who keep the opaque sides of their lanterns turned against the real world often seek each other and become followers of a leader/protector in the hope that such a leader will make their uncomfortable "moments of rest" comfortable.

Alas, such radical fundamentalist leaders also possess a lantern with an opaque side facing the outside world, magnifying the dangers that exist "out there." When you do not see the enemy clearly, the situation may be perceived as being more dangerous than it actually is. Thus, a tendency to strike out is maintained. Alternately, the extreme religious fundamentalist may turn aggression toward his- or herself in order to completely wipe out the danger behind the opaque screen, sometimes even committing suicide in order to join a god in death, in another world.

Andy Thomson drew on information from psychoanalysis, the neurosciences, cognitive psychology, and evolutionary psychology and tried to answer the question: why do we believe in god(s)? He concluded: "Religion may offer comfort in a harsh world; it may foster community; it may incite conflict. In short, it may have its uses—for good and for evil. But it was created by human beings, and this will be a better world if we cease confusing it with fact."[21] He added that "despite the political correctness of proclaiming no conflict between science and religion, the constant din of battles in school boards and educational committees" in the United States, Canada, and United Kingdom "is becoming deafening."[22] He concluded that unquestionably there is a conflict between religion and science.

Religion is here to stay, and the more regression occurs in large groups, the more members of those groups will hold on to their religion. Social scientists should feel freer and more willing to study the reasons for preoccupation with religion in large groups and the use of religion as a knife to slice off someone's hand.

# PART VIII

# THE PSYCHOLOGY OF TURKEY, CYPRUS, AND THE KURDS

# 36

# WATCHING EUROPE FROM VIENNA

## THE LINKING OF SYMBOLIC EVENTS

---

In 2002 many family members, friends, and distinguished guests gathered in Charlottesville for an academic as well as a social event to mark my retirement from thirty-eight years at the University of Virginia Medical School. I remember with gratitude and fondness all the guests' kindness and the wonderful celebration. Afterward, I stayed on at the Center for the Study of Mind and Human Interaction as an acting director for many months until a new director arrived. For a combination of reasons, this unusual center would be closed within three years.

In 2006 Austria held the presidency of the European Union and declared that year to be the Year of Mozart as well as the Year of Freud. Unusual pictures of Mozart and Freud with their eyes gazing skyward—I never figured out the possible symbolism expressed by the style of these pictures—could be seen at every tourist site in Vienna. That year I was honored to be the Fulbright/Sigmund-Freud-Privatstiftung Visiting Scholar of Psychoanalysis in Vienna and to teach political psychology for a semester as a visiting professor in the political science department at the University of Vienna. As a Fulbright scholar I had my office at the Freud Museum.

While in Vienna I tried to observe the influence that images of centuries-old historical events have on societies. This interest was initiated during the first week of my scholarship. There were six other Americans starting their Fulbright scholarships with me in Austria, all at different locations. But during our orientation program, all of us were in Vienna. One day we met an Austrian lady who had a very high position in the European Union administration. She told us all the virtues of forming this union and its bright future. As she was finishing her talk, a Fulbright scholar whom I had met only few days before, and who was aware that I was a Turkish-American, then asked the lady what she thought of Turkey's possible entrance into the European Union. The lady knew nothing about my background; to her I was just another American scholarship recipient. Her face turned purple at the question and she swore that Turkey would never be allowed to be a member of the European Union. She continued with politically incorrect remarks that implied Turks were not normal or civilized human beings.

In 1964, facing a shortage of workers, Austria had signed a bilateral agreement with Turkey to recruit Turks as guest workers for the continued postwar rebuilding of Austria. Austria stopped guest worker recruitment in the 1970s, but by 2000 there were an estimated 140,000 to 170,000 Turks living among eight million Austrians, and Turkish was the predominant minority language. This caught the attention of and induced racially inflamed sentiments among the Austrian far-right, notably by its leader Jörg Haider.[1] By 2006, the Turkish minority in Vienna and in Austria in general had become a big minority population, causing various major social and psychopolitical problems.[2]

With my Fulbright scholarship, I and my wife were given an enormous historic apartment in the heart of Vienna overlooking the front gate of St. Stephen's Cathedral at Stephanplatz. Whenever I stepped out our door I heard Turkish spoken. In 2006 it was believed that within a dozen years or so 40 percent of Vienna's population would be Muslim—mostly Turks. I could understand the EU official's frustration. The reality of having so many Turks in Vienna raised social and psychopolitical issues that became factors encouraging the reactivation of a centuries-old Austrian chosen glory: the shared image of the combined forces of the Holy Roman Empire and the Polish-Lithuanian Commonwealth that defeated the Ottoman Turkish forces on September 12, 1683, ending the second siege of Vienna by the Ottomans. During my previous visits to Vienna I had not been aware of such a reactivation. This time, however, while walking through the city visiting churches, historical places, and museums, my Austrian friends pointed out plaques on churches, monuments in parks or streets, and paintings in museums that recalled this chosen glory that had followed terror and victimization.[3]

Ottomans tried to conquer Vienna twice. The first siege of Vienna took place in the spring of 1529, when the Ottoman Empire was ruled by Süleyman the Magnificent. At that time, after occupying lands extending from Istanbul to Vienna, the Ottomans, using a huge Janissary force aided by a much smaller Christian Hungarian force, tried to enter Vienna. Reinforced three hundred-year-old walls surrounding the city and its stored food supplies ultimately caused the Ottoman forces to give up conquering Vienna. But what really evolved as a chosen glory for the Austrians was the September 12, 1683, triumph of Polish, German, and Austrian militaries under Polish King Jan III Sobieski during the Battle of Vienna that ended the two-month-long second siege of the city by the Ottoman Turks and a smaller number of Tatars who were helping them.[4] This battle is also known as the Battle of Kahlenberg, named after a hilltop north of the city. The defeat took place at a time when the fall of Vienna to the Turks seemed imminent. Forces under Sobieski were much smaller than the Ottoman forces, but using a surprise attack, they were able to drive the enemy from Vienna over a period of two days, September 11 and 12.

The defeat of Ottomans on September 12, 1683, reminds me of the September 11, 2001, tragedy since both events, even centuries apart, became key symbols representing a clash between Islam and Christianity. Sobieski's victory marked the turning point of the Ottoman expansion into Europe and the beginning of the Ottomans' withdrawal from Europe. There is evidence that images of the siege of Vienna by the Ottomans had been internalized by the terrified Viennese people and such images were transferred from one generation to the next. Earlier I wrote about how Serbs continued to drink red wine named Prince Lazar during Communist times when open preoccupation with Lazar's image was officially discouraged. The image of Lazar stayed within the Serbian population in support of the Serbian entitlement ideology, Christoslavism. The Viennese created croissants, symbolic images of the moon on the Ottoman flag, and ate them over and over throughout the centuries. The Viennese "discovery" of the croissant represented various psychological reactions to the terror created by the Ottoman Turks. We can imagine a shared regression to orality within the traumatized society that destroyed the enemy, psychologically speaking, by eating it. However, the "discovery" of the croissant most likely also stood for identification with the aggressor. Sometimes the "memory" of a historical event continues in a repressed fashion in a society, and when a new issue with the same enemy—or even another enemy—becomes inflamed, tens or hundreds of years later, the influence and the meaning of a chosen glory or chosen trauma becomes unrepressed. I do not know if the Battle of Vienna came to the mind of the EU official when she replied to my Fulbright scholar friend's question. I also do not know whether she ate a croissant for breakfast that morning!

My class of fifty-eight at the University of Vienna included students from many countries, as would be the case a year later when I taught at Bahçeşehir University in Istanbul. Some of the students at the University of Vienna were from Poland and some were from Turkey. When I lectured on concepts of chosen glory and chosen trauma, I asked the Polish and Turkish students if they would research the second siege of Vienna and the Battle of Kahlenberg as two separate teams and present their findings to the rest of the class from Polish and Turkish points of view. This project became a central and exciting focus of my visiting professorship. One morning when the Polish and Turkish students were ready—with historical data, copies of documents, paintings, clips from current Polish, Austrian, and Turkish news media and video presentations—their classmates and I witnessed a fascinating, emotional reliving of September 1683 in our 2006 classroom. Afterward, I drew upon my first profession with the presenters from opposing sides in order to erase any negative effects this exercise might have on them. The next year the whole program was recreated, again with intense emotions, by Polish and Turkish student in my class at Bahçeşehir University. Bringing to life identity issues, chosen glories, and chosen traumas was an excellent tool for teaching psychopolitical concepts. As expected, students from opposing parties interpreted history differently so they could invest narcissism into the large-group identity to which they belonged.

During my pre-2006 visits to Vienna, on several occasions, I had gone to the Kahlenberg area as a tourist and had seen the church and the little museum where paintings, drawings, and documents commemorate the defeat of the Ottomans. In 2006 during a Sunday visit to the same place with my wife, my Viennese painter friend Wolf Werdigier, and his friend, psychiatrist Regina Hofer, I had a very different experience. There is a coffee shop at this location next to a large and unattractive platform where tourists gather to look down on the city. This time I noted that I was hearing Turkish at every corner of the platform and in the open-air coffee shop. I first approached a group of six Turks, three men and three women in their mid-twenties, and introduced myself in Turkish. They were all from Vienna, second-generation Turks living in the city. I asked them why they had chosen to come to Kahlenberg on that Sunday. One young man, whose name, like mine, happened to be Volkan, looked surprised. "Don't you know why *abi* [big brother]?" he asked. "This is Kahlenberg. We were here." Wolf joined me when I interviewed fifteen other small groups of Turks. Except one young Turkish man in love and unaware of the world around him beyond his girlfriend who was visiting from Turkey, all others in the group of Turks responded to my inquiry about being at Kahlenberg on that Sunday with answers similar to young Volkan's. Wolf and I were surprised. We concluded that when the Austrian chosen glory was reactivated, Turks in Vienna seemed to respond to it. They would come to Kahlenberg on the weekends to breathe in some "Turkishness"! Ours was only an observation. I spoke about it with some Austrian psychologists and they were interested in carrying out scientific research on Turks visiting Kahlenberg on Sundays. This, however, was never done.

I began to wonder about other concrete symbols of Ottoman Turks' historical image from the sixteenth and seventeenth centuries in Austria and other surrounding countries and how local people related to them today. Talking with scholars and friends led me to visit three locations. First, I visited the second largest city in Austria, Graz. Ottomans often assaulted Graz in the sixteenth century, but only occupied it very briefly. They never took Schloßberg (castle mountain), now in the center of the city. After giving a lecture at the historic University of Graz, I was told that not many places reflecting assaults by Ottomans remain today. Then I was taken to a street not far from Schloßberg and was asked to look up at the top floor of a tall apartment building. I saw the likeness of an Ottoman Janissary hanging out of a window with one hand open. I was told, with laughter, that this "statue" represented how an Ottoman who was not civilized enough behaved at the dining table: almost flying out the window of a high building to catch a piece of meat that had been thrown from there.

The second place I visited was Prague, Czech Republic. Perhaps one of the most breathtaking downtown areas of any city in the world is the Old Town Square in Prague. At this location, mounted on the southern wall of Old Town City Hall is the huge astronomical clock that dates back to 1410. There are four figures that are set in motion hourly. These four figures represent what local people despised in the fifteenth century: vanity, death, greed as represented by a Jew, and debauchery as represented by a Turk.

Lastly I traveled to Bratislava, the capital of Slovakia. When my CSMHI friends were working in Estonia I had visited Bratislava twice, once to meet Joe Montville and another time to observe the results of Joe's peace work there. This time I saw a drastic change in Bratislava. With EU funds the old town had been renovated and more renovations were in progress. One of the popular spots in the renovated area was an outdoor café overlooking an open square full of tourists. At the entrance to this popular place, a stuffed full-size Ottoman Turk was sitting, reminding the locals and the tourists of some historical/societal memories, if they cared to think about them. I said "hello" to this stuffed man with a huge head scarf, but he did not respond to me and continued gazing at the crowd. I thought that it would be difficult, perhaps impossible, for Turkey to be accepted into the European Union.

I was not aware of the reactivation of the image of the second siege of Vienna during my visits there before 2006. I wondered why this reactivation occurred at this time. Even though it was not apparent to everyone, it was recognizable when one was watching for it. This time in Austria, there was interest in my talks on large-group identity, reactivation of chosen traumas, and ideas about Turks and related issues, and I was interviewed by various newspapers and journals.[5] Because this was the year Austria had assumed the presidency of the European Union, Europe's, and to a certain degree the world's, attention was turned toward Austria. That year during my professional meetings with Austrians I noted that they often and openly referred to themselves as the first victims of the German Nazis. This, however, seemed somewhat forced.

Elsewhere in this book I touched on my involvement in helping to end the silence in Germany about the Holocaust. Silence in Austria has not been as effectively broken as it has been in Germany.[6] With its presidency of the European Union in 2006, I thought, there was a further need to support this societal denial in order for Austria to be accepted as the "leader" of Europe. It would be the Ottomans—centuries ago—who would be the aggressors and killers, rather than the Austrians who collaborated with the Nazis. Austrians would be the victims who gloriously defeated the enemy and deserved to be the "leader" of Europe. Of course, I cannot say that what came to my mind is correct. Such thoughts, however, need to be mentioned so they can be examined more scientifically. Also, based on my experience with large-group psychology, verbalization of such ideas is useful in order to tame large-group prejudices. It is like an enemy that is more dangerous when it is unseen and less dangerous, psychologically speaking, when it is seen and then evaluated.

I am all for the maintenance and improvement of the European Union—the primary reason for its establishment was to prevent future large-group violence in a part of the world that has a long history of repeated killing in the name of identity. During one of my visits to Vienna as head of CSMHI prior to my living there for four months in 2006, I met Beatte Winkler, who was then director of the European Monitoring Center on Racism and Xenophobia (EUMC).[7] EUMC was charged with providing information on racism, xenophobia, Islamophobia, and anti-Semitism in order to help the member states of the European Union come up with appropriate strategies to deal with such issues. EUMC was located in a large building in Vienna that had been used by Nazi officials long ago. The former Nazi building had been turned into a place where humane ideals—the very opposite of Nazi racism—would be nurtured.

Beatte Winkler, originally from Germany, had gone through her personal psychoanalysis and was very interested in utilizing psychoanalytic insights in combating racism and xenophobia in Europe. I met her several times and spent some hours with her. The European Union had many committees and commissions on political, legal, economic, military, and related issues. But it had no psychological committee or commission to look into identity issues that might come up when large groups with different identities are put under one tent. Beatte and I came up with the idea that CSMHI and EUMC together might develop a program to help with potential large-group identity problems, since many European states were involved in some kind of integration. Instead of immediately dealing directly with member states, however, we wanted to see if we could help to "integrate" one location in the Czech Republic where a six-foot-high wall had been erected in the Czech town of Usti nad Labem to separate a Roma neighborhood from one of ethnic Czechs. This visible wall functioned like the "invisible wall" in Richmond, Virginia, that I described earlier. We also learned that in the Czech Republic (as well as in Slovakia and Hungary) more than half of Roma children went to special schools for the mentally disabled. In June 1999, twelve Roma families in the Czech city of Ostrava sued this city's school board and the Czech constitutional court to stop this practice.[8]

This CSMHI project would be our "entry point" into potentially larger large-group identity problems in Europe. People associated with CSMHI visited the Czech Republic several times for a year during which we contacted and spoke with leaders of the Roma communities as well as local Czech administrators to receive their help and cooperation for our psychopolitical project. We prepared steps to begin our work there under the sponsorship of EUMC. I flew to Vienna once more and went to the EUMC building to wait for Beatte to come out of a meeting with representatives from fourteen EU countries who would decide whether to fund this CSMHI/EUMC project. Beatte emerged from the meeting disappointed and informed me that the fourteen representatives could not agree among themselves about whether to support a psychologically informed project.

Associations to my work with Beatte were in my mind when in 2006 I took a train from Vienna to Budapest, Hungary, to give a talk at the European Transcultural Group Analysis (EATGA) meeting and to participate in a workshop titled "Europe: Myth and Realities."[9] Changes within Europe and the expansion of the European Union to include Eastern European states were a focus of EATGA's workshop. The program stated:

> European identity cannot be explained by national identity, stemming from historical, language, and religious affiliations. An attempt to define Europe without geographical features like the coasts, mountains, courses of rivers must fail as well. Europe geographically is no more than a peninsula connected to the big East Asian continent. Europe is consequently an idea, a process.

The workshop in 2006 strove to understand this process. One of the programs, chaired by a Italian colleague, Giovanna Cantarella, involved representatives from EU members Hungary, the United Kingdom, Austria, France, and Germany and from would-be Eastern European members. I from the United States sat in the same room, as a kind of participant observer. All of us were professionals in various fields of psychology. It was noted and acknowledged before the gathering that English would be the language used at this meeting. Giovanna asked the people present from Europe to describe how they felt about the European Union and to state how their respective countries could be helpful for its future development. For the first fifteen to twenty minutes every participant was "politically correct." All talked about the usefulness and the virtue of establishing this union, which would make Europe truly democratic. Everyone would be equal, economic gains would be shared fairly, violence would be erased, and so on. Suddenly, the French participant began to speak in French. Then she stopped and repeated, this time in English, what she had said: "Since all the European Union countries are declared equal, I do not wish this meeting to be conducted only in English. I will speak only in French!" And, she continued to speak in a high voice in French. Upon this, some others began to speak in their own languages. Soon mayhem broke out, with most participants almost screaming at one another in languages that probably were understood only by those who spoke them. The Italian chairwoman tried to stay with English and calm people down. She was not successful. After confusion and mayhem lasted an hour or so, the meeting came to an end.

Reflecting on this later, I noted how individuals who are given a task to represent their large groups—especially under conditions where no preparations are made—become spokespersons for their large groups and may give up their individual identities. The EATGA workshop also illustrated—even if only as minor evidence—that it would take some time to achieve a solid European Union identity. Then I thought that the fourteen representatives of the EU member countries had been right for not supporting the proposed CSMHI/EUMC project years earlier: focusing on large-group identity issues might have induced anxiety and opened a Pandora's box. A solid European Union identity will evolve only as economic collaborations and business and legal processes become more solidified, and then only slowly. However, as I write this chapter, I am, like everyone else, aware of the severe economic problems in Greece, Spain, and other EU countries, and they make me pause and wonder about the future of the European Union. I still hope that it will continue to exist and respond positively to the prime reason it was founded: to stop killings in the name of large-group identity.

# 37

# THE "HIJACKING" OF RELIGION AND WOMEN'S RIGHTS IN TURKEY

## ON BECOMING A SOCIETAL TRANSFERENCE FIGURE

A year prior to my Fulbright Scholar position and visiting professorship at the University of Vienna in 2005, I received a letter from John Lineweaver, a peace activist and psychotherapist from Long Island, New York. He informed me that he had just started a process to nominate me for the Nobel Peace Prize for my work examining conflicts between opposing large groups, for carrying out projects in various troubled spots in the world, and for developing psychopolitical theories. John had been in Charlottesville several times attending academic programs that were open to the public at the Center for the Study of Mind and Human Interaction. From those visits, I knew that he had been involved with societies and NGOs associated with the United Nations.

When I received his letter I did not know what to do except to thank him for thinking of me. As a member of the Carter Center's International Negotiation Network, I had met several individuals who were recipients of the Nobel Peace Prize, but I never imagined myself as a candidate for this honor. Some of my friends thought that the process John Lineweaver had started would be good for attracting attention to psychological aspects of international relations. With their efforts, and especially with John's insistence, in the end individuals and organizations from twenty-seven countries sent letters to the Nobel Peace Prize Committee supporting my candidacy. John showed me copies of some of these letters and I felt grateful for and overwhelmed by their content.

While I was a Fulbright Scholar in Vienna, officials from the Sigmund Freud Foundation, when introducing me at meetings or social gatherings, would often make reference to my candidacy for the Nobel Peace Prize. But it was only after my three-month stay in Istanbul in 2007 as a visiting professor at Bahçeşehir University and at Cerrahpaşa Medical School that the name of Nobel was attached to my name in public in Turkey. As this association was not planned, sometimes it pleased me, but most of the time it caused me some embarrassment. I became someone sought out by many newspaper reporters who wanted to interview me about my perceptions or findings about what was happening in Turkey and the world. I was also a guest on various television talk shows. Previously, for decades, I had carried out my academic and psychopolitical activities well under the radar of the popular media. My reason for allowing myself to be in the spotlight now was my strong urge to share my ideas concerning two major identity crises in Turkey and to express my opinion on women's rights.

The first identity issue involved, and still involves, the constant attempts during the last few decades to change the symbols and cultural amplifiers of "Turkishness" as they had been perceived and evolved by the founder of modern Turkey, Kemal Atatürk, and his followers. The disastrous ranking of Turkey's gender gap, I believe, was connected with this national identity issue: the World Economic Forum's "Global Gender Gap Index 2006," which assessed 115 countries covering 90 percent of the world's population, ranked Turkey 105th in gender equality right behind Algeria, Ethiopia, the United Arab Emirates, and Bahrain.

The second identity problem was, and also still is, an ethnic one. Since 1984 tens of thousands of Turkish citizens, Turks and Kurds, have died following the terrorist actions of the Kurdistan Workers' Party (PKK) and the Turkish governments' military response to it. Now millions of Kurds in Turkey, many of them peaceful citizens, have no choice but to be aware of their ethnic identity as Kurds every day of their lives. Ethnic Turks, too, due to repeated tragic events, are also exposed daily to what has become known as the country's "Kurdish question" and therefore are also aware of ethnic issues on a daily basis. As I will soon note, the initiation of these two major identity problems are connected.

In 1977 Arnold Hottinger wrote:

> Atatürk opened a wedge-shaped path of *bon sens* and even cool reason through the thick forest of Turkish politics. In the time of the Father of Modern Turkey, the end of the wedge was so wide that it seemed at first to be clearing the whole of the thicket. In the course of the decades that followed his death the broad path narrowed, and the trees and undergrowth grew tall on both sides. But the general direction of the path remains, and one can advance along it.[1]

Some years before I became a visiting professor at Bahçeşehir University, during my earlier visiting professorships in Izmir in 2003 and in Ankara in 2005, I had noticed not only that the path Hottinger spoke about was getting narrower and narrower, but also that there were efforts to start new paths in new directions and to light them with religious lamps.

It is beyond my knowledge and the scope of this book to provide here a full report on all factors influencing modern Turkish society that resulted in a highly increased investment in Islam and the use of religion for political purposes during recent decades. However, I will briefly summarize my understanding of some aspects of this development:

After the death of Kemal Atatürk in 1938, the Turkish military assumed the responsibility of protecting secularism in the country. A little over two decades later, the military began to interfere with the civilian political processes. Such interferences occurred four times—in 1960, 1971, 1980, and 1997. The 1980 Turkish military coup d'état in the long run was the most traumatic one among the four interventions. Its purpose was to do something to end the bloody conflict between the right-wing and left-wing organizations in Turkey of the 1970s, which had been marked by almost daily assassinations and an estimated death toll of 5,000. Since what was happening in Turkey in the 1970s mirrored the conflict between the United States and the Soviet Union at that time, the September 12, 1980 coup d'état under Chief of General Staff General Kenan Evren was supported by the United States. This support was also influenced by the continuing hostage crisis in Iran, which had started in early November 1979, and the Soviet War in Afghanistan, which began in late December 1979. The United States wanted a stable ally in the Middle East.

But the stability of Turkey, now under the presidency of Kenan Evren, was accompanied by a new constitution that restricted democracy, allowed selected torture, and created its own societal trauma.[2] This, in turn, resulted in more awareness of not only leftist or rightist political identities but also investments in religious and ethnic identities. The situation was further complicated when the influence of the so-called Islamic Green Belt movement was encouraged by the United States. Green is the Islamic color, and the idea of a Green Belt refers to supporting Islam on the southern borders of the Soviet Union—from Turkey to Pakistan—as a weapon to fight the Soviets. It is said that this project was initiated by President Jimmy Carter's National Security Council under Zbigniew Brzezinski.

There were neoliberal economic reforms in the early 1980s in Turkey. This too allowed various identities, such as Kurdish and religious identities, to become more public, particularly in communal processes.[3] Turgut Özal, who followed the Kenan Evren era as the president of Turkey in 1989, was of partial Kurdish decent. He died while president in 1993. Özal had worked at the World Bank, and his government opened the Turkish economy to the outside world and initiated privatization of many state enterprises. These dramatic changes were accompanied by the knowledge that Turgut Özal was the first prime minister of Turkey to have gone, before his presidency, on the hajj to Mecca. He also legalized Islamic banking in Turkey,[4] and he openly stated that Turks should stop seeing Atatürk's image as godlike and accept him as a human being.

Beginning in the 1980s, many local political leaders began to speak about their pride in Turkey's Islamic heritage and by early 1990 some would even promise that only Islamic observance would cure the country's economic problems. Turkey's polarization, which would be labeled a struggle between so-called Kemalists (named after the founder of Turkey and meaning the secularized political elite and academicians) and so-called Islamists, became more and more noticeable.[5] This polarization was concretely exhibited in the attire of many young female students. Some were determined to exhibit their commitment to Islam by covering their heads, hair, and necks with scarves and by wearing long overcoats, hiding their legs. Some highly educated city women joined them. When I was a visiting professor in Ankara in 2005, no female student with a head scarf was admitted on to state university campuses. A person high in the Ankara University administration once told me that the university was like a "walled castle" and that the Islamist politicians would never conquer it. However, I sensed that in spite of his bravado, he and other academicians would soon be silenced.

Various internal and external political processes, economic and legal developments, and military concerns combined to create a deep societal division or fragmentation in Turkey that continues today. I assume that the psychology of mourning over the loss of an empire also supported this development. As part of societal mourning citizens were ready to look back and review the loss of a sultanate and caliphate after the establishment of a secular republic in 1923.

During my 2003 and 2005 visiting professorships in Izmir and Ankara, a center-right conservative political party called the Justice and Development Party (AKP), founded in 2001, was already in power. This party has won all elections since 2002 and still has a parliamentary majority in Turkey. The electoral base of this party is in central Anatolia, the heartland of Turkey, which had been a predominantly peasant society. Since the AKP came to power, many towns and villages have gone through a kind of economic miracle, and the traditional towns and villages began to acquire modern tastes and entrepreneurship. In part because of this, the electoral support for the AKP remains strong.

According to speeches given by AKP leaders, this political party follows a conservative social agenda and liberal market economy. The party wishes to evolve a Turkish society that does not reject tradition, that has a belief in universalism that accepts localism, and that nurtures the spiritual meaning of life and a choice for change that is not fundamentalist. The party wishes to see a new generation of Turks committed to religion. The party's agenda and its extremely well-run political machinery find a good response in Anatolia and empower the party's local politicians. By 2009 it was estimated that Turkey had 85,000 active mosques. This meant "one for every 350 citizens—compared to one hospital for every 60,000 citizens—the highest number per capita in the world and, with 90,000 imams, more imams than doctors or teachers. It has thousands of *madrassa*-like Imam-Hatip schools and about four thousand more official state-run Qur'an courses, not counting the unofficial Qur'an schools, which may expand the total number tenfold."[6]

The AKP's support for the return to "traditional values" in a sense gave "permission" to many people and organizations in many localities in the country to, using a phrase of Andy Thomson, "highjack religion."[7] This was done for political purposes and put pressure on their neighbors in villages, towns, and big cities to accept and act in regressive and even sometimes bizarre manners. Even during the mid-1970s, years before AKP was founded, when another Islamist party, National Salvation Party, partnered with a secular party in running Turkey, examples of regressive events took place with government approval. For example, at that time people were hired in post offices to ink out and cover over the nipples of naked breasts in foreign magazines before these magazines were allowed to be sold.

In the 1974–1975 academic year, I served as a visiting professor of psychiatry at Ankara University and witnessed covered-over breast pictures in magazines. It was assumed that this activity would protect citizens from being "sinful"! It was done in the name of religion, just as Virginia in the United States, as I write this chapter, has passed a politically motivated law requiring women to have an invasive ultrasound before they can have an abortion. In other words, forcibly penetrating a woman for no medical reason has been mandated in the name of religion. In the mid-1970s, I should have known that "hijacking" religion would increase in Turkey, but I did not come to this conclusion at the time, because I thought that cooperation between an extremely conservative political party and a liberal one would be a temporary event.

In the mid-2000s I began reading in the news about voices in Turkey stating the following: a man and a woman dancing are encouraged by the "devil"; a woman who has an extramarital affair should be beaten with a stick in a public place; a female medical student should not even see the dead body of a man in the morgue or examine a male patient; in classrooms men and women should sit on opposite sides of the room; statues of men or women showing nakedness should be destroyed; and the required religious custom of washing one's hands, feet, and face increases red blood cells and makes one resistant to illness.

During the summer of 2006, 1,000,473 children "volunteered" to take free Koran lessons,[8] and a picture of Spider Man flying on a prayer rug was distributed to youngsters. Two girls were beaten because they walked hand in hand in a public place. More and more women began covering their heads and necks in public. During a public ceremony, young girls marched wearing headscarves. The sounds of tape-recorded calls for prayer broadcasted from minarets by someone pushing a button in an office were turned up as high as possible as if to show that the higher the noise, the greater the commitment to one's religion. Technology was being used and still is used, in a sense, by trading the traditional human call to prayer for a summons by machine. When the tape-recorded call to prayer ends, citizens and tourists hear a "tick, tick" sound as the tape recorder is turned off.

Restricted religious *tarikat*s—the general characteristics of which I described earlier—were springing back to life left and right in Turkey. I recall a cartoon published in the Turkish daily newspaper *Hürriyet*. It portrayed a man asking for directions to a store. The second man answers: "First you pass the building of Sami Efendi tarikat; then you go straight. When you come to Mahmut Efendi tarikat turn right. Then in front of you, you will see Ahmet Hoca tarikat. Then you turn left. You will reach the store you are looking for."[9] One restricted order called İsmailağa Cemaati was "reincarnating" a tradition that maintained that the best way for Muslims to live is to adopt the lifestyle of the times when Prophet Muhammad was alive. They were also involved in "religious killings" related to who was to inherit the leadership of the order after their existing leader passed away. Another restricted *tarikat* called Menzil seemed to be so generous! It allowed women with headscarves to be educated. But a former leader of this order was poisoned in 1991, survived, and died later from natural causes. In this cult too there seemed to be murders and competition for leadership. Some restricted cults such as İskenderpaşa Cemaatı were successful in investing their money in business ventures.[10]

When I resided in Istanbul for three months in 2007, a religious movement called the Gülen movement was already a globalized one with well-run schools in many countries, complete with sophisticated technological equipment. This movement is against any type of religious terrorism, but it has been very much involved in the internal and external politics of Turkey in the service of changing what is "Turkishness" and contaminating it with religion, while its absolute leader, Fethullah Gülen, a bachelor, has been living in the United States in Pennsylvania since 1998.

Fethullah Gülen is a follower of the teachings of the well-known Sunni Muslim scholar and religious leader Said Nursi, who was born to Kurdish farmers in Anatolia. The followers of Said Nursi are called Nurcu. "*Nur*" means light. They want to bring religious "light' into their lives and be enlightened. They are in favor of modernization and science as long as certain areas are kept under control and restricted according to God's giving or not giving his permission. For years, I have known a very nice and highly educated young man in Ankara with whom I met often when I went there. Many years after I got to know him I began sensing that he was going through a change. One day he was to give me a ride in his car as he had done many times before. This time I noted his hesitation to start his car. Then he quickly, as if hiding it from me, kissed a small book—I believe it was a Koran—three times and then he was able to start his car. When I realized that this very intelligent man believed God would not give his permission for us to begin our car ride before he kissed God's symbol, my heart ached, but I did not tell him how I felt about his becoming a devout Gülen movement follower. I realized that his genuine ambition to do something good for his fellow citizens would always be possible, but now also restricted, according to the nature of his God's permission.

The Gülen movement's mission, its type of *jihad*, is not to use bullets and bombs, and perhaps because of this, the movement has never come to the public eye in the United States. The Gülen movement's weapon, the hijacking of religion for political purposes and possible consequences of its use, have not been regarded as an area of concern by American politicians. The fact is, I do not have any information about how this movement became globalized and how it acquired its incredibly large amounts of money to bring "mild Islam" to Turkey and other places in the world. Were this movement's "mild" religious teachings considered suitable to American officials because they saw it as a counter to "violent" Islam, the way some came up with plans to utilize an "Islamic Green Belt" against the Soviet Union? I cannot answer this, but I am very aware of Gülen's "educational *jihad*," since it was clearly expressed in a sermon he gave in 1999 describing his mission for changing the Turkish nation:

> Now it is a painful spring that we live in. A nation is being born again. A nation of millions [is] being born—one that will live for long centuries, God willing. . . . It is being born with its own culture, its own civilization. If giving birth to one person is so painful, the birth of millions cannot be pain-free. Naturally we will suffer pain. It won't be easy for a nation that has accepted atheism, has accepted materialism, a nation accustomed to running away from itself, to come back riding on its horse. It will not be easy, but it is worth all our suffering and the sacrifices.[11]

Referring to this sermon and Gülen's other sermons, Rachel Sharon-Krespin, then director of the Turkish Media Project at the Middle East Media Research Institute (MEMRI) in Washington, DC, wrote: "What Turkey's Islamists really want is to remove the founding principles of the Turkish Republic. So long as US and Western officials fail to recognize that Gülen's rhetoric of tolerance is only skin-deep, they may be setting the stage for a dialogue, albeit not of religious tolerance, but rather to find an answer to the question, 'Who lost Turkey?'"[12]

There are also scholars who find good things in the globalized Gülen movement and even idealize it.[13] I doubt that the Austrian official with a high position at the European Union whom I met in Vienna in 2006 knew the details of what was happening in Turkey. If she became aware of the concerns I described above, she would be even more adamant about blocking its acceptance to the European Union.

While newspapers in Turkey almost daily were reporting new events happening in the name of God, people in my immediate surroundings in Istanbul during my 2007 three-month stay there seemed to be, in a certain sense, "paralyzed" in their acknowledgment of this large-group identity problem and in expressing their concerns. For example, twice a week a woman psychiatry professor would pick me up from my apartment and we would drive together for about thirty to forty minutes to Cerrahpaşa Medical School, mostly discussing her psychoanalytic cases, therapeutic technical issues, or good restaurants. At the same time we would see women covered in black cloth from head to toe walking behind their husbands in the streets in the very conservative district where this medical school is located, as if walking next to their husbands was not their human right. No reference was ever made in our car upon seeing these women in such a condition, which often would induce rage or intense sadness in me.

The then rector of Bahçeşehir University, Deniz Ülke Arıboğan, a woman, is one of the most sophisticated political scientists and university administrators I have ever met. No female student with a head cover was accepted at Bahçeşehir University. Therefore, neither was the "identity issue" problem facing Turkey "admitted" by the university! I kept wondering about the incredible gap between my psychiatrist and professional friends and the women trailing their husbands in the streets like black ghosts.[14] It was as if two types of people existed in Turkey, and they seemed miles apart. The closest similarity to this situation can be observed in today's Jerusalem, where a palpable gap exists between ultraorthodox Jews and other Israelis in the way they dress and behave.

I felt that even though I was not a Turkish citizen, the Turkishness that had been a part of me from childhood and therefore throughout my life was under attack. There were some well-known persons, both men and women, expressing their bewilderment and anxiety, but in my view their voices were not strong enough. I wanted to join them, especially on the subject of protecting women's rights. When I became a "public figure," so to speak, through the efforts of the Turkish media, I also became a "societal transference figure," meaning many individuals in the society externalized and projected aspects of themselves, their own wishes and dreads, on me and then identified me primarily according to their fantasies. In the press and on television programs, many individuals who had never met me wrote articles or made welcoming remarks about me as a scholar, as a Nobel Peace Prize nominee, and as someone helping to find solutions for Turkey's identity problems. To others I was a menace sent by a foreign force—such as the CIA or Mossad—to tear Turkey apart! Three psychiatrists—the first two are men, each whom I met only very briefly in the past and the other one a woman whom I never met—were pathologically fixated on me and their constant bizarre attacks on me via the Internet and television did not make things comfortable. On some days in the news media I was idealized in one newspaper while being rendered dangerous in another. I learned another lesson. This was about the craziness of evolving as a societal transference figure and the need to remain steady under such a situation. I thought about well-known political leaders all over the world who are forced to live their daily lives as societal transference figures, and I began appreciating their ability to tolerate misperceptions. I began to protect myself by carefully selecting my public appearances and the newspaper reporters I talked to.

I would get to know societal processes and problems in Turkey at a closer range after I agreed to give a talk at an NGO called Economic and Political Research Center (Ekopolitik) during my 2007 stay in Istanbul. The conference room was packed, but only five women, wearing headscarves, were present. These women were physically separated from the men and seated in the last row of chairs in front of a wall by the exit. Although clearly I was standing before a conservative audience, I was determined not to lose my integrity, but to speak openly and directly about my ideas and theories to this audience.

My topic was large-group identity, and I spoke about my observations in Turkey. I reminded the audience that most people in Anatolia are descendants of immigrants who had to escape from the previous Ottoman territories and come to the heartland of the country as the Ottoman Empire was shrinking. I suggested that large-group mourning over the loss of the Ottoman Empire and Ottoman glory might be taking place in Turkey and this process might be providing a psychological base for some societal and political changes and polarizations. Mourning means reviewing lost things, sorting them out, keeping or modifying some, and letting go of others. I suggested that political investment in old traditional values and a search for many aspects of Ottoman images—ranging from images of historical events to arts to old religious traditions—was taking place. There are beneficial as well as regressive aspects of large-group mourning. Reviewing the past and what had been lost and reactivating identification with these things creates a transgenerational continuity that enriches large-group identity. However, holding on to aspects of the past that do not fit realities of the present increases societal regression and creates magical thinking.[15]

While I made clear that I was not against anyone's religious beliefs or the practice of religion, I was against "hijacking" religion and reactivating magical thinking of centuries ago for political and societal propaganda and manipulation. Pointing to the situation of the five women in the room, I stated that at least half of the Turkish population is female and that treating women badly, for example, by creating a situation that forces them to sit in the back of a conference room as if they were second-class citizens, would not be good for the future of any society.

When the meeting was over I thought that I would never be invited again to Ekopolitik. I was absolutely wrong. After my talk, about a dozen individuals from the audience met with me in the office of Tarık Çelenk, the leader and general coordinator of Ekopolitik. I understood that they were people close to Turkish president Abdullah Gül's political circle. They said that they appreciated my sharing my ideas with them, and they wondered if I could be available for further talks with them.

I was hosted by the eleventh Turkish president Abdullah Gül at Çankaya Presidential Palace in Ankara for the first time in late August 2008, almost exactly one year after he had become the president of Turkey.[16] The two of us had a long and leisurely lunch. I found him to be a very kind and intelligent person. As he was scheduled to visit Armenia a couple of weeks after our meeting, this was the first topic we discussed. Turkey and Armenia had no diplomatic ties. This was in large part due to the war between Armenia and Azerbaijan over the disputed territory of Nogorno-Karabakh in the late 1980s and 1990s. Also, Armenia and Turkey were divided over the massacre of Armenians that took place as the Ottoman Empire was coming to an end. Although Turks had a different historical perspective of these events, the Armenians called these deaths genocide. President Gül's visit to Armenia would be the first by any Turkish president. The upcoming FIFA World Cup soccer match between Turkey and Armenia on September 6 had created this opportunity. Gül had accepted the invitation by his counterpart, Armenian president Serge Sargsyan. Since I had been a member of the Turkish-Armenian Reconciliation Commission in the early 2000s,[17] President Gül, I sensed, wanted to know about my psychological understanding of Armenian-Turkish relations.

My meeting with President Gül also took place after a well-known Turkish citizen of Armenian descent, Hrant Dink, had been assassinated in Istanbul on January 19, 2007. Hrant Dink was an outspoken advocate for peace between Turkey and Armenia. He was well-liked by many of his Turkish journalist friends who expressed their bewilderment, rage, and deep sadness over his death in their newspaper columns and on television. At least two hundred thousand Turkish citizens appeared at his funeral, chanting and carrying posters with the messages, "We are all Armenians" and "We are all Hrank Dink."[18]

I encouraged Gül to visit Armenia. After his visit there he would say: "I believe my visit has demolished a psychological barrier in the Caucuses."[19]

President Gül shared with me Turkey's wish to be a regional and global power.

In attempting to accomplish this, Turkey would not be a docile supplicant to the European Union or to powerful allies like the United States, but focus on improving its economy. I learned that one third of Turkey's money was being used to address Turkey's biggest problem—to combat the PKK. When we were talking about the so-called Kurdish problem, I sensed the president's compassion for everyone who had lost relatives and friends in this tragic and chronic situation. I made remarks about how a political leader can be perceived as a parental figure and wondered about the idea of his increasing his involvement in public activities and calming people's responses to tragedies, including in areas of the country where people with Kurdish ethnicity are in the majority. He then told me a couple of stories about his participation in such events. Once he asked his driver to stop the car during an official presidential visit to a predominantly Kurdish city so he could meet and speak with a Kurdish woman waving at him from the rooftop of a building. He found this brief meeting with this woman very moving.

Soon the Justice and Development Party (AKP) launched a project that would be known by different names, such as the "Democratic Initiative Project," the "Unity and Fraternity Project," and the "Kurdish Initiative." This project would seek a solution to Turkey's ethnic, especially Kurdish, problems in a peaceful way. Interior Minister Beşir Atalay, a lawyer who is the current deputy prime minister of Turkey, was in charge of this initiative. He wanted to consult intellectuals from different professions in order to gather their suggestions for this new initiative. He invited me to meet with him alone in his office and we spent three hours talking. I described the Tree Model and how its modified version might be used as part of the Kurdish initiative. He took extensive notes. I would meet with him, alone and with others, a few more times as the years passed, especially to talk about the Kurdish issue.

My attempts to be helpful regarding the Kurdish situation in Turkey became possible in a more direct way when I agreed to be a consultant to Ekopolitik and began to make plans with them to apply a modified version of the Tree Model to this protracted and deadly problem. I would do this under some conditions, which were readily accepted. I would remain as an independent academician and Ekopolitik would function as a civilian think tank. All of our activities would be recorded and available to anyone, and we would do nothing in secrecy.

Before I started to work on the Kurdish issue with members of Ekopolitik, we decided to experience together a political activity that, we thought, would not be as hot as the Kurdish issue promised to be. To this end, Ekopolitik, in collaboration with the Near Eastern University in Nicosia, had its first psychopolitical meeting in Northern Cyprus in early June 2009. This meeting brought together Turks from Cyprus and Turks from Turkey to look into problems in the Turkey–North Cyprus relationship. In the next chapter I will tell the story of my involvement with Eko-politik as a consultant on societal problems in Northern Cyprus.

# 38

# A RETURN TO NORTHERN CYPRUS

## THE PRESENCE OF INVISIBLE WALLS

After my retirement in 2002, I started spending full summers in Northern Cyprus.. During the summers of 2007 and 2008, I interviewed many young people, mostly in their late teens and some in their early twenties, as well as active and retired government officials from different political parties in order to find out how they experienced being a Cypriot Turk. I combined the data collected from these interviews with observations from my daily experiences in Northern Cyprus at family and social gatherings, markets, and places of business to explore the decades-long effects of a special type of traumatic situation: living surrounded by walls—first a concrete one and then an invisible one.

When Cypriot Greeks and Cypriot Turks—in fact Greeks and Turks in general—speak or write about what happened in Cyprus during the last five decades, they select and highlight two different events respectively as the most traumatic and devastating for their communities. Greeks rank the landing of the Turkish army on the island in July 1974 and the dividing of the island by a de facto border into northern Turkish and southern Greek sections as their most devastating societal trauma of the "Cyprus problem." When Turks speak or write about the "Cyprus problem," they go back further to 1963 and recount their horror story as originating when the Cypriot Greeks, who outnumbered Cypriot Turks four to one, forced the Cypriot Turks to live in subhuman conditions in enclaves for eleven years, geographically limiting them to 3 percent of the island. Eight years after the island was divided into two sections, the north declared its independence on November 15, 1983, and took the name Turkish Republic of Northern Cyprus (TRNC). Today around 300,000 persons are citizens of TRNC. This number includes about 160,000 people from Turkey who settled in North Cyprus after 1974. The number of Cypriot Greeks living in the southern part of the island is approaching 800,000.

International organizations imposed severe embargoes on the Turkish side of the island from the beginning of its separation from the Greek side in order to force the Cypriot Turks to go back under the Cypriot Greek–ruled Cyprus Republic. These embargoes have continued to the present day. No direct flights to the Turkish side of the island were permitted from anywhere but Turkey, and mail to and from the north could also only travel through Turkey. Cypriot Turks were not allowed to compete in international sporting events under their own flag. Furthermore, there were no major foreign investments in the Turkish side and trading directly with foreign countries became very difficult or impossible.[1] When it was established, TRNC did not have its own currency and its citizens still used the currency of Turkey. In other words, the northern part of Cyprus was inhabited by people who did not have certain typical international human rights; in a sense, they were second-class human beings.

In April 2003, after both sides agreed to ease border restrictions, hundreds of Cypriot Greeks and Cypriot Turks crossed over through selected checkpoints on the Cypriot Turk–Cypriot Greek border that for decades has been known as the "Green Line." The "Green Line" remains "open" at a few checkpoints today. In May, 2004 the European Union made a political mistake and accepted Cyprus into the European Union as a divided island. Instead of waiting and thus encouraging a comprehensive settlement, EU authorities wrongly assumed that the divided island's joining the EU would result in its reunification. Although the island became a member of the European Union, EU legislation was suspended in areas in which the internationally recognized Cyprus government (composed of Greeks) did not have "effective control,"[2] meaning in the TRNC. In fact, the government of Cyprus, meaning the internationally accepted (except by Turkey) Greek side's government, has no control over the northern side of the island. The Cypriot Turks, even though they live in the TRNC, can obtain EU passports, but only by going to the Greek side to get them. Initially some Cypriot Turks began obtaining EU passports, mostly secretly, as if by receiving such documents they would be perceived as "traitors." Now tens of thousands of Cypriot Turks have EU passports.

When the borders opened, there were moving stories of Turks and Greeks visiting their old homes, which they had been forced to abandon on the wrong side of the island after the island's division. Cypriot Turks' initial excitement over traveling south and Cypriot Greeks' excitement over traveling north after forty years of separation lasted a year or so and then faded away. The main reason for this is the fact that Turks and Greeks had lived separately for such a long time without actually seeing each other. Except for the elderly, people on both sides did not know each other. When I carried out my study in 2007 and 2008, some Cypriot Turks were going south to buy items that were cheaper in Cypriot Greek stores and also to work, and about 250 Cypriot Turkish families were sending their children to secondary schools or for higher education conducted in English on the Greek side. The Cypriot Turkish parents' justification for sending their children to schools on the Cypriot Greek side was their perception that if their children graduated from schools approved by the European Union, establishments of higher education in Europe would be more apt to accept them. I was also informed that ten to twenty much younger Cypriot Turkish children were also attending elementary schools on the Greek side where education was conducted in English. Some parents were aware that their children were, on and off, experiencing humiliations after crossing the border, but despite this they continued to send them to the south, sometimes with observable ambivalence.

Political talks between Cypriot Turks and Cypriot Greeks have continued without resolution for decades. Even though Northern Cyprus has gone through political elections in a most democratic fashion and now has its third president, the reality is that, psychologically speaking, the concrete walls that surrounded the Cypriot Turks when they lived in enclaves have been replaced by "invisible" ones since 1974. Even the opening of borders and the island's EU membership—with its many restrictions in relation to Northern Cyprus—have not change this fact. How does a society feel surrounded by an "invisible wall"?

My 2007 and 2008 study of this question was not a strictly scientific one, meaning I did not receive answers to specific questions and then measure them according to any designated methodology. By simply collecting answers to specific questions, scientific social studies become very restricted, especially since the researcher usually examines only a limited view of a large-group's horizon. Throughout this book, I presented societal observations and tried to explain them with theories. Repeated human large-group rituals in times of peace or conflict, unlike rituals of animals in the wilderness, have become sophisticated and complicated due to the development of the human brain, due to societal processes explained by intellectualizations and symbols, and due to aspects of such processes whose meanings are derived from a shared unconscious. After observations are carried out carefully and described, then scientific measurements can be applied to provide proof for limited aspects of the existence and directions of large-group movements.

Here I will not deal with the continuing conflict between Cypriot Greeks and Cypriot Turks, which for decades now only takes place at a political level without involving violence. Instead, I will try to illustrate that the Cypriot Turks' experience of living in concrete enclaves, and since 1974 in a symbolic one, continue to influence their present-day large-group identity issues. I will also try to illustrate that other external events have created more confusion about these identity issues, and this confusion has led to societal problems.

Twenty years ago I became keenly aware of the ongoing existence of the Cypriot Turks' symbolic enclave. I was in Charlottesville when I got a call from a Cypriot Turk who identified himself as a friend of a friend of mine in Cyprus. This man was on a world tour with his wife and daughter and said that our mutual friend had urged him to visit me while the family was in the United States. They had rested in Japan for a few days before coming to Florida. He was calling me from Florida, asking if he and his family could see me and my family on their way to New York, where they would catch a plane to Turkey and then to Northern Cyprus. I said that I would be happy to welcome them to our home. Two days later a very fancy car carrying the Cypriot Turkish man, much younger than I, and his family pulled up to my front door. In our living room this obviously rich man began to tell me about their fantastic travels in Japan and Florida. I was curious about their passports since I wanted to know how they could take a world tour using passports unrecognized by all countries except Turkey. He assured me that they had Cypriot Turkish passports, and indeed had traveled to faraway places. I do not know the details of how they managed to do this, but what I wish to focus on here is the emotions this man exhibited in my presence when the issue of passports came up. With great anger and sadness he described how horrible it was for them not to have identities easily accepted by others. I remember thinking that he had no right to be so upset when he had traveled around the globe in a rather luxurious fashion. They did not stay long, and later I slowly came to the realization that while showing their "unrecognized" passports at various borders, he might have had some actual difficulties and felt humiliated. Even though my encounter with this man was brief, it remained empathetically in my mind and evolved as a vivid representation of Cypriot Turks who are still living behind an invisible border. This was one of the reasons for my study that started during the summer of 2007.

That year, on the surface, the Cypriot Turks in their day-to-day lives were not preoccupied with the idea that they were still living in a symbolic enclave. Most of the time, their experiences of second-class world citizenship were denied or repressed because they seemingly had felt safe since 1974, and they, like people everywhere, had turned their attention to earning money, competing for work and prestige with others in their communities, taking care of their families, educating their children, and so on. Excitement over having been "saved" by Turkey in 1974 also was no longer a topic for discussion. Somehow, this "illegal' state had found "legal" ways to be a part, at least on the surface, of the world, and its citizens, like the rich man and his family who were able to take a world tour, could participate in many global activities.

It was difficult for citizens to picture themselves and their TRNC identity as unrecognized by the world community, especially since six universities had been established in Northern Cyprus and students from at least forty different countries were attending them and providing income to the north's economy. Tourists, too, came from many countries, went sightseeing, and visited historical castles, beautiful beaches, entertainment centers, and gambling casinos. In fact, Northern Cyprus had become a gambling center for the Middle East. Just prior to and during my study, a building boom occurred that was damaging the north's natural beauty by removing beautiful trees from the hillsides or near the beaches. Many of these houses remain unsold and unoccupied even today. All these factors, on the surface, helped to erase the shared sense of being treated as second-class citizens. Yet, seemingly endless political discussions of the "Cyprus problem" by local leaders and international bodies, reported in the news media and on television talk shows daily, continued to remind the Cypriot Turks that they were, after all, not yet recognized as equal to other human beings. The word "isolation" was the new term used by the diplomatic world to describe the Cypriot Turks' invisible enclave.

My 2007 and 2008 study in TRNC inspired an idea that I named "enclave mentality." I learned about it from my interviews with older individuals and from my daily activities. The younger generation, born to parents with this mentality, was not aware of its being an unusual societal state and therefore never thought about how it started.

While experiencing life within the *actual* enclaves, people felt close to one another; they were "brothers and sisters" facing the same unbearable fate. In their regressions, their individual psychic boundaries had become permeable to allow a kind of psychological merging, and they shared an externalizing of their fragile selves onto thousands of caged parakeets, which they took care of (see chapter 16). But their togetherness had certain peculiarities. In a society that lives in enclaves surrounded by enemies, in a broken-down, garbage-filled environment in constant fear, no one can improve his or her status without incurring others' envy and contempt. Such an act would be contrary to the obligatory psychological "merging" of the members of a victimized community living in a restricted area. To have a "shining star" in such an enclave would disturb the shared large-group identity associated with humiliation, helpless rage, magical thinking, and necessary masochistic adjustment.

An enclave mentality continues to be present even after the traumatic environment no longer exists—as happened in the rather small TRNC society. The Cypriot Turkish community still cannot tolerate a jewel in the midst of mud. The community directly or indirectly, and often without being aware of the process, attempts to sink the shining person (or organization) into the shared humiliated and shamed mess in order not to disturb the continuing enclave mentality.[3] It takes time, new historical events, or a reparative leader to change a society's shared identity and erase the older one that had been crystallized.

During the 1974 war some Cypriot Turks found valuable items (called *ganimet* in Turkish), such as large amount of money, jewelry, or other valuables, left by Cypriot Greeks escaping to the south. People wondered who had *ganimet* and, in a sense, who became jewels in the mud. Later, Cypriot Turks who had escaped from the south and thus lost their homes and properties and mainland Turks who were associated with the Turkish forces involved in the 1974 events and who were granted permission to come from Turkey as "settlers," were given properties, houses, and fields left behind by Cypriot Greeks who had fled to the south.[4] The impact of *ganimet* and property distributions infiltrated the enclave mentality, modified it, and infused it primarily with two emotions that became common in the community.

The first one was "selfishness," which was associated with an emotional withdrawal from others, as if doing so would protect the "secret" of finding *ganimet* and owning things that neighbors or relatives did not have. This "selfishness" would manifest itself in behavior patterns illustrating indifference toward people nearby, such as putting one's garbage into the neighbor's yard and throwing empty soft drink bottles and other trash from a car while driving. For decades, the government and municipalities tried to "clean up" roads and public beaches without much success, while individual owners of tourist sites had no difficulty keeping their own properties in proper fashion. I believe that this "bad habit" is also connected with keeping the "memory" of living in concrete enclaves filled with garbage. The more there is mud, the better jewels can be hidden.

The second emotion that became common within the community was envy. People who remained "poor" became envious of people who became "rich." Stories were circulated such as the one about a man who benefited greatly after the 1974 war, while his brothers remained poor. The poor brothers stopped talking with their previously loved and now rich brother. Feelings of selfishness and envy created emotional splits within the Cypriot Turks and also between native Cypriot Turks and tens of thousands of settlers who had come from Turkey and were now mostly residing in villages emptied by Cypriot Greeks who had escaped south when the island was divided.

Another external factor piggybacked on this modified enclave mentality and increased identity confusion: relentless efforts by European and American authorities and NGOs to create a new "ethnic" group, or at least a new "nation" on the island consisting of both Turks and Greeks, in an effort to find a peaceful solution for the "Cyprus problem." Soon after 1974, I was invited to participate in a couple of meetings at the Department of State, since officials involved with the Cyprus Desk wanted to meet a Turk from Cyprus and learn about Cypriot Turks. At that time I was absolutely inexperienced in international relations and large-group psychology. I remember one American diplomat's outburst at one meeting demanding that

Cypriot Greeks and Cypriot Turks get together and create a new nation. He said: "What is wrong with people who cannot get together and be a nation the way we have in America?"

For many decades the official and unofficial policy of the United States and of European countries concentrated on the creation of a "Cypriot" ("Kıbrıslı," in Turkish) identity, minimizing the existing ethnic identities of being a Turk or a Greek. Historically speaking there has never been a "Cypriot" ethnicity or nationality.[5] Nevertheless, uniting the total population under the term "Cypriotism" received much attention and energy. It is generally agreed that the term "Cypriotism" broadly refers to "the idea that Cyprus has its own *sui generis* character and thus must be viewed as an entity independent from both the motherlands of the two main communities—Greece and Turkey. This contrasts sharply with the view that dominates nationalist ideology (Greek or Turkish Cypriot) and views Cyprus as an extension of motherlands."[6] "Cypriotism" was raised by those under the illusion that quickly building a nation was possible and who considered the concept "an evolutionary process of mutual accommodation in 'societal' and 'political' culture."[7]

Since 1974 many nongovernmental American and European organizations became active on the island supporting this "Cypriotism" policy, sometimes openly and sometimes in hidden ways. There was a perception that if the divided populations on the island were linked by a common large-group identity, there would be a kind of integration of the opposing sides and even an assimilation of the Cypriot Turks by Cypriot Greeks. According to this perception, the Cyprus Republic would be able to house everyone in Cyprus in a peaceful fashion. The Cypriot Turkish population, hungry for any hope of removing the invisible wall surrounding it, has been unconsciously influenced by this chronic international wish and propaganda. The Turkish government in Turkey, at least on the surface, went along with this process since Turkey wanted to appear as a "good" country—that is, it did not want to oppose the Europeans and Americans, in the hope that Turkey's membership in the European Union would be accepted.

When I interviewed the young Cypriot Turks in 2007 and 2008, some of them seemed to perceive "Cypriotism" as their primary ethnic identity. Their personal stories reflected their unconscious refusal to identify with degraded parental figures and images of the older generation living in enclaves. Some other young persons, whose grandparents played a significant role in raising them and who repeatedly told them heroic tales of the Cypriot Turks during the struggle, were holding on to an opposite feeling of large-group identity: they were nationalistic. I heard how the grandparents defensively instilled in the latter group an exaggerated "Turkishness," which reflected a denial of humiliation, shame, and victimization. One could clearly observe split identity formation in these young Cypriot Turks.

The Cypriot Greeks were eager to go along with the political "Cypriotism" propaganda since being "Cypriot" would be equal to being "Greek." Otherwise, they would not be at all ready to put their Greek identity behind a "Cypriot" identity.[8] Being a "Cypriot" would mean that they, the Cypriot Greeks, would be in power, rule the total island, and put the Cypriot Turks once more in another invisible enclave, one called "minority status." In reality, however, to attempt a common identity for Cypriot Greeks and Cypriot Turks was to chase an unreachable goal. After all, both Greeks and Turks have their own long-idealized histories, and to create one new "nation" by fusing them is as unrealistic as it would be to create a new nation that merged Arabs and Israelis.

In April 2004, the United Nations presented a plan to the island's total population to settle the "Cyprus problem." The plan, which was put to a vote on both sides of the island, was called the "Annan Plan," since it was named after then UN secretary-general Kofi Annan. Earlier, in 1999, Álvaro de Soto, a Peruvian diplomat, had become Kofi Annan's special adviser on Cyprus, with the rank of under-secretary-general of the United Nations. A few years before he made his trip to Cyprus to talk with authorities on both sides in order to begin preparing the Annan Plan, I had met Álvaro de Soto in Peru at an international psychoanalytic meeting where both of us appeared on the same panel discussing psychological aspects of international relationships. After the panel discussion the two of us had some time together to discuss the Cyprus situation. He told me about his family background and I was impressed with his knowledge and interest in the psychological aspects of large groups. Later we communicated by e-mail.

When he visited Cyprus to start working on finding a UN solution for the "Cyprus problem," I happened to be in our Northern Cyprus home. He called me and came to our house alone with his driver. After our meeting he had an appointment to meet then Northern Cyprus president Rauf Denktaş. He did not want the president to know that he was visiting me first. I reassured him that I would not tell the president of his stopping at our house.[9] Álvaro and I met for about two hours. He wanted to know my opinion about the solution for the "Cyprus problem." I explained to him that offering a solution based on the concept of "Cypriotism" would be most unrealistic. Instead, I suggested the "Swiss-cheese-border" approach that I had been presenting at various academic meetings. Briefly, Cypriot Greeks and Cypriot Turks would look primarily after their own internal affairs while maintaining a physical border between them. This border would also function as a psychological one and thus support both sides' large-group identities. However, this border should have "holes," like holes in a block of Swiss cheese: people belonging to political, societal, artistic, and other similar organizations would be able and expected to pass through such "holes" and share their useful expertise and activities as Cypriots, and do their best together for the whole island. Then everyone would go back under his or her side's ethnic umbrella. This way there would be no space for humiliation. Such an approach would remove the Turkish side's "isolation" by creating a common Cypriot state with two opposing sides existing peacefully under certain legal conditions. I knew that at that time there was no possibility politically to imagine and spend time on a "two-state" option. I did not meet with Álvaro de Soto again or communicate any further with him about his assignment.

In the end, the Annan Plan offered a loose Cypriot bizonal bicommunal federal structure divided along ethnic lines. Even though there were areas in it not to my liking, it was something like the "Swiss-cheese" model. The plan was approved by 65 percent of the Cypriot Turks and rejected by 75 percent of the Cypriot Greeks.[10] Therefore, the TRNC, and also the invisible wall surrounding it, continued to exist. But the failure of the Annan Plan led to retraumatization of the Cypriot Turks, since the hope of removing the invisible enclave had failed.

The foreign powers' and the NGOs' direct and indirect efforts to create a common Cypriot identity continued after the failure of the Annan Plan. On March 30, 2007, a news item appeared in the Turkish daily newspaper *Milliyet.* It reported that the Cypriot Turkish government had received $69,000 from the European Union to fund its suggestion for further development of a peaceful existence between Cypriot Turks and Cypriot Greeks by modifying the social science books used in Northern Cyprus elementary schools. Accordingly, TRNC's new social science book for sixth graders no longer mentioned the chronic massive Turkish Cypriot trauma or even the Turkish military's coming to the island in 1974. It contained one picture of Kemal Atatürk, the founder of modern Turkey, while the first president of TRNC, Rauf Denktaş, was not even mentioned. Denktaş, who died in January 2012, undoubtedly was the main political figure whose name was associated with the struggle of the Cypriot Turks during their time in the enclaves and during many years following 1974. In my mind, to erase his name along with the many significant aspects of what happened to the Cypriot Turks during the long history of the "Cyprus problem" equaled erasing history. According to a high-level Cypriot Turkish official with whom I spoke, the modification of the school books had taken place in the belief that "erasing" aspects of the recent Cypriot Turkish history from their pages was in the service of not provoking enmity in Cypriot Turkish children against the Cypriot Greeks. I should also mention that Cypriot Greeks, according to this news story and according my own investigation, refused to modify their school books.[11]

I have illustrated in some of the previous chapters that study of the transgenerational transmission of massive social trauma informs us that if the impact of such trauma is denied or repressed, it will still manifest itself in various ways in new generations. The "therapeutic" way of dealing with previous generations' massive social traumas is not to deny or repress what happened to the ancestors, but to be aware of the history and the nature of the devastating events faced by the previous generations and to observe their influence on the new generations. When the historical continuity is available for new generations, they have a better chance of strengthening their large-group identity and a better chance of having a rapprochement with the offspring of their ancestors' enemies.

There is one more major external factor that further disrupted the large-group identity investments of Cypriot Turks. In the last chapter I described the process of changing "Turkishness" in Turkey. What was happening in Turkey began a similar process on the island. At one point a Turkish minister who was in charge of Turkey's Cyprus issues told me that what Cypriot Turks needed most was to have twenty more mosques built in Northern Cyprus. His sentiment was in fact put into practice on the island. For some years now, a civilian *müftü,* the person who has the authority to look after the religious affairs of Muslim communities, from Turkey and his assistants, also from Turkey, have been trying to bring "religion" to TRNC and change the native Cypriot Turks' "Turkishness." The *müftü*'s assistants, who are assigned to special districts in Northern Cyprus, have tasks such as distributing free copies of the Koran to citizens. In Northern Cyprus too the tape-recorded calls for prayer are as loud as possible. "Bringing religion" to Cypriot Turks, psychologically speaking, has further separated native Cypriot Turks from the Turks who settled on the island soon after 1974. This was due to the realistic and fantasized perception that the settlers were more religious than the native Cypriot Turks. The settlers, who are TRNC citizens, cannot go to the Greek side and obtain EU passports. This fact also induces a division within the TRNC population.

My 2007 and 2008 interviews showed that those dozens and dozens of persons I interviewed, young and old, could not present one primary large-group identity of TRNC citizens. For example, they presented various descriptions about who they thought they were: a Turk; a secular Turk as Kemal Atatürk and his followers perceived the term; a Turk who loves Turkey and experiences himself or herself as an extension of Turks everywhere; a Turk who does not love Turkey and perceives him- or herself as a different Turk than those in Turkey; a religious Turk; a Cypriot; a Cypriot who is like a Greek Cypriot; a Cypriot but different than a Greek Cypriot; a European; or a person with no large-group identity who is very lonely.

In 2007 and 2008 large-group identity confusion among the Cypriot Turks began to exhibit itself in some universities in Northern Cyprus, creating serious concerns among the university authorities. For example, it was observed that Cypriot Turkish university students had started to segregate themselves from their fellow university students from mainland Turkey. If a young man or woman from a Cypriot Turkish group started dating someone from among the students from Turkey, or vice versa, the couple would become socially isolated. Cypriot Turkish university students referred to students from Turkey as "extremely religious" or "extremely nationalistic" individuals and attempted to differentiate their large-group identity from that of Turks from mainland Turkey. This situation, according to some university authorities whom I interviewed, could conceivably lead to violence.

Thus, I welcomed my collaboration with Ekopolitik on June 4 and 5, 2009, when we brought influential Cypriot Turks and people from Turkey to look at existing problems—the continuing and modified "enclave mentality," identity confusion, societal problems within TRNC, problems between native Cypriot Turks and Turkish authorities in Turkey—and most importantly, to come up with "prescriptions," as opposed to Hal Saunders' term "ideas in the air," for solutions. Since I was conducting the dialogues, I specifically preferred the word "prescriptions" in order to induce a sense that there was no need to feel hopeless about societal problems, since they were symptoms of an "illness" caused by certain "germs," and that this "illness" could be cured with proper medication. I especially hoped that "treatment" would include influencing some authorities in Turkey to refrain from making statements that would be perceived as humiliating by the native Cypriot Turks and to stop native Cypriot Turks from feeling humiliated and unloved. Turkey had saved them, but the "motherland" no longer was being perceived as a good parent. On the other hand, Turkey, as a good parent, was demanding that her child grow up more and take greater responsibility for life, even though the child was handicapped by trauma and living in an "invisible enclave." I assumed that when the reasons for identity confusion became better known and discussed openly in public, a better and more respectful relationship between Cypriot Turks and Turkish authorities in Turkey could be established, and the sense of splitting and fragmentation within the society would become more tolerable. This was not a meeting to look into the "Cyprus problem" that referred to the Cypriot Greek–Cypriot Turkish conflict. I told the participants that we would not talk about Greeks at all.

Sixteen persons participated in the dialogue, including a representative from the TRNC president's office, former and present parliamentarians, including the former TRNC minister of foreign affairs, a former head of the TRNC high court, the leader of religious affairs, scholars, and newspaper reporters.[12] Another seventeen persons, including persons connected with both the government of Turkey and government of Northern Cyprus, news reporters, legal authorities, and heads of some civil organizations were present as observers.

It was generally agreed that this June 2009 meeting was a most unusual and important gathering. It opened a way to discuss all the issues influencing the identity problems that have been described in this chapter, not only during the dialogues but also later in public, in media, within civic organizations, and at societal and academic meetings. The content of the meeting and suggested ideas ranged from advising the persons in the Turkish government dealing with Cyprus issues to use language that would not be humiliating to native Cypriot Turks, to finding solutions to environmental problems after the psychology of "dirtying" neighbors' yards or roads were understood by the public.

The second Ekopolitik meeting in Northern Cyprus to continue the study of TRNC's internal societal issues and its relationship with Turkey took place June 28 and 29, 2011. Most participants from the first meeting were present. This time we had more well-known persons from Turkey, and five Turkish daily newspapers were represented. Second-generation TRNC citizens and descendants of those who settled in the north from Turkey soon after 1974 participated as well. All issues discussed in this chapter and during the first Ekopolitik meeting in Cyprus were carefully reviewed and once more brought to the public eye. They were openly discussed in Northern Cyprus and Turkish newspapers and were again brought to governmental authorities' attention.[13]

Decades of long negotiations between Cypriot Turks and Cypriot Greeks are going nowhere. I think, however, that in the long run a confederation with a "Swiss-cheese border" or a two-state solution will take place. More recently, the possibility of making Northern Cyprus a part of Turkey—legally and politically speaking—has been aired by some Turkish politicians. In fact, there would be no Turkish Republic of Northern Cyprus without Turkey, and Turkish troops have been stationed on the island since 1974. While our two meetings were very helpful for talking openly about aspects of large-group identity issues that had been kept in the shadows in earlier times, the "Turkishness" identity issue in mainland Turkey, until it settles down, will continue to be played out in Northern Cyprus. Forcing things on the Cypriot Turks and humiliating them, such as at the time I carried out my study in 2007 and 2008, has slowed down. I believe that bringing what was happening internally in Northern Cyprus to public awareness there and in Turkey and illuminating how people were confused and how they sometimes felt misunderstood, has played a key role in taming exaggerated emotions associated with identity confusion.

# 39

# TURKEY'S GRAND DOME

## THE "KURDISH ISSUE" IN TURKEY

About 80 million people live in today's Turkey and 99.8 percent of them are Sunni Muslims. It is estimated that 16–18 percent of Turkey's population is of ethnic Kurdish origin. There are others, an estimated 10 percent, who have different ethnic backgrounds, such as Armenian, Arab, Chechen, Georgian, Laz, and Roma. The Kurds also comprise about 17 percent of the population in Iraq, perhaps 7 or 8 percent both in Iran and Syria, and 1.3 percent in Armenia. They also live in other locations such as Azerbaijan, Lebanon, and Georgia and it is estimated that there are 30 million Kurds living in an area that includes adjacent parts of Turkey, Iran, Iraq, and Armenia. The Kurds have their own Indo-European language with various dialects and old tribal sentiments. The majority of them are Sunni Muslims.

When modern Turkey was born in 1923, everyone was given equal rights and everyone living in Turkey legally was called a "Turk." There are also many Turks living in places such as Bulgaria, Bosnia, Cyprus, Macedonia, Greece, Yemen, and Lebanon, which were old Ottoman territories. Earlier, I discussed modern-day Turks who went as guest workers to places in Europe such as Germany and Austria, just as many Kurds had done, and their descendants who live there today.

My last chapter was about the Turks on Cyprus, of which I am one. After finishing high school in Cyprus in 1950, I went to Turkey for my six-year medical education at Ankara University. During my second year there I joined an amateur orchestra as a violinist. I recall I was one of its youngest members. In addition to the long hours medical school required, I spent a lot of time with the other members of the orchestra, practicing for our concerts and sometimes visiting Ankara University's conservatory.

During my initial years in Turkey, until I adjusted my accent, my friends at the medical school or in the orchestra could easily recognize that I was a Cypriot Turk, especially when I mixed "b" and "p" sounds when speaking Turkish. My friends guessed right away that I was from "Kıbrıs" (Cyprus), since when I was asked where I came from I would say "Kıprıs."

Hearing people's accents, sometimes I could also guess if they were from the eastern Black Sea region, Istanbul, or other locations. In fact, everyone I met in my routine life spoke Turkish with a different accent. For example, three of my professors at the medical school spoke Turkish with a German accent; they were German Jews who had escaped to Turkey during the Nazi period.[1] We had no special interest in asking people why they had this or that accent or if their accents were connected with their ethnic backgrounds. During those years I never traveled to the southeastern part of Turkey, and I remained ignorant of the fact that the majority of people in that part of Turkey are of Kurdish origin and that many Kurdish children spoke their own language until they went to elementary schools and learned Turkish.

After I specialized in psychiatry in the United States and became an American citizen, I went back to Ankara during the 1974–1975 academic year as a visiting professor of psychiatry. During this time I was researching the life of Mustafa Kemal Atatürk, the founder of modern Turkey, as part of a psychobiography I was writing about him with Norman Itzkowitz.[2] The Kurds living in Anatolia fought with the Turks for the Turkish War of Independence under Mustafa Kemal's leadership. When I was doing my research, there was a general feeling that two peoples living together for centuries as Ottomans formed one people. For example, Mustafa Kemal on May 1, 1920, made the following statement at the Grand National Assembly in Ankara, about three years prior to the declaration of the new Turkey as a republic on October 29, 1923:

> There are Turks and Kurds. We do not separate them. But while we are busy defending and protecting, of course, the nation is not one element. There are various bonded Muslim elements. Every Muslim element which makes this entity are citizens. They respect each other; they have every kind of right, racial, social, and geographical. We repeated this over and over. We admit this honestly. However, our interests are together. The unity we are trying to create is not only Turkish or Circassian. It is a mixture of one Muslim element.[3]

In 1925, while Mustafa Kemal was still the first president of Turkey, a Kurdish tribal group in Anatolia, under a Kurdish clergyman, Sheikh Said, rebelled, and this rebellion was brutally suppressed. In our book on Atatürk, Norman and I did not characterize this rebellion as a Kurdish ethnic issue. This rebellion was made in the name of religion. A decade after our book was published, David McDowall studied the modern history of the Kurds. He informs us that when the new Turkish Republic abolished the caliphate in March 1924 and closed the *madrassas*, these events were like a body blow to the Kurds in Turkey. David McDowall wrote: "By stripping Turkey of its religious institutions, Mustafa Kemal [Atatürk] now made enemies of the very Kurds who had helped Turkey survive the years of trial, 1919–22."[4] The Kurds genuinely believed in the defense of the caliphate.

When I was a visiting professor in Turkey during the 1974–1975 academic year, I did not see any evidence that the Kurds in Turkey were "enemies" of the Turks of Turkey. That year another psychiatry professor happened to be my neighbor and almost every morning he drove me to Ankara University Medical School from our neighborhood. I would often share with him my findings about Atatürk's life and the interviews I had done with individuals who had known this leader during his lifetime. My professor friend was always very interested in what I told him, and in turn he shared his own recollections of what he had learned about Atatürk's life from various sources. As a small child he had actually seen Atatürk in front of the original Turkish Parliament building in Ankara. He told me more than once, his face beaming, how lucky he was because he had actually set eyes on the Great Man. Only years later I learned that my professor friend was Kurdish. In another instance, during my visiting professorship I discovered the works of Yaşar Kemal, to my mind one of the greatest Turkish novelists, whom I would meet years later and who would become a candidate for the Nobel Prize in Literature. Initially I did not know that he is of Kurdish origin.

Times are very, very different now. Earlier in this volume I made reference to Norman Itzkowitz' phrase, "the ethnic period of history." This historical development hit Turkey very hard. Now everyone in Turkey, willingly or not, is aware of other people's ethnicity, whether they have a meaningful relationship with them or meet them briefly in their daily lives. Earlier in this book I reported that 40,000 Turkish citizens, Kurds and Turks, have lost their lives since the mid-1980s because of PKK terrorist activities and the Turkish governments' military response to them.[5] PKK originally was a leftist organization—a political-ideological one based on a Marxist-Leninist model, and then it became an ethnic Kurdish one. Opposite the Sheikh Said rebellion, the PPK "rebellion" started with no links to religion. As time passed, however, the Sheikh Said rebellion would emerge as a kind of chosen trauma of the Kurds in Turkey.[6] Also, many tragic events in which Kurds were humiliated or actually hurt came to public awareness. After Atatürk's death there were events that can be considered efforts of forced "assimilation," and they left many Kurds feeling humiliated. In spite of this, *malignant* racism among Turks against Kurds in Turkey has not developed.[7] The biggest concentration of Kurds in Turkey is in Istanbul with, I understand, two million Turkish citizens of Kurdish origin living there. While some Kurdish-issue incidents have taken placed in this huge city, no tragedy that is linked to malign racism has taken place.

After having our first meeting in Northern Cyprus, Ekopolitik decided to have a meeting in Istanbul and bring together influential Turks and Kurds of Turkey to have an unofficial dialogue among themselves. I, as a consultant to Ekopolitik, would conduct this meeting and use my previous experiences with representatives of opposing groups during psychopolitical dialogues to help the Turkish and Kurdish participants learn empathically different perceptions about this major problem in their country. In earlier times I and my CSMHI team members were literally a "third party" bringing together representatives from opposing or enemy large groups. I searched within myself and concluded that if I got involved in conducting psychopolitical dialogues between Kurdish and Turkish citizens of Turkey, I would not have prejudices against the Kurds of Turkey, even though my background is Turkish. Once I was sure of this, I felt ready for this project.

Following two preparatory meetings in January, which I attended, and one in October 2009, which I did not attend, the first gathering of the Ekopolitik project named "Turkey's Grand Dome" took place on November 16 and 17, 2009. It was named after my analogy describing a large group living under the canvas of a big tent. After this first meeting, Ekopolitik became involved in a series of Grand Dome gatherings or related activities until late 2011. It considered Turkey's Grand Dome project to be a major response to the call from the AKP's "Democratic Initiative Project" or the "Kurdish Initiative," which I described in chapter 37. In fact, after the initial Turkish-Kurdish dialogues in Istanbul, the then minister of interior, Beşir Atalay, joined the members of Ekopolitik, dialogue participants, observers of the dialogue, and other guests—over one hundred persons—and listened carefully to the dialogue participants' reports and took part in a general discussion of various issues. I would meet him again at various times. Before or after Ekopolitik meetings at which I was present, the president of Turkey, Abdullah Gül, would receive Tarık Çelenk, leader and general coordinator of Ekopolitik and me and we would brief him on our progress. However, Ekopolitik officials were proud that their own civilian work on the Kurdish issue began before the government came up with a similar and highly publicized initiative.

When I became a consultant to Ekopolitik, Tarık Çelenk agreed that we would not do anything in secret during the Grand Dome project, that we would not work for the AKP, and that our findings would be open to any political party. Recalling my lecture at the Ekopolitik meeting when the five women were relegated to the back row, I also insisted that women actively take part in this project. It was clear that I could not be present at all Ekopolitik's meetings or activities under Turkey's Grand Dome project, and we needed to develop a core group of Turks and Kurds. When the members of this core group learned about and felt comfortable with each other, they would evolve as a "task group" overseeing the project's various activities along with the Ekopolitik staff and, when I could not be with them, keeping contact with me in the United States. We agreed to use ideas from the Tree Model and try to make Ekopolitik an influential nongovernmental institution whose mission was to find peaceful ways to deal with the "Kurdish problem."

One key issue that would make starting this project difficult was the existence of the other identity issues in Turkey which I described in chapter 37: the societal and political problems of modifying "Turkishness" and aligning it with religion. There was more than one type of Turk and one type of Kurd who needed to come together. Since I do not live in Turkey and actually, with a few exceptions, did not know who the influential Turks and Kurds were who would be important for this project, it was up to General Coordinator Tarık Çelenk and Director Murat Sofuoğlu from Ekopolitik to find them.[8] When we had our first meeting and for the first time met the people who were selected and who had agreed to participate in Turkey's Grand Dome project on a voluntary basis, I was very impressed by their efforts. They included "nationalist" Turks and Kurds as well as "religious" Turks and Kurds, men and women with political and societal influence.[9]

Participants made an inner circle and the observers sat outside this circle. Tarık introduced me to them. He mentioned my being a candidate for the Nobel Peace Prize, I imagine, to elevate me to a level of authority. But, in this day and age, since researching someone on the Internet is so easy and since I had become a "societal transference figure," I thought that everyone in the room already had an opinion of me. I told them that I was not an expert on the Kurdish issues and that I was there not to give any advice to them, but simply to help them talk about and understand the societal/political problems at a deeper, human level. I stated that Ekopolitik was starting a process, and that we were not getting together to come up with quick solutions at the end of a single meeting. I wanted them to just begin talking. Only then would we find "entry points" to specific topics and focus on them. Right away I apologized in advance for the occasions when I might cut short a speaker if she or he began giving a "lecture." I also told the observers not to join the participants' dialogues. I would invite them to give us their opinions at the end of each discussion period. After the meeting was over, on the evening of the second day, we would meet with the minister of interior and other distinguished guests.

Every word that was uttered during the November 16–17, 2009 meeting has been published by Ekopolitik (in Turkish) and is available for review. I believe this publication is a significant historical document illustrating how influential citizens of Turkey with various backgrounds can talk very openly and respectfully about the ethnic problems in Turkey and create a "public voice" after decades of terroristic, militaristic, and political ways of dealing with these problems. This document is a marker illustrating that a civil investment in this chronic tragedy has its own significant place.[10]

Often unexpected personal stories tell more than counting and describing historical events about the emotional state of a community or large group. During the first Great Dome meeting, a story told by Gültan Kışanak, a Kurdish politician in her early fifties, helped me understand what it was like for her, and many other Kurds, to be a citizen of Turkey.

> I was born and raised in the Bakırkoy district of Istanbul. The year was 1996 and I was still living in Bakırkoy, taking my little daughter to kindergarten on each school day. I had to hurry, because after I left her at kindergarten I had to rush to my work. One day another parent saw me. He said to me: "Gültan Hanım, if you are in a hurry I can take your little girl to kindergarten today." I had seen him at parent meetings at the school. He was a gentleman. I let him take my little girl to kindergarten. This was no problem. But when I returned home that evening my little daughter asked: "Mother, why did you leave me this morning?" I answered: "My baby, what happened?" My little girl described how while she was walking with this gentleman [he happened to be a Turk] he had asked her: "What is your name?" My little girl then told me that she had not wanted to answer the man's question. When he insisted on learning her name she ended up telling him: "Evin." My daughter was afraid that the Turkish gentleman would know that we are Kurdish when he heard her name. When I realized that this small child was afraid to be recognized as Kurdish because it might put her in danger, I understood that we are obliged to find a solution to this problem.

The Turks at the meeting suggested that when the Kurds repeat, "We are Kurdish! We are Kurdish!" they find themselves saying "We are Turkish! We are Turkish!" I helped all to realize that 40,000 or so deaths and related loses would put millions in mourning. Having so many individuals in mourning would perpetuate helplessness, guilt, and rage at a societal level and change citizens' daily relationships by constantly erasing easygoing and comfortable traditions. Due to their personal experiences, the participants could easily see this. They clearly stated that all citizens were tired of this ethnic problem, terror, and death and wanted to live in peace. Even a former member of PKK declared that he could not envision the possibility of having a separate Kurdish state and that the focus should be on finding societal political solutions that would respect all citizens and their human rights.

I wished that some of my CSMHI team members could join me in the Grand Dome process, but since everyone would be speaking Turkish during the gatherings, this was impractical. After the first Grand Dome meeting, Ekopolitik's core group of volunteers, representing both Turkish and Kurdish backgrounds, was established. It functioned as my CSMHI team had functioned when we worked in

Estonia. There would be two major differences, however: I would not be with them most of the time when they met and, unlike many members of CSMHI, no member of the Ekopolitik core group was trained in psychodynamic approaches to small- or large-group meetings.

The core group, after having two more gatherings among themselves in Istanbul, made its first trip to Hakkari in southeastern Turkey in January 2010. Hakkari is a city where most of the population is Kurdish, close to the Kandil Mountains on the Iran-Iraq border where the PPK hides. The city itself had been greatly influenced by the PKK, and police and military forces had been stationed there as well. Many Kurdish youngsters from Hakkari ended up joining the PKK and never returned home because they were captured and put in jail or because they were killed by Turkish military bombings of the Kandil Mountains. It was a very important step for the core group, with its "nationalist" Turkish members, to visit Hakkari, meet political and civilian leaders, and interact with youth groups who were not members of the PKK. This visit took place without incident.

I went to Turkey in February 2010 and, after visiting President Abdullah Gül with Tarık Çelenk in Ankara to tell him about the Grand Dome project, I met for the second time with the core group. During this meeting an interaction among three members of the core group who happened to be seated together was most moving. One member was Seydi Fırat, a Kurdish man who was born in Turkey in 1962. In 1980 he had left Turkey and spent time in Germany, Holland, and France. Then he returned to the Middle East and lived at PKK training camps in the Bekaa Valley in Syria and in the Kandil Mountains. He was involved in PKK political activities. In 1999 the PKK decided that Seydi and seven other members would surrender to Turkish authorities. Seydi did so and spent five years in jail. After his sentence he became an active spokesperson on behalf of Kurdish issues in Turkey. The second member was Mete Yarar. He was born in 1967 and was a graduate of a military school. Before his retirement from his position as a military officer in the Turkish Special Forces, he had spent over ten years in southeastern Turkey dealing with the PKK. The third member was Cevat Öneş, born in 1942. After finishing law school he joined the Turkish Intelligence Service (MIT), the Turkish version of the American CIA. He retired in 2005 from his position as assistant director of MIT. The two younger men were talking to Cevat, and both were calling the older man "*abi*" (big brother), a social custom.

Suddenly all core group members realized that not many years earlier Cevat Öneş was among the high-level MIT persons who had planned ways to kill Seydi Fırat, and that Mete Yarar was involved in carrying out the task, which obviously never took place. Now the three men were sitting next to one another in a friendly and respectful way, agreeing that the killing needed to stop and a military solution alone is an illusion. Their impressive "togetherness" was, I believe, one of the main factors that encouraged the core group to start finding consensus on "ideas in the air" or "prescriptions" for peaceful solutions to the "Kurdish problem." During a break at the beginning of this process, Seydi asked to speak with me separately. I sensed that he was in contact with Abdullah Öcalan, PKK's founder and leader, and they wanted to be sure of my intention to remain "neutral" in conducting the dialogues.

The PKK is listed as a terrorist organization not only by Turkey, but also by the United States and the European Union. After waging terrorism, or what the PKK called a "guerrilla war," against the Turkish government for fifteen years, Öcalan was captured in Nairobi, Kenya, and extradited to Turkey to face trial. Even today, how he was captured and the role of the CIA in this event remains obscure. He was sentenced to death in June 1999 and, after Turkey abolished the death penalty in October 2002, his sentence was changed to life imprisonment. Since 1999 he has been the only prisoner in a maximum security prison on the small island İmralı, located in the southern part of the Sea of Marmara. As I stated earlier in this book, I wrote a psychobiographical profile of Öcalan,[11] and I had the impression that Seydi Fırat was aware of this.

Before I became involved in Turkey's Grand Dome project, during a television appearance in Turkey, I was asked if it would be proper and useful for the Turkish government to begin direct negotiations with Öcalan to find a solution for the Kurdish problem. My answer was "no." Now Seydi wanted to know why I had given this answer. I told him that my answer would still be the same. If the public, the Turks, were exposed to Öcalan as a negotiator, there would be a huge backlash, and this itself would worsen the "Kurdish issue." I told him that any Kurdish person, like himself, who was seriously involved politically in dealing with the "Kurdish problem," should be able to consult with Öcalan if he or she wished to do so. I do not know if Seydi found a way to convey my view to İmralı that day. Nevertheless, he genuinely continued to work on finding "prescriptions" that would be supported by all participants.

First, there were "psychic realities" that had to be replaced by actual realities. For example, the "nationalist" Turks in the core group believed that during certain Kurdish political meetings the Kurds did not exhibit the Turkish national flag. They were very surprised to learn that this was not the case. It turned out, coming up with "prescriptions" would be a rather easy task once the Turkish participants were convinced that the Kurdish participants were not seeking to break up Turkey and establish their own state. All agreed that geographically separating Turkey's Turks and Kurds was not a realistic idea. Even though the majority of Kurds were located in southeastern Turkey, they were living throughout the country, two million of them in Istanbul alone. They maintained their own lives, businesses, and societal and political positions. The Kurdish participants told us that all they wanted was to remove the humiliation Kurds were experiencing. One main issue was to legally secure their human rights, especially freedoms concerning the use of the Kurdish language and to remove signs humiliating to them. In addition to opening schools where classes would be taught in Kurdish, they wanted to restore the original Kurdish names to certain towns and cities where the Kurdish population was in the majority.

A key discussion took place on how to bring people from PKK camps in the Kandil Mountains back into civil society. In October 2009, one month before Ekopolitik's first Grand Dome meeting, with the approval of Öcalan, thirty-four Kurds had left their camps in two mountainous areas and entered Turkey at a checkpoint on the Iraqi border. They were called the "Peace Group" and were accompanied by Seydi Fırat and two other Kurds who had surrendered to Turkish authorities ten years earlier. Thirty-four PKK members were given their freedom without any trial. In a public statement Beşir Atalay referred to this move as a part of the government's "Kurdish Initiative" and stated that similar events would follow. Now it was clear that the return of thirty-four PPK members did not make the positive impact that had been expected and, in fact, the Turkish public in general responded negatively to this event when they saw PKK members entering Turkey in their guerrilla "uniforms." The uniforms reminded the public of terror, death, and grief. Seydi had explained to us how the returning PKK Kurds had not had time to change into civilian garments.

At our February 2010 meeting, Seydi Fırat and core member and honorary chairman of the European Turkish Islamic Confederation, Musa Serdar Çelebi, discussed this event. They wondered why psychological advice was not sought to prepare the public for the return of the PKK members. Musa then suggested that if the returning PKK members had come to Turkey from the mountains carrying Turkish flags, the public response, especially those of nationalists, would have been very different. He asked Seydi if it would be acceptable for the Kurds to carry Turkish flags in the future when entering Turkey after they left their camps on the mountains. The answer was "yes." Then the Kurds and Turks in the room agreed on "prescriptions." The core group would discuss them further after I left Istanbul and bring them to the authorities' attention.

Ekopolitik became known in the country through news about its activities, frequent television appearances of some of the core members, and my own television interviews whenever I was in Turkey. Soon students from different universities in Istanbul, both religious and nationalistic, men and women—including women who wore a head covering—volunteered to become involved in Ekopolitik. These young persons' enthusiasm for doing something for their country was most impressive.

Ekopolitik was not able to accommodate all applicants wishing to join the organization, but they started with a dozen or so who were associated with the Ekopolitik activities and their numbers slowly grew.

In May 2010 I met with these students, gave seminars, and introduced them to psychopolitical concepts. I would repeat such teaching in the future. Also, I introduced Ayla Yazıcı, a psychiatrist and psychoanalyst practicing in Istanbul, to Ekopolitik. When I was not present, the organization benefitted from Ayla's psychological insights. I have known her for years. She became a member of the core group and also spent time passing along psychological knowledge concerning societal issues to the Ekopolitik staff and the young university students associated with this organization. She accompanied some Ekopolitik core members to Hakkari in early July 2010 and wrote a detailed report on her psychological findings.

In her report Ayla Yazıcı described Hakkari as a kind of huge "prison," as it had a single main road entering the city and there were military on all sides.[12] Many Kurds in the surrounding villages had come to Hakkari to find safety; others were forced by the military to do so in order to prevent the PKK from entering Turkey and hiding in villages. Such migrations had caused huge economic and societal problems. Ayla interviewed around ten Kurdish families and movingly described mothers' unending grief over losing their sons who had escaped to the mountains to join the PKK. Some of these families' sons were in the mountains as PKK "guerilla fighters," while other's were serving in the Turkish military.

Kurdish children and adolescents in Hakkari were negatively portrayed in the news media as bad children "who throw stones at police vehicles." Ayla was able to interview some of these children as well. She described in plain Turkish how these children identified with aggressors and how throwing stones at police vehicles was the only "game" they were able to play in such miserable surroundings. Ayla's report was distributed as widely as possible with a hope that its insights would "humanize" public perception of these kids. Twice, in 2009 and 2010, I attended Turkish Police Academy meetings in Antalya, Turkey, and spent time with police cadets, helping them understand the Kurdish children's psychological dilemma and urging the cadets to tame the local police response when they, as graduates of the police academy, were assigned to conflicted areas. Beşir Atalay was also present the second time I attended the Police Academy meeting, and once more he and I talked privately for a long time about the "Kurdish issue."

I did not meet with the Ekopolitik core group again until late July 2010. During the intervening time, no additional PKK members from the mountains came back to Turkey. Between my last meeting with the core members in February 2010 and the one in July, Ekopolitik had made three more trips to Hakkari and also branched out to Mersin on the Mediterranean coast. Mersin, a port city, is one of the richest areas of the country. Kurdish families escaping from the southeastern part of Turkey had settled in thirteen districts in Mersin, causing societal problems. Some members of the Ekopolitik core group went to Mersin, met with local leaders, attempted to "diagnose" the problems, and talked about having a major Ekopolitik gathering there in the near future.

Representatives from Hakkari and Mersin joined us when I met with the Ekopolitik core group in late July that year in Istanbul. The previous "prescriptions" were reviewed, this time with input from Hakkari and Mersin attendees. After the meeting Tarık and I flew to Ankara and briefed the Turkish president once more on our progress. I sensed that he wanted to be sure that all core participants of the Grand Dome project had indeed accepted all suggestions for a peaceful response and possible solution to the Kurdish issue that had come up during the Ekopolitik meetings. The president was aware of who these participants were. Tarık and I offered to have a meeting in his presence and he accepted.

On August 26, 2010, accompanied by sixteen core members and representatives from Hakkari and Mersin, I went to the president's summer residence in Istanbul, a house with a spectacular view of the Bosporus. I sat next to him and asked all present to speak freely. We were scheduled to meet with President Gül for only one hour and a half, but our meeting lasted three hours. Ayla Yazıcı presented some details of her findings in Hakkari. At one time I saw the president's eyes water when a young Kurdish man was describing the situation in Hakkari. This moved me tremendously. I really hoped that the government would take some action after this meeting. I left Turkey and waited for positive news, but I heard of no major initiatives.

I knew from reading the news that the Turkish political atmosphere was extremely complicated. There were various factors and power politics influencing the government, including Kurdish political organizations and opposition parties. All of them were influencing what the government could do or wanted to do about the "Kurdish issue." While all the AKP political figures I talked to were telling me how they were determined to bring "real" democracy to Turkey, they also seemed to be working on creating their version of "Turkishness" while trying to evolve Turkish power and prestige in the Middle East. The economy was improving; towns and even villages in many areas of Turkey were modernizing. At the same time, especially since 2003, many high-level military officials who allegedly were planning a Turkish secularist military coup, along with many others, such as newspersons who allegedly were supporting such a coup, were arrested and awaited trial.

One time I went to see a psychiatrist to consult with her only on clinical matters. She was not at all involved in politics. When I entered her office she asked me to leave my telephone outside with her secretary. When I asked her why, she told me that "they" were listening to private conversations through telephones, even when they were not turned on. Witnessing such fear saddened me. Yet, I was determined to continue doing what I could, however small, to help resolve the "Kurdish issue."

In early December 2010, with some core members of Ekopolitik, I went to Mersin, a city that now includes thirteen poor areas filled with Kurdish refugees and "stone throwing" Kurdish kids. We met with the governor, the mayor, political leaders from the AKP, a member of the major opposition political party, the Republican People's Party (CHP), and representatives from business and civil organizations for a Grand Dome meeting. We made public speeches and appeared on television while collecting in-depth information about the effect of the "Kurdish issue" on this city. I came to the conclusion that Ekopolitik could start projects in Mersin, such as improving police responses to "stone-throwing children." It seemed to me that starting such processes there would be much easier than starting a similar project in Hakkari. I spoke with Tarık and Murat and urged them, as I had in the past, to slowly go step by step in applying the Tree Model. I suggested strongly that two "branches" of the "tree"—Mersin and Hakkari—needed to grow properly before Ekopolitik spent time on other branches. I knew that they had already started meetings in other cities and that they were planning to visit even more areas, bouncing from one to another. I sensed that they were not listening to me. I also sensed that they needed to raise funds for their activities and therefore wanted to remain in the public eye in any way they could.

Soon after visiting Mersin, when I attended a core group meeting in Istanbul in December 2010, I was surprised that over one hundred observers from many cities were present in the huge conference room and everyone was demanding to speak. I knew that under such conditions it would be impossible to examine issues in-depth and conduct a proper and useful psychopolitical dialogue. I had to hide my extreme disappointment and, as politely as possible, did my best to let dozens and dozens of people express their opinions. I realized that to be a consultant to even a well-meaning civil organization would not be the same as having one's own trained team in control of a systematic application of one's own methodology.

After this Istanbul meeting Tarık and I quickly flew to Ankara, rushed to the presidential palace and met with President Gül. Someone in the Ekopolitik office apparently had typed seventy-six "prescriptions" that had been presented at this huge and chaotic meeting without any opportunity for discussion, and this list, without my going over it and without my "permission," was presented to the president. This embarrassed me. When news of the "76 prescriptions," including some wild ones, was widely publicized in the media as "Dr. Volkan's list" of what to do regarding the Kurdish issue, the Grand Dome project received a heavy blow, and Ekopolitik would spend considerable time correcting the misperceptions that grew from it. Once more I advise those political psychologists who will be involved in projects like the one I am describing to be aware of the negative influence of impulsive actions and of media. I had further serious talks with Tarık and, once more, I urged Ekopolitik to go slowly step by step and focus more on the trunk of the tree instead of multiplying branches that were not properly trimmed.

After I returned to the United States, I received news of Ekopolitik activities in more and more locations in Turkey, and even of Ekopolitik people going to Iraq for a meeting on the relationship between Kurds and Turks in Mosul. I felt marginalized in their way of following the Tree Model methodology, even completely lost. There was also important and positive news, such as Ekopolitik's fifth Hakkari meeting in January 2011, once more including a "nationalist" core member along with a close aid of Öcalan and a respected newspaper person. This was furthering the work on this particular branch. Ekopolitik officials were also meeting with the governor and other important individuals to increase "civilian" and humane ways of dealing with conflicts at a location with significant PKK influence.

My last meeting with some Ekopolitik members and many guests, including former lawyers of Öcalan, took place in mid-July 2011 after I gave a seminar to university students connected with Ekopolitik. General political elections had taken place in Turkey just a month earlier. AKP had won the elections once more with a great majority. In light of this, it would have been a proper time to examine the "Kurdish issue" closely and seek ways to take advantage of branches going upward, toward authorities. Once more I witnessed that the organization preferred having a crowded room over a noncrowded one where an in-depth review of important issues and finding "entry points" for making actual changes could take place. I also sensed restlessness among the Ekopolitik staff. After I returned to the United States, I heard first from the students and then from Tarık that the leadership and others associated with Ekopolitik had split and that Murat had left Ekopolitik to start his own open civil society organization. I was too sad to try to find out the reasons for this internal fight and separation and the end of Ekopolitik as I had known it. In spite of this unfortunate outcome I knew that the work they had carried out during the previous couple of years had been extremely important for Turkey. It brought a public voice to the surface, one with which previously unspoken ideas could be discussed respectfully. It showed that citizens were tired of seemingly unending terror and military actions and that there was a realistic political way to find peaceful and satisfactory solutions that were acceptable to the general public.

In September of 2011 I visited Beşir Atalay. After the last elections he had left his position as the minister of interior and had become the deputy prime minister of Turkey, overseeing various areas of government activity, still including the "Kurdish problem."

I had the impression that the minister thought of the PKK as losing power and that with additional pressure it would be more willing to follow a political path. Soon after, however, a deadly earthquake, this time a natural disaster, hit southeastern Turkey, changing the dynamics of the "Kurdish issue." Also, the Turkish government's intense involvement and interest in the outcome of the "Arab Spring" increased tensions between Turkey and Israel. These factors and the later horrifying events in Syria put the "Kurdish issue"—at least the possibility for another psychopolitical effort to deal with it—on the back burner.

Ekopolitik still exists, now without many of the previous core group and most of the university students, and I gather with less financial support. People on both sides of the organizational split continue to write polite notes to me. In early winter 2012 I received an invitation from the Ekopolitik group asking me if I would be willing to conduct a psychopolitical dialogue between ethnic Turks and ethnic Kurds from Turkey living in Germany. They had names of possible participants—over fifty of them from various social and political organizations in Germany. I declined to accept this invitation. There would be no way I could start over as a consultant to Ekopolitik using a step-by-step application of the Tree Model.

# PART IX

## EXTENDING THE FINDINGS

# 40

# THE INTERNATIONAL DIALOGUE INITIATIVE

Throughout my more than three decades of involvement in international relations, my activities took place both inside and outside meeting rooms where enemy representatives gathered. I found myself in locations where I needed to protect myself from possible radiation danger, schoolyards where I joined children in their play to observe their responses to a massive trauma, and refugee camps where people lived on top of one another. During all these times I tried to maintain an inquiring mind. I wanted to understand repeated patterns of behavior that occur when enemy representatives negotiate for peaceful coexistence. At the same time, I explored a large range of other topics that accompany large-group relationships, such as sadistic or masochistic methods to hold on to and maintain large-group identity; reactivation of shared "memories" of ancestors' traumas; and personal psychological issues of some leaders that become intertwined, directly or indirectly, with political processes. What I learned from my field studies and my theoretical understanding of these things has been reported in this book with ample examples. There is no reason to list and repeat them in this last chapter.

I became the Senior Erik Erikson Scholar at the Erikson Institute of the Austen Riggs Center in Stockbridge, Massachusetts,[1] after I retired in 2002 from both my medical school position at the University of Virginia and as director of the Center for the Study of Mind and Human Interaction. Since 2003 I have been spending some months each year in Stockbridge. In January 2006, while in my office at Austen Riggs, I received an unexpected call. It was from Frank Ochberg, a psychiatrist who had been the associate director of the National Institute of Mental Health (NIMH). Well known for his work with individuals who have experienced traumatic events, he defined the term "post-traumatic stress disorder" (PTSD). He was also involved with the Dart Foundation (Direct Action and Research Training) and was the head of the Dart Center for Journalism and Trauma. He informed me that the Dart Foundation had funds to donate to an activity for world peace before the year's end, and, even though he knew that CSMHI had been closed, the foundation was sending the money to the Austen Riggs Center to help me to start a new project.

I thought about the possibility of bringing individuals from the United States, Europe, and Russia together with persons from Israel, Iran, the Arab World, and Turkey to participate, on a voluntary basis, in a discussion on current world conflicts. If this were to happen, it would establish a group of individuals who would learn to look at international issues from different cultural, national, and religious points of view.

I got in touch with Lord John Alderdice, a psychiatrist who had joined Northern Ireland's Alliance Party in 1978 and was its elected leader from 1987 to 1998. The Alliance Party was founded in 1970, and in the 1990s it became the leading political organization attempting to end sectarian violence and find peaceful solutions in Northern Ireland. After his involvement in numerous political activities that promoted peace, John was elevated to the House of Lords at Westminster in 1996. In June 2010 he was elected Convenor (Chairman) of the Liberal Democrats in the House of Lords.

Lord Alderdice agreed to cochair these meetings if I was able to get the project started. We planned a small multinational group, independent of any government or political organization, even though we would choose some members who were active politicians in or outside their governments—after all, Lord Alderdice himself is one such person. It would be up to individual participants to apply the knowledge they had gained toward peaceful processes. Such a project also would be beneficial for the clinical psychoanalytic world, so while we envisioned having an interdisciplinary group, we also wanted to include experts in human psychodynamics who would help us scrutinize world affairs from a psychopolitical angle. Learning about the psychology of large groups and external events would teach us how events in the external world influence individuals' internal worlds.

This unusual project, which we named the "International Dialogue Initiative" (IDI), would never have gotten started without Frank Ochberg's initial funding, but it also would have gone nowhere without generous support from Bahçeşehir University in Istanbul and the Turkish Psychopolitical Association in Ankara. Deniz Ülke Arıboğan, then the rector of Bahçeşehir University and Abdülkadir Çevik, then the director of a private psychopolitical association in Ankara,[2] saw to it that the IDI had its first three meetings in Turkey. At the present time the IDI meetings are sponsored by private donors through the efforts of one of IDI's members, Ford Rowan. Ford does not raise funds for the IDI from U.S. government–linked organizations or individuals. The intent is to not disturb the IDI's aim to remain neutral.

Through my old CSMHI contacts and John Alderdice's associations with individuals in many parts of the world, we gathered participants from Turkey, Iran, Jordan, United Arab Emirates, Israel, India, Russia, Austria, United Kingdom, and United States for our initial meetings. Robi Friedman, a clinical psychologist in Haifa, Israel, who at present is the president of the International Group Analytic Society, also became a cochairperson.

Getting together twice a year, the IDI altogether has had nine meetings; three of them took place in Ankara and two of them in Istanbul. Turkey has been our preferred location since every member can travel there without difficulty. One meeting took place in Belfast and was hosted by the Centre for Psychotherapy, South and East Belfast Health and Social Care Trust. Another meeting took place at the Austen Riggs Center in Stockbridge. Our last two gatherings were in Jerusalem in January 2012 and in London in December 2012. During the London meeting I was very moved by an event: my 80th birthday was celebrated during a formal lunch at the House of Lords hosted by Lord Alderdice. At the time of this writing, our next meeting is scheduled to be held in Ankara in fall 2013.[3]

Meetings of the IDI last for two and a half days and focus on current issues, including, in various meetings, governance structures and religious archetypes in Iran, the position of women and child development in the Arab world, the Mavi Marmara flotilla incident,[4] tensions within the United States around Islam after 9/11, shifts in Middle Eastern power dynamics after the "Arab Spring," events in Syria, and "entry points" for improving Israel-Palestine relationships.

The work of the meetings begins with members presenting informally but with firsthand information about the two or three central foci of a given meeting. This is followed by a lengthy discussion, which deepens the understanding of the issues, explores the key stories surrounding a given incident from a psychodynamic point of view, and takes note of our own group processes. In this way, participants in the discussions sometimes become or are seen—often unwittingly—as representatives of their own countries. This is by design; each member is thus compelled to become an informal spokesperson for his or her large group, but at the same time maintaining individuality, thus allowing for group sentiments to be described more authentically. The ensuing dialogue may then provide insights into the imagined, emotionally textured relationships between those countries at this moment in time. This level of understanding adds potential layers of meaning to the conceptual discussion and narrative understandings emerging so far.

IDI hopes to bring attention to the importance of psychodynamic and psychopolitical findings in international and political processes. Recently the IDI was able to establish a Web site,[5] whice includes summaries of our last meetings. It also provides information about individual members' own involvement in various political initiatives in their own countries and in the international arena. Because of this, I will not detail the contents of the IDI meetings in this book.

Drawing on my and my colleagues' work at the Center for the Study of Mind and Human Interaction and the International Dialogue Initiative, I wish to make one last suggestion on what may expand the horizon and effectiveness of international conflict prevention, management, and related large-group activities. One unexpected discovery, "resistance" to acknowledging and exploring the reasons why human beings do "bad things," may interfere seriously with the results of nongovernmental peace-building or peace-maintaining activities. "Bad things" refer to several things: increased narcissistic investment into one's own large group while holding on to malignant prejudice against the Other; regression or severe splits in a society; a large group becoming stuck in a complicated mourning; and a large group performing malignant purification and hurting, torturing, and killing the Other in the name of large-group identity.

I first became aware of the tendency to not look into "bad things" during my long work with opposing groups, but also noticed such resistances among facilitators, academicians, and the general public. During the last decades, I gave countless academic and public lectures at many places around the world on my putting enemies on a metaphorical psychoanalytic couch. At such gatherings, inevitably someone directly or indirectly "accused" me of talking only about the negative aspects of human nature. They would remind me of the positive aspects of belonging to a large group and sharing its identity. If I illustrated why and how people kill in the name of religion, for example, despite the knowledge that such things have happened throughout human history, these individuals would tell me that my work was one-sided, and therefore not useful in understanding international relations. It was as if the "good" aspects of religion should prohibit us from speaking about the "bad" aspects of religion.

When I was undergoing my own psychoanalysis in the mid-1960s, one day on the couch I kept talking about good things that were happening to me and how lucky I was for finding myself in such comfortable circumstances. I recall my analyst sitting behind me bending over and whispering: "Good things have their own way of taking care of themselves." He was trying to bring an important point to my awareness: by focusing on positive things, I was staying away from examining my mental conflicts and sensing my anxiety linked to them. His words have stayed with me. Later, when people accused me of being one-sided in my study and explanation of international relations, I recalled this day on my analyst's couch and told my accusers "good things have their own way of taking care of themselves." Often after such an exchange, people would realize that I—along with my then colleagues at the Center for the Study of Mind and Human Interaction and my current colleagues with the International Dialogue Initiative—was also trying to do something "good." My analyst's words were with me while writing this book as well; I needed to examine the reasons and meanings of "bad things."

Incredible technological advances, modern globalization, worldwide economic links, opportunities for fast travel, migrations, and, above all, advances in communication tools have ushered in a new type of human civilization. During the more than three decades that I have been involved in international work, there have been drastic changes in international affairs and related issues too. Anxiety about the nuclear arms race has been replaced by the everyday reality of security checkpoints. Terrorism—the unseen enemy—has created societal regression most likely all over the world, and amazing technological inventions have made it easier to spy on enemies and friends and eliminate hostile or unwanted "targets," meaning human beings. But, human nature—for the purpose of this book, especially human nature in large groups when relating to the Other—has remained the same. No "pill" has been found or will be found to calm down excited large groups, tens of thousands or millions of persons having similar sentiments, fears, anxieties, and prejudices. Gods have not changed and never learned how to negotiate, and often large groups will evoke their gods when they kill Others.

Already in the United States and elsewhere schools and institutions have been established to teach political psychology to younger generations of students. I had opportunities to visit and lecture at many such places. Some of them pay more attention to large-group psychology than others do. There is a need for the systematic teaching of large-group psychology in its own right in universities and psychoanalytic institutions, and it is important to expose young persons who will be future nongovernmental workers in peace activities to the psychodynamic concepts that they will invariably depend on in doing serious work.

In the long run it is the diplomats, the governments, and organizations such as the United Nations that make final agreements and take legal actions. But, in this globalized world, nongovernmental organizations and political psychology are here to stay. As psychoanalyst Edward Shapiro, an IDI member, and Wesley Carr, an Anglican priest and a former Dean of Westminster in London, write, the attempt to understand large groups is a daunting prospect, and it may be "a defense against the experience of despair about the world, a grandiose effort to manage the unmanageable."[6] I join them, however, in their suggestion that to make efforts, nonetheless, is essential for large groups' psychological well-being. Elected or nonelected leaders and rulers of governments and other small or large groups will continue to spend money to manufacture or buy more bullets and bombs, or whatever new fascinating and incredible technological devices replace them. It is an illusion that "bad things" in large-group behavior will ever end. However, I am optimistic that in some specific and limited international conflicts, the more we explore and understand the psychology of the "bad things" relating to the conflicts, the more hopeful we can be about resolving them without violence.

Many books have been written on political psychology, conflict resolution, mediation in dialogue processes, and massively traumatized societies. In this book I aimed to marry the four topics and study the role that psychology plays in international processes by drawing on a broad array of conflicts and cases and by pointing to lessons with concrete examples. Further, because of my mental health training and practice and my decades of fieldwork, many of my observations made in this book about well-known historical events and deep-seated conflicts will not be found elsewhere and may be novel to many. However, what I have offered in this book is by no means a complete investigation of the psychology of international relationships. More work and time will be needed for other colleagues to continue with this investigation.

# NOTES

**Chapter 1**

1. Demetrius Julius is a former Director of Psychiatry at the Hunter Holmes McGuire Veterans Hospital in Richmond, Virginia.

2. Psychoanalysts have been interested in applying theories to large-group activities, wars, and leader-followers interactions since Sigmund Freud (1921a, 1932). Edward Glower (1947), Ernest Jones (1964), Franco Fornari (1966), Robert Waelder (1971), Alexander Mitscherlich, and Margarete Mitscherlich (Mitscherlich A. 1971; Mitscherlich and Mitscherlich 1975) all tried to open doors to psychopolitical investigations. Psychiatrists and psychologists also wrote about these topics. Therefore, "political psychology" existed in the literature decades before Anwar Sadat gave his speech at the Knesset. His speech, however, initiated a process spanning many years. This process should be considered the first *application* of political psychology in the real world that was carried out as an experimental unofficial diplomacy run by psychiatrists.

3. Sabshin 2008.

4. Volkan 1979.

5. Davidson and Montville 1981–1982. Louise Diamond and retired Ambassador John McDonald (Diamond and McDonald 1996) expanded the application of "track-two diplomacy" and came up with a new term, "multi-track diplomacy." This method does not utilize the application of psychoanalytic or psychodynamic understanding to international relations.

**Chapter 2**

1. Pinsker 2007.

2. Freud 1932.

3. Arlow 1973.

4. See Chapter 1, footnote 2.

5. Freud 1921a.

6. Anzieu 1984; Chasseguet-Smirgel 1984; and Kernberg 1980.

7. Another factor that prevented psychoanalysis from playing a significant role

in contributing to international relations again goes back to Freud. In his early efforts to develop psychoanalytic theories, Freud introduced the important role of fantasy. While acknowledging that real sexual abuse was traumatic, he focused on the stimuli that come from the child's own fantasies for the formation of psychoathology. Influenced by Freud's interest in the child's internal world, early psychoanalysis paid less attention to the role of actual seduction coming from the external world and generalized it to include de-emphasis on the role of other types of traumatic external events, including politics and international events.

8. Klein 1961.

9. Blum 1985. As Peter Loewenberg (1991) and Leo Rangell (2003) remind us, some aspects of a large-group history induce anxiety.

10. Grubrich-Simitis 1979; Eckstaedt 1989; Jokl 1997; Streeck-Fischer 1999; Volkan, Ast and Greer 2002.

11. There are too many such studies to list here (see Kogan 1995; Kestenberg and Brenner 1996 and Volkan, Ast, and Greer 2002 for reviews of studies like these).

12. Raphael Moses (1982) examined the Arab-Israeli conflict from a psychoanalytic point of view. Michael Šebek (1992, 1994) studied societal responses to living under communism in Europe. Peter Loewenberg (1995) went back to the history of the Weimar Republic and emphasized its humiliation and economic collapse as major factors in creating shared personality characteristics among the German youth and their embrace of Nazi ideology. Sudhir Kakar (1996) described the effects of Hindu-Muslim religious conflict in Hyderabad, India. Maurice Apprey (1993, 1998) focused on the influence of transgenerational transmission of trauma on African Americans and their culture. Nancy Hollander (1997) explored events in South America and later in the United States after September 11, 2001 (Hollander 2010). Mitch Elliott, Kenneth Bishop, and Paul Stokes (2004) and John Alderdice (2007, 2010) examined the situation in Northern Ireland. Samuel Erlich (2010) tried to understand the terrorist mind. For my writings on international conflicts in various locations, please see: Volkan 1988, 1997, 2004, 2006a; 2010a; Volkan and Kayatekin 2006; Volkan and Itzkowitz 1994.

13. Varvin and Volkan 2003.

14. Since Freud, many authors who are not themselves practicing psychoanalysts have referred to psychoanalysis in their attempt to understand world affairs and large-group psychology in general. They have often referred to Freud's writings, such as *Totem and Taboo*; *Group Psychology and the Analysis of the Ego*; *The Future of an Illusion*; *Civilization and Its Discontents*; and his correspondence with Albert Einstein (Freud 1913, 1921a, 1921b, 1930, 1932). However, as Ivan Hendrick (1958) noticed long ago, "psychoanalysis is misused by intellectuals, who argue its validity as if it were a philosophy, an ethical system, a set of theories; such discus-

sion . . . seems alien and unproductive to the analyst himself, whose primary convictions originate in what his patients have told him" (p. 4).

**Chapter 3**

1. Rothstein 1972, p. 147.

2. I wrote about this story in more detail in my book, *The Need to Have Enemies and Allies: From Clinical Practice to International Relationships* (Volkan 1988). See also Dayan 1981; Carter 1982; Quandt 1986.

**Chapter 4**

1. In 1900 Sigmund Freud wrote: "The unconscious is the true psychical reality; in its innermost nature it is as much unknown to us as the reality of the external world, and it is as incompletely presented by the data of consciousness as is the external world by the communications of our sense organs" (p. 613). Ronald Britton, who was interested in this topic, suggested that "*belief is to psychic reality what perception is to material reality.* Belief gives the force of reality to that which is psychic, just as perception does to that which is physical. Like perception, *belief* is an active process and like perception it is influenced by desire, fear, and expectations; and just as perceptions can be denied, so beliefs can be disavowed" (Britton 1995, p. 19).

2. Julius 1991, p. 199.

3. Julius 1991, p. 199.

4. Later Ramadan became a journalistic force to calm Egyptians when negative feelings about Israel were inflamed in Egypt.

**Chapter 5**

1. Bion 1961.

**Chapter 6**

1. Another member of the APA Committee on Psychiatry and Foreign Affairs, John E. Mack, with Rita Rogers, wrote a biography of her (Mack and Rogers 1989).

2. Sadat 1978.

3. It would take ten years for Egypt to be readmitted to the Arab League.

4. The Muslim Brotherhood was founded in Egypt in 1928 as a political group that aims to bring Islam into everyday life.

5. After being found guilty, Khalid Islambouli was sentenced to death. He was executed in April 1982.

6. Shamir and Schenker 1986, p. 177.

7. Julius 1991, p. 200.

**Chapter 7**

1. The Palestinian Liberation Organization (PLO) was founded during the first Arab summit meeting in Cairo in January 1964. Since 1969 Yasser Arafat had been the Chairman of the PLO's Executive Committee. He remained as the chairman until his death in 2004.

2. Volkan 1976.

3. Volkan 1988, 2006a.

4. Seljuk Turks conquered Palestine for ten years starting in 1070. The Ottoman Turks ruled Palestine for four hundred years from 1517 to 1917.

5. The Commission of Inquiry into the Events at the Refugee Camps in Beirut, known as the Kahan Commission (named after its chairman, the president of the Israeli Supreme Court, Yitzhak Kahan), was established soon after the Sabra and Shatila massacres. After four months, on February 8, 1983, the Kahan Report found Israel indirectly responsible for the massacres: "The decision on the entry of the Phalangists into the refugee camps was taken without consideration of the danger—which the makers and executors of the decision were obligated to foresee as probable—that the Phalangists would commit massacres and pogroms against the inhabitants of the camps, and without examination of the means for preventing this danger. . . . when the reports began to arrive about the actions of the Phalangists in the camps, no proper heed was taken of them, the correct conclusions were not drawn, and no energetic and immediate efforts were made to restrain the Phalangists and put a stop to their actions" (Kahan, Barak and Efrat 1983).

**Chapter 8**

1. At the present time Harold Saunders is director of international affairs at the Kettering Foundation. He is the author of *The Other Walls: The Arab Israeli Peace Process in a Global Perspective* (Saunders 1991a) and *A Public Peace Process: Sustained Dialogue to Transform Racial and Ethnic Conflicts* (Saunders 2001). Also see Saunders 1990.

2. Julius 1991, p. 201.

3. This story has been told in one of my previous books (see Volkan 1997).

4. Julius 1991, p. 201.

5. In 2003 Aziz Shehadeh's son Raja Shehadeh wrote a moving book about his father's murder and about living under occupation.

**Chapter 9**

1. Freud 1926b, p. 274.

2. Abraham and E. L. Freud 1965, p. 186.

3. Abraham and E. L. Freud 1965, p. 186.

4. Jones 1915, pp. 68–69.

5. Jones 1915, pp. 68–69.

6. Erikson 1956, p. 57. In everyday life, adult individuals can typically refer to numerous aspects of their identity related to social or professional status; one may simultaneously perceive oneself as a mother or father, a physician or carpenter, or someone who enjoys specific sports or recreational activities. These facets superficially seem to fit Erikson's definition but do not truly reflect a person's internal sense of sustained sameness. If a person's social or career identity is threatened, the individual may or may not experience anxiety. Anxiety is more likely to occur if the threat is connected, mostly unconsciously, to danger signals originally described by Freud (1926a): losing a loved one (a mothering person) or that person's love, a body part (castration), or self-esteem. In some cases, the anxiety is severe enough for the individual to seek treatment, but it is otherwise unlikely that changing jobs or membership in a sports club, for example, would cause severe psychological problems that change the structure of a person's internal world. On the other hand, let us consider an adult who acutely decompensates and goes into psychosis. Such an individual's unique identity is fragmenting and he or she may have an inner sense of terror and experience a sensation like a star exploding into a million pieces (Pao 1979; Glass 1989; Volkan 1995). The experience of this person helps to define the "core" identity—one that individuals are terrified of losing—and differentiates it from other social or profession-related identities. Not to have a core identity to hold on to is intolerable unless the individual utilizes primitive defenses to deal with it, such as extensive internalization-externalization relatedness, dissociation, and denial, as well as clinging to split or fragmented self-images. At times, when one cannot protect oneself and faces the loss of one's core identity, it feels like a psychological death. When Erikson referred to the aspect of identity that involves a persistent sense of inner sameness, he, I believe, was specifying core identity.

7. Akhtar 1992, 1999.

8. Salman Akhtar's description of this characteristic implies that the link occurs at the oedipal level when a child's superego is crystallized. To support this view, Akhtar refers to Chasseguet-Smirgel's (1984) remark that successful resolution of the Oedipus complex adds to the child's entrance into the father's universe. I contend that the foundation of the core large-group identity is created during the preoedipal period; oedipal influences, however important, are added later.

9. Emde 1991. Other research illustrated the role of child-mother/caretaker relationships in the development of the child's mind (see, for example, Fonagy 2001; Fonagy and Target 1997; Lehtonen 2003).

10. Bloom 2010. Also see Bloom's article titled "The Moral Life of Babies" in the *New York Times Magazine*, May 5, 2010.

11. Erikson 1966.

12. Mack 1979.

13. Moses 1982.

14. The now-classic finding on this topic was reported by René Spitz in 1965. Around the eighth month of life, infants develop an unambiguous fear of strangers, moving away from them, crying, whimpering, and showing signs of dislike. This fear of a stranger who has caused the infant no pain and whose intent is benevolent is known as "stranger anxiety." This means that the infant also begins to differentiate more clearly between people in his or her environment.

15. Kernberg 1976; Volkan 1976.

16. Stern 1985.

17. For details of Saul's case, see Volkan 2010b. Some individuals who experience traumatic events in childhood may not be able to integrate their various self-images and, instead of experiencing splitting in adulthood like Saul did, they exhibit multiple personalities (Brenner 2001).

18. Winnicott 1963, p. 75.

19. Winnicott 1969, pp. 222–223.

20. Winnicott 1969, p. 223.

21. Winnicott 1969, p. 222.

22. The key issue during psychoanalysis of an individual with unintegrated personality organization is to help the person eventually reach a "crucial juncture." The term "crucial juncture" was first used by Melanie Klein in 1946 (see also Kernberg 1976, 1984; Volkan 1987, Volkan and Fowler 2009b). She wrote: "The synthesis between the loved and hated aspects of the complete object gives rise to the feelings of mourning and guilt which imply vital advances in the infant's emotional and intellectual life. This is also a crucial juncture for the choice of neurosis or psychosis" (p. 100). It is the failure to reach natural "crucial junctures" in childhood that causes the adult to be stuck in a personality organization like Saul's.

23. Volkan 2009b.

24. Volkan 1988.

25. Itzkowitz, personal communication, 2000.

26. Erikson 1966.

27. Kakar 1996.

28. Erikson 1956.

29. Blos 1979; Volkan 1988.

30. Only through some long-lasting drastic historical event may a group of individuals evolve a new large-group identity. For example, certain southern Slavs became Bosniaks while under centuries-long Ottoman rule.

31. Loewenberg 1994, 1995.

32. Volkan and Fowler 2009a.

**Chapter 10**

1. Itzkowitz 2001, pp. 173–174.

2. Freud 1940. This splitting is not the same as that of individuals with an unintegrated self. They are called persons having borderline personality organization. Such individuals typically split their self-images and/or object images into opposite categories of "good" and "bad."

3. Freud 1917.

4. Furman 1974.

5. Wolfenstein 1966, 1969.

6. Blos 1979.

7. Tähkä 1984.

8. Linking objects and phenomena should not be confused with childhood transitional objects and phenomena that are reactivated in adulthood. Certainly there are some severely regressed adults, such as some persons with schizophrenia, who reactivate the transitional relatedness of their babyhoods and "recreate" transitional objects. A transitional object, like a child's special teddy bear, represents the first not-me, but it is never totally not-me. It links not-me with mother-me and it is a temporary construction toward a sense of reality (Winnicott 1953; Greenacre 1969). Linking objects contain high-level symbolism. They must be thought of as tightly packed symbols whose significance is bound up in the conscious and unconscious nuances of the relationship that preceded the loss. Therefore, not every keepsake or memento cherished by a mourner should be considered as a linking object possessing a significant investment of symbolism and magic.

9. Volkan 1972, 1981; Volkan and Zintl 1993.

10. After the Holocaust, psychoanalysts became interested in studying the consequences massive traumas at the hand of the Other have on individuals. William Niederland's (1961, 1964, 1968) works on "survivor syndrome" and the proceedings of a conference series under the leadership of Henry Krystal on the late sequels of massive psychic trauma in the mid-1960s are good examples of such initial studies (Krystal 1968). Psychoanalysts' Holocaust studies have continued since I began my journey into the world of politics. (For example, see Felman and Laub 1991; Laub and Auerhahn 1993; Laub and Podell 1997; Kestenberg and Brenner 1996; Brenner 2004.) I joined Gabriele Ast and William Greer in writing a book on this topic (Volkan, Ast, and Greer 2002). The reader will find references to many other psychoanalysts', including German-speaking psychoanalysts', work on the Holocaust-related clinical issues in our book.

During recent decades psychoanalysts, along with psychodynamically oriented mental health workers, cognitive behavior therapists, and others, have written a great deal about the influences of recent or current traumatic world issues (see Kogan 2004; Sklarew, Twemlow, and Wilkinson 2004; Lemma and Patrick 2010; Böhm and Kaplan 2011). Such works have enlarged our understanding of the concept of survival syndrome, but also provide reasons for various responses to massive traumas and the role of resilience.

11. Volkan 1979.

12. Kernberg 2010.

13. Volkan and Zintl 1993.

14. For my colleagues' and my studies on societal/large-group mourning, see Volkan 1988, 1997, 2004 and Volkan, Ast, and Greer 2002.

15. Volkan and Zintl 1993.

16. Volkan, Ast, and Greer 2002.

17. Volkan 1981, p. 316.

18. Kestenberg 1989, p. 391.

**Chapter 11**

1. Rabbi Meir Kahane, a United States citizen, founded the Jewish Defense League in the United States. He also founded Kach, a political party in Israel that later was banned by the Israeli government because it was considered racist. Kahane promoted keeping a "Greater Israel."

2. For a detailed examination of psychological reactions among the Cypriot Turks after the 1974 division of the island, see Volkan 1979.

**Chapter 12**

1. Volkan1993; Akhtar 1999.

2. Volkan 1990a.

3. Her story first appeared in a paper in *Journal of Applied Psychoanalytic Studies* (Volkan 1999).

4. Anzieu 1971, 1984; Chasseguet-Smirgel 1984; and Kernberg 1989.

**Chapter 13**

1. Blue Ridge Hospital had inpatient facilities for the University of Virginia's Departments of Psychiatry, Orthopedics, Neurology and Internal Medicine. On the Blue Ridge grounds, there were outpatient facilities for adult, child, and family psychiatry. The Highlands Comprehensive Epilepsy Center; Biofeedback Clinic; Forensic Psychiatry Clinic; Institute of Law, Psychiatry and Public Policy; the Sleep and Dream Laboratory; and the Center for the Study of Mind and Human Interaction were all sections of the Blue Ridge Hospital complex.

2. The head of this program was the late Raymond Ramirez from Illinois.

3. Besides receiving support from the University of Virginia and the Massey Foundation, during its existence CSMHI received grants from the William and Flora Hewlett Foundation, the Pew Charitable Trusts, the W. Alton Jones Foundation, the United States Institute of Peace, Social Development Office of the Amiri Diwan of Kuwait, International Research and Exchanges Board, and private individual donors. Of CSMHI's four years (1992–1966) working in the Baltic Republics, especially in Estonia, one part was carried out in partnership with the Carter Center's Conflict Resolution Center (CRP) in Atlanta under the directorship of former President Jimmy Carter. From 1994 to 1966 the CSMHI team, in collaboration with CRP, tried to "vaccinate" Estonia's major ethnic groups to prevent tensions from developing into dangerous domestic and/or international conflict (Neu and Volkan 1999). This project was funded by the Carter Center.

4. The first issue of *Mind and Human Interaction* came out in June 1989.

5. Besides Demetrios, Joe, Hal, and me, another participant in the Charlottesville gathering was Herbert Kelman from Harvard University, whose work on the Middle East as well as Cyprus was well known. Other participants were John Burton, James Laue, Edward Azar, Harriett Crosby, Stephen Cohen, and Richard Arndt. John Burton was a former politician from Australia who had devoted himself to conflict resolution and played a significant role shaping his country's foreign policy. Since 1985 he had been on the faculty of Conflict Resolution and Public Affairs at the Institute for Conflict Analysis and Resolution, George Mason University, Maryland. James Laue was another professor from the same George Mason institute. Edward Azar, a professor of government and politics, was the head of the Center for International Development and Conflict Management at the University of Maryland and an expert on Middle East problems. Psychologist Harriett Crosby was the cofounder and president of the Institute for Soviet American Relations in Washington, DC. She was also one of the editors of *Surviving Together*, a journal established in 1983 to cover the currents events in the Soviet Union, exchanges, trade, legislation, education programs, and media coverage. Stephen Cohen was a professor of politics and Russian studies at Princeton University and knowledgeable on the Soviet Union and its relations with the United States. Richard Arndt, a cultural diplomat who had served in various parts of the world, was at the University of Virginia from 1986 to 1989 as Diplomat-in-Residence and Director of Mid-Career Studies for the Woodrow Wilson Department of Government and Foreign Affairs. He would later become a faculty member of CSMHI. For two volumes, see Volkan, Julius, and Montville 1990, and Volkan, Montville, and Julius 1990.

6. Reagan 1983.

7. Volkan and Itzkowitz 1984, 2011.

8. See Khrushchev 1970 for details.

9. Dobrynin 1955; Tucker 1987a, b; Gaddis 1992; Matlock 2004.

10. Matlock 2004.

11. Yevtushenko 1970; Voznesensky 1986.

12. Niederland 1968.

13. My meeting with Andrei Sakharov was arranged by Viola Bernard, then a psychoanalyst from New York who was interested in applying psychoanalysis to large-group processes. Sakharov died suddenly from a heart attack on December 14, 1989.

14. Participating in this meeting, besides Richard Arndt, Demetrios Julius, Joseph Montville, Hal Saunders, and Vamık Volkan from CSMHI, were Boris Lomov and Stanislav Roschin from Moscow, Herbert Kelman, Eugene Brody (a psychoanalyst and the Secretary General of the World Federation of Mental Health), Neil MacFarlane (a professor in the Woodrow Wilson Department of Government and Foreign Affairs, University of Virginia), Robert Nelson (a Senior Correspondent for *World Monitor Television* in Boston, Massachusetts), and Blema Steinberg (a professor of political science at McGill University in Montreal and a psychoanalyst).

15. Due to my friendship with Boris Lomov, later during one of my trips to the Soviet Union my wife and I were taken to the space center near Moscow where the Soviet astronauts had some of their training.

16. After CSMHI was founded, we regularly had many American and international distinguished guests who gave lectures or joined in our discussion groups. Nechama Agmon, Rafael Moses, General Shlomo Gazit, and Mohammed Shaalan from the former APA dialogue series were among them.

17. Gorbachev 1993, p. 109.

**Chapter 14**

1. Participants at the Moscow conference: from CSMHI we were Richard Arndt, Robert Carey, Norman Itzkowitz, Demetrious Julius, Harold Saunders, Molly Turner, Vamık Volkan. Our official hosts were Andrey Brushlinsky, Director of the Institute of Psychology at the USSR Academy of Sciences; William Smirnov, Director of the Center for Political Studies of the Institute of State and Law, USSR Academy of Sciences; and Boris Shmelev, Pro-rector of the Diplomatic Academy of the Soviet Foreign Ministry. Other Soviet participants were: Anatoly Baranov, Igor Kravchenko, Vlademir Shamarov, Lubya Sydorowa, Yuri Sorokin, Sara Kamenshikova, Vlademir Vartanyan, Yuri Oleinik, Yuri Urbanovich, Nikolai Bykov, Sergei Solutsev, Anatoly Zhuzavlev, and Victor Laptev from the above three USSR organizations. Leonid Dobrokhotov of the Central Committee of the Communist Party and Alexey Petroukin with the Association for International Dialogue were also

present. Anatoly (Tolja) Golubovsky of the Institute of Art Research at the Ministry of Culture exposed us to the cultural aspects of perestroika. The next year Tolja would spend one year at CSMHI as our international fellow. The W. Alton Jones Foundation generously made CSMHI's 1990 trip to Moscow possible. I would visit Moscow twice more, without other members of CSMHI, before the collapse of the Soviet Union and the work at the USSR Diplomatic Academy.

2. Political leaders not only influence and change large-group identities as we will discuss later in this book, but sometimes they also play a role in changing the physical environment. Stalin wanted to show the world his/Moscow's power and grandiosity and he selected architects and art forms to accomplish this.

3. Obolonsky 1989.

4. While I was writing my book, *Enemies and Allies: From Clinical Practice to International Relationships* (Volkan 1988), I went to see the Berlin Wall, went through Checkpoint Charlie, and visited East Berlin.

The Berlin Wall was constructed in August 1961 by the German Democratic Republic (GDR) to keep out the "fascist ideas" coming in from West Germany. In West Germany, Mayor Willy Brandt named it the "Wall of Shame." On June 12, 1987, the then president of the United States, Ronald Reagan, uttered the well-known words in Berlin: "Mr. Gorbachev, open this gate. Mr. Gorbachev, tear down this wall!" On November 9, 1989, the Berlin Wall came down.

5. Volkan 1988.

6. This armed conflict would last until May 1994. Until now there is no formal agreement between Armenia and Azerbaijan about the fate of Nagorno-Karabakh.

7. Obolonsky 1990.

8. Volkan 2006a, 2006b.

9. Rybakov 1991. Anatoly Rybakov wrote *Children of the Arbat* in Russian in the 1960s, but the Soviet system prevented its publication until 1987.

10. See "Moscow 1990: The Psychology of Change in the Soviet Union" in the June 1990 special issue of *Mind and Human Interaction,* vol. 2, no. 1.

**Chapter 15**

1. The State Emergency Committee's members included KGB chairman Vladimir Kryuchkov, Prime Minister Valentin Pavlov, Internal Affairs Minister Boris Pugo, and Defense Minister Dmitry Yazov.

2. Golubovsky 1992.

3. Robert Tucker (1987b) stated that "political science . . . has overconcentrated on the workings of established politics and given too little systematic attention to social-political movements" (p. 16).

4. Prejudicial rituals are not "good" or "bad" in themselves. At one end of the

spectrum they help to separate one large group from another and help a large group maintain its identity. At the other end of the spectrum, prejudicial rituals may become malignant. Throughout a child's formative years she identifies in various ways with her own "type" and she encounters symbolization of the "enemy" at various levels. While modern baby and child observations indicate the existence of a psychobiological potential for separating "us" and "them," the foundation of psychologically more sophisticated prejudice occurs during the anal phase of child development, as was long ago suggested by Lawrence Kubie (1965). During the anal phase (ages 1–3), the child learns to control his muscles, including his anal sphincter. The mental mechanisms associated with this phase become a crucial part of the foundation of prejudice. They may cause the child to keep "clean and purified" elements to himself while externalizing and projecting putrefying feces-like elements (part of self, ideas, feelings) onto others. It is no wonder then that in adulthood, when speaking about shared "enemies," a level of regression may set in during which anal symbols are utilized and anal revulsion takes place.

5. Šebek 1992, p. 54.

6. Šebek 1994, p. 104.

7. Volkan 2004, 2006a.

8. On December 25 Gorbachev resigned as President of the USSR. The next day the Soviet Union was formally dissolved. The Soviet flag was gone and overnight millions of Russians found themselves in "foreign" countries. Aside from the Republic of Georgia, Estonia, Latvia, and Lithuania, all other republics joined the Commonwealth of Independent States (CIS). A new Russia replaced the USSR at the United Nations.

**Chapter 16**

1. Held 1988.

2. The conference at the University of Cape Town, from November 22 to 25 was, titled, "Memory, Narrative, & Forgiveness: Reflecting on Ten Years of South Africa's Truth and Reconciliation Commission." It also honored Archbishop Desmond Tutu's life's work on peace and reconciliation. It was organized by Pumla Gobodo-Madikizela and Chris van der Merwe.

3. Erikson 1966, p. 606.

4. Boyer 1986.

5. Murphy 1957.

6. Stein 1990, p. 118.

7. Lorenz 1967.

8. Pinderhughes 1982, p. 8.

9. Volkan 1988.

10. Smith 2011.

11. Volkan 1979.

12. Winnicott 1969, p. 224. In 2011 Warren Spielberg, who has done psycho-political work on Israeli-Palestinian issues, reported an observation that supports Winnicott's idea about the Berlin Wall. He wrote:

> Separation Wall [in Jerusalem] constructed by Israel has restricted Palestinians' ability to travel freely within their communities (the wall cuts substantially into the West Bank, sometimes dividing Palestinian farmland and towns, rather than tracing the pre-1967 borders), and even as it has generated feelings of imprisonment, threat, and outrage, provoking some Palestinians to angrily describe it as an "Apartheid Wall," it has also inspired many toward self-reliance and improvement.
>
> This observation about the Wall's unexpected silver lining is not meant to undercut legitimate criticisms of the Wall or foreclose debates over the ethics of its construction. Nonetheless, in my interviews with West Bank Palestinians I found that the Israeli security barrier has provoked many Palestinians to turn inward, to focus on their own hopes and dreams, and to build the infrastructure of their own lives complementing the work being done by the government on the community level. It has also diminished the intruding psychological specter of the threatening 'Israeli in mind' who are now seen as living 'behind the Wall.' This has given many young Palestinians some emotional respite and more internal space to imagine their own futures. (Spielberg 2011)

13. We did not wish to prepare a list of questions and collect answers for them. This type of approach would provide "scientifically" measurable results, but these results would only illustrate some surface and limited perceptions. It is difficult and perhaps impossible to measure "scientifically" peoples' unconscious and even conscious fantasies. Unconscious and conscious fantasies are best found and understood by a psychoanalytically informed approach. This fact makes it difficult to include psychoanalytic research among studies for which results are easily measurable. My approach to political psychology was to present my observations, develop theories, and let others measure aspects of such observations and theories at a later time.

14. Ast 1991, p. 102.

15. Ast 1991, p. 104.

16. Volkan 1990b, p. 3.

17. Volkan 1990b, p. 3. For a detailed account of Sabine's case, see Volkan, Ast, and Greer 2002.

18. Ohlmeier 1991; Misselwitz 2003; Maaz 1991; and Weisberger 1995. Maaz (1991), a psychotherapist, wrote: "The division of Germany and along with it most of the world into two hostile camps made it possible for individual evil and abnormality not to have to be perceived, for that were available the nefarious capitalists, imperialists and revanchists on the one side and the dangerous communists and

Bolshevists on the other (p. 85, Translated by Weisberger 1995, p. 10).

19. Rosenthal 1997 and Streeck-Fischer 1999.

20. When in June 1990 I attended the "Children in War" conference in Jerusalem, I met Liliane Opher, a child-psychotherapist who was attending from Germany. Liliane is a child of survivor-parents of the Holocaust in Romania. She told me her story and we also spoke about the situation in Germany forty-five years after the end of the Holocaust. It was obvious that even at the beginning of the 1990s there was still much silence in German society regarding the Holocaust. According to Liliane, her encounter with me motivated her to look for possibilities in Germany for how to start a project aiming to investigate the transgenerational consequences of the Holocaust for the children of the perpetrators and of the survivors and how to end the silence. She started to look for people interested in such a project. At this time there was still significant resistance toward such a project in Germany—even among psychotherapists. The unbending will of Liliane Opher led to founding PAKH in July 1995. After its establishment, PAKH started an association with Professor Karl Köhle, director of the Institute of Psychosomatic and Psychotherapy at the University of Cologne. This gave PAKH access to evaluate their work scientifically. At the present time PAKH is collaborating with Professor Köhle's successor Dr. Christian Albus.

When PAKH considered having its first international meeting sponsored by the state chancellery of North Rhein-Westphalia to end the silence about the Holocaust, Liliane Opher and her Jewish colleague Peter Pogany-Wnendt met with me in early 1996 in Frankfurt. I agreed to assist them and was able to meet a core PAKH group—besides Liliane-Opher and Peter Pogany-Wnendt, three other non-Jewish German persons, all of them psychotherapists: Johannes Pfäfflin, Bernd Klose, and Bernd Sonntag. I met with this core group in Germany four times, a few days each time, in February 1997, December 1997, February 1998, and August 1998. The members of this group were psychoanalytically trained colleagues, people with similar interests, and not enemies. However, their German and Jewish parents, grandparents, and relatives had lived in completely different circumstances. They had been enemies, victims, and perpetrators—and the next generation had carried forward this ill-starred heritage on both conscious and unconscious levels. Although in the meantime half a century had passed, they carried within themselves the inexpressible trauma of the war and of annihilation. During my meetings with them, the meeting place became a "laboratory" that allowed the core members to examine themselves and see the reflections of the Jewish-German relationships within their own internal worlds. It was after this that PAHK successfully organized the international meeting called "The End of Speechlessness?" in mid-August 1998 in Düsseldorf. This meeting opened a significant dialogue concerning the

Holocaust in German society (Opher-Cohn, Pfäfflin, Sonntag, Klose, and Pogany-Wnendt 2000; Volkan, Ast, and Greer 2002).

After the meeting, conflicts among the PAKH members, sometimes leading to strongly felt hostile emotions, would appear. The conflicts were due to the reemergence of the psychological burdens transmitted to them by perpetrators and victims of the Nazi period. Nevertheless, PAKH continued to exist. Over the years they built international contacts. For example, when I went to Africa to attend the tenth anniversary of the Truth and Reconciliation Commission, PAKH members were also present. There I met some new members. Many of them told their own family stories. My last consultation with PAKH members took place in 2008, again in Düsseldorf. At that time they were preparing to visit South Africa again in 2009 and share their experiences with colleagues who had come from other traumatized societies.

21. Wagner 1996, 1998.

22. Suzuki 1991, p. 93.

23. Volkan 1988.

24. Freud 1921b, 1930.

25. Butler 1993.

26. Volkan 1979.

27. Horowitz 1985.

28. Flores and Benmayer 1997; Hing 2004.

29. Others in Europe can be large groups with their own nation-state or internal groups such as Roma, Jews, and, especially after September 11, 2001, Muslim immigrants. Or Others may be those in "marginal places" (Shields 1991). For example, for Western Europeans a lesser-developed Eastern Europe is considered a marginal place. "Marginal places are not necessarily on geographic peripheries, of course, but rather on peripheries of a cultural system of space" (Wingfield 2003, p. 1). The *real* Others, like the Turks, who are perceived outside of European culture, may induce greater shared and individualized anxiety when they attempt to be a part of the European regional "globalization" movement.

30. Çevik 2003.

31. Liu and Mills 2006; Morton 2005; Ratliff 2004.

32. Arnett 2002; Twemlow and Sacco 2008.

33. Stapley 2006.

**Chapter 17**

1. During World War II there was also Soviet preoccupation with what the Soviets call "the Tatar-Mongol yoke" (1237–1480) (see Halperin 2009). At this time Tatars living in Crimea were accused of being Nazi collaborators. Stalin sent them into exile.

2. Also see Rogers 1990.

3. Freud 1921a.

4. Here are two more types of designs on the large-group's canvas: the first one is manufactured by the Other. Picture two large-group tents side by side. Individuals in the first tent throw mud, excrement, and refuse—that is, they externalize their "bad" images of themselves and others and project their own unwanted thoughts, feelings, attitudes, and expectations—onto the canvas of the second tent. Note that this action is taken toward the large-group identity itself, the canvas, and not necessarily toward the individuals who possess this group identity. To find an example of this type of design, we do not need to leave the United States. Maurice Apprey (1993, 1996, 1998) studied how the white-American large group's perceptions of the African-American large group had been assimilated into the African-American large-group identity experience—for example, how black-on-black crime had become a modified version of the mental representation of white-black historical interactions.

Another design standing for a large-group identity is created by "charismatic" or "transforming" leaders such as Kemal Atatürk, Vladimir Lenin, Mahatma Gandhi, and Mao Zedong. Such leaders bring hundreds of thousands or millions of people out of political isolation and into a new kind of political participation (Weber 1923; Abse and Ulman 1977; Zaleznick 1984; Volkan and Itzkowitz 2011). Sometimes these leaders go a step further: driven to meet the requirements of their own internal worlds, they reshape the external world of their followers and their subjective feelings about their large-group identity.

5. Volkan 1991.

6. Edwards 1998, p. 1.

7. Furman 1998.

8. Campbell 1998.

9. Wolfenstein and Kliman 1965.

10. Erlich 1998; Raviv, Sadeh, Raviv, Silberstein, and Diver 2000.

11. Volkan 1997.

12. Lifton and Olson 1976.

13. Volkan 1991, 2006a, 2009a. Large-group identity issues sometimes may appear in other types of massive trauma. After the 1988 earthquake in Armenia that killed or injured tens of thousands of people, Armenians refused to receive the Azeri offer for blood donations, and this tragedy, due to nature's fury, became contaminated with large-group identity issues.

14. The experience of shame and humiliation is psychologically unbearable, and affected individuals resort to various mental mechanisms to defend themselves from the influence of these affects. See Bernard, Ottenberg, and Redl 1973.

15. Niederland 1961. When a society has undergone a massive trauma, especially a chronic one, victimized adults may also endure shame, humiliation, and guilt for being unable to look after their children properly (Volkan 1997).

16. The blocking of external motor activity increases the probability of a psychological breakdown after a trauma; foxhole waiting is more damaging than active warfare (Fenichel 1945). Similarly, a person living under a totalitarian regime or occupation or under the guidelines of apartheid experiences the blocking of motor activities (such as being barred from certain locations) as well as mental activities (one cannot raise one's voice against the authorities because to do so is dangerous). This increases the sense of helplessness and causes an inability to be assertive.

To be assertive means finding "normal" or wished-for channels to act out aggression. When such channels are not available, victimized group members turn their aggression inward. This leads to an experience of helpless rage and what can be called "social masochism." The expression of direct rage toward the oppressing group remains life-threatening and psychologically impossible. Thus, on many occasions, direct rage is expressed *between* the members of the victimized group in what can be called "social sadism." Even after the traumatizing conditions are removed, the inability to be assertive may continue for a long time. Actual poverty does not disappear quickly, and this and other external factors such as the AIDS epidemic in South Africa help to perpetuate helplessness and an inability to be assertive. For example, 1996 data in postapartheid South Africa describes disturbing statistics: an average of fifty-two murders a day, a rape committed on average of every thirty minutes, a car stolen every nine minutes, and an armed robbery committed every eleven minutes (Eagle and Watts 2002). The inability to be assertive increases envy and resentment within the formerly victimized group toward those individuals who were able to "assert" themselves and become rich or important for other reasons (Šebek 1994). This in turn increases tensions in subgroups within the society, which further complicates the existing difficulties.

17. The oppressing group that limits the victimized group's actions and freedom, if it lasts long enough, becomes internalized as a shared "external superego." Earlier in this book I mentioned Michael Šebek's "totalitarian objects" (Šebek 1994). In postapartheid South Africa, perhaps we could call such internalized objects "racist objects." The shared internalization of an external superego, such as totalitarian or racist objects, does not disappear right away when policies and laws change to be more humane. It creates confusion when the oppression is lifted and when there is a new external environment. This confusion is reflected in a variety of new moral dilemmas and ethical issues. The expression of freedom can be difficult due to the continuation of the totalitarian or racist *internal* objects. New freedom and the secret wish to defeat the continuing internalized oppressive powers, and

the fear this wish induces, are combined to support a lack of respect for authority, even while this authority is still feared. The utilization of new freedom in the post-oppressive period may become corrupted.

18. Mitscherlich and Mitscherlich 1975; Volkan, 2006a.

19. Understanding transgenerational transmission of trauma at a societal level owes a great deal to studies made of the second and third generations of Holocaust survivors and others directly traumatized under the Third Reich. Many references to significant studies on this topic can be found in Kogan 1995; Kestenberg and Brenner 1996; Brenner 2001, 2004; Volkan, Ast, and Greer 2002.

20. Anna Freud and Dorothy Burlingham 1942.

21. Judith Kestenberg's term (1982) "transgenerational transportation," I believe, refers to depositing traumatized images. It is related to a well-known concept in individual psychology called "projective identification" (Klein 1946).

22. Poznanski 1972; Cain and Cain 1964; Volkan and Ast 1997.

23. For psychoanalytic case stories illustrating transgenerational transmissions, see Volkan, Ast, and Greer 2002 and Volkan and Fowler 2009b.

24. Waelder 1930; Hartmann 1939.

25. Ocak 1996; Ersoy 1998.

26. Ersoy 1998, p. 49.

27. Hollander 2010.

28. Volkan and Itzkowitz 1994.

29. In Greek "*enosis*" means "union." Here it refers to the Greek Cypriots' movement to unite Cyprus with Greece.

30. Markides 1977, p. 10–11._

31. Volkan 1996, 1997, 2002.

**Chapter 18**

1. Misiunas 1990, p. 205.

2. This meeting was conceived as part of CSMHI's collaboration, at the time in its fourth year, with the Russian (former Soviet) Academy of Sciences' Institute of Psychology and the Russian (former Soviet) Diplomatic Academy. CSMHI received funds from the United States Institute of Peace for this project.

Participants from CSMHI were Max R. Harris, the new Associate Director of CSMHI; W. Nathaniel Howell, U.S. Ambassador to Kuwait at the time of the Iraqi invasion and then Ambassador-in-Residence at CSMHI; Norman Itzkowitz, Professor of Near Eastern Studies, Princeton University; Demetrios Julius; Joseph Montville; Harold Saunders; and Vamık Volkan.

CSMHI guests from the United States: Danute Bieliauskas and Vytautas Bieliauskas. Both of them played significant roles in helping CSMHI to arrange the

Kaunas gathering due to their positions in the Lithuanian World Community. The third guest was Richard Krickus, Professor of Political Science, Mary Washington College.

From Russia: Vladimir Cherţikin, Professor, Diplomatic Academy; Yalçın Nasırov; Alexander Obolonsky; Emil Paiiyn, Director, Center of Ethno-Political Issues at Eduard Schevardnadze's Foreign Policy Association, Moscow; Stanislav Roschin; Yuri Matveevski, Senior Counselor, Russian Ministry of Foreign Affairs; Zoja Zarubina, Professor and Translator, Diplomatic Academy. Zoya was formerly Stalin's interpreter.

From Lithuania: Vygintas Gontis, Head of the Office of Information, Science and Higher Education of the Government of the Republic of Lithuania; Antanas Goštautas, Chief of Medical Psychology and Social Investigation, Kaunas Medical Academy; Halina Kobeckaite, Director General of the Department of Nationalities of the Government of the Republic of Lithuania; Egidijus Kūris, Director, Institute of International Relations, Vilnius University; and Vidmantas Pavilionis, Deputy of Supreme Council of Lithuania and Chairman of the Committee of Foreign Affairs of the Government of the Republic of Lithuania.

From Latvia: Aina Antane, Researcher, Institute of History, Latvian Academy of Sciences.

From Estonia: Triin Vihalemm, Department of Sociology, Tartu University.

From Byelorussia: Spartan Polsky, Head of the Laboratory of Ethnic Geography, Minsk Pedagogical Institute.

Max Harris and I wrote the first detailed description of the Kaunas meeting that was published in *Mind and Human Interaction* (Volkan and Harris 1992).

3. Misiunas 1990, p. 214.

4. Migranyan 1992.

5. Antane 1991.

6. Hiltzik 1991.

7. Saunders 1991b.

8. Eban 1983.

9. Misiunas 1990.

10. Volkan 2006a, 2006b.

11. This project, commissioned by Baltic Surveys, was conducted by Survey Research Center, Institute of Philosophy, Sociology and Law (Lithuania), Lasopec (Latvia), and Emor (Estonia). The results were reported in *The Baltic Independent*, April 24–30, 1992.

12. *Laisves Alejos*, the main street in Kaunas, was later named Lenin Avenue. Before we went to Kaunas it had been restored to its original name.

13. The Department of Nationalities of the Government of the Republic of

Lithuania presented a report to the CSCE Meeting of Experts on Minorities, Geneva, Switzerland, July 1–19, 1991:

> In accordance with its provisional Constitution (Articles 23, 24), the Republic of Lithuania guarantees national minorities the right to develop their culture, to practice their own religion and to perform its rites, and to use their mother tongue in accordance with the International Covenant on Civil and Political Rights (Article 27). Individuals belonging to national minorities are guaranteed legal equality and the possibility of enjoying all human rights and fundamental freedoms according to Principle Seven of the Helsinki Final Act.

14. Seventy-eight percent of eligible voters participated in the plebiscite. Ninety-one percent voted "yes." Two days later on June 16, Viktor Isakov, the head Russian negotiator in the troop withdrawal talks with Lithuania, called the demand "totally unrealistic" (RFE/RL Research Report, June 26, 1992, pp. 64–65).

**Chapter 19**

1. Volkan and Harris 1993; Thomson 1993. The Riga meeting was supported by funds from the Pew Charitable Trust, the United States Institute of Peace, the International Research and Exchanges Board, the University of Virginia's Center for Russian and East European Studies, and the Massey Foundation.

2. List of participants:

From CSMHI: Dean Robert Carey; Max Harris; Margie Howell; Nathaniel Howell; Norman Itzkowitz; Demetrios Julius; Joseph Montville; Harold Saunders; J. Anderson Thomson; Yuri Urbanovich; and Vamık Volkan.

CSMHI guests from the United States: Robert Cullen who at the time of our meeting reported from Eastern Europe for *The New Yorker*, *The Atlantic Monthly*, and other magazines; and Andreis Plakans, Professor of History, Iowa State University, Director of the Baltic Academic Center.

CSMHI guest from Sweden: Marta Cullberg, Psychoanalyst, Transnational Foundation for Peace and Future Research.

From Russia: Anatoly Golubovsky; Vera Gracheva, Counselor on Humanitarian Cooperation and Human Rights, Embassy of the Russian Federation to the United States; Vlademir Ionkin, First Secretary, Embassy of the Russian Federation to Latvia; Alexander Obolonsky; Edvard Ozhiganov, Counselor, Soviet Nationalities, Supreme Soviet of the Russian Federation; Galina Ozhiganov, Researcher, Institute of Psychology, Russian Academy of Sciences, and coeditor, *The Psychological Review*; Vladimir Podoprigora, People's Deputy of the Russian Federation and Chairman, Committee on Inter-Republican Relations, Regional Policy and Cooperation of the Supreme Soviet of the Russian Federation; Ambassador Alexander Rannikh; Stanislav Roschin; and Zoja Zarubina.

From Lithuania: Robertas Ambrazevicius, Social Psychologist of Klaipeda Municipality; Antanas Goštautas; Vlademir Jarmolenko, Member of the Lithuanian Parliament; Halina Kobeckaite; Valentinas Mite, Journalist, *Laisvoji Europa* (Free Europe); and Regina Seskuvene, Translator, Department of Nationalities of the Government of Lithuania.

From Latvia: Aina Antane; Daina Bleinere, Senior Researcher, Institute of History, Latvian Academy of Sciences; Juris Bojārs, Director, Institute of International Affairs, Latvian State University and Chairman, Democratic Labor Party; Helen Doroshenko, Translator, University of Latvia; Alexander Malcev, Director General, Department of Ethnic Affairs of the Government of Latvia; Andreis Pantelejevs, Chairman, Parliamentary Commission of Human Rights and Interethnic Relations; Indulis Ronis, Director, Institute of History, Latvian Academy of Sciences; Irena Sneidere, Senior Researcher, Institute of History, Latvian Academy of Sciences; Janis Stradins, Vice-President of the Latvian Academy of Sciences; Elmars Vebers, Project Director, Ethnic Processes in Latvia, Institute of Philosophy and Sociology, Latvian Academy of Sciences; and Rudite Viksne, Senior Researcher, Institute of History, Latvian Academy of Sciences.

From Estonia: Jevgeni Golikov, Senior Researcher, Estonian Academy of Sciences; Mare Haab, Researcher, Institute of Philosophy, Sociology and Law, Estonian Academy of Sciences; Andres Heinapuu, Member of State Assembly [Parliament] of Estonia; Mati Hint, Member of State Assembly [Parliament] of Estonia; Jaan Kaplinski, Member of State Assembly [Parliament] of Estonia; and Rein Ruutsoo, Senior Researcher, Institute of Philosophy, Sociology and Law, Estonian Academy of Sciences.

3. This story was first reported in *Bloodlines: From Ethnic Pride to Ethnic Terrorism* (Volkan 1997).

4. "Latvians to Remove the Remains of Red Army," *New York Times*, February 3, 1993, p. A6.

5. "Latvia to Rebuild National Cemetery to Past Conditions," *American Baltic News*, April 1993, p. 11.

**Chapter 20**

1. When we went to Estonia for the first time in April 1994, its population was about 1.5 million—65 percent were ethnic Estonians, 29 percent were Russians, and 6 percent had Ukrainian, Belarusian, Scandinavian, or other roots. Only those Russians in Estonia before 1940 were viewed as Estonian citizens. For practical, and perhaps political, reasons the Russian Federation would and could not initiate the return of all the Russians living in the Baltic Republics. That left roughly 170,000 people living in Estonia with no nationality. A citizenship language examination and related issues made it very difficult for noncitizens to become citizens, and the

United Nations, OSCE, and the Council of Europe were concerned about Estonia's citizenship and naturalization policies.

2. During our first visit there were approximately 2,500 Soviet troops in Estonia. By the time of our second visit there in October 1994, the withdrawal agreement had been established. Problems remained, however, since 19,000 Soviet military pensioners and their families had applied for permanent residency.

3. Discussing the border issue between Russia and Estonia was especially difficult because Russia had "ignored" the 1920 Tartu Peace Treaty. This meant that Estonia was never free and that an independent Estonian state had never existed. Estonia demanded the Russians' acknowledgement that the Soviet Union illegally annexed Estonia and that independence had been *restored* in 1991—not just established at that time.

4. Our meetings were funded by a $1 million grant made to the Carter Center's Conflict Resolution Program (CRP) by the Charles Stewart Mott Foundation. We also received funds for this purpose from the International Research and Exchange Board. After the meeting series ended, CSMHI carried out three multiyear projects in Estonia to improve peaceful coexistence between Estonians and non-Estonians living side by side in three locations in Estonia and to create models for such coexistence. For these projects CSMHI received a generous grant from the Pew Charitable Trust. We also received financial support from the United States Institute of Peace. No member of CSMHI or participant from Estonia or Russia was paid for participating in this project. The money covered CSMHI administrative activities for the project, travel and meeting expenses, and especially the initiation of three community Estonia projects in Mustvee, Mustamäe, and Klooga.

5. The total list of Baltic States project meetings:

Kaunas, Lithuania—April 1992
Riga, Latvia—April 1993
Tallinn, Estonia—April 1994
Pärnu, Estonia—October 1994
Charlottesville, Virginia—January 1995
Tallinn, Tartu, Narva and Sillamäe, Estonia—February 1995
Riga, Latvia—February 1995
Tallinn, Estonia—March 1995
Tallinn, Estonia—September 1995
Keila, Paldiski, Tartu, Mustvee, and Narva, Estonia—October 1995
Tallinn, Estonia—November 1995
Charlottesville, Virginia—February 1996
Tallinn, Estonia—April 1996

After the dialogue series ended CSMHI continued to visit Estonia over three more years to supervise three major community projects in Mustvee, Mustamäe, and Klooga.

6. The Carnegie Corporation of New York and the John D. and Catherine T. MacArthur Foundation were primary supporters of INN.

7. Twenty-three people attended this Cyprus-problem meeting. Northern Cyprus was represented by former North Cyprus foreign minister Vedat Çelik. The Greek side was represented by Glafcos Clerides. In 1993 Clerides was elected to a five-year term as president. He was reelected in 1998. (See http://www.cartercenter.org/news/publications/peace/conflict_reports.html.)

Another person who attended the Cyprus meeting was Ambassador Gündüz Aktan, then the Turkish permanent representative to the United Nations in Geneva. He would play a role in my life by expanding my psychopolitical activities. For example, when Gündüz later was the deputy minister of foreign affairs responsible for running the Turkish Foreign Ministry, some members of CSMHI, such as Joe Montville, Ambassador Howell, and I, were invited to conduct seminars on psychopolitical topics at the Turkish Foreign Ministry. Dozens of high-level Turkish ambassadors listened to us. Besides the CSMHI members, well-known historian/psychoanalyst Peter Loewenberg from the University of California, Los Angeles also took part in a seminar.

Earlier I wrote about Maurice Apprey's and my ten seminars at the U.S. Department of State. Other than those seminars, I do not know if there is any other country besides Turkey where attempts were made to introduce psychopolitical findings and concepts to high-level diplomats. Much earlier, Gündüz was a young adviser to Turkish president Turgut Özal and then ambassador to Greece. He was especially interested in the Turkish-Greek relationship, and he encouraged me to study this topic from a psychodynamic angle. Norman Itzkowitz joined me in this endeavor, and we wrote a book examining the Turkish-Greek relationship from a psychoanalytic point of view (Volkan and Itzkowitz 1994). In 2001, at the initiation of the Americans, the Turkish-Armenian Reconciliation Commission (TARC) was established. İt would bring influential Turks and influential Armenians together for unofficial dialogues on the Turkish-Armenian relationship. Gündüz was one of the original members of the Turkish team. At his invitation I joined the Turkish team, even though I was not a Turkish citizen but a Turkish-American. (The Armenian team had Armenian-American members.) I have described my observations of TARC elsewhere (Volkan 2006a).

8. The complete list of International Negotiation Network members: Jimmy Carter, 39th President of the United States; Oscar Arias Sánchez, Nobel Peace Prize Laureate, former President of Costa Rica; Eileen Babbitt, Director, Program on International Negotiation and Conflict Resolution, Fletcher School of Law

and Diplomacy, Tufts University; Tahseen Basheer, former Egyptian ambassador, former Permanent Representative to the League of Arab States (Ambassador Basheer was a participant in the APA-sponsored Arab-Israeli dialogues); Kevin Clements, Director, Institute for Conflict Analysis and Resolution, George Mason University; Javier Pérez de Cuéllar, former UN Secretary-General; Hans Dietrich Genscher, former Vice Chancellor and Minister of Foreign Affairs, Federal Republic of Germany; Tommy Koh, Executive Director, former Singapore Ambassador to the United States; Christopher Mitchell, Professor, Institute for Conflict Analysis and Resolution, George Mason University; Olusegun Obasanjo, former President of Nigeria, Chair, Africa Leadership Forum; Lisbet Palme, Director of UNICEF, Sweden; Robert Pastor, former Director, Latin American and Caribbean Program; Shridath Ramphal, former Secretary-General of the Commonwealth of Nations, Co-Chair, Commission on Global Governance; Barnett Rubin, Director, Center for Preventive Action, Council on Foreign Relations, New York; Kumar Rupesinghe, former Secretary-General, International Alert; Harold Saunders, former U.S. Assistant Secretary of State, Director, International Programs, Kettering Foundation, CSMHI Board member; Marie-Angélique Savané, former Director, Africa Division, UN Population Fund; Desmond Tutu, Nobel Peace Prize Laureate, Chair, Truth and Reconciliation Commission of South Africa, former President, All Africa Conference of Churches; Brian Urquhart, former UN Under-Secretary General for Peacekeeping; William Ury, Director, Project on Preventing War, Program on Negotiation, Harvard University; Cyrus Vance, former U.S. Secretary of State, UN, Special Envoy to the former Yugoslav Republic of Macedonia; Vamık Volkan; Peter Wallensteen, Professor, Department of Peace and Conflict Research, Uppsala University, Sweden; Elie Wiesel, Nobel Peace Prize Laureate, Professor, Boston University; Andrew Young, former U.S. Ambassador to the United Nations, Director, GoodWorks International; and I. William Zartman, Jacob Blaustein Professor of International Organization and Conflict Resolution, The Paul H. Nitze School of Advanced International Studies, John Hopkins University.

9. Today the name of this hotel is Le Meridien President. I understand that not much had been maintained since the hotel was built.

10. Volkan 2006a.

11. After leaving the Joan B. Kroc Institute for Peace & Justice, Joyce Neu became the first team leader for the United Nations' Standby Team of Mediation Experts deployed to assist special envoys of the secretary-general with peace processes. She especially traveled in various places in Africa. Often she would write and tell me about her work. Sometimes she would travel into dangerous areas to meet certain "terrorist" leaders in order to help bring an end to terrible human

tragedies. I came to think of Joyce as the bravest woman I ever met. Whenever I told her this, her response was always: "There are so many other people so much braver than I—I go in and out of conflict situations, but I don't live in them as so many humanitarian workers do, to say nothing of the incredible people who live in their own war-torn countries with no recourse to leaving or protecting themselves. My contributions, whatever they may have been, are dwarfed by those who survive these horrible wars."

12. List of participants of the Estonia dialogue series:

From CSMHI: Maurice Apprey, Margie Howell, Nathaniel Howell, Norman Itzkowitz, Demetrios Julius, Gregory Saathoff, Harold Saunders, J. Anderson Thomson, and Vamık Volkan. Yuri Urbanovich, who by then had become the International Scholar at CSMHI, came to every meeting in Estonia and was present at every meeting in Charlottesville. He participated in discussions but also served as the interpreter. Yuri's involvement in this project made the process most valuable. During the Estonia project CSMHI had a new Program Director, Joy Boissevain, and Managing Editor of *Mind and Human Interaction,* Bruce Edwards. Both Joy and Bruce accompanied CSMHI members to Estonia on many occasions. Their help was also priceless.

From the Carter Center: Joyce Neu, Senior Associate Director, Conflict Resolution Program (CRP), the Carter Center, Adjunct Associate Professor of Anthropology, Emory University, Atlanta, Georgia; DiAnn Watson, Administrative Assistant, CRP, the Carter Center. Watson did not travel to Estonia.

From Estonia (ethnic Estonians): Arno Aadamsoo, Head of Psychiatric Hospital, Tartu University; Toomas Alatalu, Member of Parliament; Mare Haab, Researcher, Institute for International and Social Studies, Tallinn; Klara Hallik, Senior Researcher, Institute for International and Social Studies, and former member of Parliament, and former State Minister in Charge of Ethnic Affairs; Arvo Haug, member of Parliament; Mati Heidmets, Dean, Social Sciences, Tallinn Pedagogical University; Mati Hint, Professor, Tallinn Pedagogical University, and former member of Parliament; Priit Järve, Director, Institute for International and Social Studies, and President's Representative on the Round Table for Minorities; Jaan Kaplinski, writer, and former member of Parliament; Paul Lettens, Advisor, Political Department, Central and Eastern Europe and Commonwealth of Independent States Division, Ministry of Foreign Affairs, and Councilor to the Prime Minister; Arnold Rüütel, Deputy Speaker of Parliament, and Director, Institute of National Development and Cooperation, and former President of Estonia; Endel Talvik, Psychotherapist, and President of the Estonian Psychoanalytically Oriented Society; and Peeter Vares, Deputy Director, Institute for International and Social Studies, Tallinn.

From Estonia (Russian speakers, both citizens and noncitizens): Hanon Barbaner, President, College of Environmental Technologies, Sillamäe; Sergei Gorokhov, Director, Institute for Social and Economic Analysis of Estonia, Narva Division, Narva; Vladimir Homyakov, Medical Doctor, and former Deputy, Narva City Council; Sergei Issakov, Member of the Parliament, Russian Faction, Tallinn, and Professor, Tartu University; Sergei Ivanov, member of the Parliament, Russian Faction, Tallinn; Iliya Nikiforov, Co-Chair, Russian Representatives Assembly, Tallinn; Georgi Perovich, President, International University of Social Sciences "LEX," Tallinn; and Alexei Semionov, Adviser, Tallinn City Government, and member of the Board, Russian Representatives Assembly.

From Russia: Viatcheslav Bakhmin, Executive Director, Open Society Institute, Moscow; Valery Fadeyev, Expert, Committee on International Affairs, State Duma of the Russian Federation; Vera Gracheva, Chief, Division of Bilateral Humanitarian Cooperation, Department of International Cooperation and Human Rights, Ministry of Foreign Affairs of Russia; Andrei Jakushev, Press Secretary, Russian Embassy, Tallinn; Aivars Lezdinysh, Member, State Duma of the Russian Federation; Marina Svirina, Analytic Researcher, Federal Assembly of the Russian Federation, State Duma of the Russian Federation; Alexandre Trofimov, Russian Ambassador Extraordinary and Plenipotentiary to Estonia; Yuri Voyevoda, Deputy Member of Parliament, State Duma, and Vice Chair, Committee on CIS Affairs and Relations with Compatriots, and Chair, Auditing Committee, Socio-Political Movement of Social Democrats, Moscow; and Andrei Zakharov, Deputy General Director, Foundation for the Development of Parliamentarianism in Russia, and former Deputy Member of Parliament, State Duma, Moscow. The following persons attended only one or two meetings:

From the United States: Richard Arndt, Past President, Fulbright Alumni Association (from CSMHI); Harry Barnes, Director, Conflict Resolution Program, the Carter Center; Hrach Gregorian, former Director of Training and Education, United States Institute of Peace, Washington, DC; George Moein, Director, Earth 2020—Center for Environmental Policy and Hazardous Materials Management Institute, University of Virginia; Joseph Montville (from CSMHI); Mary Theodore, Psychiatrist, Cornell Medical Center, Payne-Whitney Clinic, New York.

From Estonia: Peeter Tulviste, President, Tartu University.

From Latvia: Aina Antane, Senior Researcher, Institute of History, Latvian Academy of Sciences.

From Lithuania: Halina Kobeckaite, former Director, Department on Ethnic Minorities, Vilnius, and Lithuanian Ambassador to Estonia. CSMHI members visited Halina often at the Lithuanian Embassy.

From Canada: Kaspars Tuters, Psychoanalyst, Toronto; and Allan King, Filmmaker, Allan King Associates Ltd. Allen filmed our activities and also made a documentary film of our work in Estonia called *The Dragon's Egg*.

From Russia: Konstantin Kirjuhin, Consultant, Federal Assembly of the Russian Federation, Moscow; Alexander Obolonsky, Senior Researcher, Institute of the State and Law, Russian Academy of Sciences, Moscow; Mikhail Reshetnikov, Director, East European Institute of Psychoanalysis, St. Petersburg; Stanislav Roschin, Senior Researcher, Institute of Psychology, Russian Academy of Science, Moscow; Anatoly Trinova, Head of Department, Institute of Strategic Studies, Moscow; and Zoja Zarubina, Associate Professor, Diplomatic Academy; Founder and First Director of Courses for Simultaneous Interpretation, Moscow Institute of Foreign Languages, Moscow.

University students: Estonians—Andres Kalda, Katrin Kase, Keit Pentus. Russians—Ilja Denks, Pavel Goncharov, Alexei Naumov, Angelika Trusova.

I have not listed the names of participants in the CSMHI community projects in Estonia (1996–1999), but I will refer to them in the next chapter.

13. The most detailed description of the Tree Model appears in my book, *Killing in the Name of Identity* (Volkan 2006a).

One day at the CSMHI building at the University of Virginia, I was trying to explain to Steve Del Rosso, then the program director of the Pew Charitable Trust, what we planned to do in Estonia. I ended up drawing a tree on the blackboard. So, we named the intensive political/social vaccination we planned to carry out the "Tree Model."

Also see the Carter Center's special report on CSMHI/CRP's dialogue series with Estonians, Russians living in Estonia, and Russians from Russia (Neu and Volkan 1999).

**Chapter 21**

1. During the next dozen years after this very deadly shipwreck, many other conspiracy theories were put forward.

2. For those who are interested in how "disappearing fantasies" appear during psychoanalytic treatment of some individuals, see Volkan 2010b.

3. For examples, see Volkan 2006a.

4. There are diplomats such as W. Nathaniel Howell who are aware of the "playing" aspect of official diplomacy. Also the comparison between sports and diplomacy is not lost on the media, where sports metaphors abound as well, and phrases such as "Can Russia play hardball?" or "They need a new game plan" are often used in reports on international conflicts and diplomatic efforts to resolve them. One well-known event linking diplomacy and competitive sports was "ping-pong diplomacy." On April 6, 1971, the Chinese Communist government "unexpectedly"

invited the United States' ping-pong team, which was then in Japan for the 31st World Tennis Championship, to come to China. Four days later nine U.S. players, two spouses, and four officials crossed a bridge from Hong Kong, arrived in mainland China, and spent eight days there. All expenses were paid by the Chinese. They were the first Americans to visit China since 1949. This historical visit, during which the U.S. team played exhibition ping-pong matches with the Chinese team, began a new chapter between the two enemy nation-states. We now know that the United States and China had been quietly conducting back-channel talks beforehand, but ping-pong diplomacy paved the way for Richard Nixon's visit there the following year as the first U.S. president ever to visit China. During the 30th anniversary of ping-pong diplomacy, former U.S. secretary of state Henry A. Kissinger visited Beijing and played ping-pong with the Chinese vice-premier, once more symbolically linking a competitive sport with the diplomatic process.

Some NGOs attempting international "conflict resolution" seem to believe that in order to make peace between enemies—at least between their representatives who meet each other—they must "play" together. It is no wonder that some NGOs developed methodologies for conflict resolution that bring youngsters from enemy groups together to camps and playgrounds in neutral countries. These youngsters get to know each other by playing basketball, soccer, or other games. I suspect that some such NGO authorities are not familiar with psychoanalytic findings on children at play and the therapeutic benefits of such activities (for a review, see Yanof 2005); they are following their intuition, as well as the example provided by ping-pong diplomacy.

On many occasions when tensions were high between Cypriot Greeks and Cypriot Turks, high school students from each side were brought to vacation spots in the United States. Under the supervision of American facilitators they had dialogues, became involved in competitive games, and got to know each other. I know of another situation, this one involving adults, when high-level representatives, again from the two sides in Cyprus, were asked to play with toy plastic construction pieces, Legos, like small children would do, to build houses or trucks. In these situations, unlike what happened during ping-pong diplomacy, a third party forced the games on the representatives of the enemy groups. Perhaps at times such games initiated by a neutral third party were useful in breaking the ice between the enemy representatives and helped them work on a problem together. Often, however, they produce negative results. For example, the youngsters from opposing sides on Cyprus at the time could not continue to communicate with each other when they returned to the island because of the political division and the physical wall separating Cypriot Greeks and Turks. Furthermore, upon returning home some of the youngsters were perceived by their own people as traitors for playing with the enemy, causing psychological difficulties for some of them. In the case of the Lego exercise, I recall speaking with a high-level official who had participated in the exercise with an enemy representative, and he told me how humiliated he felt by being forced to behave like a little child. We can generalize and say that forcing a game on the representatives of opposing groups is like a therapist suggesting or ordering a patient to go to Disneyland to recover from his depression. It does not help.

A different type of "play" may take place during an enemy representatives' unofficial negotiation process, especially when a tense and dangerous situation exists, but it is not of the kind that can be compared to competitive sports or that which is forced upon negotiators by outsiders. This kind of play appears spontaneously within the interactions of the enemy negotiators after they unconsciously create their own *symbolic toys*. This play helps the negotiators develop empathy for the opposing group, tame the Other's realistic and fantasized sense of danger, and strengthen each group's large-group identity. As in our Estonia project, after such play more realistic and successful negotiations become possible.

**Chapter 22**

1. Jaan Kaplinski was interested in psychoanalysis and I, in turn, was fascinated to see once more how poets like Jaan "knew" things about human nature even before Sigmund Freud wrote about them.

2. Priit Järve, Director, Institute of International and Social Studies, Estonian Academy of Sciences, was appointed to replace Ants Paju. He considered CSMHI a partner as he embarked upon his new job and said that the "training" he had received during our series was an important factor in his appointment. At the same time Mare Haab, Researcher, Institute for International and Social Studies, and also a participant in the psychopolitical dialogue series, became a consultant to the Estonian minister of defense.

3. On September 14, 1995, Joyce Neu prepared a report on her observations during the language examinations. She wrote:

> These exams were among the most difficult that I have observed. Questions regarding the cultural life in Estonia were complex enough that my Estonian interpreter, who is herself a teacher, did not know the answers. . . . The aim of many of these questions was less to assess language proficiency than to ascertain the degree of affiliation with Estonian culture and perception in Estonian society.

4. With support from the Kettering Foundation, Endel Talvik and a leader of the Russians living in Estonia, Alexei Semionov, traveled to Dayton, Ohio, to participate in a Kettering training program on civic education and democratization.

5. Volkan 2006a. See also Apprey, M. (in collaboration with Krikk, V. Apprey, and Talvik) 2000.

6. The funds came from Pew Charitable Trust.

7. Neu and Volkan 1999.

8. Apprey, M. (in collaboration with Krikk, V. Apprey, and Talvik) 2000.

9. Maurice Apprey took the lead in helping to design and supervise the kindergarten project, and Margie Howell, Norman Itzkowitz, and Yuri Urbanovich joined him to make up the core CSMHI group. They worked closely with Ly Krikk and Endel Talvik. I was a participant-observer when, at the beginning and during the project, we would bring Estonian and Russian teachers together to conduct a series of psychopolitical dialogues in order to maintain a working relationship between them. In fact, when we were not in Estonia, Endel would meet with them once a week.

10. Volkan 2006a.

11. The most detailed description of CSMHI's work in Klooga and my personal observations can be found in *Killing in the Name of Identity: A Study of Bloody Conflicts* (Volkan 2006a).

12. Volkan 2006a, p. 247.

**Chapter 23**

1. Hopper 2003.

2. By inviting experts to Charlottesville, we also tried to learn about what was happening in various locations, such as certain South American countries and South Africa where CSMHI did not have projects. We also hosted Eisenhower Scholars (from South Korea and the Philippines). Eisenhower Fellowships, located in Philadelphia, was created in 1953 as a nonprofit organization. It brings mid-career professionals from many parts of the world to the United States to meet with government and nongovernment organizations for five to seven weeks in order to create a network of contacts and open international understanding and dialogues.

3. Volkan 1997, 2004.

4. In this volume I mentioned how CSMHI members conducted psychoanalytically informed interviews with many individuals from the same large group as an important part of assessing the existing shared psychopolitical processes in that large group. The reader can find a detailed example of such an interview with an Albanian woman whom I called Fazile Godo among my writing on Albania (Volkan 2004).

5. Cullen 1990.

6. Erikson 1985.

7. Volkan 1997.

8. Šebek 1992, 1994.

9. Volkan 2004.

10. Volkan 1980, 2009b.

11. Burns 1978.

12. Burns 1978, p. 16. In Burns' statement we hear an echo of Max Weber's (1923) classic description of charismatic leaders.

13. Erikson 1985.

**Chapter 24**

1. Kaufman, Rizzini, Wilson and Bush 2002.

2. Carr and Sloan 2003.

3. Frank 1988.

4. The World Bank Participation Sourcebook 1996, p. xi.

5. While writing this chapter, I benefited from Norman Itzkowitz's notes on our 1998 trip to Albania.

6. After an experience of disorganization or regression, the following signs illustrate movements toward societal well-being:

- Family, clan, and professional ties become more important in daily life than ties to political or religious ideologies and the personality of the political leader;
- Freedom of speech returns;
- Freedom of movement becomes available;
- The members of the large group begin preserving their individuality, questioning what is moral or immoral, beautiful or ugly, while developing the capacity for compromise without losing individual integrity;
- Raising new generations of children with good "basic trust" and maintaining existing traditional family structures becomes possible;
- A fair legal system and just functioning of economic and civic institutions are established;
- Religion is culturally utilized for "togetherness" and loses its power to be a tool for magical thinking, bad prejudice, or political propaganda;
- The devaluation of some groups, such as mentally or physically handicapped individuals, or women, children, or minority groups begins to disappear. Health and social care for the mentally or physically handicapped improves.
- Women, children, and minority group rights are respected;
- Sex crimes and hurting minorities decrease.

**Chapter 25**

1. For the causes of the Kuwaiti invasion by Saddam Hussein's forces; international, economic, diplomatic aspects of the First Gulf War; and the U.S. political and military issues concerning these events, see Hallion 1992 and Atkinson 1993.

During this war Iraq fired eighty-eight Iraqi-modified Scud missiles at Israel, Saudi Arabia, and Bahrain. Israel's counterattack on Iraq would have brought psychological complications to the Arab world and might have shattered the Allied coalition. Israel did not enter the war.

2. Howell 1993, p. 111.

3. Christina Smith, W. Scott Harrop, and Scott Waalkes also contributed to CSMHI's Kuwait project.

4. Howell 1993, p. 119. For the story of Ambassador Howell and the handful of Americans who remained in Kuwait surrounded by Iraqi troops and their ability to adjust in stressful conditions, see Culbertson and Howell 2001.

5. Margie Howell played a role in supporting these female institutions.

6. Interestingly, during the CSMHI members' work in Kuwait—I think even now—some *diwaniyas* had the names or nicknames of the American Universities to which the host had attended. For example, there was *The Tarheel Diwaniya*, the host of which had spent four years at the University of North Carolina at Chapel Hill in the late 1970s and early 1980s. He was still a Tarheel, following North Carolina basketball very closely. There was a small *diwaniya* called *Ohio State Diwaniya*.

7. Cheney 2011.

8. Saathoff 1995.

9. Volkan 1979, p. 159.

10. Saathoff 1995, p. 171.

11. Saathoff 1995, p. 171.

12. Saathoff 1995, p. 172.

13. Saathoff 1995, p. 172.

14. While he published M's story, Gregory Saathoff did not publish H's. I transcribe it here from Greg's notes.

15. Thomson 2000. In summarizing signs and symptoms of post-traumatic states in individuals, Thomson provides multiple examples from Kuwaitis he interviewed.

16. H never married. He maintained contact with Gregory Saathoff until 2007. He became a very rich banker. He would call Greg at least once a year and saw him when he visited the United States. In late 2007 an American friend of H called Greg to inform him that H had committed suicide. H's killing himself was attributed to his reaction to some complications in his business world, but Greg had no way of knowing if H's experiences in Kuwait after returning there as a member of the American army had left him suffering from some kind of post-traumatic stress. The one strange phenomenon that Greg kept wondering about was H's sending him yearly videos of people dying, like someone falling from a window or an airplane crash. H never explained why he was sending Greg such videos.

17. Saathoff 1996; Volkan 2000.

18. See also Volkan 1979 on children's "war games."

19. Saathoff 1996, p. 189.

20. Freud, A. 1936.

21. After the liberation and after removing Iraqi posters and billboards, the Kuwaiti government posted and broadcasted images of Iraqi atrocities. Nader, Pynoos, Fairbanks, al Ajeel, and al Asfour (1993) state that these actions increased children's post-trauma stress.

22. In psychoanalysis these developments are called "second individuation." See Blos 1979.

23. Howell 1995, pp. 168–169.

24. Howell 1995.

25. Saddam Hussein was found guilty of crimes against humanity by the Iraqi Special Tribunal after the Second Gulf War and was hanged on December 30, 2006.

**Chapter 26**

1. In November 1991 CSMHI received an invitation from Moldova and in February 1992 from Azerbaijan. Azerbaijan would renew its invitation in June 1992.

2. Eduard Shevardnadze had many positions and therefore many lives (see Shevardnadze 1991; and Ekedahl and Goodman 2001). He was the target of an assassination attempt in February 1998 by radical "Zviadists" terrorists. Later, he invited me to meet with him when I was in Tbilisi, but the day we were to meet new bloody skirmishes between Abkhazians and Georgians prevented it. I would never meet him. His presidency ended in 2003 when his previous fame and good name had faded due to allegations of corruption. He was replaced as president by Mikhail Saakashvili. On October 2012 Saakashvili's party was defeated in Georgian parliamentary elections. Most likely he will be replaced by Bidzina Ivanishvili.

3. In the summer of 1995 Joyce Neu and Yuri Urbanovich traveled to Georgia and also visited Abkhazia.

4. For its work in Georgia and South Ossetia between 1998 and 2002, CSMHI received three grants from the United States Institute of Peace and two grants from the International Research and Exchanges Board. We also used, with their permission, money provided to CSMHI for general use from the Massey Foundation and the William and Flora Hewlett Foundation for the Georgia–South Ossetia Project. Joyce Neu and Yuri Urbanovich's fact-finding tour was supported by the Carter Center.

5. For a report on Yuri Urbanovich's June 1995 and April 1997 trips to Georgia, see Urbanovich 1997.

6. For Nodar Sharjveladze's background and personal history, see Volkan 2006a. Other members included: Nino Makhashvili, child psychiatrist; Amiran Dolidze,

dramatist and screenwriter; Zurab Beberashvili, psychiatrist; Jana Javakhishvili, psychologist; Nato Sharjveladze, psychologist; David Charkviani, psychologist; Rezo Jorbenadze, social psychologist; Mamuka Erkomaishvili, teacher; and Lela Tsiskarishvili, medical student and interpreter. Manana Gabashvili, psychologist, was also associated with FDHR and was the deputy director, Regional Office of Caucasus, Norwegian Refugee Council.

7. While this city's legal name was Tskhinvali in the Republic of Georgia and was called as such by Georgians, South Ossetians referred to their city as Tskhinval. CSMHI needed to pay attention to these kinds of minor differences in order not to offend any party.

8. South Ossetian caretakers were: Venera Basishvili, Director of the Tskhinvali Youth Palace of Child Creativity; Arina Juyeva, Head, Division of Cultural Activities at the Youth Palace; Rusika Gobozova, Cultural Activities Organizer at the Youth Palace; Madina Gazzaeva, Professor of Psychology, South Ossetia State University; and Aliona Siukayeva, psychologist; and Irene Bekoeva, English teacher.

9. Our Georgian contacts included: Gela Charkviani, Special Assistant to President Shevardnadze; Avtandil Jorbenadze, Georgian Minister of Public Health; Givi Shugarov, Member of the Georgian Parliament and Chairman of the Parliamentary Group in Charge of Cooperation with the United States Congress; David Japaridze, Senior Adviser to the Georgian Minister of Refugees and Accommodations; Genrikh Mouradian, Head of Administration ("Gamgebeli" in Georgian) of Akhalkalaki region, where 96 percent of residents are ethnic Armenians; Archil Soulakaouri, well-known abstract painter who painted pictures of the civil war in which he participated and was wounded; Nina Kipshidze, art historian; Dali Pardjanadze, Dean of the Faculty of Psychology, Tbilisi State University; Valeriy Chokashvili, historian; and Alexander Rondeli, historian.

Nana Sumbadze, professor of psychology, Tbilisi State University was involved directly with our meetings with the FDRH members. CSMHI met with her separately on many occasions. In 2000, through Sumbadze I was asked to consult with the Georgian Foreign Ministry about problems involved in the proposed repatriating to Georgia of around 120,000 formerly exiled Meshketian Turks who used to live in the Meshketi region of Georgia near the Turkish border. In 1944 Stalin had exiled them, in most tragic ways, to settle in other parts of the Soviet Union. Now, they had their own civil/political organizations and the idea of their resettlement in Meshketi was in the air. Some European governments and organizations were putting pressure on Georgia to be "truly" democratic and take back the Meshketians within a year or so. Armenians living in Georgia had settled in the location where Meshketians had lived decades ago. To start a fast project to put the Meshketians back in this location without major preparations might start another major tragedy—this time between Armenians in Georgia and Meshketians—as if Georgia did not have enough problems. On the other hand, the Georgian authorities did not wish to appear to reject the suggestions from Europe. Andy Thomson joined me in preparing a written response to the European's "suggestions," in which Georgians appeared very sympathetic to the Europeans' ideas while gently explaining that they needed much more time than just a year or so to genuinely look into this matter. The Georgian Foreign Ministry, as far as I know, used our letter without making any changes to it. Nana Sumbadze has kept in contact with me and shared her research findings on various societal issues in Georgia.

Contacts in South Ossetia: Kosta Dzugayev, Chairman of the South Ossetian Parliament; Murat Dzhioyev, South Ossetian Minister of Foreign Affairs; Fatima Poukhayeva, Counselor to the President of South Ossetia.

Other contacts: Redjeb Jordania and Nicole Jordania (Redjeb is the son of Noe Jordania, President of the Democratic Republic of Georgia from July 24, 1918 to March 18, 1921. Georgia had a brief independence during this period of time, before the Soviets took over Georgia and forced Noe Jordania to flee to France); Kent Brown, former U.S. Ambassador to Georgia; Gia Tarkhan-Mouravi, UNDP, Georgia; Kent Larson, Chief, Office of Humanitarian Response/Social Transition, USAID/Caucasus; John Andrew, Head of UNHCR Mobile Team, Georgia; and Hans Dieset, Resident Representative, Norwegian Refugee Council.

10. What is described here is another example of "psychic reality," this time shared by a small group of individuals.

11. Heath 1991.

12. Since I did not work with Chechens in this location I will not give a background summary of their long history and their fights with Russians. The events I refer to here began in August 1999 when Chechens entered neighboring Dagestan, initiating a furious and deadly Russian offensive against Chechnya. In February 2000, then acting Russian president Vladimir Putin declared that the war was over, although the Chechen rebels would sporadically continue their campaign with hit-and-run attacks.

13. The Black and Caspian Sea gender identity and family violence project aimed to draw profiles of victims and perpetrators of family violence in Georgia, South Ossetia, and Turkey (with references to similar situations in Armenia and Abkhazia) through the collaborative research of participants from the above locations and experts from the Center for the Study of Mind and Human Interaction. Gender issues and family violence appear to be everywhere in the world. During our research we focused on the role of the existing extended family situations in the geographical areas of our project and cultural barriers to examining violence that is directed toward women and children.

Traditional extended family structure, by itself, does not cause family violence or dysfunction. When a society is destabilized by wars, ethnic tensions, social upheaval, urbanization, poverty, displacement of populations, or changes in the gender balance of the workforce (e.g., women obtaining a higher working status outside of the home), aspects of the family structure that once strengthened the individual and society may suddenly become harmful or destructive. Family violence or dysfunction can emerge under the pressures of social breakdown or be caused by pathological forces within the family itself; often these two causes are intertwined. Sometimes, members of a family unconsciously "pick" a specific individual, a woman or a child, to be the family scapegoat.

14. Irina Yanovskaya, Fatima Turmanova, and Gana Yanosskaya from South Ossetia accompanied Madina Gazzaeva from the Youth Palace. I would keep in e-mail contact with Irina Yanovskaya, a journalist and human rights worker until the 2008 war between Georgians and South Ossetians.

The following is a list of other participants in the IREX project from countries besides Georgia, South Ossetia, and CSMHI:

From Armenia: Dina Munukian, psychologist; Irina Tsatourian, lawyer.

From Abkhazia: Logua Khatuna, an NGO leader.

From Turkey: Işıl Vahip, psychiatrist; Müge Kocadere, psychologist; Özge Doğanavşargil, psychiatrist; Çağdaş Eker, psychiatrist; and Seval Sekin, Director, Women's Studies Center, Ege University.

From Sweden: Birgitta Johansson, psychiatrist.

From the United States: Ali Gallaher, lawyer and psychoanalyst; and Kerry Leavitt, social worker.

15. In Georgia, even before the IREX project started, breaking the taboo, CSMHI gave public talks about family violence and sexual abuse at Tbilisi University to large audiences. We also arranged a smaller meeting in the Georgian Ombudsman's conference room where the ombudsman, the commissioners of mental health, and leaders or representatives of ten NGOs dealing with civil issues were present. President Eduard Shevardnadze gave an order on February 25, 2000, for an "Action Plan on Combating Violence against Women." We were pleased that Georgian authorities listened to us. Late in 2000, the Georgian Center for Psychological and Medical Rehabilitation Center of Torture Victims (GCRT) opened, led by FDHR member Nino Makhashvili. GCRT and FDHR began collaborating and cooperating with each other. GCRT, besides serving the medical and psychological needs of individual torture victims and their families, opened the first center for abused women in Georgia and gave credit to CSMHI for helping bring the issue of violence against women out in the open. As part of the IREX program we even brought to Tbilisi a number of young South Ossetian rape victims with their moth-

ers, and at GCRT Georgian and CSMHI professionals tried their best to provide psychological counseling. GCRT also provided the South Ossetian professionals assigned to help the rape victims with telephone supervision and support from FDHR (Georgian) psychologists and psychiatrists.

16. Volkan 2006a. On January 25, 2004, Mikhail Saakashvilli became the president of Georgia after widespread protests against Eduard Shevardnadze—the so-called Rose Revolution—and was reelected in January 2008. On August 7 and 8, 2008, Georgia attacked South Ossetia and captured most of Tskhinvali, the capital of South Ossetia. I wondered, as did some of my Georgian friends with whom I corresponded, about what really made Saakashvilli take that action, since everyone knew that Russia would then intervene. Russia did intervene right away and within five days the Russian and South Ossetian military forced Georgian troops to retreat. Russians entered Georgia proper and occupied some cities and also sent their marines to Abkhazia, and Abkhazia then opened a second war front against Georgia. On August 12, especially through mediation by the French, a cease-fire took place and Russian forces left Georgia proper. Now, it appears that Georgia lost hope of keeping both South Ossetia and Abkhazia within Georgian territory.

The International Society for Health and Human Rights held an international meeting in Tbilisi on October 6–9, 2011. They asked me to give a seminar and be their keynote speaker. I arrived in Tbilisi two days before the meeting started and spent a week there. Nino Makhashvili met me at 3:00 a.m. at the airport—a new and modern one. This was my first indication that changes had taken place in Tbilisi. I was taken to my luxury hotel and was shocked when I realized that this place was the sixteen-story building where thousands of IDPs used to live on top of each other, so to speak, during my previous trips to Tbilisi. The next day I met most of my old FDHR friends. I learned that they were busy and productive, constantly working to better their society or doing peace work in Georgia and elsewhere.

**Chapter 27**

1. Kris 1943, p. 282.
2. Chakotin 1939, p. 34.
3. Jowett and O'Donnell 1992.
4. Lewis 2000.
5. Benjamin Franklin was a member of this commission.
6. Le Bon 1895.
7. Freud 1921a.
8. Le Bon 1910.
9. Lasswell 1938, p. v.

10. Brown 1963, p. 91.

11. Lasswell 1938, p. v.

12. Hitler 1925-1926, p. 180.

13. Kris 1943, p. 388.

14. Volkan 2004.

15. Lifton 1961; Buckman 1977.

16. Volkan 2009b.

17. Besides Ernst Kris (1943, 1944), Roger E. Money-Kyrle (1941), and Edward Glower (1947) examined the psychodynamics of political propaganda.

18. Kris 1943.

**Chapter 28**

1. Only after Croatia became an independent country could Eduard Klain become a member of the International Society of Psychoanalysis.

2. Volkan 1996, 1997. For more on Christoslavism, see Sells 1996, 2002.

3. Emmert 1990.

4. Early chronicles of the Battle of Kosovo did not specify the name of Sultan Murad's assassin. One version of the story says that a small group of Lazar's soldiers slipped through Turkish defenses and one was able to stab Murad. Another says Lazar himself led this group, while a 1497 account identifies Miloš Kobila (or Kobilić or Obravitch), one of Lazar's son-in-laws who had been accused of being a traitor prior to the battle, as the heroic assassin. After some time, Miloš was accepted as the actual assassin.

5. Marković 1983, p. 111.

6. Marković 1983.

7. Kaplan 1993, p. 39; also see Vulliamy 1994.

8. I wrote elsewhere about how I studied the personality of Slobodan Milosević, his and his associates' 1989 reactivation of the Serbian chosen trauma, and Serbian propaganda at the time. My studies benefited from my interviews with Horst Grabert, who was the German ambassador to Belgrade in those days and who knew Milosević well, and with Hasan Aygün, who led the Turkish embassy in Belgrade in the absence of an official ambassador. See Volkan 1997.

9. Gutman 1993, p. x.

10. Allen 1996. Also see Stiglmayer 1994.

11. My first trip to independent Croatia was supported by funds from the Soros Foundation.

12. Vukovar reverted to Croatian control in 1998. Today both Croats and Serbs make up the city's population, although to a great extent they still live separate lives.

13. Besides knowing Eduard Klain and Rudolf Gregurek, I developed a close

relationship with Croatian psychiatrists Gorana Tocilij-Šimunković and Ivan Urlic and I was available for consultations. Through Vedran Bilić I could reach younger Croat psychiatrists. Ljiljana Milivojević from Serbia was present when I was in Zagreb, and she came to most of the meetings in Dubrovnik.

14. See Wilson and Drozdek 2004 and Drozdek and Wilson 2007.

15. Volkan 2006a.

16. Jurcević and Urlić 2002, p. 234.

**Chapter 29**

1. Arnett 2002, p. 781.

2. Volkan 1993.

3. Elovitz and Kahn 1997.

4. For "culture shock," see Ticho 1971 and Garza-Guerrero 1974.

5. Akhtar 1999, 2010. For other significant contributions on the psychology of immigrants, see Grinberg and Grinberg 1989.

6. Mahler 1968.

7. Blos 1979.

8. See Dasen 2000, Schlegel 2001, and Arnett 2002 describing how adolescents are influenced by globalization. In a sense, like Akhtar 1999 and 2010, they connect the adolescence individuation process to how youngsters assimilate "global brands" (Schlegel 2001, p. 6), ranging from T-shirts to soft drinks to music and global culture as they perceive it.

9. Julius 1992, p. 56.

10. Kris 1975, p. 467.

11. Stein 1993, p. 87.

12. Volkan 2006b.

13. See: Report drawn up on behalf of the European Parliament's Committee of Inquiry into Racism and Xenophobia prepared by Glyn Ford, Luxemburg: Office for Official Publications of the European Communities, 1991; Report on Racial Violence and Harassment in Europe prepared by Robin Oakley for the Council of Europe, April 16, 1992; and Report on Elimination of Racial Discrimination: Measures to Combat Racism and Racial Discrimination and the Role of the Sub-Commission prepared by Sub-Commission on Prevention of Discrimination and Protection of Minorities. Economic and Social Council, United Nations (E/CN.4/Sub.2/1992/11), July 14, 1992.

14. Darwin 1859.

15. Some of my experiences at Cherry Hospital are reported in my introduction to my book, *Psychoanalytic Technique Expanded: A Textbook of Psychoanalytic Treatment* (Volkan 2010b).

16. See: Report drawn up on behalf of the European Parliament's Committee of Inquiry into Racism and Xenophobia prepared by Glyn Ford, Luxemburg: Office for Official Publications of the European Communities, 1991, pp. 59, 83 and Report on Elimination of Racial Discrimination: Measures to Combat Racism and Racial Discrimination and the Role of the Sub-Commission prepared by Sub-Commission on Prevention of Discrimination and Protection of Minorities. Economic and Social Council, United Nations, 1992, p. 10.

17. Members of the Committee on Neo-Racism at the Center for the Study of Mind and Human Interaction (1993) were: Maurice Apprey, Lisa Beard, Abdülkadir Çevik, William Greer, Anatoly Golubovsky, Dieter Gröschel, Max Harris, W. Nathaniel Howell, Eveline Speedie, J. Anderson Thomson, Vamık Volkan, and Yuri Urbanovich (See Thomson, Harris, Volkan, and Edwards 1995).

18. Maurice Apprey, a professor of psychiatry and a psychoanalyst, is also the Dean of African-American Affairs at the University of Virginia.

**Chapter 30**

1. This meeting was organized by World Information Transfer, a nongovernmental organization, and was cosponsored by United Nations Department of Public Information.

2. Levine 2005.

3. Akhtar 2009.

4. I described the story of conflict pertaining to these two rocks in Volkan 1997.

5. Retired Ambassador Gündüz Aktan; the former Chief of the Turkish Armed Forces General Necip Torumtay; retired Air Force General Şadi Ergüvenç; Professor of Sociology Akile Gürsoy from Yeditepe University in Istanbul; professor of International Relations Hasan Ünal from Bilkent University in Ankara; and Professor of Political Science Tözün Bahçeli, University of Western Ontario, were members of the Turkish team. Bahçeli was born in Cyprus.

6. McCarthy 1995.

7. Kemal Atatürk died in 1938. See Volkan and Itzkowitz 1984, 1994, 2011.

8. McCarthy 1995.

9. Members of the Greek team: Professor Nikiforos Diamandouros, Greek Ombudsman; Professor Thalia Dragonas from the University of Athens; Dr. Dimitris Kerides; Professor Cesar Mavratsas, Cyprus University (also a Greek Cypriot); Hellenic Air Force General George Scarlatos; and Alexis Papahelas, Editor, *To Vima*.

10. General (ret.) Necip Torumtay, Dimitris Kerides, and Alexis Papahelas did not attend the meeting in Caux. This meeting was funded by the Winston Foundation, the U.S. Information Service-Ankara, and the U.S. embassy in Athens.

**Chapter 31**

1. Dobson and Payne 1982.

2. See *Patterns of Global Terrorism: 1990*. Washington, DC: United States Department of State Publications, 9862, April 1991.

3. UN General Assembly: *Resolutions and Decisions Adopted by the General Assembly during Its Fortieth Session*. Supplement, No: 53 (A/40/53), Official Record, New York, 1986.

4. For example, see Crenshaw 1986 and Laqueur 1987.

5. CSMHI's Committee on Terrorism was also sponsored by the Office of the Turkish Permanent Representative to the United Nations in Geneva. The members of this committee were Maurice Apprey, Lisa Beard, Anatoly Golubovsky, Max Harris, W. Nathaniel Howell, Katherine Kennedy, Eveline Speedie, J. Anderson Thompson, Vamık Volkan, Carroll Weinberg, and Yuri Urbanovich.

6. From H. D. S. Greenway, "Roots of Ethnic Hatred," *Boston Globe*, December 13, 1992, p. 42.

7. UN Resolution 2625 (XXV) states: "No action is authorized or encouraged [by the principle of self-determination] which would dismember or impair, totally or in part, the integrity or political unity of sovereign and independent states conducting themselves in compliance with the principle of equal rights and self-determination of peoples and thus possessed of a government representing the whole people belonging to the territory without distinction as to race, creed or colour."

8. Mack 1979 pp. xvi–xvii.

9. See for example, Weinberg 1992; Lomasky 1991.

10. Weinberg 1992, p. 78.

11. Post 1990, p. 26.

12. Montville 1990. p.163.

13. Clark 1983.

14. Post 1990, pp. 37–38.

15. Ornstein 2012, p. 10. For more information about these terms, except for "doubling," see Akhtar 2009.

Anna Ornstein (2012) suggested that persons such as Adolph Eichmann and Joseph Mengele who planned mass murders during the Nazi period most likely used "doubling," and those persons who actually committed mass murders utilized "dis-association" and/or "disavowal." She does not write about terrorist cell leaders and actual terrorist, but what she says about "planners" and "executioners" most likely applies also to those who plan terrorism and those who actually murder people.

16. Our report was distributed at the United Nations in Geneva and was also published (Volkan and Harris 1995).

**Chapter 32**

1. Janet Reno was United States Attorney General from 1993 to 2001. She was the first female U.S. attorney general.

2. Marvick 1986.

3. Barkun 1986, 1996, 2006.

4. Balmer 1989.

5. The southern bank of Hebron is the location where the historic "Cave of Patriarchs" is located. It is believed that the tombs of Prophet Abraham and his family members are in this cave. Above this cave stands Ibrahimi Mosque (Mosque of Abraham), which has existed since 1206 and was the place where the mass murder took place. The Cave of Patriarchs also includes a section for the Jews to worship. At this historical place symbolic mental representations of two religions stand next to each other *in a concrete way*. There are rules and customs for worshipping at this location, creating a "psychological border." For example, ten days each year the entire cave is utilized by Jews and on another ten days Muslims are allowed to use it.

In February 1994 the Muslim religious holiday Ramadan and Jewish religious holiday Purim overlapped. I believe that under such a "psychological situation" certain skirmishes occurred between Muslims and Israelis and led to Baruch Goldstein's involvement in mass murder. Despite the outrageousness of this atrocity, Baruch Goldstein is seen as a martyr by some right-wing religious fundamentalist Jews. The following is written on his tombstone: "Here lies the saint, Dr. Baruch Kappel Goldstein, blessed be the memory of the righteous and holy man, may the Lord avenge his blood, who devoted his soul to the Jews, Jewish religion and Jewish land. His hands are innocent and his heart is pure. He was killed as a martyr of God on the 14th of Adar, Purim, in the year 5754 (1994)." The burial site has been turned into a small shrine.

6. Marty and Appleby 1995.

7. Barkun 1997.

8. For the classical definition of "repetition compulsion," see Freud 1920.

9. I wrote about David Koresh in *Blind Trust: Large Groups and Their Leaders in Times of Crises and Terror* (Volkan 2004).

10. Wessinger 1997.

11. Volkan 2004.

12. Why do some persons, metaphorically speaking, wrap themselves in a religious cloth and become leaders of extreme fundamentalist religious cults when mostly by chance environmental conditions help them to achieve this? CSMHI held an academic meeting on this topic in October 1995. My hunch is that because I organized a meeting on this theme, the FBI asked me in December 1995 to chair the Select Advisory Commission to the FBI's Critical Incident Response Group

(CIRG). Psychiatrist and psychoanalyst Peter Olsson was present in Charlottesville during the CSMHI meeting and other occasions. I learned from him about the psychology of what he termed "malignant pied pipers" of our time (see Olsson 2005). Another psychoanalyst, Stanley Cath, contributed a long paper on this topic to *Mind and Human Interaction* (Cath 1996). As a clinician, I never studied a cult leader in my office or on my couch. However, I worked with persons who were not psychotic, in fact who were "individuals with good professions," but who also had fundamentalist religious beliefs (Volkan 2010b). A person's holding on to religion as if his or her life depends on this clinging may have various reasons for doing so. Imagine a person who is born into an extremely religious family and community. This person may become deeply religious because that is what belonging to the family and the community demanded. But, turning to religion and hiding under its cloth usually is related to some problems in an individual's identity formation.

When I was working or visiting different mental hospitals in the United States and Turkey, I met people who identified with Jesus, Moses, or Muhammad. Religiousness has been shown to be highly prevalent among psychiatric patients, especially among those with schizophrenia (see Kroll and Sheehan 1989; G. Kirov, Kemp, K. Kirov, and David 1998; Pieper 2004). An interdisciplinary (psychiatrists, theologians, and others) team from Switzerland collected data from over one hundred patients and illustrated that "religion may be a manifestation of psychosis as well as a coping behavior that patients use to help them deal with symptoms" (Mohr, Brandt, Borras, Gilliéron, and Huguelet 2006, p. 1952).

My clinical experiences, participation in the FBI commission, and learning from colleagues helped me to understand the psychology of some cult or *tarikat* leaders.

13. Salande and Perkins 2011.

14. Weber 1999; Wessinger 1999; Moses-Hrushovski 2000; Volkan 2004; and Olsson 2005.

15. Many of the "New Religions" in Japan are also led by women. But even while this is true, as John Stratton Hawley and Wayne Proudfoot (1994) state, Japan's "New Religions" extol the return to the "Golden Age" when women were entirely dependant upon men in Japan.

16. Sivan 1985.

17. Wessinger 1999, pp. 51–52.

18. Mills 1979, p. 13.

19. For detailed information of this event, see Robert Marquand, "The Reclusive Ruler Who Runs the Taliban," *Christian Science Monitor*, October, 10, 2001, and Volkan 2004. Some people of Kandahar reportedly believe that the prophet's cloak can cure the sick and heal the lame. It had only been removed from its vault

on two previous occasions: in 1929 when King Emanullah invoked it to unify the country, and again in 1935 when authorities turned to the relic to stop a cholera epidemic in the city.

20. Volkan 2004. Also see Olsson 2008.

**Chapter 33**

1. Lewis 1990.
2. Howell 1997, p. 100.
3. Lewis 1990, p. 59.
4. For details, see: Itzkowitz 1972, p. 33.
5. Kayatekin 2008.
6. İnalcık 1987; Ortaylı 2003.
7. Yavuz 1995, p. 368. Also see Mutman 1992–1993.
8. Yavuz 1995, p. 348.
9. Kayatekin 2008.
10. Kayatekin 2008.
11. Volkan and Itzkowitz 1984.
12. Kedourie 1970.
13. Toynbee 1933–1948.
14. MacEoin 1983.
15. Landes 2001.
16. Howell 2001, p. 148.
17. Volkan 2004.
18. Olsson 2008.
19. The poem that Peter Olsson examined through a psychoanalytic lens was earlier published in the *New York Times* on April 7, 2002, called "The Travail of a Child Who Has Left the Land of the Holy Shrines." Osama bin Laden coauthored this poem with Dr. Abd-ar-Rahman (Olsson 2008).
20. Olsson 2008, p. 113. For more information about Osama bin Laden, see Bergen 2006.
21. Islam does not permit suicide. But those planners and designers of Islamic terrorism found ways to allow and even encourage suicide bombing by referring to certain passages in the Koran:

> Allah does not forbid you to deal justly and kindly with those who fought not against you on account of religion nor drove you out of your homes. Verily, Allah loves those who deal with equity. . . . It is only as regards to those who fought against you on account of religion, and have driven you out of your homes, and helped to drive you out, that Allah forbids you to befriend them. (Surah 60, Verses 8 and 9)

22. For a description of how Palestinian suicide bombers were trained, see Volkan 2004. I also described education in *madrassas* in Pakistan, which indirectly in-

cluded training in the service of future violence. Such *madrassas* existed in Pakistan before Osama bin Laden arrived in neighboring Afghanistan and before the Taliban, for all practical purposes, took control of that country. The teaching in these *madrassas* was influenced by Deobandi and Wahabi versions of extreme religious "ideology" (Rashid 2000).

**Chapter 34**

1. From President George W. Bush's speech in Ontario, California, January 5, 2002.

2. In 2005, I found a paper by a psychology professor who originally came from Iran, Fathali Moghaddam of Georgetown University in Washington, DC, and noted that he used a metaphor very similar to mine. See Moghaddam 2005.

3. Volkan 2001.

**Chapter 35**

1. See "Rev'd Up: Archbishop Desmond Tutu Looks Back, Definitely Not in Anger," by L. Duke. *Washington Post*, October 9, C1 and C8. According to Lynne Duke, Archbishop Tutu made this statement during Bill Clinton's Global Initiative Annual Meeting, September, 20–22, 2006, in New York.

2. Freud 1927, 1939.

3. Freud 1901, p. 19.

4. Winnicott 1953.

5. Winnicott 1953, p. 16.

6. Binswanger 1956, p. 115.

7. Waelder 1960, p. 59.

8. Leowald 1978, p. 57.

9. For example, see Meissner 1984, 1990.

10. Meissner 1990, p. 114.

11. Meissner 1990, p. 107.

12. Meissner 1990, p. 107.

13. Sokolowski 1990.

14. Blass 2004. An edited book by Salman Akhtar includes a psychoanalytic examination of aspects of Muslim experiences (Akhtar 2008).

15. Winnicott 1953.

16. Greenacre 1970.

17. Modell 1970.

18. Volkan 1976.

19. Erikson 1956.

20. Werner and Kaplan 1963.

21. Thomson (with Aukofer) 2011, p. 116.
22. Thomson (with Aukofer) 2011, p. 114.

**Chapter 36**

1. Jörg Haider was the leader of the Austrian Freedom Party and later chairperson of the Alliance for the Future of Austria who died in a car accident in 2008. While he was involved in politics he actually praised Nazi ideas and was anti-Semitic.

2. I learned a great deal from Esra Kilaf when I visited her on several occasions in her municipal department in Vienna, where she was responsible for integration projects and subsidies. She especially is an expert on health issues of Turkish immigrant women. See Kilaf 2008.

3. I am grateful to painter Wolf Werdigier, who helped me a great deal in understanding the reactivation of the Austrian chosen glory of 1683.

4. See Barker 1967; Shaw and Shaw 1976–1977; Halecki 1992; and Stoye 2006.

5. See, for example, Doris Helmberger, "Dann werden wir bosartig," *Die Furche*, May 4, 2006; Vamık Volkan, "Aufgeklärte Beschneidung," *Die Zeit*, May 18, 2006; Caroline Fetcher, "al-Qaida auf der Couch," *Der Tagesspiel*, June 14, 2006; Klaus Englert, "Varaus besteht das Zelt?" *Der Freitag*, June 16, 2006; von Boris Kalnoky, "Warum sich Türken und Europäer Angiften?" *Die Welt Politik*, October 15, 2007.

6. When the former secretary-general of the United Nations, Kurt Waldheim, sought election as president of Austria, for the second time, in 1986, an international controversy erupted. Waldheim was accused of lying about his military service and his knowledge of Nazi crimes. The Waldheim affair prompted the postwar Austrians' search for Austria's Nazi legacy.

7. The European Monitoring Center on Racism and Xenophobia (EUMC) was established in 1998 and lasted until the beginning of 2007. Then it evolved as the European Union Agency for Fundamental Rights (FRA). Beatte Winkler, who was the director of EUMC in March 2007, became the interim director of FRA.

8. An editorial in the *International Herald Tribune* titled "Walls for Gypsies" on October 23, 1999, compared the wall in Usti nad Labem with "Europe's 20th-century pathologies—Communism and Nazism" (p. 10). This editorial also acknowledged that when Social Democrats took over the Czech government in 1998, they began programs to change this situation, but much more work needed to be done.

9. The Budapest Workshop was primarily developed by Zsuzsa Sipos, who is originally from Hungary and is a group analyst who was connected with the Tavistock Clinic in London.

**Chapter 37**

1. Hottinger 1977, p. 81.

2. In 2012 General Kenan Evren, who had become the seventh president of Turkey after the 1980 events, faced legal charges for his role in the military coup d'état. As of this writing, his trial has just begun.

In September 2012, three hundred Turkish ex–military officers, including two former generals and a retired admiral, were sentenced to prison terms. They had been accused of activities a decade earlier to "overthrow the government by force." The public reaction to this event has been very mixed.

3. Yavuz 2003.

4. Islamic banking follows the principles of *sharia* (Islamic law). Islamic banks do not invest in business and activities considered contrary to *sharia*.

5. Also see Smith 2005.

6. Sharon-Krespin 2009.

7. Thomson 2003.

8. See article in *Milliyet,* September 12, 2006, p. 12 by A. Hasan.

9. See *Hürriyet,* September 13, 2006.

10. See *Sabah,* September 21, 2006.

11. Turkish channel ATV, June 18, 1999.

12. Sharon-Krespin 2009, p. 66.

13. See, for example, the edited book on the Gülen movement by Yavuz and Esposito, 2003. The authors in this book examine religious concepts but do not refer to hijacking religion for political purposes or its possible dangerous consequences, especially robbing women of their human rights.

14. Turkey had its first female physician in 1926, first female lawyer in 1927, first female judge in 1930, and first female pilot in 1932. When I was in medical school in Ankara in the early 1950s, one third of my class was women. The Atatürk revolution was protective of women's rights.

15. Later I also published a book in Turkish on this topic with Nuriye Atabey, then a Turkish television talk show host. See Volkan and Atabey 2010.

16. President Abdullah Gül was born in 1950 in middle Anatolia, in a city called Kayseri. He was trained as an economist and worked with the Islamic Developmental Bank in Jeddah, Saudi Arabia, from 1983 to 1991 when he started his political career as a member of the Islamist Welfare Party. He had experience in foreign affairs as a Turkish representative in the Council of Europe Parliamentary Assembly. In 2001, Gül left the Welfare Party, joined forces with Recep Tayyıp Erdoğan, the present-day Turkish prime minister, to found a new party, the Justice and Development Party (AKP). Before becoming the 11th president of the Turkish Republic he served as prime minister (only four months) in 2002–2003 and was minister of foreign affairs from 2003 to 2007.

17. Volkan 2006a.

18. In January 2012 a militant nationalist named Yasin Hilal was sentenced to life imprisonment for murdering Hrant Dink. His two accomplices were also sentenced to twelve years each. But the Armenian community in Istanbul and many liberal Turkish intellectuals were most disappointed with the Turkish government and judiciary for not investigating a wider plot.

19. See "Turkey-Armenia Relations Boosted by President's Historic Trip," *Telegraph*, September 7, 2008.

**Chapter 38**

1. Atakol 2012.

2. This is done in line with "Protocol 10 of the Accession Treaty 2003."

3. I observed this not only in the Cypriot Turkish real, and later invisible, enclaves but also in other locations in the world where refugees or internally displaced people are located (Volkan 2006a).

4. In official dialogues between representatives of Cypriot Turks and Cypriot Greeks, the land issue—who owns what land legally and how to make exchanges—is a primary obstacle to finding a "solution" for the "Cyprus problem."

5. Ortaylı 2007.

6. Khan 2002, p. 45.

7. Khan 2002, p. 44.

8. For the Cypriot Greek reaction to "Cypriotism," see Mavratsas 1997.

9. Rauf Denktaş was the President of the Turkish Republic of Northern Cyprus (TRNC) from its founding in 1983 until 2005. He was a special friend of mine. Since he and I were close, some people wondered if we discussed politics when we were alone. This was never the case. He would not ask my opinion about internal or external politics and I never offered a political suggestion to him. For me he was a wonderful family man, a photographer, a prolific writer, and a storyteller who loved his pet dogs and birds. Since I knew a great deal about his personal life, the tragedies he had gone through—losing his mother when he was a very small boy and losing three of his children when he was an adult—this made him a "hero" in my mind. He was able to sublimate his feelings over his losses and invest his incredible energy in doing things for his people who were themselves experiencing tremendous losses. While he held political power for a very long time, he was never an oppressive leader. He loved people. He used to tell me how much he envied me because I could travel freely while he, as a political figure, had to restrict his desire to travel for fun. Being around Denktaş, nevertheless, indirectly taught me a great deal about the psychology of leadership and leader-follower relationships.

10. There were reasons why the Cypriot Greeks rejected the Annan Plan, such as the prospect of a huge number of Turkish settlers receiving citizenship and Cy-

priot Greeks' doubts about Turkey's promise to withdraw its troops from the island. Also see Varnava and Faustmann 2009.

11. Later the Cypriot Turkish government stopped "erasing" this story from school books.

12. Earlier I wrote about my reasons for not getting involved professionally in Cypriot Turkish–Cypriot Greek problems. This meeting was on identity problems in the TRNC and societal and political issues between the TRNC and Turkey. Without the efforts of Tarık Çelenk and Murat Sofuoğlu from Ekopolitik, this meeting would not have taken place. The participants were: Işılay Arkan, from the Turkish-Islamic Society; Kenan Atakol, former TRNC Minister of Foreign Affairs; İsmail Bozkurt, former TRNC Minister of Culture, Scholar, Eastern Mediterranean University; Taner Erginer, former Chief of TRNC High Court; Hüseyin Gökçekuş, assistant Rector, Near East University; Hüseyin Gürşan, adviser to the TRNC president; Hasan Hastürer, news reporter; İzzet İzcan, political activist; Hasan Kahvecioğlu; news reporter; Zeliha Khasman, Chairwoman, Department of Political Science, Near East University; Sibel Siber, parliamentarian and physician; Emine Sömek, political activist; Yusuf Suiçmez, Head of Religious Affairs, TRNC; Emine Sütcü, news reporter; Fevzi Tanpınar, TRNC Foreign Press Association.

13. This time former TRNC presidential undersecretary Ergün Olgun joined us. We had well-known columnists present, such as Kadri Gürsel and academicians such as Murat Belge from Turkey.

**Chapter 39**

1. In 1933, Albert Einstein lived in France and was the honorary president of the Society for the Protection of the Health of the Jewish Population (OZE). In a letter, Einstein asked the president of the Cabinet of Ministers of Turkey "to allow forty professors and doctors from Germany to continue their scientific and medical work in Turkey. The above mentioned cannot practice further in Germany on account of the laws governing there now. The majority of these men possesses vast experience, knowledge and scientific merits and could prove very useful when settling in a new country." OZE would pay their salaries during the first year of their stay in Turkey. The letter ends as follows: "In supporting this application, I take the liberty to express my hope, that in granting this request your Government will not only perform an act of high humanity, but will also bring profit to your own country." Einstein's request was sent to the Turkish Ministry of Education, which rejected this proposal on the grounds that there were no precedents for accepting such an unusual request. But, in the long run, Einstein's request was accepted. At that time the Turkish Republic, born from the ashes of the Ottoman Empire, was only ten years old and extremely poor. Turkey had accepted some German-Jewish scholars

to come to Turkey even before Einstein's request (see, for example, the article by Feza Günergün from the Department of History of Science, Istanbul University, in the Turkish daily newspaper, *Cumhuriyet*, Science and Technology Supplement, November 3. 2006). Following Einstein's letter, thirty German-Jewish scholars and their families came to Turkey, and eventually 190 other intellectuals and their families arrived. Ultimately, over 1,000 lives were saved by this action (Reisman 2006).

2. Volkan and Itzkowitz 1984.

3. Also reported in McDowall 1996, p. 188.

4. McDowall 1996.

5. See footnote 9.

6. See also Robert Olson's interpretation of the emergence of Kurdish nationalism (Olson 1989).

7. The only time I noticed extreme prejudice against Kurds in Turkey was when I attended a meeting in Mersin, a city on the Mediterranean coast, sponsored by Ekopolitik in December 2010. A group of young Turks who were university students from Mersin exhibited deep resentment against Kurds of the same age from Hakkari, a city near the Turkish-Iranian border that is primarily occupied by Turkish citizens of Kurdish origin.

8. Tarık Çelenk was an officer in the Turkish Navy. Murat Sofuoğlu was trained as a lawyer in Turkey and graduated from the School of Conflict Analysis and Resolution, George Mason University, Virginia, before joining Ekopolitik.

9. We had seventeen dialogue participants and about thirty observers during the first Turkey's Grand Dome Project. Among dialogue participants were:

Cezmi Bayram: A specialist in science and mathematics. As a Turkish nationalist he has functioned as the leader or a member of various Turkish cultural and business organizations. He accepted membership in the Ekopolitik core group.

Murat Belge: A well-known liberal Turkish scholar and public figure who frequently appears on television speaking about political issues. He had originally studied English literature. He became a key member of the Ekopolitik core group and was a frequent consultant to Tarık Çelenk and Murat Sofuoğlu.

Bayram Bozyel: A politician and writer of Kurdish origin who in the past had spent seventy days in a Turkish military prison. He was a founder of a political party called Hak-Par that defended human rights.

Cengiz Çandar: With a degree in political science, he was an adviser to former president of Turkey Turgut Özal. He is a well-known newspaper columnist.

Musa Serdar Çelebi: He was the director of the Turkish Islamic Togetherness Association and a former politician. He lived in Germany and was also a member of the Foreign Economic Relations Board in Istanbul. He became a member of the Ekopolitik core group.

Seydi Fırat: He was a member of the political section of the PKK and lived with other PKK members in the eastern mountains of Turkey. With the permission of Abdullah Öcalan, then the leader of the PKK, he and another seven PKK members surrendered to the Turkish authorities in 1999. After spending five years in jail, he is now a member of the Peace and Democratic Solution Group, frequently lectures on Kurdish issues, and has contacts with Öcalan who, since his capture in February 1999, is the only inmate on the prison island İmralı. Fırat became a member of the Ekopolitik core group.

Ümit Fırat: A politician of Kurdish origin who was a member of the Turkish Labour Party before he became one of the founders of the first Kurdish organization in Turkey in 1969. He has been active in politically organizing citizens of Kurdish origin in eastern Turkey, and served as a member of the Ekopolitik core group.

İbrahim Kalın: He holds a doctorate degree in comparative philosophy from George Washington University in Washington, DC, and has written books on Islam. He became an adviser on international affairs to Turkish prime minister Recep Tayyıp Erdoğan.

Gültan Kışanak: Of Kurdish origin, she is a graduate of the Faculty of Communication and Public Relations, Department of Journalism, Ege University, Izmir. She became a newspaperwoman and politician and was elected as an MP in 2007. In 2011 she was reelected as a member of the Kurdish party BDP.

Altan Tan: A conservative and religious politician, architect, and newspaper columnist who wrote a great deal on the Kurdish question. His mother was Turkish and his father, who was tortured in a Turkish military prison and died, was Kurdish. He became a member of the Ekopolitik core group until he became a successful candidate for parliament in the summer of 2011.

Mete Yarar: He was a military officer in the Turkish Army Special Forces and spent over ten years in southeastern Turkey where the PKK is most active. He became a very involved member of the Ekopolitik core group.

Among the observers were:

Deniz Ülke Arıboğan: A political scientist and then the Rector of Bahçeşehir University in Istanbul, she is now a high-level administrator of Bilgi University in Istanbul. She continued to attend future Ekopolitik Turkey's Grand Dome meetings.

Ayşe Betül Çelik: She holds a degree in political science and teaches conflict resolution at Sabancı University in Istanbul.

Esra Çuhadar Gürkaynak: She is a political scientist at Bilkent University, Istanbul.

Cevat Öneş: A law school graduate, he was the assistant director of the Turkish secret service MIT (the Turkish equivalent of the CIA) prior to his retirement. Later he became a key member of the Ekopolitik core group.

Avni Özgürel: A nationalist Turk who has expertise in financial matters, he has been a prolific writer for many Turkish newspapers and also frequently appears on television and has written scripts for various documentaries. He became a member of the Ekopolitik core group.

Özdem Sanberk: A law school graduate, past Turkish representative to the European Union, and Turkish ambassador to Great Britain, he was also the former director of a Turkish civil think tank called Turkish Economic and Social Studies Foundation (TESEV). He became a member of the Ekopolitik core group.

Sema Sezer: She studied political science and is a retired member of MIT.

Halit Yalçın: A conservative Kurdish activist from Hakkari, a city with a Kurdish population near the Turkey-Iran border, he was in jail for eleven years for his political activities. He publishes books in Kurdish and is a spokesperson of Kurdish literature. He became a member of the Ekopolitik core group.

10. Full report on the November 16–17, 2009 meeting, "Turkiye'nin Büyük Çatısı" (Turkey's Grand Dome), Ekopolitik, p. 121.

11. This psychobiographical profile appears in Volkan 1997.

12. Ekopolitik also published this report.

**Chapter 40**

1. The reader can find detailed information about the Austen Riggs Center at www.austenriggs.net.

2. I am also thankful to Selçuk Börekçi, the owner of MIDI Hotel in Ankara. He provided rooms for the members of the IDI for our three Ankara meetings.

3. Cochairpersons of the IDI are:

Vamık D. Volkan, Lord John Alderdice, and Robi Friedman.

The present IDI members are:

Deniz Ülke Arıboğan (Turkey): Political scientist and former Rector of Bahçeşehir University. She is a member of the Board of Trustees of Istanbul Bilgi University and columnist at *Akşam*, a daily newspaper. On occasions she took part, with Vamık Volkan, in Turkey's Grand Dome Project (see chapter 39).

Coline Covington (United Kingdom): Jungian analyst and former Chair of the British Psychoanalytic Council. She is involved in research on the Democratic Republic of Congo.

Abdülkadir Çevik (Turkey): Former Chairperson of Psychiatry at Ankara University Medical School. He served as an adviser to the Turkish prime minister in 1992–1997. He is also Director of Ankara University's Center for the Study and Research of Political Psychology.

Gerard Fromm (USA): Psychoanalyst and Director of the Erikson Institute for Education and Research at the Austen Riggs Center in Stockbridge, Massachusetts.

He is President-Elect of the International Society for the Psychoanalytic Study of Organizations.

Anatoly Golubovsky (Russia): Sociologist, journalist, television and radio producer, and Chief Editor, STREAM Television Company, Moscow. He was an International Fellow at the Center for the Study of Mind and Human Interaction from the Soviet Union.

Hiba Huseini (West Bank): The Managing Partner of a West Bank–based law firm. Since 1994, she has served as legal adviser to peace process negotiations between the Palestinians and Israelis. She is a founding member of Al-Mustakbal Foundation, a nonpartisan organization aimed at promoting economic development and rule of law in Palestine.

İbrahim Kalın (Turkey): Chief Policy Adviser to Turkish prime minister Recep Tayyıp Erdoğan. He is a broadly trained scholar of Islamic studies and is among the signatories of the Common Word, a major initiative to improve Muslim-Christian relations.

Reuven Merhav (Israel): Former Israeli Ambassador appointed as a member of the Justice Turkel Commission to investigate the May 2010 Mavi Marmara incident off the Gaza shore. For decades he had a diverse career in the Prime Minister's Office, in the Ministry of Foreign Affairs, and in the Ministry of Immigrants Absorption. He also served as director general of the Ministry of Foreign Affairs.

Farrokh Negahdar (Iran): One of the most credible and in-demand political analysts on Iranian domestic and foreign politics and policies. He was held in prison for about ten years while he was in Iran because of his role in the student movement and also because he was a founding member of the Fadaian Organization. He is living abroad.

Alexander V. Obolonsky (Russia): Doctor of Law and Politics, and Associate Dean for Research, School of Public Administration and Municipal Management in the Higher School of Economics (HSE), Moscow. He was a Fulbright Senior Visiting Scholar in the United States and participated in the Center for the Study of Mind and Human Interaction's work in the Soviet Union and the Baltic Republics.

Frank Ochberg (USA): Introduced in this chapter.

Ford Rowan (USA): Lawyer and the Chairman of the National Center for Critical Incident Analysis, an independent research entity in Washington, DC. He is a former national security correspondent for NBC News who covered the war in Lebanon, the Watergate trials, and Three Mile Island. He was the host of the weekly PBS program, *International Edition*.

Regine Scholz (Germany): Group analyst and member of the Scientific Committee of the German Society for Group Analysis and Group Psychotherapy (D3G). She is supervisor and training analyst of the Münster Institute of Therapeutic and

Applied Group Analysis and editor of "Arbeitshefte Gruppenanalyse" and also a member of the Management Committee of the Group Analytic Society (London).

Edward R. Shapiro (USA): Psychoanalyst and former Medical Director/CEO of the Austen Riggs Center in Stockbridge, Massachusetts. He is also Clinical Professor of Psychiatry at Yale University School of Medicine, and Associate Clinical Professor of Psychiatry at Harvard Medical School. He founded the Erik H. Erikson Institute for Education and Research as a vehicle for applying the clinical insights developed at Riggs to larger social issues.

At the present time the IDI is offering scholars and political activists from Arab countries membership in the IDI since we lost our previous members from these countries. During our meetings we also have had guests from Egypt, Tunisia, and the West Bank. The IDI has three associate members: David Fromm, a lawyer from the United States; Senem Çevik, a political science specialist from Turkey; and Lee Watroba, manager of administrative support at the Austen Riggs Center.

4. The Mavi Marmara flotilla incident took place on May 31, 2010. The six-ship flotilla was attempting to break Israel's blockade and deliver humanitarian aid to Gaza. Israeli naval special forces intercepted this attempt in international waters. Some persons on the lead ship, Mavi Marmara, challenged the Israeli forces, resulting in the killing of eight Turks and one Turkish-American on Mavi Marmara. Twenty other passengers were injured.

5. Please see www.internationaldialogueinitiative.com.

6. Shapiro and Carr 2006, p. 256.

# BIBLIOGRAPHY

Abraham, H. and E. L. Freud (eds.). 1965. *A Psycho-Analytic Dialogue: The Letters of Sigmund Freud and Karl Abraham.* New York: Basic Books.

Abse, D. W. and R. B. Ulman. 1977. Charismatic political leadership and collective regression. In *Psychopathology and Political Leadership*, ed. R. S. Robons, pp.35–52. New Orleans: Tulane University Press.

Akhtar, S. 1992. *Broken Structures: Severe Personality Disorders and Their Treatment.* Northvale, NJ: Jason Aronson.

Akhtar, S. 1999. *Immigration and Identity: Turmoil, Treatment, Transformation.* Northvale, NJ: Jason Aronson.

Akhtar, S. (ed.). 2008. *The Crescent and the Couch: Crosscurrents between Islam and Psychoanalysis.* Lantham, MD: Jason Aronson.

Akhtar, S. 2009. *Comprehensive Dictionary of Psychoanalysis.* London: Karnac Books.

Akhtar, S. 2010. *Immigration and Acculturation: Mourning, Adaptation, and the Next Generation.* New York: Jason Aronson.

Alderdice, J. 2007. The individual, the group and the psychology of terrorism. *International Review of Psychiatry*, 19:201–209.

Alderdice, J. 2010. Off the couch and round the conference table, In *Contemporary Psychoanalytic Applications*, ed. A. Lemma and M. Patrick, pp.15–32. New York and London: Routledge.

Allen, B. 1996. *Rape Warfare: The Hidden Genocide in Bosnia-Herzegovina and Croatia.* Minneapolis: University of Minnesota Press.

Antane, A. 1991. Some aspects of cultural autonomy of minorities in Latvia 1920–1934 and today. Paper delivered in Oslo, Norway, September 6.

Anzieu, D. 1971. L'illusion groupale. *Nouvelle Revue de Psychânalyse*, 4:73–93.

Anzieu, D. 1984. *The Group and the Unconscious.* London: Routledge & Kegan Paul.

Apprey, M. 1993. The African-American experience: Forced immigration and transgenerational trauma. *Mind and Human Interaction*, 4:70–75.

Apprey, M. 1996. Broken lines, public memory, absent memory: Jewish and African Americans coming to grips with racism. *Mind and Human Interaction*, 7:139–149.

Apprey, M. 1998. Reinventing the self in the face of received transgenerational hatred in the African American community. *Mind and Human Interaction*, 9:30–37.

Apprey, M. (in collaboration with L. Krikk, V. Apprey and E. Talvik). 2000. From the heuristic to empirical: Integrating interethnic kindergartens. *Mind and Human Interaction*, 11:195–207.

Arlow, J. A. 1973. Motivations for peace. In *Psychological Basis of War*, ed. H. Z. Winnik, R. Moses, and M. Ostow, pp.193–204. Jerusalem: Jerusalem Academic Press.

Arnett, J. J. 2002. The psychology of globalization. *American Psychologist*, 37:774–783.

Ast, G. 1991. Interviews with Germans about reunification. *Mind and Human Interaction*, 2:100–104.

Atakol, K. 2012. *Turkish & Greek Cypriots: Is Separation Permanent*. Ankara: METU Press.

Atkinson, R. 1993. *Crusade: The Untold Story of the Persian Gulf War*. Boston: Houghton-Mifflin.

Balmer, R. 1989. *Mine Eyes Have Seen the Glory: A Journey into Evangelical Subculture in America*. New York: Oxford University Press.

Barker, T. M. 1967. *Double Eagle and Crescent: Vienna's Second Turkish Siege and its Historical Setting*. Albany: State University of New York Press.

Barkun, M. 1986. *Disaster and the Millennium*. Syracuse, NY: Syracuse University Press.

Barkun, M. 1996. *Religion and the Racist Right: The Origins of the Christian Identity Movement*. Chapel Hill: University of North Carolina Press.

Barkun, M. 1997. The Christian identity movement: Constructing millennialism on the racist right. In *Millennium, Messiahs and Mayhem*, eds. T. Robbins and S. Palmer, pp.247–260. Philadelphia: Routledge.

Barkun, M. 2006. *A Culture of Conspiracy: Apocalyptic Visions in Contemporary America (Comparative Studies in Religion and Society)*. Los Angeles: University of California Press.

Bergen, P. 2006. *The Osama bin Laden I Know: An Oral History of al Qaeda's Leader*. New York: The Free Press.

Bernard, V. W., P. Ottenberg and F. Redl. 1973. Dehumanization: A composite psychological defense in relation to modern war. In *Sanctions for Evil: Sources of Social Destructiveness*, eds. N. Sanford and C. Comstock, pp.102–124. San Francisco: Jossey-Bass.

Binswanger, L. 1956. *Erinnerungen an Sigmund Freud*. Bern: Francke Verlag.

Bion, W. R. 1961. *Experiences in Groups*. London: Tavistock Publications.

Blass, R. B. 2004. Beyond illusion: Psychoanalysis and the question of religious truth. *International Journal of Psycho-Analysis*, 85:615–634.

Bloom, P. 2010. *How Pleasure Works: The New Science of Why We Like What We Like*. New York: W. W. Norton.

Blos, P. 1979. *The Adolescent Passage: Developmental Issues*. New York: International Universities Press.

Blum, H. P. 1985. Superego formation, adolescent transformation and the adult neurosis. *Journal of the American Psychoanalytic Association*, 4:887–909.

Böhm, T. and S. Kaplan. 2011. *Revenge: On the Dynamics of a Frightening Urge and its Taming*. London: Karnac.

Boyer, L. B. 1986. One man's need to have enemies: A psychoanalytic perspective. *Journal of Psychoanalytic Anthropology*, 9:101–120.

Brenner, I. 2001. *Dissociation of Trauma: Theory, Phenomenology, and Technique*. Madison, CT: International Universities Press.

Brenner, I. 2004. *Psychic Trauma: Dynamics, Symptoms, and Treatment*. New York: Jason Aronson.

Britton, R. 1995. Psychic reality and unconscious belief. *International Journal of Psychoanalysis*, 76:19–23.

Brown, J. A. C. 1963. *Techniques of Persuasion: From Propaganda to Brainwashing*. Middlesex, England: Penguin Press.

Buckman, J. 1977. Brainwashing, LSD, and the CIA: Historical and ethical perceptions. *International Journal of Social Psychiatry*, 23:8–19.

Burns, J. M. 1978. *Leadership*. New York: Harper Torchbooks.

Butler, T. 1993. Yugoslavia mon amour. *Wilson Quarterly*, 17:118–125.

Cain, A. C. and R. C. Cain. 1964. On replacing a child. *Journal of the American Academy of Child Psychiatry*, 3:443–456.

Campbell, B. P. 1998. The hidden legacy of Jamestown: Aggression in Virginia's history. *Mind and Human Interaction*, 9:18–29.

Carr, S. C. and T. S. Sloan (eds.). 2003. *Poverty and Psychology: From Global Perspective to Local Practice*. New York: Kluwer Academic/Plenum Publishers.

Carter, J. 1982. *Keeping Faith*. New York: Bantam Books.

Cath, S. H. 1996. Cults and addiction to alternative belief systems: Psychoanalytic and psychophysiological considerations. *Mind and Human Interaction*, 7:63–90.

Çevik, A. 2003. Globalization and identity. In *Violence or Dialogue: Psychoanalytic Insights to Terror and Terrorism*, eds. S. Varvin and V. D. Volkan, pp.91–98. London: International Psychoanalysis Library.

Chakotin, S. 1939. *The Rape of Masses: The Psychology from Propaganda to Brainwashing*. Middlesex, England: Penguin Books.

Chasseguet-Smirgel, J. 1984. *The Ego Ideal*. New York: W. W. Norton.

Cheney, R. 2011. *In My Time: A Personal and Political Memoir*. New York: Threshold Editions.

Clark, R. P. 1983. Patterns in the lives of ETA members. *Terrorism*, 6:423–454.

Crenshaw, M. 1986. The psychology of political terrorism. In *Political Psychology: Contemporary Problems and Issues*, ed. M. G. Hermann, pp. 379–413. San Francisco: Jossey-Bass.

Culbertson, R. and W. N. Howell. 2001. *Siege: Crisis Leadership and the Survival of US Embassy Kuwait*. Charlottesville: Virginia Foundation for the Humanities Press.

Cullen, R. 1990. Report from Romania: Down with the tyrant. *New Yorker*, April 2:94–112.

Darwin, C. 1859. *On the Origin of Species by Means of Natural Selection, or the Preservation of Favoured Races in the Struggle for Life*. London: John Murray.

Dasen, P. 2000. Rapid change and turmoil of adolescence: A cross-cultural perspective. *International Journal of Group Tensions*, 29:17–49.

Davidson, W. D. and J. V. Montville. 1981–1982. Foreign policy according to Freud. *Foreign Policy*, 45:145–157.

Dayan, M. 1981. *Breakthrough: A Personal Account of the Egypt-Israel Peace Negotiations*. New York: Knopf.

Diamond, L. and J. McDonald. 1996. *Multi-Track Diplomacy: A Systems Approach to Peace*. Bloomfield, CT: Kumarian Press.

Dobrynin, A. 1955. *In Confidence: Moscow's Ambassador to America's Six Cold War Presidents (1962–1986)*. New York: Random House.

Dobson, C. and R. Payne. 1982. *The Terrorists: Their Weapons, Leaders and Tactics*. New York: Facts on File.

Drozdek, B. and J. P. Wilson (eds.). 2007. *Voices of Trauma: Treating Psychological Trauma Across Cultures*. New York: Springer.

Eagle, G. and J. Watts. 2002. Psychodynamic contributions to formulations of the impact and treatment of traumatic stress incidents: Part 1. *Psycho-Analytic Psychotherapy in South Africa*, 10:1–24.

Eban, A. 1983. *The New Diplomacy: International Affairs in the Modern Age*. New York: Random House.

Eckstaedt, A. 1989. *Nationalsozialismus in der "zweiten Generation": Psychoanalyse von Hörigkeitsverhältnissen* (National Socialism in the Second Generation: Psychoanalysis of Master-Slave Relationships). Frankfurt A.M.: Suhrkamp Verlag.

Edwards, B. 1998. History, myth, and mind. *Mind and Human Interaction*, 9:1–4.

Ekedahl, C. M. and M. Goodman. 2001. *Wars of Eduard Shevardnadze*. 2nd Edition. Dulles, VA: Potomac Books.

Elliott, M., K. Bishop, and P. Stokes. 2004. Societal PTSD? Historic shock in Northern Ireland. *Psychotherapy and Politics International*, 2:1–16.

Elovitz, P. H. and C. Kahn. 1997. *Immigrant Experiences: Personal Narratives and Psychological Analysis*. Madison, NJ: Fairleigh Dickenson University Press.

Emde, R. 1991. Positive emotions for psychoanalytic theory: Surprises from infancy research and new directions. *Journal of the American Psychoanalytic Association* (Supplement), 39:5–44.

Emmert, T. A. 1990. *Serbian Golgotha: Kosovo, 1389*. New York: Columbia University Press.

Erikson, E. H. 1956. The problem of ego identity. *Journal of the American Psychoanalytic Association*, 4:56–121.

Erikson, E. H. 1966. Ontogeny of ritualization. In *Psychoanalysis: A General Psychology*, eds. R. M. Lowenstein, L. M. Newman, M. Schur, and A. J. Solnit, pp. 601–621. New York: International Universities Press.

Erikson, E. H. 1985. *Childhood and Society.* New York: W. W. Norton.

Erlich, H. S. 1998. Adolescents' reactions to Rabin's assassination: A case of patricide? In *Adolescent Psychiatry: Developmental and Clinical Studies*, ed. A. Esman, pp.189–205. London: The Analytic Press.

Erlich, H. S. 2010. A beam of darkness—understanding the terrorist mind. In *Psychoanalytic Perspectives on a Turbulent World*, eds. H. Brunning and M. Perini, pp.3–15. London: Karnac.

Ersoy, M. A. 1998. Chosen traumas of the Alavis in Anatolia. *Mind and Human Interaction*, 9:38–51.

Felman, S. and D. Laub. 1991. *Testimony: Crises of Witnessing in Literature, Psychoanalysis and History*. New York: Routledge.

Fenichel, O. 1945. *The Psychoanalytic Theory of Neurosis*. New York: W. W. Norton.

Flores, W. V. and R. Benmayer (eds.). 1997. *Latino Cultural Citizen*. New York: Beacon Press.

Fonagy, P. 2001. *Attachment Theory and Psychoanalysis*. New York: Other Press.

Fonagy, P. and M. Target. 1997. Attachment and reflective functions: Their role in self-organization. *Developmental Psychopathology*, 9:679–700.

Fornari, F. 1966. *The Psychoanalysis of War*. Trans. A. Pfeifer. Bloomington: Indiana University Press, 1975.

Frank, R. 1988. Jungle accounting: Auditors in Albania pick through rubble of pyramid schemes. *The Wall Street Journal*, August, 6, pp.1,7.

Freud, A. 1936. *The Ego and Mechanisms of Defense: The Writings of Anna Freud*, Vol. 2. New York: International Universities Press, 1966.

Freud, A. and D. Burlingham. 1942. *War and Children*. New York: International Universities Press.

Freud, S. 1900. The interpretation of dreams. *Standard Edition*, vols. 4, 5. London: Hogarth Press.

Freud, S. 1901. The forgetting of names and sets of words. *Standard Edition*, 6: 15–42. London: Hogarth Press.

Freud, S. 1913. Totem and taboo. *Standard Edition*, 13:1–165. London: Hogarth Press.

Freud, S. 1917. Mourning and melancholia. *Standard Edition*, 14:237–258. London: Hogarth Press, 1957.

Freud, S. 1920. Beyond the pleasure principle. *Standard Edition*, 18:7–64. London: Hogarth Press.

Freud, S. 1921a. Group psychology and the analysis of the ego. *Standard Edition*, 18:63–143. London: Hogarth Press.

Freud, S. 1921b. The future of an illusion. *Standard Edition*, 21:5–56. London: Hogarth Press.

Freud, S. 1926a. Inhibitions, symptoms and anxiety. *Standard Edition*, 20:77–175. London: Hogarth Press.

Freud, S. 1926b. Address to the Society of B'nai B'rith, *Standard Edition*, 20:271–274. London: Hogarth Press.

Freud, S. 1927. The future of an illusion. *Standard Edition*, 21:5–56. London: Hogarth Press, 1961.

Freud, S. 1930. Civilization and its discontents. *Standard Edition*, 21:59–145. London: Hogarth Press.

Freud, S. 1932. Why War? *Standard Edition*, 22:197–215. London: Hogarth Press.

Freud, S. 1939. Moses and monotheism, *Standard Edition*, 23:1–137. London: Hogarth Press, 1964.

Freud, S. 1940. Splitting of the ego in the process of defense. *Standard Edition*, 23:271–278. London: Hogarth Press, 1964.

Furman, E. 1974. *A Child's Parent Dies: Studies in Childhood Bereavement*. New Haven: Yale University Press.

Furman, R. A. 1998. The pilgrims: Myth and reality. *Mind and Human Interaction*, 9:5–17.

Gaddis, J. L. 1992. *The United States and the End of the Cold War: Implications, Reconsiderations, Provocations*. New York: Oxford University Press.

Garza-Guerrero, A. C. 1974. Culture shock: Its mourning and vicissitudes of identity. *Journal of the American Psychoanalytic Association*, 22:400–429.

Glass, J. 1989. *Private Terror/Public Life: Psychosis and Politics of Community*. Ithaca, NY: Cornell University Press.

Glower, E. 1947. *War, Sadism, and Pacifism: Further Essays on Group Psychology and War*. London: Allen and Unwin.

Golubovsky, A. 1992. Moscow Mourns. *Mind and Human Interaction*, 3:39–42.

Gorbachev, M. 1993. On Thomas Jefferson. *Mind and Human Interaction*, 4:107–110.

Greenacre, P. 1969. The fetish and the transitional object. In *Emotional Growth*, Vol. 1, pp.315–334. New York: International Universities Press.

Greenacre, P. 1970. The transitional object and the fetish: With special reference to the role of illusion. *International Journal of Psycho-Analysis*, 51:447–456.

Grinberg, L. and R. Grinberg. 1989. *Psychoanalytic Perspectives on Migration and Exile*. Trans. N. Festinger. New Haven: Yale University Press.

Grubrich-Smitis, I. 1979. Extremtraumatisierung als kumulatives Trauma: Psychoanalytische Studien über seelische Nachwirkungen der Konzentrationslagerhaft bei Überlebenden und ihren Kindern (Extreme traumatization as a cumulative trauma: Psychoanalytic studies on the mental effects of imprisonment in concentration camps on survivors and their children). *Psyche*, 33:991–1023.

Gutman. R. 1993. *A Witness to Genocide: The 1993 Pulitzer Prize-Winning Dispatches on the "Ethnic Cleansing" of Bosnia*. New York: Maxwell MacMillan International.

Halecki, O. 1992. *A History of Poland*. New York: Dorset Press.

Hallion, R. 1992. *Storm over Iraq: Air Power and the Gulf War*. Washington, DC: Smithsonian Institution.

Halperin, C. J. 2009. *The Tatar Yoke: The Image of the Mongols in Medieval Russia*. Bloomington, IN: Slavica Publishers.

Hartmann, H. 1939. *Ego Psychology and the Problem of Adaptation*. New York: International Universities Press, 1952.

Hawley, J. S. and W. Proudfoot. 1994. Introduction. In *Fundamentalism and Gender*, ed. J. S. Hawley, pp.5–44. New York: Oxford University Press.

Heath, S. 1991. *Dealing with the Therapist's Vulnerability to Depression*. Northvale, NJ: Jason Aronson.

Held, D. 1988. Democratization and globalization. In *Re-imagining Political Community*, eds. A. Archibugi, D. Held, and M. Kohler, pp.11–27. Stanford, CA: Stanford University Press.

Hendrick, I. 1958. *Facts and Theories of Psychoanalysis*. New York: Knopf.

Hiltzik, M. 1991. No Jewish revival for Lithuania. *Los Angeles Times*, September 24.

Hing, B. 2004. *Defining America through Immigration Policy*. Philadelphia: Temple University Press.

Hitler, A. 1925–1926. *Mein Kampf (My Struggle)*. Boston: Houghton Mifflin Company, 1962.

Hollander, N. 1997. *Love in a Time of Hate: Liberation Psychology in Latin America*. New York: Other Press.

Hollander, N. 2010. *Uprooted Minds: Surviving the Political Terror in the Americas*. New York: Taylor & Francis.

Hopper, E. 2003. *Traumatic Experience in the Unconscious Life of Groups: The Fourth Basic Assumption: Incohesion: Aggregation/Massification or (ba) I: A/M*. London: Jessica Kinsley Publishers.

Horowitz, D. L. 1985. *Ethnic Groups in Conflict*. Berkeley: University of California Press.

Hottinger, A. 1977. Turkey's Search for Identity: Kemal Atatürk's heritage. *Encounter*, 48:75–81.

Howell, W. N. 1993. Tragedy, trauma…and triumph: Reclaiming integrity and initiative from victimization. *Mind and Human Interaction*, 4:11, 111–119.

Howell, W. N. 1995. "The evil that men do…": Societal effects of the Iraqi occupation of Kuwait. *Mind and Human Interaction*, 6:150–169.

Howell, W. N. 1997. Islamic revivalism: A cult phenomenon? *Mind and Human Interaction*, 5:97–103.

Howell, W. N. 2001. Killing in the name of God: Motif and motivation. *Mind and Human Interaction*, 12:146–155.

İnalcık, H. 1987. *Fatih Devri Üzerinde Tetkikler ve Vesikalar (Documents and Investigations on the Era of the Conqueror)*. Ankara: Türk Tarih Kurumu.

Itzkowitz, N. 1972. *The Ottoman Empire and Islamic Tradition*. New York: Alfred A. Knopf.

Itzkowitz, N. 2000. The demonization of the other. (unpublished manuscript).

Itzkowitz, N. 2001. Unity out of diversity. *Mind and Human Interaction*, 12:173–175.

Jokl, A. M. 1997. *Zwei Fälle zum Thema "Bewältigung der Vergangenheit"* (Two Cases Referring to the Theme of "Mastering the Past"). Frankfurt A. M.: Jüdischer Verlag.

Jones, E. 1915. War and individual psychology In E. Jones, *Essays in Applied Psycho-Analysis*, Vol. 1, pp.55–76. New York: International Universities Press,1964.

Jones, E. 1964. *Essays in Applied Psycho-Analysis, Vols. 1 and 2*. New York: International Universities Press.

Jowett, G. S. and V. O'Donnell. 1992. *Propaganda and Persuasion*. New York: Sage Publication.

Julius, D. A. 1991. The practice of Track Two Diplomacy in the Arab-Israeli conferences. In *The Psychodynamics of International Relationships, Vol. II: Unofficial Diplomacy at Work*, ed. V. D. Volkan, J.V. Montville and D. A. Demetrios, pp.193–205. Lexington, MA: Lexington Books.

Julius, D. A. 1992. Biculturalism and international independence. *Mind and Human Interaction*, 3:53–56.

Jurčević, S. and I. Urlić. 2002. Linking objects in the process of mourning for sons disappeared in war: Croatia 2001. *Croatian Medical Journal*, 4:234–239.

Kahan, Y., A. Barak, and Y. Efrat. 1983. Final Report—The Commission of Inquiry into the Events at the Refugee Camps in Beirut (authorized translation). *Jerusalem Post*, Feb. 9.

Kakar, S. 1996. *The Colors of Violence: Cultural Identities, Religion, and Conflict.* Chicago: University of Chicago Press.

Kaplan, R. D. 1993. *Balkan Ghosts: A Journey Through History*. New York: Vintage.

Kaufman, N. H., I. Rizzini, K. Wilson, and M. Bush. 2002. The Impact of global economic, political, and social transformation on the lives of children: A framework for analysis. In *Globalization and Children: Exploring Potentials for Enhancing Opportunities in the Lives of Children and Youth*. ed. N. H. Kaufman and I. Rizzini, pp.3–18. New York: Kluwer Academic/Plenum Publishers.

Kayatekin, M. S. 2008. Christian-Muslim relations: The axis of Balkans and the West. In *The Crescent and the Couch: Cross-Currents between Islam and Psychoanalysis*, ed. S. Akhtar, pp.199–216. New York: Lanham, MD; Jason Aronson.

Kedourie, E. 1970. *The Chatham House Version: And Other Middle Eastern Studies.* London: Weidenfeld & Nicholson.

Kernberg, O. F. 1976. *Object Relations Theory and Clinical Psychoanalysis*. New York: Jason Aronson.

Kernberg, O. F. 1980. *Internal World and External Reality: Object Relations Theory Applied*. New York: Jason Aronson.

Kernberg, O. F. 1984. *Severe Personality Disorders*. New Haven: Yale University Press.

Kernberg, O. F. 1989. Mass psychology through the analytic lens. Paper presented at "Through the Looking Glass: Freud's Impact on Contemporary Culture." Philadelphia, September 23.

Kernberg, O. F. 2010. Some observations on the process of mourning. *International Journal of Psychoanalysis*, 91:601–619.

Kestenberg, J. S. 1982. A psychological assessment based on analysis of a survivor's child. In *Generations of the Holocaust*, eds. M. S. Bergman and M. E. Jucovy, pp.158–177. New York: Columbia University Press.

Kestenberg, J. S. 1989. Coping with losses and survival. In *The Problem of Loss and Mourning: Psychoanalytic Perspectives*, eds. D. R. Dietrich and P. C. Shabad, pp.381–403. Madison, CT: International Universities Press.

Kestenberg J. S. and I. Brenner. 1996. *The Last Witness*. Washington, DC: American Psychiatric Press.

Khan, A. 2002. Cypriotism: Disrupted in history, forgotten in politics. *Proceedings of the Fourth International Congress on Cyprus Studies*, ed. Ü. V. Osam, pp.39–53. Gazi Mağusa, TRNC: Eastern Mediterranean University Publications.

Khrushchev, N. S. 1970. *Khrushchev Remembers*. Boston: Little, Brown.

Kilaf, E. 2008. *Turkish Immigrant Women's Health in Austria: History, Situation and Health Status*. Vienna: VDM Verlag.

Kirov, G., R. Kemp, K. Kirov, and A. S. David. 1998. Religious faith after psychotic illness. *Psychopathology*, 31:234–245.

Klein, M. 1946. Notes on some schizoid mechanisms. In *Development of Psycho-analysis*, ed. J. Riviere, pp. 292–320. London: Hogarth Press.

Klein, M. 1961. *Narrative of a Child Analysis: The Conduct of the Psychoanalysis of Children as Seen in the Treatment of a Ten-Year-Old Boy*. London: Hogarth Press, 1975.

Kogan, I. 1995. *The Cry of Mute Children: A Psychoanalytic Perspective of the Second Generation of the Holocaust*. London: Free Association Books.

Kogan, I. 2004. The role of the analyst in the analytic cure during times of chronic crises. *Journal of the American Psychoanalytic Association*, 52:735–757.

Kris, E. 1943. Some problems of war propaganda: A note on propaganda new and old. *Psychoanalytic Quarterly*, 12:381–399.

Kris, E. 1944. *Radio Propaganda: Report on Home Broadcasts during the War*. New York: Oxford University Press.

Kris, E. 1975. *Selected Papers of Ernst Kris*. New Haven: Yale University Press.

Kroll, J. and W. Sheehan. 1989. Religious beliefs and practices among 52 psychiatric inpatients in Minnesota. *The American Journal of Psychiatry*, 146:67–72.

Krystal, H. (ed.). 1968. *Massive Psychic Trauma*. New York: International Universities Press.

Kubie, L. 1965. The outgoing of racial prejudice. *Journal of Nervous and Mental Disease*, 141: 265–273.

Landes, R. 2001. Apocalyptic Islam and bin Laden. Paper presented at the Committee on International Relations, Group for the Advancement of Psychiatry (GAP). White Plains, New York. November 8–10.

Laqueur, W. 1987. *The Age of Terrorism*. Boston: Little, Brown.

Lasswell, H. D. 1938. Foreword. In *Allied Propaganda and the Collapse of the German Empire in 1918*. ed. G. G. Bruntz, pp. v–viii. Stanford: Stanford University Press.

Laub, D. and N. C. Auerhahn. 1993. Knowing and not knowing massive psychic trauma: Forms of traumatic memory. *International Journal of Psycho-Analysis*, 74:287–302.

Laub, D. and D. Podell. 1997. Psychoanalytic listening to historical trauma: The conflict of knowing and the imperative act. *Mind and Human Interaction*, 8:245–260.

Le Bon, G. 1895. *The Crowd, a Study of the Popular Mind*. London: T. F. Unwin, 1897.

Le Bon, G. 1910. *La Psychologie Politigue, et la Défense Sociale*. Paris: Flammarion.

Lehtonen, J. 2003. The dream between neuroscience and psychoanalysis: Has feeding an infant impact on brain function and the capacity to create dream images in infants? *Psychoanalysis in Europe*, 57:175–182.

Lemma, A. and M. Patrick (eds.). 2010. *Off the Couch: Contemporary Psychoanalytic Applications*. New York: Routledge.

Leowald, H. W. 1978. *Psychoanalysis and the History of the Individual*. New Haven: Yale University Press.

Levine, H. 2005. Large-group dynamics and world conflict: The contributions of Vamık Volkan. *Journal of the American Psychoanalytic Association*, 54:273–280.

Lewis, B. 1990. The roots of Moslem rage. *The Atlantic Monthly*, September 20, pp.47–60.

Lewis, B. 2000. Propaganda in the Middle East. Paper presented at the International Conference in Commemoration of the 78$^{th}$ Birthday of Yitzhak Rabin: "Patterns of Political Discourse: Propaganda, Incitement and Freedom of Speech," February 29.

Lifton, R. 1961. *Thought Reform and the Psychology of Totalism: A Study of Brainwashing in China.* New York: W. W. Norton.

Lifton, R. and E. Olson 1976. The human meaning of total disaster: The Buffalo Creek experience. *Psychiatry,* 39:1–18.

Liu, J. H. and D. Mills. 2006. Modern racism and neo-liberal globalization: The discourses of plausible deniability and their multiple functions. *Journal of Community and Applied Social Psychology,* 16:83–99.

Loewenberg, P. 1991. Uses of anxiety. *Partisan Review,* 3:514–525.

Loewenberg, P. 1994. The psychological reality of nationalism: Between community and fantasy. *Mind and Human Interaction,* 5:6–18.

Loewenberg, P. 1995. *Fantasy and Reality in History.* London: Oxford University Press.

Lomasky, L. E. 1991. The political significance of terrorism. In *Violence, Terrorism, and Justice,* eds. R. G. Frey and C. W. Morris, pp.86–115. Cambridge: Cambridge University Press.

Lorenz, K. 1967. *On Aggression.* New York: Harcourt Brace & World.

Maaz, H. J. 1991. *Das Gestürzte Volk* (The Fallen People). Berlin: Argon Verlag.

MacEoin, D. 1983. The Shi'i establishment in modern Iran. In *Islam in the Modern World,* eds. D. MacEoin and A. Al-Shahi, pp.88–108. New York: St. Martin Press.

Mack, J. E. 1979. Foreword. In *Cyprus: War and Adaptation* by V. D. Volkan, pp. ix–xxi. Charlottesville, VA: University of Virginia Press.

Mack, J. E. and R. Rogers. 1989. *The Alchemy of Survival: One Woman's Journey.* Radcliffe Biography Series. Reading, MA: Addison-Wesley.

Mahler, M. S. 1968. *On Human Symbiosis and the Vicissitudes of Individuation.* New York: International Universities Press.

Markides, K. C. 1977. *The Rise and Fall of the Cyprus Republic.* New Haven: Yale University Press.

Marković, M. S. 1983. The secret of Kosovo. In *Landmarks in Serbian Culture and History.* ed., V. D. Mihailovich, pp.111–131. Pittsburg, PA: Serb National Federation.

Marty, M. E. and R. S. Appleby. 1995. *Fundamentalism Comprehended.* Chicago: Chicago University Press.

Marvick, E. W. 1986. *Louis XIII: Making of a King*. New Haven, CT: Yale University Press.

Matlock, J. F. 2004. *Reagan and Gorbachev: How the Cold War Ended*. New York: Random House.

Mavratsas, C. 1997. The ideological context between Greek-Cypriot nationalism and Cypriotism 1974–1995: Politics, social memory and identity. *Ethnic and Racial Studies*, 20:715–725.

McCarthy, J. 1995. *Death and Exile: The Ethnic Cleansing of Ottoman Muslims, 1981–1922*. Princeton, NJ: Darwin.

McDowall, D. 1996. *A Modern History of the Kurds*. London: L. B. Tauris.

Meissner, W. W. 1984. *Psychoanalysis and Religious Experience*. New Haven: Yale University Press.

Meissner, W. W. 1990. The role of transitional conceptualization in religious thought. In *Psychoanalysis and Religion*, eds. J. H. Smith and S. A. Handelman, pp.95–116. Baltimore: John Hopkins University Press.

Migranyan, A. 1992. Russians in the Baltics. *Independent Newspaper from Russia*, vol. 2, issue 18–19, p.20.

Mills, J. 1979. *Six Years with God: Life Inside Reverend Jim Jones Temple*. New York: A & W Publishers.

Misiunas, R. J. 1990. The Baltic Republics: Stagnation and strivings for sovereignty. In *The Nationalities Factor in Soviet Politics and Society*, ed. L. Hajda and M. R. Beissinger, pp. 204–227. Boulder, CO: Westview.

Misselwitz, I. 2003. German reunification: A quasi ethnic conflict. *Mind and Human Interaction*, 13:77–86.

Mitscherlich, A. 1971. Psychoanalysis and aggression of large groups. *International Journal of Psycho-Analysis*, 52:161–167.

Mitscherlich, A. and M. Mitscherlich. 1975. *The Inability to Mourn: Principals of Collective Behavior*. Trans. B. R. Placzek. New York: Grove Press, 1967.

Modell, A. 1970. The transitional objects and the creative art. *Psychoanalytic Quarterly*, 39:240–250.

Moghaddam, F. M. 2005. The staircase to terrorism: A psychological exploration. *American Psychologist*, 60:161–169.

Mohr, S., P-Y. Brandt, L. Borras, C. Gilliéron, and P. Huguelet. 2006. Toward an integration of spirituality and religiousness into the psychological dimension of schizophrenia. *The American Journal of Psychiatry*, 163:1952–1959.

Money-Kyrle, R. E. 1941. The psychology of propaganda. *British Journal of Medical Psychology*, 19:82–94.

Montville, J. V. 1990. The psychological roots of ethnic and sectarian terrorism. In *The Psychodynamics of International Relationships*, Vol. 1, eds. V. D. Volkan, D. A. Julius and J. V. Montville, pp.163–180. Lexington, MA: Lexington Books.

Morton, T. L. 2005. Prejudice in an era of economic globalization and international interdependence. In *The Psychology of Prejudice and Discrimination: Disability, Religion, Physique, and Other Traits*, Vol. 4, ed. J. L. Chin, pp.135–160. Westport, CT: Praeger.

Moses, R. 1982. The group-self and the Arab-Israeli Conflict. *International Review of Psychoanalysis*, 9:55–65.

Moses-Hrushovski, R. 2000. *Grief and Grievance: The Assassination of Yitzhak Rabin*. London: Minerva Press.

Murphy, R. F. 1957. Ingroup hostility and social cohesion. *American Anthropologist*, 59:1018–1035.

Mutman, M. 1992–1993. Under the sign of Orientalism: The West vs. Islam. *Cultural Critique*: Winter.

Nader, K.O., R. S. Pynoos, L. A. Fairbanks, M. al Ajeel, and A. al Asfour. 1993. A preliminary study of PTSD and grief among the children of Kuwait following the Gulf crises. *British Journal of Clinical Psychology*, 32:407–416.

Neu, J. and V. D. Volkan. 1999. *Developing a Methodology for Conflict Prevention: The Case of Estonia*. Atlanta: The Carter Center.

Niederland, W. G. 1961. The problem of the survivor. *Journal of the Hillside Hospital*, 10:233–247.

Niederland, W. G. 1964. Psychiatric disorders among persecution victims: A contribution to the understanding of concentration camp psychology and its after-effects. *Journal of Nervous and Mental Disorders*, 139:458–474.

Niederland, W. G. 1968. Clinical observations on the "survivor syndrome." *International Journal of Psychoanalysis*, 49:313–315.

Obolonsky, A. 1989. Obolonsky visits Center. *Mind and Human Interaction*, vol. 1, 2:8–9.

Obolonsky, A. 1990. Resistance to Perestroika within mass consciousness. *Mind and Human Interaction*, vol. 2, 1:6,18.

Ocak, A. Y. 1996. *Babailer Isyanı, Aleviliğin Tarihsel Altyapısı: Yahut Anadolu'da İslam—Türk Heterodoksisinin Teşekkülü* (Babais Revolt, the Historical Infrastructure of Alavism: or Formation of Islamic-Turkish Heterodoxy in Anatolia). Istanbul: Dergah Yayınları.

Ohlmeier, D. 1991. The return of the repressed: Psychoanalytical reflections on the unification of Germany. Paper presented to the Sandor Ferenczi Society, Budapest, June 7.

Olson, R. W. 1989. *The Emergence of Kurdish Nationalism*. Austin, TX: University of Texas Press.

Olsson, P. A. 2005. *Malignant Pied Pipers of Our Time: A Psychological Study of Destructive Cult Leaders from Rev. Jim Jones to Osama bin Laden*. Frederick, MD: PublishAmerica.

Olsson, P. A. 2008. Ideology and aggression: Osama bin Laden. In *The Crescent and the Couch: Cross-Currents between Islam and Psychoanalysis*, ed. S. Akhtar. Lanham, MD: Jason Aronson.

Opher-Cohn, L., J. Pfäfflin, B. Sonntag, B. Klose, and P. Pogany-Wnendt (eds.). 2000. *Das Ende der Sprachlosigkeit? Auswirkungen traumatischer Holocaust-Erfahrungen über mehrere Generationen*. (The Effects of Experiencing the Holocaust over Several Generations). Gießen: Psychosozial Verlag.

Ornstein, A. 2012. Mass murder and the individuals: Psychoanalytic reflections on perpetrators and their victims. *International Journal of Group Psychotherapy*, 62:1–20.

Ortaylı, I. 2003. *Osmanlı Barışı (Ottoman Peace)*. Istanbul: Ufuk Kitapları.

Ortaylı, I. 2007. On the history of Cyprus. Keynote speech, the Sixth International Congress on Cyprus Studies, Eastern Mediterranean University, Gazi Mağusa, TRNC, October 24.

Pao, P-N. 1979. *Schizophrenic Disorders: Theory and Treatment from a Psychodynamic Point of View*. New York: International Universities Press.

Pieper, J. Z.T. 2004. Religious coping in highly religious psychiatric inpatients. *Mental Health, Religion, and Culture*, 7:349–363.

Pinderhughes, C. A. 1982. Paired differential bonding in biological and social systems. *American Journal of Psychiatry*, 139:5–14.

Pinsker, H. 2007. "Goldwater Rule" history. *Psychiatric News*, 42:15, 33.

Post, J. M. 1990. Terrorist psycho-logic: Terrorist behavior as product of psychological forces. In *Origins of Terrorism*, ed. W. Reich, pp. 25–40. Cambridge: Cambridge University Press.

Poznanski, E. O. 1972. The "replacement child": A saga of unresolved parental grief. *Behavioral Pediatrics*, 81:1190–1193.

Quandt, W. B. 1986. *Camp David: Peacemaking and Politics*. Washington, DC: The Brookings Institution.

Rangell, L. 2003. Affects: In an individual and a nation. First Annual Volkan Lecture, November 15, University of Virginia, Charlottesville, VA.

Rashid, A. 2000. *Taliban: Islam, Oil and the New Great Game in Central Asia*. London: I. B. Tauris.

Ratliff, J. M. 2004. The persistence of national differences in a globalizing world: The Japanese struggle for competitiveness in advanced information technologies. *Journal of Socio-Economics*, 33:71–88.

Raviv, A., A. Sadeh, A. Raviv, O. Silberstein, and O. Diver. 2000. Young Israelis' reactions to national trauma: The Rabin assassination and terror attacks. *Political Psychology*, 21:299–322.

Reagan, R. 1983. President Reagan's Speech before the National Association of Evangelicals. March 8, 1983.

Reisman, A. 2006. *Turkey's Modernization: Refugees from Nazism and Atatürk's Vision*. Washington DC: New Academia Publishers.

Rogers, R. R. 1990. Glasnost and the emotional climate in Eastern Europe. *Political Communication and Persuasion*, 7:247–255.

Rosenthal, G. 1997. *Der Holocaust im Leben von drei Generationen: Familien von Überlebenden der Shoah und von Nazi-Tätern* (Holocaust in the Life of Three Generations: Families of Survivors of Shoah and Nazi Perpetrators). Gießen: Psychosozial-Verlag.

Rothstein, D. A. 1972. The assassin and the assassinated – a nonpatient subject of psychiatric investigation. In *Dynamics of Violence*, ed. J. Fawcett, pp.145–155. Chicago: American Medical Association.

Rybakov, A. 1991. *Children of the Arbat*. New York: Random House.

Saathoff, G. B. 1995. In the halls of mirrors: One Kuwaiti's captive memories. *Mind and Human Interaction*, 6:170–178.

Saathoff, G. B. 1996. Kuwait's children: Identity in the shadow of the storm. *Mind and Human Interaction*, 7:181–191.

Sabshin, M. 2008. *Changing American Psychiatry: A Personal Perspective.* Washington, DC: American Psychiatric Publishing.

Sadat, A. 1978. *In Search of Identity: An Autobiography.* New York: HarperCollins.

Salande, J. D. and D. R. Perkins. 2011. An object relations approach to cult membership. *American Journal of Psychotherapy*, 65:381–391.

Saunders, H. H. 1990. An historic challenge to rethink how nations relate. In *The Psychodynamics of International Relations*, eds. V. D. Volkan, Demetrios A. Julius and J. V. Montville. Lexington, MA: Lexington Books.

Saunders, H. H. 1991a. *The Other Walls: The Arab Israeli Peace Process in a Global Perspective.* Princeton, NJ: Princeton University Press.

Saunders, H. H. 1991b. Official and citizens in international relationships: The Dartmouth Conference. In *Psychodynamics of International Relationships*, vol. II, ed. V. D. Volkan, J. V. Montville, and D. A. Julius, pp. 41–69. Lexington, MA: Lexington Books.

Saunders, H. H. 2001. *A Public Peace Process: Sustained Dialogue to Transform Racial and Ethnic Conflicts.* New York: Palgrave Macmillan.

Schlegel, A. 2001. The global spread of adolescent culture. In *Negotiating Adolescence in Times of Social Change*, eds. L. J. Crockett and R. K. Silbereisen. pp.71–88. New York: Cambridge University Press.

Šebek, M. 1992. Anality in the totalitarian system and the psychology of post-totalitarian society. *Mind and Human Interaction*, 4:52–59.

Šebek, M. 1994. Psychopathology of everyday life in the post-totalitarian society. *Mind and Human Interaction*, 5:104–109.

Sells, M. A. 1996. *The Bridge Betrayed: Religion and Genocide in Bosnia.* Berkeley: University of California Press.

Sells, M. A. 2002.The construction of Islam in Serbian religious mythology and its consequences. In *Islam and Bosnia.* ed. M. Shatzmiller, pp. 56–85. Montreal: McGill University Press.

Shamir, S. and H. Schenker. 1986. Shimon Shamir on Egypt. *Journal of Palestine Studies*, 15:177–181.

Sharon-Krespin, R. 2009. Fetullah Gülen's grand ambition: Turkey's Islamic danger. *Middle East Quarterly*, Winter: 55–66.

Shapiro, E. and W. Carr. 2006. Those people were some kind of solution: Can society in any sense be understood? *Organizational & Social Dynamics*, 6:241–257.

Shaw, S. J. and E. K. Shaw. 1976–1977. *History of the Ottoman Empire and Modern Turkey* (2 volumes). Cambridge, UK: Cambridge University Press.

Shehadeh, R. 2003. *Strangers in the House: Coming of Age in Occupied Palestine*. New York: Penguin Books.

Shevardnadze, E. 1991. *The Future Belongs to Freedom*. London: Sinclair-Stevenson.

Shields, R. 1991. *Places on the Margin: Alternative Geographies of Modernity*. London: Routledge.

Sivan, E. 1985. *Radical Islam: Medieval Theology and Modern Politics*. New Haven, CT: Yale University Press.

Sklarew, B., S. W. Twemlow, and S. M. Wilkinson. 2004. *Analysts in the Trenches: Streets, Schools, War Zones*. Hillsdale, NJ: The Analytic Press.

Smith, D. L. 2011. *Less Than Human: Why We Demean, Enslave and Exterminate Others*. New York: St. Martin's Press.

Smith, T. W. 2005. Between Allah and Ataturk: Liberal Islam in Turkey. *The International Journal of Human Rights*, 9:307–325.

Sokolowski, R. 1990. Religion and psychoanalysis: Some phenomenological contributions. In *Psychoanalysis and Religion*, eds. J. H. Smith and S. A. Handelman, pp.1–17. Baltimore: John Hopkins University Press.

Spielberg, W. 2011. A New Psychology of Hope in Palestine? *Tikkun*, June 28.

Spitz, R. 1965. *The First Year of Life*. New York: International Universities Press.

Stapley, L. 2006. *Globalization and Terrorism: Death of a Way of Life*. London: Karnac Books.

Stein, H. F. 1990. The international and group milieu of ethnicity: Identifying generic group dynamic issues. *Canadian Review of Studies in Nationalism*, 17:107–130.

Stein, H. F. 1993. The Slovak- and Rusyn-American experience: Ethnic adaptation in the Steel Valley of western Pennsylvania. *Mind and Human Interaction*, 4:83–91.

Stern, D. N. 1985. *The Interpersonal World of the Infant: A View from Psychoanalysis and Developmental Psychology*. New York: Basic Books.

Stiglmayer, A. (ed.). 1994. *Mass Rape: The War Against Women in Bosnia-Herzegonina*. Lincoln, NE: University of Nebraska Press.

Stoye, J. 2006. *The Siege of Vienna*. Edinburgh, UK: Birlinn.

Streeck-Fischer, A. 1999. Naziskins in Germany: How traumatization deals with the past. *Mind and Human Interaction*, 10:84–97.

Suzuki, P. 1991. Germany's reunification and Turkish guestworkers. *Mind and Human Interaction*, 2:90–97.

Tähkä, V. 1984. Dealing with object loss. *Scandinavian Psychoanalytic Review*, 7:13–33.

Thomson, J. A. 1993. Latvian vignettes. *Mind and Human Interaction*, 4:191–197.

Thomson, J. A. 2000. Terror, tears, and timelessness: Individual and group response to trauma. *Mind and Human Interaction*, 11:162–176.

Thomson, J. A. 2003. Killer apes on American Airlines, or: How religion was the main hijacker on September 11. In *Violence or Dialogue: Psychoanalytic Insights on Terror and Terrorism*, eds., S. Varvin and V. D. Volkan, pp.73–84. London: International Psychoanalytic Association.

Thomson, J. A. (with C. Aukofer) 2011. *Why We Believe in God(s): A Concise Guide to the Science of Faith*. Charlottesville, VA: Pitchstone Publishing.

Thomson, J. A., M. Harris, V. D. Volkan, and B. Edwards. 1995. The psychology of Western European neo-racism. *International Journal of Group Rights*, 3:1–30.

Ticho, G. 1971. Cultural aspects of transference and countertransference. *Bulletin of Menninger Clinic*, 35:313–334.

Toynbee, A. J. 1933–1948. *A Study of History* (10 volumes). London: Oxford University Press.

Tucker, R. C. 1987a. Gorbachev and the fight for Soviet reform. *World Policy Journal*, Spring:179–204.

Tucker, R. C. 1987b. *Political Culture and Leadership in Soviet Russia: From Lenin to Gorbachev*. New York: Norton.

Twemlow, S. and F. Sacco. 2008. *Why School Anti-Bullying Programs Don't Work: A Guide to Improving School Climates*. New York: Routledge.

Urbanovich, Y. 1997. Georgia in my mind. *Silk Road*, 1:18–25.

Varnava, A. and H. Faustmann, H. (eds.) 2009. *Reunifying Cyprus: The Annan Plan and Beyond*. Library of Modern Middle East Studies. London: I. B. Tauris.

Varvin, S. and V. D. Volkan (eds.). 2003. *Violence or Dialogue: Psychoanalytic Insights on Terror and Terrorism*. London: International Psychoanalytical Association.

Volkan, V. D. 1972. The "linking objects" of pathological mourners. *Archives of General Psychiatry*, 27:215–222.

Volkan, V. D. 1976. *Primitive Internalized Object Relations: A Clinical Study of Schizophrenic, Borderline and Narcissistic Patients*. New York: International Universities Press.

Volkan, V. D. 1979. *Cyprus—War and Adaptation: A Psychoanalytic History of Two Ethnic Groups in Conflict*. Charlottesville, VA: University of Virginia Press.

Volkan, V. D. 1980. Narcissistic personality organization and "reparative" leadership. *International Journal of Group Psychotherapy*, 30:131–152.

Volkan, V. D. 1981. *Linking Objects and Linking Phenomena: A Study of the Forms, Symptoms, Metapsychology and Therapy of Complicated Mourning*. New York: International Universities Press.

Volkan, V. D. 1987. *Six Steps in the Treatment of Borderline Personality Organization*. New York: Jason Aronson.

Volkan, V. D. 1988. *The Need to Have Enemies and Allies: From Clinical Practice to International Relationships*. Northvale, NJ: Jason Aronson.

Volkan, V. D. 1990a. Living statues and political decision making. *Mind and Human Interaction*, 2:46–50.

Volkan, V. D. 1990b. The question of Germany: A West German's response. *Mind and Human Interaction*, 1:2–3, 9.

Volkan, V. D. 1991. On "chosen trauma." *Mind and Human Interaction*, 3:13.

Volkan, V. D. 1993. Immigrants and refugees: A psychodynamic perspective. *Mind and Human Interaction*, 4:63–69.

Volkan, V. D. 1995. *The Infantile Psychotic Self: Understanding and Treating Schizophrenics and Other Difficult Patients*. Northvale, NJ: Jason Aronson.

Volkan, V. D. 1996. Bosnia-Herzegovina: Ancient fuel of a modern inferno. *Mind and Human Interaction*, 7:110–127.

Volkan, V. D. 1997. *Bloodlines: From Ethnic Pride to Ethnic Terrorism*. New York: Farrar, Straus and Giroux.

Volkan, V. D. 1999. Nostalgia as a linking phenomenon. *Journal of Applied Psychoanalytic Studies*, 1:169–179.

Volkan, V. D. 2000. Traumatized societies and psychological care: Expanding the concept of preventive medicine. *Mind and Human Interaction*, 11:177–194.

Volkan, V. D. 2001. September 11 and societal regression. *Mind and Human Interaction*, 12:196–216.

Volkan, V. D. 2002. Bosnia-Herzegovina: Chosen Trauma and its transgenerational transmission. In *Islam and Bosnia: Conflict Resolution and Foreign Policy in Multi-Ethnic States*, ed. Maya Shatzmiller, pp. 86–97. Montreal: McGill-Queen's University Press.

Volkan, V. D. 2004. *Blind Trust: Large Groups and Their Leaders in Times of Crises and Terror*. Charlottesville, VA: Pitchstone Publishing.

Volkan, V. D. 2006a. *Killing in the Name of Identity: A Study of Bloody Conflicts.* Charlottesville, VA: Pitchstone Publishing.

Volkan, V. D. 2006b. What some monuments tell us about mourning and forgiveness. In *Taking Wrongs Seriously: Apologies and Reconciliation*, eds. E. Barkan and A. Karn, pp.115–131. Stanford, CA: Stanford University.

Volkan, V. D. 2009a. The next chapter: Consequences of societal trauma. In *Memory, Narrative and Forgiveness: Perspectives of the Unfinished Journeys of the Past*, eds. P. Gobodo-Madikizela and C. van der Merve, pp.1–26. Cambridge: Cambridge Scholars Publishing.

Volkan, V. D. 2009b. Some psychoanalytic views on leaders with narcissistic personality organization and their roles in large-group processes. In *Leadership in a Changing World: Dynamic Perspectives on Groups and Their Leaders*, eds. R. H. Klein, C. A. Rice, and V. L. Schermer. pp.67–89. New York: Lexington.

Volkan, V. D. 2010a. Psychoanalysis and international relationships: Large-group identity, traumas at the hand of the "other," and transgenerational transmission of trauma. In *Psychoanalytic Perspectives on a Turbulent World*, eds. H. Brunning and M. Perini, pp.41–62. London: Karnac Books.

Volkan, V. D. 2010b. *Psychoanalytic Technique Expanded: A Textbook on Psychoanalytic Treatment*. Istanbul/ London: Oa Press.

Volkan, V. D. and G. Ast. 1997. *Siblings in the Unconscious and Psychopathology.* Madison, CT: International Universities Press.

Volkan, V. D., G. Ast and W. Greer. 2002. *The Third Reich in the Unconscious: Transgenerational Transmission and its Consequences*. New York: Brunner-Routledge.

Volkan, V. D. and N. Atabey. 2010. Osmanlı'nın Yasından Atatürk'ün Türkiyesi'ne: Onarıcı Liderlik ve Politik Psikoloji. (From *Mourning among Ottomans to Atatürk's Turkey: Reparative Leadership and Political Psychology*). Ankara: Kripto Yayınları.

Volkan, V. D., and J. C. Fowler. 2009a. Large-group narcissism and political leaders with narcissistic personality organization. *Psychiatric Annals*, 39:214–222.

Volkan, V. D. and J. C. Fowler. 2009b. *Searching for the Perfect Woman: The Story of a Complete Psychoanalysis*. New York: Jason Aronson.

Volkan, V.D. and M. Harris. 1992. Negotiating a peaceful separation: A psychopolitical analysis of current relationships between Russia and the Baltic Republics. *Mind and Human Interaction*, 44:20–39.

Volkan, V. D. and M. Harris. 1993. Vaccinating the political process: A second psychopolitical analysis of relationships between Russia and the Baltic States. *Mind and Human Interaction*, 4:169–150.

Volkan, V. D. and M. Harris. 1995. The psychodynamics of ethnic terrorism. *International Journal on Group Rights*, 3:145–159.

Volkan, V. D. and N. Itzkowitz. 1984. *The Immortal Atatürk: A Psychobiography*. Chicago: University of Chicago Press.

Volkan, V. D. and N. Itzkowitz. 1994. *Turks and Greeks: Neighbours in Conflict*. Cambridgeshire, England: Eothen Press.

Volkan, V. D. and N. Itzkowitz. 2011. *Atatürk/Anatürk: Yasamı, İç Dünyası, Yeni Türk Kimliğinin Yaratılışı ve Bugünkü Türkiye'deki Kimlik Sorunları* (Atatürk FatherTurk/MotherTurk: His Life, His Internal World, The Creation of the Modern Turkish Identity and Identity Questions in Today's Turkey). Istanbul: Alfa.

Volkan, V. D., D. A. Julius and J. V. Montville (eds.) 1990. *The Psychodynamics of International Relationships, Vol. I: Concepts and Theories*. Lexington, MA: Lexington Books.

Volkan, V. D. and S. Kayatekin. 2006. Extreme religious fundamentalism and violence: Some psychoanalytic and psychopolitical thoughts. *Psyche & Geloof*: 17:71–91.

Volkan, V. D., J. V. Montville and D. A. Julius (eds.) 1990. *The Psychodynamics of International Relationships, Vol. II: Unofficial Diplomacy at Work*. Lexington, MA: Lexington Books.

Volkan, V. D. and E. Zintl. 1993. *Life After Loss: Lessons of Grief*. New York: Charles Scribner's Sons.

Voznesensky, A. 1986. *An Arrw in the Wall: Selected Poetry and Prose*. eds. W. J. Smith and F. D. Reeve. New York: Henry Holt.

Vulliamy, E. 1994. *Seasons in Hell: Understanding Bosnia's War*. New York: St. Martin's Press.

Waelder, R. 1930. The principle of multiple function: Observations on over-determination. *Psychoanalytic Quarterly*, 5:45–62.

Waelder, R. 1960. *Basic Theory of Psychoanalysis*. New York: International Universities Press.

Waelder, R. 1971. Psychoanalysis and history. In *The Psychoanalytic Interpretation of History*. ed. B. B. Wolman, pp.3–22. New York: Basic Books.

Wagner, W. 1996. *Kulturshock Deutschland I*. Hamburg: Rotbuch-Verlag.

Wagner, W. 1998. *Kulturshock Deutschland: Der ZweiteBlick* (Culture Shock Germany: The Second Look) Hamburg: Rotbuch-Verlag.

Weber, E. 1999. *Apocalypses: Prophecies, Cults, and Millennial Beliefs through the Ages*. Cambridge, MA: Harvard University Press.

Weber, M. 1923. *Wirtschaft und Geselschaft (Economy and Society)*. 2 vols. Tübingen, Germany: J.C.B. Mohr.

Weinberg, C. 1992. Terrorists and Terrorism. *Mind and Human Interaction*, 3:72–82.

Weisberger, A. M. 1995. German Reunification and the Jewish Question. *Mind and Human Interaction*, 6:9–14.

Werner, H. and B. Kaplan. 1963. *Symbol Formation*. New York: Wiley.

Wessinger, C. 1997. Millennialism with and without mayhem. In *Millennium, Messiahs, and Mayhem*, eds. T. Robbins and S. Palmer, pp.47–60. New York: Routledge.

Wessinger, C. 1999. *How the Millennium Comes Violently: From Jonestown to Heaven's Gate*. New York: Seven Bridges Press.

Wilson, J. P. and B. Drozdek (eds.). 2004. *Broken Spirits: The Treatment of Traumatized Asylum Seekers, Refugees and War and Torture Victims*. New York: Routledge.

Wingfield, N. M. (ed.) 2003. *Creating the Other: Ethnic Conflict and Nationalism in Habsburg Central Europe*. New York: Berghahn Books.

Winnicott, D. W. 1953. Transitional objects and transitional phenomena: A study of the first not-me possession. *International Journal of Psycho-Analysis*, 34:89–97.

Winnicott, D. W. 1963. The value of depression. In D. W. Winnicott. *Home is Where We Start From*, eds. C. Winnicott, R. Shepherd and M. Davis. pp.74–90. New York: W.W. Norton, 1986.

Winnicott, D.W. 1969. Berlin walls. In D. W. Winnicott. *Home is Where We Start From*, eds. C. Winnicott, R. Shepherd and M. Davis. pp.221–227. New York: W.W. Norton. 1986.

Wolfenstein, M. 1966. How mourning is possible. *Psychoanalytic Study of the Child*, 21:93–123.

Wolfenstein, M. 1969. Loss, rage and repetition. *Psychoanalytic Study of the Child*, 24:432–460.

Wolfenstein, M. and G. Kliman (eds.). 1965. *Children and the Death of a President: Multi-disciplinary Studies*. Garden City, NY: Doubleday.

Yanof, J. A. 2005. Technique in child analysis. In *Textbook of Psychoanalysis*, eds. E. S. Person, A. M. Cooper and G.O. Gabbard. Washington: American Psychiatric Publishing.

Yavuz, M. H. 1995. The patterns of political Islamic identity: Dynamics of national and transnational loyalties and identities. *Central Asian Survey*, 14:3, 342–372.

Yavuz, M. H. 2003. *Islamic Political Identity in Turkey: Religion and Global Politics*. New York: Oxford University Press.

Yavuz, M. H. and J. L. Esposito (eds.) 2003. *Turkish Islam and Secular State: The Global Impact of Fetullah Gulen*. Syracuse, N.Y: Syracuse University Press.

Yevtushenko, Y. 1970. *The Face Behind the Face*. Trans. A. Boyars and S. Franklin. New York: Marek Publishers.

Zaleznick, A.1984. Charismatic and consensus leaders: A psychological comparison. In *The Irrational Executive*, ed. M. R. F. Kets de Vries, pp.122–132. New York: International Universities Press.

# NAME INDEX

# SUBJECT INDEX

# ABOUT THE AUTHOR

Vamık D. Volkan, M.D., is an emeritus professor of psychiatry at the University of Virginia School of Medicine, an emeritus training and supervising analyst at the Washington Psychoanalytic Institute, and the Senior Erik Erikson Scholar at the Austen Riggs Center in Stockbridge, Massachusetts. He served as the Medical Director of the University of Virginia's Blue Ridge Hospital and as director of the University of Virginia's Center for the Study of Mind and Human Interaction.

A founder and past president of the International Society of Political Psychology, and a past president of the American College of Psychoanalysts, Dr. Volkan has been, over the past decades, the Inaugural Yitzhak Rabin Fellow, Rabin Center for Israel Studies, Tel Aviv, Israel; a Visiting Professor of Law, Harvard University, Cambridge, Massachusetts; a Visiting Professor of Political Science, the University of Vienna, Vienna, Austria; and a Visiting Professor of Political Psychology, Bahçeşehir University, Istanbul, Turkey. He has also served as a Visiting Professor of Psychiatry at Ege University, Izmir, Turkey; Ankara University, Ankara, Turkey; and Cerrahpaşa Medical School, Istanbul, Turkey.

In the 1990s, he served as a member of the Carter Center's International Negotiation Network, headed by former president Jimmy Carter. He chaired the Select Advisory Commission to the Federal Bureau of Investigation's Critical Incident Response Group and was a Temporary Consultant to the World Health Organization in Albania and Macedonia and a Fulbright Scholar in Austria.

He is the author, coauthor, editor, or coeditor of dozens of books and the author of hundreds of book chapters and academic papers. He has served on the editorial boards of sixteen professional journals, and has received awards from numerous national and international organizations. Dr. Volkan has also given lectures and keynote addresses across the United States and in dozens of countries on every continent (with the exception of Antarctica).

The Center for the Study of Mind & Human Interaction, Blue Ridge Hospital, Charlottesville, VA

CSMHI Program Director Joy Boissevain

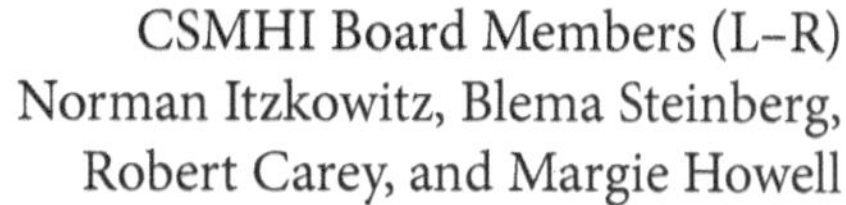

CSMHI Board Members (L–R) Norman Itzkowitz, Blema Steinberg, Robert Carey, and Margie Howell

The author with Nechama Agmon, 1984

All photos courtesy of author

With Demetrios Julius and William Davidson in Austria, 1983

With Yasser Arafat in Tunis, Tunisia, 1990

With Mayor of Bethlehem Elias Freij, 1983

Rafael Moses and Rena Moses-Hrushovski

Mohammed Shalaan and Joseph Montville in Charlottesville, VA, 1995

Welcoming Mikhail and Raisa Gorbachev in Charlottesville, VA, 1993

Stanislav Roschin, Demetrios Julius, and Boris Lomov (L–R) in Charlottesville, VA, 1992

With Zoya Zarubina, Josef Stalin's personal interpreter, 1992

Vilnius TV tower, a "hot place" where thirteen Lithuanians were killed by Soviet tanks on January 13, 1991

With Alexander Obolonsky and Molly Turner, 1989

With UN Secretary-General Javier Pérez de Cuéllar in Atlanta, GA, 1992

With President Jimmy Carter, 1994

In Dakar, Senegal, 1992

With Archbishop Desmond Tutu, 1994

With President Arnold Rüütel in Estonia, 1997

Amb. Nathaniel Howell, Joyce Neu, and Maurice Apprey in Estonia, 1995

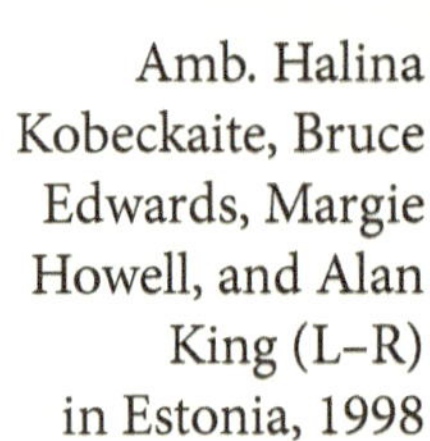

Amb. Halina Kobeckaite, Bruce Edwards, Margie Howell, and Alan King (L–R) in Estonia, 1998

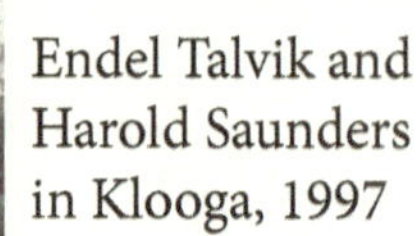

Endel Talvik and Harold Saunders in Klooga, 1997

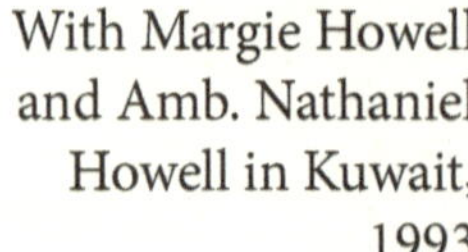

With Margie Howell and Amb. Nathaniel Howell in Kuwait, 1993

With Yuri Urbanovich and school children in Mustvee, Estonia, 1997

Visiting Josef Stalin's private train with Andy Thomson and Nodar Sharjveladze in Georgia, 2000

At Enver Hoxha's grave in Albania, 1998

With President Rauf Denktaş in North Cyprus, 2009

With President Glafcos Clerides at the Carter Center in Atlanta, GA, 1992

The author's eightieth birthday celebration at the House of Lords with Lord John Alderdice and Robi Friedman, London, 2012

With President Abdullah Gül in Turkey, 2008

www.ingramcontent.com/pod-product-compliance
Lightning Source LLC
LaVergne TN
LVHW100921110826
845155LV00035B/34

* 9 7 8 1 9 3 9 5 7 8 3 2 7 *